Praise for the first edition of

Sad Macs, Bombs, and Other Disasters

Sad Macs, BOMBS, and Other Disasters

And What to Do About Them

Second Edition

Ted Landau

Addison-Wesley Publishing Company

Reading, Massachusetts • Menlo Park, California • New York
Don Mills, Ontario • Wokingham, England • Amsterdam
Bonn • Sydney • Singapore • Tokyo • Madrid • San Juan
Paris • Seoul • Milan • Mexico City • Taipei

For Sam . . .

gone but not forgotten

Library of Congress Cataloging-in-Publication Data

Landau, Ted.
    Sad Macs, bombs, and other disasters : and what to do about them /Ted Landau. — 2nd ed.
      p.   cm.
    Includes bibliographical references and index.
    ISBN 0-201-40958-5
    1. Macintosh (Computer)   I. Title.
  QA76.8.M3L37   1995
  004. 165—dc20   95-6088
                                                           CIP

Sponsoring Editor: Martha Steffen
Project Manager: John Fuller
Production Coordinator: Ellen Savett
Cover design: Jean Seal
Set in 11 point Adobe Garamond by Pre-Press Company, Inc., Whitman, MA

1 2 3 4 5 6 7 8 9 -MA- 9998979695
First printing, June 1995

Addison-Wesley books are available for bulk purchases by corporations, institutions, and other organizations. For more information please contact the Corporate, Government, and Special Sales Department at (800) 238-9682.

Contents

Acknowledgments

As with the first edition, this second edition would never—could never—have been written without the continuing support and encouragement of my wife, Naomi, and my son, Brian. I thank them most for their understanding and patience while they put up with a spouse/father who was too often either unavailable or irritable during the time I spent hammering away at this book.

Thanks also to Carole McClendon, my agent at Waterside. Your advice is as valuable an asset as ever.

A very special thanks to all my editors at Addison-Wesley, most notably Martha Steffen, John Fuller, Ellen Savett, and Keith Wollman. Your patience with my never-ending stream of additions and corrections was exceptional. A bonus set of kudos to Keith, who worked with me on both editions and graciously allowed this edition to grow by several hundred pages without protesting too much.

A well-deserved thank you goes to Owen Linzmayer who is responsible for handling all of the hassles associated with the Sad Macs Utilities disk. Without him, I doubt there would be a disk offer.

A round of thanks also go to the magazine editors I have worked with these past years. You got me started and kept me going in this whole business. Most especially, I'm talking about Russ Ito (formerly at *MacUser*), Susan Janus (who still is at *MacUser*), Dan Littman at *Macworld*, and Bob LeVitus who, when he was editor of *MACazine*, published the first article I ever submitted.

A warm thank you goes out to all the people in the ZMac Forums of CompuServe who came through with answers to my most difficult questions—most especially to Ric Ford and Joe Holmes. Similar kudos for the help I received from the technical support staff, product managers, and public relations people at a host of companies whose products are mentioned in this book. For their help above and beyond what I had expected, a special mention for Christiane Petite at Symantec, Tom Swinford at Central Point, Keri Walker at Apple Computer, and for all of the Apple folks responsible for the Information Alley.

I especially wish to thank those people who bought and recommended the first edition of this book. It is because of your support that a second edition now exists.

Finally, I bought my first Macintosh in 1984, when almost no software was available for it and no one else I knew planned to buy one. It was a risky decision, but the Macintosh seemed worth the risk. I have never looked back since. So, to all of the people responsible for the creation of the Macintosh, thank you. Without you, there would have been no reason to write this book.

Ted Landau
May 1995

What's New in This Edition?

Since the publication of the previous edition of this book, the Macintosh landscape has changed substantially. This second edition of *Sad Macs* keeps pace with those changes. If you are familiar with the first edition, a cursory glance at the table of contents might suggest that not too much is different. Don't be misled. While the basic structure of the book remains the same, almost every section of the text has had major revisions. Almost every page has at least minor revisions. The majority of the figures have been similarly revised; many new ones have been added.

First off, two entirely new chapters have been added, one on PowerBooks (Chapter 11) and the other on Power Macintoshes and System 7.5 (Chapter 12). Problem-solving material specific to these topics is also liberally scattered throughout the remainder of the book. Chapter 11 covers a few topics (such as RAM disks, file sharing, and modems) that have relevance for any Macintosh owner that uses these features, even though the focus is on their use with PowerBooks.

In several cases, chapters have been expanded to accommodate information on hardware that was not covered as extensively in the previous edition. For example, Chapter 5 has new sections on problems with CD-ROM drives.

If software has been upgraded since the last edition, this edition reflects those changes. For example, take a look at Fix-It #7 (on SAM), Fix-It #10 (on Disk First Aid and MacCheck), or Chapter 2, Fix-It #13 and Fix-It #14 (on MacTools and Norton Utilities).

Some sections of the book were rewritten not so much to add new material but to increase the clarity of and simplify the organization of the material. Check out Chapters 4, 9, 10 or Fix-It #5 for some major examples.

Tables are now included in several chapters. Most notably, Chapters 4 and 5 have tables explaining the meaning of system error ID and Sad Mac error codes, respectively. This was the addition most frequently requested by readers of the first edition.

A few sections (especially in the first three chapters) were cut back in size. The appendix on case studies was eliminated altogether. These deletions were done partly to remove redundancies, but also just to try to keep the page count under control (which wound up increasing by several hundred pages anyway). Numerous minor errors from the previous edition were corrected.

Additionally, on almost every page, material has been updated and expanded to reflect new information on troubleshooting that I have gathered since writing the first edition. In many cases, this meant completely rewriting a given section.

Finally, as readers of the first edition are already well aware, I make mention of numerous shareware and freeware troubleshooting utilities throughout this book. While these programs are readily available from various sources (as described in the Appendix), some readers may still find it difficult to obtain them. For this reason, I now offer the *Sad Macs Utilities Disk*, a disk containing the majority of these troubleshooting utilities. Details on how to obtain this disk can be found on the last page of this book.

Overall, I am quite pleased with the results of all these changes. I believe you hold in your hands the most comprehensive book on Macintosh troubleshooting that is available anywhere.

If there is a downside to all of this change, it is how it affects the simplicity of this book. As a book designed to appeal to users of all Macintoshes, it benefits from an ability to make generalizations that are generally accurate—no matter what Macintosh you own and what system software you use. This effort is stymied by Apple's recent proliferation of hardware and software variations. These days, the chasm between users of an ancient relic like the Mac Plus and the latest Power Macintosh, while not yet the size of the Grand Canyon, is still uncomfortably large. And that doesn't even consider the special problems of PowerBook (of which there are several types) and AV Mac users. And trying to help people figure out the intricacies of System 7.5's Quick-Draw GX while not overlooking those who are still content with System 6 is yet another tough balancing act. I could go on . . . but I think you get the idea.

And still more is on the way. Apple plans major enhancements to its system software over the next months. It may already be on the shelves by the time you read this. New hardware, as always, is on its way as well.

The bottom line for writing this book is what you might expect: It ain't getting any easier. Increasingly, I am forced to give several separate explanations for a particular problem, each one specific to a different hardware or software variation. To get a feel for what I am talking about, check out Chapter 4's descriptions of the locations of power and reset buttons. It would be almost funny if it wasn't serious.

Anyway, I don't mean to sound too complaining. I enjoy learning about and writing about this stuff. That's why I wrote this book in the first place. And that's why I came back to do it again.

Preface

Who's in Charge Here?

Every Macintosh user has had this uneasy feeling at some time or other. Some rarely have it anymore; others have it every day. It's the feeling that working with your Macintosh is akin to being an apprentice lion trainer. You're never sure who is in charge. Rather than feeling in control of your computer, you feel controlled by it.

Nowhere is this more apparent than when something goes wrong—when a problem occurs that you can't figure out how to fix, when even your collection of manuals doesn't seem to have the answer. That's where this book comes in. Its goal is to put you back in charge, providing you with the information you need to diagnose and solve whatever problems you may confront.

At this point, you may be saying, "Fix *any* problem? And fix it *myself?* You must be kidding!" No, I'm not. You *can* solve most Macintosh problems yourself, regardless of your level of technical skill. Here's why I say this with such confidence:

- You don't need to know how to make hardware repairs to solve most of the common Macintosh problems. This is because most things that go wrong with your Macintosh are not hardware problems. They are primarily software problems and can be repaired directly from your keyboard, using a relatively small assortment of software tools and techniques. At most, you may need to check a few cables and switches, but that's it.

- Solving these Macintosh problems does not require any advanced technical knowledge. You do not have to be—or learn to become—a Macintosh expert. Neither do you need any programming skills. What tools and techniques you do need to know about are all designed with nonexpert users in mind.

- For many problems, everything is working fine and as it should be. The apparent problem is one of understanding. When you learn more about how your application (or the Macintosh in general) works, the unexpected will transform into the expected, and the problem is "solved." It's like discovering that the reason you are getting no sound from your TV is because someone pressed the mute button. Nothing's really wrong. That's the way it is supposed to work!

- Though this book does not specifically mention every possible problem you might have (no book could do that!), it does teach you the general skills needed to diagnose and solve even those problems that are not mentioned.

- If you follow the advice given in this book, there is virtually no risk that anything you do will harm the computer. There is certainly no key that you can press or button that you can click that will break the computer hardware.

Computer Problem Solving, Cookbooks, and Fishing

For quick answers to specific problems, you can use this book similarly to how you might use a cookbook. That is, a cookbook recipe tells you to add a teaspoon of baking powder, but doesn't tell you why the baking powder is required or why a teaspoon of baking soda would or would not be an acceptable substitute. Such an approach has an undeniable value. With a well-written cookbook, you can make very good meals even if you have no idea why the recipes work.

Similarly, this book offers "recipes" for problem solving on your Macintosh. With this book, you can solve most problems without needing to have an understanding of why the solutions work.

However, I want this book to do more than that. I hope to take some of the mysticism out of using computers—eliminating the feeling that what is going on either makes no sense or is beyond your ability to make sense of it.

This book offers you the opportunity to learn why problems occur and why the solutions work. With this information, you can go beyond the limits of the pages of this book and begin to solve most problems entirely on your own.

This is where fishing comes in. An old saying goes, "Give a person a fish and feed him for a day. Teach a person to fish and feed him for a lifetime." The cookbook explanations are the "fish" that this book gives you. The more general explanations will teach you "how to fish."

You can limit yourself to eating the "fish" if you wish. My hope is that you will want to take the next step and learn "how to fish" as well.

What This Book Is and Is Not

Perhaps you are browsing through this introduction at a bookstore, trying to decide whether this book is for you. Or perhaps you want to make sure that you clearly understand what this book does and does not cover. Fair enough. Here is an overview of what this book is and is not:

What This Book Is

- This book is designed to help you solve the common problems that occur when working with the Macintosh. Other more general information is included only when relevant to problem solving.

- This book is about many more problems than just the disasters suggested by the title. Many of the problems discussed do not even qualify as disasters. Whether it is an inability to eject a disk, empty the Trash, copy a selection to the Clipboard, or get text to print in the correct font, rest assured that these types of problems are also covered here.

- This book explains the material in as nontechnical, plain English as possible. Where it uses technical jargon, it clearly explains what it means and why you should know about it.

- This book is appropriate for everyone from near-beginners to almost-experts. In fact, it is targeted primarily for users with only minimal technical skills. It makes few assumptions about your level of expertise. However, it does assume that you are currently using a Macintosh and are at least vaguely familiar with some basic terms and concepts. For example, if I say that you need to "close a window" or "double-click that icon," or "pull down the File menu and select Save," this ideally should not sound to you as if I am talking in a foreign language.

What This Book Is Not

- This book is not a general introduction to the Macintosh. If that's all you want, check out the documentation that came with your Macintosh or any number of other excellent introductory books available in bookstores.

- This book is not designed to be a comprehensive encyclopedia of tips and hints that, while helpful and interesting, are not directly relevant to problem solving.

- This book does not cover hardware repairs, other than to indicate how to tell if such a repair is likely to be needed. Rather, the book focuses on software-based problems and solutions.

- This book does not cover problems that occur only in conjunction with optional hardware peripherals such as scanners. Instead, it limits discussions to those problems that occur with a minimum standard hardware configuration: computer, mouse, keyboard, monitor, storage devices, and printer.

- This book does not (with a few exceptions) cover problems that would occur only when you first set up your hardware. It assumes that you have already set up and successfully used the equipment.

- This book does not cover problems specific only to a single application. For example, if there is a problem specific to Microsoft Word, you are not likely to find out about it here. However, you should still be able to solve most such problems, using the more general techniques that are described.

- This book does emphasize network-specific problems. While it does cover using System 7's file sharing, this is not the book you need if you are trying to negotiate the intricacies of a large multi-user network. Solving these problems, which can be quite complex, often exceeds the skills of most of the users on the network. If your workplace uses a network, at least one person—a network administrator—should have the expertise to handle these problems.

Looking Over My Shoulder

While writing this book, I imagined at least two types of readers peering over my shoulder. They each had different, sometimes opposing, concerns. I wanted to please both of them, though this was often difficult to do.

First, I imagined the Macintosh experts, who know as much as (or even more than) I do about these subjects. Even though they are not the intended audience for this book, I still hoped to gain their approval. Yet I knew that in many cases I would be summarizing complex issues in a way that glossed over important details. I knew I would be making generalizations that would ignore the minor, but not trivial, exceptions that existed. I hoped the experts would not roll their eyes and groan at these points.

I also hoped that these experts would not find this book to be redundant, that it would not provoke comments such as, "Hey, everybody already knows this stuff. It's already been covered in two dozen other books. Why do we need to see this tired old advice yet again?" I hope that such experts understand that not everyone is as familiar with these issues as they are. And more important, I hope I have succeeded in organizing and describing these issues in a way that makes them easier to understand and more accessible than has been done before. Finally, I hope that even the expert finds a good deal more in this book than just tired old advice.

On the other hand, I also imagined the near-novice users looking over my shoulder. For them, I knew I might be assuming knowledge of basic information that they did not have. I know from experience that people can use a Macintosh for years and still have almost no idea about the basics of how the machine operates or the terms that are used to describe those operations. I always had to be careful not to assume too much.

Similarly, I didn't want to go into much more technical detail than the near-novice users really cared to know. I could hear them saying to me, "Hey, I just want to know how to get this disk working again. I don't want a whole course on how disks work." So I have tried to keep a novice's perspective on the more technical explanations, realizing that not every user has the same fondness for understanding these issues as I do.

I felt I was walking a tightrope here. I've tried to create a book that was not too technical for novices yet not too elementary for everyone else. As to whether I succeeded in this goal, you are the final judge.

How This Book Is Organized

This book has three main parts:

- *Part I: Background and Basics* deals with general background information and some problem-solving basics. This is designed to bring all users up to speed so that any relevant gaps in your knowledge get filled before you proceed.

- *Part II: Symptoms, Causes, and Cures* covers the whole range of Macintosh problems, what their symptoms are, what causes them, and what you can do to solve them.
- *Part III: Disaster Relief* focuses on specific problem-solving tools, called Fix-Its, rather than on symptoms. Each Fix-It contains all the necessary information about how and when to use it and why it works.

These three sections are followed by an appendix, called "Stocking Your Troubleshooter's Toolkit," that provides the information needed to obtain any of the troubleshooting software mentioned in this book. This is followed by two separate indexes: a symptom index and a general subject index.

On a Related Note

Throughout this book, you will find three types of text set off from the main text. Each of these has a different purpose:

TAKE NOTE ▶

These notes contain important information directly relevant to the topic under discussion. For example, they may include definitions or explanations of terms used in the main text.

BY THE WAY ▶

These notes contain more tangential information than you will find in the Take Note boxes. For example, they may list changes expected in a forthcoming version of the software under discussion.

TECHNICALLY SPEAKING ▶

These notes contain supplementary information that is at a more technical level than the rest of the book. Less technically inclined readers may choose to skip them.

See: What I Mean

This book contains numerous cross-references: Some of these references direct you to a continuation of the steps needed to solve a problem, such as, "If the system error continues to recur, see 'Solve It! Recurring System Errors,' later in this chapter." Others inform you where you can find more information about a subject, such as

See: • Chapter 8 for more details on invisible files

Still others point to the location of the initial description of a term or item.

On the one hand, the sheer number of these references may seem disconcerting at first, especially if you are in a hurry to solve a problem. However, not all of these references demand immediate attention. Many of them are only suggestions. Thus, if you can solve your current problem without needing to know more about invisible files, for example, you need not bother with that particular cross-reference.

The references to the Fix-Its are a special case. This book is deliberately designed to make frequent reference to them. They are the central location for all information on their given topic. Thus, you *should* generally check out any Fix-It references that are relevant to your problem.

However, when there is a long list of Fix-Its, you probably won't wind up needing all of them. As soon as one of them fixes your problem, you can stop. If the length of a particular list seems daunting, remember that the longer lists cover the most general cases, when the information at hand provides little or no guidance on which direction to go. Usually, if you can describe your problem more specifically, you can find more specific advice, with a narrower range of Fix-It choices, elsewhere in the book.

Your Hardware, Your Software, and This Book

The answers to the following two questions have direct bearing on your use of the information in this book. Make sure you know the answers to these basic questions before going any further.

What Model Macintosh Are You Using?

If you don't already know the name of the specific model of Macintosh you are using, find out. It's somewhere on the machine itself, usually right in front.

"Hardware" Alert: Many problems pertain only to a specific category of Macintosh model or have separate solutions for different models. This is usually discussed in the main text, as relevant. However, you will also find occasional hardware-specific alert messages with highlights like the one at the start of this paragraph. For example, these occur for Power Macintoshes and AV Macintoshes.

What System Software Version Are You Using?

If you don't already know the version of the system software you are using, find out. Even if you are unsure about what system software is, find out the version number. Here's a quick way to get an answer that is good enough for now:

- Look at the top item in the Apple menu when you are in the Finder. If it reads *About This Macintosh,* you are using System 7. If it reads *About the Finder,* you are using System 6 (or earlier!).

Almost everyone today is using some version of either System 6 or System 7. Because System 7 is required for all recently released models of Macintosh and is increasingly required for recently released software, this book focuses primarily on System 7. In any discussion of a system software feature, you can assume that the explanation applies to System 7 unless otherwise specified.

System 6 Alert: Paragraphs that pertain strictly to System 6 are highlighted like this. Despite this book's emphasis on System 7, users of System 6 can take consolation from the following:

- Despite their differences, there are many areas of overlap between the two systems. Much of what is discussed in this book does apply equally to both systems.

- Where differences between the two systems are especially relevant and significant, I try to describe the procedures for both systems.

- I have minimized the discussion of problems relevant to less commonly used features unique to System 7, such as Publish and Subscribe.

System 7.5 Alert: I will also be making distinctions between earlier versions of System 7 (7.0 and 7.1) and the more recent System 7.5.

Part I:

Background and Basics

Chapter 1 is an overview of basic computer terms, concepts, and operations. I explain the essentials of the different types of memory that your Macintosh uses, and the different types of disks used to store data, as well as some specifics about other common hardware, especially monitors and printers. I also delve into the mysteries of the System Folder.

Chapter 2 covers preventative maintenance. It begins with an overview of the causes of Macintosh problems. The next part describes the important software tools you need to make your repairs. The final part describes a general set of routine maintenance procedures designed to keep your Macintosh out of trouble.

Chapter 3 provides a set of general strategies for solving problems. With these skills, you will be ready to tackle almost any problem that comes your way, even if it is not specifically covered in this book.

Chapter 1

Macintosh Basics:
Hardware and Software

Exactly How Did I Get Here?

You turn on your Macintosh. The smiling Macintosh icon appears briefly and is soon replaced by the Welcome to Macintosh display. Eventually, this too disappears and is replaced by the desktop, a display where your disk icon appears in the upper right corner of the screen and the various files on your disk are listed in any number of windows. In one of these windows, you find the file icon for your word processor. You double-click on the file and it opens. You create a new document and save it. You quit the application and shut off the machine.

That's a typical brief session with your Macintosh.

If you are relatively new to using computers (and even if you are not), you have probably wondered exactly how all this happens. Where does the Welcome to Macintosh display come from? How does the Macintosh know what to do next? What happens when you open an application? Where was the information stored before you opened it, and where is it now? What exactly happens when you save something, and why isn't it saved automatically as you create it?

These are big questions, and they can be answered on many levels. It is a bit like the little child who asked his parent, "Where do I come from?" After the mother made several uncomfortable attempts at answering the question, the boy blurted out, "But Billy said he comes from Cleveland. I want to know where I come from."

Similarly, behind many Macintosh questions is a desire for a much simpler answer than the question may seem to imply. It is with this in mind that I attempt to answer these "big" questions. As always, the focus is limited to what you need to know to understand the problem-solving material in the chapters to come. It makes no pretense of being comprehensive.

The Macintosh's ability to strut its stuff, whether to create sophisticated page layouts or display incredibly detailed color graphics, is the result of an intricate interplay between hardware and software. If you are going to solve the problems that will confront you in your day-to-day life with the Macintosh, you need some minimal understanding of how all this works. That's what this chapter is all about.

Macintosh Models and Computer Systems

Dozens of different models of Macintosh now exist, but they can be divided into four main categories:

- **Compact Macintoshes.** These include all the models based on the original design of the Macintosh, the all-in-one box with a built-in 9-inch monitor. These range from the Macintosh Plus to the Macintosh Classics. There are no compact Macintoshes in Apple's current lineup.

- **Modular Macintoshes.** These are the Macintoshes that are simply a box. All other components, including a monitor, are purchased and added separately. Almost all Macintoshes sold today are modular Macintoshes. They range from the Macintosh II series, most LCs, the Quadras, to the latest Power Macintoshes.

- **Hybrid Macintoshes.** These describe a few Macintoshes, mostly geared toward the education market that are a cross between compact and modular Macintoshes. The computer and monitor are combined into a single unit, as in compact Macintoshes, but their overall design more closely mimics that of modular Macintoshes. The LC520 is an example.

- **Notebook Macintoshes.** These are all-battery-powered portable Macintoshes, of which there are two main types: the all-in-one PowerBooks (these contain a built-in floppy drive and have ports to connect to most external peripherals, such as an external monitor) and the PowerBook Duos (these are missing a floppy drive and external ports, but can access them via an optional "docking" accessory).

The term *computer system* typically refers to the essential combination of hardware components necessary to use the computer. For a modular Macintosh, this typically includes the computer "box" itself, a monitor, input device(s) such as a keyboard and mouse, and any disk drives. An almost essential additional component is a printer.

Apple's Performa line of Macintoshes are special versions of their standard Macs, bundled with components to form a complete computer system and usually including additional software. They are primarily marketed to home users.

Computing and Storage Hardware

The CPU and ROM

If you opened up any model of Macintosh, the most distinctive object you would see is a board full of soldered circuits. It looks sort of like the electronic equivalent of an aerial view of New York City. This is called the *main logic board* (or *motherboard*).

Many items are on this board. You are concerned now with just two of these items: the *central processing unit* (or *CPU* or *processor*) and the *read-only memory* module (or *ROM*). The expression *read-only* means that the information stored there cannot be altered in any way, it can only be read. By analogy, a compact disc is read-only, but a cassette tape is read-write.

Simply put, the CPU makes a Macintosh a computer, and ROM makes a Macintosh a Macintosh.

What you need to know:

The Processor Is the Computer

The processor is where most computations take place. Essentially, all programs are simply a set of instructions that get executed by the processor to produce the desired result.

The Macintosh User Interface Is Largely in ROM

The ROM contains the essential instructions needed to create the windows, menu bars, scroll boxes, dialog boxes, and graphics that make up what is commonly called the *Macintosh user interface.* All other programs can be designed to access this information. This is a great time-saver for programmers, since they don't have to keep reinventing the wheel. It also ensures that all programs have a similar look and feel.

Different Processors and ROMs in Different Macs

All Macintoshes have similar processors and similar ROMs (okay, Power Macintoshes are something of an exception here!). This is the main reason that all Macintoshes behave, look, and feel in such similar ways and can mostly run the same software.

However, different models of Macintosh have different versions of the same basic processor. The most important consequence of differences in these processors is differences in performance speed. Macintoshes with faster processors do *everything* faster. This is one reason why expensive Macintoshes tend to be faster than the less expensive ones: they often have faster processors. The fastest processors, of course, are found in the most expensive Macs. But these days, even a rock-bottom Mac has a faster processor than the most costly Macs of just a few years ago.

TECHNICALLY SPEAKING ▶

68040, 601, POWERPC—WHAT DOES IT ALL MEAN?

All Macintosh processors are developed by the Motorola corporation. Until recently, all Macintoshes were based on the 680x0 series of processors, with names like Motorola 68030 and 68040. Generally, the higher the number of the CPU, the newer and faster it is. More recently, Apple introduced its line of Power Macintoshes. These are based on an entirely new processor, the PowerPC chip. Different variations of these chips have names like 601 and 603. Despite this radical shift to a new processor, the Power Macintosh's can still emulate (that is, imitate) a 68040 Macintosh, allowing a Power Mac to run software designed for the older machines.

SEE: • **Chapter 12 for more on Power Macintoshes**

Similarly, different models of Macintosh have different variations in the ROM. Newer models have improved and expanded versions of the basic ROM. The most important consequence of these differences is that some features are found in newer versions of the ROM that are not present in older versions. This may limit what you can do with older hardware. For example, older models of Macintosh have limits on how many colors they can display—limits that no longer apply to the newer models.

For problem solving:

The most important thing to know is that the existence of different processors and different ROMs across different models of Macintoshes may lead to incompatibilities. For example, because of ROM and processor differences, certain programs may work fine with some models of Macintosh, but not others.

RAM: Electronic Storage

RAM stands for *random access memory*. When you hear people talking about how much memory their Macintosh has, they are talking about RAM. When a manual says that a program needs a certain amount of memory to run, it is referring to RAM.

When you first turn your computer on, the RAM contains nothing at all. The startup process consists largely of *loading* the needed information into RAM. This is because almost all program instructions must be loaded into RAM before they can be carried out.

Similarly, when you open an application, you are transferring the instructions contained within that file from its normal storage location (usually a disk) to RAM.

The hardware that determines the amount of RAM in your machine is located on the main logic board inside your computer. These hardware components are often referred to as *memory chips* or *SIMMs*, which is an acronym for "single in-line memory module"(though knowing this acronym generally doesn't help anyone understand what they do).

By the way, some Macs have separate RAM just for creating the monitor's display, called video RAM (I'll have more to say about this in Chapter 10).

What you need to know:

Measuring RAM

RAM is usually measured in megabytes (Mb). The more (or higher capacity of) SIMMs in your machine, the more megabytes of memory you have. Older Macintoshes came with as little as 1Mb of RAM (the original Macintosh had only 128K!). The minimal amount of RAM that comes shipped with most Macintoshes today is 4Mb. Eight megabytes or more is becoming increasingly common.

This RAM measurement has nothing directly to do with the physical size of the memory chip. Instead, it refers to the capacity of the chip to hold information.

These days, 4Mb of RAM is the absolute minimum needed to run System 7 (though 8Mb or more is far preferable). With less RAM, even if you can start up successfully, you will keep getting "out of memory" messages almost every time you try to launch applications.

Though some SIMMs may come soldered to your Mac's logic board, virtually all Macs have at least one RAM slot where SIMMs can be snapped in or removed. Generally, you can increase the amount of memory inside your machine by inserting a memory chip into any empty RAM slots or replacing a smaller-capacity memory chip with a larger one. With most modular Macintoshes, this can be done quite easily. You could probably do it yourself. With compact Macintoshes, it can be more tricky. You probably want a service technician to do it for you.

SEE: • Fix-It #17 for more on adding and replacing SIMMs

TECHNICALLY SPEAKING ▶

BYTING OFF MORE THAN YOU CAN CHEW

The byte is the basic unit of measurement for computer memory and storage. In particular: 1 megabyte = 1024 kilobytes (K) and, in turn, 1 kilobyte = 1024 bytes.

As a rough guideline, a page of text, single spaced, requires about 5K.

The most common size of SIMM in use today is 1Mb (though 4Mb SIMMs are gaining ground). Thus, if your machine had eight 1Mb SIMMs installed, you would have a maximum of 8Mb of RAM at your disposal!

RAM Is Fast

The *random access* in RAM means that you can almost instantly get to any portion of what is stored in RAM. Most storage mechanisms that you are familiar with are *not* random access. For example, with a cassette tape, you must fast-forward or rewind to get where you want, which can take considerable time. Even a compact disc, which has a much faster access time, technically still works on the same principle as the cassette tape.

Thus, RAM access speed far exceeds any other alternative method the computer could use. This speed advantage is the main rationale for using RAM. Without it, all computer operations would slow down immensely, if they could be done at all.

RAM Is Electrical

One reason RAM can achieve such a speed advantage is that information is stored in RAM in a purely electronic manner. Theoretically, information in RAM can be accessed at the speed at which electricity travels, which is quite fast!

Information in RAM Is Not Read-only

Information in RAM can be easily modified or erased. It's just a matter of altering the path of electrical current flow in the memory chip.

With all of these advantages, you might wonder why anyone would use something other than RAM to store data. Actually, there are two very good reasons:

RAM Is Expensive

Memory chips are expensive. The amount of RAM needed to store all the information on just one floppy disk could cost at least $50, maybe more (RAM prices tend to fluctuate more than the weather in Michigan).

RAM Is Temporary

Because RAM is electrical in nature, anything in RAM is lost forever when you turn the computer off, restart the computer, or interrupt the flow of electricity in any way (though if you use RAM disks, as described more in Chapter 11, you may know that they are a partial exception to this generalization). Thus, an unexpected power failure could result in the loss of several hours of work—if it is stored only in RAM and nowhere else! To permanently save your information, you need another form of storage, typically disks (as described in the next section).

For problem solving:

The most important thing to know is whether you have enough memory for what you want to do and what to do if you do not.

RAM limitations are generally the bottleneck that limits how much you can do at one time. Whenever you open an application, the RAM that it occupies becomes temporarily unavailable for any other use. Since everything you want to use needs to load into RAM, you can only work with as much as can fit into the available RAM.

Of course, information in RAM can be removed. The information you remove is then no longer available for immediate use, but the RAM is freed up. For example, quitting an application removes it from RAM and leaves that RAM available for another program.

Some programs may not run at all on your machine because you do not have sufficient RAM to open them, even if nothing else is running already. When that happens, it's time to buy more memory!

Disks: Physical Storage

Disks are used to store information permanently. That is, the information is retained even after the computer is turned off. This stored information on disks is commonly referred to as *software*.

Most Macintosh models have a type of disk, called a *hard disk,* built into the computer box itself. This disk is *not* in any way part of the main logic board (which holds the processor, ROM, and memory chips). A hard disk is a totally separate unit, though it connects to the main logic board. In fact, it is only a matter of convenience that it is inside the box at all. The Macintosh could work just fine without this internal hard disk, accessing instead a separate hard disk unit connected to the Macintosh on an outlet in the rear of the machine.

Still, though not technically correct, many users lump all of these components together as the internal hardware of the Macintosh. Whether in RAM, ROM, or on a hard disk, information is viewed as being stored somewhere inside the machine.

Besides a hard disk, the other most common type of disk is the floppy disk. Information on the *floppy disk* is accessed by first inserting the disk into a *floppy disk drive.* Again, almost all Macintoshes (except for some notebook models) come with at least one such drive built into the machine.

SEE: • Next section, "Types of Disks and Disk Drives," for more details

As mentioned in the section on RAM, when you *open* an application stored on a disk, you are copying its information from the disk to RAM. From here, its instructions can be sent to the processor as needed, which essentially means that the program will *run.*

Conversely, when you use an application's Save command to save a document, you are taking a copy of the document's information, which is currently at least partially in RAM, and transferring it to a disk.

What you need to know:

Measuring Storage Capacity

If RAM is normally referred to as *memory,* disk space is normally referred to as *storage capacity.* Thus, you may be asked "What is the storage capacity of your hard drive?" or simply "How large is your hard drive?" Like RAM, storage capacity is measured in *kilobytes* (K) and *megabytes* (Mb). This can be a source of confusion. When talking about megabytes, it may not be immediately clear whether someone is referring to RAM (memory) capacity or disk (storage) capacity. Once you understand the context, however, it is usually clear how to distinguish between these two alternatives.

By the way, don't expect the amount of space a file occupies on a disk to be the same as the amount of space it needs when it loads into RAM. For various reasons, the numbers may be different. A program may load only part of its instructions into RAM at one time, thus requiring less RAM than you might expect. Alternatively, a program may need a lot more space than the storage size of the file to accommodate documents that you may open with the application.

Disk Storage Is Temporarily Permanent

Disks work in a way that is metaphorically similar to cassette tape. You can write to a computer disk, just as you can record to a cassette tape. When you turn off your cassette recorder, the information remains on tape. Later, you can play back the tape, or erase it and record something else. You can do the same thing with most types of computer disks.

Thus, disk storage is temporarily permanent: Information written to it remains on the disk until you change it. That is, as with RAM, you can both read and write information to a disk. But, unlike RAM, information on disk is not stored electronically. Instead, as with cassette tape, an actual physical change to the disk occurs when you write new information to it. This is why, after you save a document to a disk, the information is retained even after you turn the computer off.

For problem solving:

The most important thing to know is that as you go through a typical computer session, a frequent two-way flow of information takes place from disk to RAM and back again. Understanding the distinctions between these two ways of holding information is often critical to isolating the causes of a problem and thus solving it.

For example, an application that cannot open because of insufficient memory is basically a RAM-related problem. An application that cannot open because the instructions stored on the disk have been damaged in some way is essentially a disk-related problem. The methods used to solve these different types of problems are, as you will see, quite different.

TECHNICALLY SPEAKING ▶

PUTTING IT ALL TOGETHER

With this information now digested, you can answer the initial questions on "Exactly how did I get here?" with more clarity.

When you turn on your machine, the processor and the ROM kick in immediately. They continue to play an essential role in all operations until the moment you shut down. Everything your computer does ultimately depends on instructions being sent to and carried out by the processor.

Almost immediately after this initial step, information (particularly from the System Folder files that I talk about later in this chapter) stored on disk (most likely the hard disk inside your machine) begins to load into RAM. As all this occurs, the smiling Macintosh icon appears briefly (indicating a problem-free start) followed by the Welcome to Macintosh display. Eventually, the desktop appears, as the program called the Finder opens.

When you launch your word processor or any other software, this too is transferred from its disk storage location to RAM, so that you can now use it (assuming you have enough RAM for

(continued)

---

that program to run). The menu bars, windows, and dialog boxes that appear are produced by information gotten from the program itself in combination with standard information accessed from the ROM (and, in some cases, from system software, as described later in this chapter). When you work on your document and save it, the information is transferred out of RAM to disk storage, so it remains there even after you turn your Macintosh off. When you quit your application, you free up the RAM it occupied, which can then be used by some other program.

Types of Disks and Disk Drives

The term *disk* refers to the actual medium that stores the information used by the computer. It is the metaphorical equivalent of the tape in a cassette tape player. The term *drive* refers to the mechanism used to read and write information to and from the disk. That is, the drive is like the tape deck. In component stereo systems, to hear the tape, you must connect the deck to a receiver and speakers. Similarly, to use information on a disk, the disk drive must be connected to the Macintosh.

Four basic categories of disks are considered here: floppy disks, hard disks, CD-ROM disks, and removable cartridges.

Floppy Disks

Floppy disks are the common denominator of Macintosh storage. Every Macintosh (except the Duos) comes with at least one floppy drive built into it. Almost all software is shipped on floppy disks (though CD-ROM disks, as described shortly, are getting more popular).

Where Is the Flop?   Looking at the hard-shell plastic case of a floppy disk, it may seem that the disk does not live up to its name. It's not floppy. This is because the term *floppy* refers to the truly flexible, thin plastic circular disk encased inside the hard plastic shell. You can see this when you slide the metal shutter back. This floppy part actually stores the information on the disk.

The metal shutter is automatically pulled back when you insert the disk into a disk drive. This gives the disk drive access to the critical floppy media.

Types of Floppy Disks   The two most common types of floppy disks in use today are 800K disks and 1.44Mb disks. These names refer to the maximum storage capacity of the disks. The 1.44Mb disks are also referred to as high-density (HD) disks.

As the front of the disk faces you with the metal slide on the bottom, 800K and HD disks have a small square hole visible in the upper right corner. On the rear side of this hole is a slide tab. When the tab is up, so that you can see through the hole, the disk is locked, which means that you cannot modify the contents of the disk in any way (see Chapter 6 for more on locked disks). HD disks include an extra hole on the upper left-hand side. There is no slide tab here; this hole is simply used by the floppy disk drive to identify the disk as an HD disk. HD disks also have the HD symbol to the side of the metal slide. Otherwise, the two types of disks look virtually identical (see Figure 1-1).

HD and 800K disks are both *double-sided* disks. This means they store information on both sides of the disk.

A third type of floppy disk is a 400K (*single-sided* or *one-sided*) disk. Single-sided disks are identical to 800K disks except that they are designed to store information on only one side of the disk. Single-sided disks are almost never used anymore.

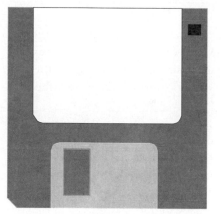 

Figure 1-1   An 800K floppy disk (left) and an HD floppy disk (right). The HD symbol is upside down here. The lock tab on both disks is in the unlocked position (you cannot see through the hole)

Types of Floppy Disk Drives   The three basic types of floppy disk drives match the different types of disks available.

The floppy disk drive that ships with Macintoshes today is the SuperDrive. This drive recognizes all three types of disks: 400K, 800K, and HD. The SuperDrive distinguishes HD disks from 800K disks by the extra hole on the HD disk.

Older Macintoshes may have 800K drives. You cannot use HD disks with these drives. If you have an ancient Mac, it may have a 400K drive. These drives recognize only single-sided disks.

Hard Disks

A hard disk, like its floppy disk counterpart, is simply a means of storing information—except that it can hold a lot more information than a floppy disk. A 40Mb hard disk (which is about the smallest size you can get today) can hold the equivalent of about fifty 800K floppy disks.

Types of Hard Disk Drives   Basically, a hard disk drive (usually referred to as simply a *hard drive*) is a mechanism that contains the hard disk storage media inside its case. The typical hard disk drive mechanism has a hard disk permanently encased inside it. You cannot remove it or insert another one. Thus, for many people the terms *hard disk* and *hard disk drive* seem synonymous, though technically they are as different as the terms *floppy disk* and *floppy disk drive.*

Most Macintoshes today come with an internal hard disk drive located inside the machine. With the proper software on this disk, no other disk is needed to get started using a Macintosh.

External Hard Drives and the SCSI Port   If your Macintosh does not have an internal hard drive or if you want to have more than one hard drive, you can add one externally. External hard drives are attached to the Macintosh via a special port in the back of the machine called the *SCSI* (pronounced "scuzzy") port, which is described further in Fix-It #16.

Why You Must Have a Hard Drive   If you think you can get by with just floppy disk drives and no hard drive, forget it. The increased speed and storage capacity of a hard drive (compared to floppy drives) make it a requirement in today's Macintosh environment. Much current software is too large to run from floppy disks, even if you're willing to put up with the much slower access speeds characteristic of floppy disks.

At the very least, you can no longer fit a fully equipped System 7 System Folder onto a floppy disk (though you can create a bare-bones one when necessary). For this reason alone, you need a hard disk.

Other Storage Devices

CD-ROM Disks   CD-ROM disks have become quite common in recent years. Most current models of desktop Macintoshes have an option to come with an internal CD-ROM drive. Alternatively, you can hook one up separately via the SCSI port.

Basically, CD-ROM disks look identical to the compact discs that are now standard in the music industry. The big advantage of CD-ROM disks is that they can hold a great deal of information for their small size—exceeding that of most common sizes of hard drives—yet at much less cost than other storage media.

However, this is offset by two major disadvantages: They are significantly slower than hard drives, and you *cannot* write to a CD-ROM disk. You purchase a CD-ROM disk with information already contained on it. This information can never be modified or deleted from the disk. Similarly, you cannot save your own files to a CD-ROM disk.

Removable Cartridges   Removable-media cartridges, as their name implies, can be inserted into and ejected from a drive, much like how floppy disks work. However, once inserted, the Mac treats a cartridge more like a fixed (noncartridge) hard disk. Different types of removable media drives work on different principles. *SyQuest drives,* for example, function very similarly to how fixed hard drives work. These are among the fastest of removable media drives, with speeds that rival those of fixed hard drives. *Optical drives,* on the other hand, work on a principle similar to how a CD-ROM drive works, except that you can write to an optical cartridge as well as read from it. Optical drives are expected to gain in popularity as their speed increases and their price comes down.

Capacities of cartridges vary as a function of the type and exact model of drive, with a maximum size generally around 250Mb (though newer optical disks now exceed 1000Mb).

TAKE NOTE ▶

WHAT ABOUT MONITORS AND PRINTERS?

In addition to the basic components described here, virtually all computer systems include some type of a monitor and a printer. I'm going to defer any description of these components for now. Check out Chapters 7, 9, and 10 for more information.

System Software

The term *system software* most commonly refers to the basic set of files included with each Macintosh. These files come preinstalled on your hard drive. They are also typically included on a set of floppy disks or a CD-ROM disk that comes with your Macintosh. Finally, you can buy system software upgrade kits independent of any hardware purchase.

A few system software files are essential for the use of your Macintosh, namely the System and Finder. Without access to them, your Macintosh typically will not even start up. Others are nearly essential, needed for routine operations such as printing. In most cases, these and related files are contained in a special folder called the *System Folder.* A disk that contains such a folder is called a *startup disk* (a topic discussed more in Chapter 5).

Many users are not familiar with what is inside a System Folder. Some users may not even be aware they have one. If this describes you, things are about to change. *To effectively solve problems on the Macintosh, understanding the basics of the System Folder and its contents is essential!*

System Software Versions

Apple periodically releases new versions, or upgrades, to its system software. Sometimes, rather than releasing a complete new version of the system software, it may release a special subset of files typically called System Updates. In either case, there are at least three reasons for doing this:

- To fix problems with the previous version of the software
- To provide support for new models of Macintosh that have been released
- To add new features that improve on the previous version

What you need to know:

The differences in features across versions is most relevant to the problem-solving issues in this book. These differences affect what problems you may have and what problem-solving tools are at your disposal.

Every time a significant revision occurs, Apple assigns it a new numerical name. Thus, people refer to system software by its version number, such as version 6.0.5 or version 7.0. The version number indicates the extent of the difference of the new version from its predecessor. Thus, changes in the number after the second decimal indicate the most minor changes. Major upgrades call for a change in the first digit.

All version numbers that begin with a 6 are usually referred to together as simply System 6. Similarly, versions that begin with a 7 are referred to as System 7. Almost every Macintosh user today should be using some version of System 6 or System 7. If you are using an earlier version, wake up. It's the nineties.

In May 1991, Apple made the most dramatic upgrade in its system software since the original release of the Macintosh. It upgraded from System 6.x to System 7.0. There are so many differences between these two systems that making general statements that apply equally to both of them is often not possible.

Most Mac users today are using some version of System 7 if only because all recent models of Macintosh require that you use it. If you still use System 6 on an older machine, I strongly recommend that you upgrade (even if it means having to buy a new Mac). Much of today's best software only runs on System 7. Upgrade disks are available from Apple dealers as well as various other sources (see the Appendix for more information).

If you are using System 7.1, note that it comes in several flavors. In addition to the basic version, there is a System 7 Pro (7.1.1) version, which includes a few additional features (most notably, a network communication feature called PowerTalk). Power Macintoshes require at least System 7.1.2. There is also a separate version for Performas, System 7.1P. For System 7.5 users, there is only one version (though you have the option as to whether or not to install PowerTalk and QuickDraw GX). Details of all of this will be covered in later chapters, as appropriate.

Apple's system software continues to evolve at a dizzying pace. Major changes are planned for the near future and may have already occurred by the time you read this.

SEE: • "Macintosh System Software" in Chapter 2, for how to tell exactly what system version you are using
       • Fix-It #5 for more on installing and upgrading system software

---

BY THE WAY ▶

THE PERFORMA MACINTOSHES AND SYSTEM SOFTWARE

Apple's Performa series of Macintoshes, prior to System 7.5, shipped with a special version of system software designed specifically for these models. Thus, purchasers of standard Macintoshes got System 7.1, while Performa users get System 7.1P (where P = Performa). The two variations are similar. In fact, for most files, the two versions are identical (or nearly so). You can run the standard System 7 software on a Performa and vice versa (though see Fix-It #5, "By the Way: Reinstalling System Software on Performas," for some cautions).

The main difference between the Performa and the standard system software is two-fold. First, the Performa software comes with some software not included in the standard system software. This includes Launcher and At Ease. These are partial substitutes for the Finder and are designed to create a more simplified interface for the user than the standard Finder-based approach. Second, it is common for Performas to ship without a complete set of system software disks. Instead, your only complete copy of the system software is what you get pre-installed on the internal hard drive. However, you do get a disk called Disk Utilities, that is useful when problems occur (it is similar in function to the Disk Tools disk that comes with the complete set of system software). You also get special utilities for backing up your hard disk's contents.

Unfortunately, these Performa oddities (especially "hiding" the Finder) often make problem solving more difficult rather than easier. Though this book does not emphasize Performa-specific problems, a few major ones will be mentioned as relevant (such as some problems using At Ease and how to reinstall the System Software if your don't have the system software disks).

Some of the special features of the Performa versions of the system software (such as Launcher) are now included as part of the general System 7.5 release.

The System and the Finder

The System File

The System file is the single most critical file in your System Folder (see Figure 1-2). The System file consists largely of instructions that complement and extend what is found in the Macintosh ROM. The information in the System file tends to be those things that are more likely to need frequent revision than what is contained in the ROM.

In some cases, certain type of files (such as fonts, sounds, or keyboard layout files) can be installed directly in the System file. These will be described more in later chapters, as appropriate.

What you need to know:

- First and foremost, your Macintosh will not run without the System file.
- Compatibility problems can occur between the system software and other software you use. Older programs may not work well with newer versions of the system software, and vice versa.

  The shift from System 6 to System 7 is a particularly radical one in this regard. However, over time, upgrades to existing software are released that resolve these problems. Even with System 7, if you are using current versions of all your software, you should have little or no compatibility problems these days.

- Files (such as sounds or fonts) that are installed in the System file are potentially accessible by any and all other applications.

System

System

Figure 1-2   The System file icon of System 7, which looks like a suitcase, and the System file icon of System 6, which looks like a compact Macintosh

---

TAKE NOTE ▶

SYSTEM ENABLERS

Starting with System 7.1, when Apple introduced a new model of Macintosh, a matching System Enabler file for that model was also introduced. This file was required in order to startup that model of Macintosh. More information about enablers (and whether or not you need one) are in various other places in this book, especially Chapter 2 (on creating an emergency startup disk, Chapter 5 (on startup problems), Chapter 12 (on enablers and System 7.5), and Fix-It #5 (on reinstalling system software).

The Finder (and the Desktop)

The Finder is the second most critical file in the System Folder. This is because the Finder creates the Macintosh *desktop*. The desktop is where you find the disk icons, the Trash, and the various windows that display the contents of all mounted disks. Actually, the words *Finder* and *desktop* are often used interchangeably. When you are in the Finder, the menu bar contains the familiar File, Edit, View, and Special menus.

BY THE WAY ▶

ICON VIEWS

You probably already know what an icon is, even if you are not familiar with the term itself. Icons are the small graphic images. Their most prevalent use is for files on the Finder's desktop.

You use the Finder's View menu to determine how files on the desktop are displayed. File icons are most easily viewed by selecting By Icon or By Small Icon from the Finder's View menu. Other views display files in a more traditional text list format. In these other views, however, you can still see icons down the leftmost column. To change the size of icons in list views, select the Views control panel (available in System 7 only), and select one of the other sizes of icon displays available for list views. However, if you use the smallest size, you will see only a bland generic icon rather than each file's custom icon.

For the discussions and figures in this book, I generally use the By Icon view.

What you need to know:

- The Finder is an essential component of system software. Except under very unusual circumstances, your Macintosh will not start up without it.

- The Finder is your main way of navigating around your disks. It is from here that you locate files, open files, copy files, and delete files. In general, you would not want to do without it, even if you could.

- The Finder is also a great problem-solving tool. Starting in the next chapter, and continuing throughout this book, I describe numerous Finder features, such as its Get Info command in the File menu, that can be used for fixing problems.

The Special Subfolders

In System 7, the System Folder depends heavily on the use of several special subfolders that now contain most of the Macintosh system software (see Figure 1-3). These folders, together with the standard files that Apple places in them, are all installed automatically when you first create the System Folder with Apple's Installer.

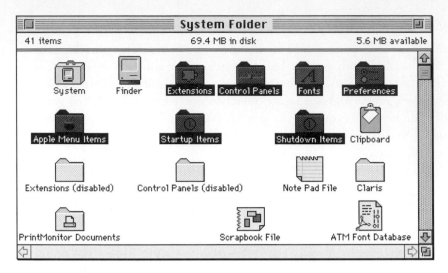

Figure 1-3 The inside of a System Folder. The highlighted folders include the special subfolders described in this chapter

System 6 Alert: In System 6, there should be no folders within the System Folder. Typically, placing a file in a subfolder of the System Folder prevents the file from working properly.

Which Item Goes Where?

One of the conveniences of System 7 is that, when you put a new item in your System Folder, you generally don't need to know which special subfolder it goes into, if any. Simply place the file destined for the System Folder *on* the System Folder icon (*not* in the System Folder window). When you see the System Folder icon highlighted, release the mouse. The Macintosh then checks if it knows where the file should go. If it does, you get a dialog box informing you of the file's intended destination and asking you to confirm that this is correct. Click OK, and you are done.

The main System Folder subfolders are named Apple Menu Items, Extensions, Control Panels, Startup Items, Shutdown Items (System 7.5 only), Preferences, and Fonts.

Apple Menu Items Folder

Any file placed in the Apple Menu Items folder appears in the Apple menu. This menu, located on the left side of the menu bar and denoted by an Apple logo, is available in almost all applications.

In System 6, this menu was reserved for a special type of file called a *desk accessory* (or *DAs*). These DAs needed to be installed directly in the System file. At one time, using DAs was the only way to have more than one program open at a time.

With System 7, while DAs still exist, the distinction between DAs and ordinary applications has blurred. In most cases, they work the same way. For example, you can now launch DAs from any location on the desktop (by double-clicking them) just as you can with an ordinary application.

Extensions Folder

The Extensions folder contains two main types of files: system extensions and Chooser extensions.

System Extensions   System extensions accomplish a variety of specialized tasks, mostly by working in the background the entire time the Macintosh is on.

SEE: • "Take Note: What's an INIT?," later in this chapter

For these type of extensions to work, they must load into memory at startup. Thus, when you first place a new system extension on your disk, it has no effect. You must restart your Macintosh before the extension can perform its function. Furthermore, during startup, the Macintosh looks for these extensions only in certain locations. The main location, of course, is the Extensions folder. However, it also checks the Control Panels folder (see below) as well as the top level of the System Folder (that is, not in any subfolder). System extensions in any other location will not load at startup and, therefore, will not work.

SEE: • Fix-It #4 for more on problems with extensions

System 6 Alert: In System 6, system extensions are usually referred to as *startup documents.*

Chooser Extensions   To understand the meaning of Chooser extensions, you first have to understand the Chooser itself. The Chooser is a desk accessory found in the Apple Menu Items folder. Its primary function, as its name implies, is to let you *choose* which printer (or networking server) you intend to use.

When you select the Chooser, a selection of icons (such as LaserWriter, ImageWriter, or AppleShare) is typically displayed on the left side of the Chooser window. Each icon represents a Chooser extension located in your Extensions folder.

The most common type of Chooser extension is called a printer driver. These files are necessary so that the Macintosh and the printer can talk to each other. Printer drivers for all of Apple's printers come with the Macintosh system software. Printers from other companies may require their own drivers.

AppleShare is a Chooser extension that has functions related to networking and file sharing (a topic I discuss more in Chapter 11). By the way, unlike most Chooser extensions, AppleShare loads into memory at startup together with system extensions.

SEE: • Chapter 7 for more on the Chooser and printing in general
• Chapters 9 and 10 for more details on the Page Setup and Print dialog boxes
• Chapter 12 on how all of this is different if you are using QuickDraw GX

The Extensions folder can also contain other types of files, technically not considered extensions, including font files and files involved in telecommunications. In System 7.5 especially, you will find an increasing amount of files in the Extensions folder that do not quite fit into either of the basic system extension or Chooser extension categories. Apple Guide documents are an example of this.

Control Panels Folder

As its name implies, the Control Panels folder holds special files called *control panels*. They are sometimes, more technically, referred to as *control panel devices,* or *cdev's*.

What do these control panels do? Many of the ones that come with the system software, such as General Controls, Mouse, and Sound, set basic preferences for the operation of the Macintosh. These include such settings as the cursor blinking rate, mouse tracking speed, and sound volume. Most remaining control panels function similarly to system extensions. That is, they perform some task(s) while working in the background, and they must be loaded into memory at startup before they can perform their task. In these cases, each control panel's window is primarily used to select among options that modify how its background activity works.

SEE: • "Take Note: What's an INIT?" later in this chapter

Several control panels that are particularly relevant to problem solving are described in more detail in the next chapter.

In System 7, control panels (as is true for DAs) open like ordinary applications. That is, you can open a control panel by double-clicking its icon, no matter where on the desktop it is located. However, you should still keep control panels in the Control Panels folder. Otherwise, control panels that function like system extensions may not load at startup. Also, for convenience, System 7 installs an alias (see the following sections for more on aliases) of the Control Panels folder and places it in the Apple Menu Items folder. This makes it easy to access control panels from the Apple menu.

System 6 Alert: In System 6, you access control panels entirely differently. A special Control Panels desk accessory is listed in the Apple Menu. To access any control panel, you must first open this DA. From here, you see a scrolling list of all control panels in the System Folder. Click the one you want to use.

Startup Items Folder

Any application or document file that you place in the Startup Items folder automatically opens as part of the startup process. Thus, if you want your word processor to be opened automatically each time you turn on your Macintosh, place the word processor file (or its alias) in this folder.

These files are distinctly different from the system extensions and control panels that load into memory at startup. Placing an item in the Startup Items folder is simply a shortcut method for getting the file to open. This folder confers no special properties on the file. Any openable file can be placed in the Startup items folder. On the other hand, system extensions, as described previously, are special types of files that must be loaded into memory at startup in order to work at all.

System 6 Alert: There is no Startup Items folder in System 6. Instead, you use a command called Set Startup, which is located in the Finder's Special menu. This is the same command you use to choose between having the Finder or MultiFinder active at startup.

Shutdown Items Folder

This feature is new in System 7.5. Complementary in function to the Startup Items folder, any applications in this folder are launched just after you select Shut Down but before the Mac actually shuts down. Personally, I don't imagine there will be much practical use for this folder (though you might like to set up some AppleScript files to run just before you shut down). Note that the Shut Down item in the Apple menu does not launch items in the Shutdown Items folder. You must select Restart or Shut Down from the Finder's Special menu.

Preferences Folder

Many programs, including the Finder, allow you to change the default settings of the program. That is, these changes are remembered even after you quit the application, and they are still in effect the next time you use it. For example, a word processor may normally open with its text ruler visible. However, you can usually select a Hide Ruler command to get rid of it. In some cases, you may even be able to set a Preferences option so that the ruler is automatically hidden from view whenever the program opens (eliminating the need to select the Hide Ruler command each time). This is a change from the default setting.

Generally, the program remembers these settings by placing the information in a special preferences file, which the program accesses whenever it is opened.

These preferences files, together with miscellaneous other accessory files, are typically located in the Preferences folder. However, preferences files can also be found at the root level of the System Folder. Occasionally, a preferences file can be located not in the System Folder at all but within the same folder as the application to which it is linked.

System 7.5 adds a dizzying array of new preferences files that work with its new system software enhancements. For example, Apple Menu Options, WindowShade, Find File, and Control Strip (to name a few) all now have matching preferences files.

Fonts Folder

The Fonts folder was a new addition in System 7.1. It is not present in version 7.0. As mentioned, fonts placed in this folder are used by applications and thus appear in Fonts menus, as if they had been placed directly in the System file in version 7.0. The folder provides a simpler and quicker alternative to having to add and delete font files from the System file.

Still More Folders

Other system software folders you may see in your System Folder include Launcher Items (used with the Launcher utility included with Performas and System 7.5) and Control Strip Modules (used by the new Control Strip utility found on PowerBooks). These, and other possible folders, will be described more later in the book, as relevant. Of course, you may also have folders, such as Claris and Aldus, that are not part of the system software at all. These are created by other applications on your disk.

The Rest of the System Folder Files

The rest of the System Folder contains items of varying degrees of significance. Some of these are part of the Macintosh system software and are installed at the same time that the System and Finder are installed. The Scrapbook File, which is used in conjunction with the Scrapbook desk accessory, is an example of this.

Is It Apple or Not Apple? You can generally tell whether a particular item in the System Folder comes from Apple by selecting Get Info from the Finder's File menu for that file. If it is part of the system software, it usually indicates this at the top of the window (where it says something like: *System Software 7.5*) and/or at the bottom next to the word *Version* (where it says that the file is copyrighted by Apple).

The remaining items in your System Folder come from other companies. They can be virtually any type of file, most commonly control panels and extensions. Some you may have directly placed there. Others were placed there by some Installer utility (similar to the Installer used by the system software) when you installed a particular piece of software. Still other files, such as some preferences files, may have been created automatically by an application the first time you launched it.

With so many possible files, if you open your System Folder now, you will almost certainly find some files that are unfamiliar to you—you have no idea what they do. For now, leave them alone. Later on in this book, especially in Chapter 2, I discuss how to decide whether you need them or not.

SEE: • Chapter 2, on using Get Info and on pruning your hard drive

Other System 7 Features

Throughout this chapter, you have seen how System 6 and System 7 handle some similar functions differently, such as installing fonts or accessing control panels. However, some entirely new functions are available in System 7 that have no comparable counterpart in System 6: These include, for example, Publish and Subscribe options, virtual memory, and new file-sharing capabilities. Most of these are either covered in more detail in later chapters or are outside the domain of this book. However, three new System 7 features are sufficiently relevant to such a variety of problem-solving situations that I describe them now: Aliases, Balloon Help, and Apple Guide.

Aliases

In the File menu of the Finder is a command called Make Alias. When you select a file (or folder) and then select this command, the Finder creates a new file that superficially looks identical to the original file. However, its name is in italics rather than plain text, and the word *alias* is attached to the end of the name (see Figure 1-4). More important, the file is as little as 1K in size. It does not contain any of the information of the original file; it is simply used as a pointer to the original file. That is, you can move this alias to anywhere else on your disk. Whenever you double-click an alias, the Macintosh locates the original file (even if it is now in a different folder) and launches it.

Minutes   *Minutes alias*

Figure 1-4
A Microsoft Word document file and its alias

Among other uses, placing a collection of aliases together in a single folder is a convenient way of having access to a variety of applications that may be scattered in a variety of different locations on your hard drive.

Of course, if you delete the original file, the alias becomes useless and double-clicking the alias does not open anything. Instead, you get an error message that says the original item could not be found. However, renaming the original file does not break the connection.

Balloon Help

In the upper right-hand corner of the menu bar, immediately to the left of the Application menu icon, is a question mark (?) icon (see Figure 1-5). This is the Guide/Balloon Help menu. To see what it does, select Show Balloons from the menu (with the Finder as the active application). Now move the cursor to various locations. You will find that balloons periodically appear, each containing a brief description of the purpose and use of the item underneath the cursor. By selecting Hide Balloons from the Balloon Help menu, you can turn this function off again.

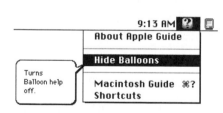

Figure 1-5
The Guide/Balloon Help menu, showing the balloon for the Hide Balloon command

Whether this feature works for applications other than the Finder depends on whether the application has been designed to support Balloon Help. Thus, Balloon Help is not available in all applications.

Apple Guide

Apple Guide is a major new feature introduced in System 7.5. It is the equivalent of Balloon Help on steroids. You access it from the Guide menu (formerly called the Balloon Help menu), where Balloon Help still remains available (see Figure 1-5). Apple Guide is an interactive help system. From a list in the main Guide window, you select the topic for which you want help (see Figure 1-6). The Guide then uses a series of HyperCard-like windows to take you step by step through the process of answering your question. In many cases, if it tells you to do something (such as "Select the Apple menu"), it further assists you by indicating on screen exactly what to do (such as by actually "circling" the Apple menu icon, as in Figure 1-7). You carry out the suggested steps while Apple Guide remains active. This is what is meant by "interactive help."

Exactly what help topics are available from Apple Guide depends on where you are. If you are in the Finder, the Guide menu will list Macintosh Guide as a selection. This is Apple's general help Guide (included as part of System 7.5). It provides information that supplements what is found in the System 7.5 printed documentation, offering advice on how to do most basic tasks on the Mac as well as a selection of troubleshooting help (see Figure 1-6 again).

Similar to Balloon Help, application developers can write Apple Guide documents specific to their application. If so, these Guides will only be listed in the Guide menu when the relevant application is active.

Overall, Apple Guide is better than any other help system I have seen. Try it out!

SEE: • **Chapter 12 for more information on Apple Guide, especially what to do if you cannot get Apple Guide to work**

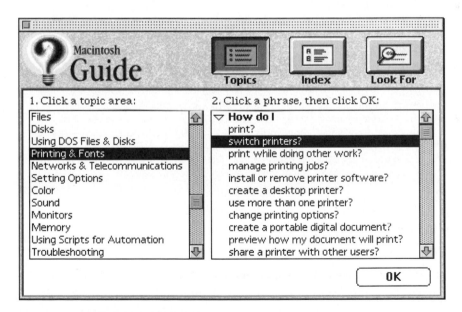

Figure 1-6   An Apple Guide window

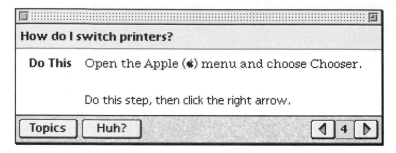

Figure 1-7 Apple Guide in action

TAKE NOTE ▶

APPLICATIONS AND DOCUMENTS

In addition to the software categories already described in this chapter, there are two other major types of files: applications and documents. Typically, applications are the programs that are used to create documents. For example, ClarisWorks is an application, while a letter that you create with ClarisWorks is called a ClarisWorks document.

This distinction can get blurry around the edges. For example, some applications never create documents (such as a utility application that is used just to check whether a disk is damaged or not). Further, many applications use accessory files (such as translator files and plug-in modules) that are a special type of document file, even though they are not created by the application. Finally, with the coming of a new technology called OpenDoc (due in 1995), this whole application-centered approach may change. The document will become the focus, as a document may contain "parts" that belong to several different applications.

Chapter Summary

This chapter gave an overview of the basic elements of Macintosh hardware. It also introduced the major components of system software, unraveling the mysteries of what is found in the System Folder. Finally, it described the types and functions of the other major categories of software: applications and documents.

It explained what each of these components do and how they work together to produce the final result that you see on your screen or printed page. A special emphasis was given to how all of this relates to problem-solving issues.

This background should be all you need to know to get started using the subsequent chapters of this book.

Chapter 2

Be Prepared: Preventing Problems

Tooling Up

For hardware repairs, you can't do much without the proper tools. It doesn't matter whether the hardware is a computer, a television, a refrigerator, or a car. You need screwdrivers, pliers, and more. The same is true for software repairs on the Macintosh—except that in this case, your main tools are electronic rather than metal. In either case, you need to gather the relevant tools and become familiar with how to use them.

Being prepared to solve problems also means trying to avoid the problem in the first place: preventative maintenance. Regularly changing the oil filter in your car can prevent the problems caused by using dirty oil. Once again, the same logic is true for computers.

That's what this chapter is all about: troubleshooting tools and preventative maintenance.

Damage Control

I talk about many different types of problems in this book, but certain themes keep recurring. For example, I make frequent references to terms such as damaged disks, corrupted files, software bugs, and software conflicts.

If these terms are not familiar to you, it can all seem a bit confusing. What exactly gets damaged? How does this damage even occur? Where do bugs come from? Here are the answers.

Damaged Files and Disks

A *damaged* (or *corrupted*) *file* means that the data contained in the file have, at least partially, been lost or incorrectly altered. The result is that the Macintosh can no longer correctly "understand" the file. This usually means that the file either will not open at all or will not function properly if it does open. In some cases, trying to use such a file may result in the Mac abruptly coming to a halt—an event typically referred to as a *system crash.*

Certain special invisible files on your disk are responsible for informing the Macintosh computer about everything else that is on a disk and how it is organized. If these files get damaged, it is often referred to as a *damaged disk.* A variety of symptoms are possible. In the worst cases, the Mac may react as if the entire disk is unreadable. If the disk is your startup disk, you may not be able to start up.

In most cases, damage to files and disks is essentially *software damage.* No physical damage to the disk itself has occurred. A reasonable analogy is a videotape of a movie that somehow had a few seconds of the film erased. The videotape machine is still fine. The actual videotape is still fine. But the movie is not fine. When you view it, the erased scene is missing. However, with computers, damaged files (the equivalent of an erased scene) can have effects beyond the "missing scene" itself. Also, in some cases, special software can be used to "fix" damaged files. At this point, our videotape analogy breaks down a bit.

Software damage can occur if a file is being saved, or even accessed, at the time of some unexpected interruption, such as a power failure or a system crash. The result is that the file is saved incorrectly. The wrong data are written to the file. Software damage can also occur because of seemingly random and unpredictable changes, of various causes, that happen over the lifetime of a disk. For example, the stored information is vulnerable to almost any sort of electromagnetic interference, and even a minor alteration can have serious consequences.

A related type of problem is referred to as *media damage* (often considered synonymous to *bad blocks*). Here, the cause of the problem is a defect in the physical disk media. For example, if a part of the surface of the disk gets marred, any file that occupies that area would be damaged. Although it is true that the file itself is damaged, the actual cause of the problem is with the disk. It takes only the smallest amount of damage to cause total loss of access to a file. Like software damage, media damage can also result in system crashes and disk crashes.

A scratch in or a flaking off of the magnetic surface of the disk are common causes of media damage. Damage may be present from the first time you use a disk, or it may occur over time. A specific event, such as an accidental bumping of the drive while it is in use, may damage the drive media. More often, particularly with floppy disks, defects occur because of no discernible cause, simply as a consequence of normal use of the disk or the disk aging.

Returning to the videotape analogy, imagine a scene in a movie suddenly appearing blurry or distorted because the tape had been stretched or crumpled in that area. The movie scene is probably irrecoverably damaged, and you can no longer use that section of the tape for future recordings (you may choose to splice it out). If the damage is severe enough, you may even have to discard the tape altogether. Still, you do not need to bring the recorder itself in for repairs. In this respect, tape damage is clearly distinct from damage to the mechanical or electronic components of the recorder.

Similarly, media damage, while technically a hardware problem, is separate from damage to the mechanisms of the disk drive itself. As with videotape damage, media damage problems can usually be resolved without requiring a trip to the repair shop. Only software tools are needed. However, media damage to a fixed hard drive, if the software techniques fail to work, will require repair or replacement of the entire drive.

Finally, a damaged disk may in fact be due to "true" *hardware damage* to some component of the disk drive. This will almost certainly require repair or replacement of the drive.

SEE: • Chapter 8 for more on invisible files
      • Fix-Its #13 and #14 for more on file and disk damage

Software Bugs and Conflicts

A software bug is simply an error made by the programmer when the program was written. Thus, it is caused by the people who created the program, not by you. There is no way that you can repair a bug yourself. The only permanent solution is to get a new version of the software, when available, that has fixed the problem. In the meantime, you may find some acceptable work-around solutions.

Bugs vary in their level of seriousness. Less serious bugs may have only a cosmetic effect on the display and can often be ignored (though caution is advised even here, as these bugs may be harbingers of serious problems). More serious bugs may entirely prevent you from using the program.

A software conflict is a special case of a software bug. Typically, what happens is that one program is written in a way that fails to take into account something that another program may do. If both of these programs are in use at the same time, they conflict with each other. A common result of such a conflict is a system crash. A conflict may also occur between a software program and a hardware component (such as a particular monitor). That is, some programs may not work when certain hardware is in use.

If all software was written perfectly, none of these bugs or conflicts would occur. Since this is admittedly very difficult if not impossible to do, bugs and conflicts do occur—all too frequently.

A Troubleshooter's Toolkit

In days of yore, solving computer problems would have required that you be a programmer and develop your own problem-solving tools. Thankfully, these days, the tools have already been designed for you. You simply need to acquire them. Many of them are free. A few require a relatively inexpensive purchase. These tools cannot solve every problem. But there are many problems you can solve without them.

The problem-solving tools (or *utilities*) described here are designed for nonexpert users who have little or no technical skills. Some of the utilities are so easy to use that they practically run themselves. Others may take a bit more effort to learn.

TAKE NOTE ▶

WHAT'S A UTILITY?

Most applications that you use probably fall in the productivity category. That is, their purpose is to allow you to do something on the computer faster, easier, and better than you could do it without the computer. Word processors, spreadsheets, and the like are typical examples.

However, some programs exist only to accomplish tasks that you would never need to do if you did not use a computer. These programs are called utilities. For example, you can get

---

utilities to help you back up your software (that is, to make a second copy that you keep in the event something goes wrong with the first copy). Unless you used a computer, you would obviously have no reason to make backups of computer disks.

Hundreds of utilities are available, to assist in almost every imaginable task, from backing up files, to undeleting files, to recovering damaged files. Some are designed to make your computer life easier. Others are designed to help solve problems. I describe many of them in this chapter.

Many beginning users balk at using these utilities. They feel that utilities are primarily for power users who have the time and interest to learn how to master them. This is not true. Every user, regardless of skill level, can learn how to use—and benefit from using—the utilities described in this chapter

Table 2-1 gives a summary of useful troubleshooting tools. It is not complete; other utilities will be mentioned throughout the book.

Make sure that your Toolkit includes at least one example of each of the following categories: data repair and recovery package, anti-virus utility, back-up utility, disk formatting utility, extension manager, and a SCSI control panel (such as SCCIProbe). A diagnostic utility, while not as essential, is desirable (use MacCheck, available for free, if you don't want to make a separate purchase).

You don't need the other utilities right away. Some you may never need. But the time to start stocking your Toolkit is now.

Table 2-1   A Catalog of Troubleshooting Utilities*

NAME(S)	USE IT TO	FOR MORE INFORMATION, SEE
Macintosh System Software		
Balloon Help and Apple Guide	Interactive help for problem solving	Chapter 1, p. 26, Chapter 12, pp. 542, 553–554
Functions built into System file and ROM and more	Rebuild desktop, zap parameter RAM, reset Power Manager (on PowerBooks),	Chapter 11, pp. 482–483, Fix-It #9, pp. 701–711, Fix-It #11, pp. 724–729
Finder	Determine pertinent information about files (such as version number), locate files, copy files, delete files, set memory allocations for files, erase floppy disks, restart, shut down, and more	This chapter, pp. 38–50, Chapter 4, pp. 109–111 Chapter 5, pp. 174–176, 189–191, Chapter 6, pp. 206–208, Fix-It #6, p. 654, Fix-It #15, pp. 770–776
Installer	Do a clean reinstall of system software	Fix-It #5, pp. 633–638
Memory control panel	Access disk cache, virtual memory, 32-bit addressing, and RAM disk settings	Fix-It #6, pp. 667–668
Startup Disk control panel	Select which disk is to be the startup disk, if more than one potential startup disk is available	Chapter 5, pp. 132–134

* Also check out Chapter 12 for more information on additions and changes specific to Power Macs and to System 7.5.

Table 2-1 A Catalog of Troubleshooting Utilities *(continued)*

NAME(S)	USE IT TO	FOR MORE INFORMATION, SEE
Monitors control panel	Adjust the depth of the display, that is, how many colors or grays are displayed	Chapter 10, pp. 416–417
General Controls control panel	Newly revised in System 7.5, it adds features for automatic locking of application and System Folder files, hiding the Finder when in the background, and more	Chapter 6, pp. 210, 214, Chapter 12, p. 540
Chooser desk accessory	Turn on AppleTalk, select printer, access AppleShare, and related functions	Chapter 7, pp. 270–277
MacCheck	Check on potential hardware and software related problems	This chapter, p. 73, Fix-It #10
Disk First Aid	Check for and possibly repair damaged disks	This chapter, p. 73, Fix-It #10
Apple HD SC Setup	Update disk driver, check for media damage, reformat disk	Fix-It #12, Fix-It #15, p. 777
Extension Manager	Manage extensions (that is, which ones are on or off at startup)	Fix-It #4, pp. 611–613
Disk Copy	Create exact copies of floppy disks (also needed to convert disk image files to a usable floppy disk format)	This chapter, p. 53, Chapter 6, p. 220, Fix-It #5, pp. 646–647, Fix-It #15, p. 772
LaserWriter Utility	Check on and/or adjust the status of a LaserWriter, download fonts, and more	Chapter 7, pp. 270–271, Chapter 9, pp. 365–366
PowerBook control panel and Control Strip	Access settings that affect battery conservation and related PowerBook-specific features	Chapter 11, pp. 464–471
Macintosh Easy Open and PC Exchange	Helps in opening files that otherwise could not be open, especially PC formatted files (included with System 7.5)	Chapter 6, pp. 229–230, 235–237, Fix-It #15, p. 775
Font/DA Mover	Move fonts and desk accessories between suitcases and the System file (only really needed for System 6 users)	Chapter 9, pp. 353–354

Data Protection, Repair, and Recovery Packages

NAME(S)	USE IT TO	FOR MORE INFORMATION, SEE
Norton Utilities for Macintosh, or MacTools	Check for and repair damaged files and disks; other functions include undelete files, optimize disks, backup files, and exactly copy floppy disks; MacTools only: virus protection	This chapter, pp. 36, 63–72, Chapter 6, pp. 213–216, Chapter 8, pp. 323–324, 335–341, Fix-It #8, Fix-It #13, Fix-It #14

Antivirus Utilities

NAME(S)	USE IT TO	FOR MORE INFORMATION, SEE
SAM, Virex, Disinfectant, or MacTools' Anti-Virus	Detect and eradicate viruses	This chapter, p. 63, Fix-It #7

Table 2-1   A Catalog of Troubleshooting Utilities *(continued)*

NAME(S)	USE IT TO	FOR MORE INFORMATION, SEE
General System Enhancement Packages		
Now Utilities or ALLRight Utilities	Manage extensions, assist in locating and launching files (plus several other functions)	This chapter, p. 37, Chapter 6, pp. 210, 230–231, Fix-It #4, pp. 611–614
Extension Managers		
Conflict Catcher II, INIT-Picker, Now Utilities, or ALLRight Utilities	Manage extensions (these have more features than Apple's Extension Manager)	Fix-It #4, pp. 611–614
Diagnostic Utilities		
Apple Personal Diagnostics	Check the functioning of your hardware and software (combines and enhances the functions of MacCheck and Disk First Aid)	This chapter, p. 70, Fix-It #17, p. 805
MacEKG or Peace of Mind	Determine whether your hardware components are functioning properly (much more extensive than MacCheck)	Fix-It #17, p. 805
Help!	Determine whether there are any known software conflicts, bugs, or related incompatibilities	Fix-It #5, pp. 632–633, Fix-It #18, p. 824
Backup Utilities		
Retrospect, Redux, DiskFit Pro, Norton Utilities, or MacTools	Back up the data on a hard disk	This chapter, pp. 57–59
Disk Format Utilities		
Drive7, Hard Disk ToolKit, Silverlining (or whatever custom utility came with your hard drive)	Update disk driver, check for media damage, reformat disk, partition disk (use instead of Apple HD Setup for non-Apple drives)	Fix-It #12, Fix-It #15, pp. 776–784
Miscellaneous Other Utilities		
CanOpener	Recover text and graphics from damaged and unopenable files	Fix-It #14, pp. 760–761
Disk Express II	Optimize disks in background	Fix-It #8, p. 695
SCSIProbe control panel	Conveniently lists and mounts SCSI devices	Chapter 5, pp. 164–166, Fix-It #16, pp. 788–795
Last Resort, Thunder 7's GhostWriter, Now Utilities' NowSave	Recover text unsaved at the time of a system crash	This chapter, pp. 70–71, Chapter 4, p. 107
Crash Barrier, Bomb Shelter, or System Error Patch	Possibly recover from a system crash without having to restart	This chapter, pp. 70–71, Chapter 4, pp. 97–98
TechTool	Rebuild desktop and zap Parameter RAM (it's better than using Apple's methods)	Fix-It #9, pp. 709–710, Fix-It #11, p. 728

Toolkit Essentials

System Software

All it takes is a glance at Table 2-1 to discover that system software is the single biggest collection of troubleshooting tools at your disposal. And with System 7.5, Apple gives you more than ever before. All of which is great news to the cost-conscious, because everyone gets system software free when they purchase their Macintosh (though you will have to pay to upgrade to any later versions).

Data Recovery Package

The system software, as wonderful as it is, is not enough. By far the next most important item on your list of acquisitions should be a data protection, repair, and recovery package. Consider one of these packages essential. These packages are a collection of several separate utilities that all share a common goal of preventing or fixing problems. At the moment, you have two main choices here: Norton Utilities for Macintosh (see Figure 2-1) and MacTools Pro. Which one of these should you get? The answer depends on whom you ask, exactly what problem you have, and which package just came out with its latest upgrade. You won't go far wrong with either of them. If your finances permit, I would actually recommend getting both of these packages. It is often the case that one of these packages can detect or fix a problem that another one cannot (even though no program consistently outperforms the other). In any case, I describe more on the use of these packages later in this chapter and in several other locations in this book, especially Chapter 8, Fix-It #13, and Fix-It #14.

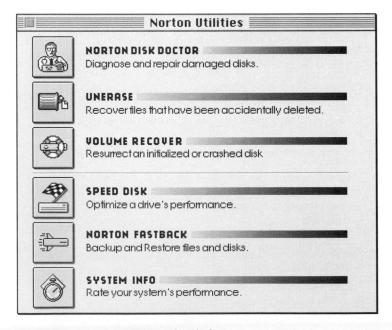

Figure 2-1 Norton Utilities main window

System Enhancement Package

Next up, I would strongly recommend getting a system enhancement package. My current favorite is Now Utilities (recently upgraded to version 5.0). Now Utilities is a kitchen-sink collection of programs that assist in troubleshooting as well as just make using your Mac more pleasant. It features programs that help locate and launch applications (Now Menus, SuperBoomerang), a startup management utility (Startup Manager), a utility that can recover text that had not been saved at the time of a system crash (Now Save) and more. In the past, you would have had to buy several single-purpose programs, costing a total of far more money, to even try to duplicate the features of Now Utilities.

Packages like Now Utilities face some new competition from Apple's System 7.5, which includes several of the features that previously led people to purchase these packages (for example, System 7.5 includes key features of NowMenus). However, I expect Now Utilities to stay ahead of the curve and remain a worthwhile investment.

System enhancement programs also describes a variety of programs, such as screen savers, not directly relevant to troubleshooting and thus not mentioned much in this book.

The Best of the Rest

Yes, you should have backup utility software (such as Retrospect or Redux) and an anti-virus program (such as SAM, Virex, or Disinfectant). But be aware that a data-recovery package may already include these features (MacTools does!). You may also want a separate disk formatting utility, such as Drive7 or Hard Disk ToolKit, though some sort of disk formatting utility certainly came with your hard drive.

Similarly, don't forget that system software already includes utilities that compete with many of these third-party single-purpose products. For example, your system software includes Apple HD SC setup, Extension Manager, MacCheck, Disk First Aid, and (for Performas) a back-up utility. However, third-party single-purpose utilities often include features and conveniences not available with either the system software or the general packages, so don't automatically rule them out.

Also consider shareware and freeware programs (such as SCSIProbe and TechTool), some of which do things unmatched by any commercial software. Apple makes a freeware utility called ResEdit. Though it was designed primarily for programmers, it can sometimes be useful as a more general troubleshooting tool. I don't go into details of its use in this book (preferring instead to focus on more end-user oriented tools). However, recognizing that some readers are already familiar with this utility, I do occasionally refer to it.

See Table 2-1 for other recommendations. Details on how to get any of the products mentioned are described in the Appendix.

Troubleshooting with the Finder

As indicated in Table 2-1, the majority of system software troubleshooting-related files are described in more detail in the other parts of this book. However, because of how often its features are referenced in the pages ahead, I have decided to describe the basic troubleshooting features of the Finder right now. Here goes.

Get Info

When in the Finder, select any file on your disk (that is, click its icon once). Then select the Get Info command from the File menu (or type its keyboard shortcut: Command-I). This brings up a window for that file called, appropriately enough, the Get Info window (see Figure 2-2). It is filled with important information.

You can also view some of the same information available from the Get Info window directly in the Finder's folder windows, if you select a non-icon view (such as By Name) from the Finder's View menu.

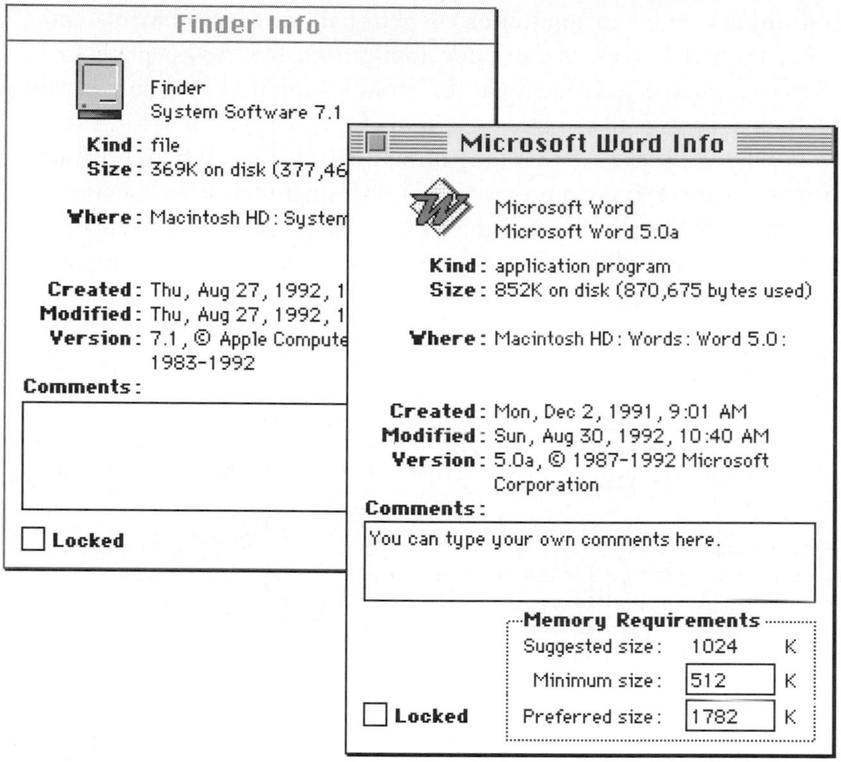

Figure 2-2 Two examples of Get Info windows

The first part of the Get Info window displays the name of the file and its icon. If the file selected is part of Macintosh system software, such as the Finder, the name should also include the version of the system software to which the file belongs (such as *System Software 7.5*).

The next line in the Get Info window is called Kind. Most commonly, it says either *application program* or *document.* If it is a document, and the Finder recognizes it as belonging to a particular application, it probably says so (such as *Microsoft Word document*). If you don't know what application created a particular document, this can be a quick way to find out. (Alternatively, turning on Balloon Help and moving the cursor over the document file's icon on the desktop also tells you the name of the creating application.)

For system software, all sorts of additional Kind names are possible, such as *desk accessory, control panel,* or *system extension.* The System file itself is listed as a *suitcase* in System 7.

The Size and Where lines refer to how much disk space the file occupies and where on the disk the file is located.

The Created and Modified lines tell you when the file was first created and the last time that it was modified (that is, changed in any way). Every time you save a document, its modification date changes. Sometimes, even applications get modified.

Thus, the modification date for an application on your hard drive may be different from the date on your backup copy of that same application. This may be just fine and normal. However, unexpected changes in the modification date may be a warning sign of trouble, such as damage to the file.

The Version number is usually relevant only for applications and system software. It identifies the particular version of a program. This information can be essential when you are trying to determine incompatibilities. For example, suppose you are told that version 2.0 of BusyWorks (a fictitious application I use in some examples) is incompatible with System 7. Here is where you can find out if you are using the problematic version 2.0.

BY THE WAY ▶

FINDING THE VERSION NUMBER

Sometimes, the programmers forget to include the version information in the Get Info window. In that case, if you need to know the version, you should be able to find it by launching the application and then selecting About <name of program> from the top of the Apple menu. The window that then appears usually indicates the version number.

The Comments box may contain any text, including whatever you care to type there. Most often, it is empty.

The Locked check box is used to lock the file. This simply prevents the file from being deleted when you place it in the Trash and select Empty Trash. You can still delete a locked file either by first unlocking it (by unchecking the check box) or by holding down the Option key when you attempt to empty the Trash that contains the locked file.

TAKE NOTE ▶

LOCKING FLOPPY DISKS

On floppy disks, you can lock the entire disk, which prevents you from adding, deleting, or even modifying any and all files on the disk. Even holding down the Option key while you select Empty Trash does not allow you to delete a file from a locked disk. The only way to delete a file from a locked disk is to unlock it first.

To lock a floppy disk, slide up the tab, located in the upper right-hand corner (as the front of the disk faces you) of the disk, so that you can see through the hole. Sliding it back down unlocks it again.

SEE: • **Chapter 6 for more on deleting locked files**

For an application, the lower right-hand corner of its Get Info window has an area called *Memory Requirements* (refer to Figure 2-2 or 2-3).

It includes three numbers: Suggested size, Minimum size, and Preferred size. These numbers refer to the amount of memory (RAM) that the program occupies when it is opened.

The default values of all three numbers are initially set by the application itself. The Suggested size can never be altered. This is the recommended amount of memory needed to run the program under normal conditions.

The user can alter the remaining two values simply by typing a new number in the appropriate box. You can increase or decrease these values at any time, as long as the application itself is not currently open. If it is open, just quit the application and then make the change.

The Minimum size is the minimum amount of memory the program must be able to access in order to open. This number can be set to less than the Suggested size (helpful for those times when memory is tight), but I would generally avoid doing this. If you do, some of the program's features may not work, or serious problems (such as system crashes) may develop. If the program's default Minimum size is already set lower than the Suggested size, certainly don't set the Minimum size any lower.

You can set the Preferred size for considerably more than the Suggested size. Whenever a program opens, it uses its Preferred memory size, if that much free memory is available. This can be helpful for those applications, such as graphics and multimedia programs, that generally run faster or can work with larger documents when they have additional memory available.

If, when you open an application, the available free memory is less than the application's Preferred size (as might happen, for example, if other applications are already open), the application uses whatever free memory still remains. However, if the free memory is less than the Minimum size, the program does not open at all. Once an application launches, its memory allocation cannot change until the next time you use it, even if more memory frees up while you are running the application.

Thus, on a given launch, the amount of memory occupied by an application can vary anywhere between the Minimum and the Preferred size, depending on the available memory at the time you launch the application. If you don't like this degree of uncertainty, you can guarantee that the program always uses the same amount of memory by setting the Minimum size and Preferred size to the same number. Otherwise, to find out exactly how much memory an open application is using, you have to check in the About This Macintosh window (as described in the next section).

In most cases, you will probably do just fine if you leave the memory values the way they were initially set by the program's publisher. However, some adjustments may occasionally be required. For example, an application's memory allocation includes the amount available to the application plus all its open documents. For some programs, you may need to increase the Preferred size in order to be able to open several documents at once or to open a single large, complex document.

On the other hand, if you plan to have several applications open at the same time, you may want to use a smaller value for any one application's Preferred size. Doing so increases the amount of memory left over for the other applications to use. Of course, the greater the amount of memory hardware inside your machine, the more leeway you have in making these adjustments. Deciding on the best settings may take some experimentation.

Overall, knowing how to work with these settings is an important technique for solving numerous memory-related problems.

SEE: • Chapter 6 and Fix-It #6 for more on memory management

In System 7.0, this memory area of the Get Info window is designed a bit differently than in System 7.1/7.5. The area is simply called *Memory* and there are only two settings: Suggested size and Current size (see Figure 2.3). Often, the default values of these two numbers are identical. The Suggested size works the same as in System 7.1/7.5. The Current size is how much memory the program actually occupies when you launch it. To shift from a minimum to a preferred maximum value (or anywhere in between), you must change the Current size as desired. System 7.1/7.5 provides greater flexibility by essentially splitting the Current size setting into two separate settings: Minimum and Preferred.

```
┌···Memory Requirements ···········           ┌···Memory ···········
  Suggested size:   1024    K                  Suggested size: 1,024  K
  Minimum size:    [512    ] K                  Current size:  [1782 ] K
  Preferred size:  [1782   ] K                └··········································
└·····················································
```

Figure 2-3   From Microsoft Word 5.0's Get Info windows: the Memory Requirements box in System 7.1/7.5 and the Memory box in System 7.0

System 6 Alert: In System 6, Application size is the term used to describe Current size. Otherwise, it works identically to System 7.0.

Power Macintosh Alert: If you have a Power Macintosh, you may also see a note at the bottom of the screen concerning virtual memory. The significance of this is explained in Chapter 12 and Fix-It #6.

You may find other items in a Get Info window. For example, if the file is an alias, a button called *Find Original* locates the original file that the alias represents. If the file is a document, you are likely to see a check box for *Stationery pad*. If checked, this means that, if you launch the file from the Finder, it opens to an untitled copy of the file, rather than the original file itself. However, this System 7 feature does not work with all applications. If it doesn't work, it will open a document in its ordinary format.

About This Macintosh . . .

If the Finder is the active application, the first item in the Apple menu is *About This Macintosh* (see Figure 2-4). Select this item, and a new window opens. From this window, you can learn the name of the Macintosh model you are using (in case you didn't already know it). It is still another location where you can get the exact version number of the system software you are using.

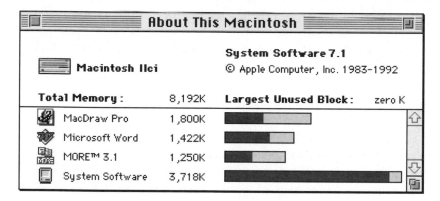

Figure 2-4 The About This Macintosh window shows the amount of memory allocated to all open programs

More important, it tells you the settings for Total Memory and Largest Unused Block. The Total Memory is equivalent to the amount of RAM you have installed in your computer.

The Largest Unused Block is essentially how much of that RAM is currently not in use and therefore available for use by other applications. However, sometimes the Largest Unused Block size may be less than the total amount of unused memory (as explained in Fix-It #6).

The remainder of this window contains a series of bar graphs that indicate the memory usage of every currently open application plus the system software. The number after each file name is the memory allocation for that file. In System 7.1, this value can range from the application's Minimum size to Preferred size, as listed in the Memory Requirements area of the application's Get Info window. For example, in Figures 2-3 and 2-4, the memory allocation for Microsoft Word is 1422K, larger than its minimum size (512K) and smaller than its Preferred size (1782K). This is because Word was the last of all the programs listed to be opened and this was all the memory left at that time. If 1782K or more of memory were available, Word would have used the full 1782K. In System 7.0, the situation is simpler. The memory allocation is always equal to the Current size for that application, as set in its Get Info window.

The last line is always for the system software. It lists the combined amount of memory currently used by the System file, the Finder, and various other system software (as well as third-party extensions and control panels). Its size varies depending on what system software version you are using, how many extensions and control panels you have installed, and (in System 6) what desk accessories you have open. It is in a state of constant flux.

By the way, in Figure 2-4, since the size of the Largest Unused Block is zero, this implies that the sum of the memory allocation of the four items listed should be approximately equal to the Total Memory value of 8192K. The actual sum is 8190K.

The bar graphs also indicate how the memory is currently allocated within each application. The total length of the bar (light- and dark-shaded areas combined) represents the total amount of memory assigned to that application (that is, it is the graphical equivalent of the number to the left of the bar). The dark-shaded portion of the bar represents how much of that memory is currently in use by the application.

For example, every time you open an additional document within an application, you use more of the memory allocation for that application. This means the light area of the bar graph gets smaller.

When the light-shaded portion of the bar gets very small, you are approaching the memory limits of the program. At this time, you may be unable to open any more documents (without first closing other currently open ones). Further attempts to tax the application's use of memory in this (or any other) way result in *out of memory* alert messages.

Also, be aware that even if a program is not using most of its assigned memory at the moment, that memory cannot be used by any other program. It sits there waiting for the program to use it, until you quit the application.

If you want to know precisely how much the shaded and unshaded areas of each bar represent, select Show Balloons from the Balloon Help menu and then move the cursor over a bar. A balloon appears that gives you the size of the darker-shaded area (see Figure 2-5).

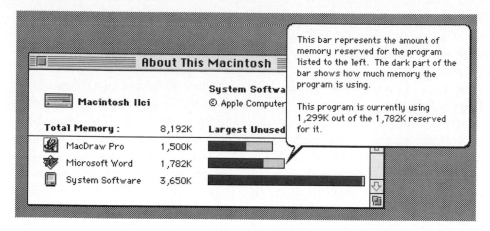

Figure 2-5   Using Show Balloons to find out how much memory each program is using

System 6 Alert: In System 6, the name in the Apple menu is called About the Finder and the display is somewhat different. In particular, the System and the Finder are listed as separate items, rather than as a single system software line.

Window Headers

Underneath the title of each window in the Finder is a line that lists three items: the number of *items* in the window, the amount of space currently occupied *in disk,* and the amount of disk space currently *available* (see Figure 2-6). The number of items listed varies depending on how many items are in the selected folder. The other numbers refer to the entire disk and are the same no matter what folder is selected. The last two items, if added together, should yield the total size capacity of the disk. Thus, if you are using an 80Mb hard drive, adding these two numbers together should come close to 80 (though it may be a few megabytes less or more). This information is useful, for example, when you are trying to determine whether you have sufficient space available for an operation that you are attempting, such as copying files to the disk.

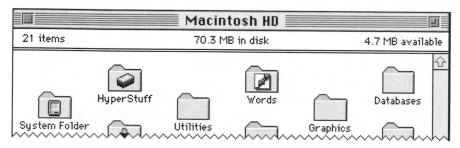

Figure 2-6   The top of a window, showing the window header information just below the title

This header information is initially missing when you are using a non-icon view. However, in System 7, you can still get this information to appear, even in these non-icon views, by selecting the Show Disk Info in Header option from the Views control panel.

By the way, hidden within the window title is a feature useful to locate where on the disk you are and quickly navigate to a related location. To access it, hold down the Command key when you click the name of the window in the header. This brings up a pop-up menu showing the hierarchy of folders starting from the current folder and working backward to the root level (see Figure 2-7). Selecting any folder immediately takes you there. (Also aiding in your navigation and preventing screen clutter, if you hold down the option key when opening a folder, the window that contains the folder will close as the new one opens.)

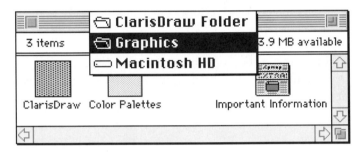

Figure 2-7 The pop-up menu that appears when you click a window title while holding down the Command key

The Find Command

The Find command is available from the Finder's File menu. It is an essential tool for finding a file that you cannot otherwise locate or to check if a certain file even exists on your disk.

The nature of the Find command varies depending on the version of the system software you are using. The following is an overview of each version.

SEE: • Chapter 6, "When You Can't Locate a File," for a step-by-step example of using each of the two different System 7 Find functions

• System 7.0/7.1
  You select Find (Command-F) from the Finder's File menu. This brings up the window shown in the top of Figure 2-8. Simply type the name of the file you are searching for and click the Find button. Remember, you do not have to type the entire name; just type any portion of the name (such as BusyW for Busy Works) and it will eventually find all files that contain that portion.

  When it finds its first matching file (or folder), it opens the window containing that file and the file itself is highlighted. If this is not the file you want, select Find Again (Command-G). It will continue to search for matching files, displaying each in turn, until all have been found.

For more extensive search criteria, select the More Choices button. This opens the window shown in the bottom of Figure 2-8. From here you can search on criteria other than name (such as date created, kind, and size) as well as specifying more specific limits on a criteria (such as name starts with, name ends with, or name contains). You can also limit the search to specified volumes. If you select the *all at once* button, you get a listing of all searched files with the ones that match the criteria highlighted.

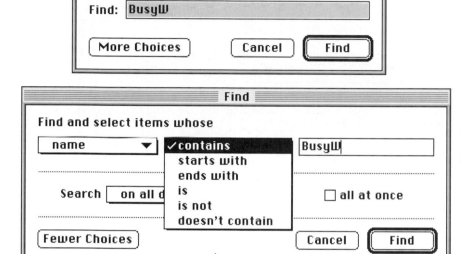

Figure 2-8 Two views of the Finder's Find window, accessed by selecting Find from the File menu

- System 7.5

  An expanded Find capability is included with System 7.5. It is a desk accessory called Find File (based on a freeware utility called FindPro), available from the Apple menu. However, if you have the Find File Extension installed in the Extensions Folder, selecting Find (command-F) from the Finder's File menu will also bring up this desk accessory. Otherwise, selecting Find brings up the same window as in System 7.0/7.1. Actually, even with this extension installed, you can still get the old Find function by holding down the Shift key when you select Find or Find Again.

  The new Find File accessory is somewhat similar to the More Choices view of the previous version. But behind this similarity are significant new features (see Figure 2-9). First, it has two important new search criteria: File Type and Creator (the meaning of these criteria is explained more in Chapter 8 and an example of using them is described in Fix-It #2). Second, the function of the More Choices button has changed. It now opens up additional selection criteria rows, allowing you to search on multiple criteria at one time (such as all files less than 128K that were last modified after December 31, 1993). You can have as many as eight rows.

A more dramatic change is that, after you select Find, the search results are displayed in a Find File Results window (no more need for Find Again!) (see Figure 2-10). The top part of this window lists every file and folder that matches the selected criteria. Double-click on any given listing and it will launch the file or open the folder. With System 7.5's drag-and-drop, you can even directly drag the name from the Results window to any location on your disk (such as the Desktop or the Trash) and the file will be immediately moved there. The bottom of the Results window lists the hierarchical location of the currently selected file. Again, double-clicking any folder directly opens that folder. Personally, the advantages of the Results window have sold me on using this new Find File over the previous version.

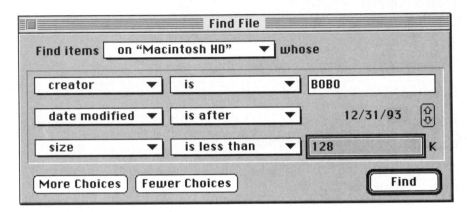

Figure 2-9   The Find File desk accessory in System 7.5

Name	Size	Kind	Last Modified	
Repair Items	4K	ClarisWorks document	8/15/94	1:03 PM
Sad Macs Figs. II-d	90K	ClarisWorks document	7/9/94	4:06 PM
Ted's Post-Its	12K	ClarisWorks document	8/10/94	10:14 AM
Thank You Card	21K	ClarisWorks document	6/5/94	5:23 PM
Thank You Card/inside	3K	ClarisWorks document	6/12/94	10:38 AM
Thank you Notes 2	13K	ClarisWorks document	6/25/94	2:58 PM

Desktop Folder
 Sad Macs 2nd
  Misc. Stuff
   Sad Macs Figs. II-d

Found 22 Items

Figure 2-10   The Find File Results window

System 6 Alert: In System 6, the Finder does not include a Find command. Instead, there is a Find File desk accessory, only available in the Apple menu. It is a much simplified variation of the System 7.5 Find File desk accessory.

BY THE WAY ▶

HIDDEN SEARCH OPTIONS IN FIND FILE

Hold down the Option key while accessing the Name pop-up menu. If you do, you will get four additional attributes that you can select as search criteria: name/icon lock (searches for locked files and icons); custom icon (searches for files that have a custom icon); visibility (can search for invisible files); and contents (searches for text within a file, up to 30 characters).

The Erase Disk and Empty Trash Commands

The Erase Disk and Empty Trash commands are found in the Finder's Special menu. The Erase Disk command is primarily used to reformat floppy disks. That is, the entire disk is erased and recreated as if you had started with an unformatted disk.

The Empty Trash command deletes only the files currently in the Trash. Thus, it is more selective than Erase Disk. To place a file in the Trash, you drag the file's icon to the Trash icon until the Trash icon is highlighted. Then release the mouse button. The Trash can icon bulges to show that it contains file(s).

In System 7, the Trash is never actually emptied until you select Empty Trash. In System 6, there is the same Empty Trash command. However, the Trash also gets emptied automatically after various actions, such as when you select Shut Down or when a floppy disk is ejected.

In either case, until the Trash is emptied, you can remove files from the Trash. Just double-click the Trash icon to open up its window and drag the file out again.

SEE: • "Protect Against Accidentally Deleted Files" later in this chapter
• Fix-It #15 for more on erasing disks

The Restart and Shut Down Commands

Under most circumstances, do *not* use the on/off switch in the back of your machine to turn off or restart your Macintosh. Use the Restart or Shut Down command instead.

Restart essentially turns off your machine momentarily and then immediately restarts it again. This may be useful, for example, when you add system extensions to your System Folder. These extensions require that the Macintosh be restarted before they can work.

Shut Down turns your machine off—period. In most Macintoshes, the Shut Down command completely shuts off the machine. No further action is necessary. However, in certain Macintosh models, selecting Shut Down results in a message that says *It is now safe to turn off your Macintosh.* You then have to turn off your machine by using the on/off switch.

These commands do some final cleanup, updating, and proper closing of files before turning off your machine. Using the on/off switch without first selecting Shut Down bypasses these actions and may result in the loss of data and possibly damaged files.

SEE: • **Chapter 4 for more on restarting and shutting down**

Preventative Maintenance

As is often the case, you can avoid big headaches later on by enduring some small headaches now. This is what preventative maintenance is all about: Solving problems before they happen.

I am certainly sympathetic to those who abhor routine maintenance. I am one of them. Whenever I purchase a piece of equipment, such as an air conditioner or a microwave oven, one of the first things I check out is how long I can happily ignore cleaning it, replacing parts in it, or anything else that might take up more than five seconds of my time.

Thankfully, there isn't much cleaning maintenance necessary with your Macintosh—aside from occasionally cleaning dust and dirt out of your mouse or floppy disk drive (as described in Fix-It #17). The rest is either common sense (don't spill coffee on your keyboard) or more for aesthetics than to prevent any real problem (such as wiping dust off the monitor screen).

However, there is another form of maintenance—electronic maintenance. This is the focus of the remainder of this chapter. True, it can be just as tedious as any other kind of maintenance. But ignoring these procedures can seriously hamper the performance of your computer and (without wanting to sound too alarmist) possibly result in the irrecoverable loss of invaluable data.

Have an Emergency Startup Disk Ready

If your one and only hard drive is your startup disk and it develops a serious problem, you will not be able to use it to startup the Macintosh. Similarly, several troubleshooting utilities cannot make alterations or repairs on the current startup disk—which will be a problem if your current startup disk is the one that needs repairing. For these reasons, you need to have a special emergency startup floppy disk (or disks). Having one of these ready *before* trouble strikes is wise preventative maintenance.

Emergency Startup Disks You Already Have

You probably already have one or more emergency startup floppy disks. The system software's Disk Tools disk is one example (Performa users get a similar disk called Disk Utilities). Disk Tools includes Disk First Aid and Apple HD SC Setup. If your system software came on 1.44Mb HD disks, Disk Tools has a minimal System 7 System

Folder on it. However, if your system software came on 800K disks, the System Folder on the Disk Tools disk is a System 6 System Folder. This will be unusable on most recent Mac models (as they require System 7). In this case, you want to create your own customized System 7 Emergency Toolkit disk as an alternative.

Utility packages, such as Norton Utilities and MacTools, also include special Emergency Startup Disks for making disk repairs, as do most anti-virus utilities and disk formatting programs. These packages now also include special utilities used to create your own variation on their basic startup floppy disk. These do-it-yourself utilities solve the problem of a basic startup disk possibly not having the Enabler needed for your machine (as explained more in a moment).

Problems Creating Your Own Emergency Startup Disk

Even if you already have an emergency startup disk, you may want to create your own customized disk, so that you can include software not on the prepackaged disks or combine utilities from other disks in a way that is more convenient for you. However, you will confront two major problems in trying to do this:

There Isn't Much Room to Spare on a Floppy Disk   Once you add a System and a Finder to a floppy disk, there will only be a few hundred K, at most, left over for your utilities. In fact, with System 7, you must use a HD floppy disk to create a startup disk at all. The 800K disks are simply too small.

One solution to this problem is to create a startup disk that does not include a Finder. Doing this is not as simple as just deleting the Finder from the disk. It requires a bit of special finagling, as I will describe shortly. While this does saves space, you will probably be able to use these disks only to launch a single program at startup. There will be no way to transfer from one program to another. Nor will you be able to go to the Finder's desktop (which can be essential for solving some problems that require accessing files on your disk—such as if you want to get to the Startup Disk control panel on your hard disk to change its setting—though you can always use your system software's Disk Tools disk for these occasions). Still, for doing disk repairs or virus detection, even having access to one program can be useful. And in some cases, such as if trying to mount a disk on the desktop would result in a crash, it can be preferable not to have a Finder. The emergency startup disks included with Norton Utilities and MacTools, for example, are both set up this way.

The main other alternatives include:

- Create a series of emergency startup disks, each with different utilities on them (assuming that no one utility is too large to fit on a floppy disk).

- Have one floppy disk with a System Folder, and place the needed utilities on a second (and third or more, if needed) floppy disk. However, unless you have two floppy disk drives, using multiple floppy disks will lead to a lot of disk swapping.

- Create a System 6 startup disk, assuming you have access to System 6 software and that your model of Macintosh can run on System 6. System 6 software takes up less room than System 7, leaving more space for utilities.

- If you have two or more fixed hard drives (or if you have a removable cartridge drive), you can start up from one hard disk to repair another.

- Your Mac may have come with the system software on a special CD that can function as a startup disk (see Chapter 5 for more on using CD-ROM disks as startup disks). If so, and you have an Apple CD-ROM drive, startup from the CD-ROM disk and use a floppy disk that contains utilities not on the CD-ROM disk, as needed.

If Your Macintosh Needs a System Enabler File, an Emergency Startup Disk Will Not Work Without It   If you are using System 7.1, all current models of Macintosh require a System Enabler file in the System Folder. This is a special file that contains information needed for a successful startup that is specific to your model of Macintosh. Different models of Macintosh use different enablers. There are now a dozen or so different enabler files. This has turned out to be a major headache for makers of utilities, such as disk recovery packages, that supply their own emergency startup disks. These disks used to come with no enabler files on them. Thus, if your Macintosh needs an enabler, you would not be able to use these floppy disks for startup, at least not without some modification.

The latest version of Norton Utilities includes a startup disk that has a limited selection of Enabler files on it. However, if your needed Enabler is not on this disk, don't despair. And don't worry if you have MacTools. Both Norton Utilities and MacTools include special features that will create an Emergency Startup Disk (installing their own software on it), customized with your correct Enabler (taken from what is in your startup disk's System Folder). For example, the one in Norton Utilities is called Startup Disk Builder. If you use these options, be sure to start with a freshly formatted floppy disk. This ensures the maximum amount of free space on the disk. Also, make sure that there is not more than one enabler file in your startup disk's System Folder. Otherwise, the program may not know which one to copy to your floppy disk.

Otherwise, you may be able to add an Enabler to an existing emergency disk. To do this, make a duplicate copy of an Emergency Startup Disk (don't risk altering the original!). Especially if the original Emergency Startup Disk is a Finderless disk, be sure to make an *exact* copy of the disk. Simply dragging files from one disk to the other, using the Finder, does not make an exact copy and will not work! Then manually add the System Enabler from your startup disk's System Folder to the floppy disk copy.

SEE: • "Take Note: To Make an Exact Copy of an Entire Floppy Disk," later in this chapter

Finally, you can usually use the Disk Tools disk that came with your Macintosh. It should already include the correct System Enabler for your particular model.

If you regularly try to fix problems on a variety of different Macintosh models, such as in an office environment, you may want to have a collection of all the current enabler files. This will allow you to quickly find and add whatever enabler file you may need for a particular Macintosh. For such cases, Apple maintains a disk with all the current enabler files on them. This disk is available for downloading from major online services. This disk also lists which enabler file goes with which model (which is important, since the names of the enabler files often give no clue as to what model they are for). System Update disks typically also include an updated set of Enablers.

System 7.5 Alert: In System 7.5, you will not need an Enabler for any models released prior to System 7.5 (the needed information has been incorporated directly into the rest of the system software). You will need a Enabler file for models released after System 7.5 was released.

SEE: • **Chapter 5 for more on Enabler files and related startup disk issues**

TAKE NOTE ▶

TO MAKE AN EXACT COPY OF AN ENTIRE FLOPPY DISK

Most times, you copy a file by dragging the file's icon to the disk icon (or any folder window) of the destination disk. However, there is a special method for copying an entire floppy disk from the Finder. Simply drag the icon of the disk you wish to copy to the icon of your desired destination disk. A prompt asks you whether you want to replace the contents of the destination disk with that of the source disk. Click OK.

However, particularly in System 7, this procedure does not make an exact duplicate of the original disk. The name of the disk isn't replaced, the location of the files and folders on the new disk do not match those on the original disk, and any invisible files are not copied.

To truly make an exact duplicate copy of a floppy disk, you need to use a copy utility. Apple makes such a utility, called Disk Copy. Although it is free (and available from the usual sources, as described in the Appendix, "Stocking Your Troubleshooter's Toolkit"), it is not included with most versions of the Macintosh system software (it does come with the CD-ROM disk version of System 7.5). Norton Utilities and MacTools include utilities with a similar ability, called Floppier and FastCopy respectively.

Use these utilities whenever you want to make a copy of a disk. It is the only way to be sure that your copy is an exact duplicate of your original disk.

SEE • **Fix-It #5, "Take Note: "Why Can't I Open the System Software I Just Downloaded?," for more details on how to use Disk Copy**

Create Your Own Startup Floppy Disk

Bearing in mind all of the problems just described, you are now ready to make your own customized System 7 Emergency Toolkit startup floppy disk.

Ideally, you should have at least the following utilities on your Emergency Toolkit startup disk(s): an anti-virus utility, a disk repair utility, a disk formatting utility, a backup utility, a disk optimizing utility, and an SCSI utility (such as SCSIProbe).

Once you have created your Emergency Toolkit disk, always keep it locked. This way, you can use it to check for viruses without having to worry about infecting the Toolkit disk itself.

There are two main methods to get a viable System Folder on to a floppy disk.

Method #1: Use the System Folder on the Disk Tools Disk   Copy the System Folder on the Disk Tools disk (that came with your system software disks) to a blank floppy disk. Add whatever applications you want to the disk, assuming there is room. If this works, it is the simplest possible method.

Method #2: Create Your Own Minimal System Folder   This requires using the Installer utility from your system software disks. This may give you an even smaller System Folder than found on the Disk Tools disk. If it doesn't, it has no advantage over Method #1.

By the way, System 7.5 comes with a newly designed Installer. It looks completely different from the old one and is easier to use, with more control over what you can install (see Fix-It #5). Unfortunately, as of this writing, the Minimal System install option for System 7.5 creates a System Folder too large to fit on a floppy disk. Presumably this will be fixed eventually. In the meantime, you can still create a floppy startup disk from the System Folder on the Disk Tools disk.

On the assumption that you will eventually be able to use the System 7.5 Installer, the steps that follow include instructions for both types of Installers (instructions for the older method are given in parentheses).

1. Start with a 1.44Mb HD disk. The 800K disks are not big enough. Name it Emergency Toolkit or something similar.

2. Launch the Installer from your system software disks (floppy or CD-ROM). For Macs that need an Enabler, you typically start with the Install Me First disk. In other cases, it will probably be the System 7 Install 1 disk.

3. From the Installer, use the Switch Disk button until the name of the floppy disk you are using is the selected disk. Click Eject Disk. (This step is unnecessary if you are running the Installer from a CD-ROM disk.)

4. Insert your intended startup floppy disk, thus making it the selected destination for the installation.

5. From the pop-up menu at the top of the window, select Custom Install. (If you are using the older style Installer utility, click the Customize button.)

6. Click the triangle at the left end of the System Software line. This opens up a list of options. Select *Minimal System for this Macintosh only.* (If you are using the older style Installer, scroll to the line that says *Minimal Software for <name of your Macintosh model>.*)

   For more flexibility in using your disk with a variety of Mac models, you could alternatively select the option for *any* Macintosh, but this will require more disk space. And the resulting disk may still not work on other Macintosh models, if you don't have a needed Enabler file for a given model. There is not a great solution to this problem!

7. Click Install. Unless you were using a CD-ROM, expect considerable swapping of disks in and out of the drive during this process. When the installation is done, quit the Installer and return to the Finder.

8. You can now copy to the disk as many utilities, of your choice, as space will allow. For example, I was able to fit Apple HD SC Setup and Disk First Aid (from the Disk Tools disk), as well as Virex (an anti-virus utility) and SCSIProbe.

    If necessary, you can set up additional custom Emergency Toolkit disks to hold other utilities. To start this process, copy the System Folder from your first Toolkit disk to your second one. You don't need to use the Installer again.

System 6 Alert: To create a System 6 Emergency Toolkit disk, if you are starting with System 6 software disks, follow the same procedure as outlined in the preceding steps. If you are starting with System 7 software on 800K disks, just copy the Disk Tools disk (it has a System 6 System Folder on it). Discard everything from inside the System Folder except the System, the Finder, and the General control panel. Then start adding (or deleting) your desired utilities. If you have the System 7 software on HD disks, these do not include the System 6 System Folder. In this case, the only way you can set up a System 6 System Folder is if you have access to the System 6 software from other disks you possess or you can obtain such disks from other sources.

A Finder-less Startup Floppy Disk

You can squeeze even more utilities onto a single startup floppy disk by getting rid of the Finder. I already mentioned that this is how some commercial utilities make their startup emergency disks. While there are several ways to do setup Finder-less startup disks, what follows are two of the simplest and best. The idea in both cases is to "fool" the Macintosh into thinking that a substitute application is the Finder. Otherwise, the Mac will look for the real Finder at startup and, failing to find it, refuse to start.

    Both methods assume you are starting with a floppy disk that has a System Folder on it already (created by using one of the methods described in the previous section).

Method #1: Renaming an Application as the Finder   This works well if you only need to run a single application from the startup disk.

1. Move the System file and an Enabler file (if one is needed) from the System Folder to the root level of your disk (that is, not in *any* folder). Discard the rest of the System Folder.

2. Copy any single application you want to your disk and rename it *Finder*. This file should also be at the root level of the disk.

3. Restart with the floppy disk inserted. It should directly launch the application you renamed as Finder. You won't be able to quit from it or go to other applications. You will need to restart again when you are done. Otherwise, it should work fine.

System 7.5 Alert: This method will probably not work with System 7.5. In order to accomplish this trick in System 7.5, you have to change the type and creator codes of the application to match that of the Finder (as explained more in Chapter 8, "By the Way: Other Types of Finder-less Startup Disks").

Method #2: Using ShortFinder This requires using a shareware utility called Short-Finder. The main advantage of ShortFinder is that it takes up hundreds of K less disk space than the real Finder.

1. Move the System file and an Enabler file (if one is needed) from the System Folder to the root level of your disk (that is, not in *any* folder). Discard the rest of the System Folder.

2. Copy ShortFinder to the floppy disk and rename it *Finder*. Copy to the floppy disk any other applications you wish to use, until you run out of room. All files should be at the root level of the disk.

3. Restart with the floppy disk inserted. It should directly launch ShortFinder. From there, you should be able to launch other applications, by selecting *Launch Application* from its File menu.

TECHNICALLY SPEAKING ▶

GETTING FANCY WITH SHORTFINDER

With ShortFinder, you can even setup a floppy disk so that you can leave the System and Enabler files (and any other system software files you wish, such as extensions and control panels) in the System Folder, starting up almost as if you were using the real Finder. As with the Finder itself, you can access multiple applications with ShortFinder set up this way. However, to do this, you have to change ShortFinder's type and creator to match that of the real Finder. I describe exactly how to do this in Chapter 8.

Save and Back Up Your Work

Saving your work simply means using the Save command to save a file to disk. Backing up your work means making a copy of the file to a separate disk location.

    Regularly saving and backing up your work is Preventative Maintenance Rule #1. It supersedes every other rule by a wide margin. It cannot be emphasized enough. It is critically important. Save often. Back up everything. Regularly. Am I making myself clear? The dire consequences of almost every type of disaster that could possibly befall you can be avoided if you frequently save your files while you work and back everything up when you are through.

Almost everyone has a horror story about how their only copy of an important document, representing weeks of work, was lost or destroyed just before it needed to be printed out. Don't add your name to that roster. Save the document. Back it up. It can happen to you.

I wouldn't have to emphasize this advice so vigorously if it weren't ignored so routinely—even by people who should know better. Why is this? The usual culprits are time and money: People complain that it either takes too much time to back everything up or costs too much money to buy the equipment needed to do it at a reasonable speed.

But ask anyone who has ever lost any critical data (maybe it's happened to you already). Ask them about the time and/or money it cost to replace those data. Then reconsider your attitude.

Save Your Work ... Often

The simplest of all methods of preventing disaster is to make generous use of the Save command (found in the File menu of almost all applications). Remember that unsaved data exist only in RAM (that is, electronic memory). This means it disappears into digital hyperspace if there is an unexpected (are there any other kind?) system crash or power failure. Yes, hours of unsaved work could vanish in an instant—unless you have already saved it.

So, when you are working on a file, save it frequently—at least every ten minutes. Alternatively, if your program has an *autosave* feature, you can use it. An autosave function automatically saves documents, without giving any prompting or requiring any input from the user, at any specified interval. Some people like this idea. Personally, I prefer to do my saving the old-fashioned way. If I am experimenting with some strange formatting, I would not want it to be saved automatically, before I decided whether I preferred to revert to the previous format. Still, for some people, autosaving could be just the ticket.

If your program does not include a built-in autosave function, some utilities allow you to include this function in virtually any program. NowSave, one of the utilities included as part of Now Utilities, can do this.

SEE: • Chapter 6 for more on the use of the Save and Save As commands
         • "Protect Against Loss of Data Due to System Crashes" later in this chapter

Make Regular Backups

Don't Depend on Just the Finder and Floppy Disks   Copying files from one disk to another (such as from your hard disk to a floppy disk) via the Finder is a quick and easy backup method. However, it is not an effective way for backing up an entire hard disk (what is called a *global* backup). There are several reasons for this:

• At least some files on your hard disk are likely to be larger than can fit on a single floppy disk. The Finder cannot split a file across more than one floppy disk.

- When you want to restore a single file, the Finder is not an efficient mechanism to locate a file that may be stored on any one of several dozen floppy disks that contain your backup files.

- Your disk probably contains important invisible files that the Finder does not copy.

Use Special Backup Software and Hardware   There are software utilities specifically designed for backing up your files. They overcome the limitations of the Finder. They make global backups relatively easy, keeping track of what goes where (so that you don't have to). They can split large files across disks and can quickly identify what disk contains a particular file you are seeking.

The previously mentioned utility workhorses, MacTools and Norton Utilities, both contain decent backup utilities. Other popular alternatives include Retrospect, Redux, and DiskFit. For global backups, using one of these utilities should be considered essential.

Instead of backing up to floppy disks, it is far more manageable (not to mention less time-consuming) to backup to a special backup device. These include an additional fixed hard drive, a removable cartridge drive, or a tape drive.

Devise a Good Backup Strategy

How, how much, and how often should you back up your files? Everyone has their own recommendation for the best way to accomplish the most with the least amount of hassle. Here are the two most important things to do.

Back Up All Personal Document Files   Your personal files, such as manuscripts and illustrations, are your unique creations and are thus irreplaceable. Back them up frequently (as in every time you modify them) and maintain multiple backups if feasible. This *can* be done by just using the Finder and floppy disks, if the files are not too large or numerous. This should be done in addition to any global backups.

Maintain a Global Backup of Your Hard Drive(s)   Ideally you want to use special backup software that can create a *mirror image* global backup. This can be used to recreate your entire hard drive, down to every customized preference file and every invisible file, with all files and folders in their original hierarchical location. This will be a tremendous time saver if you ever have to reformat your hard drive. If you work on your computer almost every day, update this backup at least once a week, more often if you make frequent major changes to the contents of the drive.

After doing an initial global backup, your backup software/hardware may provide the option to do either an *incremental* or *archival* backup on subsequent updates. An incremental backup backs up only newly added and modified files (deleting the old version of any modified files). Archival backups work similarly except that they never delete anything, not even files that have been modified or deleted since the last backup. This allows you to revert to versions prior to the most recent version, if desired.

Helpful hint: Try a restore *before* you have a problem.   Try restoring some files to your hard disk using your specialized backup software. If you are willing to take the risk, even try a global restore. Doing so may reveal that the restore fails because of procedural problems, problems that you can now easily address and fix. However, if you wait until the crisis occurs, it may be too late.

Prune Your Hard Drive

Delete Unneeded Data and Application Files

As you back up your hard drive, you won't want to keep useless and outdated files. That's why you should periodically go through your hard drive and delete these un-needed files.

If you never delete anything, you probably still have that 1988 letter to your Aunt Millie sitting in some folder somewhere. Get rid of it. In fact, delete any applications and documents that you rarely or never use. If you haven't used them for the last six months or more, get rid of them. Maintain a copy of them on floppy disks, if desired. But get them off of your hard drive.

Why bother getting rid of these files? First, it will be easier to locate files, since you won't have to wade through "garbage" files. Second, depending on your work habits, this can also have the benefit of freeing up a surprising amount of space. If you already have a nearly full disk, the extra space can allow you to add other more important files. Even if you don't need more space, a nearly full hard disk is subject to all sorts of minor problems. For example, certain activities, such as printing, may create temporary files in order to work. There needs to be enough free disk space to hold these files. I'm getting ahead of myself a bit here, but too little empty disk space hastens fragmentation of the files on your disk, which can slow down your Mac. Conversely, discarding unneeded files prior to rebuilding your desktop leads to a more compact Desktop file, which will speed things up.

> SEE: • "Give Your Macintosh a Tune-up," later in this chapter, for more on fragmented files and rebuilding the desktop

Overall, for hard drives of 100Mb or less, at least 5 percent, and preferably 10 percent, of your hard drive should remain unused. For larger-capacity hard drives, try to keep at least 5Mb to 10Mb of unused space at all times. Need to know how much free space you have left? Remember, the current amount is usually visible in the upper right corner of any open Finder window on your disk.

Delete Items from the System Folder

Extraneous files in the System Folder can be a huge waste of space. Here's what to look for.

Application-Related Files   For example, suppose you decide to discard a word processor you have been using in favor of another one. You may forget that your old word processor included a special dictionary file, for use with its built-in spelling checker, that is still buried somewhere in your System Folder. After a while, you can build up quite a collection of these unneeded files. Similarly, delete preferences files for deleted applications. The Preferences Folder is often a rich source of files that can be deleted.

If the initial placement of an application on your disk required an Installer utility, your System Folder may have many application-related files that you did not even know existed. Once the application is deleted, these can all be removed as well.

System Software Files   Similarly, when your system software was installed on your hard drive, it probably installed many files that you never use. For example, if you find a printer driver (such as StyleWriter or ImageWriter) for a printer that you do not have or use, delete it. If you are not on a network with other users, you can delete any control panels or extensions that deal with file sharing (such as Network, Network Extension, File Sharing Extension, File Sharing Monitor, or Sharing Setup).

The same thing is true for any extensions, control panels, and Apple menu items that you no longer use. Get rid of them. This often has the side benefit of reducing the amount of memory occupied by the system software, freeing up more RAM for other uses.

Delete Mystery Files

What if you don't even know what a file is doing? How do you know if it is safe to delete it? For applications and documents, this is usually easy to solve. Just open them and see what they are.

If a data document cannot be opened, it probably belongs to an application that is no longer on your drive. Similarly, many System Folder files cannot be opened from the Finder under any circumstances. You may have trouble identifying the purpose of these files.

In these cases, select Get Info for the mysterious file. Check for any information there that might give you a hint about the source and purpose of the file. This may tell you all you need to know to make a decision about deleting it. Otherwise, if Get Info at least identifies the origin of the file, you can presumably go to the relevant documentation for more help.

Also try turning on Balloon Help and placing the cursor over the mystery item. This is particularly useful for system extensions. If you are unlucky, you will get the generic message that simply says the file in question is an extension (see Figure 2-11, left). If you are lucky, you may learn exactly what the extension does (see Figure 2-11, right).

System extension

This file adds functionality to your Macintosh. To add this file's functionality to your Macintosh, place the file in the Extensions folder and then restart the computer.

Now Toolbox

Network extension

This file allows you to set network options using the Users & Groups and Sharing Setup control panels.

Network Extension

Figure 2-11 Balloon help messages may (right) or may not (left) help you identify a mystery file

BY THE WAY ▶

WHAT'S WITH FOLDERS NAMED DUPLICATE ITEMS AND DEINSTALLED?

Occasionally, in our System Folder, you may find folders with names like Duplicate Items *or* Deinstalled 4/10/95. *These folders were created at the time you ran an Installer utility of some sort (such as when upgrading your system software). In many cases, Installers replace existing older versions of software with the newer versions. However, in some cases (as a protection to you in case you still want to preserve the older version), it will move the older version to a special folder it creates and give the folder a name like* Duplicate Items. *In general, if you discover this folder, you can probably delete it and its contents, because you already have other versions of its contents somewhere else (such as in the Control Panels folder). This is another way to free up some disk space.*

Similarly, if you find a file called Installer Cleanup, *you can delete it. It is a temporary file that should have been automatically deleted when you quit the Installer.*

SEE: • Chapter 6 for more on opening and identifying files

Other Ways to Save or Get More Space

If you discard all unneeded files and there is still not enough free space on your hard drive, you have two alternatives:

• Replace your hard drive with a larger one (or just add another one).

• Use an automatic compression utility.

The rationale behind increasing your hard drive space is obvious. Compression utilities may require a bit more explanation.

Compression utilities reduce the size of files stored on your disk by eliminating "redundancy" in the file's data. When you really need to use the file, the compression utility uncompresses it to its normal state, without any data loss. There are currently two main types of compression utilities. One is *file-level compression,* exemplified by programs like AutoDoubler or StuffIt SpaceSaver. These utilities are system extensions that work in the background to automatically compress files on your disk in the background, while you work on other tasks. They then automatically decompress the file when you attempt to launch it. With file-level compression you can select which files and/or folders on your disk you wish to compress. The alternative is *disk-level compression,* exemplified by programs such as Stacker, eDisk, or Times Two. This operates at the disk driver level (described more in Fix-It #12) to compress files even before they are written to the disk. It decompresses them when you use them. It actually fools your Macintosh into thinking that your disk drive is much larger than it really is. You have no option to select which files to compress. The utility always compresses everything. Many users claim disk-level compression is more subject to compatibility problems than file-level compression, but other users find them reliable. (Personally, I would not trust disk-level compression. Among other things, it can become a problem if and when you have to upgrade your disk driver.)

With either method, the utility's operation is quite transparent; that is, it happens without your issuing any commands or even being directly aware that it is taking place. These compressed files can take up as little as 50 percent of the original size of the disk, so this can free up a lot of space.

Still, this technique is not for everyone. The compression and decompression procedures, although fast, do take up extra time. In particular, disk-level compressors always compress a file as soon as you close it, which can introduce a substantial time lag. File-level compressors, on the other hand, usually wait to compress a closed file until the Macintosh is idle, making the wait less noticeable. Finally, should you lose access to the decompressing program for any reason, the compressed files may be rendered useless.

BY THE WAY ▶

ARCHIVAL COMPRESSION UTILITIES

For just occasional compression of a few infrequently used files, for archival storage of files, or for transmitting files across networks and modems (where reduced size means less transmission time), consider manual archival compression utilities (such as DiskDoubler Pro, StuffIt Deluxe, or Compact Pro). These are really a variation on file-level compression. However, they compress files only when you launch the application and specifically issue a command from within the utility itself. In some cases, you can also make self-extracting compressed files that can be compressed even without the utility. Archival compression and decompression times are typically much slower than with the automatic utilities, which is one reason why you wouldn't want them for files you use regularly. On the plus side, they manage to compress files down to a smaller size than the automatic utilities.

By the way, StuffIt includes a neat feature, called DropStuff and Expander, that allows you to automatically compress or decompress a file simply by dragging the file's icon over the relevant StuffIt icon.

Install Protection Utilities

Typically, protection utilities are control panels and system extensions that can do their intended job only if they are installed on your startup disk before a problem occurs. Thus, getting them installed is part of preventative maintenance. None of these utilities is essential. Still, depending on your work situation, all are worth considering.

Protect Against Virus Infections

To protect yourself against computer viruses, you need to use an anti-virus utility. The most popular ones are Symantec Anti-virus for Macintosh (SAM), Virex, and Disinfectant. They are all good. Disinfectant has the advantage of being free. MacTools also includes an anti-virus utility that is competitive with these separate utilities.

Of course, these utilities can be used at any time to check for and eradicate an existing virus infection. However, when properly set up, they can also monitor your disk and block a virus infection before it occurs. That's why I mention it here as part of preventative maintenance.

SEE: • **Fix-It #7 for more details on checking for viruses**

Protect Against Accidentally Deleted Files

Have you ever unintentionally deleted a file or deliberately deleted a file that you subsequently wished you had back? Sure you have. Luckily, utility packages such as the Norton Utilities and MacTools provide a means of recovering files that have been deleted via the Finder's Empty Trash command.

These utilities accomplish their magic because when you empty the Trash, you do not really immediately remove the file from the disk. Only its name is removed from a special area of the disk (where the computer looks to find out what is on your drive). The file data remain on the disk, intact, until it is overwritten by a new file. Undelete utilities can find these deleted files, even though the Finder cannot, and restore them to their undeleted condition.

However, eventually you will write new information over that area of the hard drive, and then the file will be unrecoverable. Thus, these utilities work best if you use them as soon as possible after deleting the file. You should not depend on this method as a guaranteed method of recovering deleted files!

While these utility packages have some ability to recover deleted files, even without first installing their special protection features, they work best with these features installed. So do it.

Norton Utilities Norton Utilities uses a control panel called FileSaver:

1. To set FileSaver in motion, place it in the Control Panels folder.
2. Open the control panel and click the On button (if it isn't already on).
3. Select Fewer Choices (if it is not already selected).

Advanced users may want the greater customization control possible with the More Choices option. If so, check out the Norton Utilities manual for details.

4. Click the check box next to the name of each mounted volume that you wish to protect (see Figure 2-12).

5. Close the control panel and restart.

6. When you need to undelete files, launch Open UnErase from the Finder (or alternatively select UnErase either from Norton Utilities' main menu window or from the Utilities menu). Details on using UnErase are given in Chapter 6.

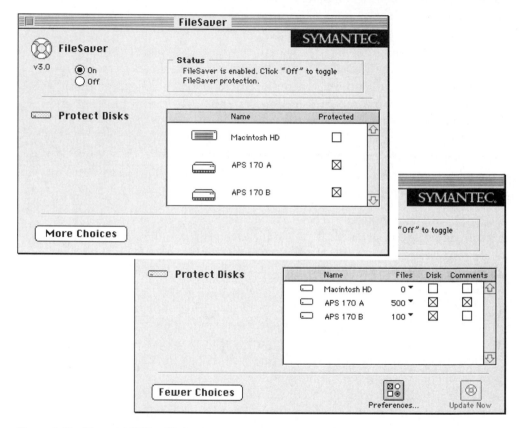

Figure 2-12 Norton Utilities FileSaver control panel. Left: the More Choices display. Right: the Fewer Choices display

MacTools Pro   MacTools Pro uses an extension called MacTools TrashBack:

1. To set TrashBack in motion, place the extension in the Extensions folder and restart the Macintosh. This was most likely done automatically when you first installed MacTools Pro. If not, the extension may be in a folder called "Move these to System Folder" located in your MacTools Pro folder. If so, move the extension to the System Folder, as the folder's name suggests. Otherwise, you will need to return to the MacTools Pro Installer to install TrashBack.

2. Launch MacTools Pro's Clinic application. From the top row of buttons in the Clinic window, click the Undelete button. From the dialog box that next appears, click the TrashBack button (see Figure 2-13, left). This finally results in the opening of the TrashBack window.

Alternatively, assuming the TrashBack extension is installed and active, a Trash-Back item is added to the bottom of the Finder's Special menu (see Figure 2-13, right). If you select it, you are taken directly to the TrashBack window. Actually, selecting this command takes you to a separate TrashBack application, called Mac-Tools TrashBack App, stored in a folder called Support Files, located in the Mac-Tools Pro folder. If you delete this application, the Special menu's TrashBack command will not work. On the other hand, when the application is present, you can also choose to directly launch TrashBack from the App, rather than from the Finder menu command.

3. Click the Options button from the row of buttons along the top of the Trash-Back window. From the list of TrashBack options, make sure you have selected "Enable TrashBack protection" (see Figure 2-14). If you want TrashBack to protect removable hard drive cartridges, uncheck the item that says "Don't protect files on removable drive." TrashBack will now automatically enable protection for all hard disks, even ones that get mounted at some later time (but not floppy or RAM disks).

If you next click the Recover Options button, you will be presented with choices as to where you want recovered items to be placed. In particular, you can choose between having all items stored in a folder called Recovered Items or having all items returned to their original location.

4. To undelete files, locate the items you want to undelete in the directory listing of the TrashBack window. Click to the left of each item's name to place a check mark in front of it. Checking a folder automatically checks all items contained in the folder. Finally, click the Recover button at the bottom of the window.

If you did not have TrashBack turned on when you deleted a file you now want to recover, you can still possibly undelete it. In this case, you must use MacTools Pro Clinic and, after clicking the Undelete button (as described in Step 2), select one of the other two options (File Scan or Text Scan) listed in the dialog box that next appears, rather than the TrashBack option.

All of this is described more in Chapter 6, as part of a general discussion of how to undelete files. Otherwise, check the MacTools Pro manual for explanations of remaining buttons and options, as needed.

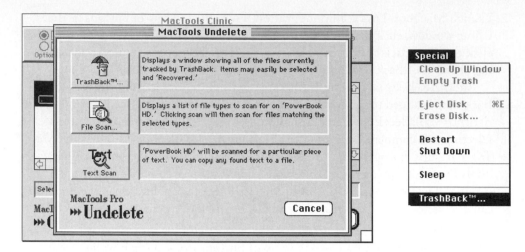

Figure 2-13   Left: the dialog box that appears after selecting Undelete from MacTools Clinic;
Right: MacTools Pro's TrashBack command in the Finder's Special menu

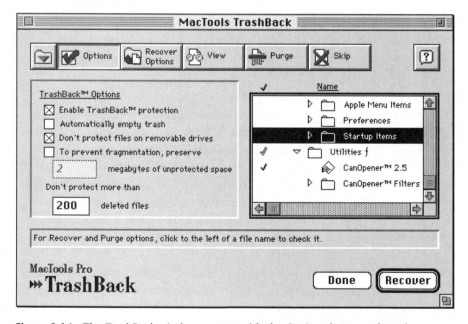

Figure 2-14   The TrashBack window as seen with the Options button selected

TRASHBACK'S INVISIBLE PROTECTION FOLDER

TrashBack stores deleted files in a special invisible folder. Normally, you have no access to this folder. However, the folder becomes visible if you startup with the TrashBack extension off or if you turn off TrashBack's enable protection option. If you have done this, look for a folder called TrashBack Protected Files, located at the root level of each protected disk (inside the folder will be other folders, such as one called TrashBack Temporary Items and another called Deleted Files). Files deleted while the extension is off are not placed in the Protected Files folder. Ordinarily, if you come across this folder, just leave it alone. However, when TrashBack is off, all files in the TrashBack folder contribute to your occupied disk space, just as if the files were not deleted (which, in fact, is technically true). The result is that you will probably have significantly less Mb listed as available on your disk when TrashBack is off. Don't worry. If need be, you can go to the TrashBack folder and directly delete files by moving them to the Trash (this is functionally similar to using TrashBack's Purge option). While this will eliminate the ability of TrashBack to later recover these files, it will make your available disk space listing more accurate. Otherwise, you will have to wait until you restart with TrashBack on once again.

Some applications may list the invisible TrashBack folder (and its deleted files) in their Open dialog box, just as if the files had not been deleted. This can happen even when TrashBack is on (though this seems to be less likely with the current version of TrashBack). You may even be able to open such "deleted" files. If you think you may be viewing the TrashBack folder, just click the Desktop button in the Open dialog box to take you out of there. Some Find utilities (including the Finder's Find command) may also list these invisible folders/files, though surprisingly most do not.

TWO VERY DIFFERENT VERSIONS OF TRASHBACK

MacTools first introduced TrashBack in MacTools 3.0. This 3.0 version worked very differently from the version included with the more recently released upgrade, MacTools Pro. The most notable difference is in the working of the Special menu's TrashBack command. In MacTools 3.x, if you selected the TrashBack command, it resulted in the appearance of a hierarchical menu listing all deleted items currently tracked by TrashBack. Simply moving the mouse to select one of these items immediately undeleted it, returning the item to its original location. You did not need to open the TrashBack application. This was the height of convenience and I am sorry to see that Central Point abandoned this feature. However, I am sure they did so because of the all-too-frequent compatibility problems it had. Numerous other extensions had problems working with TrashBack. Actually, TrashBack 3.x was itself incompatible with System 7.5.

This first incarnation of TrashBack also automatically placed its invisible TrashBack folder on RAM disks. This presented a problem when you tried to delete the RAM disk, since a RAM disk cannot be deleted when there are any files on it. The presence of the TrashBack folder thus prevented deleting the RAM disk, even though it would appear that the disk was empty. You could get around this problem in several ways, including simply selecting the Finder's Erase Disk command (assuming you knew to try this), but it was still confusing to unwary users.

This is only one of many ways in which MacTools 3.x and MacTools Pro are different. This text emphasizes almost exclusively MacTools Pro.

TrashBack can retrieve undeleted files even after a disk has been optimized (a process described in Fix-It #8). Norton Utilities does not do this as well. This is because TrashBack works by maintaining an invisible TrashBack folder that essentially contains all of the supposedly undeleted files (see "Take Note: TrashBack's Invisible Protection Folder"). They are only really deleted when there is no other free space available for whatever other activity you are trying to do. Undeleted files in the Trash-Back folder are not overwritten when a disk is optimized. Norton Utilities' FileSaver, in contrast, creates a special invisible file that essentially keeps a record of the location of files that have been deleted but does not protect them from being overwritten during a disk optimization.

Two final important points to remember: First, if you wait until you need to recover a file before you install FileSaver or TrashBack, it will be too late. The critical point here is prevention. The undelete features of Norton Utilities and MacTools work best if their associated control panel or extension is installed before you need to use it! While you still may be able to recover files even without this prior installation, you are severely hurting your chances. Second, only files that have been saved can be undeleted. These utilities are not useful for recovering work that was lost because of a system crash that occurred before you saved the file.

SEE: • "Protect Against Loss of Data Due to System Crashes" later in this chapter
      • Chapter 6 for more on undeleting files

Protect Against Crashed or Accidentally Erased Hard Disks

Disk Crash   A disk crash is when you have lost all access to your disk and its contents. Usually, the disk does not even appear on the desktop. If the disk is your startup disk, you may even be temporarily unable to start up your Macintosh.

Accidentally Erased Hard Disk   An event almost as traumatic as a crashed disk would be to accidentally erase your hard drive. It's hard for me to imagine how this could occur by accident. To do this, you would first have to inadvertently select Erase Disk from the Finder's Special menu. Then you would have to click OK to the prompt asking if you really want to do this. Making this mistake even harder to make, the Macintosh prohibits you from erasing the current startup disk (which is often your one and only hard drive). Still, I suppose it may happen to some poor soul somewhere.

Having Norton Utilities' FileSaver or MacTools' TrashBack installed (as described in the previous section) prior to the crash or accidental disk erasure will facilitate any recovery.

However, Norton Utilities' FileSaver includes a special recovery feature that is not available with MacTools: Norton Utilities can quickly restore an entire disk in one step, rather than via a file-by-file selection. This feature is similar to restoring a disk from a global backup, except it's much faster and you don't need the separately stored backup files. The effectiveness of this recovery feature depends on having the relevant invisible files (maintained by FileSaver) periodically updated. The more recently they have been updated, the better the recovery. This updating is done automatically at certain predetermined times. To modify the default update options (such as "At Restart/Shut Down"), select More Choices, then click the Preferences button and select "Protection Preferences" from the pop-up menu. You can also Update the files at any time by clicking the "Update Now" button (or select "Update FileSaver Files" from the Options menu of Norton Utilities' main menu window).

Older versions of MacTools included a similarly functioning utility called Mirror. However, Mirror was dropped from version 3.0 and later versions of MacTools. This was done because Central Point (owners of MacTools before Symantec took it over) contended that this type of recovery was only a rarely needed option, likely to cause more problems than it could solve (for reasons explained more in Fix-It #13, "Take Note: Use Backups Instead of Restore or Recover"). So if you insist on having this type of volume recover protection, you will have to go with Norton Utilities. It's gone from MacTools.

SEE: • Chapter 5 for more on disk crashes
• Fix-It #13 for more on repairing and restoring disks
• Fix-It #14 for more on file recovery
• Fix-It #15 for details on formatting disks

Protect Against Disk Damage

The most critical use of MacTools and Norton Utilities is to repair a damaged disk. In some cases, damage to a disk causes few, if any, symptoms at first. Eventually, symptoms worsen and a disk crash may ultimately occur. To prevent the more serious symptoms from developing, both of these packages have options to periodically scan disks for potential problems—while they are still minor—automatically and in the background. If a problem is spotted, an alert message appears on the screen informing you of the problem and typically suggesting a course of action (such as "There is a problem on the disk . . . Run Norton Disk Doctor"). These background scans only scan during idle activity, so as not to slow down your other work.

These automatic scans are far from an essential preventative measure. However, I have found them useful. Here's how to set them up.

Norton Utilities Simply install FileSaver (as explained in Steps 1 through 5 of "Protect Against Accidentally Deleted Files"). That's all you really need to do. However, with the More Choices option selected, you can modify when a scan is initiated and exactly what it scans for.

MacTools Pro To accomplish a similar sort of protection with MacTools, you need to place its AutoCheck application in the Startup Items folder. You then select the timing of the automatic background scans by setting AutoCheck options (accessed by clicking the Options button from MacTools Pro's Clinic window and then clicking the AutoCheck button, as seen in Figure 2-15). AutoCheck checks for most, but not all, of what DiskFix checks; so it is not a total substitute for DiskFix. New to Mac-Tools Pro, AutoCheck can now "auto-repair" problems that it detects, eliminating the need to separately access DiskFix.

Apple Personal Diagnostics   Apple Personal Diagnostics, though more of a diagnostic utility than a repair utility, does have some repair functions (see Fix-Its #10 and #17), including an automatic background scan option. You set this up by installing the Automated Diagnostics extension and then selecting the Automated Diagnostics button from within the Apple Personal Diagnostics application.

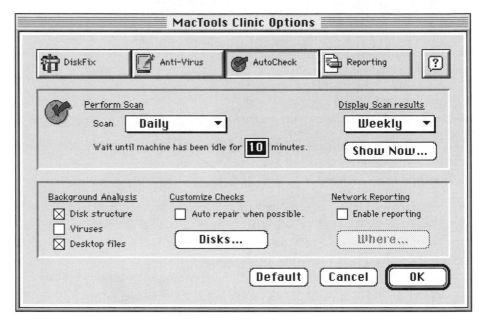

Figure 2-15   MacTools Pro's AutoCheck settings

Protect Against Loss of Data Due to System Crashes

Following some sadistic logic, a system crash or bomb seems to occur most often when you are in the middle of some important task.

Yes, even if you take all the previous precautions, there will probably come the day when you have been working for an hour or so on some important document, so engrossed in what you were doing that you forgot to save your work. Suddenly, you remember. You are about to select Save, when WHAM!—the infamous system bomb appears. Or maybe there is just a brief power failure. Whatever the case, all your work is lost.

Recovering from a system crash is usually as simple as restarting your computer. This gets you up and running again, but it does not resurrect any data that were unsaved at the time of the crash. The probability of recovering this unsaved work is almost zero—unless you have previously installed certain protection utilities (and even then, the probabilities may not be all that good!).

Saving Text Data After a System Crash NowSave is a control panel included as part of Now Utilities. With version 4.0 or a later version of Now Utilities, you can set NowSave so that it saves all text input to a special continually updated file, no matter what application you are using to type the text. If a system crash or power failure occurs, this file has a copy of all of your work up to (or almost up to) the point of the interruption.

This feature has its limits. For example, text is saved in the order you typed it, which may not be the order it appears in the document. However, in times of crisis, whatever is saved may be worthwhile.

Other similar alternatives include Last Resort and the GhostWriter option of Thunder, a spelling checker.

Recovering from a Crash Without Loss of Data Crash Barrier is a control panel that, when installed, supposedly increases your chances of recovering from a system crash. If it succeeds, it ideally returns you to where you were just prior to the crash. You then have a chance to save your data before proceeding further. Freeware utilities, Bomb Shelter and System Error Patch, have a similar basic function.

How often do these utilities really allow you to recover from a crash and save your unsaved data? Some say only very rarely. Others claim to find them helpful. Personally, I don't use any of these utilities. Still, even if they work only once or twice a year, they may be worth it for those times. Don't expect miracles and you won't be disappointed.

Using an Autosave Function An autosave function, which is another feature of NowSave, can be viewed as a means of protecting you against loss of data after a system crash. That's assuming it automatically saves your data just prior to a crash and that you ordinarily would not have manually saved the data at that point.

SEE: • Chapter 4 for more details on system errors, including more on using these utilities

Give Your Macintosh a Tune-up

The following quintet of procedures should ideally be done on a regular basis, even if your machine seems to be running smoothly:

- Defragment your disk.
- Rebuild your desktop.
- Run Disk First Aid and/or MacCheck.
- Replace the System file.
- Stay up-to-date.

Think of them as the equivalent of giving your car a tune-up. I do these operations at least three or four times a year, more often if it seems warranted. While I am sure many people have merrily gone along without ever having done any of these things, I don't recommend doing so. Again, better safe than sorry.

These procedures are more than preventative measures. You can also use them to solve problems after they happen. Thus, I discuss these procedures again, from a more specific problem-solving perspective, in Part III, especially Fix-Its #1, #5, #8, #9, and #10. To avoid repetition, I delve into most details in these later Fix-Its. For now, I simply present an overview.

Defragment Your Disk

It may surprise you to learn that when you write a file to your hard drive, the file may be split and saved in several sections, scattered across your drive. This typically occurs when there is not enough disk space in a single unused chunk to hold the entire file. While not a problem by itself, if too much fragmentation exists, you may see a slow-down in performance or an inability to open a file. At the very least, less file fragmentation tends to improve chances of recovering files after a disk crash.

You usually defragment a disk by using a special disk-optimizing utility. In Norton Utilities and MacTools, the optimizing utilities are called Speed Disk and Optimizer, respectively. Another alternative utility is called Disk Express II (available separately or as part of a package called AlSoft Power Tools). The advantage of Disk Express II is that it can be set to automatically defragment your disk in the background, whenever your computer is idle, rather than waiting for you to do it manually all at once.

By the way, whenever you reformat your hard drive and restore files from your backup copies, you have also defragmented the files on your disk.

SEE: • Fix-It #8 for details on how to defragment a disk

Rebuild Your Desktop File

Rebuild your desktop. Rebuild your desktop. This is almost a mantra of Macintosh problem solving. It is usually one of the first things recommended, no matter what your problem is. It is as if to say, "Well, even if it doesn't do anything, it can't hurt to try."

So what does it really mean to rebuild your desktop? The Desktop file(s) are invisible files that the Finder uses to keep track of information required to create the Finder's desktop display. Basically, rebuilding your desktop means to update or replace your existing Desktop file.

Rebuilding the desktop is a useful tool for solving a variety of problems, especially those related to the functioning of the Finder (such as an inability to launch files). However, it is also useful as a maintenance measure, even if you don't suspect anything is wrong at the moment.

The basic way to rebuild the desktop is: hold down the command and option keys just prior to the mounting of a disk (hold them down at startup for the startup disk), until an alert box appears asking if you want to rebuild the desktop. Click OK.

SEE • Fix-It #9 for more on how to rebuild the desktop
• Chapter 8 for more on invisible files, including the Desktop files

Run Disk First Aid and/or MacCheck

Disk First Aid is included with all versions of the system software and with every Mac that is sold (it's on your Disk Tools disk). MacCheck has had a more limited distribution, shipping with some systems (mostly Performas) but not others. Both are available from online services. If you don't have MacCheck, don't worry. It is the less important of the two utilities. Disk First Aid is the real workhorse. It is a repair utility designed primarily to detect and fix problems caused by corruption of special invisible files, the Directory files, that keep track of the overall organization of your hard drive.

Though there are competing utilities that detect and fix more problems, these have the distinct advantage of being free. Also, since they come from Apple and especially since Disk First Aid is frequently upgraded, they sometimes get the scoop on fixing a newly discovered problem. Thus, they are a good place to start, even if they do not turn out to be your last stop.

Although these utilities are most often used after a problem has been discovered, I also recommend using them periodically, even if nothing appears to be wrong. This is especially true for Disk First Aid. When I run Disk First Aid for a maintenance check, I have been surprised by how often it reports that a repair is needed—even though I did not suspect a problem existed.

SEE • Fix-It #10 for how to use MacCheck and Disk First Aid
• Fix-It #13 for more on using other utilities to check and repair disks
• Chapter 8 for more on invisible files, including the Directory files

Replace the System File

The System file is the most essential and probably most complicated file on your disk. Unfortunately, it is also one of the most frequently modified. The Macintosh modifies the System file quite often, as part of the Mac's normal operation. You get no special notification that this has happened, so you may not even be aware of it. With every modification, there is a chance that an error will occur and that the System file will be corrupted. This can lead to a variety of problems whose cause may not be easily diagnosed as due to a corrupted System file. Sometimes, these problems may not even appear until weeks after the damage first occurred. Thus, it is usually a good idea to replace the System file every 3 or 4 months, even if you are not yet experiencing any symptoms. The easiest way to do this is if you keep a special backup copy of your

System file (that you are confident is not damaged) maintained for just this purpose. Otherwise, you will have to reinstall the System file from your system software disks, using the Installer utility.

SEE: • Fix-It #5 for how to reinstall system software

Stay Up-to-Date

Periodically, check sources (such as the ones described in Fix-It #18) to find out if Apple has recently released any new or upgraded system software files that you should install. If so, install them. This can solve problems you may be experiencing, but couldn't figure out the cause of. It can also help you to avoid some of the problems before they ever show up on your machine.

Most especially, note that Apple periodically releases extensions, such as its System Updates, that fix bugs known to exist in its system software (see Figure 2-16). Read Me files that come with these utilities describe precisely what problems these Updates fix. If you have any of the symptoms described, be certain to install the Update. Each Update incorporates all the enhancements of the previous updates for that version of the system software, so that you never need to have more than one Update file in your System Folder. Unfortunately, these Updates often cannot be used with the special versions of system software used (prior to System 7.5) with Performas. For Macintoshes that require an Enabler file, these System Updates also include the latest versions of these files.

SEE: • Fix-It #5 for more details on installing System Updates and Enablers

System Update

As a rule, also stay current with your non-Apple software, especially checking for maintenance releases that fix bugs uncovered in previous versions.

Figure 2-16
The System Update 3.0 extension, the centerpiece of the System Update 3.0 disk

BY THE WAY ▶

WHAT EXACTLY DOES A SYSTEM UPDATE UPDATE?

System Update 3.0 *In mid-1994, Apple released System Update 3.0, designed for users of System 7.1 (you don't need it if you are using System 7.5, which already builds in all of these fixes). It fixed and enhanced literally dozens of aspects of the system software, far too many to list here. However, to give you a flavor of what you get when you use these updates, here is a selected list of the more significant improvements that you get with Update 3.0 (taken from the Update's Read Me file):*

- Updates the Memory control panel to version 7.3. This new version prevents a potential crash during boot if the RAM disk was set too large. Also, this control panel now opens with 32-bit addressing on.
- Corrects a problem that potentially allowed the system to become corrupted during a power failure or a crash. This corruption would prevent the Macintosh from restarting.
- Fixes a problem where a Power Macintosh, Quadra 840AV, or 660AV may hang if a CD-ROM disk is inserted when file sharing is on and a large file is being transferred.
- Fixes a problem that prevented the Macintosh Plus from using any system software newer than 7.1. Users wishing to upgrade to newer system software must also delete the Finder Preferences file from the Preferences folder and restart.
- Corrects a problem that caused some programs to quit unexpectedly or caused the computer to freeze when you attempted to open programs over the network. This includes/replaces all of the functionality of Network Launch Fix (and the Installer will delete it).
- Fixes the "About This Macintosh" box so the memory usage line does not get drawn outside of the box's bounds.
- Fixes a problem with throwing away folders that are on an AppleShare volume. Sometimes when attempting to empty the Trash, the Finder would warn that the folder contained items in use and could not be deleted. The Finder will now properly delete such folders.
- Updates the Standard File package to include many fixes and enhancements. The most significant fix corrects a crash problem when more than 20 volumes are mounted. The most significant enhancement is the use of color icons.
- Includes Apple HD SC Setup version 7.3.1,. This new version fixes a crash problem version 7.3 has when run on Macintosh models that do not support virtual memory.
- Corrects problems ejecting floppy disks when the computer is shut down on Macintosh IIsi, IIci, IIvx, IIvi, Macintosh Quadra 700, and Macintosh Quadra 950 computers.
- Prevents fonts from being needlessly locked in memory during the boot process. This frees up memory on affected machines.
- System Update 3.0 also includes enhancements from System Update 2.0.1, Hardware System Update 2.0, and Hardware System Update 1.0.

System 7.5 Update 1.0   In March 1995, Apple released a new four-disk update specific to System 7.5: System 7.5 Update 1.0. It includes a System 7.5 Update file, an updated Finder 7.5.1., and an assortment of other file updates. The first thing you will notice after installing the Update (and restarting) is that the familiar "Welcome to Macintosh" startup screen is replaced by a new "MacOS" screen. There are many fixes and enhancements included with this update.

- It fixes a potential crash problem when pasting large blocks of data.
- The Power On key on the keyboard now can be used to turn the computer off as well as on.
- For PowerBook models 160, 165, 165C, 180, and 180C, pressing the Power button automatically launches items in the Shutdown Items folder and shuts down the computer.
- You no longer have to turn off file sharing in order to eject a removable disk or CD-ROM.
- A new version of Apple Guide runs native on the Power Macintosh and is compatible with At Ease.
- A new version of WindowShade fixes a potential crash problem that occurs when memory is very low.
- A new version of Stickies launches reliably, even when a note is collapsed.

Chapter Summary

This chapter began with an overview of some of the common terms (such as damaged files and software bugs) that are used to describe problems you may have with your Macintosh.

From here, I covered the various tools you need in order to be an effective troubleshooter. These ranged from the Finder and other components of the system software to several more specialized utilities, especially packages such as Norton Utilities and MacTools.

Finally, I considered a range of activities you could do to help prevent problems from occurring, or at least to be better prepared for their inevitability. These included regularly backing up all your files, installing protection against viruses, rebuilding your desktop, checking your disk with Disk First Aid, and several more.

Chapter 3

Problem Solving: General Strategies

Uh-oh . . .

Something has gone wrong with your Macintosh. You are sitting and staring at your screen, trying to figure out exactly what has happened and (more important) what you can do to fix it. That's exactly what you are about to find out.

Five Steps to Solving Macintosh Problems

1. Read Alert Box Messages

Often, after something unexpected has occurred with your Macintosh, an alert box error message appears. Often these messages contain valuable information.

> **TECHNICALLY SPEAKING** ▶
>
> **WHAT'S AN ALERT BOX?**
>
> *An* alert box *pops up on your screen to warn you or inform you about the consequences of what you have just done* (Your file has been successfully transferred) *or what you are about to do* (Erasing the disk will permanently erase all data on it. Do you still want to erase it?). *It is usually accompanied by either the "! in a triangle" icon (which means "caution") or the "hand in a stop sign" icon (which is more serious and means "stop and read this before proceeding"). Examples of these icons are in Figures 3-1 and 3-2.*
>
> *Usually, you cannot do much in response to an alert box message other than click an OK or Cancel button.*
>
> *Alert boxes are a normal and expected part of the Macintosh's operation. Their appearance doesn't necessarily mean that you have any problem. However, when you do have a problem, they are particularly likely to appear. In such cases, they are often referred to as* error messages.
>
> *A terminology note: A cousin to the alert box is the* dialog box. *A dialog box usually appears after you've selected a command from a menu. For example, the box that appears after you select Print from the File menu is a dialog box. Dialog boxes are distinguished from alert boxes both by the different functions and by the fact that dialog boxes usually have many more options than the one or two choices typical of an alert box.*

The alert box may inform you of an action you need to take *(Please select Page Setup before printing your document)*. It may also inform you why you cannot perform a command you requested *(The disk cannot be erased because the disk is locked)*. Or it may tell you what has just gone wrong *(The application unexpectedly quit)*. In any case, it can also provide advice on how to successfully carry out the command or fix the problem.

For example, let's suppose you have an application that does not open when you try to launch it and you get the message shown in Figure 3-1.

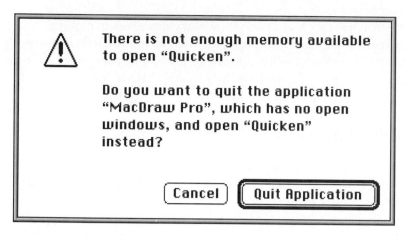

⚠ There is not enough memory available to open "Quicken".

Do you want to quit the application "MacDraw Pro", which has no open windows, and open "Quicken" instead?

[Cancel] [Quit Application]

Figure 3-1   An alert box indicating that there is insufficient memory available to open Quicken

This alert box offers a suggested solution to the problem and, in this case, provides a button for enacting that solution. In System 7, these messages are generally much more helpful than they were in System 6.

The alert box in Figure 3-2 is another example. It not only tells you why you could not empty the Trash, but it gives you a *keyboard shortcut* needed to quickly solve the problem. This keyboard shortcut works faster than having to go to the Get Info window of each locked file and unlock it.

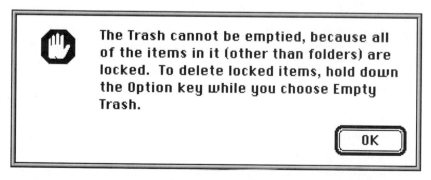

🖐 The Trash cannot be emptied, because all of the items in it (other than folders) are locked. To delete locked items, hold down the Option key while you choose Empty Trash.

[OK]

Figure 3-2   An alert box that may appear when you try to empty the Trash

What if you don't understand the meaning of the alert box message or if it doesn't offer any useful advice? This is where the rest of this book can help. This book describes dozens of alert box messages and how to deal with them. You can look up any particular error message in the Symptom Index at the back of this book. This book does not list every possible alert message you might get. No single book could do that. But it does describe and explain the most important and most common alert messages you are likely to encounter.

One final note: Alert boxes that accompany some of the more serious problems you can get, such as a system crash or an unexpected quit, often include esoteric information about the cause of the problem (such as *An error of Type 3 occurred*). While I generally recommend ignoring this information, as it is rarely helpful for most users, I do describe its meaning in some detail in Chapter 4.

2. Check If the Problem Repeats

Clearly, not all problems can be solved by reading error messages (especially so if your problem did not result in any error message!). Still, the solution to your problem may be close at hand, often just a few mouse clicks away.

First off, many Macintosh problems are one-time-only occurrences. They happen for reasons that may never again be exactly duplicated and that no one will ever fully understand. So, before you run off and spend hours trying to solve a problem, make sure you really have a problem to solve: See if you can get the problem to recur.

If the problem involves an application, quit and relaunch it. If the problem involves a floppy disk, eject and then reinsert it. And so on. Then check if the problem recurs.

If your problem is a system crash or other equally debilitating event, you will have to restart the Macintosh before you can check if the problem recurs. Even for less serious errors, it is usually good advice to restart the Macintosh before checking for a recurring problem. A restart solves a surprising array of problems all by itself. But beware: A restart may sometimes only appear to solve a problem. The symptoms may return again the next day or the next week.

If the problem does not recur, be happy! You probably had one of those once-in-a-lifetime unknown causes that may never happen again. Chalk it up as one of life's cosmic mysteries. If it does continue to recur, you have more work to do.

3. Isolate the Cause

Macintosh problems have many possible causes, but relatively fewer specific symptoms. For example, a system crash (a symptom) can result from hundreds of different possible causes. Your job is to progressively narrow the range of possible causes of your problem, until you succeed in isolating the precise cause. While the general problem-solving strategies described here are useful to apply no matter what the specific nature of your problem, they are most critical for those times when you are trying to diagnose and solve problems on your own, on those occasions when seeking help did not provide the answer.

SEE: • Chapter 4, "Solve It! Recurring System Errors," for more detailed strategies on diagnosing recurring system errors

Look for Recent Changes or Unusual Circumstances

Suppose that while you are trying to save a BusyWorks word processing document, a system crash occurs. You have saved many documents with BusyWorks before and have never had a system crash. What's going on? Usually, some recent change to your software or hardware is precipitating the crash. The culprit may be a newly added system extension or a recently connected hardware peripheral. The problem may even be due to a change you recently made in existing software, such as changing an application's default preference setting or turning on a new option in a control panel. Thus, if you are aware of any recent changes to your computer system, focus your search on them.

If you don't know of any recent changes to your computer system, consider whether any unusual circumstances, not previously duplicated, could have caused the problem. For example, perhaps you were trying to save a particularly long BusyWorks document when the crash occurred. If you had never before tried to save a document that long, perhaps the size of the document is the problem.

Assess the Specificity of the Problem

Suppose you cannot open a particular document file currently stored on a floppy disk. What's the cause? The problem could be with the particular file, the particular application used to open the file, some related file stored in the System Folder, the floppy disk that contains the file, or even the disk drive hardware.

Often, the exact symptom or error message (if one appears) helps you choose among these possibilities. Otherwise, you need to assess the specificity of the problem. Thus, to see if the problem is specific to that file, try opening another file. To see if it is specific to that application, try opening files in other applications. To see if it is specific to that disk, try using other disks. I think you get the point by now. There are no exact rules here. In the end, isolating the cause of a problem is often more of an art than it is a science.

TAKE NOTE ▶

RISK MANAGEMENT

Whenever you try to fix a problem, there is at least a small risk that what you do will somehow succeed only in making matters worse. Always look for ways to minimize this risk. For example, as stressed in Chapter 2, always back up your files before you attempt to fix a problem.

In general, try the simplest, easiest, and most-likely-to-be-successful techniques first. Then proceed to the more powerful, difficult-to-use, more time-consuming, lower-probability-of-success ones, if necessary. This not only saves you time and hassle, it is also generally safer. The more powerful techniques tend to be the riskier ones.

4. Go for Help

You needn't wait to try this step until you have exhausted all your attempts to isolate the cause in the previous step. Similarly, you don't always need to go for help before you can go on to the next step and solve the problem. These last three steps can be thought of as more parallel than sequential. You can skip from one to the other in whatever order gets you to the solution the fastest.

Check an Application's Built-in Help

If the problem is specific to a particular application, and the application has built-in help, check it out. The location of the help file will vary from application to application. Sometimes it is a separate program. Sometimes it is accessed from within the application, under the Apple menu. Other times, it may be found in the Balloon Help menu. If you are using System 7.5, check if there is a special Apple Guide document for the application.

Also be sure to check both your hard drive and the application's original disks for any Read Me files. These often contain important late-breaking troubleshooting information.

Check the Manual!

I know. At best, people use the manual for a while when they first start using a new program and then never glance at it again. Whole sections of the book remain untouched by human hands. Many Macintosh users are proud of how much they can accomplish without *ever* looking at the manual. The fact that they can accomplish anything at all is touted as evidence of how easy the Macintosh is to use.

And yes, most manuals are not fun to read. They are reference books, after all, not science fiction adventures.

Despite all of this, I am telling you to read the manual. Check whatever manuals, for hardware or software, that seem potentially relevant to your problem. No, you don't have to read the whole thing cover to cover. Just check for the part relevant to the problem you are having. Check the opening pages of the manual, the ones that discuss how to install the program. Vital details about where files should be located and possible incompatibilities are found here. Check the troubleshooting section, if there is one. Use the index, if necessary. You will be amazed how many problems you can solve this way. Sometimes, you will even discover helpful tips that make it easier to complete your task, regardless of any problems you may be experiencing.

If a feature of a program doesn't work the first time you try it, don't immediately assume there is a problem with the program. Often the problem is that you did not correctly understand how to use the program. Reading the manual will almost invariably solve this type of problem.

Call Technical Support

Almost all companies maintain a phone number to help answer your technical questions. The number should have been included somewhere in the documentation that came with the program.

Technical support should not be used as a substitute for reading manuals or generally developing your own problem-solving skills. However, it can be helpful in providing information about undocumented features or recently discovered bugs in the software—information not readily available anywhere else. The company may even be able to supply an updated version of the software that fixes the bug.

SEE: • Fix-It #18 for more on dealing with technical support and other outside sources of help

Consult This Book

This is an obvious bit of advice. After all, solving problems is the purpose of this book.

5. Fix the Problem

Identifying the cause of a recurring problem is often the most difficult and time-consuming step in this whole procedure. However, it obviously is not the last step. You next need to fix the problem so that it no longer recurs.

I can make broad generalizations here. Problems unique to a particular application are usually solved by replacing or upgrading the application. Symptoms that span across most applications are usually caused by system software. This is especially likely if the problem involves activities, such as printing, that depend heavily on system software files. Solutions to these problems often involve replacing system software files. System extensions and control panels can also be involved here. Problems that affect the entire disk are usually due to damage to special invisible files on the disk. You should try to repair these files, if possible. If they can't be repaired, you will probably have to reformat the entire disk.

The Troubleshooter's Cure-Alls

As an alternative to searching for a precise cause of and solution to a given problem, many experts suggest working your way through a familiar list of likely cures, supposedly guaranteed to fix almost any problem you might encounter: Rebuild the desktop, do a clean reinstall of your system software, turn off all your extensions, run Disk First Aid, and so on. It certainly can't hurt to try at least some of these procedures. Indeed, doing this is sometimes a useful way to discover what has gone wrong.

Still, to just follow these procedures blindly will often result in your wasting time trying things that have little or no hope of helping you. Sure, I describe these all-purpose panaceas, in extensive detail, in the Fix-Its section of this book. But this book does much more. The chapters that follow present a series of specific diagnoses and treatments for a broad range of Macintosh problems. They also show how to understand what went wrong, so that you can begin to more intelligently solve problems on your own.

Avoiding Problems

Get to Know Shortcuts

Almost anything you can do with the Macintosh, you can do in more than one way. For example, do you want to close a window on the desktop? Simply select the Close command from the Finder's File menu. Or click the close box in the upper left corner of the window. Or use a keyboard shortcut—in this case, command-W (this shortcut is listed in the File menu next to the word Close). Other shortcuts are more obscure and can be found only by consulting an application's manual.

The Command (⌘), Option, Control, Shift, and Escape keys, in combination with other keys, often produce a variety of strange and wonderful results and shortcuts, depending on which application you are using.

Familiarity with at least the more common of these shortcuts is invaluable in negotiating many problem-solving tasks, not to mention making your daily work with the Macintosh considerably more pleasant. Check the manuals of your applications for details, or simply explore on your own and see what happens.

Go Exploring

Having mentioned the topic of exploring, it is worth discussing a bit more. The design of the Macintosh, with its pull-down menus and point-and-click approach, encourages exploring. This is because the design minimizes the need to memorize anything or type in long and obscure commands. Take advantage of this. Even if you never look at an application's manual, spend some time exploring its menus and dialog boxes. Try out potential shortcut commands.

You may feel like you do not have the time to spend on this sort of frivolity. However, time spent exploring can be an investment repaid several times over in avoiding future frustrations. Often the biggest benefit of exploring is the pleasant surprise of discovering that there is a way (often an easy way) to do something that you thought was impossible. It is the "I didn't know you could do that" reaction. This, in itself, can be considered a form of problem solving.

Still, if you are a relatively inexperienced user, this may sound like dangerous advice—like advising a novice tightrope walker to practice without a net. However, with a little common sense, the risks are minimal at best. Here's some commonsense advice to use while exploring.

Work Only with Duplicates

Work only with a duplicate copy of any important document (or use a document that you don't care if you lose). That way, even if the document gets deleted or corrupted in some way, it does not matter. Even if your entire machine crashes and you have to start all over again, no harm is done.

Use Undo

Remember that most actions can be reversed by the Undo command and that (usually!) no changes are saved until you select Save from the File menu. When in doubt, undo.

Use Cancel

Almost all potentially "dangerous" operations on the Macintosh, such as erasing a disk, are preceded by a warning and an opportunity to cancel. If you get too anxious about what you might be about to do, just select Cancel.

Chapter Summary

This chapter described general strategies for solving problems, regardless of what the specific symptoms are. It described five basic steps in solving problems: reading alert messages, checking to see if the problem repeats, isolating the cause, seeking help and (finally) fixing the problem. These guidelines are a blueprint for what follows in the remainder of this book. They are also useful for those situations not specifically covered in this book.

Finally, the chapter concluded with a brief plea lauding the value of learning about and exploring the nuances of your Macintosh.

Part II:

Symptoms, Causes, and Cures

When preventative measures are not enough and a problem occurs anyway, this is the section to turn to first. Here, you will find a listing of symptoms that cover a broad range of both the most common and the most serious problems you are likely to confront, together with step-by-step instructions for what to do to solve them. Again, the solutions require only a few simple software tools and no particular expertise on your part.

Chapters 4 and 5 cover those problems that are the most disruptive to your use of the Macintosh.

Chapter 4 covers system errors (also called system crashes), typified by the infamous bomb alert box. Chapter 4 walks you through exactly what to do after specific system errors. It may surprise you to learn that you can often do more than simply give up and restart your Macintosh.

Chapter 5 covers what is probably the most anxiety-provoking problem to confront any computer user: a total inability to start up the machine. The Macintosh may successfully turn on, but the startup sequence may never begin or never reach a successful conclusion. Chapter 5 also describes what to do for any crashed disk, whether it is a startup disk or not. The chapter concludes with a look at a few other general disk-related problems, such as problems with ejecting floppy disks or shutting down the Macintosh.

From launching applications to printing documents, Chapters 6 through 8 explain what can go wrong and how you can make it right again.

Chapter 6 covers the most common and yet most frustrating file-related problems: Are you having trouble locating a particular file? Or if you do locate it, do you find that it refuses to open? Maybe there is insufficient memory to use the Clipboard. Perhaps you want to copy or delete a file, but the Macintosh refuses to let you do it. If you are having any of these problems, Chapter 6 guides you to a solution.

Even after you have successfully completed and saved your masterpiece, your problems may not be over. You probably want to print out your work. This introduces a new host of potential problems. **Chapter 7** is devoted to what to do when you cannot get a document to print.

Chapter 8 is a more technical look at some of the Macintosh's more esoteric, yet still comprehensible and certainly useful, topics: file types, creators, and attributes. As always, the focus remains on how you can apply this knowledge to solve problems.

Chapters 9 and 10 are devoted to problems specific to the two most common categories of document files: text and graphics. Whether it's dashing off a memo or writing a novel, whether it's creating a chart in a spreadsheet or creating a full-page ad for a magazine, virtually every Macintosh user spends most of their time with these two prime functions.

Chapter 9 covers text problems. Although most likely to crop up when using a word processor, text problems can appear when you are using any application that contains text, including spreadsheets and databases. The chapter begins with an overview of the different categories of fonts and how they determine the appearance of your text. It concludes with a description of common text-related problems and their solutions.

Chapter 10 deals with those graphic-related problems that can confront even the most nongraphic of Macintosh users. It begins with an explanation of the different types of graphics files and the basics of how your computer displays grayscale and color documents. It concludes with a collection of common graphics-related problems and how to solve them.

Chapters 11 and 12 cover problems that are specific to PowerBooks, Power Macintoshes, and the latest versions of the system software.

Chapter 11 deals primarily with PowerBook problems. It also briefly covers problems related to file sharing, with a focus on sharing between a PowerBooks and a desktop Macintosh.

Chapter 12 describes the problems unique to Power Macintoshes. It also covers problems specific to System 7.5, with a special focus on QuickDraw GX.

As you go through these chapters, you will find frequent references to other parts of the book, particularly the Fix-Its from Part III. Part II emphasizes the diagnosis of a problem and, in general, how to go about solving it. The Fix-Its describe, more specifically, the tools used to solve these problems. By analogy, if this were a book on home repairs, Part II might tell you that the squeak in your flooring is caused by a loose floorboard and that you have to hammer in some nails to fix it. Part III, in contrast, would explain what hammers are and the general techniques for using them. So, if any explanations in these chapters seem less than complete, check out the Fix-Its for the rest of the story.

Chapter 4

System Errors:
Living with the Bomb

The Mac's Worst-Kept Secret

If you are new to the world of computers, you may think that a *system crash* is the sound your computer makes after you have thrown it to the floor in frustration. No, that's not it exactly—though a series of system crashes can certainly get you thinking about sending your Macintosh into free fall. Actually, a system crash refers to any time your computer's processing gets so messed up that it stops whatever it was doing and no longer responds to further user input.

What to do when you have this type of system crash, or any other of several related *system errors,* is the subject of this chapter. System errors are the Macintosh's worst-kept secret. Most software manuals barely mention the possibility that system errors can occur. Yet they do occur, all too frequently.

If (or more realistically, when) you get any sort of system error, it is the equivalent of seeing a "road closed" sign at the end of a long stretch of highway. There's no going forward, and you will have to spend some time heading back before you can make progress again.

I am not going to delve much into what causes these system errors. My goal is simply to explain how to rid yourself of them. Still, it may make you feel better to know that system crashes are not the result of some mistake on your part. It is either the result of faulty hardware or (much more likely) damaged or less-than-perfectly designed software. Your freedom from guilt is at best only a small consolation when a system error does occur. This knowledge doesn't save any of your data or eliminate any of the frustration.

Helpful hint: No software is perfectly designed.　Therefore all software is potentially a source of a system error. Trust no one. But wait! Don't get overly alarmed by this warning. Programming for the Macintosh is not the easiest thing in the world to do, and it is almost impossible to anticipate every potential circumstance that might lead to a system crash—especially, when they have to contend with the ever-growing number of Macintosh models, a dizzying assortment of potential peripherals, and a seemingly endless variety of software, all of which may be combined in a nearly infinite number of permutations. The real surprise is that, most of the time, things work just as expected.

Your immediate concerns are probably the following:

- What permanent damage has been done to the machine, if any?
- What data have I lost, if any?
- How do I get the Macintosh working again?
- How do I prevent the system error from occurring again?

The answer to the first question is good news. System errors never cause any permanent damage to your hardware. A system crash can result from damaged hardware but it will never cause it. And while a system crash may damage (or, as it is sometimes called, corrupt) your software (particular anything you were using at the time of the crash), it is much more likely that everything on your disks is still okay. In general, you should be able to get your Macintosh up and running again in a matter of seconds.

The answer to the second question is potentially bad news. Barring a few exceptions to be discussed shortly, everything you were working on at the time of the crash that had not been previously saved to disk is forever lost in space, never to be seen again. If you spent the last hour writing the opening chapter of your next novel and never saved it—it is probably gone forever. Actually, any file open at the time of the crash, saved or unsaved, is at some risk of damage.

Helpful hint: Save frequently.   Saving is your greatest protection against the worst-case scenarios of a system crash. So, if you are planning to spend the day working on your Great American Novel, don't forget to use the Save command every few minutes.

The answers to the remaining two questions depend on the cause of the system error. The main thing you will do after most system crashes is to restart the Macintosh. Happily, in many cases, after you restart, the system error does *not* recur. This is because the specific combination of events that led to the system error will not be repeated. Even if you think you are repeating what you did prior to the system error, the Macintosh may see it differently. However, sometimes a system error occurs repeatedly. In these cases, you must track down the cause of the error, so you can find a way to prevent its recurrence.

Solve It! A Catalog of System Errors

TAKE NOTE ▶

SOLVING SYSTEM ERRORS IN A HURRY

This chapter provides extensive details about what to do in the event of a system error—more than you are likely to find in any other single source. Still, if you have a system error right now and want quick advice on what to do, you don't have to wade through this whole chapter to find it. So here's a quick summary of what to do:

1. *If you get any system error dialog box, jot down any error code that appears in it, just in case it proves to be useful later on.*

2. *Regain control of your machine. Try a forced quit (press Command-Option-Escape). If this does not work, restart your Macintosh either by clicking the Restart button in the system error dialog box, pressing the Reset button (or using an equivalent keyboard command, if your model supports this feature), or by simply turning the Macintosh off and then back on again.*

3. *Assuming the Mac started successfully, check the Trash for recovered files that may contain unsaved data.*

4. *Return to what you were doing prior to the error. If the error does not recur, forget about it for now. It may not happen again. Resume your work.*

(continued)

5. If it does recur, and it is limited to the use of a specific application or document, the software may be damaged. Replace the software from your backups. If replacing a program, you may also want to delete any preferences files related to that program, as reinstalling does not typically create a new preferences file.

6. If the error still recurs, you probably have a software bug in the application or a conflict between the application and a system extension, control panel, system software, or hardware. Contact the manufacturer of the application for advice. Otherwise, try to resolve the conflict yourself. For example, check for: INIT conflicts by restarting with INITs disabled (hold down the shift key during startup); disk damage by using Disk First Aid; system software problems by reinstalling the system software.

7. If none of this helps, or you are uncertain about how to do any of the previous steps, then you do need to wade through the rest of this chapter. Even if the previous advice did help, browse through this chapter at some later point. What you learn will better prepare you for your next system error.

System Crashes

 ### Symptoms:

The Bomb Alert Box Appears

The bomb alert box (see Figure 4-1) is the best-known of all system errors. The alert box includes an icon of a bomb, as well as a text message apologizing for what has just occurred (*Sorry, a system error has occurred.*). Users typically refer to this unhappy event by saying "My computer crashed" or "My Mac just bombed."

This is not a warning that your computer may explode. But it does mean that your Mac's activity has come to a grinding halt.

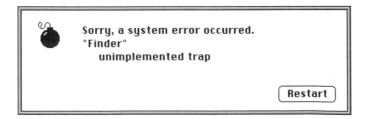

Figure 4-1   A system bomb alert box from System 6 (top) and System 7 (bottom)

Breakup of Screen Display

The other type of system crash is so severe that the Macintosh cannot even muster the strength to put up the bomb alert message. Instead, the screen display may break up into an unintelligible mess, complete with flashes of light and crackling noises. This is less common on the newer models of Macintosh. Despite the pyrotechnics, it is still a system crash. Again, no permanent harm has been done to your machine.

 Causes:

Most crashes are due to a software bug or conflict between two active programs. Bad memory management is the likely immediate culprit in most of these cases.

System crashes can also have some hardware-related causes. These include defective memory chips, defective power supply, and SCSI device problems.

 What to do:

Understanding System Error Alert Box Messages (Or What the Heck Is a "Bad F Line Instruction" Anyway?)

Besides offering its apologies, the bomb box error message typically provides a description of the cause of your crash. You are not likely to be impressed with these descriptions. Depending on whether you are using System 6 or System 7, and the exact circumstances of the system error, these descriptions are one of two types. Either it defines the problem by name (such as *bad F line instruction* or *unimplemented trap*) or by number (such as *ID = 02* or *an error of Type 1*). Not very informative, is it? On a scale of understandability, it ranks slightly lower than the instructions for how to calculate depreciation on your tax return.

The truth is, this information was not meant to be easily understood by the masses. It was meant for programmers to understand, so that they can figure out why their programs are crashing. Most of the time, the numbers simply mean that there is a mistake (or "bug") in the program that needs to be fixed (for example, this is what typically causes a *bad F-line instruction* or *unimplemented trap* message). Correcting a program's instruction code is not something you can do yourself. This is why the ID information is almost always of no value to you.

If, despite all this, you are still curious about what the error code numbers mean, there are several places that list their translation. Unfortunately, the translation usually is not much more illuminating than the error code itself. For example, you will learn that an error of ID 1 is a *bus error* and an error of ID 2 is an *address error*. Still, Table 4-1 lists several common error codes, together with a more non-jargonese explanation of what they mean and what you might do about them. Otherwise, check out the Help files included with Apple's MacCheck utility (see Fix-It #10) for a more complete list of error codes. Another source are shareware utilities, such as System Errors or MacErrors. Theoretically, understanding these error codes might sometimes help you track down the cause of a repeating system error. But even this assumes that you can trust the error code to be accurate. Unfortunately, a system crash can so mess things up that the Macintosh may put up a code that doesn't really describe the true cause of the problem . . . in which case, the information is once again useless.

Helpful hint: Don't waste much time trying to interpret the error message. Understanding these messages *never* helps in the immediate crisis of recovering from the crash. It only rarely helps in diagnosing the ultimate cause of the crash. At best, jot down the number for later reference, if needed.

By the way, these same error codes may appear in alert messages resulting from other types of system errors, as described in upcoming sections of this chapter (as well as in other chapters, especially Chapters 5 and 6). In the most benign cases, the message may simply inform you why you can't do what you are trying to do (such as copy a file or open an application) but will otherwise let you proceed with using your Mac. In the worst cases, you have a "fatal" system crash (the focus of this section!). In all cases, the codes have the same meaning as they do here (see Figure 4-2 and Table 4-1).

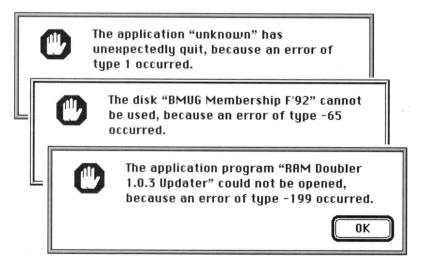

Figure 4-2 System error ID numbers as they appear in a variety of different types of alert messages. In case you are curious, Type 1 means a "bus error," -65 means "read/write requested for an off-line drive," and -199 means "map inconsistent with operation." Aren't you glad you asked?

Table 4-1   Some Common System Error Codes*

ID/ERROR NAME	WHAT IT MEANS	WHAT TO DO**
01/ Bus error and 02/ Address error	Most often due to a software bug, extension conflict, or insufficient memory assigned to an application. More rarely caused by an SCSI problem or even a defective logic board. Technically, the problem is usually that a program has tried to access memory that either doesn't exist or is inaccesible.	If problem is specific to one application, try increasing its memory size (Fix-It #6). Otherwise, call manufacturer to find out about a possible bug. If error happens across many applications, replace system software (Fix-It #5). See Fix-Its #4, #16, and #17 for more on extension conflicts, SCSI problems, and logic board problems, respectively.
03/Illegal instruction	Most likely a software bug. Technically, Macintosh is trying to execute an instruction not in its processor's vocabulary.	Problem is usually specific to a single application. Contact manufacturer for information about a bug-fixed upgrade.
04/Divide by zero error	A mistake in the program code has caused the program to attempt to divide a number by zero. Since this is impossible, the system error results.	Problem is almost assuredly specific to the program in use. Contact manufacturer for information about a bug-fixed upgrade. Also, see Fix-It #4 to check for possible extension conflicts.
09/Line trap (A-line) error and 10/F-line instruction error and 12/Unimplemented trap of core routine (operating system)	Typically an extension conflict or a software bug. For example, a program may assume that the Mac's ROM contains information that is only found in newer Macs, and thus bombs when run on an older model. Technically, it typically means a call was made to the Macintosh's ROM for an entry that doesn't exist or to a debugger that is not installed.	Problem is usually specific to a single application. Contact manufacturer for information about a bug-fixed upgrade. Also, see Fix-It #4 to check for possible extension conflicts. For error 10 (or related error, "floating point coprocessor not installed,") see especially Fix-It #1, No Math Coprocessor.
11/Miscellaneous hardware exception error	An error generated by the processor and not covered by IDs 1 to 10. Exact cause unknown, though could mean a hardware failure. This error is more common on Power Macintoshes. In this case, it is typically due to corruption of the 68040 emulator as it loads into RAM.	Problem is usually specific to a single application. Contact manufacturer for information about a bug-fixed upgrade. Also, see Fix-It #4 to check for possible extension conflicts. Reinstalling system software (Fix-It #5) may help. Otherwise, you may have hardware-related problems (Fix-Its #16 and #17).

*Most other positive number error codes imply either a bug in an application (especially likely with IDs 5–8, 15, 16, or 26) or a damaged file, particularly the System file (especially likely with IDs 17–24 or 27). Negative number error codes have a variety of specific, usually technical, meanings. See a utility such as Mac-Check or MacErrors for a more complete list, if needed.

**Refer to main text for more complete explanations of suggested actions.

Table 4-1   Some Common System Error Codes *(continued)*

ID/ERROR NAME	WHAT IT MEANS	WHAT TO DO
25/Out of memory and 28/Stack ran into heap	While this should be caused by an application running out of memory, Macintosh may be "fooled" by other cause into thinking there is a memory problem.	Increase application's memory allocation (see Fix-It #6). Otherwise, seek more general solutions as described in this chapter.
-34/Disk is full	Not enough room on the disk (typically occurring when trying to save a file to a disk). Otherwise, disk may be damaged.	Delete or transfer files on the disk to free up more room for what you are trying to do. Otherwise, try to repair disk (Fix-Its #10 and #13).
-39/End of file	Indicates a discrepancy between the actual and expected size of a file. Usually means the file is hopelessly corrupted.	If it is an application, replace it and its preferences file (if any). See Chapter 6 (on deleting files) and Fix-Its #2 and #3 (on replacing application and preferences files). For a data file, recover data, if possible, then delete it (see Fix-It #14). Otherwise, try replacing the System and Finder (see Fix-It #5) and/or check for disk damage (see Fix-Its #10 and #13).
-43/File not found	A file you are trying to use could not be located.	Unless the file is really missing, it probably means you have disk damage (see Fix-Its #10 and #13).
-97/Port in use	Most likely a problem with a serial port (printer or modem) connection. Possibly a problem with an SCSI device.	Turn off the serial port peripheral device and turn it back on again. Restart the Mac. Try again. If problem persists, zap Parameter RAM (see Fix-It #11). Otherwise, check for disk driver (Fix-It #12) or other SCSI problems (Fix-It #16).
-108/Out of memory	While this should be caused by an application running out of memory, Macintosh may be "fooled" by other cause into thinking there is a memory problem.	Increase application's memory allocation (see Fix-It #6). Otherwise, seek more general solutions as described in this chapter.
-127/Internal file system error	Usually due to a corrupted Directory.	Try repairing the disk with Disk First Aid (Fix-It #10) or other repair utilities (Fix-It #13). Otherwise, reformatting the disk will probably be required (Fix-It #15).
-192/Resource not found	Usually due to a corrupted application.	If it only happens with one application, it is probably corrupted. Replace it.

Restart the Macintosh

There is no way to completely undo the effects of a system crash or other serious system error! It would be wonderful if you could simply select an Undo command and return your Macintosh to exactly where it was prior to the crash, with all your data still intact, but this is not possible. Even if it was, the crash might recur a few moments later.

Here's what you can do: Restart the Macintosh. To do this, try the following solutions. If one doesn't work, or it is not applicable, try the next one, until you are successful.

- **Click the Restart button in the System error alert box**
  System bomb alert boxes usually include a Restart button. Clicking this button, as its name implies, should restart the Macintosh just as if you had selected Restart from the Finder's Special menu. However, this button works at best only about half the time.

effect, so don't expect too much from it. Another extension, called System Error Patch *works similarly. It bypasses the error box altogether, sounding three beeps and directly quitting the offending application. It seems marginally more reliable than Bomb Shelter, though the current version of System Error Patch has a minor bug that causes the Mac to bypass the dialog box that appears after you select Shut Down in certain mostly older Mac models (the box that tells you that you can safely shut off your machine).*

    The best of these extensions is Crash Barrier *(of course, it is the only one that is not freeware). If it works, it should interrupt the normal system error message and bring up its own dialog box. This should increase your odds of being able to recover from a system crash, without having to restart and with only a minimum (or no) loss of data. With luck, you may even be able to resume the application that was active at the time of the crash and save any unsaved work! Without luck, Crash Barrier is no better than using a forced quit.*

    If you have a system freeze (described later in this chapter), Crash Barrier is not automatically invoked. However, you can access it by pressing the Interrupt button (as described in the next section) or by using a special combination of keys as defined by Crash Barrier.

    In the unlikely case that these buttons actually do return your computer to active duty, my recommendation is to immediately save any unsaved work and select Restart from the Finder's Special menu. Otherwise, you are at imminent risk of having a second system crash.

If the Restart button does work, you probably notice that it takes longer for the Welcome to Macintosh screen to appear after a system crash restart than after using the Finder's Restart command. This is largely the result of the startup sequence partially compensating for the lack of cleaning up (including saving and closing all files, updating Directory files, and so on) that would have normally been done after you selected Restart or Shut Down from the Finder.

BY THE WAY ▶

SYSTEM 7.5 AND THE SHUT DOWN WARNING MESSAGE

If you restart after a system crash with System 7.5 (or really any time you shut down other than by using the Shut Down command), you will probably get the message seen in Figure 4-3 during your next startup sequence. In this case, it is simply telling you what you already know: that you did not restart in the normal fashion. If you don't want to keep seeing this message, you can turn it off by unchecking Shut Down Warning in the newly designed General Controls control panel.

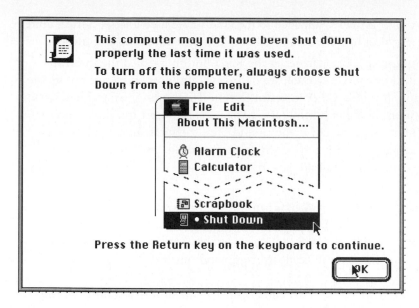

Figure 4-3 In System 7.5, this message may appear after restarting following a system crash

- **Press the Reset button (not the Interrupt button)**

  The Reset Button The Reset button is (in most Macintosh models) an actual physical button located somewhere on the case of your Macintosh (as opposed to the onscreen buttons described in the previous section). It is one of a matched pair of buttons (see Figure 4-4). It is the one of the pair that is identified by a triangle symbol (though on my old Macintosh Plus, it identified by the word "Reset").

  Pressing the Reset button restarts the Macintosh in the same way as if you had clicked the bomb box's Restart button. However, unlike the Restart button, the Reset button is "a sure thing." It always works (at least it has never failed for me). Press it and you have restarted your Macintosh.

Figure 4-4
The Reset and Interrupt buttons on the front of a Macintosh IIci. The Reset button is the one with the triangle symbol, while the Interrupt button has the circle symbol

Helpful hint: The Reset button is designed to be used after system crashes. It is not the ideal way to routinely restart your Macintosh. Use the Finder's Restart command for routine restarts. The Finder's Restart command has the advantage of prompting you to save all unsaved work before it restarts. Also, there is a small chance that restarting with the Reset button may cause some software damage to files on your disk (especially if you press the button while something is being written to a disk). This has never actually happened to me (and I have used a Reset button quite often), so the risk must be quite small. But why take it at all, unless you must?

The Interrupt Button   The partner to the Reset button is called the Interrupt button (identified by a circle symbol; see figure 4-4). In most cases, just ignore the Interrupt button. It is rarely, if ever, useful to you. If you press it by accident, when you meant to press the Reset button after a system crash, don't fret. Just press the Reset button next. Alternatively, if you should press the Interrupt switch by accident, when nothing is actually wrong with the Macintosh, you should be able to return to where you were, with no data lost, by typing G immediately followed by pressing Return.

One notable problem you may have with using the Reset or Interrupt buttons is to find them. The hardware designers at Apple apparently amuse themselves by devising new ways to hide the location of this button. And, with some Macs, there are no buttons. You have to use keyboard commands instead.

SEE: • "Oh Where Oh Where Did My Reset Button Go?" for help on accessing the Reset function on your particular Macintosh

BY THE WAY ▶

OH WHERE OH WHERE DID MY RESET BUTTON GO?

Oh for the good old days, of say four or five years ago . . . when there were only a half dozen or so Macintosh models and they all were designed fairly similarly. Now, explaining even the most simple of features can be a daunting task. Case in point: the location of the Reset and Interrupt buttons.

In the oldest Macintoshes (such as the Macintosh Plus), these buttons came as a separate piece of plastic (referred to as the Programmer's Switch) that you installed on the side of the case (the left side as it faced you). In subsequent modular Macintoshes (such as the IIci), the switch was similar but was installed on the front of the unit. If you have any of these models, you may not find this switch installed at all. This means that you, or whoever first set up the Macintosh, never bothered to install it. If you can no longer find it stashed away somewhere, your only recourse is to call Apple to see if you can order a replacement. If you do eventually find the missing switch or purchase a new one, follow the instructions in your manual as to how to install it (or get some outside help, if needed).

On more recent desktop models, the two buttons typically come preinstalled (so you don't have to bother to install them) on the front of the unit. That is, unless they aren't. On some models (such as the Power Mac 6100/60), they are on the back of the machine. If you don't find them anywhere, it is probably because your model uses special keyboard commands to serve the same function. For example, on LC models, pressing and holding the Command-Control-Power keys should act as a reset button. On some of these models, to substitute for the Interrupt button, try pressing Command-Power (or alternatively try Control-Power or Command-Control-Shift-Power). If these don't work, there is probably no equivalent for the

Interrupt button on your Macintosh (in which case, if you really want to, you can still add this capability via a freeware extension called Programmer's Key). On many recent Mac models, these keyboard equivalents work even if the Mac has separate physical buttons. Try it out.

By the way, a potential problem with a keyboard Reset command is that a system crash might mess things up so much that the keyboard Reset command won't work. However, this happens only very rarely.

Oh, I almost forgot the PowerBooks. PowerBooks of the 100 series (except the PowerBook 100) have their buttons recessed on the back panel. You need something like an unbent paper clip to get in there and press these buttons. Hardly convenient. For the PowerBook 100, the buttons are on the side of the machine. As far as I am aware, PowerBook Duos and 500 series PowerBooks have no Reset or Interrupt buttons. For these you must use the keyboard command equivalents.

No doubt, Apple will find still more ways to locate these buttons on future models. If you are still having a problem finding your Reset button, check with the manual that came with your machine.

SEE: • Chapter 11, "Restarting a PowerBook After a System Error," for more on PowerBooks

TAKE NOTE ▶

POWER ON, POWER OFF

There are two types of Power buttons on Macintoshes. Some Macs have only one of these buttons, some have both. One is usually on the rear of the machine (though sometimes it is on the front) and can turn the Mac both on and off. The other one is on the keyboard. The keyboard button is in the upper right-hand corner of the keyboard and usually has a triangle symbol on it (yes, it's similar to the symbol on the Reset button). The keyboard button does not work on all Mac models. If it does work, it usually can only turn the Mac on, not off. This can all get a bit confusing as both buttons are referred to with the same name: Power button. I usually try to distinguish them by referring to the keyboard button as the Power On button and the other button as the Power on/off button.

For those who need to know, here are some more specifics: Most compact Macs, have a rocker on/off switch in the back. When you select Shut Down, you are soon greeted with a message that says to turn off that switch. Reverse the position on the rocker switch to turn the Macintosh back on. Some models (such as the Power Macintosh 6100/60) work similarly except there is an on/off button on the front of the machine rather than a rocker switch on the rear. You also have to separately turn off the monitor, even if it is plugged into the Macintosh!

On most Macintosh II, Quadra, Power Mac, and other later models of Macintosh, selecting Shut Down turns off the Macintosh without any further action needed. The Power On button on the keyboard, turns the Mac back on again. However, in most cases, these Macintoshes also have an on/off push button in the rear of the machine. On some models, the on/off button may have a slot in it. The slot should be horizontal. If it is vertical, this means that the Macintosh automatically restarts itself after any loss of power. This is great if your Macintosh is an unattended file server on a network, but it is less than ideal for any one else. If you seem to have this problem, use a screwdriver to turn the slot to the horizontal direction.

On some Macintoshes (such as the Color Classic and the LC520), you will find some new wrinkles in on/off schemes. Here, you have to switch the on/off rocker switch in the back to the on position and also press the Power button on the keyboard to get the Macintosh to turn on. Fortunately, you can simply leave the rocker switch in the on position all the time,

(continued)

simplifying this procedure. Similarly, on these models, you no longer have to select Shut Down from the Finder's Special menu in order to turn the Macintosh off. Hitting the Power button does the same thing. This is an improvement from most other models where the keyboard button can turn the Macintosh on but not off. System 7.5 Update 1.0 now adds this feature to almost all Mac models.

The PowerBooks have their own special attributes. The 100 series PowerBooks and the Duos have a Power on/off button on the rear of the machine. The Duos also have a Power On button on the keyboard. If your Duo is in a Duo Dock or MiniDock, there is also an on/off button on the rear of the dock. For the 500 series PowerBooks, there is a Power On button on the keyboard, identified by a circle symbol with a vertical bar inside it. The 500s do not have a separate on/off button.

Apple now has control panels, called Energy Saver (one version for the CPU and another for the monitor) and Auto Power On/Off, that allow you to schedule the Macintosh to shutdown or startup automatically. However, these only work on selected models of Macintosh. Auto Power On/Off works on almost all Macs that can be turned on from the keyboard's Power button.

Finally, new in System 7.5, there is a Shut Down desk accessory in the Apple menu. This allows you to select Shut Down without having to return to the Finder's Special menu.

SEE: • **Chapter 11, "Restarting a PowerBook After a System Error," for more on PowerBooks**

• **Turn the Macintosh off and then back on**

If the reset button should ever fail to work, locate the Power on/off button for your Macintosh (see: "Take Note: Power On, Power Off," for its location) and turn off your Macintosh altogether. Wait about 10 seconds (to make sure that everything has really shut down). Then, depending on your model of Macintosh, either press the Power on/off button again or press the Power On button on your keyboard. Doing this will initiate a restart that is similar to using the Reset button. That is, it does not do the cleanup (such as saving and closing all open files) that is done after using the Finder's Restart command.

At this point, you may well wonder: why bother with the Reset button at all? Why not always use the alternative of turning the Macintosh off and then back on again? Won't this do pretty much the same thing as the Reset button? The short answer is, "Yes it will." So go ahead and turn the Macintosh off and on again to restart it after a system crash if you want.

Still, the official view is that using the Reset button is preferred because by not actually shutting down the system, it places less strain on the computer's electronic circuitry, thereby prolonging the life of the components. It may also extend the life of the on/off switch (though you would have to be having a lot of system crashes for this to be relevant). Personally, I believe that this threat is highly exaggerated and would not worry about it too much. Nevertheless, I use the Reset switch whenever possible. Why take chances, especially when (on most models) the Reset switch is more conveniently located than the on/off switch?

Finally, if the on/off switch should fail to initiate a restart (an extremely unlikely possibility), unplug the Macintosh from the wall outlet. Wait a few seconds and plug it back in.

See if you can start normally now. If not, you probably have a hardware problem. Start by checking Chapter 5 for how to deal with startup problems. Otherwise, contact Apple or an authorized Apple dealer for what to do.

BY THE WAY ▶

WHEN NOT TO TURN ON OR OFF YOUR MACINTOSH

- *Don't turn the Mac on during a thunderstorm. If a power failure occurs during the storm, the Macintosh should restart itself when power returns. This is the equivalent of using the on/off switch under normal power conditions. However, during a storm, the return of power may be accompanied by a power surge that could damage your hardware (even if you are using a surge-protected outlet). Since a power failure may be only momentary (too short for you to react to it by turning the Macintosh off), your safest action is to turn off and unplug the Macintosh until the storm is over. Then you can turn the Mac back on.*
  I have ignored this advice myself many times, and nothing has ever happened. You'll make your own decision on what risks you wish to take.

- *Never turn the machine off (or hit the Reset or Interrupt buttons) while the Macintosh is reading from or writing to a disk. You may damage the data files currently in use.*

- **Special case: PowerBooks and restarting after a system error**
  For most 100 series and Duo PowerBooks, if you want to use the Power (on/off) button to restart your PowerBook after a system crash (as you likely will especially with the 100s because of their difficult to access recessed Reset button): hold in the Power button (on the rear of the machine) for around 5 seconds before letting it go. Doing this is called a *hard shutdown*. If you let go of the button too soon, pressing the button may have no effect. After the PowerBook turns off, press the Power button again to restart.

  On these PowerBooks, a brief press of the Power button initiates what is called a *soft shutdown*. The soft shutdown is equivalent to having selected the Shut Down command from the Finder's Special menu (which will not work after a system crash). This will only work at those times that the PowerBook is running normally and the Shut Down menu command would have also worked.

  Since the 500 series PowerBooks have no on/off button, if you can't get a 500 series PowerBook to reset after a system crash, try pressing Command-Option-Control-Power On. If this fails, your only alternative is to remove the batteries and disconnect AC power temporarily.

SEE: • Chapter 11, "Restarting a PowerBook After a System Error," for more details

- **Special case: RAM disks and restarting after a system crash**

  There is an important exception to the just described cavalier attitude about using a hard shutdown to restart a PowerBook after a system crash: Doing this may result in the loss of the contents of a RAM disk. You may think that any type of restart would have the same result. But you would be wrong. Surprisingly, selecting the Restart command or using the Reset button preserve the contents of the RAM disk (though you still lose your unsaved work in the rest of RAM). However, after any type of shut down, the RAM disk's contents are lost.

  By the way, you can increase your odds of saving a RAM disk's contents, even after a shut down, by using software such as Apple's PowerBook File Assistant (included with System 7.5) or Connectix's Maxima RAM disk utility.

  Finally, note that a RAM disk's contents are typically saved after a restart on most desktop Macintoshes that have the RAM disk option, not just on PowerBooks.

SEE: • Chapter 11 and Fix-It #6 for more on RAM disks and these related utilities

Recover Unsaved Data After a Restart

Okay, you're back in the saddle again. You've successfully restarted your Macintosh and returned to the Finder's desktop. What now? If you didn't lose any unsaved data or didn't care about what you did lose, just return to whatever you were doing before the crash and hope that it doesn't happen again. In the meantime, be careful to save your work frequently.

You can also try to recover any data that weren't saved prior to the crash. I know. This sounds almost impossible. It also seems to contradict my own previous statements that unsaved work at the time of a system crash cannot be recovered—because unsaved work is present only in RAM, and information in RAM (other than perhaps RAM disk contents) evaporates when you restart the Macintosh. Despite this, you may yet be able to recover some "unsaved" data.

A word to the wise before you start trying the options about to be described: They are really only good for rescuing text data and even then they are often unsuccessful. Even if they do work, they typically only save part of your data or save them in a form that requires deleting unwanted text, rearranging paragraphs and reformatting (fonts and margins and so on) before it resembles how it appeared originally. This all takes time. If you only lost a small amount of work, you are often better off simply starting from scratch and redoing it. However, for those times when you really are desperate, try the following.

Check for Temporary Files   Many (but far from all!) programs create temporary files (sometimes called work files) that hold part or all of a document's data while the document is open. Ordinarily, you are unaware of the existence of these files. The software manual may not even refer to them. This is usually okay, because these temporary files should be automatically deleted when you quit the program. You never see a trace of them. However, after an unexpected quit, a forced quit, or a reset after a system crash, these temporary files typically do not get deleted and remain somewhere on your hard drive.

These temporary files may contain data from the document you were last working on before the crash, even if you had not yet saved the data!

Often, temporary files are invisible. That is, you would never see them on the Finder's desktop or in most Open or Save dialog boxes. This is to prevent you from using them inadvertently during normal operation of the Macintosh. For example, deleting a temporary file while the application that is using it is still open (assuming the Macintosh lets you do this) could cause a system crash! The downside, however, is that this invisibility makes these files more difficult to find when you do want to use them.

Some temporary files on your disk may be remaining from system errors that are now ancient history. These will obviously be of no value to you in recovering data from your current system error. Ideally, you are looking for the one temporary file that contains data from the document you were working on at the time of the system error. Often, you can figure this out by the name of the file. Their names tend to give away their origin and nature (such as Word Work File for Microsoft Word 6.0 temporary files or—a bit harder to decipher—ALDTMP for Aldus PageMaker temporary files). To be certain that you ferreted out all of these files, look for both visible and invisible temporary files.

SEE: • Chapter 8 for more on invisible files and folders

• **Look for visible temporary files (check the Trash!)**
  After a system crash, the first place to look for visible temporary files is in the Trash! I'm not kidding. If you are using System 7, the system software creates a special folder called *Temporary Items*. Any programs that are written to be aware of this folder place their temporary files into this folder. This folder, and the files within it, are normally invisible.

  However, after a system crash and a subsequent restart, the Macintosh automatically places all the items in the Temporary Items folder into a new folder called *Rescued items from <name of your disk>*. This folder is visible and is placed in the Trash (see Figure 4-5). It contains the files that were in the invisible Temporary Items folder at the time of the system error. On Power Macintoshes, the folder may simply be named *Temporary Items*.

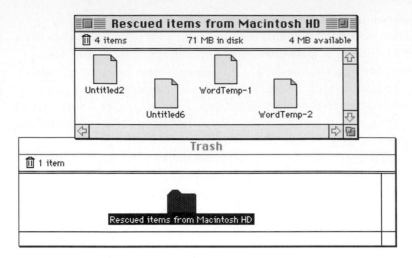

Figure 4-5 A Rescued Items folder, normally found in the Trash following a restart after a system error

The Macintosh places the Rescued Items folder in the Trash for a good reason. Deleting these files is usually the best way to deal with them. Still, the point of all this discussion is that these rescued files may contain some of your unsaved data. So, if you find the Trash can bulging immediately after a restart, double-click the Trash icon to open its window. If you find a Rescued Items folder in the Trash, remove it and place it in any other location. The temporary files in the folder should all be from applications that were open at the time of the system error, so it should be relatively easy to check for one that is useful to you.

Occasionally, there may be visible temporary files on your disk that do not make it to the Trash. They are typically either in your System Folder or in the same folder as the application that was active at the time of the crash or at the root level of your disk. You can use the Finder's Find command to help locate these temporary files, if necessary. If you are unsure of what the name of the temporary file might be, try search words such as *Temp* or the name of the application itself. Or even better, search by creator (as explained in Chapter 8).

• **Look for invisible temporary files**
If you are having trouble locating the temporary file you want, it may be because it is invisible. These files can still appear in the Open dialog boxes of some applications. For example, Microsoft Word can do this (as described in the following paragraphs). Otherwise, your main hope of finding invisible temporary files is by using a special utility that lists them. Norton Utilities and MacTools can both do this. For text data files, these utilities may be able to extract and save the text to a separate visible file, using the same technique you would use to recover text from a damaged file. Alternatively, these utilities can change the invisible file to a visible file. However, the probability of successfully recovering any data from these files is fairly low. So, unless the lost data are important, don't feel compelled to learn how to do this.

SEE: • Fix-It #14 on extracting data from damaged files
• Chapter 8 on changing an invisible file to a visible one

- **Recover data from temporary files**

  Once you have located the appropriate temporary file by any method, open it to view its contents. To do this, your best bet is to open the application that was in use at the time of the crash. See if it lists the relevant temporary file in its Open dialog box. If so, open it.

  Some applications may not list their temporary files as openable. Others may do so, but only after a bit of fiddling. For example, to see temporary files listed with Word, select the All Files option from the List Files of Type pop-up menu in the Open dialog box. Otherwise, for text files, try any other application you have that can read text files. In general, select the option that shows the broadest range of file types.

  If you are successful in opening the temporary file, you may find some useful data in it, even if it is only a partial recovery. If so, edit and save the data as with any other file. If there is any garbage data along with the real data, you can cut them. You have the best chance of successful recovery with text files. With graphics or other specially formatted files, you have little or no chance of recovery.

  Temporary files that remain on your disk after a system error are not used again as temporary files. Rather, the program creates a new temporary file the next time one is needed. Thus, if there is nothing worth saving in these recovered temporary files (which unfortunately is all too often the case), delete them. Otherwise, they remain on your disk, taking up space. And as long as you are doing this, you might as well delete any other old temporary files that you find.

  However, delete these temporary files only when the program that created them is *not* open. This is to be sure that you do not accidentally delete a temporary file that is currently in use, which (as mentioned above) can lead to a system crash.

Use Special Recovery Utilities   You can recover text by using utilities such as Now Utilities' NowSave, Last Resort, or Thunder 7's GhostWriter feature. These were first described in Chapter 2. To briefly review, these utilities record each keystroke that you make as you type. The resulting text is automatically saved in a special file typically stored in your System Folder. This is done every minute or so, without your having to select any command. This is separate from any autosave function you might have. Autosave saves the actual file you are using. These utilities save data to a separate file, even if the file itself was not saved. After a system crash, locate these special files and open them in a word processor. With luck, you will find your unsaved text. The recovered data may not be in perfect shape (some data may be missing or garbled), but it should be far preferable to having nothing at all. On the other hand, if you remember to use the ordinary Save command often enough, these utilities will probably not be of much extra benefit.

Helpful hint: These extension utilities only work if you install them prior to a system crash.

SEE: • Chapter 2 for more details on these recovery utilities

What If the System Error Keeps Recurring?

After completing all the previous advice, you can typically return to what you were doing prior to the system crash and continue your work. Most often, another crash will not occur. But what if it does? What, most especially, if it keeps recurring every time you get back to the same point? Ah yes. If this unfortunate event happens to you, you will have to spend some time trying to determine the source of the error. The only other alternative is to stop doing whatever caused the system error. Sorry.

To solve recurring system error problems, skip to the last section of this chapter.

SEE: • "Solve It! Recurring System Errors" later in this chapter

System Freezes

 ### Symptoms:

The Macintosh appears to lock up. Without warning, everything on the screen display comes to a complete halt. If it was an animated cursor, like the watch cursor, all animation has stopped. At best, the cursor may continue to respond to the mouse, but you can't get it to do anything. Menus do not drop down, applications do not open. Typically, keyboard input has no effect either. At worst, everything, including the cursor, refuses to move or respond to any input. For the moment, your computer screen has become little more than an expensive paper weight.

When any of this happens, you have a system *freeze* (also called a *hang*).

 ### Causes:

A freeze is almost always caused by a software bug. But identifying the program that contains the bug can be tricky. The bug can be in the application, or it can be in the system software, or it can be a conflict between two programs that are active at the same time. Most often, the bug is related to problems with the way a program is trying to access RAM memory.

Damaged files, particularly damaged System, Finder, or font files, may cause a freeze. A damaged Directory may similarly lead to a system freeze. Trying to defragment a disk with a damaged Directory can result in a system freeze. A loosened and disconnected cable can cause the same symptoms as a freeze, although no system error has occurred.

What to do:

Try to Save Your Work (Press Command-S)

Despite the system freeze, you may still be able to save your unsaved work. Presumably, you cannot actually select the Save command from the File menu because of the freeze. However, sometimes the Macintosh responds to certain keyboard input even though it seems frozen. By pressing Command-S (the keyboard shortcut for Save), you may be able to save whatever document you were using at the time of the freeze. Otherwise, it is almost certain to be lost. In either case, you still have a (semi?) frozen Macintosh that needs to be remedied.

Try a Forced Quit (Press Command-Option-Escape)

To do a forced quit, press the Command-Option-Escape keys all at the same time. An alert box should appear at this point. Its message asks if you want to do a forced quit of the active application and tells you that any unsaved changes in that application will be lost (see Figure 4-6). Since you have few other alternatives at this point, go ahead and do it.

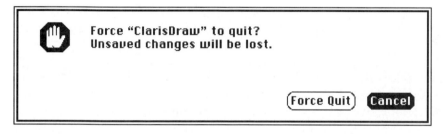

Figure 4-6   The forced quit alert box

This should return you to the Finder's desktop. The Macintosh should be functioning fairly normally now, except that the application you were using has been closed and any unsaved work is lost. Still, if you had other applications open at the time, besides the active one, you should be able to return to them and save any previously unsaved documents in these other applications.

By the way, a forced quit is designed to work primarily after either a system freeze or an endless loop (as described in the next section). I have never seen it work following a system crash (where the bomb alert box appears), but it can't hurt to try.

If the Forced Quit Succeeds . . .

- **Try (again) to save your work**
  Assuming the forced quit succeeds in bringing your Macintosh back to life, immediately save any unsaved work still open in other applications. Otherwise the danger is that another error may occur again soon, because you have not fixed whatever caused the first error to occur. You may even be able to recover unsaved data from the application that led to the freeze, either by searching for temporary files or by using other special recovery utilities.

SEE: • "Recover Unsaved Data After a Restart" in the section on System Crashes earlier in this chapter

• **Select Restart from the Finder's Special menu**

To be honest, I have recovered from a freeze with a forced quit and then continued using my Macintosh for several more hours without any problem. However, this is a risk. You can try it, but don't blame me if it soon leads to another freeze or crash.

Instead, restart the Macintosh. This usually "corrects" the problem that led to the system freeze. The best way to restart is to simply select the Restart command from the Finder's Special menu (see Figure 4-7). This ensures that all files are properly updated, saved, and closed before the actual restart occurs. This prevents any accidental loss of data and minimizes the (admittedly unlikely) chance of damaging files.

Some other utility programs may contain a similar Restart command. If this command is more convenient, you can use it instead of the Finder's command. If you select Shut Down from the Finder (or from the Shut Down desk accessory), and then turn your Macintosh back on, this is almost identical to selecting Restart.

Figure 4-7
The Restart command highlighted in the Finder's Special menu

TECHNICALLY SPEAKING ▶

TO SLEEP . . . PERCHANCE TO POWER DOWN

If you have a PowerBook, and you select Sleep from the Special menu, the computer appears to shut down. But it hasn't. Power to the hard drive is essentially cut off (to preserve battery power). But enough current is maintained so that the information in memory is preserved. On most PowerBooks, pressing any key (except Caps Lock) will awaken the PowerBook. On some models, you must press the Power On key. The hard drive then spins up, the screen brightens, and all returns to normal.

SEE: • Chapter 11, on PowerBooks, for more details

If the Forced Quit Fails to Work . . . Restart

Unfortunately, sometimes the forced quit trick fails to work. Instead, when you click the Force Quit button, your system freeze worsens from the type where you can still use the cursor, to the type where now even the cursor is frozen. Or the freeze may develop into a system crash. In some cases, the forced quit dialog box never even appears. In any of these cases, your main recourse is to restart the Macintosh, as previously described for a system crash. That is, hit the reset button or the Power (on/off) switch.

SEE: • "Restart the Macintosh" and "Recover Unsaved Data After a Restart," in the section on System Crashes, earlier in this chapter

If the Freeze Recurs

After restarting, you will usually be able to continue your work without another freeze occurring. However, if the freeze recurs after restarting, you will need to try to figure out the cause.

• **Check for disconnected cables**
If the freeze reappears immediately upon startup, your best bet is to check the keyboard cable, especially if your mouse is connected to the keyboard rather than to the back of the Macintosh. In this case, a loose or defective keyboard cable prevents both keyboard and mouse input from having any effect. I call this a *false freeze.*

A disconnected cable does not halt any operation in progress (such as a printing process), but otherwise mimics a true system freeze. It is not a true freeze because the processing of information has not been disrupted.

If other cables, such as a printer cable or the SCSI cable (most commonly used for connecting an external hard drive), become disconnected, this can precipitate a true freeze.

Always turn off the Macintosh before reconnecting any disconnected cables you may find. This is especially true for the keyboard and SCSI cables. Otherwise, reconnecting the cable may cause permanent damage to the Macintosh's circuitry.

Even if you do reconnect a cable while the computer is running and nothing adverse happens, it may not by itself restore the Macintosh to normal. You still probably have to restart the Macintosh.

• **Check whether a cable, keyboard, and/or mouse may need a repair**
It is always possible that a cable, mouse, and/or the keyboard have suddenly gone belly up. This too may mimic a freeze that appears immediately upon startup. If this is the case, try to swap your keyboard and cables for other ones, if other ones are available (remembering to turn off your Macintosh before removing or connecting any cables). If replacing components eliminates the freeze, you need to replace the defective components.

INTERNAL HARDWARE PROBLEMS CAN CAUSE SYSTEM FREEZES

Problems with the internal hardware of the Macintosh, typically faulty components on the logic board, can cause repeated system freezes. In many cases, these problems are specific to a particular model of Macintosh.

For example, in early versions of the PowerBook 540c, a flawed chip on the logic board would cause intermittent freezes. Call Apple at 1-800-SOS-APPL to get a free fix for this.

Similarly, Macintosh 630's have a hardware problem that can result in periodic freezes during long SCSI transfers (such as when copying large files from one hard disk to another). Apple has released an extension (available on online services), called 630 SCSI Update, that fixes this.

More generally, be aware that defective RAM can be a cause of frequent freezes.

SEE: • Fix-It #16 on SCSI devices and Fix-It #17 on hardware repairs for more on problems with cables and other hardware

• **Replace the System, the Finder, Finder Preferences, and/or Enabler files**
This is particularly likely to work if the freeze only occurs when in the Finder or when doing system-related activities. For example, a freeze could occur whenever a floppy disk was inserted into a disk drive. Similar situations include freezes that occur when copying files or emptying the Trash.

Replace the System, the Finder, Finder Preferences, and/or Enabler files to attempt to correct these problems.

SEE: • Fix-It #2 on replacing Preferences files
• Fix-It #5 for more on replacing system software

• **Replace damaged font files**
If a freeze occurs whenever you try to launch a particular application, a damaged font file may be the cause. Claris Corporation specifically mentions this as a potential cause for freezes with its software (ClarisWorks, FileMaker, MacWrite Pro, and so on). Damaged font files may also cause a freeze to occur when printing. The solution is to identify the damaged font and replace it from your backups.

SEE: • Chapter 9 for more on identifying and replacing damaged font files

• **Turn off virtual memory or other memory enhancing utility**
Freezes are often due to memory-related problems. If you are using virtual memory or a utility such as RAM Doubler, turn it off. RAM Doubler is especially known as a possible cause of freezes while running communication and/or networking software.

- **Otherwise . . .**

   If a system freeze occurs whenever you try to mount an external hard drive, try to repair the disk. If that fails, reformat the disk.

   SEE: • **Fix-It #13 on disk repairs**
   • **Fix-It #15 on reformatting a disk**

If none of these suggestions solves the problem, it's time to look elsewhere.

SEE: • **"Solve It! Recurring System Errors" later in this chapter**

Endless Loops

Symptoms:

The symptoms of an endless loop appear, at first, not to be symptoms at all. Everything appears perfectly normal. Usually, whenever a process promises to take more than a few seconds to complete (such as a complex transformation in a graphics program), the cursor (most often an arrow) changes. Typically, it shifts to a watch cursor with rotating clock hands or a spinning beach ball. This is perfectly normal. It is the Macintosh's way of telling you to wait a minute.

During this time, the cursor continues to move across the screen in response to movement of the mouse. However, all other activity is temporarily disabled. It remains this way until the task is completed, at which time the regular cursor (usually the arrow) reappears.

The signal that you have a problem is that the task never seems to reach completion. The watch cursor appears destined to remain on the screen until at least the turn of the century. Welcome to endless loops! Be especially suspicious of an endless loop anytime a task is taking much longer to complete than expected (for example, saving a document should almost never take more than a few seconds).

A similar situation occurs when the computer's activity is monitored by a progress bar on the screen (as occurs when copying disks from the Finder). The dark part of the bar continues to grow as the activity moves to completion. If the progress bar seems to stop, no longer showing any sign of progress, you may be caught in an endless loop.

At a practical level, the endless loop is a first cousin to the system freeze. Your course of action will be similar in both cases.

Causes:

Before taking any action, consider that you may not be in an endless loop. The Macintosh may be doing something that takes a very long time to complete. For example, depending on your printer, it can take more than ten minutes to print one page of a complex PostScript graphics document.

The other alternative is that you *are* in an endless loop. This is typically due to a software bug that causes the program to attempt the same action repeatedly—and indefinitely.

What to do:

Break out of the Loop with Command-Period

Often, a long delay here does not mean that you have a freeze. It just may be that the operation really takes an unusually long time to finish. To check for this, press Command-period (holding both keys down together). This is an almost universal command for canceling an operation in progress. Hold the keys down for several seconds before letting go. Wait a few more seconds to see if the operation halts, typically indicated by the progress bar (if any) disappearing and/or the animated cursor being replaced by the arrow cursor. If nothing seems to happen, try again. Continue retrying for at least a minute before giving up.

If canceling does work, you either halted a normal but slow process, or (less likely) you have a forgiving program that was able to break out of an endless loop with this technique.

BY THE WAY ▶

CANCELING A COMMAND

This Command-period technique is useful anytime you wish to halt an operation that you no longer want to do, even if there is no suspected endless loop. It does not always work, but it is worth a try whenever you need it. Depending on the operation in progress, it may take as long as a minute or so before the operation is canceled.

Retry the Procedure

If you were able to break out of the loop, retry the procedure a second time. Wait even longer before resorting to Command-period.

If it is just a slow process, it may reach completion this time. If the problem was an endless loop, it may have been a one-time-only problem, and it will not repeat.

Otherwise . . .

If you cannot break out of the endless loop, treat this exactly as if it were a system freeze. In particular, try a forced quit (hold down the Command-Option-Escape keys). If this doesn't work, restart the Macintosh.

SEE: • "System Freeze," earlier in this chapter, for more details

Whether or not you can break out of the endless loop, if it continues to recur, you will have to figure out the cause.

SEE: • "Solve It! Recurring System Errors" later in this chapter

Unexpected Quits

 ### Symptoms:

An application abruptly and inexplicably quits, returning you to the Finder. Often, you see an alert message informing you that the application *unexpectedly quit.* (Does this mean that there are quits of this sort that the Macintosh *expects* to happen?) This is the most benign of system errors described in this chapter, because the system continues to function after the unexpected quit (see Figure 4-8).

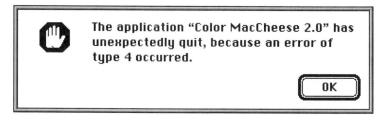

Figure 4-8   The unexpected quit alert box

 ### Causes:

Unexpected quits are usually due to software bugs that affect memory management. Typically, less memory is available than the program needs. Ideally, the program should detect this and warn you of the problem. However, when the program is not written carefully enough, an unexpected quit happens instead.

If this happens, you can consider yourself lucky in a way. Unexpected quits occur only in System 7 or under MultiFinder in System 6 because, in these cases, the system can return you to the Finder (which is always open). Under the ordinary Finder in System 6, the Finder is not open when you are using another application. In this case, a memory-management problem would simply lead to a system crash (see the section on "System Crashes" earlier in this chapter).

What to do:

Interpreting System Error Codes . . . Again

As seen in Figure 4-8, an unexpected quit alert box often indicates the type of error that led to the unexpected quit (such as an error of "Type 4"). These numbers refer to the same codes as used for system crashes. While trying to figure out exactly what these mean is not likely to be helpful, you can check Table 4-1 for guidance. Sometimes, the alert box often says the cause of the quit is of a type "unknown," making it irrelevant to look up the meaning of the error code.

Save Data in Open Applications

As with almost all system errors, any unsaved data that were open in the application that unexpectedly quit is almost certainly lost. However, you should still be able to save any data in other applications that remain open. You may even be able to recover unsaved data from the application that led to the unexpected quit, either by searching for temporary files or using other special recovery utilities.

SEE: • "Recover Unsaved Data After a Restart," in the section on System Crashes, earlier in this chapter

Restart the Macintosh

To restart, select Restart from the Finder's Special menu. You can probably continue using your Macintosh without restarting. To be safe, however, you should restart first because once this problem occurs, the probability that it will recur increases until you restart.

Actually, if you want to return to the problem program, it may be necessary to restart. For example, I have occasionally had a program that would no longer relaunch immediately after an unexpected quit. It simply quit again whenever I tried to launch it. Restarting the Macintosh cleared up this problem.

Increase Preferred Size of Memory Requirements

The immediate cause of some unexpected quits is insufficient memory assigned to the application. This can be the case even if you arc using the default assignments given to the application. So, if the unexpected quit persists, after a restart, try increasing the Preferred Size of the application's memory from the file's Get Info window.

SEE: • Chapter 2 on Get Info window and Fix-It #6 on memory problems, for more details

If the Unexpected Quit Occurs During Launch

Unexpected quits often occur in the middle of using an application. Sometimes, they occur as a program is first launched, preventing you from successfully opening the program. If this happens, and the previous solutions have been unable to solve the problem, try removing the application's preferences file from the preferences folder and, if that fails, replacing the application itself. While a damaged application file may be the cause of any unexpected quit, it is more likely a cause if the quit occurs during launch.

SEE: • Fix-Its #2 and #3 on replacing applications and their related files

Otherwise . . .

Sometimes, an unexpected quit will develop into a system freeze or a system crash before you can successfully restart. If so, refer to the previous sections on those topics for what to do.

Finally, if the unexpected quit continues to recur, despite all the previous attempts at a solution, you need to track down what else may be the cause.

SEE: • "Solve It! Recurring System Errors" later in this chapter

The Finder Disappears

Symptoms:

The desktop seems to vanish. All disk icons and folder windows disappear. Sometimes the menu bars on the top of the screen disappear. At the same time, the Macintosh appears to freeze.

Causes:

Basically, this is still another variation on the freeze or endless loop, and it has similar underlying causes. In this case, however, it is more likely that something is amiss with the Finder and/or System files.

What to do:

Wait a Minute

Occasionally, the Finder will reappear by itself, if you wait a minute or two. If this happens, I would still be suspicious about a more serious error occurring soon. Restart to be safe.

Try a Forced Quit (Press Command-Option-Escape) and Restart

If the Finder does not return on its own, try a forced quit. Occasionally, as with a generic system freeze, a forced quit may return you to a fully functional desktop.

If the forced quit does succeed, rather than immediately resume your work, you should save any unsaved work and restart the Macintosh. Restart by selecting the Restart command from the Finder's special menu. If the forced quit does not succeed, use the Reset button to restart. In either case, the Macintosh should return to normal following the restart.

SEE: • "System Freezes," earlier in this chapter, for more details

Replace the Finder and Its Preferences File

If the problem keeps recurring, replace the Finder and its preferences file.

SEE: • Fix-It #2 on problems with the Finder preferences file

Otherwise . . .

If the Finder continues to vanish, replace or upgrade the entire system software. If even that doesn't work, it's time to look for more esoteric causes.

SEE: • Fix-It #5 on replacing system software
       • "Solve It! Recurring System Errors" later in this chapter

Solve It! Recurring System Errors

If you have been directed to this section, you presumably have a recurring system error. If the error does recur, you probably want to eliminate it. This requires using diagnostic guidelines as follows:

Seek the Cause of a Recurring System Error

Suspect recent changes to the contents of your disk (such as a new system extension added or an upgrade to the system software) as the most likely culprits for a recurring system error. In general, the most common cause of system errors are software conflicts or incompatibilities, software bugs, or damaged software.

What Circumstances, If Any, Reliably Cause the System Error?

To check to see if a system error recurs, first try to *exactly* duplicate the precipitating situation (for example, reopen all applications and documents that were open at the time of the error).

System errors can be quite finicky about when they will or will not recur. For example, perhaps the error occurs only when you select Check Spelling immediately after you select Save. Or it may be that it happens only when you select the command while a specific graphics application is also open. Or it may occur only when a specific INIT is in use. Or it may occur only when many applications are open and memory is running low. You don't really know for sure whether a system error will recur until you repeat the exact circumstances.

What Variations in Circumstances, If Any, Will Eliminate the System Error?

If you do get the system error to reliably recur under a specific set of circumstances, your next step is to determine how altering those circumstances affects the error. For example, suppose a crash occurs after selecting Check Spelling from your word processor. Does it happen regardless of what documents, other applications, and other extensions are open and/or in use at the same time? Are there other commands that will also result in the same type of system error? Does the error recur when you are working with other documents and/or trying similar procedures with other applications?

If the error recurs only whenever a specific document is open, it suggests a problem with the document. If the error happens across all documents within an application, the problem is most likely with the application. If the error keeps recurring during the launch of the program, it usually means damage to the application (or one of its accessory files). If it happens across several applications, it is most likely an extension conflict or a bug or incompatibility in the system software.

Whatever happens, hopefully you can narrow down or isolate the cause of the system error via this approach.

What If the System Error Recurs at Unpredictable Intervals and Situations?

System errors that occur at unpredictable intervals or in apparently unrelated situations are the worst-case possible scenario. If nothing else, it is hard to know if and when the problem has gone away.

The single most likely cause of these types of system errors is an INIT conflict. The second most likely cause is corrupted system software, particularly the System file or the Finder. A corrupted font file can also cause system errors. Damage to the Directory, the Desktop, or the disk driver is also a possible cause. SCSI connection or other hardware-related problems may similarly lead to system errors. Computer viruses are yet another cause of wide-spread system errors. Check out the next section of this chapter ("Fix It So That the System Error Does Not Recur") for a complete list of possible causes and where to go to find out what to do about them.

SEE: • Chapter 3 for more on general problem-solving strategies

Fix It So That the System Error Does Not Recur

Once you have narrowed down the cause as much as possible, it's time to do something to fix the problem. A list of suggestions is given in this section. Don't worry if you do not entirely understand all of the terminology (such as *device driver* or *SCSI*). The terms are explained in more detail in the indicated Fix-Its.

SEE: • Chapter 11 for more on system errors with PowerBooks

Check for Hardware and/or System Software That Are Incompatible with the Application in Use

If the system error is specific to a particular application, check its manual for any troubleshooting advice. In particular, check for any mention of incompatibilities between the application and either the particular hardware or any version of the system software you are using. For example, an application may crash when launched on an AV Macintosh. A game may crash if you try to run it with the monitor set to black-and-white instead of color. In general, new versions of an application sometimes do not work with older versions of the system software. Similarly, older versions of the application sometimes do not work with newer versions of the system software.

SEE: • Chapter 11 on PowerBook problems and Chapter 12 on Power Macintosh problems
• Fix-It #1 on incompatibilities between software and hardware
• Fix-It #5 on system software problems

Install the Latest System Update (Fixes System Software Bugs)

For example, if you are using System 7.1, be sure to install System Update 3.0. It fixes literally dozens of problems, several of which may lead to freezes or crashes. For example, it "corrects a problem that potentially allowed the system to become corrupted during a power failure or a crash. This corruption would prevent the Macintosh from restarting."

SEE: • Chapter 2, "By the Way: What Exactly Does a System Update Update?," for more on what this update and System 7.5 Update 1.0 do

Check for Software Bugs in the Application

If you suspect a bug in the application, your only recourse is to find some work-around, avoid using the offending software, or get a bug-fixed upgrade to the software (if one is available). Call the software manufacturer to find out about known work-arounds and upgrades. Often, publishers release minor maintenance updates just designed to fix bugs. Sometimes, they will only send you these updates if you call to complain. So call and complain. Remember, you cannot fix buggy software yourself.

SEE: • Fix-It #18 for more on using technical support

Turn Off Selected Options from Memory and Turn Off Sharing Setup Control Panels

Turn off File Sharing from the Sharing Setup control panel. Similarly, turn off 32-bit Addressing (for Macs other than Power Macintoshes) or turn off the Modern Memory Manager (for Power Macintoshes) from the Memory control panel. Also from the Memory control panel, turn virtual memory off or reduce its size. For example, Apple reports that setting virtual memory to larger than 20Mb results in a error of type -250. These are all common sources of conflicts.

SEE: • Fix-It #6 on the Memory control panel

Check for INIT Problems

Turn off all your INITs (files that load into memory at startup). To do this in System 7, restart the Macintosh while holding down the Shift key. Continue to hold down the key until the desktop appears. If this procedure eliminates your system error, you have an INIT problem.

Be especially wary of extensions that actively process information in the background, such as Disk Express II or the prevention checking features of MacTools, Norton Utilities, and Apple Personal Diagnostics (see Chapter 2).

Be especially careful never to use two extensions that do essentially the same thing, such as two screen savers. This is almost a sure way to cause problems.

SEE: • Fix-It #4 on INIT problems

Check for Memory Allocation Problems

Whether a software bug is the ultimate cause or not, the immediate cause of many system errors is a memory problem. Usually this means that an application or extension is trying to grab some memory that, for one reason or another, it can't have. Memory problems are almost always the cause of an unexpected quit.

Some recurring system errors can be solved simply by allocating more memory to the application via its Get Info window (to access this, select the application icon and press command-I). For starters, try increasing the Preferred size by several hundred K (assuming you have the memory to do so). Other related solutions are covered in the relevant Fix-Its.

SEE   • Chapter 12 on Power Macintosh problems and memory
        • Fix It #4 on problems with INITs
        • Fix It #6 on memory management problems

Check for Damaged Document Files

If a crash occurred while a document file was open, you may find that, not only did you lose what had not been saved prior to the error, but your entire document is now corrupted. It either does not open at all or it just displays random gibberish.

If these problems occur, the crash may have been the cause of the damage to the file. Alternatively, the damage may be the cause of the crash, in which case trying to open the document will surely cause the crash to recur.

In either case, the preferred solution is to delete the damaged file and replace it with a copy from your backups. This, by itself, may solve the system error problem. If you do not have a backup of the file, you can try to repair the file or at least recover data from it before you discard it. For starters, if you can open the file (most often you cannot), try copying the document to a new file, using the Save As command. Otherwise, do the following.

SEE: • Fix-It #14 for more on recovering data from damaged files

Check for Other Damage

A mixed bag of related causes fall into this area:

- **System software (System, Finder, Enablers, Finder preferences, and so on)**
  Replace the System, Finder, and Enabler files if you have backups. Delete the Finder Preferences file (drag the file to the Trash, restart, then empty the Trash). Make sure you are using matching and most recent versions of all system software files and that they are designed for your model of Macintosh. If there is any doubt, do a clean reinstall of the entire system software.

  By the way, if a freeze occurs while using the Scrapbook desk accessory, this is more likely due to damage to the Scrapbook File (located in the root level of the System Folder) than to the Scrapbook desk accessory itself (located in the Apple Menu Items folder). Delete the File (after recovering items from it, if needed, using a utility such as Can Opener, as described in Fix-It #14). Similarly, for problems with the Clipboard, delete the Clipboard file, if you find one in the System Folder. In either case, the Mac will create a new replacement file when needed.

- **Application preferences**
  An application's preferences file may be damaged. To fix this, locate and delete the file. Go to the Preferences Folder, located in the System Folder, and locate the Preferences file that appears to match the problem application (such as Panorama Prefs for Panorama or Word Settings for Microsoft Word). Delete this file. The program will automatically make a new one when you next launch it. You may have to reselect any customized preference settings you may have made, if desired.

- **Font files**
  A font file may be damaged. Claris particularly cites this as a reason that you may have trouble launching its applications. Also suspect font-related problems, among other possible causes, if you have system errors occur only when trying to print.

- **Directory**
  Check for damage to the Directory files on your disk. If you find Directory damage and it cannot be repaired, you have to reformat the disk. You could even check for a damaged Desktop file by rebuilding the desktop.

- **Media damage**
  With any type of damaged file, there is the possibility of associated media damage. If so, the disk will probably have to be reformatted.

SEE: • Chapter 7 on printing problems
       • Chapter 9, "Damaged Font Files," for how to detect and replace a damaged/corrupted font
       • Fix-It #2 for problems with preferences files
       • Fix-It #3 for replacing application and accessory files
       • Fix-It #5 for replacing system software
       • Fix-It #9 to rebuild the desktop

- **Fix-It #10 to run Disk First Aid, checking for damaged disks**
- **Fix-It #14 for more on damaged files**
- **Fix-It #13 to do more checks for damaged disks**
- **Fix-It #15 for reformatting the disk**

Check for More than One System Folder on the Startup Disk

Though opinions on this issue remain divided, there remains concern that the presence of two or more System Folders on the same startup disk could cause system crashes. Personally, I believe that the potential for this to cause problems is highly exaggerated. Still, to be safe, if you find more than one System Folder on your startup disk, delete all but one of them. By the way, the one that is currently considered the active System Folder is the one that has a mini-icon of a Macintosh on its folder icon. You can't entirely delete this folder from a disk while it is currently the active startup disk. You must startup from another disk first.

SEE: • Chapter 5 and Fix-It #5 for more on multiple System Folder problems

Check for Multiple Copies of Applications and Related Files

Though it is only rarely a source of system error problems, make sure there are not two different versions of the same application on your disk. If possible check for files related to the application that may have two versions in the System Folder (such as two slightly differently named Preferences files). If you find any out-of-date files, delete them. Use only your newest version.

Check for Viruses

A virus becomes more likely if you are having frequently recurring system errors that show no predictable pattern. It is especially likely if the problem begins immediately after you've added a potentially infected file to your disk.

SEE: • Fix-It #7 to check for viruses

Check for Problems with the Hard Disk's Device Driver

The device driver is software contained on a hard disk that is needed for the Macintosh to recognize and interact with the disk. It is contained in an area of the drive that is normally inaccessible to the user. It may become damaged. Also, an older version of the driver may be incompatible with newer versions of the system software and newer models of Macintosh. In such cases, the driver needs to be replaced or updated.

SEE: • Fix-It #12 to update the disk device driver

Check for Hardware Problems: Cable Connections, Peripheral Devices, SIMMs, and Logic Board

This is an especially likely cause if you are having frequent system crashes and/or ones that occur at apparently random and unpredictable intervals. A system error does not create a hardware problem, but it may be the symptom of an existing hardware problem.

Defective SIMMs are a prime cause of frequent system crashes (assuming that you can start your Macintosh at all!). Persistent Type 1 and Bad F line errors are sometimes caused by nondefective but dirty SIMMs. If you have the skill, remove the SIMMs and clean them (as described more in Fix-It #17). Otherwise, seek outside help.

If you are having frequently recurring system errors that seem to occur only when a specific external hard disk (or other peripheral device connected via the SCSI port) is in use, this signals a problem with how these devices are connected.

Crashes that occur in a variety of contexts (such as whenever you launch an application or try to empty the Trash) may indicate a defective logic board.

Hardware problems tend to cause system freezes more often than they cause system crashes. Especially consider, as mentioned, whether you might have a false freeze (that is, an apparent freeze due to a defective keyboard, mouse, or keyboard cable).

While some hardware-related problems can be easily fixed by even an unskilled user, others will require a trip to the repair shop.

SEE: • Fix-It #16 to check for problems with SCSI devices and connections
      • Fix-It #17 to check if hardware repairs or replacements are needed

Seek Outside Help

If none of the preceding suggestions has helped, and you haven't already done so, it's time to seek outside help.

SEE: • Fix-It #18 for more information on getting outside help

Chapter Summary

The first major section of this chapter described five different categories of system errors: system crashes, system freezes, endless loops, unexpected quits, and disappearing Finder. Next, it described specific remedies for each case.

The second major section explained what to do if a system error keeps recurring. In particular, it explained how to determine the cause and then take the necessary action to eliminate the error. This will frequently involve following advice covered in more detail in other chapters of this book.

Chapter 5

Startup and Disk Problems: Stuck at the Starting Gate

Unpleasant Topics

Sad Macs. Dead Macs. Crashed disks. Unreadable disks. Damaged disks. These are the unpleasant topics of discussion for this chapter. Although the emphasis is on those times when you can't even start your Macintosh, this chapter is also about disk-related problems that can happen at any time.

These problems tend to fall into one of three categories. Some problems are specific to the startup process. Disks with these problems cannot act as startup disks but may otherwise function normally. More generic problems, such as an inability to mount a disk, cause problems whether the disk is used as a startup disk or not. Finally, some fairly serious problems have little or nothing to do with startup. For example, files and folders may begin to vanish from your disk.

Inevitably, some of these problems are caused by damaged hardware. Once again, however, many of these problems are entirely due to software-related causes. And even some hardware problems, such as those related to SCSI connections, can be remedied without requiring any repairs. The point is that there's a lot of simple stuff you can do to solve these problems on your own. So let's get going.

Understanding the Startup Sequence

What Is a Normal Startup Sequence?

For most users, the startup disk is usually an internal hard drive. Assuming this is the case for you, here's how a normal startup sequence proceeds:

1. Turn on your Macintosh. I am assuming you already know how to do this. If you have any questions, check the section in Chapter 4 on turning your Mac on and off.

2. The Macintosh immediately begins a series of diagnostic tests that check the condition of the hardware. Since we are describing a normal startup, I will assume no problems are found.

    In this case, the Macintosh plays its normal startup tone. That's the sound you hear every time you turn on your Macintosh. These days, the tone may be a single note or a chord, depending on what type of Macintosh you are using (this is yet another example of how Apple continues to make life difficult for those of us who would like to be able to describe these matters without needing to cite numerous exceptions and variations!). The Power Macs have added an entirely new startup sound not heard on any previous models.

3. You may or may not briefly see the appearance of a disk icon with a ? inside it.

4. The Macintosh checks all available disks (in a prescribed order, to be described shortly) to see if any of them are startup disks (typically, this means a disk with a valid System Folder on it). If it finds one, you briefly see the (smiling) happy Mac

Figure 5-1
The smiling happy Mac icon, a sign of a successful startup

icon (see Figure 5-1). The Macintosh has now passed all of its initial diagnostic tests.

5. The Welcome to Macintosh screen (or other custom startup screen, if you use one) appears next. During this time, enablers, system extensions, and control panels load.

You can usually identify this activity by the sequential appearance of small icons along the bottom of the screen. These are the INITs loading (see Chapter 1 and Fix-It #4). If you don't have any INITs that use these icons, or if their icons are turned off, you won't see them.

6. Finally, the Finder's desktop appears. The startup disk icon appears in the upper right corner. This means the disk has *mounted.*

The term *mounted* is used to describe all volumes, not just the startup disk, that appear along the right border of the desktop. For example, you can have both a floppy disk and your internal hard disk mounted at the same time. The icons for both disks would then appear on the desktop.

The icons for other disks, if there are any, appear beneath the startup disk icon. That is, the startup disk is *always* the disk that is initially at the top of the stack of disk icons (see Figure 5-2). Of course, you can change the icon's location with the mouse, though this does not affect which disk is the startup disk.

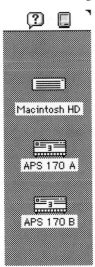

Figure 5-2
When your reach the desktop, the topmost disk icon (Macintosh HD, in this case) will always be the startup disk

7. If you have placed any files in the Startup Items folder, these are launched next, and the startup sequence concludes.

What Is a Startup Disk?

Without a startup disk, your Macintosh will not start up. That's why it's called a startup disk. To qualify as a startup disk, the disk typically needs a valid System Folder. While there are ways to create startup disks without a "politically correct" System Folder (a few such methods are described in Chapters 2 and 8), I will be ignoring these unusual startup disks in this chapter.

A valid System Folder is one that contains at least a System and a Finder (and an Enabler file, if needed for your Mac model). Usually, a valid System Folder can be identified on the desktop by a miniature

System Folder

Figure 5-3
A blessed System Folder has a miniature Macintosh icon on it

Macintosh symbol on its folder icon. A folder with this icon is called a *blessed System Folder* (see Figure 5-3).

The contents of the blessed System Folder on the current startup disk determines what fonts, sounds, system extensions, control panels, and Apple menu items are in menus and available for use. The Macintosh ignores information from any other System Folders that may be present.

A working startup disk also needs a valid set of *boot blocks.* This refers to a special invisible (to you!) area of the disk containing information that the Macintosh checks at startup to initially determine the status of a disk. The boot blocks get their name from the fact that the startup process is sometimes referred to as "booting your computer" (which in turn comes from the expression "pulling yourself up by your own bootstraps").

Most of the time, you can be blissfully unaware of the boot blocks. Creating and writing to the boot blocks is normally handled automatically behind the scene. Boot blocks are created when you first initialize a disk. Whenever you change the startup status of a disk, by adding a System and Finder for example, the Macintosh modifies the disks' boot blocks accordingly. It's only when things go wrong that you may need to be aware of boot blocks.

What Determines Which Disk Is the Startup Disk?

Suppose you have two hard drives connected to your Macintosh, each with a valid System Folder on it. Now suppose you start your Macintosh with both hard drives running. How does the Macintosh decide which disk to use as the startup disk?

Default Rules for Selecting a Startup Disk

The Macintosh will check the following locations, in the order listed, until it finds an appropriate startup disk.

Floppy Drive(s) The Macintosh first tries to start up from an internal floppy drive, if it finds a startup disk there, and then from an external floppy drive (if any).

CD-ROM Drive Apparently, automatically checking the CD-ROM drive for a possible startup disk at this point only occurs with certain Macintoshes (see "By The Way: CD-ROM Startup Disks").

CD-ROM STARTUP DISKS

Certain CD-ROM disks, such as the Power Macintosh CD-ROM disk included with all Power Macintoshes, can be used as startup disks. That is, if they are present in a CD-ROM drive at startup, the Mac can potentially start up from it. However, there are qualifications and limitations to getting this to work!

Of course, a CD-ROM startup disk needs the expected blessed System Folder on it. But to act as a startup disk, a CD-ROM disk needs more. This is because you normally cannot access a CD-ROM drive until after the CD-ROM driver extension has loaded. CD-ROM startup disks include special instructions that allow them to get around this problem. As of this writing, CD-ROM startup disks are only made by Apple (because the needed special instructions involve a technique that Apple has kept secret).

Further, CD-ROM startup disks will probably only work with Apple brand CD-ROM drives and then only on certain models of Macintosh. Probability of success also increases if you are using an internal, rather than an external, CD-ROM drive. However, these disks can still be mounted as a non-startup disk on any Macintosh with a CD-ROM drive (Apple brand or not, internal or external).

To try to get a CD-ROM disk to act as a startup disk, either select it as the startup disk from the Startup Disk control panel (and restart) or hold down the Command-Option-Shift-Delete keys at startup. In either case, if the method is successful, the internal drive should still automatically mount as a secondary disk (see "By The Way: The Internal Drive May Still Mount When Using Command-Option-Shift-Delete," later in this main section). However, I have found that these techniques may fail to work if you have an external hard drive with a System Folder on it. In this case, the external drive becomes the startup disk. In this case, if you must startup from the CD-ROM disk, you will need to start up with the external drive off or disconnected from the SCSI port.

The situation is improved with Power Macs. Apple initially claimed that they should start up from a CD-ROM startup disk as long as the disk is in the drive at startup (similar to how startup floppy disks work), regardless of the control panel selection or external hard drive. However, Apple now says you need to hold down the C key immediately at startup to get a Power Mac (or 630 series Mac) to recognize a CD-ROM startup disk. In either case, this useful Power Mac attribute makes it especially easy to use these disks as startup disks in emergencies, such as when your startup hard drive crashes.

There are other potential problems with using a CD-ROM startup disk on a Power Mac. The CD-ROM may not eject when you shut down the Mac, perhaps causing it to be the startup disk again when you restart. If this happens, you can get the disk to eject by holding down the mouse at startup, just like for floppy disks. You can also press the eject button immediately at startup. If you have any problems restarting a Power Mac that had just previously used a CD-ROM as a startup disk, do a soft restart (by holding down Command-Control-Power) or press the reset button. This should cure the problem.

Startup Disk Control Panel Selection   A choice here overrides what would otherwise be the default choice (as explained in the next section).

Internal Hard Drive   This is the normal default startup device. It is where you start up from if no floppy disks or CD-ROM disks are present at startup and no changes have been made in the Startup Disk control panel.

External Hard Drive(s)　This is the default choice only if there is no internal hard drive in your Macintosh. If there is more than one external hard drive, all with System Folders on them, the Macintosh will select one to be the startup disk, based on the SCSI ID numbers of the drive. The drive with the highest ID number (starting from 6 and working down to 0) becomes the default startup disk.

　　If, by this point, the Macintosh has failed to find a startup disk anywhere, it will return to the beginning and try again.

SEE:　• **Fix-It #16 for information about SCSI device ID numbers**

The Startup Disk Control Panel: Changing the Default Startup Selection

You can change the Macintosh's default startup disk by using the *Startup Disk control panel* (see Figure 5-4). To use it, simply click on the icon for the disk you want to assign as the startup disk. You could use this, for example, to switch from your internal to your external drive as a startup disk. The selected disk will be used as the startup disk the next time you restart (assuming that there is a valid System Folder on the selected disk).

Figure 5-4
The Startup Disk control panel

This control panel lists all mounted hard disks and CD-ROM disks. Thus, with this control panel, you can select a CD-ROM disk to be the startup disk on almost any Mac, not just Power Macs (but see "By The Way: CD-ROM Startup Disks," for some possible problems here).

　　If the selected disk is not present at startup (such as an external drive that is no longer connected or a CD-ROM disk that is not reinserted at startup), the Macintosh will return to its default search procedures.

　　Finally, don't confuse this control panel with the Startup Items folder discussed in Chapter 1. The Startup Items folder contains files that you want to be automatically opened at startup. The Startup Disk control panel is used to select a particular disk to be the startup disk.

The Startup Disk control panel cannot be used to assign a floppy disk as the default startup disk. Actually, if a floppy startup disk is present, it is selected as the startup disk in preference to any hard disk, regardless of the setting in the Startup Disk control panel. However, the Startup Disk setting is retained and will be used the next time you start up without a floppy disk present.

System 6 Alert: In System 6, the control panel equivalent to Startup Disk is called Startup Device.

Older Macintosh Alert: These control panels do not work on a Macintosh Plus or earlier Macintosh models.

Partition Alert: If you have divided a hard disk into separate partitions, and both partitions contain System Folders, you cannot use the Startup Disk control panel to select which partition is used as the startup disk. One partition is considered to be the default startup partition and will always be the selected one. Usually, it is the partition whose name comes first when listed in alphabetical order. So you would think that to switch the default startup partition, all you need to do is rename your hard drives appropriately. However, I have found this to be unreliable. In general, you can assume that the preferred partition is the one that appears at the top of the stack of icons on your desktop, regardless of their names.

If you want to startup from a non-default partition, there are a number of things you can try. First, your disk formatting utility may have an option to let you assign which partition is to be the startup partition (Apple HD SC Setup does not have such an option!). If your utility can do it, this is the most reliable method. A quicker method, which almost always works, is to select the desired startup partition via a freeware utility from Apple, called System Picker. Just launch it and select which partition you want to use. (By the way, System Picker modifies your boot blocks. This means that if you have used any other utility to change your boot block data, as is discussed occasionally in other parts of this book, System Picker will erase those changes. Just so you know.)

If you still are unsuccessful, go to the partition that you do not want to act as startup disk, and place the Finder in another folder (such as in the Control Panels folder). This "unblesses" the System Folder. Now, when you select the disk from the Startup Disk control panel, the remaining "blessed" partition should act as the startup disk. If you really don't care to save the System Folder, you can even delete it entirely. (If you have more than two partitions you may have more work of this sort to do!)

None of these methods are guaranteed to work. But I have had success with them. Much of the variation in success seems to depend on differences among different disk drivers (see Fix-It #12). You'll have to experiment a bit to see what works for you.

Starting with an Alternate Startup Disk

If you are having any problems starting up your Macintosh, a usually critical step is to try to restart the Macintosh using an alternate startup disk. The logic is that if the problem is specific to the original startup disk (rather than the Macintosh hardware), you should be able to startup successfully with the alternate disk. I'm assuming here that your normal startup disk is a hard disk, either internal or external.

Start Up with an Alternate Hard Disk

If you have two (or more) hard disks connected to your Macintosh, and you are unable to start with the one you normally use for startup, you can try to switch to one of the other ones (assuming it has a valid System Folder).

There's one problem with using an alternate startup disk. Since the Macintosh will not start up at the moment, you cannot access the Startup Disk control panel to change the default setting.

 What to do:

Bypass the Internal Drive If your current startup disk is your internal hard drive, and you have at least one external hard drive, you can bypass the internal drive at startup and attempt to start up from an external hard drive instead. To do this:

1. Restart your Macintosh, typically by using the Reset button.

SEE: • Chapter 4 for more details on restarting

2. Hold down the *Command-Option-Shift-Delete* keys immediately after restarting. Hold these keys down until the Welcome to Macintosh screen appears. Release the keys. The Macintosh should now start up from the external drive (assuming it has a System Folder on it). If you have partitions on the disk that each have separate System Folders, see the Partition Alert in the previous section of this chapter for more information.

Bypass the External Drive   If your default startup disk is an external hard disk (which will not start up) and you also have an internal hard disk, the solution is even simpler. Restart the Macintosh with the external drive turned off. The Macintosh should now restart from the internal drive. When startup is complete, turn the external drive back on.

Mounting the Problem Drive   With either type of bypass, the bypassed disk will not appear on the desktop when startup is finished (though see "By The Way: The Internal Drive May Still Mount When Using Command-Option-Shift-Delete"). To get it to appear, you have to mount it manually. There are several control panel utilities you can use to do this. One popular one is a control panel called SCSIProbe. To manually mount disks with it is usually as simple as clicking its *Mount* button. If SCSIProbe fails to work, you will probably have to use a repair utility to mount the disk.

SEE: • "A Hard Disk Won't Mount" later in this chapter for more details
       • Fix-It #16 for more on SCSIProbe, especially on using it to mount disks at startup

---

BY THE WAY ▶

THE INTERNAL DRIVE MAY STILL MOUNT WHEN USING COMMAND-OPTION-SHIFT-DELETE

Typically, when using the Command-Option-Shift-Delete (COSD) technique to bypass an internal drive at startup, the internal drive does not mount. However, when doing this in System 7.0.1 or later, the internal drive may mount. The reason for this is that a patch in the system software causes the Mac to do a second check for connected SCSI devices later in the startup sequence, mounting any devices that it finds. (This patch was intended to prevent large-capacity slow-starting drives from being bypassed during a normal startup.) When using the COSD shortcut, the result is that the drive mounts at the second check, despite being bypassed at the first check. Whether or not this happens depends on which Macintosh model you are using and the size of your hard disk. (There is also a way to accomplish a similar effect, with any Macintosh, using SCSIProbe, as described in Fix-It #16.)

Normally, if this happens to you, it is not a problem, as you would just as soon have the internal drive mount anyway. However, if it is important not to have the internal drive mount at startup (because it precipitates a crash, for example), you can still bypass the internal drive altogether. The way to do this is to both reset (zap) the PRAM and use the COSD shortcut. This works because the second check uses information about connected SCSI devices that is stored in the Parameter RAM (PRAM).

(continued)

Start Up with an Emergency Floppy Disk

For many users, their startup hard disk is their only hard disk. If it fails to start, the only alternative is to use a startup floppy disk (or perhaps a startup CD-ROM disk, if available). Actually, in emergencies, many users will start up with a floppy disk (containing their needed repair utilities) regardless of their hardware setup.

Here is where the default rules for selecting a startup disk help. Recall that the Macintosh uses a floppy disk as a startup disk, if one is present, regardless of what hard disks are also present and what default rules are in effect. This automatically allows you to use a floppy disk as the startup disk simply by inserting it into your floppy disk drive at startup (with Power Macs, you can also do this with CD-ROM startup disks).

Most often, in these problem situations, you should use an emergency startup disk that contains repair utilities (as described in Chapter 2). Remember, that your floppy startup disk must have the appropriate enabler (if your model of Macintosh needs one) and must use System 7 (if your model of Macintosh only runs on System 7).

 What to do:

Start Up from Your Emergency Disk Hopefully, you have already obtained or created such a disk. You obviously cannot create one on a Macintosh that won't start up!

SEE: • **Chapter 2 for how to prepare or obtain an emergency startup floppy disk**

1. Restart your Macintosh, typically by using the Reset button.

SEE: • **Chapter 4 for more details on restarting, if needed**

2. *Immediately* after restarting, insert your Emergency disk. The disk should now be the startup disk. If you wait too long to insert the floppy disk, the Macintosh again attempts to start up from the problem hard disk—and you may have to begin all over again.

Bypass Hard Drives at Startup   Even when using a floppy disk as a startup disk, the Macintosh still tries to mount any hard drives that it finds during the startup sequence. Sometimes, the same problem that prevented a hard drive from acting as a startup disk may cause similar problems when the Macintosh attempts to mount it as a secondary drive. In these cases, you need to bypass the hard drive at startup, preventing it from mounting altogether.

To do this, use essentially the same techniques as described in the previous section. Thus, if you are using an external hard drive, turn it off before restarting with a floppy disk. After startup has completed, turn the external drive back on. For an internal hard drive, hold down the Command-Option-Shift-Delete keys while restarting.

Assuming the startup is now successful, you will find that the bypassed drive is not mounted on the desktop (that was the idea after all). So you now need to mount it in order to try to fix the problem. Again, as described in the previous section, you can try to mount the disk manually. If this fails, other solutions, including using repair utilities to mount the disk, are detailed later.

SEE: • "A Hard Disk Won't Mount" later in this chapter

Solve It! When Your Macintosh Won't Start Up

Welcome to every Macintosh user's worst nightmare. You turn on your Macintosh and nothing happens. Or maybe all that happens is that your screen turns dark except for a ominous-looking Sad Mac icon. Or maybe you keep getting system crashes before the startup sequence is over.

If any of these things happens to you, don't panic. All is not lost—at least not yet. You are about to go on a tour of the startup sequence, stopping at every place where something can go wrong and learning what to do in each case. You will soon see that the vast majority of startup problems can be completely and easily fixed right from your keyboard.

The Macintosh Is Dead

 ## Symptoms:

You turn on the Macintosh and absolutely nothing happens. There is no bong, no whirring of the hard drive, no status lights go on, no nothing.

 ## Causes:

This is such an unlikely occurrence that it often means something embarrassingly simple to fix is the cause (such as your Macintosh is not plugged in). Otherwise, it does imply a major hardware failure (such as a dead power supply).

 ## What to do:

Are All Cables Plugged In and All Switches Turned On?

Make sure all cords are securely plugged into their respective receptacles. I know. This seems almost too elementary to include. But check just the same. If you are using an outlet that is controlled by a wall switch, make sure the switch is on. If you are using a separate power strip, press its reset button.

 If you are starting the Macintosh from the keyboard Power On button, make sure that the keyboard cable is actually connected to the Macintosh (though to be safe, turn off the Macintosh before attempting to reconnect any cables). If your model of Macintosh requires that an on/off switch be on before the keyboard button will work, make sure the switch is on.

Check the Battery

I discuss PowerBooks more specifically in Chapter 11. But obviously, if you are trying to start up from battery power, it won't work if your battery is dead. Plug the Power-Book into an AC outlet to see if it starts. If so, it means that your problem is specific to the battery. You will need to recharge it. If it won't hold a charge, replace it. If it is a relatively new battery and it won't hold a charge, check Chapter 11 for some other things to try.

Substitute Cables and Components

If you can start the Macintosh from the Power on/off button in the rear of the unit, but not from the Power key, it's time to suspect a defective keyboard or keyboard cable. If so, try swapping the keyboard or keyboard cable (if you have a second one available) to see if that gets things moving. If it does work, you have isolated the problem. Be thankful it is not inside the Macintosh itself. The solution is to repair or re-place the faulty component.

SEE: • Fix-It #17 for more on ADB ports

Visit the Repair Shop

If nothing has worked, or if you have already determined that you have a hardware problem, take your Macintosh to an authorized service location to have it checked out. End of story.

SEE: • Fix-It #17 for more on diagnosing hardware repairs

Sad Macs and Unusual Startup Tones

Symptoms:

The Sad Mac Icon

The (frowning) sad Mac icon appears at startup (see Figure 5-5). The screen turns black except for the sad Mac in the center. It is the inverse of the happy Mac that normally appears.

Figure 5-5
The sad Mac icon appears above a sequence of numbers (and letters A–F)—sort of an Unwelcome to Macintosh greeting

Unusual Startup Tones

A sad Mac is typically accompanied by un-usual startup tones (that is, tones other than the ones you normally hear almost immedi-ately after turning on or restarting your Mac). These tones have various pessimistic-sounding names, such as *Chimes of Death* or *Chords of Doom*. It may be a single note (of a different pitch from the usual one), a chord (again different from what you normally hear), a progression of as many as four notes, or the sound of a car crash (new to Power Macs).

A sad Mac may occur without unusual startup tones, and, conversely, these tones may appear without a sad Mac occurring. In any of these cases, all progress comes to a halt. The startup process stops.

Causes:

These symptoms occur when the Macintosh's initial diagnostic tests, which occur at startup, discover a problem that prevents the startup from continuing further.

You may have heard that this only happens if you have a serious hardware problem. This is a myth. The truth is that the vast majority of sad Mac problems are either software problems or minor hardware problems (such as replacing a cable) that you can fix yourself.

Still, these symptoms can also signal serious hardware problems with your Macintosh. The damage could be to the Macintosh itself (a component of the main logic board), a card or memory chip plugged into the main logic board, a disk drive (especially if it is your startup hard disk), or any other peripheral device. A rare cause is a stuck Interrupt switch.

Software damage to the Directory area of the disk could also lead to a sad Mac. Other less ominous causes include a nonsystem disk in the default startup drive or an incompatible System file on the startup disk.

In general, if the Macintosh can start up from another disk than the one that first caused the sad Mac, you probably do not have a hardware problem. Conversely, if the sad Mac appears immediately after turning on the power even before trying to access a disk, you most likely *do* have a hardware problem.

What to do:

Decode the Message

Sad Mac Codes Decoded   If you already read the chapter on system errors, you know that I don't recommend wasting much time trying to interpret the system error ID messages. The same is true for the string of letters and numbers that you find underneath the sad Mac icon . . . with a couple of exceptions.

Beneath the sad Mac should be two rows of eight digits (the code is in hexadecimal, which means that the digits can range from 0–9 and A–F). Check out the last digit of the first row. If it's an F, it almost certainly means that your problem is software related. Sad Macs caused by software problems are most often accompanied by an arpeggiolike four-note startup tone. These are all good signs because, as you will see shortly, it means that you can probably fix the problem yourself. If you have a Mac

Plus or older model, there will be only one row of six digits. In this case, if the first two digits are 0F, these too indicate a likely software problem.

Otherwise, the problem is probably hardware related. In particular, the most common hardware cause for the appearance of the sad Mac icon is a problem with memory chips (SIMMs). This is especially likely to be a cause if the sad Mac first appeared soon after you added SIMMs to your machine. Some error codes specifically indicate a SIMM problem. In some cases, they even suggest where the problem SIMM is located (though I won't be going into this level of detail here). Apple's MacCheck utility provides a list of sad Mac error codes and what they mean. Otherwise, Table 5-1 lists a few of the more common or easy-to-interpret codes.

Table 5-1   Some Common Sad Mac Error Codes*

ERROR CODE**				WHAT IT MEANS	WHAT TO DO
xxxx0001 xxxxxxxx				ROM test failed. The Macintosh ROM has a problem.	Take the Macintosh in for repair.
xxxx0002 xxxxxxxx xxxx0003 xxxxxxxx xxxx0005 xxxxxxxx	or or	xxxx0002 xxxxxxxx xxxx0004 xxxxxxxx	or or	RAM test failed. At least one SIMM is defective or not seated properly.	Check if SIMMs are inserted correctly. Otherwise, if possible, get a replacement SIMM and use it to replace existing SIMM to determine which one is defective. Replace the defective SIMM. Otherwise, take the Macintosh in for repair.
xxxx0008 xxxxxxxx				ADB failed. ADB refers to Apple Desktop Bus. These are the ports where the mouse and the keyboard connect to the Macintosh. Either an ADB device or the ADB section of the logic board is defective.	Check if ADB devices are correctly plugged in. Otherwise, take the Macintosh and all ADB devices in for repair.
xxxx000A xxxxxxxx				NuBus failed. This refers to the special NuBus cards (such as graphics cards) and the NuBus slots on the logic board that hold these cards. A NuBus card or a NuBus slot is defective.	If you can, try removing the NuBus cards to see if that solves the problem. If so, the faulty NuBus card needs to be replaced. Otherwise, take the Mac in for repair.
xxxx000B xxxxxxxx				SCSI chip failed. The section of the main logic board (that controls the SCSI port and the devices connected to it) is defective.	Take the Mac in for repair.

Codes are different for Mac Plus and older models and for the Macintosh Portable. Other special codes exist for PowerBooks and Power Macintoshes. Check MacCheck (see Fix-It #10) for a more complete, though relatively unhelpful, list of Sad Mac codes.

** an "x" in the codes listed here means any digit from 0 to F.

Table 5-1   Some Common Sad Mac Error Codes *(continued)*

ERROR CODE	WHAT IT MEANS	WHAT TO DO
xxxx000C xxxxxxxx	Floppy drive chip (called IWM chip) failed.	This is more likely a problem with the chip on the logic board that controls the floppy drive than with the floppy drive itself. You can check in Fix-It #17 for some suggestions on fixing floppy drives, but most likely the Mac will need a re-pair.
xxxx000D xxxxxxxx	Chip controlling the serial and modem ports (called SCC chip) failed.	Guess what? You will most likely need a hardware repair.
xxxx000F 00000001	Bus error. Most likely a soft-ware error.	Try solutions indicated in text.
xxxx000F 00000002	Address error. Most likely a software error.	Try solutions indicated in text.
xxxx000F 00000003	Illegal Instruction. Most likely a software error.	Try solutions indicated in text.
xxxx000F xxxxxxxx	Most likely a software error.	Try solutions indicated in text.

How Soon After Startup Does the Sad Mac Appear?   In addition to the sad Mac code itself, you can sometimes glean useful information from closely following the exact moment that the sad Mac appears. This can indicate what diagnostic test failed, thus precipitating the sad Mac. In particular, the Macintosh's logic board and the SIMMs are among the first items tested. So if you get a sad Mac almost as soon as you turn the Macintosh on, problems with them are the likely cause. A hardware repair looms likely. On the other hand, if the sad Mac appears shortly after the hard drive begins to start working, a problem with the hard drive or with the SCSI connections is more likely (though software causes are possible here too). If the sad Mac appears even later in the startup sequence (such as after the Welcome to Macintosh message appears), software problems are by far the most likely cause. These are also the ones most likely to have the error codes that end with an F on the first row.

Error Tones Decoded   For nonnormal startup tones, the exact notes and their pat-tern is often indicative of the cause of the problem. However, trying to learn how to make use of this information is probably more trouble than it is worth. This is be-cause Apple keeps changing both the normal and nonnormal startup tones as it comes out with different models, making useful generalizations practically impossible. First, for example, the sound that means a memory problem on AV Macs is not the same sound that you will hear if you have a memory problem on a Macintosh IIci. Even the normal startup sound is quite different on different Macintoshes. Second, interpreting some of the tones requires that you identify the note (such as whether it is a C or an

F), which you may not be able to do. Finally, older Macintoshes (Macintosh SE and earlier models) do not have error tones. So, unless you are the type of person who enjoys memorizing the names of every episode of *Gilligan's Island,* I don't recommend bothering to learn about the different tones. You are unlikely to ever confront this symptom anyway.

Here's my best rough guide to interpreting these tones. A single tone of a different pitch from usual or any two-note sequence generally means a problem with defective SIMMs. A four-note chord (or other unusual sound, such as a car crash) indicates an unknown problem that, as indicated, most often turns out to be a software problem (though a hardware cause remains possible).

If you have a PowerBook, an eight-note tone typically means a problem with a memory expansion card.

Helpful hint: Don't waste time trying to figure out what the different sounds mean. Try the simple things to fix regardless of what sound you get. If they don't work, you're going to be taking your Macintosh in for repair anyway.

Restart the Macintosh

Restart Again with the Same Disk as a Startup Disk   Maybe the sad Mac will vanish when you restart (but don't bet on it!). To find out, press the Reset button. If the sad Mac goes away, you can probably forget about it for now. If you really have a problem, it will return soon enough.

SEE: • Chapter 4 for more details about restarting

Restart with an Alternate Startup Disk   If you do get the sad Mac icon after your initial restart, it's time to try to restart with an alternate startup disk.

SEE: • "Starting with an Alternate Startup Disk," earlier in this chapter, for more details

By the way, if you were already trying to use a floppy disk as the startup disk, it may appear to be stuck in the drive. That is it does not come out when you restart. If this happens, hold down the mouse key before you restart. Continue to hold it after you restart, until the floppy disk ejects. If you also have a connected hard drive, your Mac should now try to start from this drive. If the software on the floppy disk was the problem, this may cure your sad Mac all by itself.

If the Macintosh Successfully Restarts from an Alternate Startup Disk

You probably have a software problem. As stated, this is especially likely if the first line of the sad Mac error code ended in an F. There are a number of solutions to try. The first three solutions listed here only work if the problem disk appears as a secondary disk on the Finder's desktop after restarting. The remaining solutions are worth trying whether or not the problem disk mounts.

After each attempted solution, restart the Macintosh with the original startup disk to see if the problem is solved. Continue until one solution succeeds.

Reinstall the System Software   You may have a corrupted System file. To check for this, reinstall a fresh copy of the System file or (even better) do a clean reinstall of the entire system software.

Upgrade the System Software   If the version of the system software on your emergency startup disk is different from the version on the disk that generated the Sad Mac, it may be that problem is specific to the system software version on your problem disk. In particular, you probably have an incompatibility between an older out-of-date version of the system software and your current (presumably newer) hardware. In this case, the solution is to upgrade to a more recent version of the system software.

Note especially that newer Macs will not run System 6 at all. Many models now require at least System 7.1!

SEE: • Fix-It #1 on incompatibilities between hardware and software

Rebuild the Desktop   Apple says this is worth trying, but I have never seen it work.

Zap the PRAM   I have actually seen this work, especially for problems with external drives.

Update the Disk Driver   A sad Mac could also be caused by a corrupted or out-of-date disk driver. Try reinstalling the driver by using your disk formatting utility (such as Apple HD SC Setup). Upgrade to the latest version of the disk driver available.

Repair the Directory   Your Directory files or boot blocks on the problem startup disk may have gotten corrupted. To repair this, use the appropriate utilities on your emergency startup disk(s). Start with Disk First Aid. Then try Norton Utilities, Mac-Tools, or whatever comparable utility you have.

Even if the disk did not mount from the Finder, the more heavy-duty repair utilities, such as MacTools or Norton Utilities, may be able to mount it. If repairs fail, these utilities may still be able to recover files from the disk, as needed.

Check for SCSI problems   If the problem disk is an external SCSI-connected disk, you may have a problem with its connection to the Macintosh. It may be with conflicting SCSI ID numbers, improper termination, or defective cables. Or an SCSI device may need to be repaired. SCSI problems loom particularly likely if the problem first appears immediately after adding a new SCSI device to your computer.

In one special case, Apple reports that a sad Mac may occur if a removable media drive is on at startup and a cartridge is present in the drive (which would seem to preclude using such a cartridge as a startup disk!). This is especially likely if you are using Macintosh PC Exchange.

SEE: • "Technically Speaking: The Sad Mac Makes a Visit" later in the chapter

Reformat the Disk   If all else fails, this is your almost-never-fails last resort.

SEE: • Fix-It #1 hardware and software incompatibilities
      • Fix-It #5 on reinstalling system software
      • Fix-It #9 on rebuilding the desktop
      • Fix-Its #10 and #13 on repairing damaged disks
      • Fix-It #11 on zapping the Parameter RAM
      • Fix-It #12 on updating the disk device driver
      • Fix-It #15 on reformatting
      • Fix-It #16 on SCSI problems

If the Macintosh Does Not Restart from an Alternate Startup Disk

This is more likely to mean a hardware problem, though don't despair quite yet. Try the following.

Check for System Software Problems   You may have an out-of-date version of system software that is incompatible with your current hardware. This assumes that the software on your emergency startup disk is the same out-of-date version as on your normal startup disk, which is why you could not startup with the emergency disk. This is an unlikely possibility, but I mention it just for the sake of completeness. In this case, you will need to obtain a set of system software disks for the most recent version and use them to update your system software.

SEE: • Fix-It #5 on updating system software
      • "Technically Speaking: The Sad Mac Makes a Visit" later in the chapter

Check for SCSI Problems   You may have a problem with your SCSI devices and/or connections. Turn off your Mac, disconnect the SCSI cable from the back of the machine, and restart. If you restart successfully now (presumably from your internal drive or startup floppy disk), you have an SCSI-related problem. You may be able to fix this yourself, though ultimately it may require something as extreme as reformatting your external drive.

In one special case, Apple reports that a Sad Mac may occur if a removable media drive is on at startup and a cartridge is present in the drive (which would seem to preclude using such a cartridge as a startup disk!). This is especially likely if you are using Macintosh PC Exchange.

SEE: • Fix-It #16 for SCSI problems

Check for Hardware Problems   If all else has failed, you probably have a hardware problem. The most likely hardware cause is an improperly mounted or defective SIMM. This is almost certain to be the case if the sad Mac error code or startup tones indicates a SIMM problem.

If the problem is an improperly mounted SIMM (it may have gotten loose), you may be able to solve this yourself by reseating the SIMM chip in its respective slot on the main logic board inside the Macintosh. If the small clip that holds the SIMM in place, on some models of Macintosh, is broken, this will need to be replaced. Otherwise, you probably have a defective SIMM that itself will need to be replaced.

If you have a modular Macintosh, you can usually do most of this yourself, by removing the lid of the Macintosh and directly examining the SIMMs. Of course, this assumes you would recognize SIMMs if you saw them. In any case, I am aware that many readers of this book will not feel inclined to open up their Macintosh and start fiddling with the SIMMs. Many Macintosh users seek the help of others here. The most sure-fire alternative is to take your Macintosh to a qualified service technician to have it checked out.

SEE: • Fix-It #17 for more on SIMM-related and other hardware problems

---

TECHNICALLY SPEAKING ▶

THE SAD MAC MAKES A VISIT

Here are two cases of sad Mac problems I have had. Neither involved hardware problems. The first was solved almost immediately. The second took more effort.

- *I once tried to start up with a 400K floppy disk that had an ancient System Folder on it, using my Macintosh IIci. I didn't use my hard drive as a startup disk because I knew that the game on the floppy disk was incompatible with the system software on my hard drive. Unfortunately, the sad Mac icon appeared rather than my game. After my initial shock, I noticed the F in the sad Mac code that indicated a probable software problem. I assumed (correctly, as it turned out) that the System Folder on the game disk was incompatible with my hardware. Reluctantly, I understood that the game was destined to be unusable on my machine.*

  I gave up and hit the Reset button on the Programmer's Switch, intending to return to my hard drive as a startup disk. However, things didn't work as I had planned. The floppy disk did not eject. Instead, the Macintosh again tried to start from the floppy disk and the sad Mac reappeared. To solve this problem, I held down the mouse button immediately after restarting, keeping it down until the floppy disk ejected. At last, the Macintosh started up normally using my internal hard drive as the startup disk.

- *A sad Mac appeared the first time I started up my Mac after connecting a new external hard drive. The exact code was uninformative, other than suggesting a non-hardware cause (code = 0000000F; 00000001). Obviously suspecting the newly added hard drive as the root cause, I restarted with it off. Everything started okay. I then turned the drive on and tried to mount it using SCSIProbe (as described later in this chapter and Fix-It #16). This led to a system freeze. Next I tried to mount it using MacTools (see Fix-It #13). It eventually succeeded, but only when I used its Load Emergency Driver option. At this point,*

The ? Disk Icon or a Reappearing Happy Mac

Symptoms:

Figure 5-6
The blinking ? icon—a sign of trouble if it doesn't quickly go away

The ? disk icon remains on the screen indefinitely (see Figure 5-6) or the happy Mac icon appears and disappears and reappears in an endless loop.

Causes:

The most common cause is that the Macintosh cannot locate a valid startup disk. If so, the Macintosh sits and stares at you with the blinking question mark (?) disk icon. It is asking you to insert a startup disk and waiting until you do so. For example, this happens if you turn on your Macintosh without a floppy disk inserted and no hard drive connected.

If the ? disk icon persists even when a supposed startup disk is available, you have a more serious problem. Usually, the problem is with the startup hard drive. Either the disk is not connected properly (which can easily happen with an external hard drive), the software on the disk is damaged, or a hardware repair is needed.

A cycling happy Mac icon indicates similar causes, especially damaged software. Other possible causes include incorrect SCSI connections or corrupted Parameter RAM.

What to do:

Try each of the following items, in turn, until one is successful in getting your Macintosh to start up. Remember to turn off all the devices before disconnecting or reconnecting any cables.

If Your Startup Disk Is an External Hard Drive: Check Connections

Make sure that the external drive is connected properly to the Macintosh. Make sure the drive is on and plugged in to a power outlet. Check that all cables are firmly connected. Restart.

SEE: • Fix-It #16 on SCSI problems

If Your Startup Disk Is an Internal Drive: Disconnect Any External SCSI Devices and Restart

Disconnect the SCSI cable from the back of your Mac. If this succeeds in getting your Mac to startup, you probably have either an SCSI connection problem or a hardware problem with one or more of your external SCSI devices.

SEE: • Fix-It #16 on SCSI problems

Check Indicator Lights

Most hard drives have one or two indicator lights on the front of the unit (the light is built into the front panel of the Macintosh if it is an internal drive). If there are two lights, one usually indicates that the drive is on, while the other only goes on if the drive is being accessed (reading or writing). If there is only one light, it is usually an access light. In either case, the light should go on, at least intermittently, at startup. If it does not, it means that the drive is not functioning. A hardware repair looms likely.

Restart the Macintosh

Restart Again with the Same Disk as a Startup Disk   Hopefully, the problem disappears. If so, your troubles may be over. If the problem returns later, however, you may have an intermittent problem, such as *stiction.*

SEE: • "A Hard Disk Won't Mount" later in this chapter

Restart with an Alternate Startup Disk   If the previous restart did not work, try restarting with an alternate disk, preferably a floppy disk. Continue to the next step.

By the way, if you are starting up from a floppy disk, you can still change settings of some control panels on your hard disk. This may be useful at times. For example, you could change the setting of Startup Disk from an external drive (if that is its current setting) back to an internal drive for your next restart.

SEE: • "Starting with an Alternate Startup Disk" earlier in this chapter

Check for System Folder Problems

If you can get the Macintosh to start up with an alternate startup disk, check to see if the problem disk has mounted and is now present as a secondary disk (its icon is shown below the startup disk icon on the Finder's desktop). Most likely it will be there. If so, check for the following problems (restart the Macintosh, using the problem disk as the startup disk, after each attempted solution, to see if the problem is solved).

Make Sure a System Folder Is on the Problem Disk   Okay, presumably you already know that a System Folder is there. But just in case, check anyway. If there isn't one already there, install a System Folder and start again.

SEE: • Fix-It #5 on installing system software

Make Sure There Is Only One System Folder on the Disk   Multiple System Folders (or, more technically, more than one copy of the System file and/or Finder) on your startup disk are not likely to cause startup problems, especially if you are using System 6.0.7 or later. Still, to be safe, it is good practice to delete all but the intended startup System Folder from your disk (unless you deliberately want to maintain multiple System Folders for some reason). If you are unsure whether additional System Folders are present, you can use the Finder's Find command and search for the word *Finder* or *System.*

SEE: • Fix-It #5 on system software problems for more details

Bless the System Folder If Necessary   From the Icon View in the Finder, check to see if the System Folder has the mini-icon of a Macintosh on it. This is the indication that you have a blessed System Folder. The Macintosh typically does not accept a disk as a startup disk, even if it appears to have a valid System Folder on it, unless it is shown as a blessed System Folder (that is, with a mini-icon of a Macintosh on the folder).

SEE: • "Understanding the Startup Sequence" earlier in this chapter

Normally, all System Folders are blessed folders. Occasionally, however, a problem may develop where an apparently valid System Folder is not blessed. For example, the utility System Picker unblesses otherwise valid System Folders. Similarly, if you remove the Finder or System file from a blessed System Folder, it will become unblessed. Replacing these files will "rebless" the folder.

Also, an unblessed System Folder may be a warning signal that there is more than one System Folder on your disk. *This is because a disk can have one and only one blessed System Folder on it,* which is the one that the Macintosh actually uses when it starts up from that disk.

If the System Folder isn't blessed, open the System Folder to check if the essential files (System file and Finder) are really there. If they are, remove the System file from the System Folder. Close the folder and open it again. Then replace the System file and close the System Folder again. This usually reblesses the System Folder. You should now see the mini-icon of the Macintosh on the folder.

Whether the mini-icon appears yet or not, try restarting now with this disk as the startup disk. The disk will most likely start up without further problems.

TECHNICALLY SPEAKING ▶

BOOT BLOCK PROBLEMS

Some startup problems can be attributed to corrupted or incorrect data in the boot blocks. This is technically why an apparently valid System Folder may appear as unblessed. Such a disk does not start up properly.

In some cases, the procedure described here for blessing the System Folder fixes a boot block problem. Otherwise, you may have to resort to special utilities that repair boot blocks. Norton Utilities and MacTools can do this. If there is a boot block problem, these utilities find it, report the problem to you, and fix it. If they cannot fix the problem, your last resort is to reformat the disk.

SEE: • **Chapter 8 on boot blocks and Fix-It #13 on disk damage for more details**

Replace the System and the Finder   If the previous steps have not worked, the System file or the Finder may be damaged. Replace these files. You might also try replacing any needed System Enabler and the Finder Preferences file.

SEE: • **Fix-It #5 for replacing system software**

Check for Startup Partition Problems

If your startup disk is divided into partitions, only one of those partitions can normally act as the startup disk. If you place a System Folder on another partition and try to select it as the startup disk (via the Startup Disk control panel), it will not work. In some cases (depending on your particular disk driver and especially if the only available System Folder is on the partition that cannot act as the startup disk), the result may be that you get the cycling happy Mac. If this happens, do the following.

Select a Different Startup Disk   To do this, first start up from a floppy startup disk. Then, if needed, install a System Folder on the partition that can act as a startup disk. Next, select that disk (or any other valid startup volume) as the startup disk from the Startup Disk control panel. (If you had used System Picker originally, you may need to use it again to select a new startup disk.) Restart.

Update Your Disk Driver   Alternatively, switching to a different disk driver may eliminate this cycling happy Mac problem altogether, allowing you to start up from the previously problematic partition. In general, however, you will keep these and other related problems to a minimum by using the disk driver from the utility that was used to format your disk and by using the same utility for all of your mounted volumes.

SEE: • "The Startup Disk Control Panel: Changing the Default Startup Selection," earlier in this
          chapter, for more details
        • Fix-It #12 on disk drivers

Zap the PRAM

This is a special type of memory that is preserved (by a battery inside the Macintosh) even after the Macintosh is shut off. Some of the data stored in PRAM relate especially to SCSI connections. If the data stored in PRAM become corrupted, they can cause problems with a hard disk mounting. Zapping the PRAM restores the data to their default value and should solve this problem.

SEE: • Fix-It #11 on zapping the Parameter RAM

Make Disk Repairs

If none of the preceding solutions worked, or if the problem disk did not mount when starting up with the alternate startup disk, or if you could not startup at all when using an alternate startup disk, try the following.

"Repair" and Defragment the Disk   If you get the blinking question mark icon immediately after restarting after a system crash (or other improper shutdown), you may have something called the Disk Check bug. What is happening is that the Macintosh's startup diagnostics are mistakenly reporting a damaged disk, even though the disk is fine.

To fix this, use a repair utility, such as MacTools' DiskFix or Norton Utilities' Disk Doctor, to "repair" and mount the disk. This disk will now work normally.

To prevent this from happening in the future, defragment your disk. Continue to defragment it on a regular basis.

To see if you are even susceptible to this particular bug, run a freeware utility called Disk Bug Checker. Also, Hardware System Update 2.0.x (for System 7.1) or later corrects this bug so that it will no longer occur. Neither should it occur in System 7.5.

SEE: • Fix-It #8 on defragmenting disks
        • Fix-It #13 on repairing disks

Last Resort   If none of the previous solutions worked, it's time to check for other disk damage, corrupted data, or a hardware problem. For starters, try running Disk First Aid.

SEE: • "A Hard Disk Won't Mount" later in this chapter

The X Disk Icon Appears

Symptoms:

Figure 5-7
The X disk icon usually means that there is no System Folder on a floppy disk

You should see the X disk icon only if you are trying to start up from a floppy disk. At the beginning of the startup process, the floppy disk is ejected and a disk icon with an X in the center appears (see Figure 5-7).

If you do not have any startup hard disk connected to the Macintosh, the blinking ? disk icon returns and the startup process halts.

Causes:

This is usually no cause for concern. It simply means that the Macintosh did not find a valid System Folder on the floppy disk and so could not start up. The disk is otherwise likely to be a normal, perfectly okay Macintosh disk.

These days, this is a relatively rare problem, since you almost never use a floppy disk as a startup disk anyway (except in emergency or other special situations). Normally, if you do get this icon, it is because a floppy disk was unintentionally present in a drive at startup.

What to do:

Do Nothing . . . At First

If you have a startup internal or external hard disk connected to your Macintosh: Do nothing. The Macintosh will start up normally from the hard disk after ejecting the floppy disk.

If you do not have a hard disk connected, you need to do something. Start up with an alternate startup floppy disk.

SEE: • "Starting with an Alternate Startup Disk" earlier in this chapter

Check the Problem Floppy Disk Once startup is complete, reinsert the problem floppy disk, ejecting the alternate startup floppy disk, if needed.

Check for a System Folder There almost certainly isn't one, but check anyway. If there is no System Folder (and you want one on the disk!), install a System Folder on the disk. Then try to start up from the disk again. It should work.

SEE: • Fix-It #5 on installing system software

Make Sure the System Folder Is Blessed If there is a System Folder, you do have some problem with the disk. It may simply be that the System Folder is not blessed. To check for this, follow the guidelines described previously for blessing System Folders. Most of the time, if it is a valid System Folder with no damaged files, simply opening and closing the System Folder should get it blessed.

SEE: • "The ? Disk Icon or a Reappearing Happy Mac" earlier in this chapter

Check for Disk Damage For more general advice on problems with floppy disks, including dealing with a possibly damaged disk:

SEE: • "A Floppy Disk Won't Mount" later in this chapter

A System Error Occurs Just Prior to or While Welcome to Macintosh Appears on the Screen

Symptoms:

A system error occurs while the Welcome to Macintosh screen—or any substitute startup screen you may use instead—is visible. The system error may be a freeze (where everything just stops dead), a crash (with the bomb message perhaps appearing), or a spontaneous restart (where the whole process begins again and crashes again at the same spot). A variety of other error messages are also possible.

If you get the system bomb error message at this point and you are using System 7, the message may offer advice on how to proceed next: *To temporarily turn off extensions, restart and hold down the Shift key.*

If you are using certain startup management utilities, such as Now Utilities Startup Manager (as described more in Fix-It #4), when you restart after a startup crash caused by an INIT conflict, you may get a special message, as shown in Figure 5-8.

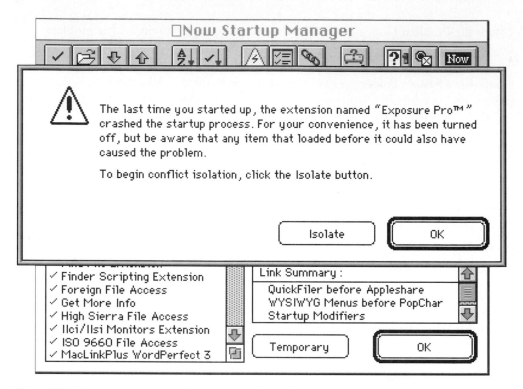

Figure 5-8   A message at startup from Now Utilities' Startup Manager

 Causes:

This almost always means a problem with a system extension or control panel that loads at startup (previously referred to as INITs). The loading of these files corresponds to the appearance of their icons along the bottom of the screen.

Otherwise, the problem is probably with the system software. In some cases, the PRAM may be corrupted. Occasionally, improper SCSI connections may be the cause.

A spontaneous restart at startup is most likely due to an INIT problem. Otherwise, it may be due to more general causes as described later in this chapter.

SEE: • "Problems with Restart, Shut Down, or Sleep" later in this chapter

A Mac that requires a system enabler file will not start up successfully if it does not have its appropriate system enabler in the startup disk's System Folder. Actually, any time you try to start up with a version of software incompatible with your current hardware, you should get an error message informing you of this (in worse cases, you may get a system crash or a sad Mac instead).

What to do:

Try each of the following until you find a solution that works.

Do You Have the Correct and Latest Version of the System Software, Especially the Enabler File?

Suppose you get a message something like the one in Figure 5-9, that seems to imply that you need to upgrade your system software: *This startup disk will not work on this Macintosh model. Use the latest Installer to update this disk for this model. (System 7.x does not work on this model; you need a newer version that does.)*

> **This startup disk will not work on this Macintosh model. Use the latest Installer to update this disk for this model. (System 7.1 does not work on this model; you need a newer version that does.)**
>
> [Restart]

Figure 5-9   This message, or one like it, may not always mean what it seems to be saying

If you are using out-of-date system software (such as System 6 on a Macintosh that requires System 7), the obvious solution is to update it, as the message suggests.

A message like this may also mean that you are using a version of the system software customized for a Macintosh model different from the one you are now using. For example, if you have an external drive with system software customized for a Mac Classic and then attach it to a Quadra, you will have problems. The solution here, once again, is to reinstall the system software, using either the version for your current model or the custom "any Macintosh" option.

SEE: • Fix-It #5 on installing system software

Oddly enough, you may also get this message even when you are using the correct and latest version of the system software. In this case, it probably means that the appropriate Enabler file is missing from your System Folder. In order to fix this, you need only to reinstall the Enabler file itself. Here's what to do:

1. Press the Restart button in the alert box.

2. Startup from another startup disk (ideally, one with a System *and* Finder) that is known to work with your Mac (such as your Emergency Toolkit disk). Locate the needed Enabler file on this disk and copy it to the System Folder of your problem disk. One exception: the Power Mac Enabler on a floppy disk cannot be used on a hard drive. In this case, skip to step 3.

    By the way, these Enabler files are periodically updated. The one that came with your Mac may no longer be the latest version. Apple maintains a file, with a name like *System Enabler Info,* that lists the latest Enabler version for each Mac. This file, as well as the Enablers themselves, are available from on-line services.

3. If you do not have another normal startup disk, start up using the Install Me First disk that came with your Macintosh model. Select *Custom,* rather than *Easy Install.* Scroll to the bottom of the list. There should be an option with a name like *Update Universal System* or *Updates System Software for Any Macintosh.* Select this option. It will install the correct enabler as well as some additional control panels. It will not replace your System and Finder.

System 7.5 Alert: This Update option is not currently available in System 7.5. This makes sense since Enablers were not needed for the initial release of System 7.5.

SEE: • Fix-It #5 on installing system software

Test for an INIT Problem

If missing or out-of-date system software does not seem to be the cause of your problem, restart with your INITs off. With System 7, you can easily do this by restarting while holding down the Shift key. When the Welcome to Macintosh screen appears, the words *Extensions Off* should appear directly below the words *Welcome to Macintosh.* This means that you have bypassed the INITs. You can now release the Shift key. If an INIT was the source of the problem, you should now start up successfully.

System 6 Alert: In System 6, to bypass the startup disk's INITs you need to start up using an alternate startup disk.

Determine the Problem INIT

If the previous step indicated an INIT problem, you now want to determine which INIT is the source of the problem. If you have several INITs, this may not be at all obvious.

SEE: • Fix-It #4 for more details on how to solve INIT problems

Once you isolate the problem INIT, the most common solution is to stop using it by removing it from your System Folder. You should then be able to restart successfully using the original startup disk.

A related possibility is that you don't have enough memory to load all of your INITs. This is likely only if you are running a large number of INITs with a relatively low amount of memory (2.5Mb or less). If so, you have to remove INITs from the System Folder until you have reduced the number enough to allow the startup to proceed. There is no specific INIT that must be removed in this case. However, the amount of memory needed by an INIT varies. Thus, one INIT may require as much memory as three or four other INITs combined. Some startup management utilities (see Fix-It #4 again) list the RAM usage of each INIT.

Zap the PRAM

Some of the data stored in PRAM relates especially to SCSI connections. If the data stored in PRAM become corrupted, it can cause problems with a hard disk mounting. Zapping the PRAM restores the data to its default value and should solve this problem.

SEE: • Fix-It #11 on zapping the Parameter RAM

Replace or Reduce System Software

If there is no INIT or PRAM problem, the system software may be damaged. Be especially wary of a System file that has suddenly substantially increased in size for no apparent reason. Reinstall your system software.

It is also possible that your system software is just fine but that you do not have sufficient RAM to load it all at startup (even with extensions off). This becomes a more likely possibility if you are using System 7 on a machine with 2Mb or less of memory. You may be able to reduce memory needs at startup by reducing the number of sounds located in the System file (reducing the number of fonts may also help, especially in System 6). Otherwise, you either have to switch back to System 6 (if you are using System 7) or add more memory to your machine.

Finally, if for some reason, you have a System Folder with a System file but no Finder, the Mac may startup successfully, but will crash at the point that the Finder would normally load. The solution is to restart with another disk and install a copy of the Finder into the System Folder.

SEE: • Fix-It #1 on incompatibilities between hardware and software
      • Fix-It #5 for how to replace system software
      • Fix-It #6 on increasing memory availability

Check for Other Problems

Otherwise, check for other file or disk damage, SCSI connection problems, or a hardware problem.

SEE: • "A Hard Disk Won't Mount" later in this chapter

Problems While Launching the Finder and the Desktop

 ## Symptoms:

The loading of INITs has completed, the Welcome to Macintosh screen has disappeared, and the Macintosh is now ready to launch the Finder and create the desktop. Instead—just when you thought it was safe to start using your Macintosh—something goes wrong.

Typically, problems here are signaled by the appearance of an error message. The message may appear at any time from just prior to the appearance of the desktop to just before the end of the entire startup sequence (as the disk icons appear on the right side of the screen).

If the error occurs prior to the appearance of the disk icon for the startup disk, the startup disk is the likely source of the problem. If the error occurs after the appearance of the startup disk's icon but before the appearance of the icon of any other disk that may be mounting as part of the startup sequence (such as a second hard drive), the problem is probably with the secondary disk.

Possible error messages include: *Can't load the Finder, The desktop file could not be created, The disk is damaged,* and *The disk <name of disk> needs minor repairs.* More rarely, you may get a message that says that the disk is *unreadable* or that it is *not a Macintosh disk.*

Occasionally, rather than an error message, a system freeze or system crash may occur, typically just before the startup disk icon would appear on the screen.

Causes:

Usually, the *Can't load the Finder* error message is a one-time glitch. The exact reason it happened may never be clear. Otherwise, it is most likely due to defective Finder and/or System files.

The other messages typically signal damage to system software or to the Desktop and/or Directory files (the critical invisible files that allow the Macintosh to interact with the disk). Sometimes it is an SCSI-related problem.

SEE: • Chapters 2 and 8 for more details on these invisible files

What to do:

Can't Load the Finder

A message that says *Can't load the Finder* (see Figure 5-10) may appear near the end of a startup sequence (sometimes with an -41 system error ID code). Here are four potential solutions to this problem.

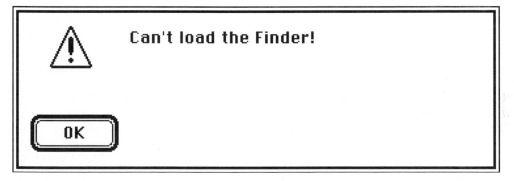

Figure 5-10 If you get this error message, simply restarting the Macintosh usually solves the problem

Restart Restart the Macintosh (typically by using the Reset button). Wait to see if the Finder loads correctly on the next startup sequence. If the startup is successful, the problem may not recur. Otherwise, try restarting again with Extensions off. This may succeed because it reduces the amount of memory needed by the system software, leaving more memory for the Finder. In this case, it may mean that you cannot use so many extensions without adding more RAM. If the problem still recurs, you need to start up using an alternate startup disk and proceed to the next potential solution.

Replace the Finder and the System File   Replace the Finder and the System file. It makes sense to be extra cautious and also replace the Finder Preferences and Enabler file (if one is needed) at this point.

SEE: • Fix-It #5 on replacing the Finder and the System file

Check for Disk Damage   Use utilities such as Norton Utilities or MacTools. In particular, there may be a problem with the boot blocks, since they contain information that tells the Macintosh which file on the disk is considered the Finder.

SEE: • Fix-It #13 on using Norton Utilities and MacTools

Wrong Boot Block?   If the problem disk is a copy of a floppy disk, and you made the copy using the Finder, make another copy using a utility such as Disk Copy. If the original floppy disk has customized boot blocks, the Finder does not copy them to the new disk. This could cause a startup problem when you use the copy. Disk Copy will copy customized boot blocks.

SEE: • Chapter 2, "Take Note: To Make an Exact Copy of Entire Floppy Disk"

The Disk Needs Minor Repairs

You may get a message saying *the disk needs minor repairs* (see Figure 5-11). This occurs most often with floppy disks. Here's what to do.

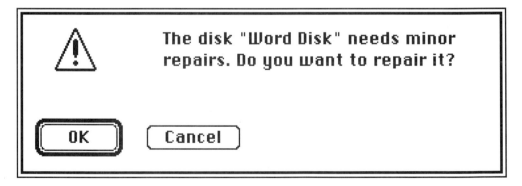

Figure 5-11   Clicking OK here usually remedies the minor repair problem

Click OK   Clicking OK usually repairs the problem. If all goes well, the startup sequence is successfully completed and your problem is over. The minor repairs message may be restricted to System 6, as I never see it anymore.

Rebuild the Desktop   Clicking OK to this message appears to fix minor damage to the Directory files, as well as make repairs to the Desktop file(s). So, if clicking OK failed to work, try rebuilding the desktop.

Check for Viruses   If the minor repairs message keeps recurring, it may indicate that you have a particular virus called INIT-29. Run an anti-virus utility to check for this.

SEE: • "A Floppy Disk Won't Mount" later in this chapter
       • Fix-It #7 on eliminating a virus
       • Fix-It #9 on rebuilding the desktop

The Desktop File Could Not Be Created

Rebuild the Desktop   If you get this message, it may mean that the Desktop file is damaged. Rebuilding it should fix it.

Check for Other Damage   There may be damage to the Directory files or SCSI problems.

SEE: • Fix-It #13 on repairing damaged disks
       • "A Hard Disk Won't Mount" and "A Floppy Disk Won't Mount," in the following sections, for more general advice

Unreadable or Damaged Disk

If you get a message that the disk is unreadable, not a Macintosh disk, or is damaged, the problem is usually with secondary disks mounted during the startup, not the startup disk itself. If the problem had been with the startup disk, it would probably have caused a symptom at an earlier point in the startup process.

For Unformatted Disks   If one of these messages does appear, and you are using a disk for the first time, it may mean that it was never formatted. If so, format it. If it is a floppy disk, accept the alert box's offer to initialize it.

SEE: • Fix-It #15 on formatting disks

For Formatted Disks   If the disk has been formatted previously, don't reinitialize the disk! For floppy disks, you may simply be using the wrong type of disk drive for the disk. If so, the disk is still fine. Otherwise, for floppy or hard disks, try repair utilities to remedy the problem. Reformatting may ultimately be necessary.

SEE: • "A Hard Disk Won't Mount" and "A Floppy Disk Won't Mount" in the following sections
       • Fix-It #15 on formatting disks

For RAM Disks   This unusual situation is described in detail in Chapter 11.

SEE: • Technically Speaking: An 'Unreadable' RAM disk" in Chapter 11

Cursor Alternates Between a Watch and an Arrow (or All Icons in a Window Are Missing)

The alternating cursor is usually caused by the Finder having a problem trying to display the contents of windows that are automatically opened at startup. You probably also have a system freeze.

To solve this, restart and hold down the Option key until the Finder mounts (if you want, you can wait to press the key until just after the Welcome to Macintosh message disappears). This forces the Finder to close all open windows and should resolve the problem. When startup is over, you should be able to re-open the windows without further symptoms.

A related symptom, basically due to the same cause, is if all the icons are missing from the display of an open window at startup. Sometimes, just closing and reopening the window will solve the problem. Otherwise, leave the window closed and restart.

For Any Other Symptom, Including System Errors

Start by Restarting a Few Times   See if the problem fixes itself. If it does and things now seem normal, run Disk First Aid just to be safe. It may spot damage that was causing the problem.

SEE: • Chapter 4 for more on system errors
        • Fix-It #10 on MacCheck and Disk First Aid

Rebuild the Desktop   Restart the Macintosh and hold down the Command-Option keys until a message appears asking whether you want to rebuild the desktop. You get a separate message for each disk to be mounted. Click OK for the suspected problem disk(s).

SEE: • Fix-It #9 for more details on rebuilding the desktop

Did You Deinstall At Ease Improperly?   If you use Apple's *At Ease* program, it is important that you use its Installer utility to deinstall it. To do this, you select the Installer's Customize option and then, holding down the Option key, click the Remove button. If you remove the At Ease extension any other way, such as by simply dragging it out of the System Folder, your disk will crash at startup. The other main solution at this point is to do a clean reinstall of your system software.

SEE: • Fix-It #5 on reinstalling system software

AT EASE IS NOT ALWAYS THAT EASY

The reason that removing At Ease without using the Installer will cause a system crash at startup is because At Ease modifies the boot blocks so that the Mac looks for At Ease rather than the Finder at startup. With At Ease gone, the Mac doesn't know what to start up with. Using the Installer to deinstall At Ease fixes this problem.

On a related front, if you have password-protected your disk with At Ease and you forget your password, you can still start up with a floppy disk. Then delete the At Ease Preferences file in the Preferences Folder of the System Folder. This eliminates the password protection, allowing you to start up from the hard disk again. However, with the enhanced security options used by At Ease for Workgroups (a special version of At Ease for large multiuser environments), you can be prevented from accessing the At Ease startup drive even if you start up from a floppy disk. At Ease accomplishes this feat by modifying the disk driver (it works only with the Apple driver or Drive 7). This is similar to how most dedicated security utilities work. If you forget your password in these cases, you will need to update the disk driver, which should eliminate the password protection. If this should fail to work, you will need to reformat the disk to use it again.

There are numerous other problems associated with At Ease. Especially common are problems making copies of floppy disks from the Finder while At Ease is on. At Ease can also cause improper rebuilding of the desktop. If you are having such problems, disabling At Ease is a good way to begin looking for a solution.

SEE: • **"By the way: Ejecting CD-ROM disks while using At Ease," later in this chapter, for still another At Ease problem**

SEE: • **Fix-It #12 on disk device drivers**

Check for Damage If these techniques do not work, you have to start up with an alternate startup disk. Then check for other disk damage (including media damage), corrupted data, or a hardware problem.

SEE: • **"A Hard Disk Won't Mount" and "A Floppy Disk Won't Mount" in the following sections**

Solve It! Generic Problems with Disks

A Hard Disk Won't Mount

Symptoms:

• A hard disk won't mount, even when it is not the startup disk. This is typically referred to as a *crashed disk.* Most often, no error message or any other indication of a problem occurs. The disk's icon simply does not appear on the desktop. The operation of the Macintosh otherwise proceeds normally.

- In some cases, an error message appears, indicating why the disk cannot mount. Most commonly, the error message appears that says the disk is damaged, unreadable, or that it is not a Macintosh disk.

- In the worst cases, you may get a system crash.

Note: If the problem disk you are trying to mount is your current startup disk, thereby preventing you from starting up, begin in the preceding section.

SEE: • "When Your Macintosh Won't Start Up" earlier in this chapter

 ## Causes:

The most common cause is damage to critical invisible files needed for the Macintosh to interact with the disk: the Directory and the device driver (see Chapter 8 for background on the Directory and related invisible files). Otherwise, if it is a new drive, the disk may not yet be formatted or the drive may be incorrectly connected.

Hardware problems are also possible. This is especially likely if the hard drive appears to make less noise than usual or if its indicator lights do not go on or flash as expected. Also suspect hardware damage if symptoms appear shortly after you've jostled a hard drive while it was in use.

 ## What to do:

If an error message appears, skip ahead to the section relevant to that message. Otherwise, try the following.

Check Power and Connections

For external drives, make sure the drive is actually on and plugged in. Make sure all cables are firmly connected (remember to turn the Macintosh off before reconnecting loose cables).

Restart or Try to Manually Mount the Drive

If you are starting up from an internal drive and a secondary external drive did not mount automatically as expected, the problem may simply be that you did not turn the hard drive on in time for the Macintosh to recognize its presence. Similarly, external hard drives that are turned on after startup is over do not automatically mount. These problems are usually easy to solve. Just select Restart. Everything should now mount as expected. In the future, remember to turn on the external drive a few seconds before turning on the Macintosh.

SEE: • "Take Note: Where Is My External Drive?," earlier in this chapter, for more on
        this problem

Otherwise, try to manually mount the drive. The easiest way to do this is to use a special control panel, such as one called SCSIProbe. Alternatively, you can usually use the formatting utility that came with your hard drive (except for Apple's formatting utility, Apple HD SC Setup, which has no mount function).

To use SCSIProbe, open its control panel window. Ideally, you should see the name of your hard disk present in its list, even if the disk was not mounted. From this window, click the Mount button (see Figure 5-12). This should mount the drive. If so, your problems are probably over. The drive should mount as expected next time.

If SCSIProbe does not even indicate that your drive is present, you can try SCSIProbe's Update button to see if that gets SCSIProbe to recognize the presence of your drive. If it does, now click Mount, to see if you can get the disk to mount. Again, if this works, your problems are over.

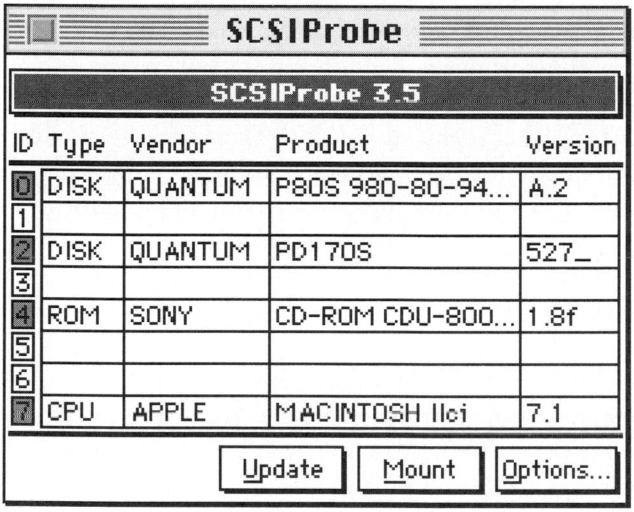

Figure 5-12   SCSIProbe. Click the Mount button to mount a hard disk without having to restart the Macintosh

SEE: • Fix-It #16 for more details on using SCSIProbe

Check for SCSI-Related Problems

If you have external SCSI devices, particularly if you have more than one, check for SCSI-related problems such as SCSI device ID conflicts and improper termination. The best way to start this search is to try to start up with all SCSI devices detached. Do this by shutting down, detaching the SCSI cable from the back of the Macintosh, and restarting. If things now go well, suspect an SCSI problem.

Be especially suspicious of SCSI-related causes if you have made recent changes to your SCSI connections. In many cases, these problems cause a system crash at startup, typically immediately after the Welcome to Macintosh message appears.

Also, if you have more than one hard drive, Apple's official recommendation is that they all use the same device driver. This may require shifting to a new driver on one or more of your drives or even reformatting disks. However, I have never seen a problem result from ignoring this advice.

SEE: • Fix-It #12 for more details on disk device drivers
     • Fix-It #16 for details on these SCSI-related problems

Special Case: Problems Mounting Removable Media Cartridges

A removable cartridge, such as used with a SyQuest drive, should mount automatically when you insert it. However, my experience is that this does not always occur. Success seems to depend on a variety of factors, such as whether you started up with extensions on or off, whether certain options are selected from an SCSI mounting control panel (such as SCSIProbe or Drive7's Mount Cache), whether the drive was turned on prior to startup, whether the cartridge was inserted at startup, and more.

For example, the APS PowerTools control panel (included with APS drives) has "AutoMount" and "Support This Device" checkboxes. Selecting these options should increase the odds that your cartridge mounts when inserted. Check your utility's documentation for details. Just remember that no icon appears on your desktop until a cartridge is inserted in the drive. In that regard, I have also found that when I select Restart, sometimes a cartridge automatically ejects and sometimes it does not. If it does eject, be sure to reinsert it or it will not reappear on your desktop when the restart is complete.

Occasional problems with an inserted cartridge that does not automatically mount can almost always be solved by mounting the cartridge manually. To do this, use an SCSI mounting control panel and click its Mount button. If you are trying to use a cartridge as the startup disk, make sure the drive is on and the cartridge is inserted before you turn on your Mac. (However, having cartridges inserted prior to startup can sometimes be the cause of problems, including a sad Mac. So if you are unsuccessful in mounting a cartridge in this way, give up using it as a startup disk and insert it after startup is over.)

Problems mounting a removable cartridge can especially occur when you eject a cartridge and insert a different one. Problems are most likely to happen if the new cartridge uses a different disk driver than the previous cartridge (this can happen if they were formatted by different utilities). Control panels, again such as SCSIProbe and Drive7's Mount Cache, are designed to solve these conflicts. Definitely use one of these utilities if you are having problems mounting removable media drives. As an immediate solution, simply restart.

By the way, these utilities work either by getting the Mac to switch to the new disk's driver or by using a universal driver that works with virtually all formats. In the latter case, it is recommended (though not possible for intended startup disks) that you do not have any cartridge inserted in a drive until after startup (otherwise, the driver contained on the disk is installed in memory instead of the control panel's universal driver; these may not be the same).

Finally, if you insert a cartridge and get a message that says the disk is "not a Macintosh disk," the disk may simply be a new unformatted disk. If so, do not click the Initialize button. This will format it improperly. Instead, use your disk formatting utility to format the disk. If the disk is already formatted, you may have a damaged disk (see next section). SyQuest cartridges, in particular, are susceptible to damage from dust, which is why you should always eject them from the drive and store them in their case when not in use. Never open the cartridge's metal shutter.

SEE: • Fix-It #12 for more details on disk device drivers
• Fix-It #15 on formatting disks
• Fix-It #16 for more on these SCSI-related problems (especially "Take Note: Mounting Removable Media Cartridges with Different Drivers")

Check for Damaged Files and Disks (Disk Is "Unreadable" or "Not a Macintosh Disk")

If none of the previous solutions work, you probably have damaged files on the disk, most likely the Directory files. This is especially likely when you get the message that says that the disk is *unreadable* or *not a Macintosh disk*. Check for this with repair utilities, such as Disk First Aid or MacTools. You may also have the Disk Check bug, as described previously in this chapter in the section on getting a blinking question mark on startup. If so, after the disk is repaired, defragment the disk.

SEE: • Fix-It #10 and #13 on repair utilities
• Fix-It #8 on defragmenting a disk

If these fail to work, round up the usual suspects. Especially try zapping the PRAM.

SEE: • Fix-It #7 on viruses
• Fix-It #9 on rebuilding the desktop
• Fix-It #11 on zapping the Parameter RAM
• Fix-It #12 on updating the hard disk device driver

After you try each Fix-It, restart your Macintosh to check whether it has remedied the problem. If any of them succeeds, your problem is over. Unfortunately, if the Finder cannot mount your disk, it probably means that most of these techniques do not recognize the drive either. But it's worth a shot.

Reformat

If all else has failed, reformat the entire drive and start over (but if you are desperate to try to recover unbacked-up files from your disk, check the next section before you reformat). Assuming you have backups, restore them to your disk.

With these sort of problems, it often pays to reformat even if previous attempted solutions seem to have fixed the problem. Otherwise, problems may soon return. Reformatting is often necessary for a permanent solution.

SEE:　• Fix-It #15 on formatting disks

Hardware Problems: Stiction and Beyond

If reformatting fails, you probably have a hardware problem. If you couldn't even begin to reformat because the disk showed no signs of life, you almost certainly have a hardware problem. In particular, suspect hardware trouble if the drive is either making no noise or not making its usual noises when you first turn it on. Similarly suspect a hardware problem if the hard drive's indicator light(s) are not going on as expected or are not flashing on and off as it typically does.

Usually, a damaged hard disk cannot be repaired. It will need to be replaced instead. This can, and often does, mean the loss of all data on your disk. However, there are a few glimmers of hope even here.

Stiction　　Stiction refers to a hardware problem whereby the drive gets physically stuck at startup and is unable to reach its normal spinning speed. The result is that the Mac never starts up at all. A sharp slap to the side of the drive case can sometimes get it going again (but the problem will return the next time you try to start up). If this happens, immediately back up all your data.

A stiction problem is most severe when the drive is first turned on. So, as a temporary fix, do not ever turn the drive off. The Mac will probably continue to run fine as long as you leave it on.

As with other hardware damage to a disk, stiction cannot be repaired. Replacing the disk is the only permanent solution. However, the temporary fixes should at least allow you to recover any needed data from the disk before replacing it.

Power Supply　　For external hard drives, the problem may be in the power supply, a separate component from the disk itself. Once it is replaced, your hard drive will function normally again, and all data on your disk will still be there unharmed.

Otherwise, for internal drives, there is a slim chance that the problem is with the connection cable from the drive to the logic board. This should be fixable. Finally, if all else fails and you have important unbacked-up data on a damaged disk, try a repair shop that specializes in recovering data from problem drives. Some of these places, such as DriveSavers (1-800-440-1904), advertise nationally. You can mail them your drive. They may succeed where you could not. Do this *before* you try to reformat the disk.

SEE:　• Fix-It #17 on dealing with hardware problems

A Floppy Disk Won't Mount

Symptoms:

Upon inserting a floppy disk into a disk drive, one of the following things happens:

- The disk drive makes no sound, as if it does not recognize that the disk has been inserted. Obviously, the disk does not mount.
- The Macintosh appears to recognize the disk and attempts to mount it, but ultimately a system freeze occurs.
- An error message appears informing you that the disk cannot be mounted. The most common messages say that the disk is damaged, unreadable, or that it is not a Macintosh disk. Usually, you are given the option to initialize the disk.
- An error message appears telling you that the disk needs minor repairs.

If you are trying to use the floppy disk as a startup disk, you should start with the section earlier in this chapter.

SEE: • "When Your Macintosh Won't Start Up" (especially the topic on the X disk icon) earlier in this chapter

Causes:

The causes vary depending on which of the symptoms you have. In general, similar to what was true for hard disks, the problem is usually due to damage to the files used by the Macintosh to recognize and interact with the disk, particularly the Directory. If the disk cannot be easily repaired, you have a *trashed disk*.

The problem can also be caused by physical damage to the disk or the disk drive.

TAKE NOTE ▶

IF YOU CAN'T GET A DISK TO INSERT

A disk that won't insert is probably due to a stuck or bent shutter, the metal piece at the bottom of the floppy disk. If it doesn't freely slide, it is stuck. If you can't free it, remove it (to do this, bend it open as if you are trying to straighten a paper clip). Then insert the disk and, if it mounts, immediately copy all data on it to another disk. Discard the problem disk.

If you know that your disk has a stuck or bent shutter, do not even try to insert it into a drive without first removing the shutter. Otherwise, even if you succeed in inserting it, you may have even greater problems getting it to eject again. A disk with a bent shutter can even damage the drive itself.

What to do:

For the "Disk Needs Minor Repairs" Message

If you get an error message saying the disk needs *minor repairs:*

Click OK The error message includes an OK button. Click it. This usually repairs the problem.

If Clicking OK Doesn't Succeed You may have a corrupted Desktop file. To check for this, you can completely delete and create a new desktop, rather than simply re-build it, as explained in Fix-It #9. Otherwise, check for a damaged disk by using Disk First Aid and/or other repair utilities. Finally, some viruses will cause this message to appear. So check for virus infections using your anti-virus utility.

> SEE: • Fix-It #9 for more on rebuilding the desktop
> • Fix-Its #10 and #13 on disk repairs
> • Fix-It #7 on viruses

For the "Disk Is Unreadable" or "Is Not a Macintosh Disk" Messages

You may also get error messages that say the disk is unreadable or not a Macintosh disk. Typically, the alert box asks if you want to initialize the disk (see Figure 5-13).

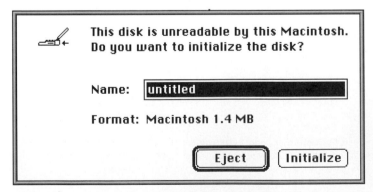

Figure 5-13 *Disk is unreadable* message from System 7.1 (top) and System 7.5 (bottom). Don't give up—your disk may be perfectly okay

For Unformatted Disks The messages that the disk is unreadable or is not a Macintosh disk appear when you insert an unformatted floppy disk. This is perfectly normal. If this happens, simply click Initialize (or Two-Sided) to format the disk.

SEE: • Fix-It #15 on formatting and Fix-It #5 on installing system software

For Formatted Disks If the disk has been formatted previously, don't reinitialize the disk! The disk may be perfectly fine. Reinitializing it loses any chance you have of saving the disk or recovering any data from it.

Click Eject instead. Then make sure you are using the right type of disk for the right type of drive. For example, do not insert an HD disk into an 800K drive; 800K disk drives cannot read HD disks and treat them as unreadable, even though they are perfectly fine. If this happens, eject the disk and insert it into an HD drive. All will be fine. Copy the data to 800K disks, if desired. This is just one of several similar problems you may have with inserting the wrong type of floppy disk into the wrong type of disk drive.

SEE: • Fix-It #15 for the other reasons why a floppy disk may not mount

Otherwise, proceed to "After You Eject the Disk" later in this section.

For PC (DOS)-Formatted Disks PC (DOS) computers can now use the same disks that Macintoshes use—except they are formatted differently. If you insert a disk formatted for a PC machine, you will also likely get the "unreadable" disk message. Again, don't initialize the disk, and don't ever try to repair it with any Macintosh disk repair utilities. Most likely, the disk is just fine and anything you do to it will risk destroying data on the disk. The solution to this is to use an extension such as Macintosh PC Exchange (now included as part of System 7.5). With this extension, a DOS disk will mount on the Finder's desktop just as if it were a Macintosh-formatted disk. Also note that PC Exchange (together with Macintosh Easy Open) will assist you in opening PC-format files that may be on the PC disk (see Chapter 6 for more on this).

By the way, even with Macintosh PC Exchange installed, the Mac will not recognize "improperly formatted" PC disks. In particular, it will not recognize double-sided (720K) disks formatted as HD (1440K) disks or HD disks formatted as double-sided disks. In this case, you need to go back to the PC machine and get the needed files onto a properly formatted disk.

For the "Disk Is Damaged" or "Disk Error" Messages If you get an error message saying the disk is damaged, it probably is. You may have a choice whether you want to eject the disk or initialize it (see Figure 5-14). Alternatively, there may simply be an OK button to eject the disk, with no opportunity to initialize it.

Figure 5-14 "Disk is damaged" (left) and "disk error" (right) messages—don't accept any offer to initialize the disk here

Click Eject Don't reinitialize the disk if offered! You may be able to repair the damage. Reinitializing it loses any chance you have of saving the disk or recovering any data from it.

Click *Eject* instead. Proceed to "After You Eject the Disk" later in this section.

If No Error Message Appears

In some cases, you don't get an error message. The disk simply does not mount. The Macintosh acts as if you never inserted the disk.

Eject the Disk Try to eject the disk by pressing Command-Shift-1 (internal or lower drive) or Command-Shift-2 (external or upper drive). If you cannot get the disk to eject with this method:

SEE: • "A Floppy Disk Won't Eject" later in this chapter

Otherwise, proceed to the next section, "After You Eject the Disk."

After You Eject the Disk

Hope for the One-Time Glitch Lock the disk (to protect against any possible further damage). Reinsert the disk. See if it mounts now.

Do this a few more times, if needed. Sometimes, a minor misalignment in the disk drive causes problems that disappear on the next insertion. This may be a problem with some disks but not others.

Floppy disk drives can get pretty finicky about what disks they accept. It might help to briefly shake the disk or rotate the metal circle on the back side of the disk before reinserting it. PowerBook floppy drives seem particularly prone to these types of problems. Here, you may have success by inserting the problem disk into another Macintosh, mounting it, ejecting it, and then reinserting it into the PowerBook.

If reinserting succeeds in mounting the disk, your disk may be okay. However, it often means that you have media damage on the disk. As a precaution, especially if the problem occurs repeatedly with the same disk and not with others, I would copy files on the disk to another disk and then repair or replace the problem disk as described shortly.

Restart (with Extensions Off)   Sometimes restarting alone will solve this problem. More rarely, an extension may prevent the reading of a floppy disk. So, to be extra safe, when you restart, hold the Shift key down, to keep extensions off. Now try to mount the disk.

SEE: • Fix-It #4 for more on dealing with extensions

Special Case: AV and Power Macs   AV Macs and Power Macs (and possibly other new models by now) use a new floppy drive controller that, because it is more sensitive to inaccuracies, may result in problems reading 800K disks that were mass-produced. To try to solve this, try any or all of the following: startup with extensions off, zap the PRAM, or use another Macintosh to copy the data on the 800K disk to an HD disk.

Replace or Repair   If reinserting or restarting fails to get the disk to mount, you probably have damaged files and/or damaged hardware.

- If you have a backup copy of the disk, throw the damaged disk out. Even if you were to succeed in repairing the disk, your best bet would be to discard the disk. Otherwise, it will probably cause problems again sometime soon. Better safe than sorry. Use your backup copy to make a new backup copy.

- If you do not have a backup of the disk, and the data on the disk are *not* important, throw the damaged disk out. You could try to successfully reformat the disk. However, I prefer to simply throw the disk out. Disks are cheap enough that I would not risk using a defective disk twice. Certainly, if you try to reformat the disk and get the *Initialization failed* message, it's time to discard the disk.

SEE: • Fix-It #15 for more on formatting disks

- If it is important to save the data on the disk that are not backed up, try to repair the disk. When your attempted repairs are completed, try to mount the disk again and see if it mounts successfully. If it doesn't mount, try to recover files from it to another disk.

SEE: • Fix-It #10 and Fix-It #13 on disk repairs
       • Fix-It #14 on file recovery

- Finally, you may have a problem with the disk drive itself, even if you do get the disk to mount. To check for this, insert other disks into the disk drive. Insert the problem disk into other disk drives. If a specific drive fails to recognize virtually every disk that you insert, but those same disks work fine when inserted into other drives, this is the classic pattern implying a hardware problem with the drive. At best, the drive is just a little dirty. At worst, it is beyond repair.

SEE: • Fix-It #17 for more on hardware problems

If the same disk causes problems in other drives, it may mean a physical problem with the disk itself (such as a stuck or bent slide shutter, as described in "Take Note: If You Can't Get a Disk to Insert" earlier in this chapter), rather than the drive.

A Floppy Disk Won't Eject

Symptoms:

You attempt to eject a floppy disk from its drive, using the standard methods, but it does not eject.

Causes:

Many times, the problem is software-based. For example, the problem may be due to insufficient memory available to permit the disk to be ejected (more of a possibility in System 6 than in System 7). If so, you should get an error message that describes this as the problem. Various bugs in the system software can also cause this problem.

In other cases, the problem has a physical cause. Possible causes include a damaged disk or a defective disk drive. However, it may be as simple as a disk label that has come partially unglued and is jamming the eject mechanism.

In any case, unless the problem is a recurring one, understanding the cause is not necessarily critical. More important is figuring out how to remove the disk. Regardless of the cause, the methods for removal remain the same.

What to do:

For the sake of thoroughness, I review both the standard and nonstandard ways of ejecting a disk. It may surprise you to discover how many different ways there are.

Standard Methods for Ejecting a Disk

From the Finder   First select the disk by clicking its icon on the Finder's desktop. Then try either of the following:

- Select Eject Disk (from the Special menu of the Finder) or type Command-E (the command-key equivalent of Eject Disk, as listed to the right of the command). These both do the same thing.
- Drag the icon of the disk to the Trash (no, this does not erase any data on the disk!), select Put Away from the File menu, or type Command-Y (the command key equivalent of Put Away). These all do the same thing.

There is an important difference between these two procedures (see Figure 5-15). After you use Eject Disk, a dimmed image (called a *shadow*) of the disk icon remains on the screen. This means that, technically, the disk is still mounted and information about the disk remains in memory. Thus, you can still refer to the disk for purposes of copying, moving, or otherwise working with files on that disk. The Finder will request that the disk be reinserted if it is needed (see more about this in the next section).

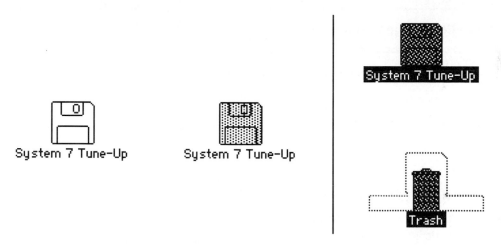

Figure 5-15 Left: A typical disk icon (left) changes to a shadow disk icon (right) after selecting Eject Disk. Right: Dragging either type of icon to the Trash removes the icon from the desktop altogether (and ejects the disk if it is currently inserted)

After you select Put Away, the disk image disappears entirely. The disk is un-mounted and is no longer in memory. The Finder acts as if the disk no longer exists.

System 6 Alert: The Put Away command does not eject disks in System 6. However, try pressing Command-Option-E, holding the Option key down a bit longer than the others. This should work just like System 7's Put Away command.

From Within an Application   If you are in an application, such as a word processor, select the Eject button from its Open or Save dialog box (see Figure 5-16). This is the same as selecting Eject Disk from the Finder.

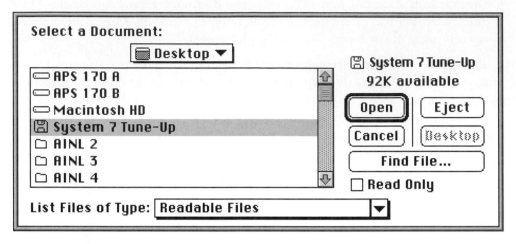

Figure 5-16   Click the Eject button in this Open dialog box to eject the selected disk

From Any Location   Press Command-Shift-1 (for internal or lower internal drive) or Command-Shift-2 (for an external or upper internal drive). This is also similar to selecting Eject Disk from the Finder.

Nonstandard Methods for Ejecting a Disk

All of the preceding methods assume that there is no problem with the disk that would prevent it from being ejected normally. If none of those standard techniques work, it is time to get more serious. Try the following.

Restart Your Macintosh   This by itself may eject the disk. It should work for any disk that does not have a System Folder on it.

Restart While Holding the Mouse Button   Restart the Macintosh holding down the mouse button until the disk ejects. This should eject a disk even if it has a System Folder on it.

SEE: • "By the Way: The Sad Mac Makes a Brief Visit," earlier in this chapter, for an example of using this method

Actually, this is a general technique to get the Macintosh to bypass and eject a floppy disk that is present in a disk drive at startup, whether the disk is causing a problem or not. However, it does not seem to work on PowerBooks (using the track-ball or trackpad button here, since there is no mouse).

The Low-Tech Approach

If the disk is physically damaged or somehow stuck in the drive, none of these techniques may work. It is then time to try to eject it by inserting a straightened paper clip into the little hole to the right of the drive slot. Ideally, the Macintosh should be off before you try this.

Gently push straight in until the disk ejects. If you have to push too hard, stop. The disk or metal disk slide shutter may be damaged or caught in such a way that further force would damage the drive rather than eject the disk. It is time for a trip to the repair shop.

Reinserting the Disk

Before You Reinsert the Disk   Check whether the disk has a torn label that may be getting stuck in the drive. If so, remove the label. Check if the slide shutter is bent. If so, you may be able to straighten it. Or you can remove the shutter altogether.

SEE: • "Take Note: If You Can't Get a Disk to Insert" earlier in this chapter

Reinsert the Disk   If you can reinsert the disk successfully, congratulations. If the problem recurs, get the disk to eject again. Insert other disks to determine whether it is a problem with all disks or just that one. If the problem is just with that disk, you probably have to discard it. Before discarding, copy files from it to another disk, as needed.

SEE: • Fix-Its #13 and #14 on disk repairs and file recovery for problems recovering files

If the problem occurs with all disks, you may have a problem with the system software. Make sure you have installed the latest System Update for your version of the system software, as these updates may have fixes that solve the problem (for example, see "By the Way: Floppy Disks That Do Not Eject at Shut Down"). Otherwise reinstall the system software.

SEE: • Fix-It #5 on system software

As a last alternative, you may have a problem with the disk drive itself. Take the drive in for repairs, as needed.

SEE: • Fix-It #17 on hardware problems

Special Cases

Files on the Disk Are "in Use"   You cannot use the Put Away command if any file on the disk is currently open or in use (see Figure 5-17). If you try, you get an alert message informing you of this fact. The simplest solution here is to close all open files from the disk and try again. More specifically, you could go to the Application menu and see which applications from the problem disk are currently open. Close just those applications.

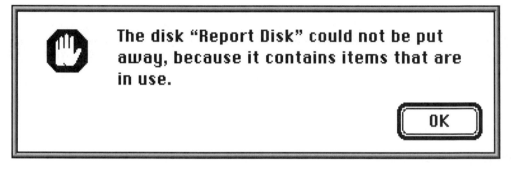

The disk "Report Disk" could not be put away, because it contains items that are in use.

OK

Figure 5-17   A disk cannot be ejected when applications or documents on the disk are currently open (also see Figure 5-21)

Insufficient Memory to Eject a Disk   When you try to put away a disk, the disk may not eject because, according to the error message that appears, there isn't enough memory available to move the disk to the Trash. The easiest thing to do is to quit an open application. This frees up enough memory to allow the disk to eject. If the problem occurs frequently, consider increasing the memory capacity of your machine by adding more SIMMs.

SEE: • Fix-It #17 on hardware problems

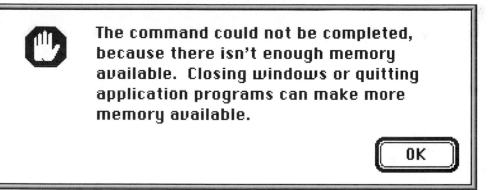

Figure 5-18   The Finder is having problems because of insufficient memory

Repeated Requests to Reinsert a Floppy Disk

Symptoms:

- You eject a floppy disk using the Finder's Eject command, meaning that the disk is still mounted. However, you are immediately (or soon) asked, via an alert box message, to reinsert the same disk.

You reinsert the disk and once again eject it. The request to reinsert appears again. This sequence appears likely to continue indefinitely (see Figure 5-19).

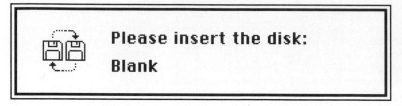

Please insert the disk:

Blank

Figure 5-19   The Mac requests that you reinsert a disk

- In a similar situation, the Macintosh may eject a disk and ask that another named disk be inserted. You insert what you believe to be the requested disk. However, the computer immediately ejects the inserted disk and asks that it be reinserted. There seems to be no end to this repetitive cycle.

 Causes:

If you eject a disk using the Finder's Eject command, the disk remains mounted and the shadow (dimmed) icon of the disk remains on the desktop (as described in the previous section). This shadow icon may similarly remain if an application automatically ejects a disk as part of its normal activity.

So far, this is all perfectly okay. In fact, it may be necessary that this happen for certain operations, such as when making a disk-to-disk copy with only one floppy drive. In this case, the computer automatically and repeatedly ejects the disks and asks you to insert the other one until the copying is finished. The number of swaps it takes to complete the copying varies depending on how much you are copying, what system software version you have, how much memory you have, and what model of Macintosh you are using. A similar situation can occur when you are using Installer utilities.

However, even when you are not copying or installing, you may find that the Macintosh unexpectedly asks you to reinsert a disk with a shadow icon. Usually, this is because it needs to update information on the disk or otherwise access data from the disk (such as if you try to launch an application from a disk that is not inserted). Other times, it may seem to be asking you to reinsert the disk for no apparent reason.

In most cases, reinserting the disk ends the problem. If two floppy disks are involved, several swaps back and forth may be required before the system comes to rest. All of this is normal. The problem occurs when the swapping back and forth never seems to end. Or when the Macintosh repeatedly spits out the disk that you insert and then asks you to reinsert the same disk. The exact cause is often vague, but the problem is usually attributable to bugs in the system software.

What to do:

Make Sure You Are Inserting the Requested Disk

It may be that you are inserting the wrong disk, and that is why it is being rejected. The Macintosh may want Disk 1 and you are inadvertently inserting Disk 2. The obvious solution is to find Disk 2 and insert it.

To Break out of the Cycle, Try Pressing Command-Period

Press Command-period several times. On your last press, hold down the keys until the request to insert a disk goes away (or until you give up in despair). It may take a minute or more for this to happen.

Alternatively, pressing Command-period may lead to another message saying that your command could not be completed. If you click OK to that message, the insert disk message may reappear. If so, press Command-period again. Do this several times if necessary. At some point, you should break out of this cycle.

Unmount the Disk or Close Windows

If you manage to break out of the cycle, go immediately to the Finder and drag the shadow icon of the problem disk to the Trash (assuming you don't need the disk mounted). This should make the icon disappear and prevent any further recurrence of this looping. Sometimes, the Mac does this for you automatically.

Actually, this is a good preventative measure to do for any shadow disk icon that you know you are finished using. Routinely unmounting these floppy disks can prevent these problems before they start.

On the other hand, if you want the disk to remain mounted, close any open windows from the disk. That way, if you make any changes to the contents of these windows from within applications, the Finder will not need to update the screen display, which would require you to reinsert the disk.

Restart

If none of the above seems to work, treat this as a system error. Restart the Macintosh. Normally, after restarting, the problem does not recur. If the problem occurred while using an Installer utility, restart with extensions off and try again.

SEE: • **Chapter 4 for more on system errors**

A CD-ROM Disk Won't Mount

 Symptoms:

- You insert a CD-ROM disk into a CD-ROM drive, but the disk icon never appears on the desktop. No error message appears. The disk tray may even eject the disk.

- When you insert a CD-ROM disk, the Macintosh displays the message that *This is not a Macintosh disk. Do you want to initialize it?*

 Causes:

There are a number of possible causes. First, the driver software or related extensions may not have been installed. Second, there may be a problem with SCSI connections. Third, the drive itself may be damaged.

By the way, if you are trying to use the CD-ROM startup disk as a startup disk, remember that you may have problems doing this on some models of Macintosh.

SEE: • "Default Rules for Selecting a Startup Disk" earlier in this chapter

 What to do:

Make Sure the Disk Is Inserted Correctly

Insert the disk label side up. While you are at it, make sure that the disk is seated correctly so that the tray can completely close. And make sure the disk is clean. Otherwise, the tray may automatically eject the disk instead of mounting it.

Make Sure the Drive Is Turned On Before You Start Up

If you are using the Apple CD-ROM driver and you have an external CD-ROM drive, the drive must be turned on at startup for the driver extension to load (it doesn't matter whether a disk is in the drive or not). If you turn the drive on after startup, and then insert a disk, the disk will not mount. No icon will appear. The solution is to turn the drive on and restart.

This is not a problem for internal drives, as they are turned on whenever you turn on your Mac. Similarly, some other CD-ROM drivers, such as DriveCD, avoid this problem.

Make Sure the CD-ROM Driver Is Installed in the System Folder

Similarly, if the CD-ROM driver extension is not installed, you will typically not be able to use the drive. For Apple drives, the name of the extension is *Apple CD-ROM*. This must be loaded at startup, as with all extensions, for you to use your CD-ROM drive (see Figure 5-20).

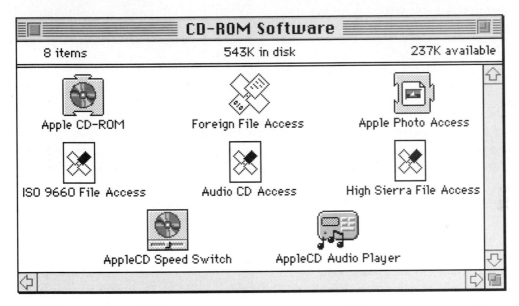

Figure 5-20   Apple's CD-ROM driver and related files. All, except Speed Switch and Audio Player, are extensions that may be needed to mount a given CD-ROM disk

Make Sure You Have Foreign File Access and Other Related Extensions, as Needed

To mount a non-Macintosh formatted CD-ROM disk, such as an audio CD or a photo CD, special extensions such as Foreign File Access and Apple Photo Access (and possibly other relevant access files) must be present and be loaded at startup (see Figure 5-20). Photo CD disks also need QuickTime 1.5 or later. Otherwise, when you insert a "foreign" disk, you will get the message that says that *This is not a Macintosh disk.*

Otherwise, Check for Miscellaneous SCSI and Related Hardware Problems

Especially make sure that you do not have an SCSI ID number conflict.

SEE: • Fix-It #16 (especially "Take Note: CD-ROM Drivers and Problems Mounting CD-ROM Disks"), for more on CD-ROM drivers, including non-Apple drivers and other SCSI-related problems
      • Fix-It #17 on other hardware problems

A CD-ROM Disk or Removable Cartridge Won't Eject

 Symptoms:

When you select Put Away, Eject, or an equivalent command to eject a CD-ROM disk or removable cartridge, it does not eject. Typically, an error message appears that gives you some clue as to why it will not eject.

 Causes:

The most common reason that these disks cannot be put away is that the file is "in use." In the same way that you cannot delete a file that is currently open, you cannot eject these disks if they contain a file that is currently open. You will get a message that says *The disk <name of disk> could not be put away, because it contains items that are in use* (see Figure 5-21).

The second most common reason that these disks will not eject at all is if file sharing is on. If a CD-ROM or removable cartridge is mounted at startup, with file sharing active, you will not be able to eject the disk. Sometimes this problem can occur even if the disk is mounted after startup. In either case, you will get a message that says *The disk <name of disk> could not be put away, because it is being shared* (see Figure 5-21). There is really no good reason to justify this restriction. Most people consider it a bug in Apple's system software. Apple apparently agrees. This problem can be eliminated altogether by installing System 7.5 Update 1.0. Of course, if you keep file sharing off all the time, you need not be concerned about this possibility. It is also possible that the disk is somehow physically stuck in the drive.

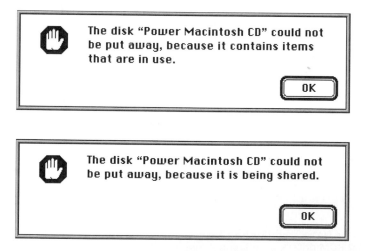

Figure 5-21 Messages that may appear when you are trying to eject a disk. The top one can occur with any type of removable disk (floppy, CD-ROM, or cartridge). The bottom message will not occur with floppy disks

SEE: • Chapter 11 for more on file sharing in general, especially as it applies to **PowerBooks**

 What to do:

Use the Put Away Command

The Put Away command (Command-Y) or simply dragging the icon of the disk to the Trash are the main ways to eject a CD-ROM or removable disk (the same as for a floppy disk).

Remember, for a removable cartridge (such as a SyQuest), ejecting a disk may be a two-step process. After you drag the disk icon to the Trash, the disk may spin down and partially eject. Otherwise, you may have to additionally press a stop button to get the drive to spin down. In either case, after the drive has spun down, you may have to slide a lever to get the cartridge to completely eject. Do not do this until you are certain that the drive has spun down (often a light goes off to indicate that spin down is complete). Otherwise, you could damage the disk. Check with your drive's manual for details.

Also be careful not to eject a removable cartridge (by any method) without first dragging its icon to the Trash. Otherwise, when you insert another cartridge, the Mac may think it is the one you just ejected—with the result that it damages the Directory of the second cartridge.

Eject the Disk Rather than Put Away the Disk

If Put Away does not work, you can often still eject the disk (Command-E), leaving its disk image on the desktop. If ejecting is good enough for what you want to accomplish at the moment, then do it. You can also try ejecting a CD-ROM with the Eject button on the AppleCD Audio Player if you have that installed in your Apple menu.

If you still cannot get the disk to eject (or if you must actually put away the disk), proceed to the next steps.

If a File on the Disk Is "In Use," Quit the Relevant Application(s)

If you cannot eject a disk because you get the "in use" error message, quit any and all applications that are currently open on the problem disk or that use documents that are on the problem disk. The disk should now eject.

If the Disk Is "Being Shared," Turn File Sharing Off

1. Select the Sharing Setup control panel (refer to Figure 11-18, bottom).

2. Click the Stop button in the File Sharing section.

3. If you get a dialog box that asks "How many minutes until file sharing is disabled," simply leave it set at zero if you are only sharing files among your own computers (such as between your PowerBook and desktop machines). Otherwise, set it for a time sufficient to let others connected to your machine disconnect before you turn file sharing off.

4. Wait briefly for file sharing to be turned off. The Stop button will now read Start.

5. You should now be able to eject the disk. Afterward, if desired, you can select the Start button to turn file sharing back on.

Other Ways to Eject a CD-ROM Disk

1. If you have a CD-ROM drive, such as external Apple CD-ROM 300 drives, with an eject (open/close) button, press it. You should find this button on the front of the drive.

2. If that fails to work, turn the drive off and then on again (or, for an internal CD-ROM drive, restart the Mac), and then immediately press the eject button, repeatedly if necessary. For Macs like the Power Mac 6100 that do not automatically turn off when you select Shut Down, try pressing the eject button when the "power off" message appears.

3. Otherwise, try holding down the mouse button at startup. The disk may eject.

4. If it doesn't, start up with extensions off. Now try the CD-ROM drive's eject button.

5. If that fails, turn off the drive, take a large straightened paper clip and insert it into the small hole to the right of the eject button. This should cause the disk to pop out.

6. Otherwise, follow the instructions that came with your particular drive. If nothing works, you may have a damaged CD-ROM drive. Take it in for repair.

SEE: • "By the Way: CD-ROM Startup Disks," earlier in this chapter, for related information

Other Ways to Eject a Removable Cartridge

For most drives, when standard methods fail, remaining choices are basically similar to the methods for CD-ROM disks just described. In particular, shut down the Mac and press the drive's Stop/Eject button. If that fails, insert a unbent paper clip into the small hole near the drive opening (usually provided as a fail-safe for when nothing else works). Check your drive's manual for details.

BY THE WAY ▶

SELECTING RESTART OR EJECT WHEN A REMOVABLE CARTRIDGE IS THE STARTUP DISK

If you are using a removable cartridge as a startup disk:

- *If you select the Eject command for the removable cartridge, you are likely to get in to an endless loop of the computer asking you to reinsert the cartridge and then spitting it out again. Restarting will be the only way out of this.*
- *Selecting the Restart command from the Finder's Special menu will cause the removable cartridge to eject, typically resulting in your Mac shifting to the internal drive as your startup disk. To avoid this, select Shut Down rather than Restart. Then, reinsert the cartridge and wait for it to spin up. Finally, turn your Mac back on. The cartridge will now remain as your startup disk.*

A Hard Disk Gets Unmounted

Symptoms:

- A disk icon of a hard disk can become unmounted. Typically, this means that the desktop icon of the hard disk is either removed or becomes a dimmed shadow icon.
- In some case, an undimmed hard disk icon may remain on the desktop, but you are unable to access anything on the disk. Attempts to do so may lead to a variety of problems, including system errors.

SEE: • Chapter 4 for more on system errors

Causes:

Removing a Disk Icon

If you drag the icon of a hard disk to the Trash, the disk is unmounted and its icon disappears from the desktop (unless the disk is the current startup disk, in which case the disk cannot be unmounted).

As with the similar unmounting of a floppy disk, the Macintosh no longer has any memory of an unmounted hard disk. This is not a problem by itself. However, it does mean that you no longer have access to anything on that disk until it is remounted.

Dimmed Hard Disk Icons

Normally, the Eject Disk command is not accessible when a hard disk is selected. Thus, a dimmed (or shadow) hard disk icon should never occur for a nonremovable (fixed) hard disk (though it may occur for a removable media cartridge, such as SyQuest and Bernoulli drives).

If it does occur, its cause is usually unclear. Usually, some sort of software bug has caused the Macintosh to become confused so that the Macintosh is aware of the presence of the hard disk but does not think that it is currently accessible. A corrupted System file might be the ultimate cause. Whatever the cause, this could spell trouble if you try to access anything on the disk.

Turning the Power Off

If you turn the power off on an external hard drive *after* you have dragged its icon to the Trash, this is not necessarily a problem. However, to be safe, I would usually recommend against doing this. For example, if you have several devices attached to a SCSI chain (as discussed in Fix-It #16), turning off one of the devices can prevent the others from working.

However, if you turn the power off *before* dragging the disk's icon to the Trash, you have essentially unmounted the drive without informing the Finder of this fact. This is a definite no-no. Problems are likely to ensue.

 What to do:

Drag the Disk Icon to the Trash

If you have turned the power off on an external hard drive without first dragging its icon to the Trash, immediately drag the disk icon to the Trash. Do not try to work with any folders, windows, or files from the disk. Doing so will probably lead to a system crash. It may also cause corruption of the hard disk's Directory so that it no longer mounts at all.

If you have files that are currently open and in use from that disk, you may have problems no matter what you do. Dragging the disk icon to the Trash may not be enough to save you.

Your best bet is to save what open files you can (to another disk, obviously) before a system crash occurs, and then restart. If you don't need to save any files, simply restart.

Drag a Shadow Icon to the Trash

Similarly, if the disk icon appears dimmed, your best bet is to drag the shadow disk icon to the Trash, unmounting the disk before any other problems develop.

Otherwise, some particularly perplexing symptoms may appear. For example, you may get an alert message to reinsert the hard drive, which of course cannot be done. You can try to get this message to go away by pressing Command-period, as you would do for a floppy disk. If this does not work, you have to restart the Macintosh, as you would after a system error, by pressing the Reset button or by turning the Macintosh off and on again.

SEE: • Chapter 4 for more on system errors

Even if you do not get the reinsert message, if you ignore this situation, a system crash is likely to occur soon. Restart to be safe.

Remount Any Unmounted Disk

Whatever the cause of the unmounting, if you want to use the disk again, you have to remount it. To do this without restarting, you have to do it manually, using a utility like SCSIProbe. Otherwise simply restart the computer, using the Finder's Restart command. This should remount the disk.

SEE: • "A Hard Disk Won't Mount" earlier in this chapter
• Fix-It #16 for more on using SCSIProbe

Problems with Restart, Shut Down, or Sleep

Symptoms:

- You select either Restart or Shut Down from the Finder's Special menu. The shut-down process begins normally but is halted by a system error. You may get an error message or you may simply get a freeze.

- A similar problem may occur when selecting Sleep on PowerBooks (though see Chapter 11 for more general problems with the Sleep command).

- When selecting Shut Down, the Macintosh spontaneously restarts rather than shutting down.

- A spontaneous restart occurs for no apparent reason at any time during an otherwise normal work session.

Causes:

When you select Restart or Shut Down, the Macintosh attempts to save and close all currently open documents and quit all currently open applications before actually shutting down. It also does a final update of the Directories of any mounted disks. If for any reason (usually a bug somewhere in the software) the Finder cannot close a given file, the shutdown process halts. This could be caused by a problem with an application, extension, or control panel. It could also be due to corrupted system software or directory damage.

Corrupted PRAM may also cause an inability to shut down. Finally, you may have a hardware problem, such as a stuck Power On button on your keyboard or a bad power supply.

 What to do:

Quit Any Open Applications

Sometimes the Mac cannot automatically close an open application during a shut down or restart. If you go to the application and manually select its Quit button, this may let the operation proceed. If not, do the following.

Restart (by Using the Reset Button If Needed)

If you had a spontaneous restart, and your Mac successfully restarted afterward, your problem may be over already. Check it out by trying Restart. If things go smoothly, congratulations. It was probably the old one-time glitch.

Otherwise, especially for a machine that refuses to shut down or restart, treat this as a system error. You have to restart your computer by using the Reset button or by turning the computer off and on again. The problem is unlikely to recur after you restart.

SEE: • Chapter 4 for more on system errors

Check for INIT problems

If the problem does recur, check for INIT-related problems. For example, I had an anti-virus utility that prevented me from shutting down normally until I rearranged its loading order. Similarly, I had some fax software (FaxSTF 3.0) that prevented me from shutting down normally whenever its control panel INIT was active.

As mentioned earlier in this chapter, INITs are an especially likely cause of a spontaneous restart if the restart occurs during startup (that is, while INITs are loading). However, not all of these restarts signal a problem. For example, some startup managers restart the Mac if you use them to change the status of any INIT that loads before the manager itself.

In the worst-case scenario, if continued spontaneous restarts prevent you from completing a startup, try starting up with extensions off. This is almost guaranteed to work. Then determine the offending INIT.

SEE: • Fix-It #4 on solving INIT problems

Replace the Finder Preferences File

If the Macintosh fails to restart after selecting the Restart command from the Finder's Special menu, it may be due to a damaged Finder Preferences file. To fix this, restart (using the reset button if needed) with Extensions off (by holding down the Shift key during startup). Go to the Preferences folder in the System Folder and drag the Finder Preferences file to the Trash. Restart again (using Reset if needed) and empty the Trash.

SEE: • Fix-It #2 for more on preferences files

Replace the Open Application and/or the System Software

If the problem does recur, and if it always seems to involve the same application, you may have a defective copy of the application. Replace it. If this does not work, contact the company to see whether there is a bug in the software that has been fixed by an upgraded version. Otherwise, do a clean reinstall of the system software.

SEE: • Fix-Its #2 and #3 on replacing application software
      • Fix-It #5 on system software

Zap the Parameter RAM

SEE: • Fix-It #11 for how to zap the Parameter RAM

Check for Disk Directory or Hardware Problems

Run the usual repair software (Disk First Aid, Norton Utilities, and/or MacTools) to check for Directory problems. The most likely hardware cause is a stuck Power On button. To check for this, restart with the keyboard detached. For this, or other suspected hardware problems, take the Mac in for repairs.

SEE: • Chapter 11 for more on PowerBooks and sleep problems
      • Fix-Its #10 and #13 on disk repairs
      • Fix-It #17 for more on possible hardware problems

Files Missing from the Desktop

 ## Symptoms:

- The most common situation is when many or most files on a particular disk (floppy or hard) seem to have vanished from the desktop. These files are not listed in any Open or Save dialog boxes. Continued use of the disk may lead to system crashes. You can usually tell that something is wrong right away because the indication of the amount of disk space in use (as shown in the window header of any window from that disk when using an icon view) indicates that much more disk space is in use than is accounted for by the files that are still visible.

- A special case is when files and/or folders have vanished from the desktop but are still accessible from within applications and seem intact when accessed this way. The disk behaves normally in all other respects. This is an especially likely symptom if you are using System 7.0 or 7.0.1.

 ## Causes:

The problem is almost always due to damage to the invisible Directory or Desktop files that keep track of what is on the disk.

SEE: • Chapters 2 and 8 for more details on these invisible files

The special problem that crops up in early versions of System 7 is apparently due to a long-standing obscure bug in the Macintosh hardware (ROM) that rarely appeared until System 7.

 ## What to do:

Close and Reopen the Window

Sometimes, especially if the problem is limited to one or a few newly copied files, the file(s) are really there and perfectly okay. It's just that the Finder may not have been updated properly and thus does not yet display the files. Usually, simply closing and reopening the window that contains the files will get the files to display.

Otherwise, use the Finder's Find function to search for the files. This will similarly force the Finder to update its display.

SEE: • "Cursor Alternates Between a Watch and an Arrow (or All Icons in a Window Are Missing)" earlier in this chapter
   • Chapter 6, "When You Can't Locate a File," for more on locating a single missing file

If even this fails, it's time to consider more serious possibilities.

Use Disk First Aid

Recent versions of Disk First Aid (shipping with System 7.1 or later) are especially good at solving these problems. Try it.

SEE: • Fix-It #10 on using Disk First Aid

Upgrade or Tune-up

If you are using System 7.0 or 7.0.1, you can avoid the special case problem before it appears. Do one of the following.

Upgrade to System 7.1 or 7.5   System 7.1 or later includes a fix that prevents this problem.

Install the System 7 Tuner 1.1.1   Get a disk called the System 7 Tune-Up disk. Using the Installer on the disk places, among other things, the System 7 Tuner extension in the Extensions folder of your System Folder. The Tuner contains a "patch" to prevent this missing files problem. It works even if you start up with extensions off. A quick way to tell if the Tune-up is installed is to select the About This Macintosh window. If a bullet dot appears next to the name of the System Software version, then the Tune-up is installed.

    However, a far preferable solution is simply to upgrade to System 7.1 or later. In fact, you may find it difficult to even locate this tune-up disk anymore.

SEE: • Fix-It #5 for details on upgrading system software and using tune-up disks
       • Appendix for how to obtain upgrades and tune-up disks

Too Late for a Tune-up?

A system upgrade or installing the Tuner are preventative measures. They will not eradicate the problem if you are already having the symptoms. In this case, try one of the following suggestions.

Use Find   Here again, use the Finder's Find command to search for the name of the missing file (if you can recall it). If it locates the file, this often makes the file visible again, at least temporarily.

Rebuild the Desktop   Rebuilding the desktop can sometimes solve this problem, again at least temporarily, especially if you delete the Desktop file before rebuilding it.

SEE: • Fix-It #9 for how to delete the Desktop file

Once you succeed in recovering whatever vanished files you could, by either method, install the Tuner or upgrade your system software (to at least version 7.1) immediately, before files vanish once again.

Check for Damage to the Disk

If damage is discovered, repair it, or recover data from the disk as appropriate. If the damage cannot be repaired, you need to reformat the disk. Reformatting is probably a good idea even if you think you fixed the problem. If it is a floppy disk, you should probably discard it instead.

SEE: • Fix-It #13 on disk repairs and Fix-It #15 on reformatting

The Macintosh's Speed Is Unexpectedly Slow

 Symptoms:

- The primary symptom here is that many operations across most or all of your applications are running slower than is typical for your particular Macintosh model. This commonly includes delays in opening files, saving documents, menus dropping down, and/or responses to mouse clicks. Other symptoms include increased time to copy or delete files and slow redrawing of the screen.
- Sometimes delays may be restricted to particular applications or situations, usually ones that are processor-intensive, such as running QuickTime movies.

 Causes:

Having operations run in the background generally slows down the speed of your machine. Using up almost all of your available RAM also tends to cause slow downs. Operations that require frequent disk access, such as compressing and decompressing files, will also slow down the Macintosh. More unusual causes revolve around problems with system software or even with the drive itself.

Though some of the causes listed here may not fit perfectly into the scope of this chapter, I include them here anyway. The list of solutions is by no means exhaustive, but it covers the most common problems. Some solutions require giving up certain features to gain a speed benefit. You'll have to decide if the trade-off is worth it.

What to do:

BY THE WAY ▶

WHAT IS THE EXPECTED SPEED OF YOUR MACINTOSH?

If your Macintosh suddenly starts performing at a snail's pace, you will undoubtedly notice this. But what if you have a new Macintosh and you have no idea how fast your machine should perform? Is there some way of finding out whether it runs as fast as is typical for its model? Yes, there are a variety of commercial and shareware utilities that do this. Apple Personal Diagnostics (a commercial program) and MacBench (a freeware program) are two examples. These are discussed in a bit more detail in Fix-It #17. The new version of Norton Utilities has a similar feature.

Try any or all of the following, in the general order listed here, until you get the speed you expect:

- Quit any applications you do not need to keep open.

- Stop any background applications or processes, such as PrintMonitor, or communications software that is downloading a file in the background.

- Turn off file sharing. Do this by selecting the Sharing Setup control panel and clicking the Stop button in the file sharing section.

SEE: • "A CD-ROM Disk or Removable Cartridge Won't Eject," earlier in this chapter, for more on how to turn off file sharing

- Turn off an unneeded extensions and restart. Several extensions, particularly those that modify general system function, such as Now Menus (part of Now Utilities), will noticeably slow down the Macintosh. The cumulative effect of several of these extensions can be substantial.

  By the way, one function of most anti-virus extensions is to check a file for viruses when it is launched. This can significantly extend the time to complete the launch. Some versions of SAM were particularly prone to this problem and would cause inordinately long launch times.

- Add certain extensions. If this seems to contradict the previous advice, you are right. The resolution of this paradox is that I am talking here about just a certain few extensions that are designed to speed up specific operations, particularly those of the Finder. Included here would be utilities such as CopyDoubler and SpeedyFinder.

  However, here's an exception to the exception: System 7.5 improved the Finder's speed of copying files and emptying the Trash (as compared to System 7.0/7.1). With System 7.5, speed-enhancing features of utilities such as CopyDoubler and SpeedyFinder may no longer be needed.

- Turn off virtual memory if you are using it (with the possible exception of if you are using a Power Macintosh). Similarly, if you are using a memory-enhancing utility, such as RAM Doubler, turn this off. Typically, this will require that you restart the Macintosh.

SEE: • Chapter 12 on Power Macintoshes and virtual memory

- Turn off any automatic compression utility you are using. This is more important for disk-level compression than for file-level compression (see Chapter 2, the section "Other Ways to Save or Get More Space," for an explanation of this distinction).
- Lower your display depth, using the Monitors control panel. All other things being equal, your Macintosh will perform faster when displaying in black and white, for example, than when displaying in 256 colors. If you don't need the color display, you can speed things up by switching to black and white.

SEE: • Chapter 10 for more on setting the display depth

- Defragment your disk and rebuild the desktop.

SEE: • Fix-It #8 on defragmenting
       • Fix-It #9 on rebuilding the desktop

- Reduce the number of files on your disk, especially if you have folders that contain hundreds of files in them. This tends to overwhelm the Mac's operating system and slows things down.
- Turn off Calculate Folder Size in the Views control panel.
- If you are using a PowerBook, open the PowerBook control panel. Uncheck the Reduce Processor Speed and Allow Processor Recycling options.

SEE: • Chapter 11 for more details on finding and using these options

- If you are using a 68040 Macintosh, check the Cache Switch control panel. Make sure it is on.

SEE: • Fix-It #1 for more on the disk cache

- Users of AV Macs may experience a slowdown caused by excessive hard disk access. For System 7.1, recent versions of relevant System Enablers (such as Enabler 088) partially fix this. Otherwise, try a freeware extension called sAVe the Disk.
- For problems when running multimedia programs (such as some games), particularly those that make use of QuickTime or Sound Manager, get Apple Multimedia Tuner. This free extension often enhances the performance of these applications.

- Update your disk driver. Especially, if your Macintosh uses SCSI Manager 4.3, make sure you have an upgraded disk driver that is compatible with this new manager.

SEE: • Fix-Its #12 and #16 for more on SCSI Manager 4.3 and upgrading the disk driver

- Check if your hard drive was formatted with the proper interleave. This is an unlikely issue these days, especially for internal drives that came with your Macintosh, but you can still check it easily enough.

SEE: • Fix-It #15 on formatting a hard disk and what interleave is all about

- Otherwise, it's time to check whether you have a hardware problem with your hard drive.

SEE: • Fix-It #17 on hardware problems

- As a long-term issue, hardware additions (such as adding more RAM, a coprocessor, or an accelerator card) can increase the overall speed of your machine. Of course, moving up to a faster Mac (a 68040 or Power Mac) will also help.

Frequent System Crashes and Other Disk-Related Quirks

 ## Symptoms:

In this scenario, the disk apparently mounts successfully, but as soon as you attempt to work with it, you notice serious problems, such as:

- Multiple copies of the icon for a mounted hard disk appear scattered across your desktop. Continued use of the Mac is likely to result in a system crash. This unusual symptom is a SCSI-related problem, as described later in this section.
- Frequent system crashes occur at erratic and unpredictable intervals (but only when the problem disk is the startup disk).
- System crashes occur shortly after you attempt any sort of access to a specific disk, such as trying to open an application or document on the disk.

Other strange symptoms may appear. The critical diagnostic clue in almost all these cases is that the problem is specific to one particular disk but involves almost all general activity related to that disk. These are all one step short of a total disk crash. If the problem is left unattended, you may soon find that the disk does not mount at all.

Causes:

The problem is almost always due to software damage to the Directory or related invisible disk files or to media damage to the disk itself. Other possibilities include a virus, corrupted system files, SCSI problems, or hardware that needs to be repaired. Again, depending on the nature of the damage, it is often repairable entirely by software techniques.

What to do:

Check for Damage

Check for damage to the disk and repair it if possible. Start by using Disk First Aid. Then try the more industrial-strength repair utilities.

SEE: • Fix-It #10 on Disk First Aid and Fix-It #13 on other repair utilities

Check for Viruses

SEE: • Fix-It #7 on viruses

Startup Disk Problems

If the problem occurs only when the disk is the startup disk, you should probably try replacing the system software files. Also consider possible problems with INITs that loaded at startup. You can even try rebuilding the desktop.

SEE: • Chapter 4 for more details on system errors
       • Fix-It #4 on INIT problems
       • Fix-It #5 on replacing system software
       • Fix-It #9 on rebuilding the desktop

Hard Disk Problems

If the problem is with a hard drive (as opposed to a floppy disk), update the hard disk's device driver. If you have multiple disk drives connected, try to have all disks use the same driver.

Also check for general SCSI-related problems, especially if your symptoms include multiple copies of the hard disk icon appearing across your desktop. This symptom typically indicates a SCSI ID conflict.

SEE: • Fix-It #12 on disk device drivers and Fix-It #16 on SCSI problems

If All Else Fails

If none of the previous steps has worked, recover essential files from the disk, if possible.

SEE: • Fix-It #13 on recovering files from damaged disks

After recovery, if it is a floppy disk, discard it. If it is a hard drive, reformat it. Make sure your reformatting utility is a current version.

SEE: • Fix-It #15 on reformatting

If the problem persists after you've reformatted a hard disk (or, for a floppy disk drive, when you use other floppy disks), you may have a hardware problem with the drive itself. If you have not already done so, this would be a good time to seek outside help.

SEE: • Fix-It #17 on hardware problems and Fix-It #18 on seeking outside help

Chapter Summary

This chapter described the basics of a normal startup sequence, from the moment you turn on your machine until the desktop appears and the startup process is completed. It then described the various things that can go wrong with this process, from the appearance of the infamous sad Mac icon to a persistent blinking ? disk icon to an inability to load the Finder and more. It explained the causes of these various problems—both hardware and software—and what you can do to remedy them.

Finally, the chapter covered some general disk problems not specific to the startup process. These included problems mounting disks, problems ejecting disks, and problems restarting or shutting down the Macintosh.

When You Can't Find, Open, or Otherwise Use a File

It's the Little Things

Maybe you want to open a file but you can no longer remember where on your disk it is located. Or maybe when you do finally find it, the Macintosh refuses to open it. Or maybe when you later try to delete the file, the Macintosh says "no dice." These are the sorts of problems that are the subject of this chapter. If the previous chapter focused on problems that affected your use of an entire disk, this chapter narrows the focus to those problems that are limited to your use of a specific file. You will most likely confront these problems in one of two situations:

- When you are using an Open or Save dialog box from within an application to locate, open, or save a file.
- When you are using the Finder to locate, open, copy, or delete files.

As familiar as these procedures are to most Macintosh users, there are some potential misunderstandings about their use I should clear up before going any further. Then we'll go on and describe the problems you are likely to confront.

Understanding Opening and Saving

Open and Save Dialog Boxes

The Open or Save dialog box appears after you select the Open, Save, or Save As commands from the File menu of most applications.

To briefly review, using these commands is a two-step process:

1. **Navigate to the desired location.** The folder name (it may also be a volume name or simply the Desktop) listed above the scroll box is the name of the folder whose contents is currently displayed in the scrolling list. Double-click any folder listed in the scroll box, and you shift to display the contents of that folder. That folder's name then becomes the one listed above the scroll box. Conversely, select a folder's name from the pop-up menu that appears when you click the name of the currently open folder, and you retreat back to the location you selected (see Figure 6-1). Use these techniques to move to the desired location.

2. **Open or save.** You've arrived at your desired destination. If you are in an Open dialog box, click Open to select the desired file. If you are in a Save dialog box, enter a name for the file (after first clicking in the rectangle where a name is entered, if necessary) and click Save.

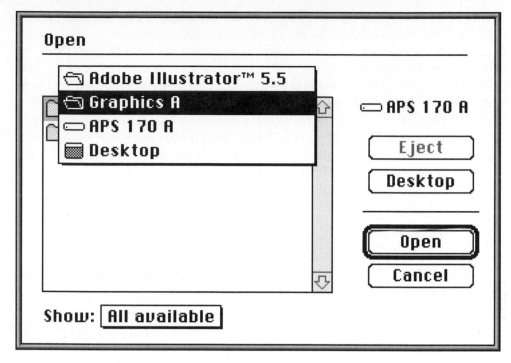

Figure 6-1   Navigating in an Open dialog box: Choose an item from the pop-up menu to go to the selected location

Opening Files from the Finder

You can also open most files (applications or documents) directly from the Finder, either by double-clicking the file's icon or by single-clicking the icon and then selecting Open from the Finder's File menu.

With applications that support *drag and drop* (and many do not), you can drag the icon of a document over to an application icon. If the application can read that type of document file, the application icon will highlight. Release the mouse button and the file will open.

If you use any of these methods to open a data document, the application needed to open the document launches followed by the document itself.

Using Save Versus Save As

When you are saving a document for the first time, the Save and Save As commands do the same thing. The difference emerges when you want to save changes to a previously saved document.

In this case the Save command simply overwrites the previous version and replaces it with the newly modified version. You get no dialog box or alert message when this happens. This also means that (unless you have a backup copy) the previous version is gone forever! It can't even be undeleted (as described in Chapter 2).

The Save As command prompts you to save the document as a separate file with a different name. As a result, you wind up with two documents: the original file and the modified file. After you do this, if you have not closed the document at the same time, you are now working with the modified document—not the original one.

Be careful not to unintentionally overwrite a file with Save As. When you are using Save As, if you give the document the exact same name as the file you are currently using, you get an alert message asking whether you want to replace the original document. If you click Replace, you essentially wind up with what you would have gotten if you'd simply selected Save instead (see Figure 6-2). If you expected to wind up with two separate documents, you will be sadly surprised.

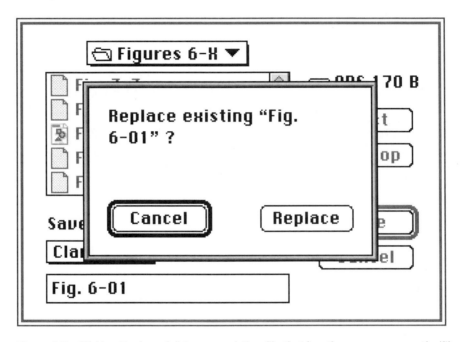

Figure 6-2   Clicking Replace deletes any existing file that has the same name as the file you are about to save

If you get the Replace alert, even though you have changed the name of the file, it means that some other file with the same name is already at that location. Clicking Replace overwrites that file and replaces it with the current one. Before doing this, make sure you are not deleting a file you still want.

Finally, remember that until you save it, it ain't saved! Don't be nervous about making sweeping changes to your document and then not being able to return to the original version. Until you select Save, you can always get back to the original version simply by closing the document (click No when asked if you want to save it) and then reopening it. A Revert to Saved command, if your program has one, does the same thing. And, of course, if you save your sweeping changes to a new file using Save As (rather than Save), the original version remains available. The only problems you may have here is if your program autosaves documents even if you do not select Save.

Solve It! Problems with Files

When You Can't Locate a File

Symptoms:

You are looking for a file that you are fairly certain should be on your disk, but it does not seem to be there. More specifically, one of two situations is likely.

Can't Find It in the Finder

You look for a file from the Finder, navigating through all the folders on the desktop, but you are unable to locate the file. Usually, these missing files are document files. You are less likely to lose track of an application, but it can happen.

Can't Find It in an Open Dialog Box

You are using an Open dialog box from within an application and cannot get the document to appear in the list.

Causes:

Admittedly, in some cases, a file may really be missing from your disk. But before you assume this has happened, calm down. Almost always, the file is present somewhere on your disk—and it is perfectly okay.

The most common cause of apparently lost files is—to put it bluntly—you. Here are typical examples of what can happen. More details are given in the What to do section that follows.

- You incorrectly recall what you named the file.
- The file was inadvertently saved to an unintended location.
- The file was moved rather than copied.
- You are looking for the file in the Open dialog box of the wrong application.
- The file was inadvertently deleted.

What to do:

Avoid Saving Files to Unintended Locations

When you first use Save or Save As to save a new file, the application you are using may select a default folder to place the file. This location may not be where you intend to save the file. If you do not notice this and simply click the Save button, the file winds up buried in a location you might never think to look. In some cases, you may even save it to a floppy disk when you intended to save it to your hard drive (or vice versa).

When you are using Save for the first time (or whenever you are using Save As), check the pop-up menu above the list of files in the dialog box to see if the currently selected folder (and disk) location is the one that you want to use. Change it if it is incorrect. Then save the file.

Don't Inadvertently Move a File Instead of Copying It

Moving a file is when you drag a file to a different folder on the same disk. Doing this transfers the file to that new location. There is still only one copy of the file on your disk.

Copying a file is when you move a file to a different disk. In this case, you wind up with two copies of the file: one on the original disk and another on the destination disk.

If you forget this distinction, you may expect to find a moved file still in its original location. Hint: You won't.

BY THE WAY ▶

COPYING ON THE SAME DISK

If you want to make a second copy of the same file in a different folder of the same disk, you can do it. Just hold down the Option key as you drag the file. To make a second copy of a file at exactly the same location as the original, use the Duplicate command (Command-D) from the Finder's File menu.

Look for a File from the Finder

Use the Finder's Find File Command　If you cannot easily find a particular file, save yourself the headache of searching manually through every folder on your hard drive. Use the Find command instead (as first described in Chapter 2):

1. Select Find from the Finder's File menu.

2. Restrict the search range, if desired, by selecting a choice from the pop-up menu to the right of "Find items."

3. Type in the name of the file you are looking for (such as Board Minutes) and click the Find button. If you are not sure of the exact name of the file, type in a portion of the name only. Thus, maybe you don't recall whether you named the file Board Minutes or Meeting Minutes. No problem—just type Minutes or even Min, and it locates every file that contains that segment of text.

4. If it finds a file with a similar name that is not the one you are seeking, type Command-G (which is the equivalent of Find Again), and it looks for the next file that contains the selected text as part of its name. Keep doing this until you find the file or completely search the disk.

System 7.5 Alert: Using Command-G is not necessary with the Find File feature in System 7.5. It displays a complete list of all found files.

If none of this works, it may be that you gave the file a totally different name from what you recall. Perhaps you called it October Notes. The Find command can still assist you here. All you need to do is remember some critical aspect of the file, such as what day you saved it. Let's assume that you know that you saved the file yesterday.

1. To find the file, once again select Find from the Finder's File menu.
2. This time, click the More Choices button (if it isn't already selected).

System 7.5 Alert: This step is not necessary if you are using the Find File function in System 7.5. Here, the More Choices button is used to setup searches based on multiple criteria, not to access more options for doing a single-criterion search.

3. Select Date Modified from the first pop-up menu (the one that probably says Name when you first open the dialog box) (see Figure 6-3).
4. The current date should appear. Click on the day. Use the arrow buttons that now appear to change the date back to yesterday (or whatever date you want).
5. To find all files created on a single day (or created from that day forward), select *is* (or *is after*) from the middle pop-up menu.
6. Click Find. For the pre–System 7.5 Find function, the first matching file will appear. Use Command-G to search for more files, if the first one found is not the one you are looking for. For System 7.5, just look in the Results window for the file you want. If the correct file appears, you can hopefully recognize it by its name at this point.

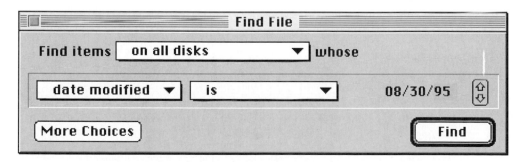

Figure 6-3   Using System 7.5's Find File to find all items created on a specific day

Modify the Finder's Window Displays

Close and Reopen the Folder Window   There is an apparent bug in some versions of system software such that the Finder does not properly update information about files listed in open windows until after the window is closed. This could lead to a file temporarily listed with an older, incorrect modification date. In the most extreme cases, it can mean that a file appears to be missing altogether. Simply closing and reopening the window usually corrects this problem.

BY THE WAY ▶

WRONG MODIFICATION DATES

If all of your recently saved documents have incorrect modification dates, usually much older dates than they should be, you may have a weak or dead battery in your Mac. The correct date is maintained in PRAM via the battery. Check the date in the Date and Time or General Controls control panels. If it is wrong, reset it. If the corrected setting is lost again after you reset, try zapping the PRAM. If that doesn't work, you probably need to replace the battery. This problem may also be caused by a corrupted System file. If PRAM fix fails, replace the System file.

SEE: • **Fix-It #5 on reinstalling system software**
SEE: • **Fix-It #11 on zapping the Parameter RAM**

Select Clean Up by Name   Sometimes, if you are using an icon view, a file is located in the extreme corners of a window, far from the other files, almost inaccessible by normal scrolling. To quickly solve this, hold down the Option key and then select the Clean Up command from the Finder's Special menu. What is normally the Clean Up Window command will now most likely read Clean Up by Name (though depending on your most recent selection from the View menu, it may read Clean Up by Size or by Date, and so on). Clean Up by Name moves all icons close together, sorted in alphabetical order.

Use View by Date (or Other Non-Icon View)   Selecting a non-icon view can help locate a file lost in a crowded folder. For example, if you know that a file you want was just saved earlier in the day, View by Date should bring it to the top of the list.

BY THE WAY ▶

SEARCHING WITHIN A TEXT FILE

If you are searching for a text file and you can't remember anything helpful about its name or date, specialized utilities can search for text files based on the actual content within the file. One popular example is called Gofer. With one of these utilities, you could search for any file that contained, for example, the expression "academy award" anywhere in the document itself, not just in the title. Microsoft Word, via its Find function, has this capability built into the program, but it can only search for files that Word can read—utilities like Gofer work with all files.

Look for a File from an Application's Open Dialog Box

In general, if you are having difficulty locating a file from an Open dialog box, go to the desktop (Finder) to look for it. Otherwise, when using the Open dialog box, consider the following.

The Application Is Not Supposed to List the File   An application's Open dialog box usually lists only those data files that can be opened by that application. So, for example, don't look for a database document from your word processor's Open dialog box. Make sure you correctly recall what application you used to create your document.

You Are Not Using the Application You Think You Are Using   When you select Open from a File menu, make sure you have the correct application. That is, make sure your intended application is the active application. There are several ways to do this.

- **Check the Application menu (System 7)**
  This is the menu at the far right of the menu bar (see Figure 6-4). The active application is the one with its icon displayed in the menu bar itself. Additionally, the menu lists all open applications, with a check mark in front of the active one. If the checked application is not the one you want, select the one you want instead.

Figure 6-4
The Application menu, with ClarisDraw as the active application (indicated by its icon in the menu bar and the check mark next to its name in the menu)

- **Check the Apple menu**
  Alternatively, the first line in the Apple menu almost always says *About <the name of the active application>*. If it is not the one you want, you can use the Application menu to shift to the correct one.

- **Examine the menu bar**
  The menu bar contains the menus of the active application. If you are familiar with an application's unique menus, you may recognize what application is currently active just by examining the menu bar briefly.

- **Click a window**
  If the application you want to use has any open windows, clicking any one of its windows makes it the active application.

TAKE NOTE ▶

SYSTEM 7.5, NOW UTILITIES, AND MORE: HELPING YOU FIND YOUR WAY

Many novice users get frustrated by what happens when they accidentally click in the desktop background while working within an application. Typically, this causes the active application to shift from whatever they were using to the Finder. Windows may disappear or move to a back layer. The user may have no idea what has happened, may not realize they are no longer in their word processor, or whatever, and may have some difficulty figuring how to return.

All of this is solved in System 7.5, with a new option called Finder Hiding. This makes the Finder inactive while an application is running, so that you remain in that application even if you click outside its windows. To activate this, uncheck "Show Desktop when in background" from System 7.5's new General Controls control panel. This feature complements the Hide Others and Hide <application name> commands in the Application menu.

By the way, other third-party utilities, such as NowMenus' "Auto-Hide application windows" option, have a similar function.

A related new feature in System 7.5 is WindowShade. With this control panel installed, when you click the title bar of any window, the entire window (except the title bar) disappears (like a window shade rolling up!). This can reduce screen clutter when you have several applications, each with their own windows, open at once.

System 7.5 also includes an option, accessed from the General Controls control panel (and borrowed from Performa system software), to save all documents to a single folder called Documents, no matter what the application. This will help prevent saving documents to unexpected locations, making later finding these documents easier.

A new control panel in System 7.5, Apple Menu Options, adds Recent Applications, Recent Documents, and Recent Servers hierarchical menus to the Apple menu. The listings in these menus are based on folders, stored in the Apple Menu Items folder, where the Mac places aliases of the relevant recently used items. Since selecting a listed item opens the item, you can use these menus to quickly access desired files.

Now Utilities' NowMenus provides a similar, more full-featured, version of this idea. Its menu can be totally separate from the Apple menu. Also, if you place an alias of your hard disk's icon in the Apple Menu Item's folder, NowMenus will create a hierarchical menu of everything on your disk, nested five levels deep (bearing in mind that the more items NowMenus needs to keep track of, the more RAM NowMenus uses). New to version 5.0, Now FolderMenus will pop up a hierarchical menu of folders, subfolders, and files off of any folder listed in an Open or Save dialog box, as well as from any folder icon in the Finder, or from a folder's window header. PopUp Folder is another utility that does this. You have to see these utilities in action to truly appreciate them.

SEE: • **"Take Note: Files Locked by the Performa or by System 7.5's General Control Panel," later in this chapter, for more on this control panel**
   • **Chapter 12 for more on System 7.5 in general**

Check the Open Dialog Box's Settings Many applications have options to selectively filter which files get displayed in its Open dialog box (see Figure 6-5). If you select a translation filter that does not match your missing file, the file will not be listed. To maximize your chances of success, make sure the most general option for reading files (such as *All Available*) is selected. If the file is at all readable by the current application, it is now listed.

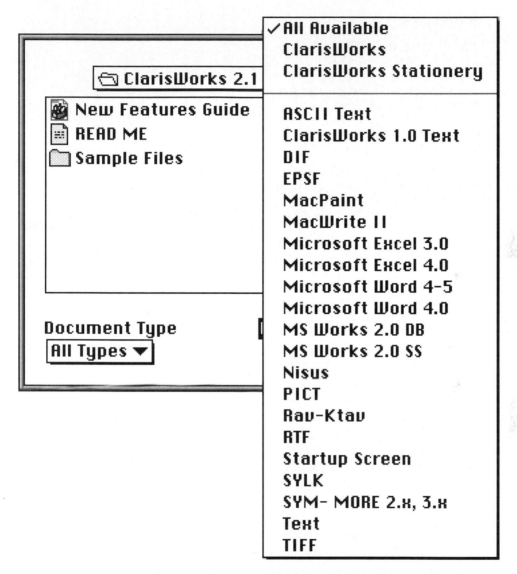

Figure 6-5 Some of the file format translators available with ClarisWorks—select one, and only the files that match that format are displayed in the Open dialog box

Check for Unusual File Names   For example, if a blank space precedes the name of the file, this causes it to sort alphabetically at the top of the list in an Open dialog box. If you look for the file based on where it should be, given the first real letter of its name (which, for a file named Zoo Animals, would be at the bottom of the list), you will not find the file.

The solution is to check the entire file list when a file does not appear in its expected location.

Check the Desktop "Folder" Normally, all files on a disk are listed as "inside" that disk. Thus, if you click the Desktop button in an Open dialog box, you see the names of all currently mounted disks/volumes. Double-clicking a disk name results in a list of all the folders and files at the top level of the disk. These are the same items you would see from the Finder, in the window that would open if you double-clicked the disk icon.

In System 7, however, a file that is located directly on the desktop—that is, not in any window but directly on the background area where the Trash and disk icons are found—is not listed as being inside the disk. These files are listed at the desktop level alongside the names of the mounted disks. All the items on the desktop are listed in this one list, regardless of what disk contains the item.

If you fail to realize this, you may search in vain for a file by restricting your search to those files and folders inside the disk window. Instead, the file may be relaxing quietly at the desktop level.

System 6 Alert: System 6 has no Desktop button in its Open and Save dialog boxes. This is because it does not maintain a separate Desktop Folder (see: "Technically Speaking: The Desktop Folder"). All files on the desktop are treated as if they were at the root level of the startup disk (that is, the same level as the files and folders in the window you see when you double-click the disk's icon).

If the File Was Inadvertently Deleted

If after trying all of the preceding suggestions you still cannot find your file, it is time to consider that it is really missing. One way this might happen is if you inadvertently deleted the file. Maybe you discarded a folder that contained the file you want, not realizing that the file was inside it. Whatever the reason, the file is now gone. Here's what you can do about it.

Wait! First Make Sure You Really Deleted the File   Remember, in System 7, the Trash is never emptied until you specifically select the Empty Trash command from the Finder's Special menu. Even if you restart the Macintosh, the items in the Trash remain and the Trash can icon continues to bulge. So, if you haven't yet emptied the Trash, just double-click the Trash icon. A window opens up with your items still there. Drag them out of the Trash, and you are back in business. This trick can also work in System 6 if you are lucky enough to try it before the Finder decides to automatically empty the Trash.

Undelete the File   If you really have deleted the file, don't despair yet. All is not lost. You may yet be able to recover the file. This is because when you delete a file, the Macintosh does not erase the data immediately. It simply frees up the space so that it can be overwritten with new data as needed. If you have only recently deleted the file, and you have not added too many new files since, the file may still be intact on your disk.

Utilities, such as Norton Utilities and MacTools Pro, can recover recently deleted files. As first described in Chapter 2, these utilities work best if you have previously installed special extensions that the utility uses to keep track of what you have deleted (FileSaver and TrashBack, respectively).

SEE: • Chapter 2 for more on installing and using these control panels

If you are using Norton Utilities:

1. Run Norton Utilities and select the UnErase option (turn File Sharing off if requested to do so). You can also directly launch UnErase using the Open UnErase application in the Norton Utilities folder.

2. From the next dialog box that appears, select the disk(s) that you believe may contain the deleted file(s). Then click the Search button. A list of files appears (see Figure 6-6). If desired, click the View Contents button to view the content's of a selected file. For text files, this can help you figure out whether the file is truly the one you want to recover.

3. Assuming that the FileSaver control panel was installed prior to when you deleted the file(s) you want to recover, the desired file(s) should be listed. Select the files (using shift-click to select more than one file) and then click the Recover button. Files are saved to the location you specify.

4. If FileSaver was not installed in time, click the Search Again button in the UnErase window. From the dialog box that appears, select options as described in "Technically Speaking: Undeleting Files Without First Installing the Special Invisible Files." These will create a list of files in the UnErase window that can then be recovered.

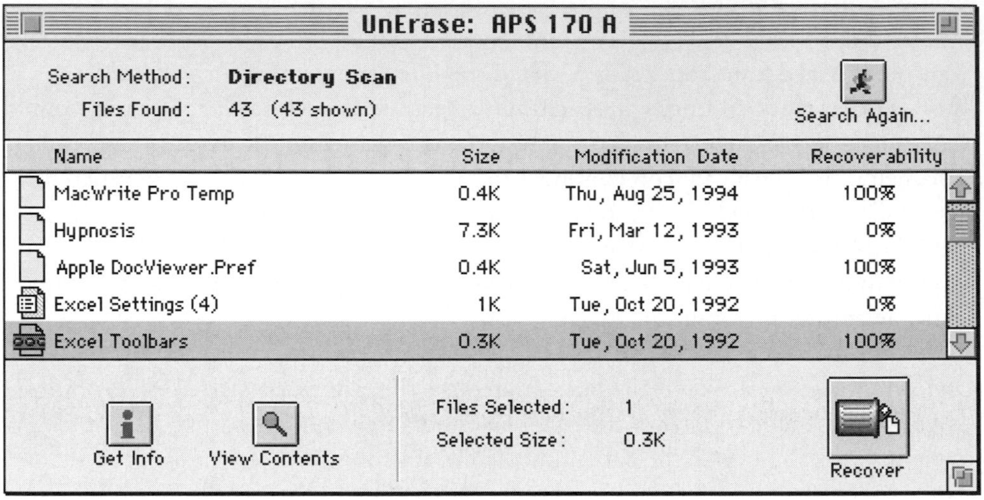

Figure 6-6   Norton Utilities' UnErase window

SEE: • **Fix-Its #13 and #14 for more on using UnErase**

If you are using MacTools Pro:

1. If TrashBack is installed and enabled, select the TrashBack command from the Finder's Special menu. This will bring up a window that lists all files currently tracked by TrashBack (refer to Figure 2-14). If desired, click the View button to view the content's of a selected file. For text files, this can help you figure out whether the file is truly the one you want to recover. Otherwise, simply click to the left of the name of each file you want to undelete so as to place a check mark next to its name. Then click the Recover button. Files are saved to the location you specify.

2. If TrashBack was not installed or enabled, launch MacTools Clinic. Select the disk from which you wish to undelete files and click the Undelete button. From the dialog box that next appears (refer to Figure 2-15), click the File Scan button.

   You are then presented with a dialog box from which you can select what types of files you wish to search for. To search for all types of files, click the Check All button and then click the Scan button (though when I tried it, I got the same result by simply clicking the Scan button, leaving all types unchecked).

You will then be presented with a list of files that your can recover (see Figure 6-7), similar to how TrashBack works. These may include applications as well as documents. Click the View button to check on the contents of any file, if desired. Again, click to the left of the name of each file you want to undelete so as to place a check mark next to its name. Then click the Recover button. Files are saved to the location you specify.

If even this fails, return to Clinic, click Undelete again, and then click the Text Scan button.

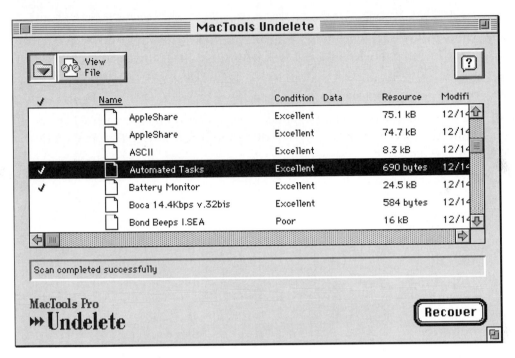

Figure 6-7   MacTools' Undelete window, used when TrashBack was not enabled

TECHNICALLY SPEAKING ▶

UNDELETING FILES WITHOUT FIRST INSTALLING THE SPECIAL INVISIBLE FILES

If you have not installed FileSaver or TrashBack (or some comparable utility from a competing product) prior to when you need to undelete a file, all is still not lost. Packages such as Norton Utilities and MacTools Pro include other options to help recover files. In particular:

- *The* file scan *or* file pattern scan *method searches for specific types of documents that the utility is designed to recognize (such as Excel documents and MacWrite documents). Both Norton Utilities and MacTools Pro give you options to specifically select which applications' documents you want to search for. With MacTools Pro, if you want to search for a type of document not listed, you can add its type (check MacTools Pro's manual for details).*

(continued)

- *The* text scan *method can recover segments of text from a deleted text document (such as a word processing file). Usually, you cannot recover more than a few paragraphs of text this way, particularly if the document is fragmented (see Fix-It #8 on defragmenting your disk). But this still may be better than nothing. You enter a string of text that you want to search for and then initiate a scan of the disk for any document that contains that string. Choose this option only as a last resort.*
- *Norton Utilities' UnErase also includes a third option,* Directory-scan. *If you haven't installed a utility like FileSaver or TrashBack, this is your best chance of recovering a file intact. Choose this one first.*

  With MacTools, you access these options by clicking the Undelete button from MacTools Clinic. With Norton Utilities, click the Search Again button in the UnErase window.
  In general, these methods are less reliable than the method that depends on a preinstalled extension. So don't depend on these alternate methods. They are only for those times when you are really desperate.

Two important caveats to bear in mind when you are trying to undelete files are that some files may be only *partially recoverable* and that recovered files may appear in a *generic* file format.

- **Some files may be only partially recoverable**
  Eventually, an erased file is written over by a newly created file. The erased file is then gone forever. In some cases, only part of an erased file may have been over-written. These files may still be partially recoverable, something that is mainly useful only for text files. Your undelete utility typically lists the recoverability of each deleted file. If you have problems opening a partially recovered file, refer to "When You Can't Open a Document" later in this chapter.

- **Recovered files may not open properly**
  When you double-click a recovered document file, even if it appears 100% recovered, it may result in the error message that says the creating application could not be found. Usually, you can still open the document if you select it from within the application using its Open dialog box. If you then save the document to a new name using Save As, the new document should then behave as normal.

SEE: • "When You Can't Open a Document," later in this chapter, for more details
       • Chapter 8 on file types and creators for more technical information

If None of the Preceding Steps Succeeds in Locating the File

The File May Be Missing Because of Problems with the Disk Itself   This is the last, and most unhappy, possibility. It often means that you have problems that go beyond the immediate loss of one file. Sometimes these problems are repairable, usually requiring a utility such as Norton Utilities or MacTools.

SEE: • Chapter 5, the section entitled "Files Missing from the Desktop"
       • Fix-It #13 on fixing damaged disks

Otherwise, It Is Probably Lost for Good   It's time to give up. I hope it was nothing critical or, if it was critical, I hope you had a backup copy.

When You Can't Launch an Application or Control Panel

Symptoms:

You try to open an application or control panel (or desk accessory) from the Finder, usually by double-clicking its icon, but the application does not open. Usually, an error message appears that gives an indication as to why the file did not launch. Often, it also offers advice on how to solve the problem.

In the worst cases, a system error may occur. In this case, refer to Chapter 4, which covers system errors.

Causes:

Insufficient Memory to Launch an Application

The most common reason an application does not open is because there is less available RAM (memory) than the application requires. Whether you have as little as 1Mb of memory or as much as 32Mb, you can still reach the limits of your machine. Each time you open an application, you occupy some of that RAM memory. As you keep more and more applications open at the same time, you eventually have too little left over to open still one more application.

Actually, some applications require so much RAM that they may not open on your machine even if no other applications are open (other than the Finder, which stays open at all times).

In any of these cases, you probably get an error message informing you that the problem is due to insufficient memory (see Figure 6-8).

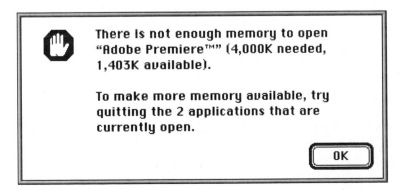

Figure 6-8   Here's what happened when I tried to open Adobe Premiere with less than the necessary amount of memory still available

Sometimes, an application starts to open but then quits in midstream, accompanied by a message that says that the program *unexpectedly quit* (a problem described in more detail in Chapter 4). This is also usually a memory-related problem.

Miscellaneous Other Causes

More explanation of these causes is given in the What to Do section. By the way, many of the following causes apply to documents as well as to applications, control panels, and desk accessories.

- A control panel setting is incompatible with the application.
- Cannot open a file from its alias.
- Cannot open a file because it is in a compressed or disk image format.
- Cannot open a file because you have the "wrong" Macintosh.
- Too many files are currently open.
- Cannot open damaged files.

 What to do:

Insufficient Memory or Unexpected Quit

If an error message offers advice on what to do to remedy this problem (such as in Figure 6-8), generally follow its advice. Otherwise, try each of the following, as needed:

- Quit currently open applications, to free up more memory. Then try to launch the application again.
- Restart the Macintosh and try again to relaunch the application.
- Restart the Macintosh with all unneeded extensions/control panels (INITs) disabled. This reduces the amount of memory allocated to the system software, freeing up more memory for your application. This is a work-around solution (since it means that you no longer have the benefit of the disabled extensions/control panels), but it at least may allow you to launch the problem application. The simplest approach here is to disable all INITs by holding the Shift key down at startup. If you need a particular INIT to remain enabled while using the application in question, you will instead need to selectively disable INITs.

SEE: • Fix-It #4 on disabling extensions

- You may have to decrease the problem application's Preferred memory size (called Current size in System 7.0). This is done from the application's Get Info window. If none of the previous suggestions work, there are several other similar memory-related solutions.

SEE: • Chapter 2 on the Get Info window
• Fix-It #6 on memory management problems for more potential solutions

Incompatible Control Panel Settings

One common example of an incompatible control panel setting is a program that requires a color depth setting different from your current setting (such as needing 256 colors when you are using 16 grays). Usually, you get an error message that explains this problem when you try to launch the application (see Figure 6-9). In other cases, problems may be due to incompatibility with virtual memory or 32-bit addressing options in the Memory control panel.

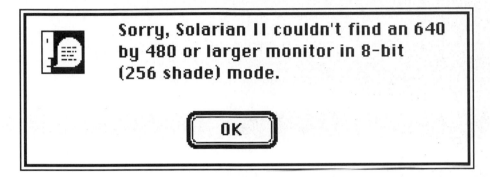

Sorry, Solarian II couldn't find an 640 by 480 or larger monitor in 8-bit (256 shade) mode.

OK

Figure 6-9   The game Solarian II does not open when you are running in black and white—if you try, you get this error message

For color depth problems, assuming that you have the appropriate hardware to adjust the color depth as needed, the obvious solution is to change the setting by using the Monitors control panel.

For Memory control panel problems (or similar sorts of problems with any other control panel), you probably have to turn the relevant control panel options off.

SEE: • Chapter 10 on displaying color
• Fix-It #1 on hardware incompatibilities
• Fix-It #5 on system software problems
• Fix-It #6 on memory problems

Cannot Open a File from Its Alias

Aliases are one of the popular new features of System 7's Finder (see Chapter 1). Occasionally, you double-click an alias file, but the file does not launch. Instead, you get a message that says the original file cannot be located (see Figure 6-10). Usually, this is because the original file has been deleted or renamed.

The easiest solution is to discard the alias file, find the original application, and create a new alias. Several utilities (such as one called Alias Director) are available to help facilitate this process.

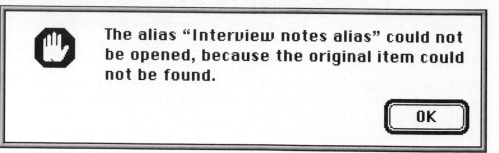

The alias "Interview notes alias" could not be opened, because the original item could not be found.

OK

Figure 6-10   Here's what you see if you try to open a file from its alias, but the original file is missing or cannot be located

You also cannot open a file from its alias if the original file is on a disk that is currently not mounted, such as a CD-ROM disk or a shared disk (accessed via file sharing). To access these files, you have remount the needed disk.

BY THE WAY ▶

ALIAS (AND PREFERENCES FILE) LINKS LOST AFTER RESTORING OR TRANSFERRING DATA TO A DISK

If and when you reformat your hard drive and restore your files from your backups or if you transfer the entire contents of your disk to a new disk (such as you might do after purchasing a new hard disk), it is possible for most or all existing alias links to be broken. In the worst cases, the alias may actually wind up linked to a wrong original. All of this is less likely to occur if you make sure that the new or reformatted disk volume has the same name as the original disk. Similarly, make sure you assign the same name to the volume in the Sharing Setup control panel. Finally, try not to relocate any files that have aliases associated with them until after you have used the alias to launch the file. If you still have problems, there is no easy solution left. You will have to check out and recreate all affected aliases.

In some cases, you may have a similar problem with an application losing its link to its preferences file. Again, in this case, you may have to delete the original preferences file and recreate your preference settings (see Fix-It #2 for more details).

Cannot Open Because File Is in a Compressed or Disk Image Format

This problem is most likely to occur as a result of downloading files from an online service. These files are often stored in a compressed format. They need to be decompressed before they can be opened. Unless they are stored as self-extracting files, you need special utilities to do this. One popular freeware utility of this sort is called *StuffIt Expander.*

Similarly, sometimes you will download an entire disk, such as an Apple System Update disk. Most often, these are stored in a special disk image format that requires a special utility, such as Apple's Disk Copy, to convert the files to a usable form. I discuss this a bit more specifically, as it applies to upgrading system software, in Fix-It #5 (Take Note: "Why Can't I Open the System Software I Just Downloaded?").

Finally, if you use *SpaceSaver* and start up with extensions off, all your compressed files will now display the StuffIt icon. You will have to separately expand each compressed file (using a utility such as Expander) before you can use it. A similar situation exists with AutoDoubler and other background compression utilities.

Cannot Open a File Because You Have the "Wrong" Macintosh or System Software

This is becoming an increasingly common problem, particularly for control panels from Apple system software. Many of these control panels are designed to work only with certain models of Macintosh (such as just on PowerBooks or just on Power Macs) or with other optional hardware. Some only work with certain versions of the system software (such as System 7.5 or later). Apple's Installer may mistakenly install these files on your Mac even though they do not work with it. If so, when you try to open it, instead of opening you will get a message like the one in Figure 6-11.

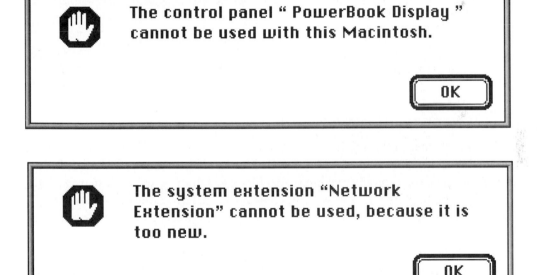

Figure 6-11 Examples of messages that may appear when you try to open a control panel that does not work with your model of Macintosh and/or your version of the system software

However, before giving up, make sure that the control panel is in the Control Panels folder in the System Folder, restart and try again. Sometimes, this type of message appears when you try to open a control panel that was not loaded at startup (such as one that you added since the last time you started up). After restarting, the problems go away.

You can have the same sorts of problems with applications. That is, versions of an application that are written specifically for a Power Mac will not run on other types of Macintoshes (see Chapter 12). Similarly, many applications only work with certain versions of the system software (such as 7.0 or later).

TECHNICALLY SPEAKING ▶

CANNOT OPEN A CONTROL PANEL BECAUSE NO INITS BIT IS CHECKED

On one strange occasion, upon trying to open a control panel, I got a message that said it would not open because it had not been loaded at startup. This typically means simply that the control panel had been disabled via an extension management utility (as described in Fix-It #4). However, in this odd case, I knew it had not been disabled. Even odder, when I checked my extension manager's listing, the control panel was not even there anymore! Yet, when I checked in the Finder, the control panel file itself was clearly in the Control Panel folder within the System Folder. What was going on?

What had happened was that a conflict between two other extensions had caused an unusual result: the NO INITS bit on several of my control panels was incorrectly checked. This meant that the Macintosh, and my extension manager, no longer considered these files as ones to be loaded at startup. After determining and eliminating the conflicting extensions, I used a utility called Get More Info to uncheck the bit. After that, things worked fine.

SEE: • Chapter 8 for more on the NO INITS bit and Get More Info

---

Too Many Files Are Currently Open

The Macintosh has a limit to how many files can be open at one time. This limit is defined in an invisible area of your disk called the boot blocks (described more in Chapters 5 and 8). Typically, the limit is 40 files (though in System 7, it may expand more if needed). Normally, you will not come up against this limit (though some applications keep more files open than may be apparent because of their use of invisible files). If this does become a problem, the easy solution is to close some currently open files and try again. However, if you frequently have this problem, there is a freeware utility, called Up Your FCBs, that can permanently change the limit. I would use this utility with caution, as raising the limit too high may lead to other problems.

Cannot Open Damaged Files

If a file is damaged, there may be no error message when you try to open it. It may just fail to open. Or you may see an (often cryptic) error message. Or a system error may occur. If you suspect a damaged file:

- Try again, as always. Just in case it opens fine the second time.

- Otherwise, usually, there is only software damage. In these cases, the best and easiest solution is to replace the application, its preferences file, and (if necessary) any of its accessory files.

SEE: • Fix-It #2 on preferences files and Fix-It #3 on accessory files

- Sometimes an application may not open because of a damaged font file, rather than a problem with the application itself.

SEE: • Chapter 9 for more on locating and replacing damaged font files

- For control panels, if you get a message like the top one in Figure 6-12, it may simply mean that the control panel did not properly load at startup. To check, make sure the control panel is in its correct folder (that is, not disabled) and that you did not start with extensions off. Then restart normally. The control panel will probably open now. Otherwise, the message is probably accurate.

- If you are having trouble opening the Scrapbook (see Figure 6-12, bottom), it is just as often due to a corrupted Scrapbook File (stored in your System Folder) as due to a problem with the Scrapbook desk accessory itself. If the File is corrupted, you may or may not be able to recover data from it (using a program such as Can Opener). However, if you just remove the Scrapbook File from the System Folder, you will at least be able to use the Scrapbook again (albeit with an empty Scrapbook File). If you don't need anything inside the damaged Scrapbook File, just delete it. While you are at it, replace the Scrapbook DA as well—just to be safe.

  However, if you are using System 7.5 and you get a message such as "Sorry, this disk is full or the system is out of memory," you may really have a memory problem. In this case, you can actually increase the Scrapbook's Memory allocation via its Get Info window (as discussed more in Chapter 12, "Solve It! System 7.5 Problems").

- If you get an error message that says something like *Unable to read from disk,* this suggests possible media damage, typically in the area of the file you are trying to open. In this case, before replacing the damaged file from your backups, you should check for and repair any media damage. This usually requires reformatting the disk.

- Otherwise, check for more general damage (such as to system software) that may be causing problems beyond the file in question.

Figure 6-12 Top: Trouble opening a control panel that may or may not be damaged. Bottom: This message often implies damage to the Scrapbook DA or to the Scrapbook File

SEE: • Fix-Its #13 and #14 on fixing damaged files and media damage
       • Fix-It #15 on reformatting disks

TECHNICALLY SPEAKING ▶

A FEW WORDS ABOUT SOUND AND SOUND FILES

- *Sound file formats.*   In System 7, sounds can exist as independent files on the desktop, much like font files. If you double-click a sound file, the Macintosh will play the sound. If you have sound files that do not work this way, it is probably because these files are not in the standard format. Unfortunately, because Apple failed to provide any standard format prior to System 7, there are a variety of different formats that your sound file could be. Fortunately, there are several shareware utilities that can easily convert most sound formats to the System 7 standard format. The one that I use most often is called Sound Extractor.

- *Damaged sound files.*   If you still cannot get a sound file to play when you double-click it, the file may be damaged. In this case, a utility such as CanOpener may be able to recover the sound. Also, for those of you familiar with the basics or using Apple's ResEdit, try to open the sound resource using ResEdit. If the file is damaged, ResEdit will identify this and offer to try to fix it for you. If it succeeds, you should then extract the sound resource to a new file.

SEE: • Fix-It #14 for general information on fixing damaged files

- **Sound Manager 3.0 and the Sound control panel.** Apple has expanded and improved the Mac's sound capabilities via an extension called Sound Manager 3.0. It has similarly upgraded the Sound control panel (see Figure 6-13). If you do not have these items, the upgrades are included as part of System Update 3.0 as well as System 7.5 (Actually, Sound Manager is built into System 7.5's System file and a separate extension is no longer needed). The control panel has several new options, including a pop-up menu with four main choices: Alert Sounds, Sound In, Sound Out, and Volumes. A detailed description of how all of these options work are beyond the scope of this book. However, a few common situations where you would use these features are described in the next sections.

- **Accessing alert sounds.** You select an Alert sound from the Sound control panel. Other applications, such as alarm clock utilities, may similarly access the list of alert sounds. The sounds listed here are determined by what sound files have been installed directly into the System file (see Figure 6-13). Though System 7.1 and later now uses a Fonts folder, rather than installing fonts into the System file, there is no equivalent Sounds folder. However, there are several third-party utilities (such as Now Fun! or SoundMaster) that can bypass this restriction, allowing you to access sound files from anywhere on your disk and use them as alert sounds. These utilities additionally allow you to attach these sounds to almost any sort of event (such as Empty Trash or Eject Disk). There is also a way to access sound files that are not in the System file without requiring any specialized software: change the file's type and creator to match that of a font suitcase. After this, simply place the sound file in the Fonts folder and the System will correctly access it as a sound, listing it as a potential alert sound.

SEE: • Chapter 8, "Add Alert Sounds Without Installing Them in the System File," for details on how to do this

- **Alert sound volume.** With the new Sound control panel, the volume of alert sounds is regulated by two different volume controls. The main one is the slider visible when Alert Sounds is selected from the Sound control panel's pop-up menu. The other control (assuming you are using the built-in speakers) is the slider for Built-In volume, accessed by selecting Volumes from the pop-up menu. The Built-In volume sets the level for all sounds going to the built-in speaker, not just alert sounds. If you are not getting the sound level you expect by adjusting one of these sliders, try adjusting the other instead. For example, try keeping the Alert Sounds volume turned up to its maximum and instead adjust the Built-in volume. In any case, if the Built-in volume is set to zero (or if the Mute checkbox below the volume slider is checked), you will get no alert sounds (or any other sounds from the built-in speaker) no matter what the volume setting of the Alert Sounds slider. If either slider is set to zero, the menu bar will flash when an alert sound would have otherwise occurred. Also, be aware that if you have a cable plugged into the sound-out port (the one with the speaker icon over it), sound will be directed through that port rather than to the built-in speaker (even if you have not made a separate selection from the sound-out section of the Sound control panel). This again can mean that you will be unable to hear alert sounds. If none of this seems to solve the problem, it is possible that the wire from the logic board to the built-in speaker may have come loose. If you have a Mac whose insides are easily accessible, you can probably check and fix this yourself. If all else fails, you may need a logic board repair.

- **Application sounds.** If you are having problems with hearing sounds other than alert sounds, such as ones used in games, again check the setting of the slider(s) in the Volumes section of the Sound control panel. Also, some applications may be incompatible with the new Sound Manager, with the result that they will not play any sounds. If you suspect this may be the case, try removing the Sound Manager (not possible with System 7.5) and restarting. If virtual memory is on, this can distort sounds, especially in games and QuickTime movies.

(continued)

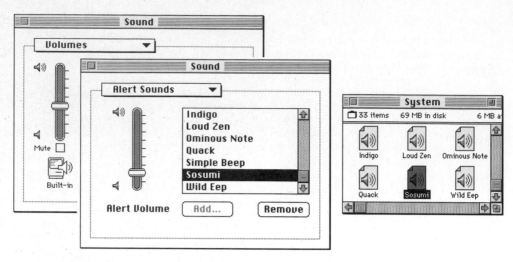

Figure 6-13 The Volumes and Alert Sounds sections of the Sound control panel (left) and the alert sound files themselves, as installed in the System file (right)

CD Audio   *Most Macintosh models (other than AV and Power Macs) cannot play stereo sound from CD-ROM disks (or from ordinary audio CDs) through the Mac itself. To hear this sound, you will have to attach external speakers or headphones directly to the external CD-ROM drive. For AV and Power Macs (at least those with internal CD-ROM drives), you can play stereo sound through the Mac's internal speakers (though the quality will not be great) if you first make the appropriate settings in the Sound control panel. In particular, select Sound In from the pop-up menu, then click the Options button. From the Options window, select the Internal CD icon and click the Playthrough checkbox to get the x to appear (remember to uncheck Playthrough when you no longer wish to access CD audio). Then select Volumes from the pop-up menu to access and adjust the Built-in volume setting (make sure the Mute button is not checked).*

PlainTalk Speech   *Apple's new speech input and output technology is loosely referred to as PlainTalk. Macintoshes can now talk to you via MacinTalk 2, MacinTalk 3, or MacinTalk Pro (originally called PlainTalk Text-to-Speech), all part of Apple's text-to-speech PlainTalk technology. However, to do this you will need the Speech Manager extension (which has a version of MacinTalk built in to it) and assorted other "voice" files (on AV Macs, Speech Manager is in ROM). Understanding the differences between these different versions of MacinTalk can lead to more confusion than I can possibly disentangle here. However, if you use an Installer utility to install all this software, it will generally turn out okay. Check a PlainTalk manual for more details. To finally hear the speech output, you will also need an application that supports this feature (Apple included this support in SimpleText; check out its Sound menu).*

Conversely, AV Macs and all Power Macs can obey your commands, when spoken into a microphone. However, this requires other components of Apple's PlainTalk software as well as a PlainTalk compatible microphone. If you intend to use either of these technologies, make sure you have the needed software and read instructions carefully for proper installation and use.

When You Can't Open a Document

Symptoms:

You attempt to open a data document, either directly from the Finder (usually by double-clicking the file's icon) or from within an application (using the Open dialog box). In either case, the result is the same: The file refuses to open. Typically, you get an error message indicating the cause of the problem. In the worst cases, a system error may occur.

Alternatively, the file may open, but only part of the file's contents remain or the file displays random gibberish rather than the correct data. (More minor display problems, such as incorrect use of fonts or colors, are not covered here. For solutions to these problems, refer to Chapters 9 and 10.)

Causes:

Reasons that you cannot open a document file include:

- The Macintosh cannot find the application needed to open the document (there are several possible reasons for this, as detailed in the following What to do section).
- The file is in PC/DOS format and/or on a PC/DOS formatted disk.
- Insufficient available memory.
- The file is not intended to be directly opened (for example, extensions).
- The document (or its application) is damaged.
- Many of the same reasons that prevent you from launching an application (refer to the previous section for advice on these causes).

What to do:

If a Document's Application Can't Be Found by the Finder

You double-click a document file from the Finder, but, instead of the file opening, you get an error message that says that the file could not be opened because the application program that created it could not be found (see Figure 6-14).

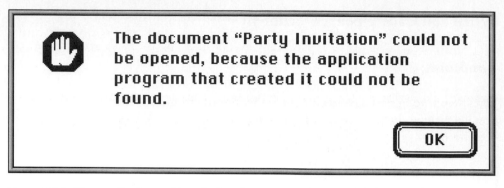

Figure 6-14 The *application could not be found* error message

System 6 Alert: In System 6, the message says that it cannot do this because the application is "busy or missing."

What exactly is going on here? What's happening is this: The Finder "knows" to which application a document belongs (see Chapter 8 for an explanation of how it knows this). For example, it knows that Excel documents belong to the Excel application. When you try to open an Excel document, the Finder searches the disk until it locates the Excel application. It then launches the application followed by the document. However, if the Finder cannot locate the creating application, nothing opens. Instead, you get the error message just described. What to do about this depends on exactly why the Macintosh could not find the needed application. There are several possibilities.

The Creating Application Has Been Deleted or Is Not Currently Accessible   You create a document file using a particular application. For whatever reason, you later delete that application from your startup disk. Or perhaps you have received a document from a colleague that was created by an application that is not on your disk. When you try to launch such documents, you probably get the *application could not be found* error message.

The most obvious solution to this problem is to install the needed application on to your disk. If you are uncertain what the needed application is, try opening the file from within any application you have that is likely to be of the same category (such as using a word processor for text files of unknown origin). You may get lucky and hit on the right application (or at least find one that can successfully import the file). Also, the Kind line in the file's Get Info window (see Chapter 2) may indicate the name of the document's creating application.

Finally, you should be aware of several utilities that can assist in your efforts to open a document:

- **Use TeachText/SimpleText**
  New in System 7, if TeachText or SimpleText is on your disk (it comes with Apple's system software), when you try to open certain text or graphics files (plain TEXT

or PICT documents) that would normally lead to the *application could not be found* error message, you may instead be given the option to open the file in TeachText/SimpleText (see Figure 6-15). This at least allows you to view the contents of the file.

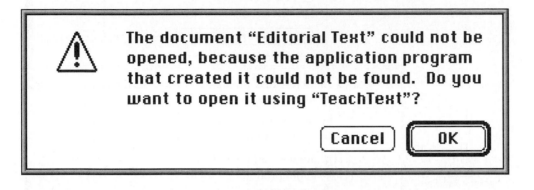

Figure 6-15 Similar to the message in Figure 6-14, these messages appear if the file that cannot be opened with its intended application can still be opened with TeachText or SimpleText

SEE: • Chapter 8 for more on the types of files (TEXT and PICT) that can be opened this way

• **Use Macintosh Easy Open**
This Apple utility is now included as a standard part of System 7.5. It is also available with other-third party utilities, such as Access PC. With Easy Open, when you try to open a document whose creating application is missing, you get a window listing all other available applications that can open the document (see Figure 6-16). You can select which one to use to open the document. On subsequent occasions, the substitution application will be remembered and it will open automatically, without the dialog box. If desired, you can later delete a particular substitution pair from Easy Open's "memory" by using the Easy Open Setup control panel (see Figure 6-16).

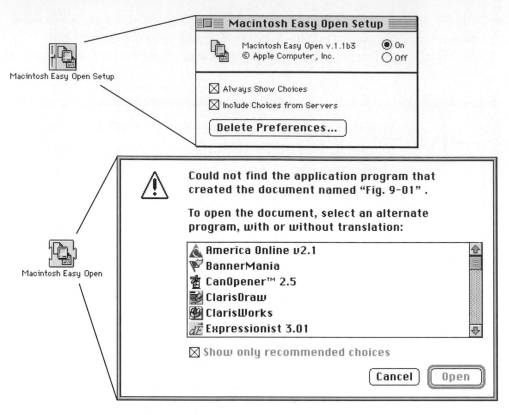

Figure 6-16 Top: Macintosh Easy Open Setup control panel (used to delete previously created pairing preferences); Bottom: With Macintosh Easy Open extension installed, the dialog box shown here appears, rather than the one in Figure 6-14, if the file cannot be opened with its intended application but can still be opened with TeachText or SimpleText. With additional translator files installed this dialog box also appears for other types of files.

The bare-bones version of Easy Open only recognizes TEXT and PICT documents, making it not much more effective that the basic System 7 alternative just described. However, with appropriate translators, such as the MacLink ones (a set of which come with System 7.5) or Word for Word, it will work with a variety of other document types, including documents created by PC applications.

If you have a related utility, called Easy Open Document Converter (not available with System 7.5), this converts a document from one format to another at the Finder level, without even needing to open the document or the application.

- **Other utilities to the rescue**
  Suppose you want to be able to double-click WordPerfect files in the Finder and get the Mac to automatically open Word. Easy Open can do this, as just described. But other utilities provide similar solutions. Now Utilities' NowMenus control panel is one example of this (see Figure 6-17).

The document "Party Invitation" could not be opened, because the application program that created it could not be found.

Pick An Application...   OK

Figure 6-17 The same alert message as in Figure 6-14, except the Pick An Application button is added because Now Utilities' NowMenus is running

After one of these is installed, when you try to open a document for which the Finder does not recognize the creating application, these utilities intercept the normal *application not found* error message and give you an option to open the document with another application. If you do so, they remember this link, if desired, so that the next time you try to open any document of that format, the alternative application opens automatically without bothering you with any alert message.

BY THE WAY ▶

CREATE DOCUMENTS THAT ANYONE CAN OPEN

If you plan to give a document to other users that may not have your creating application, you can help them out by saving the document in a way that lets them open the document, no matter what application you used to create it. However, this does require special software that all users must have, such as Acrobat and Common Ground. For example, with Acrobat, you can save any document as an Acrobat document. Then any user who has an Acrobat reader can open the document. You can similarly use the new portable document (PDD) feature of System 7.5's QuickDraw GX.

The Creating Application Has Been Replaced with an Upgraded Version   When a new version of an application is released, the format of its document files may be changed. Even if this happens, the new version should retain its ability to read files created by its earlier versions, opening the files and converting them to the new format.

However, sometimes this does not work. For example, suppose you are using Busy-Works version 3.0, but you have a file created by BusyWorks 2.0. The file should open in BusyWorks 3.0 without a problem. But in this case, when you try to open the 2.0 document file from the Finder, you get the *application not found* error message.

- **Use the Open command**
  The key here is to *not* try to open the file from the Finder. Open the creating application first, then try to open the document using the application's Open command. If the program is at all capable of reading its older version's files, this should work.

- **Check for special commands**
  Alternatively, you may find that the application itself has a special command for opening files of earlier versions. There may even be a separate special converter utility needed to convert old versions of files to the new version's format. Check the manual for any mention of this.

- **Import to another application**
  You could also try the previously described importing alternative. That is, try to open the file from the Open dialog box of another application that has a translator capability for BusyWorks 2.0.

- **Use the older version**
  Finally, if all else fails, you could reinstall the deleted older version of the application (assuming you have retained a copy of it—which is usually a good preventative measure). Delete the newer version. Open the document with the now reinstalled older version.

The Document Was Created by a Newer Version of the Application than the One You Are Using   This is sort of the reverse of the previous situation. This case is a bit less likely. It usually would happen only if you get a file from someone else. For example, perhaps a friend gives you a document created by BusyWorks 3.0, but you are still using version 2.0.

The result is that when you try to open the document from the Finder, you get the *application not found* error message.

If this happens, be careful about shifting to the standard alternate approach of trying to open the document from within the application itself (BusyWorks 2.0 in this case). This may succeed on occasion. However, more likely it won't. Usually, the name of the document does not appear in the Open dialog box's file list. Even if it is listed, don't rejoice yet. When you open it, you may find that the document has lost its formatting or contains garbage data (in addition to the actual data). In the worst case, just trying to open the document may result in a system crash!

The crash can occur because the application successfully gets partway through opening the document and then suddenly discovers it isn't in the expected format. Not knowing what else to do at this point, it decides to crash the system. I have seen this happen when trying to open MacWrite II files with an earlier version of MacWrite.

- **Upgrade**
  The easiest (though not necessarily the fastest or cheapest) solution is to upgrade to the new version of the application.

- **Save in a different format**
  Alternatively, you can see if the person that gave you the file can save the file in a format readable by your version. That is, BusyWorks 3.0 may have an option to save the file in version 2.0 format.

- **Import to another application**
  If you have new versions of other applications, you may find that one of them has a translator file for BusyWorks 3.0. You can use this application to open the file.

BY THE WAY ▶

AVOID MULTIPLE VERSIONS OF THE SAME APPLICATION

When you upgrade to a new version of an application, be sure to delete the previous version from your hard drive. Otherwise, when you try to launch a document created by the application, it may incorrectly launch the old version rather than the new one.
*   In any event, I would be cautious about opening two different versions of the same application at the same time. While doing this can often work just fine, it could just as easily cause problems, including a system crash.*

The Correct Version of the Creating Application Is Present, Yet the Document File Still Does Not Open from the Finder   This is not supposed to happen. It indicates something has gone wrong. Sometimes this happens to a file you have undeleted. Usually, if this does occur, you also find that the customized icon for the document is lost and that only the blank generic blank document icon is present. To try to solve this:

- **Use the Open dialog box**
  Launch the creating application and try to open the file from within its Open dialog box. If this works, create a copy of the document as a new file with a different name. Quit the application and delete the now unneeded original file. Most of the time, this remedies the situation.

  If the custom icon does not yet appear, select Get Info for the file. This should get the Macintosh's attention and update the icon display. Otherwise, it will probably display correctly after your next restart.

- **Rebuild the desktop**
  If the preceding steps are unsuccessful, try rebuilding the desktop. The Desktop file stores information about the links between documents and applications. Errors in the Desktop file data can prevent the document from opening. Rebuilding the desktop usually fixes this.

SEE: • **Fix-It #9 on rebuilding the desktop**

NOWMENUS CAN LAUNCH THE "WRONG" APPLICATION OR PREVENT QUITTING FROM AN APPLICATION

As mentioned in the main text, Now Utilities' NowMenus (as well as several other competing utilities) can be set up so that when you double-click a WordPerfect file, for example, it launches Microsoft Word rather than WordPerfect. This is fine if that's what you want to do (because you don't own WordPerfect). However, if you inadvertently create such a link (or if you later buy WordPerfect but forget that you made the link), you may be frustrated by the Mac's apparently strange insistence that all WordPerfect documents launch into Word. If this happens, check out the substitution list in NowMenus and delete the undesired link.

Diverging a bit here, NowMenus can cause even stranger problems because of its ability to reassign command key equivalents. For example, if you want Command-R to be the equivalent to the Replace command, rather than Command-H, you can use NowMenus to do it. However, beware! This will override whatever Command-R did previously, if anything. This problem is made worse by how easy it is to accidentally make these assignments with NowMenus. For example, I once, by mistake, reassigned Command-Q (normally used to quit the application) to some rarely used function. From that point on, I could not use Command-Q to quit the application. Instead, nothing happened. It took me quite a while to figure out what was going on.

If None of the Preceding Steps Work   If none of the preceding steps work, and you are willing to get technical in search of a solution, check for problems with the file's type, creator, and Bundle bit settings.

SEE: • Chapter 8 for explanations of these terms and what to do

WHAT TO DO ABOUT LOST ICONS

One day you start up your Macintosh and notice that some or all of the creative customized icons that you are used to seeing on your desktop are missing. This can happen even when there is no problem correctly launching a document. What can you do? Many times this is solved simply by selecting Get Info for the file in question and/or restarting. Otherwise, this problem is most often solved by rebuilding the desktop. If this doesn't work, it may be that you are dealing with special custom icons not affected by a rebuild. This is certainly the case if the icon in question is for a folder, rather than a file. Otherwise, for a document file, it is possible that the creating application needed to maintain the document's icon is no longer on your disk. Details on solving all of these problems are covered in Fix-It #9. Less likely but still possible, you may have an incorrect Creator code (as explained in Chapter 8, "Type and Creator Code Problems"). Finally, the problem may be related to Directory damage, usually a relatively minor problem with what is called the "bundle bit," though sometimes it is due to more serious damage. MacTools and Norton Utilities can typically fix bundle bit as well as other Directory problems (as mentioned in Fix-It #13).

An Application Does Not Import a Document File, Even Though the Application Has a Translator Available for the File's Format

For example, suppose you try to open a Microsoft Word file from within the Open dialog box of BusyWorks. You select the *All Available* or *Microsoft Word* option from the pop-up menu that lists the types of readable files. Yet either the file you wish to open does not get displayed in the dialog box or, if it does appear, it does not open when selected.

The most likely cause for this is that the importing translation filter is not an exact match for the file you are trying to import. In particular, the filter may be specific to a different version of the file's creating application from the one used to create the file (such as trying to open a Microsoft Word 6.0 file with a Microsoft Word 3.0 translator).

In a related example, Microsoft Word has a Fast Save format option. You can check this option from the Save As dialog box. Doing this is supposed to speed up the process of saving documents. However, files saved with Fast Save may not be recognized by another application, even if the other application does recognize Word files saved in the normal format. Similarly, different types of TIFF document formats exist. A particular translator maybe able to open some formats but not others.

The general solutions to these problems are to resave the document file in a format that matches the filter, get a filter that matches the file (check if the company that makes your application has one available), use another application that can successfully import the file, or give up on this approach altogether.

BY THE WAY ▶

IF SYSTEM 7 STATIONERY PAD OPTION DOES NOT WORK . . .

You check the Stationery Pad option in a document's Get Info window. Yet when you double-click the document, it still opens as an ordinary document, not as stationery. The problem may simply be that the application in question does not support this System 7 option. If so, there is nothing you can do about it. However, many word processors have their own stationery feature, separate from the System 7 feature. You could use this instead.

The File Is in PC/DOS Format and/or on a PC/DOS-Formatted Disk

This is really a special case of the previous section on problems importing files. Many Macintosh applications (such as Microsoft Word and WordPerfect) can read files saved in a PC format (as used on IBM PCs and compatibles), especially those files created using a PC version of their software. However, to successfully do this may require some special preparation.

Make Sure the Macintosh Can Read the PC-Formatted Floppy Disk   When you first acquire PC files, they will probably be on a PC-formatted disk. Fortunately, if set up properly, the Macintosh can mount and read files from these disks just as if they were Macintosh-formatted disks. First, all PC 3½-inch floppy disks are HD disks, so you need a SuperDrive to mount them (since older 800K drives can not read HD disks). Second, you need a special INIT, placed in your System Folder, that is used to recognize PC-formatted disks. With System 7.5, Apple includes such an INIT: the Macintosh PC Exchange control panel. (You can also separately purchase this or other competing utilities, such as AccessPC.) With PC Exchange installed (see Figure 6-18), an inserted PC disk will mount on the desktop as a disk icon in exactly the same manner as a Macintosh disk. Files on the disk will be represented by file icons, again just as with a Macintosh disk. Files can now be copied back and forth to your hard drive or any other disk. This is a much better alternative to Apple's former attempt at PC compatibility: Apple File Exchange.

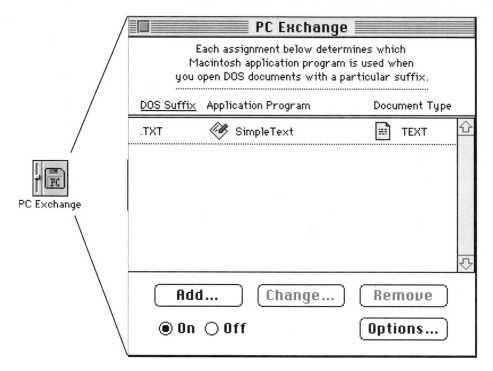

Figure 6-18   The PC Exchange control panel

SEE: • Fix-It #15 for more on formatting disks

Make Sure the Application Can Read Files Formatted by the Application That Created It on the PC   Some applications have "built-in" translators for reading PC-formatted files. For example, WordPerfect for the Macintosh can open files created by the PC versions of WordPerfect. To access these documents, the most reliable method is to open them from within the application, not by double-clicking the document from the Finder. However, with PC Exchange installed, you may be able to open the document directly from the Finder. Specifically, PC Exchange will match a DOS suffix in a document's name to a particular Macintosh application, as set in the PC Exchange control panel window. Of course, this only works well if the application in question can read the PC-formatted file. Other competing utilities, such as AccessPC, have a similar capability.

Opening PC-formatted files directly from the Finder, regardless of their name, is further enhanced if you use Macintosh Easy Open (also included as part of System 7.5) (refer to Figure 6-16).

Check for the Correct Suffix If you are trying to import DOS-formatted files (such as a PC Works 2.0 file to Microsoft Works 3.0), make sure the document file has the correct suffix (such as file.*wrk*)—that is, the suffix that would be assigned to that file on a DOS machine. Without the suffix, some Macintosh programs cannot recognize the file when you try to open it later—even though they list a file translator for that format.

Insufficient Memory to Open the File

Sometimes, even if you can open the application itself, you cannot get it to open a document. This is common if the document is especially large (particularly common with large graphics files) or if you are trying to open several documents at once.

This is usually a memory-related problem. When you are using System 6's Multi-Finder or System 7, each application is allocated a specific amount of memory (as determined by the memory size setting in the application's Get Info window). This amount of memory must contain the application itself plus any documents that you open within that application. If opening a document would require more than this allotted amount of memory, you cannot open it (even though the memory setting was sufficient to open the application itself). If this occurs, you usually get an error message accurately describing this problem (see Figure 6-19).

The same sort of error may appear if you try to cut or copy a large selection to the Clipboard. These errors can occur no matter how much memory you have installed in your system. It is a function of the amount of memory assigned to an application, not of the total amount of available memory!

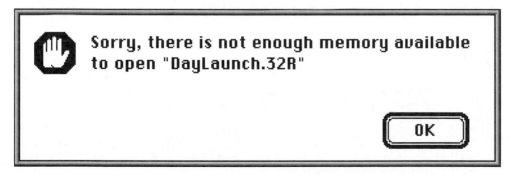

Figure 6-19 This message appeared while I was trying to open a document with a graphics application

Close Other Documents   The easiest solution is to close other open documents within the application, if any. See if the document now opens.

Increase Application's Memory Allocation   You can increase the problem application's memory Preferred size (called Current size in System 7.0) from the settings in the application's Get Info window.

SEE: • Fix-It #6 on memory management problems for details

Other Solutions   Reduce the size of your system software memory allocation (by turning off extensions at startup) or add more memory hardware.

The File Is Not Intended to Be Opened

Some files are not intended to be opened from the Finder. For example, After Dark is a screen-saver utility. In particular, it replaces your display with some amusing alternative after several minutes of inactivity. It uses numerous plug-in modules to let the user choose what alternative appears on the screen. Each module is a separate file. Still, if you double-click any of these files, it does not open After Dark. Instead, you get the *application could not be found* message. You can only access these modules by first opening the After Dark control panel directly.

Similarly, many System Folder files are not intended to be openable (such as the Finder itself and most extension files). If you try to open these files, you get a message like the ones shown in Figure 6-20. There is nothing particular to do in such cases. The files are not supposed to be opened. So don't try.

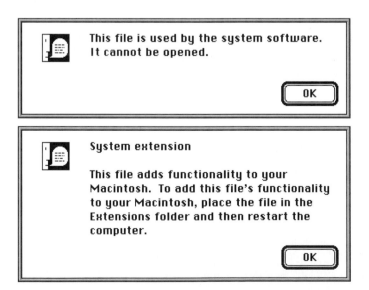

Figure 6-20   Top: If you try to open the Finder (by double-clicking its icon), it won't open—this message appears instead; Bottom: This message appears if you try to open a system extension

On a related note, you cannot use an application to open a file that is already opened in another application. For example, you cannot simultaneously open a graphics document in ClarisDraw and ClarisWorks. If you try, you will get an error message telling you that it cannot be done.

Opening a Document from the Finder When the Application Is Already Open

You try to open a document file from the Finder for an application that is already open. Instead of opening the file, you get a message saying either that you can't open the document because the application is in use or just that the document could not be opened.

For example, you double-click a BusyWorks document file from the Finder when BusyWorks is already open. Instead of shifting to BusyWorks and opening the document, you get an error message instead (see Figure 6-21). Technically, this should not happen. You should be able to open the file in this way. However, some programs may give you problems with this. The solution here is simple. Open the document from within the application, using the application's Open dialog box.

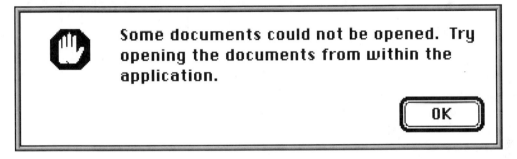

Figure 6-21 This message may appear when you are trying to open a document from the Finder for an application that is already open

Opening a Document File from the Finder Succeeds, But It Launches the Wrong Application

You create a text file in BusyWorks. The next day, you double-click that file to open it. But rather than the file opening in BusyWorks, it opens it in TeachText or perhaps in Microsoft Word.

What happened? Some programs save their documents as plain text files (see Chapter 8 for more on this). This is common for some programs that are not really word processors but that produce text reports of some sort. In such cases, if the document is launched from the Finder, it often opens in a generic text application (such as TeachText). This is only a problem if you don't want this to happen for some reason.

Actually, I just as often have the reverse problem. I save a file in a plain text format, expecting it to launch into SimpleText the next time. But instead it opens into the creating application (which may take a lot longer to open).

A related situation is if you saved the file (inadvertently?) in a format other than the application's default format (such as saving a BusyWorks file in Microsoft Word format). In this case, trying to open the file from the Finder causes it to launch Word rather than BusyWorks. (Actually, if Word is not on your disk, the file may not open at all—and you get the *application could not be found* message, described earlier in this chapter.)

If a text document does open in the "wrong" application, it is also possible that text formatting (such as the font, the size of the text, the line breaks, and margins) are different from when you saved it.

SEE: • Chapter 9 for more on text-formatting problems

To get a file to open with the desired application, the solution is usually simple. Open the document from within the application, using the application's Open dialog box, rather than from the Finder. If this does not work, you can fiddle with the document's creator code (see Chapter 8 again). Otherwise, there is not much else you can do.

The Problem May Be with the Application, Not the Document

If a particular application refuses to open most or all appropriate documents, the application itself may be damaged or there may be a software bug involved. To check for this, replace the application software. If this fails, you may still be able to open the document(s) in another application that can read files created by the problem application.

Damaged Documents That Can't Be Opened

When none of the preceding solutions opens a document (or, if it does open, much of the data appear garbled or lost), the document itself may be damaged. In most cases, the simplest solution is to revert to a backup copy of the file, assuming you have one. If this works, delete the problem copy. Make a new backup copy. You are back in business. If you do not have a backup copy, you can try several options that may repair or recover data from the damaged file.

SEE: • Fix-It #14 on fixing damaged files

If you got an error message such as *Unable to read from disk,* this usually means media damage to the area of the disk where the file resides. This damage has to be fixed even if you can recover or replace the file.

SEE: • Fix-Its #13 and #14 on fixing damaged files, including media damage
       • Fix-It #15 on reformatting

If, after trying this and all of the previous suggestions, you still cannot open the file, there is little or no hope of saving it. Just delete the problem file and go on with your life.

When You Can't Delete a File or Folder

Symptoms:

You place a file or a folder in the Finder's Trash. You select Empty Trash from the Finder's Special menu, but the item does not get deleted.

Usually, you also get an alert message explaining why the Trash was not deleted. It may say, for example, that *The Trash cannot be emptied . . . because . . . items in it are locked* or *The item <name> could not be deleted because it contains items that are in use.*

Causes:

Exact causes vary depending on the error message you get.

- Locked files or files on locked floppy disks cannot be directly deleted. They need to be unlocked.

- Files that are currently open (or in use) cannot be deleted until they are closed. This makes sense. Deleting an open file would be like erasing a videotape while you are in the middle of watching it. Similarly, the System and the Finder on the startup disk cannot be deleted because they are always in use.

- In rarer cases, problems with the system software, damaged files, or damaged disk media may prevent a file or folder from being deleted.

SEE: • Chapter 8 on the invisible Trash folder

BY THE WAY ▶

EXCEPTIONAL TRASH BEHAVIOR

Normally (as discussed previously), you cannot have two files or folders of the same name in the same location. If you try to do this, the Macintosh asks if you want to replace the existing file (or folder) with the new one. However, the Trash is a partial exception to this rule. If you place an item in the Trash when the Trash already contains an item of the same name, the Macintosh renames one of the items (by appending the word copy to the end of the name). Both can then coexist in the Trash—while they await your decision to delete them. You get no message alerting you to this name modification.

What to do:

Make Sure the File or Folder Is Really in the Trash

If you can still see the file/folder on the desktop, near the Trash, it is *not* in the Trash. To get it in the Trash, drag it until the cursor arrow covers the Trash and the Trash icon turns black. Then release the mouse. Now select Empty Trash.

If the File or Folder Is on a Floppy Disk, Check if the Floppy Disk Is Locked

A disk is locked if the sliding tab, located in the upper corner on the rear side of the disk, is positioned so that you can see through the hole. Ordinarily you cannot even move an item from a locked floppy disk to the Trash (see Figure 6-22). Certainly, nothing can be written to or deleted from a locked floppy disk.

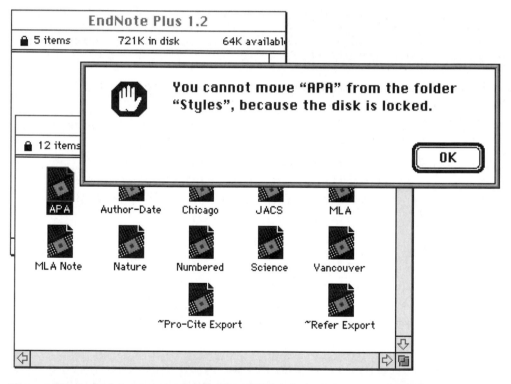

Figure 6-22 Padlock icon means that the floppy disk is locked; the error message appeared when I tried to move a file on this disk

For a floppy disk that is already inserted, you can check if it is locked without having to eject it. If it is locked, any window from the disk displays a small icon of a padlock in the upper left corner of the window (see Figure 6-22).

To unlock the disk, eject the disk and slide the tab down. Reinsert the disk. You can then delete the file.

Check If the File Is Locked

A file is locked if the Locked box in the file's Get Info window is checked (as described more in Chapter 2). If you are viewing files by any view other than an icon view, locked files will have a padlock symbol at the end of its listing line (see Figure 6-23).

If a file is locked, you can still place it in the Trash. However, when you try to delete it, you get a message informing you of the situation (see Figure 6-23). The message tells you that the solution to this problem is to hold down the Option key while you select Empty Trash. This allows locked files to be deleted. Actually, in some cases of files that refuse to delete, it may pay to hold down the Option key even if the file is not locked (or to deliberately lock the file and then try to delete it with the Option key held down).

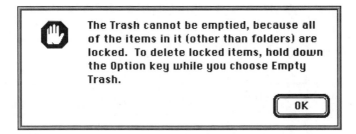

Figure 6-23   Top: The padlock symbol appears next to the locked Script Editor file; Bottom: The message that appears if you try to Empty Trash with a locked file in the Trash

System 6 Alert: In System 6, you need to hold down the Option key while dragging a locked item into the Trash. Otherwise, the file does not go into the Trash. Once it is in the Trash, however, you can delete the file without receiving any further messages. Alternatively, you can go to a file's Get Info window and uncheck the Locked box. The file is now unlocked and may be deleted.

SEE: • Chapter 2 for more on using the Get Info command

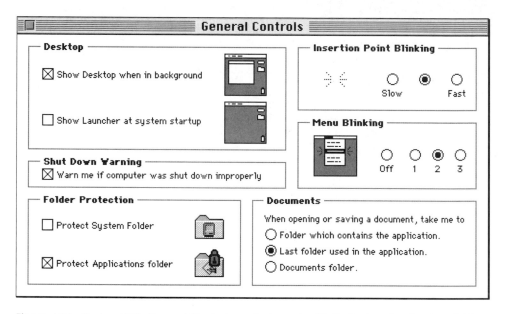

Figure 6-24   System 7.5's General Controls control panel, with its Protect Applications folder option checked

Folders Locked via the Sharing Command

If you use System 7's file sharing, you probably know that you can restrict users' access to files, preventing them from modifying your files in any way. You do this via the checkboxes in the dialog box that appears after selecting Sharing from the Finder's file menu (see Figure 6-25). However, at the bottom of this dialog box is a lesser known option that can even limit your own ability to modify a folder on your disk.

To see this in action, turn file sharing on, select any folder, then select the Sharing command. At the bottom of the dialog box, note the checkbox option called *Can't be moved, renamed, or deleted.* If this is checked, the folder cannot be moved, renamed, or deleted by anyone, including yourself, whether accessing it directly or via file sharing— but only as long as file sharing is on. If you try, you will get a message that the folder can't be moved to the Trash because it is locked. The only solution for this is to select the folder, go the Sharing dialog box, and uncheck this option.

However, assuming that you otherwise have access, you can still remove individual files from the folder and delete them separately.

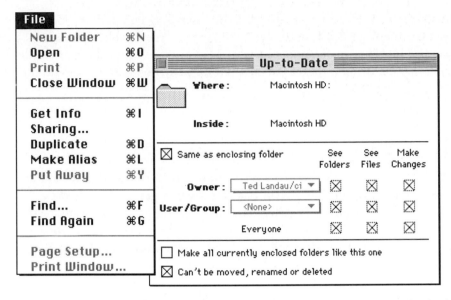

Figure 6-25   Locking a folder via the Sharing command. It only works when File Sharing is on

SEE: • Chapter 11 for more on file sharing

Check If the File Is Currently Open or in Use

Any application or document file that is currently open cannot be deleted. If you try to do this, you get an error message instead (see Figure 6-26). If you get this message, click Continue to delete any other files that may be in the Trash. Then:

For Applications   If the file to be deleted is an application, quit the application. Then select Empty Trash again. The file should now be deleted.

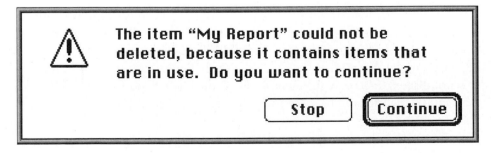

Figure 6-26   This message appears if you try to delete a file that is currently open

For Documents   If the file is a document, it is usually sufficient to just close the document file. Then return to the Finder and select Empty Trash again. If this doesn't work, try quitting the aplication that created the document. Then try to trash the document.

For Essential System Folder Files   If the file is an essential system software file on your current startup disk (such as the System, the Finder, or an Enabler file), you cannot delete it. To do so, you have to restart the Macintosh using an alternate startup disk. Then drag the file to the Trash and delete it. Normally, you only want to do this if you are about to replace these files.

SEE: • Fix-It #5 on replacing system software files

For Other System Folder Files (Extensions, Control Panels, Fonts, and so on)   If the file is a startup extension or control panel on your current startup disk (or for any other unknown type of file in your System Folder), you may get an error message saying that it cannot be deleted. This often happens if the file gets loaded into memory at startup (an INIT). In this case, drag the file out of the System Folder. Then restart the Macintosh. You should be able to delete it. You don't need to use an alternate startup disk.

SEE: • Fix-It #4 for more on deleting INITs

Folders That Remain "In Use" Unexpectedly

Suppose you are working on a file called Daily Report #6. After printing the file, you decide to delete it. In fact, you have a whole folder of daily reports that you now are ready to delete. The folder is called Articles 2. Knowing that you cannot trash an open file, you remember to close the Daily Report #6 file (but you do not quit the application you are using). You then drag the entire folder to the Trash.

When you select Empty Trash, you get an alert message saying that the Articles 2 folder could not be deleted because it contains items that are still in use (see Figure 6-27). When you check the folder, it is empty. Every file in the folder was in fact deleted. But the folder itself was not. How can anything in it be still in use? What's going on?

The problem is that the Macintosh considers a folder to be in use until you quit every currently open application that has opened any of the files that were within that folder (even if the files have since been closed). In this case, if the word processor (Word, for example) that was used to create the Daily Report file is still open, the folder is not deleted, even though you have closed the Daily Report #6 file. The odd thing is that the file itself can be successfully deleted. To delete the folder:

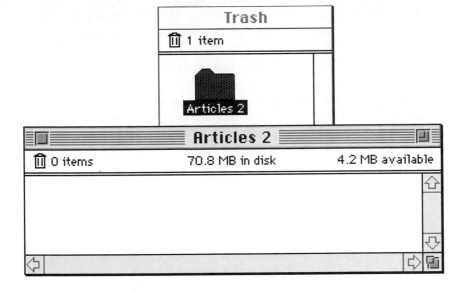

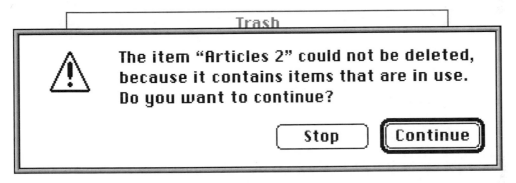

Figure 6-27 The folder Articles 2, now in the Trash, is empty (top); even though the folder is empty, it does not get deleted when Empty Trash is selected, instead an error message appears (bottom)

1. Click Stop or Continue.

2. Quit the relevant applications (Word in the previous example).

3. Then select Empty Trash again. It should work now.

An Invisible File in the Folder?   A relatively rare problem is if a folder contains an invisible file that is "in use." In this case, the Macintosh will not delete the folder until you either remove the invisible file or quit whatever application is causing the file to be "in use." The best way to check this is with a utility, such as Norton Utilities or DiskTop, that lists invisible files.

Special Case: Deleting Folders from an AppleShare Volume   If you are using System 7.1, make sure you have installed System Update 3.0. This fixes a problem with deleting folders that are on an AppleShare volume. Without this update, the Finder may prevent deleting folders by falsely claiming that the folder is "in use."

SEE: • Chapter 11 for more on connecting Macs via AppleShare

The Folder from Hell Problem

Occasionally, you may have a folder that is empty but refuses to be deleted no matter what you try. Everything in the folder can be deleted, but the folder itself does not go away. Even after you quit all open applications, even after you restart the Macintosh, even if you hold down the Option key while emptying the Trash, the folder refuses to be deleted. Trying to move or delete the folder may produce various strange symptoms and error messages, such as a -127 error. Often, this problem begins as an aftereffect of a system crash.

This type of folder has been referred to as the *folder from hell.* The most likely cause of this problem has to do with the special Directory files that the Macintosh uses to keep track of what is on the disk.

SEE: • Chapter 8 for more on the Directory files

Without getting too technical here, the problem is the result of a discrepancy between different areas of the Directory files as to how many files and folders are contained within the problem folder. Because of this confusion, the Macintosh winds up acting as if there is still an "in use" file or folder inside the problem folder, even though there is not. Thus, it does not allow the folder from hell to be deleted. This can be an especially difficult problem to solve. Here's how to try.

Rename the Folder   Then try to trash it. It's unlikely to work, but easy to try.

Create a New Folder with the Same Name   The easiest solution, if it works, is to create a new folder with exactly the same name as the problem folder. Make sure you create it in a different location (such as within a separate folder) from the problem folder, or you will not be able to give the new folder the same name (since two folders at the same location cannot have identical names). Then drag the new folder to the same location as the problem folder. The Macintosh asks you whether you want to replace the problem folder with the new one (see Figure 6-28). Click OK. Now try to delete this replacement folder. If it works, the folder from hell is gone!

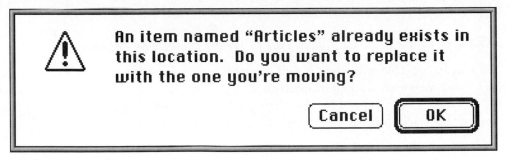

An item named "Articles" already exists in this location. Do you want to replace it with the one you're moving?

Cancel   OK

Figure 6-28   Click OK to try to delete a folder from hell

Utilities to the Rescue   Disk First Aid or the other repair utilities (such as MacTools or Norton Utilities) can usually fix this problem. A special shareware utility, called HellFolderFix, is specifically designed to combat this problem. However, it only works in System 6. This problem may also be caused by a bug that appears to be limited to version 7.0 (not 7.0.1 or later), with file sharing in use. The bug also typically prevents renaming of folders, including the hard disk icon itself, in addition to possibly preventing deleting of a folder. In this case, special utilities such as Apple's Rename Rescue or a shareware utility called UnlockFolder may fix the problem.

SEE: • Fix-It #10 on Disk First Aid and Fix-It #13 on other repair utilities

Deleting Damaged Files

Sometimes you will have trouble deleting a damaged file. Often, when you try to do so, you will get an ID = -39 error message. Damaged font files and font suitcases seem particularly prone to this sort of problem. If this happens, try any or all of the following:

Create a New File with the Same Name   Create a new file, of any type, with the same name as the problem file. Drag the dummy file to the location of the problem file. The Macintosh should ask whether you want to replace the problem file. Click OK. If it successfully replaces the problem file, now try to delete the dummy file. It should work.

Drag the file out of the System Folder   If the file is in your System Folder, such as a font file, try dragging it out of the System Folder and then restarting. Then try to delete the file. For a problem font file, you may have to first drag out the entire Fonts folder.

Restart with Extensions Off   Hold down the shift key at startup. Now try to delete the file. This, again, is useful for problem font files, especially if you are using an extension such as Suitcase.

SEE: • Chapter 9 on damaged font files for more specific advice on this problem

When All of the Preceding Steps Fail to Delete the File or Folder

You may have problems that go beyond an inability to delete a file or folder. It's once again time for a more scattergun approach.

Restart the Macintosh   If you haven't already done so, restart your Macintosh. This alone may solve the problem.

Rebuild the Desktop   Rebuild the desktop. Then try to delete the file or folder again.

SEE: • Fix-It #9 on rebuilding the desktop

Start Up from Another Disk   If this does not work, try restarting from an alternate startup disk. Try to delete the file or folder now.

Try a Finder Alternative   You may be able to delete the file or folder using a utility such as DiskTop rather than the Finder.

Attempt to Repair the Disk   If you haven't already done so, run Disk First Aid and, if necessary, any other disk repair utility you have (such as MacTools and Norton Utilities). Repair any problems that are discovered.

SEE: • Chapter 5 for more details on disk-related problems
• Fix-It #10 on Disk First Aid and Fix-It #13 on other repair utilities

Reformat the Disk   If the problem persists, reformat the entire disk. First back up the disk, reformat it, and then restore the contents of the disk from your backups. This should almost always solve the problem.

SEE: • Chapter 2 on Apple HD SC Setup
• Fix-It #15 on reformatting disks

If None of the Preceding Steps Work   If none of this works, there is probably some file (most likely in the System Folder) that you are reintroducing to the disk (when you restore the disk from your backup) that is causing the problem. You can continue to search for this problem file by yourself—by testing for INIT conflicts, for example. But if your patience begins to wear thin at this point, seek some outside help.

SEE: • Fix-It #4 on problems with system extensions and control panels
• Fix-It #18 on seeking outside help

When You Can't Rename a File or Folder or Volume

Symptoms:

You try to rename a file in the Finder, but you are unable to get the I-beam cursor to appear and the text remains uneditable.

Causes:

Most often, there is nothing wrong. You just need to follow correct procedures to get the I-beam to appear. Otherwise, for volume names, the problem may be that file sharing is on or you are experiencing an unusual system software bug.

What to do:

1. To get the I-beam to appear, from an icon view, click once in the area where the name of the file is (not the icon). Then wait for the name to highlight and the I-beam to appear. Otherwise, you can click in any part of the icon and press the Return key. You should now be able to edit the name. Remember a name cannot be more than 31 characters long or contain a colon (:).

2. For files: if the previous step fails to work, the file may be locked. Select Get Info and uncheck the Locked box, if it is checked.

3. Some files have locked names even if their Get Info box is not locked. This is because a special file attribute called *Name Locked* has been checked. This typically would only occur for certain system software files, such as the System and Finder. If for some reason you need to rename these files, you will have to uncheck this attribute and then restart.

   SEE: • Chapter 8, "What Are Finder Flags (Attributes)?," for more details

4. For volume names (such as hard disks) and/or for folders that cannot be renamed: turn file sharing off. (Alternatively, for folders only, select the folder, then select the Sharing command from the Finder's File menu and make sure that the *Can't be moved, renamed, or deleted* option is unchecked.) This will usually solve the problem. Otherwise, you may have a rare bug that apparently afflicts only System 7.0 (not 7.0.1 or later). In this case, special utilities such as Apple's *Rename Rescue* or a shareware utility called *UnlockFolder* may fix the problem.

5. Otherwise, this may be a symptom of a more general problem of a damaged file or disk.

   SEE: • Fix It #10, #12, and #14 for more on fixing damaged files and disks

When You Can't Save or Copy a File

Symptoms:

Saving a File

You try to save a file from a Save dialog box, but you are unable to do so. Usually, you get an error message such as *Disk is locked; there is not enough room on the disk* or *Disk is full* (see Figure 6-29).

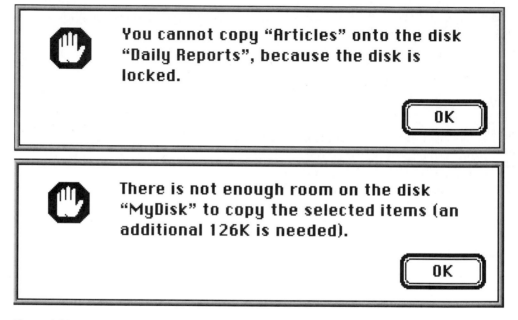

Figure 6-29 Messages that appear when you try to copy files to a locked disk or to a disk with less unused space left than is needed for the file(s) to be copied

Copying or Replacing a File

You try to copy a file (to another disk or to another folder on the same disk), but the copy does not complete successfully. Instead, you get an error message. In some cases, it may say that you cannot copy or replace the file because it is *in use* or because you do not have *access permission*. In more serious cases, it may say *The file couldn't be read and was skipped (unknown error)* or some other similar message (see Figure 6-30).

Figure 6-30 Ominous messages such as these may appear when you try to copy files from the Finder

Causes:

In most cases, the cause is evident from the error message and easy to solve. If you try to save a 100K file to a floppy disk that only has 20K of empty space left, you get an error message saying that you cannot do this. Similarly, you cannot copy or save anything to a locked floppy disk. Files that are open cannot be replaced and sometimes cannot be copied.

More rarely, you may be unable to save a file from within an application, even though the disk is unlocked and there seems to be sufficient space available. This probably means there is a bug in the application software.

The most troublesome problem is when you get the message that the file you are trying to copy could not be read or could not be written, usually referred to as *disk errors*. This sometimes happens when you are trying to copy too many items at one time. Otherwise, it almost always means a problem with defective disk media, commonly referred to as bad blocks. If the file cannot be read (read error), it means that the damage is to the area of the disk where the file now exists. If the file cannot be written (write error), it means the damage is to the area where the Macintosh is trying to create the copy. If you are trying to make a copy from one disk to another, *read errors* refer to the source disk and *write errors* refer to the destination disk.

Sometimes you get a message that says a file could not be *verified*. Functionally, this is similar to a write error. It means that the error went undetected when the file was first written, but was caught when the disk was rechecked (as is normally done by the Finder prior to completing a copy operation to a floppy disk).

Write (and verification) errors are definitely the lesser of two evils. It means that your file is still intact and that the damage is in a presently unused area of the destination disk. Read errors mean that the damage is to the area presently containing the file. In this case, the file is almost assuredly damaged, perhaps beyond repair.

What to do:

For Problems with Locked or Full Disks

Follow the Advice in the Alert Message These problems are usually remedied simply by paying attention to the alert message that appears. Thus, if the message indicates that the disk is locked, unlock the disk. If the message indicates that the disk is full or that there is not enough room, you either have to go to the Finder and delete some other files from the disk (to free up more space for the file to be saved) or save the file to another disk.

SEE: • "When You Can't Delete a File or Folder," earlier in this chapter, for more on locked disks

For "Disk Is Full" Message When Disk Is Not Full If you know that the disk is not full or think that it should not be full, despite the message, try restarting and/or rebuilding the desktop. This alone may cure the problem. Also check for temporary files that may have unexpectedly stayed on your disk (if you use PrintMonitor, especially check in the PrintMonitor Documents folder in your System Folder). Otherwise, you probably have a damaged disk. Try to repair it. If you use MacTools' TrashBack, your disk is likely to appear to fill up if you start up with TrashBack off (as described in Chapter 2). The solution is either to purge TrashBack's files or restart with TrashBack on.

SEE: • Fix-It #9 on rebuilding the desktop
      • Fix-Its #10 and #13 on repairing disks

BY THE WAY ▶

DON'T TRY TO SAVE A FILE THAT IS CURRENTLY IN THE TRASH

Don't open and select the Save command for a file that is in the Trash. Why anyone would want to do this is unclear to me, but apparently people occasionally try this. Doing this can lead to system crashes and other assorted problems. Using Save As (and saving it to a new location) is okay, but using Save is not.

MOVING FILES ON A LOCKED DISK TO THE DESKTOP

If you try to move (or copy) a file on a locked disk (floppy or CD-ROM or whatever) to another folder on that same disk, you will correctly get a message that says you cannot do it because the disk is locked. However, if you instead try to move a file from the locked disk to the desktop, you will get the somewhat strange message seen in the top of Figure 6-31. Here the Mac is telling you that, while you cannot move the file to the locked disk's desktop (because the disk is locked), it will copy the file to your startup disk (if you wish) and place it on the startup disk's desktop. Often, this is what you are trying to accomplish anyway. If so, click OK. Otherwise, for floppy disks, an alternative is to unlock the disk (CD-ROM disks, of course, can never be unlocked).

In one strange case, when I tried to move a folder on my hard drive to the desktop, I got the message seen in the bottom of Figure 6-31. It seemed to indicate that the desktop itself was locked. Since there was no reason to expect this to be the case, I suspected that some software on the disk was damaged. Rebuilding the desktop did not help. Ultimately, the problem turned out to be due to Directory damage. I was able to fix it using MacTools.

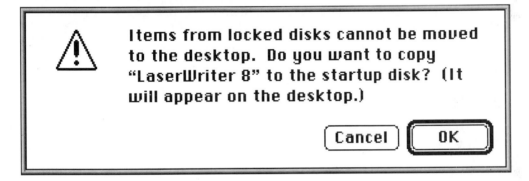

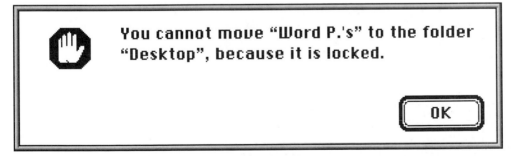

Figure 6-31   Top: This message appears when moving a file to the desktop of a locked floppy disk; Bottom: This message turned out to be due to Directory damage

For Files That Are "In Use" and "Illegal Access Permission"

If you try to replace a file that is currently open or in use, such as by copying a new file with the same name to the same location as the open file, you will be unable to do this. Instead, you will get the same sort of "in use" alert message as occurs when you try to delete such a file (see Figure 6-32, top). This is because replacing the file requires deleting the original version. For application and document files, the obvious solution is to close the open file. For control panels and extensions that are in use, drag the "in use" file out of the System Folder to the Trash. Then move the new copy to the intended location. You may have to restart before you can delete the file now in the Trash.

SEE: • "Check If the File Is Currently Open or in Use" in "When You Can't Delete a File or Folder," earlier in this chapter, for more details
• Chapter 9 for special problems replacing a font file

In some cases, if you try to copy a file that is currently open, you will get a similar "in use" message (see Figure 6-32, middle). However, if you are trying to transfer an open file across a network, via file sharing, you may instead get a message that says you have "illegal access permission," even if you do have proper access permission. For me, this seemed to occur especially if I was using a copy utility called CopyDoubler (see Figure 6-32, bottom). In either of these situations, the simple solution is to close the document (or quit the application) and then make the copy.

However, when using file sharing, a message that says you do not have the proper "access privileges" may really mean what it says. I discuss this issue in Chapter 11.

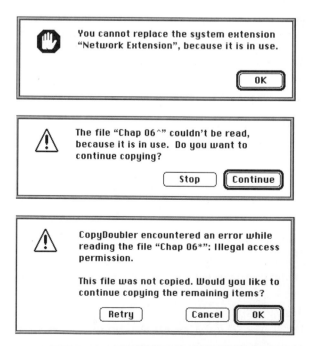

Figure 6-32 One of these messages may appear if you try to replace or copy a currently open file

SEE: • "Take Note: Files Locked by the Performa or by System 7.5's General Control Panel," earlier in this chapter, for another example of an access permission problem
• Chapter 11 for more on file sharing and illegal access permission

For Problems Due to a Disk Error

Disk errors refer to those situations when, while trying to save or copy a file, you get an error message that says that the file could not be read or could not be written. If you were trying to copy more than one file, click the Continue button in the error message. This copies any of the remaining files (assuming they are not having a problem themselves). Otherwise, you can click Cancel and do the following.

Try to Copy Files Again, in Smaller Groups If Appropriate   Check which file(s) did not copy. Try again to copy the file or files that were not copied successfully the first time. Then try one or two more times. Sometimes the problem was a short-lived glitch, and one of your next tries will be successful.

This is especially worth doing if you were trying to copy several files at one time. This can overwhelm the Finder's processing and/or memory capacity, causing the disk error to occur. You may even get a separate error message indicating that there is insufficient memory to copy the files. In these cases, copying one file (or at least a fewer number of files) at a time should solve the problem.

For Floppy Disks, Use a Special Copy Utility   If you get an error message that the disk could not be read, while trying to copy files from a floppy disk using the Finder, try instead to make the copy of the entire disk using a special copy utility. Disk Copy is a utility from Apple that can be used for this purpose. Norton Utilities includes a similar program called Floppier; MacTools has one called FastCopy. These sometimes work when the Finder fails.

Alternatively, you may be able to copy files from a damaged floppy disk using Apple File Exchange software (included on System 7 software disks prior to System 7.5), even though that is not the main purpose of this software.

If This Does Not Work

• **Read errors**
A read error often means that the file is hopelessly damaged. Your best bet is to replace the file with a backup copy. If you do not have a backup copy, you may still be able to repair or recover data from the disk.

SEE: • Fix-It #14 on rescuing damaged files

• **Write (or verify) errors**
If a write error (or a verification error) occurs, try copying the file(s) to a different disk. This should work fine, since a write error indicates that the problem is with the original destination disk.

You should then back up all unbacked-up files that already exist on the disk that generated the write error. You may get read errors as you try to do this, indicating that some files on the disk are themselves damaged. Try to recover data from these files, as needed.

SEE: • Fix-It #14 on rescuing damaged files

For both read and write errors, in addition to any attempt to repair files, check for bad blocks: Disk errors of either sort almost always mean there are bad blocks on the disk, usually due to media damage (as first described in Chapter 2). The damage is on the source disk for read errors and on the destination disk for write errors. If you detect any bad blocks, you probably have to reformat the disk.

If the disk is a floppy disk, you are probably better off discarding it instead of reformatting it. For the price of a floppy disk, why take chances? Even if you had a read or write error that appeared to vanish after repeated attempts to copy a file, do not trust the disk. If the media is bad, the error will return again! Be happy you were able to copy the file first. Get rid of the disk.

By the way, by using repeated copy attempts, even if you are eventually able to copy a file that had triggered a read error, open the file to make sure it is okay. Sometimes, the file is damaged even though the Finder does not report an error.

If the damaged disk is your only copy of an application disk, contact the manufacturer for a replacement. If you are a registered user of the software, you can usually do this for a nominal fee.

SEE: • Fix-It #14 on damaged files
      • Fix-It #15 on reformatting

BY THE WAY ▶

DISK ERRORS WHEN USING APPLE'S RESTORE UTILITY

If you get a disk error when restoring files to a disk using the Restore utility (included with Performas), you can probably ignore it. For some reason, this happens when it encounters locked files, but the restore will still proceed unhindered.

When the Going Gets Weird . . .

 ### Symptoms:

While you are using an application (or control panel or desk accessory), something unexpected happens—something not covered by or not explained by any of the previous sections of this chapter.

This could be anything: a command that ceases to function (especially one that previously functioned just fine) or a dialog box that doesn't come up when requested. Or it could be anything else that seems to run counter to what the software's documentation (or common sense) says should happen.

This is a catch-all category that also summarizes many of the suggestions made earlier in this chapter. Though it is hard to generalize here, the list tends to run from the easiest to solve and most common causes toward more complex causes.

Causes:

The common causes include hardware incompatibilities, software bugs, missing accessory files, corrupted files, INIT conflicts, and memory problems.

What to do:

Scroll, Close, Quit, Restart

An impressive variety of problems with an application can be solved by simply scrolling the current display off the screen and then scrolling it back again (to find that everything wrong with the display has been corrected), or by closing a window or document and then reopening it, or by quitting the application and then relaunching it. Or finally, by simply restarting. Give these a try before proceeding further.

TAKE NOTE ▶

FLASHING ICONS IN THE MENU BAR AND UNEXPECTED ALERT NOISES

If you suddenly see a flashing icon in the menu bar, especially in the Apple menu, or if an alert sound keeps going off repeatedly for no particular reason, these are both usually requests to get your attention. What is probably going on is that some application, working in the background, needs you to do something (such as respond to an error message). To find out which application is making this request, go to the Application menu on the right side of the menu bar. The application in the list that is preceded by a diamond symbol is the application you want. Select it. You will soon see what needs to be done.

The only other likely possibility here is that some extension function is the cause of a flashing icon. For example, Apple's Alarm Clock desk accessory will do this when an alarm goes off. Similarly, Retrospect will do this when it is time to run a scheduled backup. In these cases, the program is not listed in the Application menu. You simply have to know what the program is by the nature of the icon.

If the Problem Results in a System Error of Any Sort

Check Chapter 4 for the information on your particular type of system error. Return to this section only if Chapter 4 fails to provide a solution.

Check for Hardware Incompatibilities Between Your Hardware and the Application in Use

SEE: • Fix-It #1 on incompatibilities between hardware and software

Check for Damage to or Other Problems with the Application's Preferences File

SEE: • Fix-It #2 on problems with preferences files

Check Whether One of the Application's Accessory Files Is Missing or Mislocated

SEE: • Fix-It #3 on missing or mislocated accessory files

Check Whether the Application or Any of Its Accessory Files Are Damaged

Start by replacing just the application file from a copy on the original disk. To do this, first delete the suspected defective file before making the new copy. If this does not solve the problem, reinstall the application together with all its accessory files. If the program has an Installer utility, use it (if it requires the use of an Installer utility, you may not have the prior option to replace only the application).

As always, when dealing with potentially damaged files, check for possible media damage to the disk itself. If the original application disk is damaged, you may still have an undamaged version of the files on your regular backups.

SEE: • "When You Can't Save or Copy a File" earlier in this chapter
       • Fix-It #14 on damaged files

Consider Whether the Problem Is Due to a Bug in the Application

There is no way you can repair a bug yourself. This must be done by the manufacturer of the software in the form of a bug-fixed upgrade of the application. If you suspect a bug, you should call the company's technical support personnel to check it out. They may already know about it and be able to tell you what to do.

SEE: • Fix-It #18 on calling technical support and getting upgrades

In general, make sure you are using the latest version of the application, especially if you are using a version of the system software that was released after the version of the application you are using. Newer versions tend to fix bugs and conflicts from earlier versions.

How convoluted can a bug get? Pretty convoluted. For example, this description of reported bugs in a popular word processing program (which I leave unnamed, since it has already been fixed) appeared in the May 1992 issue of *Macworld* magazine: "It . . . strips certain . . . characters (including em dashes and curly quotes) from a file when exporting to MacWrite format. Crashes may occur when checking grammar or during other memory intensive activities on the Plus and SE (not the Classic), even with adequate memory available."

BY THE WAY ▶

PROBLEMS WITH RUNNING IN THE BACKGROUND

A program that continues to work even when it is not the active application is said to run in the background. System extensions and many control panels do this, as first described in Chapters 1 and 2. Some applications do this as well. For example, the Finder in System 7 can complete a copy operation in the background. PrintMonitor (see Chapter 7) runs in the background. Background-acting programs make it seem like two things are happening at once, but it is really an illusion. What actually happens is that background activities time-share, grabbing time whenever the foreground application is sufficiently idle.

Depending on the nature of the background activity, you may or may not notice an overall slowing down of the foreground activity as the background action proceeds. For example, cursor movements can become jerky or dialog boxes may take longer to appear. In the most extreme cases, a conflict may occur between a foreground and a background activity, with the result that one or both of the programs cease to function. A system crash may even result.

If you suspect that a problem is due to a background processing conflict:

- ***Pause your foreground activity briefly.*** *Some background activities halt while you type and resume again when you pause. Thus, if you take a brief rest, the background activity is given priority and completes faster. When you resume, you are no longer bothered by a slower response time and jerky cursor movements. Transient problems with PrintMonitor can be avoided this way. Doing this makes practical sense only if the background activity does not take too long to complete.*

- ***Turn off the background activity temporarily, if such an option is available.*** *For example, for control panels, there is usually an on/off button in the control panel window. Turn it back on when you are no longer using a foreground activity that conflicts with the background processing.*

Otherwise, you have to forgo the background processing altogether, either by keeping the potential background activity in the foreground until it is completed, or (when all else fails) by not using the background-processing program.

Check for INIT Conflicts

INIT conflicts are a common cause of almost any problem you may have with an application or control panel.

SEE: • Fix-It #4 for detailed procedures on how to identify and resolve INIT conflicts

INIT problems can cause difficulties either with using an application or with using the INIT itself. INITs that modify either the normal functioning of the Finder or basic system functions (such as Open and Save dialog boxes) are especially likely culprits. The control panels of Now Utilities are a prime example here. Surprisingly, problems with Now Utilities can often be fixed simply by replacing the preferences file associated with the problem control panel (located in the Now Utilities Preferences folder that is inside the Preferences folder of the System Folder). RAM Doubler, CEToolbox (used by QuickKeys), ATM, and virtually any fax software are among many other common INITs that are prone to causing problems. Similarly, be wary of any extensions that actively process information in the background, such as Disk Express II or the prevention checking features of MacTools, Norton Utilities, and Apple Personal Diagnostics. Finally, be careful never to use two extensions that do essentially the same thing, such as two screen savers. This is almost a sure way to cause problems.

In most cases, these INITs are regularly updated to resolve identified problems, so make sure you have the latest version. With ATM, try turning off (or on) the options in the ATM control panel, particularly the "Substitute for missing fonts" checkbox to see if that fixes the problem.

In general, check the ReadMe files that come with these programs to find out about any already known conflicts. If you have access, check on-line services for problems reported by other users (often accompanied by answers from the publisher of the software). If you are still stumped, call the program's technical support line.

Installer Alert: Installer utilities (used to first install a given software product on your hard disk) generally don't get along well with INITs. If an Installer utility fails to work correctly for any reason, restart with extensions off (holding down the Shift key at startup) and try again. You will likely be successful now.

SEE: • Chapter 9 for more on ATM
       • Fix-It #2 on preferences files
       • Fix-It #18 on calling technical support and getting upgrades

Check for Memory-Related Problems

Insufficient available memory is yet another leading cause of problems. In these cases, you will most likely get an error message that tells you the general nature of the difficulty.

SEE: • Chapter 4 for resolving memory problems that lead to a system error, such as a freeze or unexpected quit
       • Fix-It #6 for more general advice on solving memory-related problems

Check for System Software Problems

Some problems with applications can be solved by reinstalling the system software. This is particularly advised if you get an error message that says needed system resources are missing.

Also, install the latest System Update available. For example, if you are still using System 7.1, be sure to install System Update 3.0. It fixes literally dozens of problems, some of which may seem application-specific but are really due to the system software. Also, consider upgrading to a newer version of system software, if you are not yet using the most recent version.

SEE: • Chapter 2, "By the way: What Exactly Does a System Update Update?"
 • Fix-It #5 on system software problems

If All Else Fails, It's Time to Round Up the Usual Suspects

The cause may extend beyond the problem application itself. For example, check for a possible virus infection. Check for damage to the invisible Directory files. Let your particular symptoms guide you as to which Fix-Its seem most relevant. Try those first. For example:

SEE: • **Fix-It #7 to check for viruses**
        • **Fix-Its #10 and #13 to check for damage to the Directory files**
        • **Fix-It #9 to rebuild the desktop**

Chapter Summary

After briefly reviewing some basics about opening and saving files, this chapter took a tour of the major problems that can occur when working with files, especially applications and data documents. In particular, the chapter focused on problems in locating a file, launching an application, opening a document, deleting a file or folder, and saving or copying files.

One major topic not mentioned here was problems with printing files. This is the subject of the next chapter.

Chapter 7

When You Can't Print

The Paperless Office?

In the prophesied paperless office of the future, there will be no need for printed output. However, quite the contrary is true today. Printing is one of the most common and critical of all computer activities. For most tasks, the job isn't done until you print it out—which means that if you have a problem printing, you have serious trouble.

This chapter focuses on just one of the many possible printing-related problems you could have. But it is a big one: the failure of a document to print—either because the printing never gets started or because it stops before it is finished.

Many other types of printing problems are either mentioned only in passing or not mentioned at all in this chapter. So, if you are looking for the answer to one of these problems, let me be clear about what is *not* covered in this chapter:

Formatting Problems   If the printer spits out your document but the document's appearance is not what you expected, don't look here for help. These sort of problems are the domain of Chapters 9 and 10.

Problems Specific to Non-Apple Printers   Although all printers work similarly on the Macintosh, each has unique options. I stay as general as possible here, addressing those issues and problems that are common to all printers. However, when I do need to be specific, I focus on Apple's PostScript LaserWriters. This is because they are the most popular printers currently sold for the Macintosh and because other Macintosh printers tend to have fewer options and therefore fewer specific problems. Information about other Apple printers (non-PostScript LaserWriters, StyleWriters, ImageWriters) will crop up occasionally. However, if you are looking for advice specific to a Hewlett-Packard or other non-Apple printer, you won't find too much help here. Sorry.

However, many non-Apple laser printers use the same LaserWriter driver as do Apple laser printers. If this is the case for your non-Apple printer, you will find this chapter to be more directly relevant.

Problems with the Printer Itself   This chapter covers some general problems related to printing hardware, such as proper connection of the printing cables. Aside from that, this chapter largely avoids a discussion of hardware-related problems (such as paper jams or replacing the toner). Instead, the focus, as is true throughout this book, is on software-related problems. Check your printer's manual for troubleshooting advice concerning your particular printer's hardware.

DIFFERENT TYPES OF PRINTERS

Three major categories of printers are commonly connected to Macintoshes: dot-matrix, inkjet, or laser printers:

- *Dot-matrix printers. A dot-matrix printer uses a series of small pins to hammer against an inked ribbon. Which pins are hammering at a given moment determines what is printed on the paper. These printers are no longer popular, except for printing stencils or forms that have multiple copy layers. The ImageWriter is Apple's dot-matrix printer.*

- *Inkjet printers. Inkjet printers work by shooting ministreams of ink from a cartridge onto the page. Apple's StyleWriters and Hewlett-Packard's DeskWriters are two popular examples. Color inkjet printers are the least expensive way to create decent color output.*

- *Laser printers. Laser printers use a printing method similar to that of a photocopier. The quality of laser printer output is the best of any of the printer types described here. For Macintosh users, Apple's LaserWriters are the most common example of this type of printer.*

This chapter focuses primarily on laser printers, though much of the information applies to any type of printer.

Your Dialog Boxes May Vary

Printer drivers (to be described in more detail shortly) are the files in your Extensions folder with the names of printers. Generally, you want to make sure that you have the driver whose name matches the model of printer you are using.

The information in Page Setup and Print dialog boxes, accessed from most File menus, is determined by what printer driver you use. Unfortunately, making sweeping generalizations about these dialog boxes and other printer-related commands is becoming nearly impossible. One obvious reason for this is that with the proliferation of different printers, differences in the appearance of the dialog boxes is similarly proliferating. However, even if you stick with the same printer, these dialog boxes and commands may vary, sometimes dramatically, because there may be more than one printer driver that you can use with a given printer. Here are two especially important examples of this.

LaserWriter Versus LaserWriter 8

Until 1993, the standard LaserWriter printer driver, the one used for PostScript LaserWriters, was called simply LaserWriter. While minor differences occurred as the system software version changed, it remained remarkably the same for several years. In 1993, Apple and Adobe jointly released a major upgrade to the LaserWriter driver called LaserWriter 8. It was designed primarily to take advantage of new features available in Adobe's latest version of the PostScript language, called *PostScript Level 2*.

It also increases printing speed with some printers. Using PostScript Level 2 also requires a printer that has the Level 2 instructions built-in. Older LaserWriter models, and even some newer ones, do not have this (check with your printer's manual to find out about your particular printer). Thus, users of these older models would gain little by upgrading to LaserWriter 8. There are also potential problems that might result from upgrading because of incompatibilities between LaserWriter 8 and some existing software.

Thus, LaserWriter 8 is not considered as a universal replacement for the standard LaserWriter driver. In fact, both drivers are still included with System 7.5 and you can choose which one you want. So if you suspect that a problem is due to the LaserWriter 8 driver, try shifting to the older LaserWriter driver instead. Also, when installing LaserWriter 8, be sure to do so using the Installer utility, following all directions on any ReadMe files or in printed documentation.

More recently, as applications and the LaserWriter 8 driver itself are upgraded, incompatibility problems have diminished. At the same time, some applications (such as Adobe Illustrator) now require LaserWriter 8 in order to work properly. Thus, users are increasingly shifting to LaserWriter 8 no matter what LaserWriter printer they have.

QuickDraw Versus QuickDraw GX

In order to display or print almost anything, all Macintoshes depend on something called QuickDraw, built into the Macintosh ROM and to some extent into system software. In 1994, Apple released QuickDraw GX, an optional upgrade to Quick-Draw. It is included with System 7.5, though you can use System 7.5 without it. You decide whether to install it or instead go with the standard non-GX version of Quick-Draw.

Among its other features, QuickDraw GX includes a complete overhaul of the Macintosh printing software. Everything is different. Each printer will need a separate GX version of its printer driver. Thus, LaserWriter users now have to contend with LaserWriter GX in addition to the aforementioned LaserWriter and LaserWriter 8. The Page Setup and Print dialog boxes for LaserWriter GX are completely redesigned from either of the two previous drivers, with many new options.

I expect that, in the short run, many users will choose to ignore QuickDraw GX. This is because it takes up a significant amount of disk space, increases the minimum RAM you need just to run your system, and many of its features only work if you are using an application that has been rewritten to be "aware" of QuickDraw GX. Because of this, I am putting off a discussion of QuickDraw GX and its associated print-related dialog boxes until the more general discussion of System 7.5, in Chapter 12.

And so . . .

The result of all of this is that, for the descriptions of LaserWriter printing in this chapter, I will almost exclusively focus on the LaserWriter 8 driver. However, for a point of comparison, Figure 7-1 shows how the Page Setup dialog boxes differs across the three versions of the LaserWriter driver.

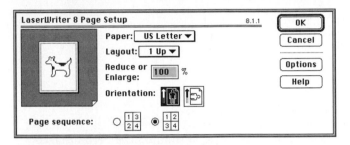

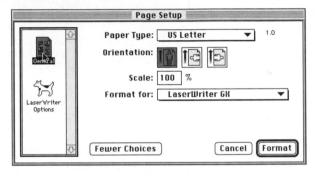

Figure 7-1   The Page Setup dialog boxes of LaserWriter (top), LaserWriter 8 (middle), and LaserWriter GX (bottom)

BY THE WAY ▶

WHAT EVER HAPPENED TO . . . ?

If you have upgraded from System 6 to System 7, you may have noticed that two files present in System 6, LaserWriter Prep and Backgrounder, are no longer found in System 7. These files have been combined into System 7's LaserWriter driver and Print Monitor, respectively. If you do find them in your System Folder, you can ignore them or delete them.

However, these files are still used in System 6. So when you change or upgrade the LaserWriter driver and PrintMonitor in System 6, be sure to replace LaserWriter Prep and Backgrounder as well.

If you are using QuickDraw GX, you may additionally note that PrintMonitor is now missing. Again, this is as it should be. The functions of PrintMonitor have been rolled into the new GX print architecture.

SEE: • Chapter 9 on PostScript printers and text printing
       • Chapter 10 on PostScript printers and graphics printing
       • Chapter 12 for more on QuickDraw GX

When Things Go Right

Before looking at how things can go wrong when printing a document, let's start by looking at what normally happens when things go as expected. The three steps to no-hassle printing are as follows:

1. Select the Chooser.
2. Select Page Setup.
3. Use the Print command.

Step 1: Select the Chooser

The Chooser is a desk accessory that is an essential part of the Macintosh system software. It's almost certainly already on your startup disk. It should have been installed when your System Folder was initially created. If it was not, you should get it on to your startup disk now.

 When to use it:

You use the Chooser, as its name implies, to tell the Macintosh which printer to use when printing. Even if you have only one printer connected to your Macintosh, you still need to use the Chooser, at least once, to initially identify that printer for the Macintosh. After that, the Macintosh remembers your choice. You do not have to use the Chooser again unless you want to change your selection.

 What to do:

Select Chooser from the Apple Menu

This opens up the Chooser window, from which you make the other selections in this section.

LaserWriter Utility and wait until it finishes reading information from your printer. Now you can select commands. For example:

1. *To change the name of a LaserWriter printer as it appears in the Chooser, select Name Printer from its Utilities menu. Enter the name you want to use.*

2. *To put a stop to the startup page that spits out every time you turn on your LaserWriter, select Set Startup Page from the Utilities menu, and check the Off button.*

Among other things that LaserWriter Utility can do is: (3) provide a list of what PostScript fonts are built into your LaserWriter (as detailed in Chapter 9, "How to Identify a PostScript Font," (4) manually download fonts to the printer (also detailed in Chapter 9, "Technically Speaking: Automatic Versus Manual Downloading").

TAKE NOTE ▶

WHAT IS APPLETALK?

AppleTalk refers to a method of networking computers and peripherals together so that, for example, several users could all share the same printer. It is the equivalent of the language that is used to send information over the network. It is a language that all Macintoshes understand. To make an AppleTalk network connection:

1. *Make sure the hardware you want to connect to the network is all AppleTalk-compatible. Every Macintosh computer comes with built-in AppleTalk support. However, not all printers do. For example, the LaserWriter LS does not support AppleTalk, but the Personal LaserWriter NTR does. The manual that came with your printer should provide this information. Otherwise, check with your dealer.*

2. *Connect the hardware. Usually, this is done via special networking cables. Apple's cabling system is called LocalTalk. Other companies make competing cabling systems that connect via the same ports. A popular LocalTalk alternative is PhoneNet, which uses ordinary phone wire to make connections. It is still basically a LocalTalk system.*

   On one end, the cable is connected to the Macintosh, typically through the serial port. If your Mac has two serial ports, AppleTalk is available only via the printer port, not the modem port. So AppleTalk printers can never be connected through the modem port (even though non-AppleTalk printers can typically be connected through either port). If your Macintosh has only one serial port, it supports AppleTalk.

   On the printer end, connect the cable to the serial port. Just remember (especially for PhoneNet-like systems), the cable connected to the end device at each end of the chain may need a special terminating resistor, plugged into the empty slot in the phone plug.

   In some cases, you may have the option of connecting over an EtherNet network rather than LocalTalk. If so, you will have a special EtherNet port that you use instead of the serial port. Check with your manual or seek outside help for details on setting up a EtherNet network. While details of using EtherNet are beyond the scope of this book, most of what is in this chapter applies equally well to either type of network.

3. *Turn on the AppleTalk option (select Active) from the Chooser.*

4. *Open the Network control panel and select the appropriate icon. Most likely, it will have "LocalTalk Built In" as its default selection. As you are probably using LocalTalk, this is just fine. Leave it as it is. If you are using EtherNet or some other type of networking protocol, you will need to select that option.*

SEE: • **Chapter 11 for more on networking**
      • **Fix-It #17 for more details on cable connections**

Make AppleTalk Active or Inactive

Thus far in this book, I have minimized discussion of networking issues. However, we must make an exception here. Here's why: Certain printers, most notably the majority of Apple's LaserWriter models, require the use of an AppleTalk network in order to work—even if it is just one Macintosh connected to one printer.

Historically, this is because when the LaserWriters were first released, they were so expensive that no one expected them to be used by just one person. Today, however, individually owned LaserWriters are common.

- **For AppleTalk printers, AppleTalk should be active**
  For AppleTalk printers, you need to turn on AppleTalk before you can print anything. Do this by clicking AppleTalk's Active button, located in the lower right-hand side of the Chooser window (see Figure 7-2).

  By the way, occasionally, the AppleTalk Active button may read "Active after restart" indicating that AppleTalk will not be active until you restart. This is especially common after system crashes. Just restart, as it requests, and all will be fine.

- **For non-AppleTalk printers, AppleTalk should be inactive**

TECHNICALLY SPEAKING ▶

APPLETALK ON AND OFF?

If you have a non-AppleTalk printer, you may still want your Macintosh connected to an AppleTalk network for other reasons (such as file sharing). In this case, you can connect the printer through the modem port and connect to the network through the printer port. AppleTalk is now turned on for the network even though AppleTalk is not used by the printer. Actually, with an option called GrayShare or ColorShare, available with some non-AppleTalk Apple printers (or with PrinterShare included with System 7.5), you can access a non-AppleTalk printer over a network (as long as the computer that the printer is connected to is on and is connected to the network).

By the way, some printers can be used with or without AppleTalk. For example, you can use an ImageWriter II on an AppleTalk network if you add a special card (available from Apple) to the printer and select the AppleTalk ImageWriter printer driver (as opposed to the standard ImageWriter driver).

Select a Printer by Clicking a Printer Driver Icon

You tell the Macintosh which printer you intend to use by selecting one from the display of printer icons on the left side of the Chooser dialog box. Normally, you select the icon that corresponds to the particular printer currently connected to your Macintosh.

These icons represent the different printers you can use (as well as possibly some networking options, such as AppleShare, which I will ignore for now). What printers

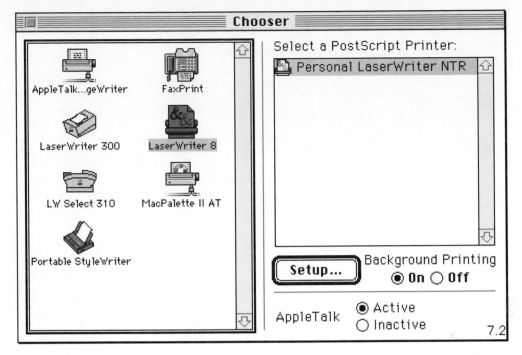

Figure 7-2 The Chooser, with the LaserWriter printer driver selected: Note that the name of the printer (NTR) is shown and selected, Background Printing is on, and AppleTalk is active

appear in the Chooser window is determined by which printer Chooser extensions (also called *printer drivers*) are located in the Extensions folder of your System Folder. If the icon you are looking for is not present, you need to add that printer driver to the Extensions folder before you can proceed. Printer drivers for all Apple printers are included as part of the system software (though you will need the latest version of the system software to have the drivers for the latest printers).

SEE: • "The Macintosh Can't Find the Printer," later in this chapter, for more details

Note especially that the LaserWriter/LaserWriter 8 drivers are used only for Post-Script LaserWriters. Non-PostScript LaserWriters, such as the Personal LaserWriter 300, have separate drivers. In a few cases, such as with the LaserWriter Select 310, even a PostScript LaserWriter has its own unique driver.

At the risk of stating the obvious, selecting a particular icon only lets you use that printer if it is physically connected to your Macintosh. The icon has no magical qualities.

Select Printer-Specific Options

- **Non-AppleTalk printers: Printer or modem port**
  If you selected a non-AppleTalk printer, you usually have an option to select an icon representing one of the *serial ports:* either the *printer port* or the *modem port* (see Figure 7-3). Select the icon that matches the port where the cable from your printer is connected. You can check the rear of your Macintosh to find out which port this is. Each port has an icon over it that matches the icon in the Chooser display. Despite their different names, the ports are almost identical. A non-AppleTalk printer can be successfully connected to either port.

  If your Mac has only one serial port (some PowerBooks now come this way), it acts as a combined printer and modem port. In most cases, you should select the modem port icon from the Chooser even though you are using a printer. If you have an internal Express modem, you may also have to change a control panel setting. If your Express Modem is version 1.5 or later, select Use Express Modem from the Express Modem control panel. If the modem is an earlier version, select Internal or Normal from the PowerBook Setup control panel.

- **AppleTalk printers: Select a printer name**
  If you selected an AppleTalk printer, the name of the printer should appear now in the scrollable box on the right-hand side of the dialog box—but again only if the printer is currently turned on and properly connected! Click the name of the printer you are using, if it is not already selected. Unless you are on a network with several printers, there should be only one name listed. For example, as seen in Figure 7-2, after you select the LaserWriter printer driver, the name *Personal Laser-Writer NTR* appears already selected.

- **LaserWriter 8 driver: Click the setup button**
  After you click the LaserWriter driver icon, a Setup button will appear in the Chooser window. If this is the first time you are using LaserWriter 8 with this printer, you should select the Setup button before you try any printing. To do this,

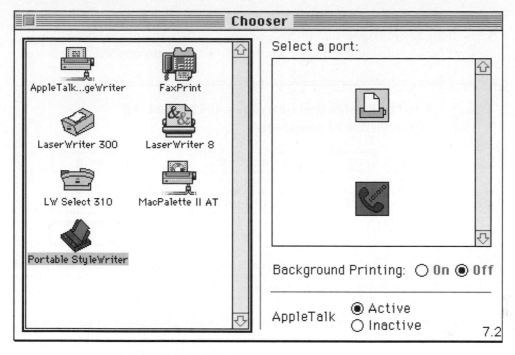

Figure 7-3 The Chooser with the ImageWriter driver selected; note the option to select either the printer port or the modem port

click the name of the printer (as listed in the right-hand side of the Chooser) and then click the Setup button.

(If no printer name is listed in the Chooser or if you have not yet selected a name, the Setup button will be dimmed and therefore unusable. Since a printer's name only appears here if the printer is connected and turned on, you must connect and turn on a printer before you can select Setup for it. If it is important for you to get around this restriction, try a freeware utility, called LaserWriter Patch, that alters the driver so that the Setup button is never dimmed).

If you are using LaserWriter 8.2 or a later version, after you select Setup the driver will automatically determine the correct setup for your selected printer. A series of messages will briefly appear on the screen. When they are gone, you're done with Setup. You only need to do this once for a given printer, not every time you reselect that printer. If a Setup has already been completed for a given printer, an icon for that printer will appear to the left of its name (as is the case for Laser-Writer NTR in Figure 7-2). If you see this icon, there is no need to bother with Setup unless you wish to make changes to the current settings. If you do reselect Setup after having already previously setup the printer, you will get the dialog box shown in Figure 7-4 (you can also get this dialog box the first time you select Setup by holding down the Command-Option keys).

One of the buttons in this dialog box is Auto Setup. Clicking this does exactly the same thing as what automatically happened the first time you selected Setup. Unless you are having some problem, there would usually be no reason to select this button.

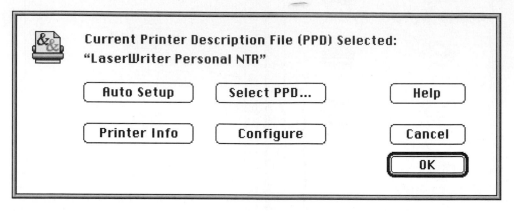

Figure 7-4 The Setup dialog box of LaserWriter 8.2

However, if you are using LaserWriter 8.1.1 or an earlier version, selecting Setup takes you to the Setup dialog box even if you are selecting Setup for the first time. In this case, you need to click Auto Setup to get a setup to take place.

You may well wonder what Setup is doing. Here's the scoop: If you properly installed LaserWriter 8, there will be a folder within your Extensions folder called *Printer Descriptions.* Within this folder are a collection of files, called *PostScript Printer Description (PPD)* files that cover every different model of LaserWriter that uses the LaserWriter 8 driver (or at least all those models available at the time your version of LaserWriter 8 was released). Non-Apple laser printers may come with their own PPD file that you can install. When you setup a printer, the Chooser automatically ferrets out the PPD file for your printer and loads it. Additionally, your printer itself is checked for what options it may have available, such as whether an optional paper tray is installed. All of this information is then used to configure your Page Setup and Print dialog boxes to specifically match your printer and its options.

If you never select Setup at all (or if there is no PPD file that matches your printer), the LaserWriter 8 driver will probably default to a PPD named General (also referred to as the Generic setup). If you have a choice, avoid the Generic setup. You will almost certainly be better off by selecting your printer-specific Setup.

Most of the time, Auto Setup will work fine. However, if needed, you can manually override its selections. To do this, click the Select PPD button (if you are using LaserWriter 8.1.1 or an earlier version, you will first need to select the More Choices button to access this and other buttons). This will bring up a scroll box listing all the PPD files in your Printer Descriptions folder. Just choose the particular PPD for your printer. It is possible to select a PPD file other than the one that matches your particular printer. If you do so, you may find options in the Print dialog box that your printer doesn't support (or supported options may be missing). However, when you simply select Print, the document should print out okay. Still, I wouldn't recommend doing this—and can't think of any reason you would want to do it.

Next, if desired, click the Configure button to access selection settings for certain printer-specific options. The remaining button in the Setup dialog box is "Printer Info." It doesn't allow you to change anything, but gives you a description of your printer's characteristics (such as its resolution, its installed memory, whether it supports PostScript Level 2 or not, and so on) that you may find informative.

Whatever you do, after you are done, close the Setup dialog box.

BY THE WAY ▶

SETUP FOR OTHER PRINTERS

Some other printers drivers, in addition to LaserWriter 8, also include a Setup button. However, what you will find there will be quite different. For example, for printers such as the StyleWriter II and the Color StyleWriter, this is where you activate Apple's non-AppleTalk printer sharing feature. There are no separate PPD lists to be found here.

- **Background printing: On or off**
  Background printing will appear as an option only if your printer supports this feature. Almost all models of LaserWriter do support it. You turn background printing on or off via buttons in the Chooser dialog box (see Figure 7-2).

  This useful feature returns control of the Macintosh to you very soon after you select Print, even before the first page is actually printed. The printing process continues in the background while you return to your other work. Thus, you can continue editing your document or work on a different application without halting the printing process. You can even select additional documents to be printed. They will just be added to the waiting queue.

  Without background printing, you would have to wait until your print job was completely finished before you could use your computer for something else. Since this could take many minutes, background printing can often be a big time-saver. However, turning background printing off usually speeds up the total time until completion of a given print job—which may be relevant if you are in a big hurry to get the job done. It may also occasionally be necessary to turn it off to prevent certain problems (as described later in this chapter). Still, for most users, background printing is definitely the way to go.

  Using background printing requires the presence of the PrintMonitor extension in the Extensions folder (with the exception of using QuickDraw GX, which no longer needs PrintMonitor). PrintMonitor is the application that actually carries out the background printing. Normally, you do not need to interact with PrintMonitor in any way. The program handles everything automatically as soon as you select Print.

SEE: • "A Special Case: Printing with PrintMonitor" and "Problems with Background Printing and PrintMonitor," later in this chapter

Step 2: Select Page Setup

The Page Setup command brings up a dialog box that is important for formatting a document so that it matches the requirements and limitations of the selected printer. Thus, the options listed in this dialog box differ depending on which printer you are using. Different applications may also add their own custom options to this box.

 When to use it:

As with the Chooser, you need not select Page Setup prior to every print request. You need only select it after you change printers (from the Chooser) or whenever you wish to change any of its options from their current settings.

 What to do:

Working with the Page Setup Dialog Box

1. Select Page Setup from an application's File menu (see Figure 7-5).

2. Make modifications to any of the options listed, if desired. For example, most Page Setup dialog boxes include a Paper option, for selecting among different sizes of paper. An Orientation option shifts printing from portrait to landscape, as indicated by the icons. A Reduce or Enlarge option does what its name implies, changing the size of the entire printed output. For most common printing tasks, you should not need to change any of the default settings.
   If you are using LaserWriter 8:
   a. Click on the picture of the "dogcow" and you will see the detailed specifications for the paper size you selected.
   b. The Layout option lets you choose whether 1, 2, or 4 pages of your document will be printed on each printed page.
   c. Click the Help button to get a brief description of all the different options.

3. If your Page Setup box includes an Options button, clicking it brings up a window with further options. For LaserWriters, these options are described in more detail in Chapters 9 and 10. To return to the main dialog box, click OK when finished making these selections.

4. Click OK. This is sufficient to reformat the document to match the requirements of the selected printer.

SEE: • Chapter 9 on Page Setup commands and text printing
• Chapter 10 on Page Setup commands and graphics printing

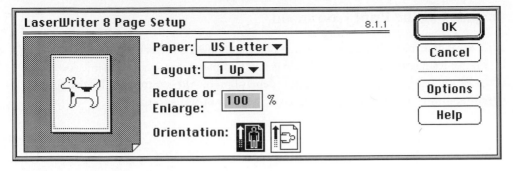

Figure 7-5   The Page Setup dialog box for LaserWriter 8, as selected from SimpleText

When Changing Printers

If you change printer drivers from the Chooser, then whenever you quit the Chooser, you automatically receive a message telling you to select Page Setup (see Figure 7-6). If you get this message while an application is open, simply select Page Setup from within the application and click OK. That's it.

If no application (other than the Finder) is open at the time the Chooser message appears, you can usually ignore the message. Applications should adjust to the newly selected printer automatically when the applications are launched (though see Chapter 9 for some problems that may occur).

By the way, if you get a message that says that you cannot use Page Setup because you have never selected a printer, go to the Chooser and select a printer, as the message suggests.

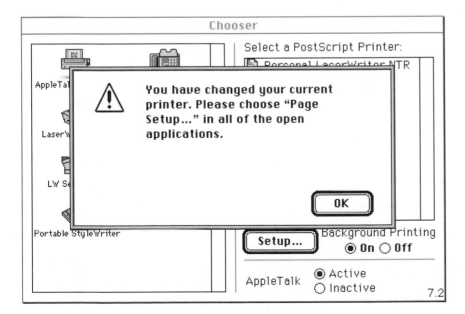

Figure 7-6   If you change printer drivers, the Chooser (when you go to close it) automatically alerts you to select Page Setup

Step 3: Use the Print Command

The Print command brings up a dialog box that is used to select such options as how many copies you want to print and what range of pages you wish to print. As with Page Setup, its options differ somewhat depending on the printer you are using. Different applications may also add their own custom options to this box.

 When to use it:

This is the only step that is essential to do every time you wish to print something.

 What to do:

Working with the Print Dialog Box

1. Select Print from the application's File menu. This brings up the Print dialog box (see Figure 7-7).

2. Make modifications to any of the options, if desired. In particular, if you want more than one copy of a document or if you only want to print a selected subset of the total number of pages, make those selections. Otherwise, for most printing tasks, you will not need to make any other changes.

   Unlike Page Setup, most selections here are not saved when you close the dialog box. They revert to their default option each time you select Print. Thus, even if you change the number of copies from 1 to 3, it will return to 1 the next time you select Print.

   If you are using LaserWriter 8:

   a. If an option you expect to find is missing, you may not have installed the appropriate PPD file (see "Step 1: Select the Chooser").

   b. If you are using an earlier version of LaserWriter 8 than version 8.2, the selection you make in the Destination box (Printer, File, or Fax) will be retained the next time you select Print. If you forget about this, you may inadvertently create a disk file when you had intended to print the document. Starting with version 8.2, the dialog box always defaults to Printer.

TECHNICALLY SPEAKING ▶

LASERWRITER 8 PRINT OPTIONS

This chapter does not explore the details of most options in Page Setup and Print dialog boxes (they are covered more in Chapters 9 and 10). However, because of the new features and added complexities of the LaserWriter 8 Print dialog box, I will describe its options in more detail here (see Figure 7-7). Remember, you can click the Help button in any LaserWriter 8 dialog boxes to get a graphic summary of what the buttons do.

First note that the available options in the Print dialog box will vary depending on which PPD is selected. The dialog boxes in the figures here are based on a LaserWriter NTR.

The Copies and Pages options are pretty much self-explanatory and common to virtually all printer drivers. From the pop-up menu for Paper Sources, you can select from among different paper input locations (such as manual feed tray as opposed to a paper cassette). Auto Select will pick whatever source currently has paper (defaulting to the cassette, if available). You can even select to use a different source for the first page from the remaining pages, useful for manual feeding of a letterhead sheet.

The Destination options allow you to choose whether you want to send the document to the Printer or create a file saved to the Disk. If you use the Disk option, the Print button changes to a Save button. If you select Save, you will get a Save dialog box that offers still more options, including whether to save the file as a PostScript file or an EPS file (see Chapter 10 for more on EPS), whether to include the font information for your document as part of the file (selecting None for a text document may mean that the document will print in an incorrect font), and whether you want the file to be Level-1 compatible or not. One use of the Disk option would be to save the print job as a PostScript file so that you can later print it to any PostScript printer, without needing either the original document or its creating application. Another use would be to import a selection from a program that cannot save in EPS format to a program that does support the EPS format. Finally, if your printer has a fax card (such as the LaserWriter 810F), a Fax option is included as a Destination choice. If you select the Disk or Fax options, you may want to consult other sources to get more instructions on how to use them.

Clicking the Options button opens a new window that lets you select among options such as Black and White or Color/Grayscale printing (which is in the main dialog box of the standard LaserWriter driver) and whether you want a cover page or not (useful for separating documents printed out at the same time). You can also choose whether or not you want a report of any PostScript errors that might occur while printing (though these error reports will not be all that informative to most users, I would probably still select either the Summarize on Screen or Print Detailed Report options if you are retrying a print job that failed the previous time). Finally, other options specific to your particular PPD may appear at the bottom of the window. For example, you may have a choice of printing resolutions, as well as FinePrint and PhotoGrade settings. Consult your printer's manual for details.

Click the Help buttons contained in the dialog box for a brief explanation of most of these features. By the way, if you do not have any documentation on the LaserWriter 8 driver, Adobe has a booklet available that briefly explains its features. Contact them for how to obtain it.

3. Click OK. The document now prints.

SEE: • **Chapter 9 on Print commands and text printing**
      • **Chapter 10 on Print commands and graphics printing**

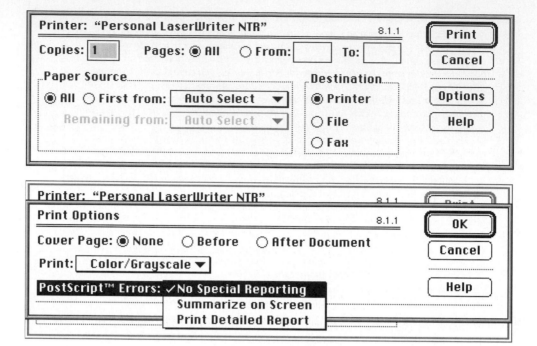

Figure 7-7   Top: The Print dialog box for the LaserWriter 8 driver, as selected from SimpleText. Bottom: the Options window of the Print dialog box

What Happens Next

After you select the Print command, printing is handled automatically by the Macintosh. Initially, you will see a message on the screen that tells you that the document is printing, usually with instructions that you can cancel the print job at any time by holding down the Command-period keys.

If you are printing to a LaserWriter, this message is typically followed by the appearance of a second separate message window that informs you of the progress of the print job. The exact messages vary depending on what LaserWriter you are using and what you are attempting to print. But there are generally three or four basic stages:

1. *Looking for <name of printer>* or *Waiting for <name of printer>*. This message means that the Macintosh is searching for the printer currently selected from the Chooser. If the printer is on and properly connected, it will be found.

2. *Initializing.* This message, if it appears at all, appears only during the first print job after turning on the printer. Essentially, information from the Macintosh, mainly from the printer driver, is sent to the printer to establish how the printer and the Macintosh communicate.

3. *Starting job* and *Preparing data.* The Macintosh and printer are working to get the document (referred to as a *print job*) ready to be printed.

4. *Processing job.* This is the final stage before your printed output begins to appear. Here is where the PostScript instructions are finally interpreted. For long documents, the printer may alternate between *preparing data* and *processing job* messages several times before finally printing.

With LaserWriter 8, you typically first see a window that tells you it is "spooling" the pages to be printed (even if background printing is off). This is then replaced by a similar window that progressively lists the "starting job," "preparing data," and "processing job" messages, as it indicates which page is currently being printed. During the starting job phase, you will typically briefly see a "creating prolog" message followed by an indication of all fonts that are being "downloaded," if any (see Chapter 9 for more on downloading fonts).

If your document prints without a problem, you can happily ignore all these messages. However, if a problem interrupts the printing process, it can be diagnostically useful to know exactly where in the printing process the interruption occurred.

A Special Case: Printing with PrintMonitor

PrintMonitor is a special type of application used in conjunction with background printing. After you select the Print command, and assuming that background printing is on, PrintMonitor is automatically launched and begins to oversee background printing operations. The first step is typically the creation of a special PrintMonitor spool file (see "PrintMonitor Documents Folder," later in this section, for more on this). On screen, an alert box will appear indicating the page-by-page progression of this spooling, which should average about a few seconds per page for text documents (actually, this process takes considerably longer—and requires more disk space—than it does with the old LaserWriter driver, a potential disadvantage of LaserWriter 8 if you frequently print large files).

After this, control of the Macintosh is returned to you and printing begins. Then, after the print job is through, PrintMonitor automatically quits. Normally, that is all there is to it.

However, while PrintMonitor is active, its name will appear in the Application menu (that's the one in the upper right corner of the menu bar). If spooling has just completed, you may have to wait several more seconds before the PrintMonitor name first appears. In fact, it may briefly seem as if your Mac has frozen as it waits for Print-Monitor to gear up. Don't worry. Just wait a bit longer and all will be fine again.

Once its name does appear, you can select PrintMonitor as you would any other application. If you do, it opens the PrintMonitor window (see Figure 7-8).

Note that PrintMonitor usually quits (its name is removed from the Application menu, unless you have its window open) before all your output has been printed. This happens when all the information needed to finish the printing job has been sent to the printer's memory. After that, the Mac itself is no longer involved.

PrintMonitor works fine whether or not you select it from the Application menu. So why would you ever select it? Here's why.

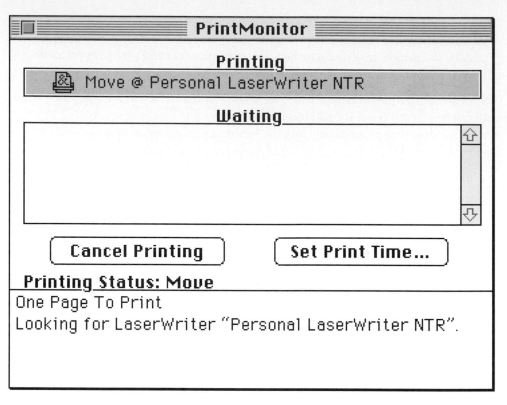

Figure 7-8   The PrintMonitor window: The information in the box under the word Printing
indicates that the LaserWriter is about to print the document named Move

Monitor Your Printing

Selecting PrintMonitor allows you to follow the progress of the print job. The messages that would normally have appeared on the screen (if you were *not* using background printing) are instead shifted to the PrintMonitor window. If you have several jobs queued to be printed, you can determine what they are and the order in which they will print. So, if you want to see any of this, select PrintMonitor.

Cancel Printing

If you have queued up several print jobs at once, you can also cancel any waiting print jobs from the PrintMonitor window. Just highlight the document name you want to cancel from the list in the Waiting box (there aren't any listed in Figure 7-8). Then click Cancel Printing. This is the only way to cancel a print job at this point. Using Command-period to cancel a print job is *not* an option once PrintMonitor takes over.

Do *not* go to PrintMonitor's File menu and select Stop Printing. If you do, this will stop the current and all subsequent print jobs. To undo this, you will have to return to the File menu and select Resume Printing.

Error Messages

PrintMonitor alerts you when any sort of printing error occurs (see Figure 7-9), even if you haven't select the PrintMonitor window. Exactly how PrintMonitor alerts you (such as whether a general message appears on the screen or whether you see only a flashing icon in the menu bar) is determined by preferences settings that you select, via the Preferences command in PrintMonitor's File menu (see Figure 7-10).

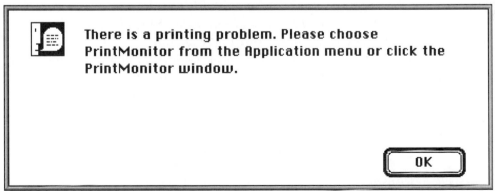

Figure 7-9 Two ways that PrintMonitor may alert you of a problem: a diamond next to its name in the Application menu (top) or an alert message that appears on your screen (bottom)

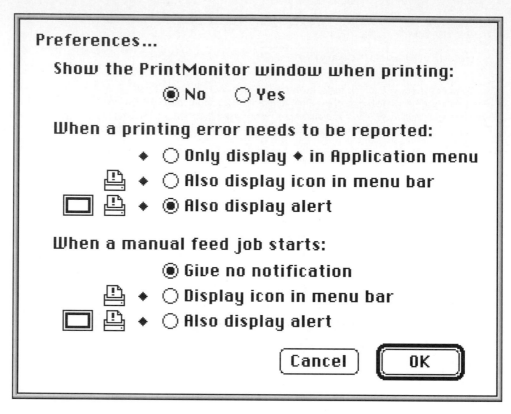

Figure 7-10   PrintMonitor's Preferences window

If you get one of these alerts, you need to select PrintMonitor to see the specific error message. Most of the likely messages are described in the next sections of this chapter. With background printing off, the error message would have appeared directly on the screen, without any need to use PrintMonitor.

Again, with LaserWriter 8, you have additional control over how PostScript errors (which are one category of possible printing errors) are reported through the PostScript Errors pop-up menu in the Options window of the Print Dialog box (see "Technically Speaking: LaserWriter 8 Print Options" earlier in this chapter). Whatever setting you select here, PostScript errors are still reported in the PrintMonitor window.

Quitting PrintMonitor

When you are done working with PrintMonitor, don't close its window (and certainly don't select Stop Printing from its File menu—which brings all printing to a halt). These choices do not make you quit PrintMonitor. To exit, simply go to another application, either by using the Application menu or by clicking in any window from another application. PrintMonitor looks after itself and quits when it is done.

PrintMonitor Documents Folder

PrintMonitor creates a folder in your System Folder, called PrintMonitor Documents, where it holds temporary "spool" files that it uses to carry out the printing. These files are essentially copies of the documents to be printed, created at the time you selected Print. Thus, the printed output always reflects the state of the document at the time Print was selected. Any changes you make to the document after selecting Print are not included in the pending printout, even if you make the changes before the document is actually printed. A file in the PrintMonitor Documents folder is automatically deleted when the print job is completed.

Solve It! When Things Go Wrong

Most of the time, if you have followed the preceding three steps—select the Chooser, Page Setup, and Print—your printing proceeds without any further problem.

Then there are those remaining times, when the printer simply refuses to cough up your request. The following sections detail the myriad of reasons that a printing request may fail and what you can do about it.

General Advice

The advice in this section should solve the majority of your printing problems. If you don't succeed, try the more specific solutions offered in the next sections. If you are using PrintMonitor, refer especially to the section later in this chapter, called "Problems with Background Printing and PrintMonitor."

Try Again

If at first you don't succeed, try again. This is the standard advice for almost any type of problem you may have with your Macintosh. It certainly applies to printing problems. Maybe you had a one-time glitch and the problem will not repeat itself.

If simply selecting the Print command a second time does not work, quit the application, relaunch it, open the document to be printed, and try yet again. If even this does not work, consider the following common situations and what to do about them.

Respond to Any Error Message That Appears

The Mac may seem to freeze briefly before an error message appears. Don't worry; the error message will usually show up in a few moments.

If the error message includes a *Try Again* button, use it. This button automatically retries the printing attempt.

If the error message only has a button such as *Cancel Printing* or *OK,* click the button. Follow any obvious advice (such as adding paper if the message says that the printer is out of paper). Then, if needed, return to the application you were using and reselect *Print* from the application's File menu.

If background printing is on, you may need to select PrintMonitor to see the specific error message, as explained earlier in this chapter (see Figure 7-9).

Restart the Computer if a System Crash or a Similarly Serious Problem Occurs

If a system crash occurs (as described more later in the chapter), you will need to restart the computer before you can retry printing. Once you have completed the startup, return to your application and repeat the printing request.

SEE: • **Chapter 4 for details on restarting**

Free Up Memory

If it is practical to do so, before trying to print a second time, close all open applications and documents not needed for the printing to proceed. This frees up additional RAM, which may solve the problem. More specific memory-enhancing procedures are described later in this chapter, as relevant.

Reinitialize the Printer

If none of this works, turn off the printer, wait about 10 seconds, then turn it back on again. This *reinitializes* the printer. That is, the information from the Macintosh that establishes the link between the printer and the Macintosh is sent again. This often clears up the problem all by itself. After the printer startup is over, you also might as well check the Chooser to make sure you have selected the correct printer driver. Then try printing again.

The Macintosh Can't Find the Printer

Symptoms:

You select Print from the application's File menu and one of the following events happens (see Figure 7-11):

- The Print dialog box does not appear. You immediately get an error message that says the Macintosh *can't open printer.*
- The Print dialog box appears. You click OK. However, then you get the message that the Macintosh *can't open printer.*

- You may get a message that says the printer *can't be found* or *is not responding.*
- An error message of any other sort appears instead of the Print dialog box.

In all these cases, the result is that no printed document ever appears. The good news is that probably nothing is wrong with the printer. Even better, the solutions here tend to be quick and easy.

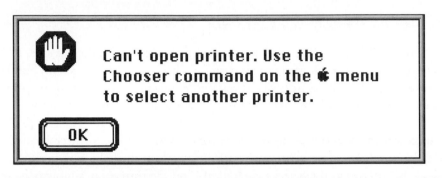

Figure 7-11   Examples of error messages that may occur after you select Print, if the Macintosh cannot locate or access the selected printer

 Causes:

Typical causes are that the Macintosh cannot locate the printer driver, that the wrong printer driver is selected, or that the printer is not properly connected. If your printer requires an AppleTalk connection, it may be that AppleTalk (or PrinterShare, for those printers that can use this option) is not turned on or that the wrong printer name is selected. The wrong port (printer as opposed to modem) may be selected. Corrupted Parameter RAM (PRAM) can also cause this problem.

Often, especially in System 7, you may get an error message that describes the likely cause. For example, it may say *Use the Chooser to make AppleTalk active* or that the ImageWriter's *Select light is off. Please push the select switch.* If you get this sort of helpful advice, follow it.

What to do:

Try Again

Follow any relevant suggestions from the previous General Advice section.

Make Sure the Printer Is Ready to Print

Make Sure the Printer Is Turned On   It never pays to overlook the obvious. If the printer is not on, turn it on. If it doesn't turn on, check that it's plugged in. Similarly, make sure the power cord is firmly connected to the printer. You'll know the printer is on when either its status lights are on or the printer at least makes some noise.

For ImageWriters: Make Sure the Select Switch Is On   This is a switch located on the ImageWriter itself directly below the off/on switch. If the light next to the Select switch is off, this means the Select switch itself is off. To turn it on, simply press the switch. You must have paper fed through the printer to get the Select switch to turn on.

For LaserWriters: Make Sure You Did Not Select the Print Command Too Soon After Turning the Printer On   If you select Print too soon, the Macintosh does not recognize the presence of the printer. Wait for the printer to complete its startup cycle. It takes about a minute. You can usually tell this has happened when the printer status lights stop flashing. At this point, reselect the Print command.

Non-AppleTalk Printers: Try Plugging the Printer Cable into the Other Serial Port Assuming you are a single user with a Macintosh and a printer, a cable connects the Macintosh to the printer. This cable usually runs from one of the serial ports on the Macintosh (usually the printer port) to the appropriate port on the printer (there is usually only one port that fits the cable you are using).

   If your non-AppleTalk printer is currently plugged into the printer port, switch it to the modem port—or vice versa. This may help if one of the ports is damaged (which ultimately requires a hardware repair to fix). You will also have to change the port selection from the Chooser.

Make Sure You Are Using a Correct Cable   If you have never used this printer and/or connecting cable before, there is a chance that you are trying to use an incorrect cable. For example, the cable for connecting a modem to the Macintosh may look identical to the one used to connect a non-AppleTalk printer. But they are not necessarily the same. You may not be able to use a modem cable for printing—or vice versa. Similarly, the cable used to make an AppleTalk connection is different from the standard serial cable used for non-AppleTalk printers (see "Take Note: What Is AppleTalk?" earlier in this chapter). If you are uncertain whether your cable is correct, take your cable to an Apple dealer (or other knowledgeable source) to check it.

Make Sure the Cable Is Firmly Plugged In and Not Damaged   Check if the printer cable is loose. Reconnect it if needed. Make sure no pins on the plug are bent or missing. To be certain that a cable is not defective, switch it with a different one that is successfully working with another printer, if possible. If this solves the problem, then the original cable was damaged.

SEE: • Fix-It #17 for more on cable problems

After Completing the Previous Checks, Try Printing Again   Even if you didn't find anything amiss, try again anyway. Printing may proceed successfully. If the document still fails to print, proceed to the next step.

Check the Chooser

Incorrect settings from the Chooser are a common source of problems at this point in the printing process.

If You Cannot Locate the Chooser in the Apple Menu   In System 7, this means that the Chooser is not in the Apple Menu Items folder. If necessary, locate it (either elsewhere on your disk or on a backup disk) and place it in the Apple Menu Items folder in your System Folder.

System 6 Alert: The Chooser should have been installed as a desk accessory in your System file. If it is not listed in the Apple menu, use the Font/DA Mover to check the System file and install the Chooser there, if needed.

BY THE WAY ▶

AN EXCEPTION TO THE RULE

If you are using a font/DA manager, such as Suitcase (you folks know who you are!), desk accessories such as the Chooser need not be installed in the System file (of System 6) or the Apple Menu Items folder (of System 7). They can be anywhere on your disk. If such is the case with the Chooser, and if Suitcase is turned off, the Chooser will not appear in the Apple menu. The solution, of course, is either to turn Suitcase back on or to install the Chooser in its normal location.

Once you have installed, located, and selected the Chooser, do the following.

Make Sure the Correct Printer Driver Icon Is Selected   Thus, if you are using a LaserWriter printer, select the LaserWriter (or LaserWriter 8) icon. If the correct icon is not present, it means that the printer driver for your printer is not present in the Extensions folder. To correct this, locate the correct driver from your Macintosh system software disks (or, if you are using a non-Apple printer that has its own driver, locate this driver), and place it in the Extensions folder.

If You Are Using AppleTalk, Make Sure It Is Active If it isn't, you get a message to this effect when you try to print a document (see Figure 7-12).

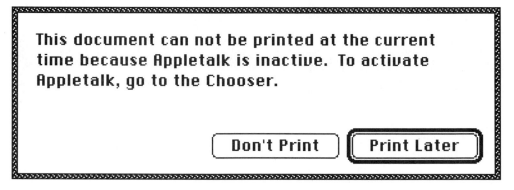

This document can not be printed at the current time because Appletalk is inactive. To activate Appletalk, go to the Chooser.

Don't Print   Print Later

Figure 7-12 If AppleTalk is off when trying to use a printer that requires AppleTalk, you get a message like this

If You Are Using AppleTalk, Check That the Name of Your Printer Is Listed and Selected The name should appear after you select the printer driver icon, assuming the printer is already on.

SEE: • "When Things Go Right" earlier in this chapter

If no name appears, it means that the Macintosh does not recognize the presence of the printer. For laser printers, assuming that you have already checked that the printer is on and connected properly (as described previously), it usually means you haven't waited long enough for the printer to warm up after turning it on.

To solve this problem, quit the Chooser (even though this step probably isn't necessary). Wait a minute. Then select the Chooser again. The name should now appear. Select it if it is not already highlighted.

By the way, note that the top line of the Print dialog box gives the name of the currently selected printer. This may be different from the name of any printer that is now available on your network. For example, if you have a PowerBook and print to one printer at work but another at home, you may be at home, but your PowerBook may still list your workplace printer as the selected one. In this case, the Macintosh will claim that it cannot find the selected printer. To solve this problem, again simply select the Chooser and select the name of any currently listed printer.

LaserWriter 8 Problems: If you get an error message that says *The LaserWriter 8 Preferences file may be missing or damaged . . . ,* this most likely means you have not selected the Setup command for your printer. Go to the Chooser, select the printer driver icon, select the printer name, and then click the Setup button. As a last resort for this or related problems, go to the Preferences folder, locate and delete the Laser-Writer 8 Prefs file, then go to the Chooser and select Setup for your printer.

TAKE NOTE ▶

FINDING YOUR PRINTER NAME: WHEN A SHUT DOWN IS BETTER THAN A RESTART

If the Chooser refuses to list your AppleTalk printer's name no matter what you do, sometimes the magic of a restart will do the trick. Try it. However, I have occasionally found (particularly with PowerBooks) that even if a restart fails to work, a Shut Down and subsequent Restart will succeed.

For Non-AppleTalk Printers: Check the Port to Which the Printer Cable Is Connected Make sure the selected serial port icon is the one that has the printer cable connected to it. That is, if the icon is for the printer port, make sure the cable is in the printer port and not the modem port. Also, it may help simply to turn the printer off and then on again. If you are connected to the printer port, make sure AppleTalk is turned *off.*

SEE: • "When Things Go Right," especially the list item "Non-AppleTalk printers: Printer or Modem Port," earlier in this chapter, for more advice, including advice concerning PowerBooks with only one serial port

If you are trying to use PrinterShare (or GrayShare or ColorShare) to print to a computer connected to another Macintosh, remember that the computer that the printer is connected to must be on as well as the printer itself. Unlike with AppleTalk, it is not sufficient that just the printer be on. Also, in order for the printer to be shared, the Share This Printer option must be turned on for that printer. This is done through the Chooser: Select the printer's icon and then click the Setup button to see this option. Using this feature also requires that the printer be connected to the modem port, not the printer port.

Try Printing Again If you have successfully navigated your way through the Chooser dialog box, close the Chooser, reselect Page Setup if needed, and reselect the Print command. The document should now print.

Investigate Other Possibilities

If none of the preceding suggestions worked, consider any or all of the following, as appropriate.

The Wrong Version of the Printer Driver   Generally, you should use the version of the printer driver that matches the version of your System file and Finder (see later in this chapter "Take Note: Mixing Versions of Printers, Printer Drivers, and Other System Software," for an exception to this). In this regard, also check if you have more than one System Folder on your disk. If so, you may be starting up from the wrong System Folder, which may be using a wrong version of the printer driver.

SEE: • Fix-It #5 on system software problems

A Corrupted Printer Driver   The printer driver may be damaged. To check for this possibility, replace it with a copy from your backups. For example, if you are trying to print using a LaserWriter, replace the LaserWriter driver extension in the Extensions folder. Use the printer driver from your original Macintosh system software disks.

Corrupted Parameter RAM (PRAM)   The PRAM, a special area of memory (as described in detail in Fix-It #11), contains information necessary for the serial ports to work. If the PRAM becomes corrupted, information cannot get sent through the serial ports (printer and modem) to the printer. The PRAM then needs to be reset (or *zapped,* as it is often called) before printing can proceed.

SEE: • Fix-It #11 for how to zap the Parameter RAM

Hardware Problems   If none of the previous suggestions work, a hardware problem looms likely. It's time to take your printer (or perhaps your Macintosh itself) in for repairs.

SEE: • Fix-It #17 on hardware problems

Printing Halts with No Error Message

Symptoms:

The printing process does not even begin, or it begins but then stops in midstream. In either case, no error message occurs. Everything else seems to be operating as normal. It is simply that a long time has passed and the printer is producing no output.

Causes:

It may be that everything is fine and that the document just needs a long time to print. Otherwise, an *endless loop* type of system error has probably occurred.

SEE: • Chapter 4 for more on endless loops and related system errors

In the latter case, the document never prints out, no matter how long you wait. If this happens with a LaserWriter, you are likely to notice that the print job seems to be stuck forever in the *preparing data* or *processing job* phase.

The ultimate causes of such system errors are the typical ones: software bugs or damaged files (see also the next section for more on these causes). Occasionally, the problem may be due to insufficient RAM, either in the Macintosh or (in the case of laser printers) the printer itself.

What to do:

If You Are Using PrintMonitor

If you are using PrintMonitor, you usually regain control of the computer before the first page prints out. If so, you can check the PrintMonitor window to make sure no message is waiting there. To do this, select PrintMonitor from the Application menu.

For example, if you selected the Manual Feed option from the Print dialog box, you may see a message telling you to insert the next sheet of paper so that printing can proceed. If no message appears, select Cancel Printing to stop any potential endless-loop printing process. Also make sure you have not selected Stop Printing. If you have, go to PrintMonitor's File menu and select Resume Printing.

If You Are Not Using PrintMonitor

If you are not using PrintMonitor, you are probably stuck with some sort of *Now printing* message on the screen. Press Command-period to try to cancel the printing. Press it a few times. Wait a minute or so to give it a chance to cancel the process.

Do a Forced Quit or Restart the Macintosh

If neither of the previous procedures has any effect, you can try a forced quit (press Command-Option-Escape) of the application. Otherwise, you have to restart the computer.

SEE: • Chapter 4 on forced quits and restarting

Reinitialize the Printer

In any case, once you regain control of the Macintosh, reinitialize the printer: Turn off the printer, wait a few seconds, and turn it back on again.

Try to Print Again

Return to your application and select the Print command a second time. See if it works now.

SEE: • "General Advice" earlier in this chapter

TECHNICALLY SPEAKING ▶

WHAT ACCOUNTS FOR PRINTING SPEED?

Speed of printing is hard to predict because it depends on so many different factors. Similar to automobile mpg, your printing "mileage" may vary.

The first factor is the printer itself. Usually, a printer is rated in terms of pages per minute (ppm). This represents the approximate maximum rate that the printer can produce its output. Most popular printers are in the range of 4 to 10 ppm. The ppm rating is primarily a function of the physical limits of the actual printing machinery. However, printers rarely meet this theoretical maximum.

For example, for laser printers (especially PostScript laser printers), real printing times are also influenced by any computer processing hardware built into the printer. Thus, the faster the processor in the printer can get the information to the printing machinery, the more likely the printer can live up to its ppm maximum. Similarly, the greater the amount of RAM in the printer, the faster that printing generally proceeds.

Speed is also influenced by events that take place before the information ever reaches the printer. The specific version of the printer driver can have an effect. Newer versions often include improvements designed to enhance printing speed.

Sometimes the printing application itself has an effect. Thus, two different word processors may print similar documents at different rates.

The nature of the document itself has a major effect on speed. Simple formatted text usually prints the fastest. Heavily formatted text and (especially) complex graphics slow the operation down considerably.

You can speed up printing somewhat by turning background printing off—but then you lose the advantage of more quickly regaining control of the Macintosh. As always, free lunches are hard to find!

For LaserWriters: Is It a Complex Document?

If the document still fails to print, don't automatically assume that you have a system error. Consider whether you simply have a document that takes a long time to print.

For laser printers, where an entire page is printed at once, it is not unusual to have to wait a considerable amount of time before the printing of the page begins. Particularly if the page contains large or complex graphics, it would not be unusual for it to take ten to fifteen minutes, or even more, for the laser printer to spit it out.

So if you are printing something new and different, where you don't have experience with how long it should take, give it a chance before assuming the worst. If everything else seems to be working normally (for example, the green status light on the printer is blinking as expected), go away for a while. By the time you return, it may print.

For LaserWriters: Check the Status Lights

There is typically one status light that turns on when you are out of paper. Another light indicates a paper jam. Attend to these problems as necessary. Check the manual that came with your printer for how to remove jammed paper. If both lights are on at the same time (or are flashing in any way), it almost certainly means a hardware repair is needed.

SEE: • Fix-It #17 for more general information on hardware problems

If None of the Preceding Steps Work

If none of this works, treat the problem as a more general system error. Continue to the next section.

BY THE WAY ▶

OUTPUT TOO LIGHT, TOO DARK, STREAKED, OR SMEARED?

- *For LaserWriters.* When the output becomes too light or prints with streaks, it probably means that you need to replace the toner cartridge. Too light or too dark output can also be adjusted by changing the print density control, a knob located on the printer (location varies with different models).

- *For inkjet printers.* Too light an output means that you need to replace the ink cartridge. Remember, for color inkjet printers, one color may run out before the others. So, if only certain colors are printing incorrectly, this too means that you should replace the cartridge. Inkjet-printed output can smear more easily than laser-printed output, though newer inks are less susceptible to this problem. Still, be especially careful not to get inkjet output wet. For color inkjet printers, even though they can print on plain paper, using special coated papers usually yield better results. Finally, some Hewlett-Packard color printers do not have a separate black ink. Instead, they produce black by combining its three colored inks together. This results in a black that is more like a muddy brown. Having separate black ink is better.

Printing Halts Due to a System Crash, PostScript Error, or Other Printing-Related Error

 Symptoms:

Printing halts as a result of any of the following:

- A system crash occurs, usually generating the system bomb error message.

SEE: • Chapter 4 for more general information on system errors

- An error occurs that says *the serial port is in use.*

SEE: • Chapter 11, on file sharing and Apple Remote Access, for more on this problem

- A specific printing-related error occurs, usually indicated by a printing-related error message. For example, with PostScript LaserWriters, it is common for the message to read *PostScript error.* Usually, additional text follows. Sometimes, this text indicates the precise source of the problem (such as too many fonts in use). More commonly, you cannot make any sense out of the often cryptic content of the message—and it is probably not really worth trying (see Figure 7-13). It may have nothing directly to do with PostScript anyway. Often a corrupted font is the cause.

SEE: • Chapters 9 and 10 for more on PostScript

- An error message appears suggesting a problem with incompatible printer software or system software.
- If you are using PrintMonitor, you may get a message that suggests that PrintMonitor itself is the cause of the problem (such as a lack of sufficient memory for PrintMonitor to work).

These events may happen even before the first page is printed, or it may occur at some point in the middle of a print job. Particularly for LaserWriters, a print job may successfully begin and then halt at a particular page because of a problem specific to the contents of that page.

Remember that the Mac may seem to freeze temporarily prior to the appearance of a printing error message. This is normal. Just wait and the Mac will probably "unfreeze" shortly and the error message will appear.

Many error messages will cite insufficient memory as a cause. However, this message cannot be entirely trusted. Often, something else is the true cause.

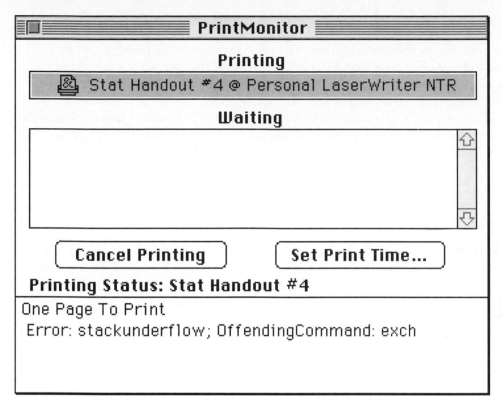

Figure 7-13   A PostScript error, as reported in PrintMonitor

Causes:

There are two likely candidates as the source of all of these problems: software bugs or corrupted software.

Bugs in the Relevant Software

Technically, any software that is active at the time of printing could be the offending party. This could include any INIT or the System file itself. However, the most likely candidates are the printer driver, the PrintMonitor file (if background printing is on), any other non-Apple background printing software you are using, or the application that issued the Print command.

Sometimes the problem may represent an interaction between one of these files and some particular characteristic of the document to be printed, such as the type of font used or a specific graphic element. The bug may be such that the problem occurs only with a specific model of printer, or it may affect all printers.

As is always the case with software bug problems, there is no way to eliminate the bug yourself. That must await a future upgrade to the product. However, some common work-arounds may allow you to print a document, despite the presence of the bug.

Corrupted Software

In this case, the problem is that one of the files involved in the printing process has become corrupted. The most likely guilty parties are the same ones as for software bugs, especially the printer driver or PrintMonitor. Additionally, the document itself or font files that the document uses may be corrupted.

The exact events that caused the damage may never be known. However, it doesn't really matter. The important thing is to recognize the problem and to replace the damaged file with an intact copy from your backup disks.

SEE: • Chapter 2 on damage control

Other Causes

Other possible causes include the wrong printer driver selected, insufficient memory available, insufficient unused space on the startup disk, and corrupted PRAM. Damaged cables may also cause a PostScript error.

 What to do:

Try Printing Again

SEE: • "General Advice," earlier in this chapter, for specific guidelines

If trying again fails to work, try to determine the exact cause of the problem, as described in the following sections. Unless the specific error message you receive offers guidance as to what to do first, there is no particular recommended order for trying these solutions. All other things being equal, try the ones you find easier to do and less disruptive first. I begin with two suggestions that are the most often successful. After that, try the subsequent suggestions until one works.

Replace Potentially Corrupted Files

If a printing problem is caused by a damaged file, replacing the file should solve the problem. To check for this, do the following.

Replace Printing-Related Files   Use your backup disks as a source of uncorrupted copies of these files. In particular, replace the printer driver, the PrintMonitor file (if you are using background printing), and the application file and its accessory files.

By the way, damage to PrintMonitor is a particularly common occurrence with System 7.0.x. The permanent solution, after replacing the PrintMonitor file, is to install Tune-up 1.1.1 (see Fix-It #5 for more on tune-ups and updates) or upgrade to System 7.1 or later.

Replace the Document File   If a document file is corrupted, you will probably notice this as soon as you open the document. The content of the file will probably be partially missing or garbled in some way. In fact, the document may not even open at all. Sometimes you may be "lucky" (in terms of finding a cause) and get an error message indicating a damaged document (see Figure 7-14). However, even if everything seems normal, you may still have damage that somehow prohibits printing of the document. It's worth a try to replace the document with a (hopefully uncorrupted) backup.

Otherwise, you may find that you only have trouble printing a specific page or paragraph. While this could indicate a corrupted font, it may also mean problems with the document itself. You may be able to fix this by simply deleting the problem text and retyping it.

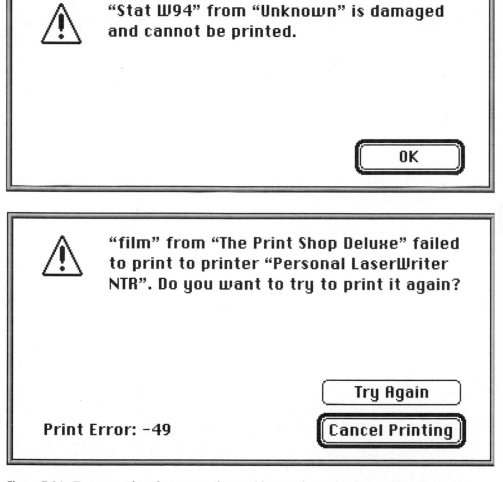

Figure 7-14   Two examples of messages that could mean that a printing problem is due to a damaged document

Replace a Potentially Corrupted Font File   If a font file becomes damaged, documents that contain that font may display correctly on the screen but do not print (this is a particularly likely possibility for TrueType fonts, but it occurs for other font types as well). If a printing problem seems specific to the presence of a particular font, suspect this as the cause. In such a case, you need to replace the corrupted font file (for PostScript fonts replace both the printer font and the screen font).

Shift to a Different Font   While replacing a corrupted (or otherwise problematic font) is the recommended course of action, sometimes you may be too rushed to want to bother or maybe replacing the font didn't solve the problem. In these situations, an obvious work-around is simply to shift to a different font. For example, I once had a case where printing in Palatino Bold Italic lead to a PostScript error but printing the same text in plain Palatino worked just fine. Shifting fonts does not eliminate the ultimate source of the problem, but it at least gets your document to print.

Retry Printing   Retry printing after each replacement. See if the printing problem goes away.

SEE: • Fix-Its #2, #3, #5, and #14 for more on replacing damaged files
      • Chapter 9, "Damaged Font Files," for specifically how to detect and replace a damaged or corrupted font

Zap the PRAM

Try this especially if you got the message that said printing was unsuccessful because "the serial port was in use." If you get system errors while in the Chooser, zapping the PRAM often solves that problem as well.

SEE: • Fix-It #11 on zapping the Parameter RAM

Check the Printer Driver

Make sure the printer driver you selected from the Chooser is the one that matches your printer. The wrong selection can result in a variety of unusual error messages (such as messages that mention a Ready button when printing to a StyleWriter).

Shift to a Different Version of the Printer Driver and/or PrintMonitor File

As a general rule, you want all your system software files to be from the same version. Thus, whatever version of the system software your System and Finder come from, choose your printer driver (and Chooser) from the same source.

However, if problems persist despite the matching of printing software, try any or all of the following procedures.

Use Another Version of the Driver   If you own more than one version of the printing software, try using either a newer or an older version (at least as a temporary fix to continue printing). If it fails to work, or even seems to make things worse, return to the original version.

In particular, LaserWriter users, try switching from the LaserWriter to the LaserWriter 8 driver (or vice versa). You can keep both in your Extensions folder at the same time, switching back and forth from the Chooser as needed.

Also, try to use the latest version of LaserWriter 8, as it should contain fixes for bugs found in previous versions. However, a few applications may not work with the latest version. For these cases, you may succeed by using a previous version (such as downgrading from LaserWriter 8.2 to 8.1.1).

Match Printer Driver and PrintMonitor   If you change versions of the LaserWriter driver, change the PrintMonitor file as well, so that these two files are the same version.

Reinitialize Laser Printers After Changing Drivers   If you change drivers while a LaserWriter is on and then try to print a document, you probably get an alert message that says that the printer has already been initialized with an incompatible version of the driver and you are asked whether you wish to reinitialize it (see Figure 7-15). This is perfectly normal. Click OK. The printer reinitializes and your document will print. This message no longer seems to occur with LaserWriter 8.

This message may also appear if you are sharing a printer on a network and some other user initialized the printer with a different version of the driver from the one you are using. Again, click OK and your document will print. To avoid repeated occurrences of this message, however, make sure everyone on the network is using the same version of the driver.

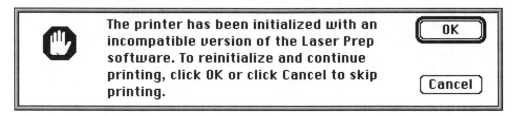

Figure 7-15 Message that appears if your printer has already been initialized with a printer driver different from the one you are now using

LaserWriter 8 Users: Make Sure You Used the Installer Utility When Upgrading to LaserWriter 8   Whether upgrading from LaserWriter to LaserWriter 8, or from one LaserWriter 8 version to another, make sure you use the Installer utility on the system software or printer driver installer disk. Don't just drag the driver from the floppy disk to your Extensions folder. For one thing, you need to upgrade PPD files as well as the driver. Also, the Installer utility may perform operations that would not be duplicated by simply copying files.

Check the Printer Cable

Check if the printer cable is loose. Reconnect it if needed. Make sure no pins on the plug are bent or missing. To be certain that a cable is not defective, switch it with a different one that is successfully working with another printer, if possible. If this solves the problem, then the original cable was damaged. Make sure you are using the right cable.

Turn Off Certain Printing-Specific Options

Some of the following suggestions apply only to certain types of printers.

Turn Off Fractional Character Widths   A Fractional Character Widths checkbox option, if your active application includes this feature, is usually found in a modified Page Setup dialog box (see Figure 7-16), though in some applications it may be in a separate Preferences dialog box or even directly in a menu (check the manual of your application to determine where it is located). Making changes to this option affects only the current application. Fractional Widths settings in other applications have to be adjusted separately, as needed.

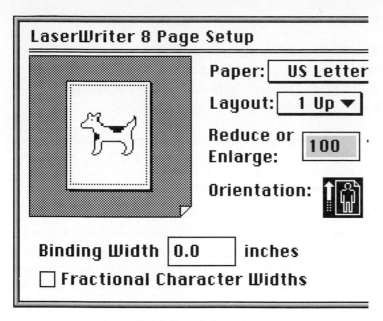

Figure 7-16   A Fractional Character Widths check box, as located in WordPerfect's Page Setup dialog box

For high-resolution printers, such as LaserWriters and StyleWriters, checking this option should improve the appearance of printed text by adjusting the spacing between letters. But this option may also cause problems that prevent the document from being printed. For example, I once got a PostScript error while trying to print a particular page of a document with Microsoft Word. Turning off Fractional Widths solved the problem.

Thus, if you are having printing problems and Fractional Character Widths is checked, uncheck it. Try to print the document again.

SEE: • Chapter 9 for details on what the Fractional Character Widths option does

If you are using Adobe Type Manager (ATM), you may have problems when using Fractional Widths (as described more in Chapter 9). If so, you should turn Fractional Widths off. On the other hand, when using SuperATM (an enhanced version of ATM), Adobe specifically advises keeping Fractional Widths settings on. Ultimately, you may have to experiment a bit here to see which works best—on or off.

Turn Off Faster Bitmap Printing   This option is found in the Page Setup box of the LaserWriter driver. It is been eliminated from the LaserWriter 8 driver dialog box (see Figure 7-1). Some documents refuse to print with this option turned on. In this case, if Faster Bitmap Printing is checked, uncheck it. Try to print the document again. Actually, I would avoid ever using this option. It causes more problems than it solves (if it indeed solves any problems at all). Maybe that's why it was dropped from LaserWriter 8.

SEE: • Chapter 10 for more on what the Faster Bitmap Printing option supposedly does

Turn Off Unlimited Downloadable Fonts   This option, also found in the Page Setup box of LaserWriter drivers, can sometimes be the cause of a PostScript error. So if it is on, try turning it off and see if it solves the problem. However, as described shortly, sometimes turning it *on,* rather than *off,* will solve a problem.

SEE: • Chapter 9, "A Document Prints with a Different Font from the One Displayed," for more on this option

Eliminate TrueType Fonts from Your Document

Change TrueType font text to a non-TrueType font, ideally a PostScript font. Normally, it should not be necessary to do so. However, some versions of the LaserWriter driver and some applications still have problems with TrueType fonts. Also, the original LaserWriter and LaserWriter Plus models have general trouble with printing True-Type fonts because they don't have enough memory to accept the needed information to be passed to the printer.

If your printing problems seem limited to documents that contain TrueType fonts, shift to another type of font. Try printing again. If it prints now, you have solved the immediate problem. For the future, if you have a choice between a PostScript or a TrueType version of the same font, you can delete the TrueType version and use the PostScript version instead. The best long-term solution here is to hope that Apple and/or the maker of your application release a bug-fixed upgrade so that you can once again use the font as desired.

TrueType fonts can occasionally cause other, less serious, printing-related problems, as described in Chapter 9.

BY THE WAY ▶

WHAT'S TRUETYPE? WHAT'S POSTSCRIPT?

If you do not know a TrueType font from a PostScript font, have no idea where these files are located, and don't have a clue about how to tell what type of font you are using, check out Chapter 9. It explains all of this in great detail.

Make Sure Enough Free Space Exists on Your Disk

In many cases, printing requires the formation of temporary files that may take up a significant amount of disk space. For example, this is true whenever you use the ImageWriter (except in Draft mode) or whenever PrintMonitor background printing is turned on (as explained in "PrintMonitor Documents Folder," earlier in this chapter).

The computer always looks for this free space on the startup disk, so it doesn't matter if there is a lot of extra room on any other mounted disk. Unless you are doing a lot of background printing or unless your drive is filled almost to capacity, this is unlikely to pose a problem on a hard drive, as enough free space is almost always available. It is more likely to happen if a floppy disk is your startup disk (itself a rare event these days).

If such problems occur, you usually get a specific error message informing you of the problem (see Figure 7-17). However, if you are using PrintMonitor, the error message may say that you are out of memory, even though the real cause is insufficient disk space.

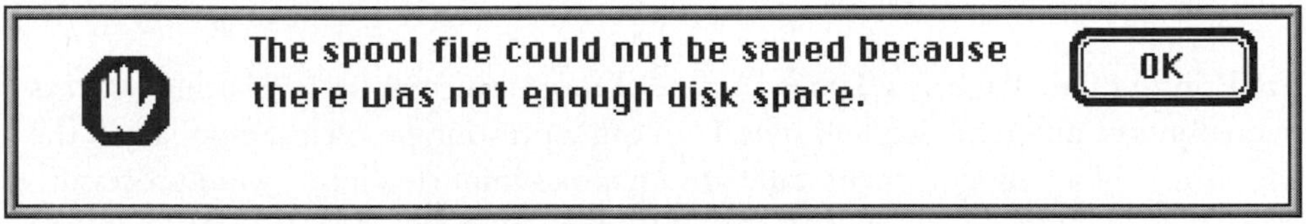

 The spool file could not be saved because there was not enough disk space.

Figure 7-17 This message may appear when printing a large document with background on and too little free space on your disk

In any case, the solution here is either to delete files from the disk until you have freed up sufficient space or to use a different startup disk that has additional space already. Then try printing again.

By the way, if you are saving a PostScript print job to a disk file, rather than sending it to the printer, again make sure there is enough disk space available to hold the file.

Check for Insufficient Memory and Related Problems

Does Your PostScript Printer Have Enough Memory?   PostScript printers have their own RAM memory. The amount installed varies with different printers. If your document requires more memory than is available you will get a PostScript error. Be especially wary of this problem if the error is listed as a "limitcheck error" or "VMerror." In some cases, additional RAM can be added to your printer. If so, doing this is the best long-term solution for frequent memory-related PostScript errors. Also, printers that use PostScript Level 2 do a better job of handling memory than was done with the previous PostScript versions. Otherwise, try any of the following suggestions, as may be relevant.

Try Printing One Page at a Time   A page of text with complex formatting (such as many fonts of different sizes and styles) can cause printing problems, especially if the page is part of a long document. Similarly, graphics imported into a word processor from draw programs, such as MacDraw or Canvas, may not print—especially if the graphic includes many grouped objects.

Too many fonts is an especially likely problem with PostScript LaserWriters if you are using fonts that are not built into the LaserWriter's hardware. Such fonts must be downloaded to the printer's memory before you can print the document. If you have many of these fonts, you can run out of memory to hold them, which then causes problems with printing.

If only those pages with complex formatted text or graphics do not print, try printing that page by itself. Thus, if the problem page is page 5, enter 5 to 5 in the *Pages From: . . . To:* area of the Print dialog box (see Figure 7-7).

Turn On Unlimited Downloadable Fonts   Turning on this option (accessed by clicking the Options button in PostScript LaserWriter Page Setup dialog boxes) may similarly help solve problems with too many fonts in a document.

SEE: • Chapter 9, "A Document Prints with a Different Font Than Is Displayed," for more on this
        option

Simplify the Document   If the previous solutions do not work, simplify your page layout, if possible. In particular, if you are using many fonts on the same page, modify the text to reduce the total number of fonts. For problems with graphics combined in a word processing document, cut the graphic from the word processing document and try to print it separately from the text. Sometimes just reimporting the graphic may solve the problem.

Actually, bugs in the printer driver may cause PostScript errors when certain special effects are in use, no matter how much memory you have in your printer. For example, rotated objects with rounded corners or selection of both Invert Image and Smooth Graphics (selected from the Page Setup dialog box) for the same document, have been reported to lead to PostScript errors. To cite one specific case, PageMaker 5.0 documents containing rotated text do not print correctly with earlier versions of LaserWriter 8.

There is nothing you can do about these errors except avoid using the problem effects or upgrade to a newer (hopefully less buggy) printer driver.

Change the Format of a Graphic   If the problem appears to be with printing a specific graphic object, sometimes saving it in a different format (such as shifting from PICT to TIFF) may eliminate the problem.

SEE: • Chapter 10 for more on graphics formats

Turn On 32-Bit Addressing   This sometimes solves memory-related PostScript errors (though it may sometimes cause other problems, as described in Fix-It #6).

Turn Off RAM-Using Options from the Page Setup Dialog Box   In particular, turn off Larger Print Area. Also turn off Smooth Text and Smooth Graphics.

Make Sure Sufficient Memory Is Allocated to the Application   Though insufficient application memory is not a common cause of a printing problem, if nothing else seems to be working, try increasing the Preferred (or Current) Memory allocation, from the Get Info window of the application you are using. This is likely to help only if you are having a problem trying to print very long or complex documents.

SEE: • Chapter 2 on the Get Info command and Fix-It #6 on memory problems for more details

Make Sure Sufficient Memory Is Allocated to PrintMonitor   This is discussed in more detail in the next section. As an alternative, print with Background printing off.

Problems with Background Printing and PrintMonitor

This section is relevant only if you are using background printing, particularly as used with LaserWriter drivers. Printing problems related to background printing may or may not be accompanied by an error message. So to check if background printing is the cause of your problem, try each of the following suggestions until one works.

Don't Do Anything Else While You Are Trying to Print   Don't continue working with your application (actually, it may help to quit the application altogether as soon as the job is sent to the printer). Don't try to copy files. Don't do anything that may use additional memory, until the printing is completed. For example, stop any other nonprinting-related background processing that may be going on at this time (such as a telecommunications program that is working in the background).

All of this minimizes the chance that the problem is caused by overloading the processing capacity of the Macintosh. Of course, this also negates the advantage of using background printing. But hopefully, you won't be required to do this very often. In general, you should be able to carry out other tasks while background printing is in progress. If this does not solve the problem, keep going.

Remove Documents from The PrintMonitor Documents Folder   If you get a error message with a Try Again option, but selecting Try Again simply leads to the return of the same message, Cancel printing the next go round. Then go to the PrintMonitor Documents folder in your System Folder. Delete any documents you find there. You will now have to reselect Print for whatever documents you were trying to print. However, they may successfully print now.

Turn Background Printing Off Altogether   Go to the Chooser and turn off background printing. Try to print the document again. If you can now print the document, PrintMonitor is likely at least a partial cause of the problem. To further isolate the cause, turn background printing on again, as needed, and try the following.

Check for a Conflict Between PrintMonitor and the Application (or Document)
If the problem appears only when you are using background printing in a particular application, a conflict is a likely possibility. You may not be able to do anything about this immediately, other than keep background printing off when using this application. However, the problem may occur with some documents but not others, so it may pay to turn background printing back on and print a different document, just to check. If you can successfully print most documents, you can turn background printing off only for those rare documents when it is a problem.

TECHNICALLY SPEAKING ▶

PROBLEMS WITH EMBEDDED FONTS

A special problem can occur with background printing of a document that uses fonts that are embedded directly in the document or the printing application, rather than somewhere in the System Folder (a subject I discuss in more detail in Chapter 9). All you need to know now is this: The System is aware of an embedded font only while the document or application that contains the font is open. This means that if you close these files before PrintMonitor is finished printing your file (normally an okay thing to do), PrintMonitor cannot find the embedded fonts when it needs them. This has been known to cause serious problems, including system crashes.

Thus, you should avoid using PrintMonitor with files that have embedded fonts. But how do you know whether a file has such fonts? Well, you can use Apple's Font/DA Mover to check (again, see Chapter 9 for details). If you find embedded fonts, remove them and transfer them to the System file (or Fonts folder), where they can be accessed by PrintMonitor.

However, turning background printing off temporarily also solves this problem. If you are unfamiliar with embedded fonts, you may prefer this simpler, more general solution.

Check for a Damaged or Incorrect Version of PrintMonitor   I already mentioned, in previous sections of this chapter, the possibility of a damaged or incorrect version of the PrintMonitor file. If you haven't already done so, replace the file with a copy from Macintosh system software disks that match the system software version on your startup disk.

Check for Insufficient Memory for PrintMonitor   You may get an error message that says the document did not print because PrintMonitor did not have enough memory. The message may say that it will try to print again when more memory is available (see Figure 7-18). If so, click OK and close any unneeded documents, applications and/or desk accessories. Close any open Finder windows. Printing should now proceed.

Alternatively, the message may offer to allocate more memory to the PrintMonitor application. If so, let it. Click OK and try printing again by selecting Print.

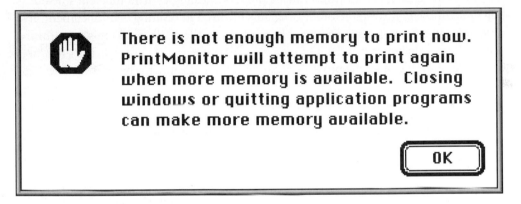

There is not enough memory to print now. PrintMonitor will attempt to print again when more memory is available. Closing windows or quitting application programs can make more memory available.

OK

Figure 7-18   A message indicating that not enough memory is available for PrintMonitor to work

Check for Free Space on Your Startup Disk   As already mentioned (see "Make Sure Enough Free Space Exists on Your Disk" earlier in this chapter), a document may not print in the background if there is too little free disk space to create the needed spool files (stored in your PrintMonitor Documents folder). Making matters worse, if this problem occurs, you may get an error message that erroneously says the problems is due to insufficient memory. In either case, if there is very little free space left on your disk, delete some files from your disk. Then try printing again. Alternatively, for multi-page documents, try printing the document in smaller segments, waiting until each one is finished before you try the next one. Or simply turn off background printing.

Otherwise . . .   With any other error message that suggests a problem with Print-Monitor, manually increase PrintMonitor's memory:

1. Locate PrintMonitor in the Extensions folder, select it, and then select Get Info from the Finder's File menu.

2. Its preferred (or current) memory size is probably 80K. Whatever the amount is, increase it by another 50 to 100K. This assumes you have enough memory available to accommodate this increase.

3. Try printing again. It should work.

4. If it still doesn't work, as a sort of last resort, you can try increasing the Finder's memory allocation. This too may help PrintMonitor. In System 7, the easiest way to do this is with a utility called Finder Fixer (described more in Fix-It #6).

SEE: • **Chapter 2 on Get Info and Fix-It #6 on memory management, as needed**

Widen the Search to More General Causes

If all of the preceding fails to work, you are probably dealing with an inherent software bug or conflict in one or more of the programs involved in printing your document. It's time to begin a more general diagnostic hunt to isolate the cause. To do this, try printing using different documents and applications, to determine exactly how specific the problem is. For example, does the problem occur with some documents but not others?

SEE: • **Chapter 3 for general strategy guidelines**
• **Chapter 4 on general guidelines for system error problems**
• **Chapter 6 for a more general discussion of file-related problems**

More specifically, do the following.

Resolve Conflict with the Application   Most likely, the problem is caused by the application making the print request. Often, the application turns out to be incompatible with the particular printer you have. Usually, the only immediate work-around is to stop using the problem application, at least for the moment.

SEE: • **Fix-It #1 on incompatible software and hardware**
• **Fix-Its #2 and #3 on other application-specific problems**

Resolve Conflict with an INIT or System Software   Similarly, there may be an INIT conflict or a more general problem related to the system software. You may ultimately need to turn off your INITs, replace your entire system software, and/or change your hardware. (For example, SuperATM reportedly causes problems when you print to a Personal LaserWriter NT. The simplest solutions here are either to upgrade your printer to an NTR or not use SuperATM.)

SEE: • **Fix-It #4 on problems with system extensions and control panels**
• **Fix-It #5 on system software problems**

Call Technical Support   Call the technical support line for the company that makes the problem software. If you have not been able to find a good work-around solution, they may have one to suggest. Or they may have a newer version of the program available that fixes the problem. Though upgrading may be more expensive than a typical work-around, it is generally the best and most permanent solution.

For example, I once read an article in which the author spent three pages explaining why a particular SuperPaint 2.0 document would generate a PostScript error every time he tried to print it. He eventually found a work-around for the problem, of which he was quite proud. But the real culprit turned out to be a bug in SuperPaint 2.0 that had been fixed in version 3.0, which was already available. Upgrading would have quickly and easily solved the problem.

SEE: • Fix-It #18 on calling technical support

Round Up the Usual Suspects   If no special problem file can be identified, start rounding up the usual gang of suspects in search of still more general causes. These include rebuilding the desktop and running Disk First Aid. Problems with PRAM, as mentioned earlier in this chapter, are another common source of printer-related problems. See the appropriate Fix-Its for details.

SEE: • Fix-Its #7 to #13 to check out the usual suspects

Hardware Problems   Finally, if all else has failed, it's time to assume a hardware problem as the cause, most likely with the printer. Take the printer (and, if need be, the Macintosh itself) in for repairs.

SEE: • Fix-It #17 on hardware problems

Chapter Summary

First, this chapter explained the implications of recent changes in print technology, especially LaserWriter 8 and QuickDraw GX (though a full discussion of QuickDraw GX is deferred until Chapter 12). Then, because so many printing problems stem from a lack of understanding of basic printing procedures, this chapter reviewed these essential steps: selecting options from the Chooser, using Page Setup, and selecting Print. For those people who use background printing, I also described how to work with PrintMonitor.

From here, I covered the range of problems that can cause a document either to fail to print entirely or to halt before it is finished. I described what to do if the Macintosh can't seem to find your printer, if printing seems to get caught in an endless loop, if system crashes occur, or if any of a variety of more specific error messages appear. In the last case, solutions focused on checking for and replacing potentially damaged or incorrect versions of printing-related files. Special consideration was also given to problems with PrintMonitor.

Chapter 8

Getting Under the Hood: The Invisible Macintosh

Peeking Under the Hood

This chapter takes you inside the workings of the Macintosh more than any other chapter in this book. Still, understanding and using the material in this chapter does not require any special software or any particular skills other than those already described. So, stick around. Don't rush or skip to the next chapter.

If you make an effort to master this material, you will be amply rewarded. For example, it can aid in solving problems locating or opening files, as described in Chapter 6. It will be immensely helpful in understanding problems with graphics formats, as described in Chapter 10. It bears on how applications import and export files of different formats (as discussed in several chapters). Finally, it allows you to do some neat tricks that you will meet for the first time in this chapter.

File Type and File Creator

How Kind

Every file on your disk is assigned a particular kind. The kind is a brief description of the general category to which the file belongs. Thus, all application files have a kind called *application.* Similarly, the kind for a document created by Excel is *Microsoft Excel document.* Note that for document files, the kind description not only lists the general category *(document),* but also identifies the application that created the document (in this case, *Microsoft Excel*).

As first presented in Chapter 2, you can easily determine the kind for any file by selecting Get Info for that file and reading its kind description (see Figure 8-1). You can also see the kind for all files in a folder at one time by switching to a non-icon view, such as By Name or (even better!) By Kind.

This kind information can help you to identify an unfamiliar file. The Finder similarly uses this information to identify files. For example, if a file's kind is *application,* the Finder knows it can be opened directly and does so when you double-click it. On the other hand, if it is a system extension, the Finder knows that it cannot be opened at all and belongs in the Extensions folder. If it is a document, the Finder uses the kind to determine what application is launched along with the document when you double-click it. Thus, a problem with a file's kind is one reason you can have difficulty opening a document. This problem, briefly alluded to in Chapter 6, is described more fully here.

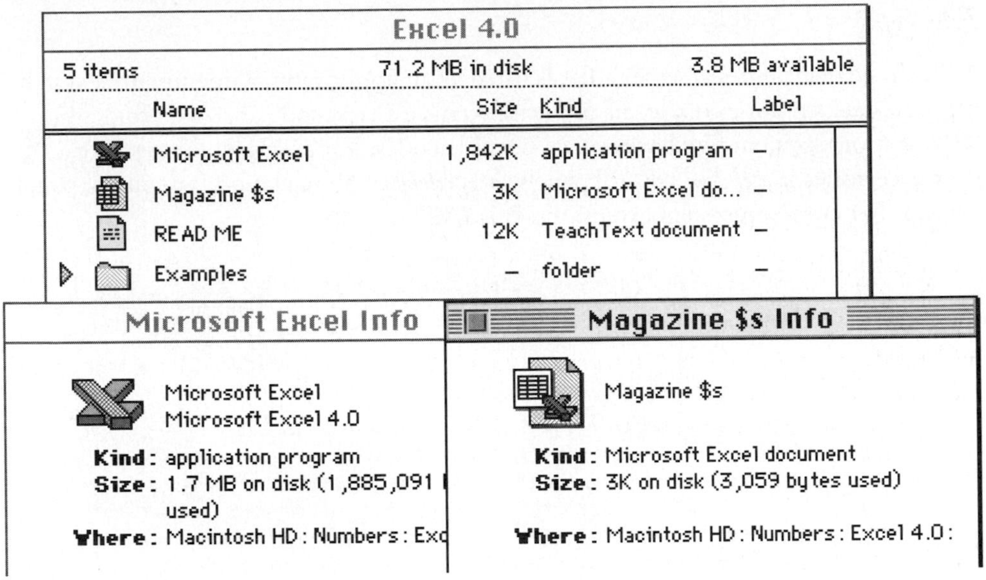

Figure 8-1 Where to find a file's kind: in a By Kind view of a folder's contents (top) or in the Get Info windows (bottom)

Kind and the Desktop File

How does the Finder identify a file's kind? The initial answer is that the needed information is stored in an invisible Desktop file (System 7 actually has two separate Desktop files). Every time you add a new file to your disk, the Desktop file is updated to include the kind information for that file. In fact, the Desktop file is the Finder's storage site for virtually all of the information listed in Get Info windows, including what icon a file should have.

SEE: • Fix-It #9 for more on the Desktop file

So where does the Desktop file get this kind (and other related information) in the first place? Each file on your disk contains this information about itself in a special area of the file reserved for this purpose. When a file is first copied to a disk, this information is copied to the Desktop file where it is then accessed by the Finder as needed. Applications are the primary source of this information, providing the needed icons and document-linking data for all the application's accessory files and documents.

Finally, exactly what information is used to determine a file's kind? A file's kind is determined by two four-letter codes assigned to and initially stored with each file. These are referred to as the file's type and creator codes.

File Type

A file's type determines whether a file is listed as an application, a document, a system file, or whatever. For example, all applications have a type code of *APPL* (for *APPL*ication). System files have several possible codes. For example, the type for desk accessories is *dfil.* For control panels, it is *cdev* (an abbreviation for *c*ontrol panel *dev*ice). For common system extensions, it is *INIT.*

TECHNICALLY SPEAKING ▶

INIT REDUX

In Chapter 1, I used the expression INIT to describe programs that must load into memory at startup in order to work. In particular, this lumped together system extensions and most control panels. Here, based on the type code, it seems that only system extensions should be considered INITs. This is true, in a sense, but it is also true that control panels that load into memory at startup (and not other control panels) contain the equivalent of an INIT within their program. This is the basis for using the term INIT to group these control panels and extensions together.

SEE: • **"Finder Flags (Attributes)" later in this chapter and Fix-It #4 for more details**

For documents, virtually an infinite number of possible type codes is available. Each application uses a unique type code that it assigns to documents that are saved in its unique format. These type codes are determined by the developers of the software. For example, the type code for MacWrite Pro data documents is MWPd. Thus, all MacWrite Pro data documents created in MacWrite Pro are given a MWPd type (related documents will probably have a different type; for example MacWrite Pro stationery has a type sWPd). As another example, the type code for Microsoft Word 4.x/5.x documents is WDBN (it's W6BN for Word 6.x documents).

The type information determines what files get displayed in an application's Open dialog box. Thus, MacWrite Pro recognizes files of the MWPd type as being MacWrite Pro documents. Similarly, MacWrite Pro's file-translation feature, if installed, would determine that files of the WDBN type should be interpreted as Word files.

File Creator

The creator code is used to *bundle* (or link) an application and all the documents that it creates. Thus, an application and its documents generally have the same creator code. For example, the creator code for both the MacWrite Pro application and a MacWrite Pro document is: MWPR. For Microsoft Word, it is MSWD. Creator codes, like the type codes, are selected by the software developer.

The creator code is used primarily at the Finder level. For example, it is what tells the Finder that a MacWrite Pro document was *created* by the MacWrite Pro application. This, in turn, tells the Finder to launch MacWrite Pro when you double-click a MacWrite Pro document. It also determines what icon the Finder assigns to a newly created MacWrite Pro document.

For documents, the kind description in the Get Info window is determined primarily by the file's creator, not the file's type.

Programs can often save files in several different formats. When MacWrite Pro saves a file in Microsoft Word format, for example, it assigns Word's document type and creator codes to the file. Thus, when it is finished, there is no way to tell that the file was originally created in MacWrite Pro and not in Word. When you next double-click this file from the Finder, it launches Word, not MacWrite Pro (assuming Word is on your disk somewhere). Had it changed only the file's type but not the creator, double-clicking the Word file from the Finder would launch MacWrite Pro (because of its MacWrite Pro creator). MacWrite Pro would then correctly interpret the file as a Word file (because of its Word type) and translate it.

To solve problems involving type and creator codes, you need to know what a file's codes are and, if necessary, be able to change them. The next section describes how to do this.

Type and Creator Code Problems

 Symptoms:

One or more of the following symptoms occurs.

Application Could Not Be Found

You are unable to open a document from the Finder because you get an error message that says the application program that created it could not be found. This could happen for many reasons that do not directly relate to type or creator problems (as covered more in Chapter 6). The best tip-off that you have a type/creator problem is if you get this error message even though the creating application is presently on a mounted disk.

Wrong Kind

The kind for a data document, as listed in the Get Info window, is listed as *document* (when it should be something more specific, such as *MacWrite Pro document*). Although a kind of just *document* is the correct listing for some files, this is usually not the case for data documents such as word processing files.

Wrong Icon

A file, most often a data document, does not display its correct icon in the Finder. Typically, it displays a generic (blank-page) icon instead. You will often find this to be the case with documents that have *document* as their kind, as just described. If this is the only symptom you have, you can often ignore it (unless the aesthetic loss bothers you). But if it is linked to a problem opening the file, you probably want to fix it.

TAKE NOTE ▶

ASSIGNING ICONS

Most file icons in the Finder are custom icons. Generally, an application and all its accessory and data document file icons share a similar appearance that helps identify them as belonging together.

If no custom icon is present, the Finder instead assigns it one from its standard set of generic icons. The generic document icon, for example, is simply a blank rectangle with a corner turned down. Thus, these generic icons can be perfectly normal, even if they are rarely seen these days.

However, occasionally a file that has previously displayed a custom icon may unexpectedly appear with a generic icon. This is usually a sign of at least minor trouble.

 Causes:

As is true for software in general, the area of a file that contains the type and creator codes can become corrupted. These codes can also be mistakenly altered by other programs. Finally, for various reasons, the Finder may have difficulty correctly interpreting a file's type and creator information. More specifically, the following situations can occur.

A File's Type Code or Both Its Type and Creator Codes Are Missing or Corrupted

This situation is relatively rare, but it can happen. Files without type or creator codes can often be quite difficult to open, especially from the Finder. They may not even open from within the creating application. Happily, restoring the proper codes is a quick way to restore the document to working condition.

A Document File's Creator Code Is Missing or Corrupted

Be especially suspicious that a document is missing its creator code if you get the message that *the application program that created it could not be found,* even though you know the application is on a currently mounted disk. Restoring a document's proper creator code reestablishes the link between the document and its creating application, allowing the Finder to identify the file and open it.

The Creating Application Is Missing

Even if a document has its correct type and creator codes, it cannot be opened from the Finder if the creating application is not currently on a mounted disk. In fact, if the creating application has *never* previously been on the same disk as the document, the document may display a generic icon rather than its correct custom icon.

Bundle Bit Problems

Occasionally, a document has its correct type and creator codes and the creating application is on a mounted disk, but the Finder still fails to recognize the link between the application and the document. Technically, this is not a type or creator problem. This is most often due to the application's Bundle bit being set incorrectly (as described more in the section on "File Attributes," later in this chapter) or more serious file damage.

Multiple Versions of the Same Application on Your Disk

If you have two different versions of the same application on your disk, you may find that one of them displays the wrong icon (typically using the icon associated with the other version). Similarly, its documents may display the other application's document icons or may display only the generic blank page icon.

What to do:

For the fastest and easiest route to success, try the following suggestions in the order given.

Try the Simpler Solutions

Copy the Creating Application to a Mounted Disk   If the creating application is *not* on any mounted disk, you can solve most of these problems easily enough by copying it to a mounted disk. This assumes that you know what the creating application is and that you have access to it. Not only should this allow you to open problem documents directly, but it usually fixes any icon display and related problems (after you restart).

Open the File from Within the Creating Application   If the creating application *is* on the disk, you can usually solve the problem by trying to open the file from within the application's Open dialog box rather than from the Finder. If this works, save a copy of the file with a new name, quit the application, and delete the original file. This usually solves the problem.

Open the File with Another Application   Otherwise, you can try to open the file from within another application already on your disk, one that can import the problem document file.

SEE: • Chapter 6 for more details on these solutions

Rebuild the Desktop   This fixes a variety of wrong icon and related problems. If you have two different versions of the same application on your disk, get rid of one of them before you rebuild.

SEE: • Fix-It #9 for details on rebuilding the desktop

Use a Repair Utility   Run Norton Utilities' Disk Doctor or MacTools' DiskFix (or FileFix) to check for incorrect Bundle bit settings and/or minor problems with other file attributes. This is all done automatically as part of the utility's routine disk-checking procedures (as described in Fix-It #13). If a problem is detected, the utility alerts you and asks if you wish to fix it. Say yes.

Viewing and Editing Type/Creator Codes

To view and edit the type and creator codes, you can use Norton Utilities for Macintosh or MacTools. Many other utilities also let you do this. Two others, both mentioned later in this chapter, are DiskTop and Get More Info. The former is a desk accessory that is an especially good tool for doing virtually any of the functions described in this chapter. The latter is a shareware extension that is especially convenient when you want to quickly access the codes of a single file.

BY THE WAY ▶

CHANGING A FILE'S TYPE HAS ITS LIMITS

Other than correcting for a lost or damaged type code, there is rarely (though I'll provide a couple of exceptions later in this chapter) any reason to consider modifying a file's type. Changing a type code does not change the underlying format of a document. For example, changing a document's type code from WDBN to MWPd does not magically change a Word document into a MacWrite Pro document. Instead, it only leads to confusion. On the other hand, as described here, changing a file's creator can be useful even when it is not lost or damaged.

Editing type and creator codes is how, for example, you can restore a missing or corrupted code. Also, if the creating application is unavailable to you, you can use these utilities to change a document's creator to that of another application, one that is available. Assuming that the other application can import files of the document's type, you would now be able to double-click the document from the Finder and have it launch with its newly assigned application rather than its originally intended one. Other utilities (such as NowMenus and Macintosh Easy Open) accomplish this same goal in a simpler manner (as mentioned in Chapter 6). However, sometimes directly altering the creator code is the only thing that works.

Several specific examples of the potential usefulness of editing a file's creator and type codes will be described shortly. But first, let's see how to use utilities to actually make these changes. A general warning: before attempting to make any of these changes, make sure the file is closed.

With the Norton Utilities

1. Open Norton Disk Editor (either from its Finder icon or by selecting it from Norton Utilities' Utilities menu). This should lead to a dialog box with a pop-up menu of all mounted disks.

2. Select the disk you want and click Open. This opens a window with a directory listing of all files and folders on the disk, including invisible ones. Double-click a folder to reveal the contents of the folder.

3. The Type and Creator codes for each file are already listed in columns to the right of the file name. To edit any of these codes, select the desired file and then click the Info button at the top of the window (see Figure 8-2). This opens up a new window that lists the Type and Creator (among other things) of the file. From here, you can modify the code by typing in a different one.

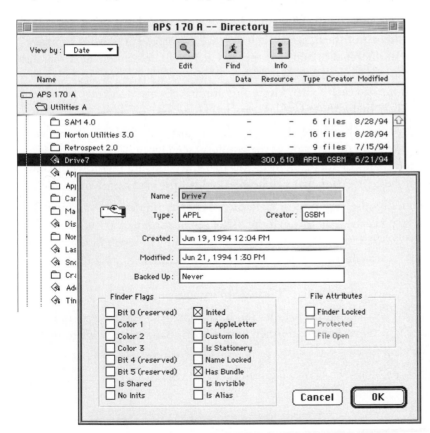

Figure 8-2 Norton Disk Editor shows the type and creator codes of the Drive7 application

BY THE WAY ▶

A GREAT FEATURE OF MACTOOLS DISAPPEARS

If you are familiar with versions of MacTools prior to version 3.x, you will notice that one of the major applications from the earlier versions is missing in version 3.x: DiskEdit. This was a great utility that allowed you to access a variety of the features that I describe in this chapter, including editing a file's Type and Creator, file attribute bits, boot blocks, hex code for the entire disk, and more. In some ways, it was superior to the comparable features found in Norton Utilities. Unfortunately, Central Point (before it was taken over by Symantec) decided to drop this application from version 3.0. However, two important features, editing file Type and Creator and viewing invisible files, are still available through FileFix. The remainder of DiskFix's features can no longer be accessed in any manner via MacTools. Pity.

With MacTools Pro

1. Open the MacTools Clinic application. Then click the FileFix button from the row of buttons at the top of the window. This opens up the FileFix window. From here, making sure the File Info button is selected, your display should look similar to what is shown in Figure 8-3.
2. From the scrolling list on the right-hand side of the window, locate and select the desired file. To the left of the name of each disk is a triangle. These work similarly to the triangle's in the Finder's non-icon views. Clicking on a triangle next to a disk name results in a sublist of all files and folders at the root level of the disk. Further triangles appear next to each folder. Using this approach, you can eventually locate any file on the disk, including invisible ones.
3. When the desired file is highlighted, its type and creator will appear in the appropriate editable boxes on the left side of the window (see Figure 8-3). If the boxes contain question marks or are blank, it means that the codes are unknown. Below these boxes will be a checkbox that will be checked if a file is currently invisible.
4. You can now modify the Type and/or Creator codes by typing in different one(s).

   Alternatively, you can scroll through the list of application names above the Type and Creator boxes. Selecting the name of any application will result in the current file's Type and Creator shifting to match that of documents belonging to the selected application.

   You can also change the selected file's invisibility status.
5. Click Save to save any changes. That's it. You have changed the file's type and creator. Click Done when you are finished with all the changes you wish to make.

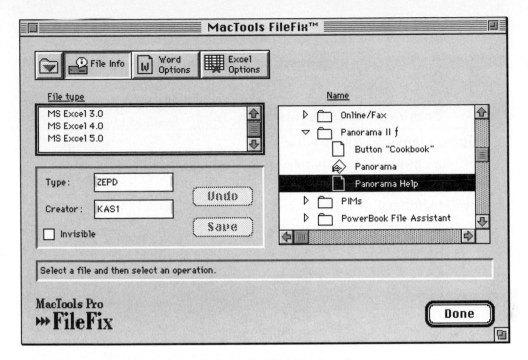

Figure 8-3 MacTools Pro's FileFix window, with File Info selected

With Get More Info

1. Before using Get More Info, install it in the Extensions folder and restart the Macintosh.

2. Accessing Get More Info works similarly to accessing the Finder's Get Info window. For ordinary Get Info, you select a file and then press the Command-I keys (or select Get Info from the Finder's File menu). To use Get More Info, select a file and hold down the Option-Command-I keys (or hold down the Option key while selecting Get Info from the Finder's File menu).

3. This opens up a new window that lists the file's type and creator, as well as several other attributes of the file (see Figure 8-4). From here, you can modify the code by typing in a different one. Click OK when you are done.

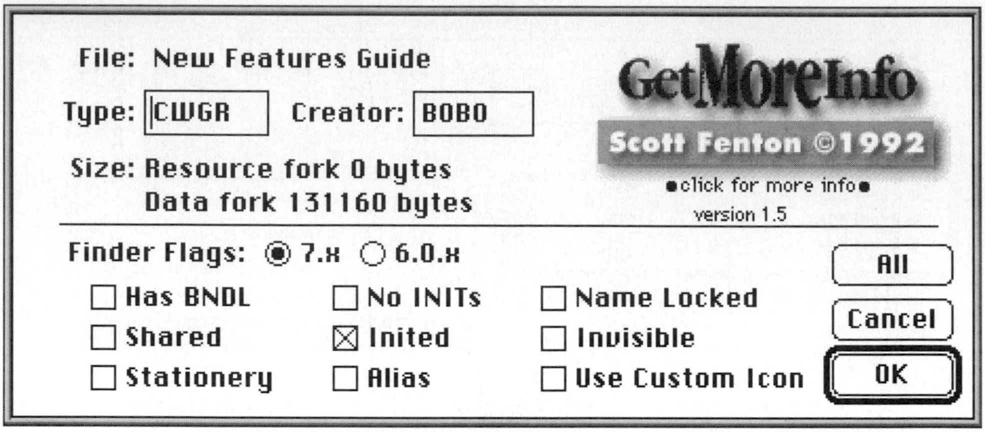

File: New Features Guide

Type: `CWGR`   **Creator:** `BOBO`

GetMoreInfo

Scott Fenton ©1992

●click for more info●

version 1.5

Size: Resource fork 0 bytes
Data fork 131160 bytes

Finder Flags: ◉ 7.x ○ 6.0.x

☐ Has BNDL   ☐ No INITs   ☐ Name Locked

☐ Shared   ☒ Inited   ☐ Invisible

☐ Stationery   ☐ Alias   ☐ Use Custom Icon

[All]

[Cancel]

[OK]

Figure 8-4   Get More Info shows the type and creator codes of a ClarisWorks document file

Most other competing utilities work in a similar manner to those described. For example, DiskTop works very similarly to Norton Utilities. You simply open DiskTop, navigate to the file you want, and then select Get Info from the DiskTop menu (or type Command-I). This brings up a window where you can edit the type and creator.

No matter which utility you use, when you return to the Finder, you may find that the Finder does not appear to recognize that you made a change. For example, the file may still show its old, incorrect, icon. If so, select Get Info for the file. This gets the Finder's attention and forces it to update its information. If this still fails to work, restart. As a last resort, rebuild the Desktop.

Identifying the Correct Creator Code

The just cited ability to alter a file's creator or type is not of much value if you do not know what creator or type code you need to enter. For example, perhaps you want to restore a missing creator code to a Microsoft Excel document file but you have no idea what the creator code is. Usually, this is not much of a problem. If you have an existing Microsoft Excel document on your disk, you can use any of the utilities just described to check what its codes are and then apply them to the problem document. Note that use of uppercase and lowercase makes a difference in these codes. Copy codes exactly!

If you have no document to use as a guide, your best bet is to try MacTools' File-Fix, since it provides a built-in list of common file codes. As explained, you simply select the name of the suspected creating application in the scrolling list (as shown in Figure 8-3), and FileFix will automatically fill in the correct codes for that application. Just make sure the version of the application on your disk matches the version listed in FileFix. Sometimes an application's creator and type codes are changed when an upgrade is released.

TEXT and PICT Formats: Type and Creator Issues

Some file formats (file types) are *generic.* That is, they are not associated with a particular application, but are recognized by most applications of a given category.

The most common example of this is a format called *(Plain) Text.* This format is recognized by virtually every word processor, as well as many other types of applications that work with text. Thus, even if a word processor has no special translator files, it typically can still read Text format files.

Using the Text format facilitates transfer of text data across many different types of applications. For example, even spreadsheets and databases can save their data as text files as well as read text files created in other applications. However, there is a cost to this universal acceptance: Text files do not retain any of the special formatting options (such as font styles or pasted-in graphics) available, for example, when you save a word processing file in its application-specific format.

Graphics formats have a whole collection of generic file formats. Each one has different qualities. Unlike text applications, many graphics applications do not have a unique format for saving documents. Instead, they depend entirely on the generic formats. This makes it much easier to transfer graphics information from one graphics application to another, since it is likely that both applications recognize the same generic formats.

Probably the most common generic graphic file format is called PICT. Almost every graphics application can read and save PICT files. It is the graphic equivalent of the plain Text format.

SEE: • Chapter 10 for more on PICT and other generic graphics formats

Documents with Text and PICT formats are identified by the appropriate type. Thus, the file type for plain text documents is TEXT, and the file type for PICT documents is PICT.

No single creator code is associated with these types. Normally, when you save a file in one of these formats it is assigned the creator of the application used to save it. Thus, the next time you double-click a PICT file from the Finder, it should launch the graphics application used to create the file (such as MacDraw or Canvas). Similarly, if you create four different PICT files, each created by a different application, double-clicking each document launches a different application—even though they are all PICT documents. The same idea applies to TEXT documents.

As a result of all this, you can't trust icons to identify PICT or TEXT files, as each type of file may have any of several different icons, depending on the application that created them.

TAKE NOTE ▶

TEACHTEXT VERSUS SIMPLETEXT

TeachText is a bare-bones word processor that comes as part of Apple's system software. Because of its widespread availability, many companies use TeachText documents for their ReadMe and related files. More recently, Apple replaced TeachText with SimpleText. It comes included with all Power Macintoshes and with System 7.5. This new processor, while it is still sparse in features (you still can't open files greater than 32K or paste graphics via the Paste command), at least now allows you to vary the font and size of text, as well as allowing multiple documents to be open at once. Fortunately, the Type and Creator of SimpleText documents remains exactly the same as for TeachText documents. Still, as a precaution, once you shift to SimpleText, you should remove any copies of TeachText from your disk.

However, if the creating application is not on your disk, the Finder will not launch a TEXT or PICT file when you double-click it. In this situation, as discussed for documents in general, you instead typically get an error message that says that the file did not open because the application program that created it "could not be found." In System 7, however, if you have TeachText (or its more recent replacement, SimpleText) on your disk, the Finder additionally asks whether you want to open the document using TeachText (see Figure 8-5).

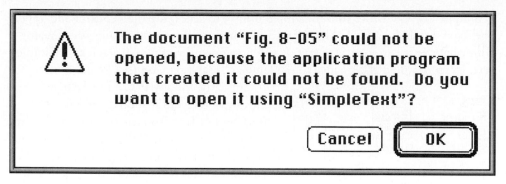

Figure 8-5 This message appears when you try to open a TEXT or PICT document for which the creating application cannot be found

Remember, all of this only affects opening the file from the Finder by double-clicking. All applications that can read TEXT files can recognize and open the file from within the application itself. In fact, once the document is open, you can use Save As to save the document, and it should acquire the creator (and type) code of the application you are using. Otherwise, if you wish, you can directly change the creator code of the TEXT document using the methods described in the previous section.

Alternatively, as described in Chapter 6, utilities such as NowMenus or Apple's Macintosh Easy Open, can be used to automatically make substitutions of this sort, so that whenever you double-click a text file, for example, it might be set to automatically open ClarisWorks.

SEE: • Chapter 6 for more on problems with opening files

Five More Good Reasons to View or Change a File's Type/Creator

If you are still not convinced that a working knowledge of how to edit Type and Creator codes is of value to you, here are a few more practical examples that may change your mind.

Get Documents to Open in TeachText/SimpleText by Default

Here's the deal. You save a text document in a communications program like CompuServe Information Manager or America Online. The next time you want to double-click the text document, you would prefer it to open directly in TeachText or SimpleText (which launch rather fast) instead of the slower launching communications software. Unfortunately, it doesn't. What to do?

Simple. Use Get More Info (or similar utility) to access the file's Creator and Type. The Type should be **TEXT.** That's fine. Leave it alone. However, change the Creator from whatever it currently is to **ttxt.** It will now open directly in TeachText or Simple-Text. Its icon should also change to the familiar TeachText icon (see Figure 8-6).

Yes Edit   No Edit   Picture

Figure 8-6
TeachText/SimpleText icons for editable text files (left), uneditable text files (center), and PICT files (right)

Similarly, for any **PICT** file, change its creator to **ttxt** and it should open in Teach-Text/SimpleText. You can't edit it from there, but you can view it. By the way, these are the type of PICT files that are created by your Macintosh when you take a picture of your screen by typing Command-Shift-3 (try it!).

Make Uneditable TeachText/SimpleText Documents Editable

Did you ever get those uneditable TeachText documents, the ones with the newspaper icon (see Figure 8-6)? If you even try just to copy any text from that document (never mind actually altering any of the text!), TeachText/SimpleText gives you an alert message that says you cannot do it. What to do?

Easy enough. Change the file's Type this time (not its Creator). While the file is closed, change its Type from **ttro** to **TEXT.** Presto, you now have an editable Teach-Text document. Its icon will change accordingly.

By the way, with editable TeachText/SimpleText documents, you can copy and paste text, copy graphics, but not paste graphics. To get graphics into a TeachText document requires using a utility like ResEdit.

Fit More Utilities on an Emergency Toolkit Floppy Disk

In Chapter 2, I described how to make your own Emergency Toolkit startup disks. One method involved using a utility called ShortFinder as a substitute for the real Finder. This utility, because of its small size compared to the Finder, frees up more disk space for you to add other utilities: version 1.5 of ShortFinder only takes up 30K, while the Finder takes up more than 450K, giving you another 420K or so.

The method I described in Chapter 2 required that all files be at the root level of the startup disk. I promised that I would later reveal how to create a startup disk with ShortFinder and still keep all relevant files in a true System Folder. Here's how:

First, delete the original Finder from you startup floppy disk. Now copy Short-Finder there instead, placing it in the System Folder. To be really cute, rename Short-Finder to Finder. Now (and here's the key step), use Get More Info (or similar utility) to change ShortFinder's Type and Creator to match that of the original Finder. In particular, change its Type from **APPL** to **FNDR,** and its Creator from **sFdr** to **MACS.** When you are done, ShortFinder's icon should change to that of the real Finder (see Figure 8-7). The disk should now function just fine as a startup disk!

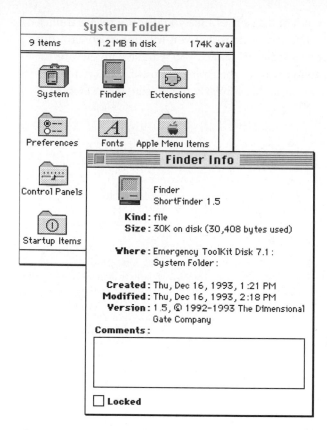

Figure 8-7   ShortFinder "disguised" as the Finder in the System Folder of a startup floppy disk (take a close look at the top of the Get Info window—and the Size of the file)

This ShortFinder trick is the only technique, of which I am aware, that will let you launch more than one utility from a Finder-less floppy startup disk! If you need to save even more space (or don't want to use ShortFinder for any reason), and you don't need to run more than one application from the floppy disk, you can use an almost identical method to create a totally Finder-less startup disk. In this case, simply assign the FNDR and MACS codes to whatever single troubleshooting application you wish to access at startup. Combine this with a System file and you have a startup disk. These two files needn't even be in a System Folder, just leave them loose at the root level of the floppy disk. Actually, as described in Chapter 2, if you do place the files at the root level of the disk, you may not even have to bother with changing the application's Type and Creator. Just renaming the application to Finder may work (though apparently not in System 7.5).

When you start up with these types of disks, they take you directly to the application serving as a Finder substitute. The downside is that you will not be able to shift to any other application (unless you used ShortFinder), you will have no view of the Finder's desktop, and will you have no access to the Apple menu. If you try to quit from the application, the Macintosh treats this similarly to a Restart/Shut Down.

BY THE WAY ▶

OTHER TYPES OF FINDER-LESS STARTUP DISKS

Some commercial Finder-less startup floppy disks, such as those that come with MacTools Pro, may be created by the same Type/Creator method described here for ShortFinder, except that they use their own utility (such as DiskFix) rather than ShortFinder. In other cases (such as with recent versions of Apple's Installer disks), these startup floppy disks are not created by changing the application's Type/Creator. Instead, these disks are created by altering the floppy disk's boot blocks (a term explained more later in this chapter) so that the Macintosh is instructed to start up with an application other than the Finder. That is why the application on these disks does not have to be renamed "Finder" even though it is at the root level of the disk. Beyond this, these disks have no system software except a System file. Like most other Finder-less disks, the Finder-substitute application is the only one that can be opened.

While you can create your own custom disks of this type, using Norton Utilities or DiskEdit (from MacTools 2.x), I will pass on describing the details here. I recommend using the Type/Creator method instead.

In any case, as I described in Chapter 2 ("Take Note: To Make an Exact Copy of an Entire Floppy Disk), if you make a copy of these boot block-altered disks from the Finder, the copy may not work as a startup disk. This is because the Finder does not copy the modified boot blocks. Instead, use a special copy utility such as DiskCopy.

Add Alert Sounds Without Installing Them in the System File

Open up the Sound control panel and you'll see a list of all the alert sounds you can select. This same list is also used by a variety of programs for various purposes, such as for selecting the alarm sound in appointment/reminder programs. The sounds in this list come from the sounds installed directly in the System file. To install a new sound, you simply drag the sound file to the System file icon. But suppose you would like to add new sounds in the same way that you can add new fonts in System 7.1 or a later version simply by placing the sound in a folder, like the Fonts folder, rather than having to install it directly in the System file? This would have the advantage of allowing you to modify your sound list without having to modify the System file each time (which reduces the risk of damage to the System file).

Can this be done? Yes. The trick solution here is to change the file Type and Creator of the sound file to match that of a font suitcase file. In particular, change its Type from **sfil** to **FFIL** and the Creator from **movr** to **DMOV**.

Actually, if you have multiple sounds stored in a sound suitcase file, as provided with utilities such as Now Fun!, you can change the entire sound suitcase into a font suitcase. Dragging this lone file to the Fonts folder will now add all the sounds in one step.

Search for a File Based on Its Type or Creator

The Find function in the Finder of System 7.1 or earlier cannot search for files based on their Type/Creator. However, this ability was added to the Find File function of System 7.5. For users of earlier versions of the system software, there are a host of competing utilities that also provide this function, such as DiskTop (via its Find command), Norton Utilities' Fast Find, or FindPro (a shareware utility that, in fact, is the basis of System 7.5's new feature). With this ability, you can search by Creator to easily locate every file on your disk created by a specific application.

True, with most Find utilities, you can probably instead search by Kind to accomplish the same thing as a search by Creator, but I trust searching by Creator as more reliable. Also, System 7.5's new Find File feature limits what you can use as input for Kind, making a search by Type/Creator the only viable alternative in many situations. For example, to find all ClarisWorks documents, you might decide to search for all files whose Kind contains the word **ClarisWorks.** Unfortunately you can't do this with System 7.5's Find File. Instead, search for all files with a creator equal to **BOBO.**

One notable reason to do this type of search, as described in Fix-It #2, is to search for a hard-to-locate preferences file.

Finder Flags (Attributes)

What Are Finder Flags (Attributes)?

Finder flags describe a set of "on-off" characteristics that have been separately assigned to each file (and folder) on your disks. These flags are also often referred to as a file's *attributes* or *bits*. They determine important aspects of how the Macintosh (especially the Finder) interacts with a given file (such as whether it is invisible and whether it loads at startup or not). Normally, these flag settings are handled without any user involvement. You may not even be aware that these flags exist. However, as you will soon see, you can examine and modify these flags by using the special utilities already described in this chapter. Here are four common examples of Finder flags that you might have reason to check on or modify.

The Invisible Bit

If a file's (or folder's) Invisible bit box is checked, it will not be visible on the Finder's desktop. Normal access to these files is thus prohibited. The Desktop file is a common example of a normally invisible file. Unchecking this bit for an invisible file will make the file visible on the Finder's desktop. You can similarly turn any ordinary visible file into an invisible one, by checking this bit.

Of course, if a file is already invisible, you may wonder how to find it so that you can change its flags. Don't worry, I'll explain that shortly.

SEE: • "Invisible Files and Folders" later in this chapter

The Bundle Bit

The Bundle bit is usually turned on for applications. This informs the Finder to check the application for information about linked document files, including what icons to assign to documents that the application creates. Programs like Norton Utilities or MacTools, when used to check for disk problems (as described in Fix-It #13) can detect and correct Bundle bit errors (that is, a Bundle bit set to off that should be on, or vice versa). A shareware utility called Save a BNDL also fixes these errors. This can sometimes help restore the correct icon to a document file. Unless you are sure you know what you are doing, you should depend on these utilities to fix Bundle bit problems, rather than altering the Bundle bit yourself.

The NO INITs Bit

The NO INITs bit is relevant mainly for certain control panels. If a control panel is designed to act as an INIT (that is, if it loads into memory at startup along with system extensions), this bit is unchecked. Otherwise, it is checked. You can use this bit to determine for certain which control panels (or extensions) are INITs and which are not.

Normally you should not alter this bit yourself. However, in Chapter 6 (see "Technically Speaking: Cannot Open a Control Panel Because NO INITS Bit Is Checked"), I described one case where certain control panels could not be opened because their NO INITs bit had been inadvertently checked. This caused the Mac not to load these control panels at startup, and so they would not work. The solution (after discovering how this had happened in the first place) was to recheck the NO INITs bit and restart.

SEE: • Chapter 1 and Fix-It #4 for more details on INITs

The Name Locked Bit

This bit, when checked, prevents the name of the file from being changed from the Finder, regardless of whether the Get Info Locked box is checked or not. This is the reason you cannot change the name of the System, Finder, or Enabler files, for example. If you turn this bit off and then restart(!), you will be able to change the name of these files.

However, you might instead simply make a copy of the file (since the copy does not have its locked bit set). You can then change the name of the copy.

Viewing and Editing Finder Flags

One of the conveniences of the Macintosh design is that you can easily turn these flag settings on or off without having to know any special programming skills. Just one click of a mouse can turn an invisible file into a visible one. Still, you don't want to make these changes recklessly. Normally, these flags are set on or off by the developer of the software (or, in some cases, by the Finder), and there is no reason to change them. Nevertheless, a few of these attributes, such as the ones just described, can be relevant to certain problem-solving issues. Even if you don't change them, it pays to know how to check on them.

So, to access the list of flags/attributes for a file, you use the same familiar utilities (and similar procedures) that you used to check a file's type and creator: Norton Utilities, MacTools, or Get More Info (as well DiskTop or other competing utilities). Here are the exact procedures.

With Norton Utilities

1. Open Norton Disk Editor (either from its Finder icon or by selecting it from Norton Utilities' Utilities menu). This should lead to a dialog box with a pop-up menu of all mounted disks.

2. Select the disk you want and click Open. This opens a window with a directory listing of all files and folders on the disk, including invisible ones. Double-click a folder to reveal the contents of the folder.

3. Select the desired file and then click the Info button. This opens up a new window (see Figure 8-2) that lists the file's attributes (as well as its Type and Creator as described).

4. Check or uncheck a particular attribute as desired. Older versions of Norton Utilities presented slightly different lists of attributes depending on whether you selected those for System 6 or System 7. This feature has been dropped from version 3.x.

By the way, you can also get a similar list of information from Norton Disk Doctor. Select *Get Info* (for volumes) or *Get Info for . . .* (for files and folders) from Disk Doctor's File menu.

With MacTools   The latest version of MacTools no longer has the option to list a file's attributes other than the Invisible bit. This bit, as described, is accessed from FileFix using the same procedure used to access the Type and Creator. In earlier versions of MacTools, you could access all attributes via the DiskEdit utility.

With Get More Info   The basic procedure is the same as for getting a file's Type and Creator. One disadvantage of Get More Info is that, since it works from the Finder, you cannot use it to select invisible files.

1. Select the desired file from the Finder's desktop and type Option-Command-I. The list of file attributes appears (see Figure 8-4). Its list is somewhat different from the list in Norton Utilities, but they both list the key attributes described in this chapter.

2. Check or uncheck a particular attribute as desired. The list of attributes differs slightly depending on whether you select those for System 6 or System 7.

Invisible Files and Folders

Lurking on your disk are invisible files and folders. These include the Desktop files, the Desktop Folder, files created by certain extensions and control panels (such as by FileSaver or by AppleShare), the Temporary Items folder, the Trash Folder, and more.

System 6 Alert: Some invisible folders, such as the Trash and Desktop Folders, are specific to System 7. If you use a disk under System 6 that was previously formatted under System 7, these folders usually lose their invisibility and appear as normal visible folders. If so, ignore them. They will be correctly invisible again when you return to System 7.

Normally, you access invisible files and folders indirectly. Thus, you can rebuild the invisible Desktop file without ever opening it or in any way viewing it. However, there are occasions when you may want to directly view or modify these invisible files and folders. The next section describes how to do this.

SEE: • Chapter 2 for more on FileSaver
       • Chapter 4 for more on the Temporary Items Folder
       • Chapter 11 for more on ApppleShare
       • Fix-It #9 for more details on Desktop files

BY THE WAY ▶

TWO TYPES OF DESKTOPS

By the way, a distinction is usually made between the Finder's desktop (which refers to the display of windows and icons that the Finder creates) and the invisible Desktop file(s). By convention, the word desktop, when used for the Finder desktop, is not capitalized. For Desktop files, it is capitalized.

Viewing and Editing Invisible Files and Folders

With Norton Utilities or MacTools Pro You can view invisible files and folder with Norton Utilities or MacTools, using the same basic procedures described previously for accessing Type/Creator and attributes. That is, for The Norton Utilities, open a disk with the Norton Disk Editor (see Figure 8-8). For MacTools Pro, open the Clinic application and click the FileFix button. From the window that appears (see Figure 8-3), locate the file/folder you want from any currently mounted disk. In either case, a complete list of files and folders, both visible and invisible is displayed. To see the contents of a given folder, open the folder, as indicated for each application.

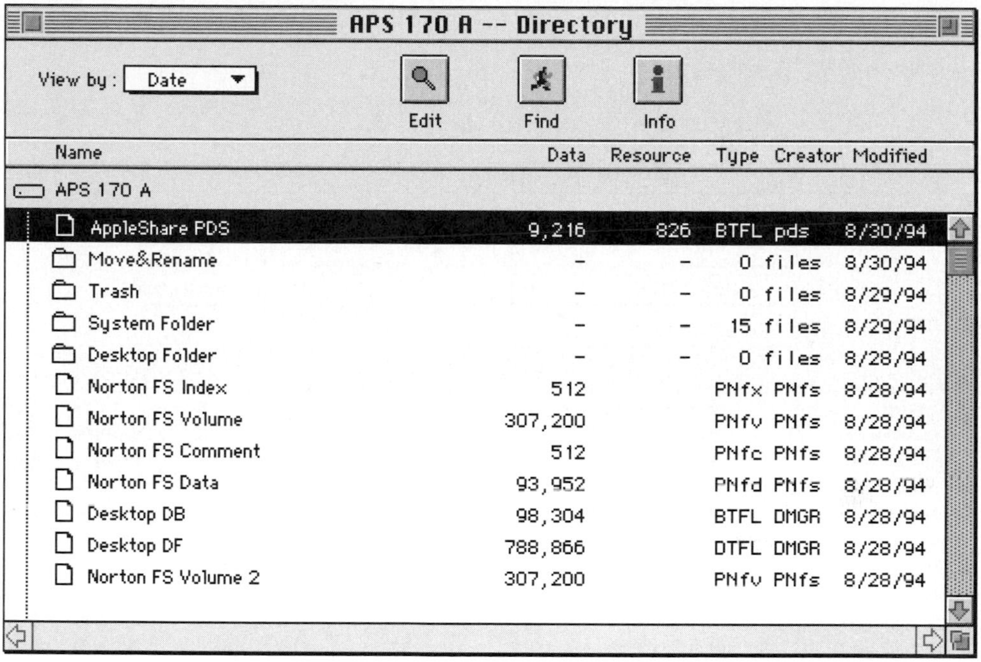

Figure 8-8 A view from Norton Disk Editor; all of the files and all of the folders listed here (except the System Folder) are invisible on the desktop

These utilities list *all* files, but they do not make it immediately obvious which ones are normally invisible. If you are familiar with the file you are looking for, such as the Desktop file, this may not be a problem. Otherwise, the only sure way to determine if a file is normally invisible is to select the file and check if its Invisible bit is turned on (as previously described in the section on "Finder Flags (Attributes)."

These utilities typically list only the name and location of these files. You cannot use them to open the file and examine its contents. Similarly, you cannot directly delete any of these invisible files from these utilities. To do any of this, you must first make the file visible, by unchecking its Invisible file attribute. You can then access the file from the Finder. A shareware utility called InvisiFile works similarly.

With DiskTop DiskTop deserves special mention here because you *can* use it to directly launch any files or delete invisible files from its listing window. This useful utility, as mentioned, also allows you to modify Type/Creator and file attributes as well as search by Type or Creator.

1. Open DiskTop. A list of the contents of all mounted disks will be displayed. Double-click a volume or folder name to reveal its contents.

2. The listing should include both visible and invisible files. If invisible files are not listed, select Preferences from the DiskTop menu. Check Technical from the Level options. Return to the file listing. Invisible files and folders will now be listed there.

3. To delete an invisible file or folder, simply select it and click the Delete button, located near the top of the window (see Figure 8-9).

4. Or, to launch any file, just double-click it.

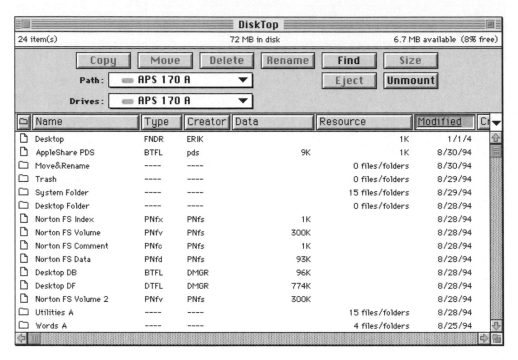

Figure 8-9   DiskTop, still another utility that lists invisible files and folders; but this one lets you copy, move, delete, or rename them

With System 7.5's Find File   System 7.5 has a new Find File feature (as described in Chapter 2). Open it, hold down the Option key, and select the Name pop-up menu. This will bring up four additional options at the bottom of the menu. Select "visibility" is "invisible." Then click the Find button. This will give you a list of all invisible files and folders on your disk. You will not be able to open or edit any of these files (and perhaps not even move them). If you try you will get a message such as *Unable to open <file name> because it is invisible (or is inside an invisible folder)* or *An unexpected error occurred, because the original item could not be found.* However, there is not a quicker, more convenient way to get a list of these files.

By the way, also convenient, another of these special options (name/icon lock) identifies which files have their Name Locked bit turned on.

Special Case: Viewing the Contents of the Desktop Folder and Trash Folder

By definition, an invisible folder is not displayed on the Finder's desktop (though it may appear in Open and Save dialog boxes). Similarly, none of the contents of an invisible folder are visible on the desktop (even though the invisible bits for each item in the folder are not turned on).

However, the special Desktop Folder and Trash folder are exceptions to this generalization. The contents of the Desktop Folder *are* visible. They are seen as the files and folders on the desktop (those items not in any folder nor in the root-level window of a volume). Similarly, just double-click the Trash icon to open a window that displays all items currently in the Trash folder. Think of the Trash can as a special folder icon.

Each disk maintains its own set of these invisible Desktop and Trash folders. For example, if you use MacTools Pro's FileFix or Norton Disk Editor to open the Trash folder on a given disk, it only lists those files that are currently in the Trash from that particular disk. In contrast, if you double-click the Trash icon on the desktop, it lists all files placed there from all mounted disks. If you eject a floppy disk, any unemptied items from that disk remain unemptied but disappear from the Trash folder window. They return to the Trash the next time you insert the disk.

Viewing and Editing *Really* Invisible Files and Folders

The Directory and Boot Blocks

Some files are so invisible that they do not even appear in the main listings of utilities like MacTools or DiskTop. In part, this is because these special files are not files in the same sense as typical documents and applications. A disk's *Directory* and *boot blocks* are two examples of this. However, you can sometimes use other special features of these utilities to view, and even alter, the contents of these files.

SEE: • Chapter 5 for more information on startup disks and boot blocks
       • Fix-Its #10 and #13 for more information on the Directory

Viewing the Directory and the Boot Blocks

With Norton Utilities

1. Open Norton Disk Editor (either from its Finder icon or by selecting it from Norton Utilities' Utilities menu). This should lead to a dialog box with a pop-up menu of all mounted disks.

2. Select the disk you want and click Open. This opens a window with a directory listing of all files and folders on the disk, including invisible ones.

3. Pull down the Objects menu. You will see a list of objects that include the Boot Blocks and the different components of the Directory (such as Extents B Tree). Figure 8-10 shows the window that appears if you select Boot Blocks. Note that

near the top of the window is an explanation of the function of the selected component (MaxFiles in this case). This explanation shifts accordingly each time you select a different component.

By the way, the Directory object (the last one in the Objects menu list, as seen in Figure 8-11) is something of a misnomer. It refers to the default listing of the contents of the disk, as seen in Figure 8-8, not to the actual Directory files.

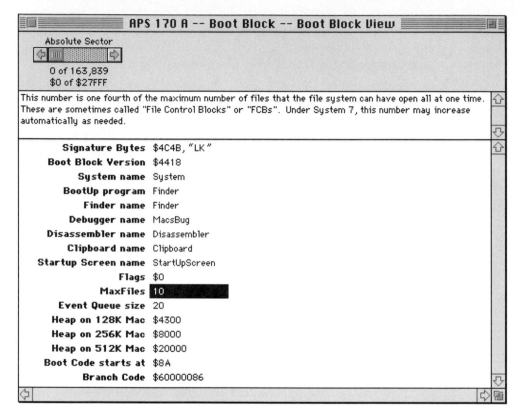

Figure 8-10   Norton Disk Editor's view of a disk's boot blocks

It's technically possible to use Norton Utilities to modify any of this boot block and Directory information. To do so, select the View in Hex or View in ASCII commands from the Display menu. You can now directly modify the data. By the way, you can get a similar hex or ASCII listing for any ordinary file on your disk by selecting the file name (when in the Directory view) and clicking the Edit button. But unless you are following detailed instructions or are generally skilled in how to work with hex code, I would not mess with any of this. Thankfully, you will rarely, if ever, need to edit this information, or even understand more about it than the minimum I have presented here. Refer to Norton Utilities documentation for more help if you really want or need to try this editing. MacTools' DiskEdit, unfortunately now extinct, could similarly view and edit this information—and in a way that made making changes easier to do.

Special Case: The Disk Driver and Related Low-Level Data

A hard disk's *driver descriptor map* (related to the *disk driver* first installed when you initialize a disk) and *partition map* (similarly determined when you format a disk) are often referred to as in the *low-level* areas of the disk. These areas allow the Macintosh to first interact with a hard disk, identify critical components of its operation, and maintain information about disk partitions.

These areas are located physically separate from the rest of the disk and, as such, are inaccessible from every function in Norton Utilities or MacTools that I have so far described. In fact, Norton Utilities' manual draws the distinction between the *logical disk* (what we have been working with so far) and the *physical disk* (which includes these additional areas). In essence, this is what is implied by saying these areas are at a low level. Normally, you interact with them only indirectly, such as via a disk formatting utility.

However, if you are really determined, you *can* see the Driver Descriptor Map and Partition Map with Norton Disk Editor. They are listed at the top of the Objects menu (see Figure 8-11). Normally these menu items are grayed out, but you can make them active (leaving the other items grayed out). Doing this requires a special procedure involving holding down the Command and shift keys when selecting a volume from Disk Editor's Open pop-up menu (after first selecting the "Scan SCSI Bus" command). This brings up a list of the additional names of the physical disks (such as Quantum drive) that you can open. Check the Norton Utilities manual for details.

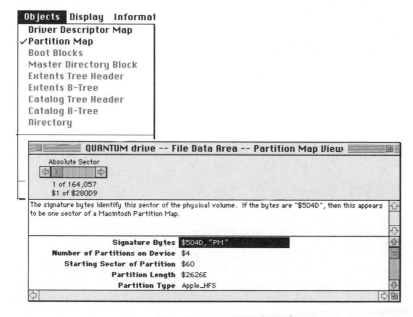

Figure 8-11   Norton Disk Editor finds friends in low places

I only mention all of this for the sake of completeness. Typically, you would have no reason to ever work with these areas.

SEE: • Fix-It #12 for more details on disk device drivers
     • Fix-It #15 for more details on partitioning and disk formatting

Chapter Summary

This chapter focused on an understanding of a file's type and creator. These settings affect how the Finder recognizes files, assigns icons to files, and links applications and documents. The type and creator can even determine whether a file can be opened. This chapter described how to view these codes as well as how and when to modify them. It described, in more detail, two of the most important file types: the generic TEXT and PICT types.

This chapter also described other Finder flags (or bits), such as the Invisible bit and the Bundle bit, that similarly affect how the Finder (or the Macintosh operating system in general) interacts with files.

Finally, this chapter surveyed the variety of invisible files and folders that exist on a Macintosh, from the Desktop files to the Temporary Items folder to the Directory and device drivers. It described how you can locate and view these files. Many of these invisible files and folders are mentioned in more detail in other chapters, as they apply to the specific problem-solving techniques discussed there.

Chapter 9

Fonts and Text:
Write and Wrong

The Write Stuff

No matter what else you do with your Macintosh, sooner or later you use it to write something. It may just be a note to a colleague or a caption added to an illustration. Or it may be a full-length manuscript. Whatever it is, you are using the text capability of the Macintosh. And what a capability it is! The various and varied ways you can alter the appearance of text on the Macintosh is one of the computer's most impressive features.

These text features and the applications that use them, most notably word processors, are the focus of this chapter. In most of these applications, changes to text are made by selecting items from the Font, Style, and Size menus (see Figure 9-1). For example, you might start by selecting a basic font appearance from the choices in the Font menu (such as Times or Helvetica). Then, you can decide on the style (such as *italics* or **bold**) and size (such as smaller or larger) of the font. A quick trip to the menu bar can change "**this**" to "*this*." Equally impressive is that when you finally print your text, the output looks virtually identical to what appeared on the screen, sometimes even better! This is the basic *what you see is what you get (WYSIWYG)* appeal of the Macintosh.

Figure 9-1   Typical Font, Style, and Size menus

What's even better is how easy it is to do all of this. Most people can create and print their text documents with little or no hassle and without the slightest understanding of how any of these font miracles happen. This is good, because understanding Macintosh's methods for displaying and printing fonts is about the most convoluted topic covered in this book.

Most of the time, the Macintosh succeeds in hiding this complexity from you. However, eventually something unexpected happens. Perhaps the line breaks on the printed copy do not match what appeared on your screen. Or maybe your document inexplicably displays with a different font from the one you expected. Or worse.

Resolving these sorts of problems, which is the topic of this chapter, *does* require that you learn at least a little about how all of this works. So, take a deep breath and let's go.

QuickDraw GX Alert: QuickDraw GX is a new technology that is included with System 7.5 (though it can also be used in System 7.1). It is an optional feature. That is, you can use System 7.5 without installing QuickDraw GX. QuickDraw GX affects almost everything about the display and printing of text and graphics. I say a lot more about QuickDraw GX in Chapter 12. Unless otherwise indicated, this current chapter assumes you are not using QuickDraw GX.

Font Basics

Font Files Versus Font Suitcases

Font Files

A font file is the term used to describe a particular individual font as it appears on the Finder's desktop. It can be moved or copied just like any other type of file. Most font files will have icons such as the ones on the left of Figure 9-2. Thus, Times 12 is an example of a font file.

Figure 9-2
Font file (left) versus font suitcase (right) icons

All characters in a font look related, and this basic design is called the typeface of the font. All fonts of the same typeface have the same general name and are said to belong to the same *family.* Thus, Times 10, Times 12, Times (bold), and so on are all part of the Times family of fonts, even though they are a different size and/or style. The Macintosh can tell which fonts belong to the same family because of special information contained within the font files. Sometimes, because it is common practice, the word font is also used to refer to the entire family rather than just a single file (as in, "Select the Times font from the Font menu").

Font Suitcases

It is possible for several font files to be combined into one superfile called a *font suitcase* (see Figure 9-2). In System 7, to see the contents of a suitcase file, simply double-click the file icon. This will open up a new window that lists all of the individual font files stored in the suitcase. In most cases (some exceptions are listed in the following sections), you can modify the contents of a font suitcase simply by dragging a font file out of or into the suitcase.

A font suitcase can contain just one font file, or it can contain several font files (such as all sizes of New York). The fonts in a suitcase do not have to be of the same family. For example, New York and Geneva fonts can be combined into one suitcase.

System 6 Alert: Modifying the contents of a font suitcase in System 6 requires a special utility called Font/DA Mover (see "By the Way: Font/DA Mover and Other Font/DA Management Utilities").

Where the Fonts Are

Just because a font file is on your disk somewhere doesn't mean it will show up on your Font menus. To be in Font menus, it has to be in a special location in your System Folder.

Many new Macintosh users—especially if they work with only one application—are surprised to discover that the available fonts are not part of the application itself. Instead, applications get their font listing from the System Folder. Since all applications' font listings are generated in the same way, the same set of fonts is available to all applications running under that startup disk. Thus, if you were to shift from a word processor to a spreadsheet, you would almost always find the same font listing.

You can choose from thousands of possible fonts. The Macintosh system software includes a basic set of fonts that are automatically installed when you first create a System Folder on your hard disk. However, these are only a tiny sample of what is available (even though they are probably all that most people ever use). Other fonts are available from Apple as well as from many other companies.

How Can You Tell What Fonts Are Installed in Your System?

One way, of course, is to open your System Folder and check directly (assuming you know where to look, as I will describe shortly). However, a much simpler solution is to open the Key Caps desk accessory (it comes with Macintosh system software disks). Its Key Caps menu lists all currently installed fonts. Actually, the Font menu of most word processors and related applications would have the same menu.

Locating, Adding, and Removing Fonts from Your System Folder

To add a new font to or remove an unwanted font from your Font menu requires installing or removing fonts from their relevant System Folder location. How to change which fonts are in your System Folder varies depending on what version of the system software you are using. Here's what you need to know (except for special issues that pertain only to PostScript fonts, which will be described later in this chapter).

Fonts in System 7.1 and System 7.5

Font files are located in a special folder within the System Folder called Fonts (see Figure 9-3). The Fonts folder can contain both single font files and font suitcases. The Macintosh will deal with both of them appropriately. The Fonts folder must remain in the System Folder in order for applications to access its contents.

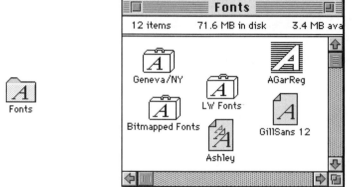

Figure 9-3   A Fonts folder containing both suitcase files and individual font files

Font and suitcases files can be dragged to or from the Fonts folder, similarly to how any other set of files and folders on the desktop would work. Alternatively, for adding a font or suitcase file to the Fonts folder, you can drag the file onto the active System Folder icon. This moves the font directly to the Fonts folder, after first giving you an alert message (see Figure 9-4, top).

You can add font files or suitcases to the Fonts folder, whether or not any other applications are open. However, if applications are open (other than the Finder), you will typically get an alert message warning you that the added fonts will not be available to any open applications until after you quit and relaunch them (see Figure 9-5, top). On the other hand, if you try to replace a font file with another file of the same name while applications are open, you *cannot* do it (see Figure 9-5, middle). Similarly, you cannot simply remove a file from the Fonts folder while any applications are open (see Figure 9-5, bottom). Sometimes you can remove a font file from a font suitcase within the Fonts folder, even though applications are open, but I have found that this doesn't always work. The solution in each of these cases, of course, is to quit all open applications before you try to make these changes.

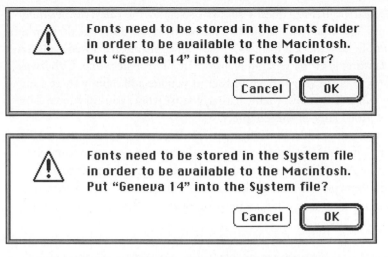

Fonts need to be stored in the Fonts folder in order to be available to the Macintosh. Put "Geneva 14" into the Fonts folder?

Cancel   OK

Fonts need to be stored in the System file in order to be available to the Macintosh. Put "Geneva 14" into the System file?

Cancel   OK

Figure 9-4 Similar messages that appear when you drag a font file to the System Folder icon in System 7.1/7.5 (top) and System 7.0 (bottom)

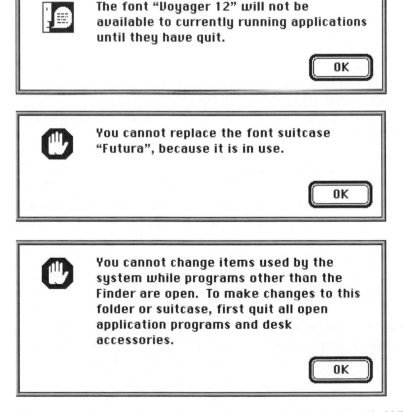

The font "Voyager 12" will not be available to currently running applications until they have quit.

OK

You cannot replace the font suitcase "Futura", because it is in use.

OK

You cannot change items used by the system while programs other than the Finder are open. To make changes to this folder or suitcase, first quit all open application programs and desk accessories.

OK

Figure 9-5 Messages that appear when you try to add (top), replace (middle), or remove (bottom) a font file to a Fonts folder while applications are open

Helpful hint: The system software doesn't always behave by the rules. Sometimes you get these alert messages when you shouldn't. Sometimes you don't get them when you should. For example, to replace a font, even with all applications closed, you may have to remove the existing font file separately and then add the new one. Otherwise, you may get the *font is in use* message. Beyond that, if you are still having these font problems, restarting will usually solve them. If that doesn't work, you may have damaged font files (as described later in this chapter).

The Fonts folder was a new addition in System 7.1 that was not present in earlier versions of the system software. Previous versions, as described next, store fonts directly in the System file. Actually, a few critical fonts needed for the Macintosh's menus, windows, and message boxes are still located in the System 7.1/7.5 System file, although you will not find them there when you open the System suitcase. The Finder keeps their listing "invisible."

SEE: • "Technically Speaking: Searching for Reserved Fonts in System 7," in the "Font Menu Problems" section, later in this chapter, for more on these invisible fonts

Overall, using a Fonts folder simplifies most font management tasks. Less frequent need to modify the System file also reduces the risk of possible damage to the file. However, in a few situations, such as replacing a font currently in the Fonts folder, the Fonts folder approach can be a bit tricky. For example, it is possible to have two copies of the exact same font file in the Fonts folder at the same time (you could not do this with fonts installed into the System file itself). One way this could happen is if duplicate font files are contained in two different suitcases. Surprisingly, this usually doesn't cause any problems. Still, you want to be careful here. For example, you wouldn't want to add a duplicate file when you are trying to replace an existing file that you suspect is corrupted.

SEE: • "Damaged Font Files," later in this chapter, for more details

Technically, fonts can still be stored in the System file, rather than the Fonts folder (see "By the way: Font/DA Mover and Other Font/DA Management Utilities"). Fonts in the System file are recognized and used just as if they were in the Fonts folder. Similarly, any fonts you find in the System file can be removed by opening the System file window and dragging the font files out. However, the Finder no longer lets you add new fonts to the System file. Instead, it insists that you place them in the Fonts folder (see Figure 9-6).

In this regard, if you upgraded from System 6 or 7.0 to System 7.1/7.5, check whether there are any fonts still remaining in your System file. If they are duplicated in your Fonts folder, drag the unneeded fonts from the System file to the Trash and delete them. Otherwise, drag the nonduplicate fonts to the Fonts folder.

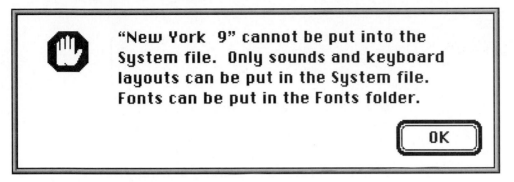

Figure 9-6 This message appears in System 7.1/7.5 if you try to add a font to the System file by dragging the font file directly to the System suitcase icon

Fonts in System 7.0.x

In System 7.0.x, there is no Fonts folder. Instead, font files are stored directly in the System file. Appropriately enough, the System file icon is a suitcase (and as such is sometimes referred to as the System suitcase). It works just like a font suitcase. Double-click it, and it opens up a window with a list of installed fonts (see Figure 9-7).

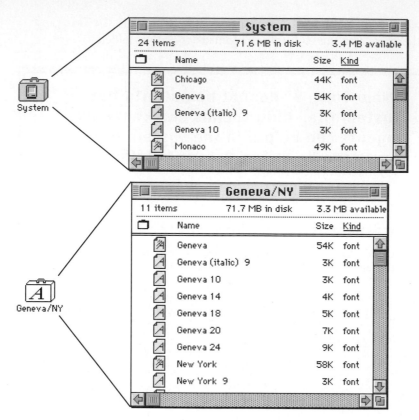

Figure 9-7 Opening a System suitcase (top) and a suitcase file (bottom) to view the font files within each

To add a font file to the System file, simply drag the file to the System Folder icon. After receiving an alert message (see Figure 9-4, bottom), the Macintosh will directly install the font(s) into the System file. If you do this with a font suitcase, it will first empty the suitcase, moving the fonts to the System file, and then delete the suitcase.

Alternatively, you can drag a font file directly to the System file icon. Or you can open the System file's window (by double-clicking the System icon) and drag a font file into the window. Any of these procedures will install the new font. To remove a font, open the System file's window and drag out the desired font to any other location on your disk.

You can neither add nor remove fonts in System 7.0 while any applications other than the Finder are open. (In System 7.1 you can add, but not remove, fonts with other applications running.)

If you want to move only part of the contents of a font suitcase to the System file, this is no problem either. Double-clicking the suitcase icon opens up its window, showing all the font files inside. These can now be moved individually to the System file.

Fonts in System 6.x

System 6 Alert: In all versions of System 6, similarly to System 7.0, fonts are stored directly in the System file. However, you cannot see the contents of the System file by double-clicking it. Instead you need the Font/DA Mover utility. When you open Font/DA Mover, it automatically shows a list of all the fonts stored in the System file of the startup disk (see Figure 9-8).

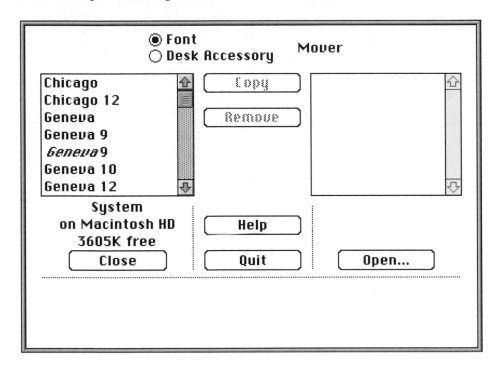

Figure 9-8   Font/DA Mover

Similarly, fonts are transferred from suitcase files to the System file by using Font/DA Mover. Font/DA Mover can also remove a font from the System file or copy it to a separate suitcase file. System 6 users should refer to the manual that comes with their software for more details on using Font/DA Mover, if necessary.

BY THE WAY ▶

FONT/DA MOVER AND OTHER FONT/DA MANAGEMENT UTILITIES

In System 6, font files cannot exist as separate files on the Desktop. They must either be in the System file or in a font suitcase. Moving them from one location to another requires a utility called the Font/DA Mover. This utility performs a similar function for desk accessories (DAs) and DA suitcases. Font/DA Mover can also create new empty suitcases or modify existing ones.

(continued)

In System 7, you no longer need Font/DA Mover. Actually, except for convenience and organizing, you don't really need suitcase files either. As a result, Font/DA Mover is no longer included with System 7 software.

In System 7, desk accessories function almost like independent applications and are typically stored in the Apple Menu Items folder. If you do still have DAs stored in a DA suitcase file, dragging the suitcase to the System Folder icon will automatically empty the suitcase and place the enclosed DAs into the Apple Menu Items Folder. Similarly, fonts are stored either in the System file or the Fonts folder and, in either case, can be moved without Font/DA Mover, as explained in the main text.

About the only use for Font/DA Mover in System 7 would be to create new suitcases if you have no existing suitcase files on your disk anywhere. Just make sure you are using Font/DA Mover version 4.1 or later. Earlier versions will not work properly with System 7. The latest version can be obtained from various on-line services and user groups (see Appendix).

Although you cannot use the System 7.1 Finder to install fonts directly into the System file, you can still get fonts into the System file if you really want. However, it requires either the use of Font/DA Mover or booting from a System 7.0 startup disk. But why bother? There is little or no advantage to bypassing the Fonts folder.

By the way, System 6 and System 7.0 users can access font files not stored in the System file. To do so, you use any of several third-party utilities, such as the well-known and aptly named Suitcase. These utilities can track fonts anywhere on a disk and allow them to be used as if they were installed in the System file. They have at least one possible advantage even in System 7.1/7.5: you can use them to open or close specific suitcase files on a temporary or permanent basis without having to move anything into or out of the Fonts folder. Still, for most System 7.1/7.5 users, the advantages of these utilities are probably not enough to justify their purchase. However, if you do use Suitcase, note that you should not use Suitcase to access any font file that is in the Fonts folder. Use one method or the other, but not both.

The Different Types of Fonts

The different categories of fonts described in this section do not refer to the appearance of the font (such as whether it is plain or decorative), but rather to the *technology* the Macintosh uses to create a font, both for screen display and for printing.

The Macintosh's multiplicity of font technologies is evidence of a sorry state of confusion—the result of historical compromises, competing interests, and changing technology. It is certainly *not* the result of a deliberate strategy to make the Macintosh easier to use. As end users, we simply have to make the best of this less-than-great situation.

Bitmapped Fonts

Bitmapped fonts (sometimes referred to as *fixed-size fonts*) are so named because each character is made up of a collection of dots (or *bits*) that create the appearance of the font (see Figure 9-9). It is an exact representation of the font, including its size. As such, a separate set of instructions is needed for each different size of a font. Thus, a bitmapped font *family* (such as New York) typically would include a collection of separate font files, each representing different font sizes (such as New York 9, New York 10, New York 12, and so on), where each number refers to the *point size* of the font as listed in the Size menu.

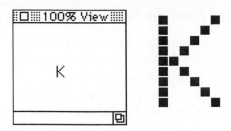

Figure 9-9
A bitmapped letter K, enlarged to show its underlying bit (dot) structure

Most bitmapped fonts come in a small set of standard sizes. The most common point sizes are 9, 10, 12, 14, 18, and 24. This is why the Size menus of many applications list only these sizes and do not include odd sizes such as 13 or 17. Larger sizes of fonts (greater than 24 point) are similarly rare. This is mainly because, as the font sizes get larger, the amount of disk space needed to store the larger bitmap files increases dramatically.

Estimating Font Sizes and Styles: The Jaggies

For bitmapped fonts, if you select a font size, such as 13 or 17, for which you do not have a corresponding font file installed, you get the *jaggies*. What happens is that the Macintosh tries to approximate the appearance of the font by estimating shape information from sizes that are installed. Unfortunately, the Macintosh cannot do a very good job of this estimation, and so the font appears with an unpleasing jagged look (see Figure 9-10, top example).

New York 14 point with jaggies.

Bitmapped New York at 14 point.

TrueType New York at 14 point.

Figure 9-10
Screen displays of different font types; jaggies occur (top line) when bitmapped New York 14 point is displayed without the 14 point size installed

Technically, the Macintosh uses the same sort of estimation when you select different font styles (such as **bold** versus *italics*). However, the changes necessary to effectively alter a style are generally simpler than what is needed to change a size. Thus, the Macintosh does a much better job of estimating the appearance of different styles than it does for different sizes. That is why you generally don't need separate bitmapped font files for each different style (although separate bitmapped font files for different styles do exist and can improve the appearance of the font over using the estimated style).

At one time in the Mac's history, bitmapped fonts were the only kind there was. Even today, they produce the sharpest screen displays of any type of font, especially at smaller point sizes (12 points or less). Still, because of the jaggies problem as well as their low resolution for printing (bitmapped fonts are designed at 72 dots per inch (dpi) while current laser printers commonly print at 300–600 dpi), they have largely been replaced by newer font technologies, as explained in the next sections.

SEE: • Chapter 10 for details on the meaning of resolution and dpi

How Do You Know What Sizes of Bitmapped Fonts Are Installed?

A quick way to find out what sizes of bitmapped fonts are installed is to select the Size menu of a text application (see the Size menu in Figure 9-1). Here you may see some numbers in plain type (9) and others in outline style (10). The outlined numbers mean that the current System file contains the bitmapped font file for that particular size of the selected font and can therefore produce a smooth display. Attempts to use those sizes not in outlined numbers will generally result in jagged fonts on the screen.

Of course, which sizes are installed, and which are not, may change each time you select a different font. It depends on which sizes for that particular font are installed in the appropriate System Folder location.

The other sure way to check this information, of course, is to directly inspect the contents of the System Folder itself, to see what font files are located there.

By the way, if all the sizes listed in a Size menu are outlined, even odd sizes that are definitely not installed as bitmapped fonts, it is because you are using a TrueType font (described in the next section).

Outline Fonts: TrueType and PostScript

Outline fonts (sometimes referred to as *variable-size,* or *scalable, fonts*) are an alternative to bitmapped fonts. Essentially, with outline fonts, the shape of each character is initially derived from a mathematical formula that describes the curves and lines that represent the character, rather than by the dot-by-dot mapping of bitmapped fonts. For example, an outline font would derive the letter O from the basic formula for a circle (the exact formula differs from font to font, accounting for the different variations in the letter O for each font). This information is then converted to the pattern of dots necessary to display or print the character, a process called *rasterizing.*

BY THE WAY ▶

OUTLINE FONTS VERSUS OUTLINE STYLE

The term outline, *as applied to outline fonts, has nothing to do with the outline display style of a font. The former refers to a method of generating font characters. The latter refers to the appearance of a particular style of font as selected from a Style menu.*

As their name implies, scalable font files are not restricted to a specific size. In fact, with only a single outline font file, you can select *any* font size you want and *not* have a problem with the jaggies.

While bitmapped fonts may look better on a typical monitor, outline fonts usually look far superior in printed output. This is because the resolution of outline fonts is *device independent.* This means that they take advantage of whatever resolution is available in the output device. They are not tied to a 72-dpi (or any other) resolution, as are bitmapped fonts. The appearance quality of outline font text thus improves as the resolution of the printer increases. Laser-printed output, even though it is still a collection of dots constructed similarly to how fonts are displayed on a screen, has a resolution of at least 300 dpi. Since most monitors are limited to about 72 dpi, the appearance of fonts on the monitor display can never match what you can achieve in the printed output from laser printers or any other comparable higher-resolution printer.

SEE: • **Chapter 10 for more on resolution**

There are two basic types of outline fonts on the Macintosh: TrueType fonts and PostScript fonts.

TrueType Fonts

TrueType fonts are an outline font technology developed by Apple. Several TrueType fonts ship with System 7 software disks. TrueType and bitmapped versions of the same font generally look similar (which is what you would expect, of course), but some differences are noticeable (compare the samples in Figure 9-10).

Only one TrueType font file is needed to display and print all possible sizes. Similarly, you only need the same solitary font file to create the different styles of the font (such as bold or italics). However, you may occasionally see TrueType fonts with separate files for different styles (such as Futura Bold and Futura Italic). If you install these additional files, they will be used when you select the Bold or Italic styles from the Style menu. Otherwise, the Macintosh will estimate the style from the plain text font file information, as it typically does with bitmapped fonts. This is directly comparable to the situation with PostScript fonts, as described in "Technically Speaking: All in the Family"). Possible problems with how all these variations are listed in Font menus are described in the section "Font Menu Clutter" later in this chapter.

System 6 Alert: TrueType fonts are used almost exclusively with System 7. However, they can also be used with some versions of System 6 (6.0.7 or later), but only with the addition of a special TrueType INIT system extension. Do *not* use this extension with System 7. If you do, you will get an error message that says TrueType is "already installed."

How to Identify a TrueType Font Versus a Bitmapped Font?

The standard set of bitmapped fonts that ship with the Macintosh include the familiar "city" fonts, such as Geneva, New York, Chicago, and Monaco. However, some TrueType fonts use the exact same name and have the same general appearance. In fact, both types of fonts may be contained within a single suitcase file. So how do you know which is which?

Identifying Fonts from the Finder   If you go into the System folder and look at the icon of the font file, you can see that a bitmapped font icon has one *A*, while a True-Type font icon has three overlapping *A*'s (see Figure 9-11). Similarly, if you double-click a font file, it opens up to display a sample of what the font text looks like. Bitmapped fonts show only a sample in their single fixed size. TrueType fonts show samples in three different sizes (see Figure 9-11).

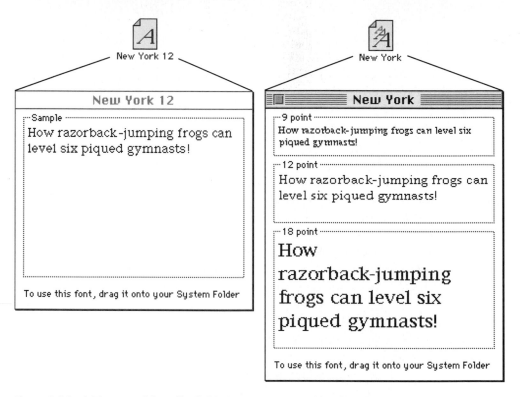

Figure 9-11   A bitmapped font file (left) versus a TrueType font file (right)

Even their names give them away. Bitmapped fonts are always named with a number representing their size (New York 12). TrueType fonts are named without any number (New York).

QuickDraw GX Alert: In QuickDraw GX, PostScript font icons and Get Info windows look just like the ones for TrueType fonts. This can be confusing! Check out Chapter 12 for more information.

Identifying a TrueType Font from Within Applications   You can usually distinguish the presence of a TrueType font from directly within a text application. First, select the font in question from the Font menu. Then check the Size menu. For TrueType fonts, all sizes in the menu should be in outline style and, if there is an Other size option, the word *Other* is also in outline style (see Figure 9-12). If only bitmapped font files are present, only installed sizes are outlined, and the word *Other* is never outlined.

PostScript Fonts

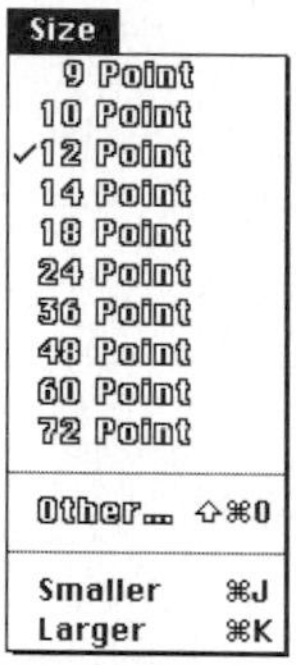

Figure 9-12
The Size menu for a TrueType font

PostScript outline fonts, which predated the arrival of TrueType fonts by several years, were originally developed by a company called Adobe. They instantly became an essential ingredient of high-quality output on a Macintosh. In fact, one of the reasons that Apple developed TrueType fonts was that it did not want Adobe, or any other company, controlling such an important part of the Macintosh technology. TrueType was Apple's answer to PostScript fonts.

TAKE NOTE ▶

WHAT IS POSTSCRIPT?

PostScript is a page-description language that describes the location and appearance of text and graphics output, usually to a PostScript printer. When you use a PostScript printer, text and graphics (as displayed on your monitor) are translated into PostScript instructions. These instructions, in turn, are used to create the image of each page. The information needed to interpret these instructions and create the final printed output is built into the hardware of a PostScript printer.

PostScript printers can print text created with any type of font. However, to take maximum advantage of PostScript's capabilities, you need special PostScript fonts. Most PostScript printers have a set of PostScript fonts built into the hardware. Other PostScript fonts can be downloaded from the Macintosh. Details are described in the main text.

Similarly, while a PostScript printer can print any graphic you see on the screen, it is at its best when printing graphics that directly utilize PostScript instructions (you need special software to create these graphics, as described more in Chapter 10).

The vast majority of Macintosh PostScript printers are laser printers. However, not all laser printers include PostScript. For example, the LaserWriter LS and LaserWriter Select 300 are not PostScript printers. Dot-matrix and inkjet printers are generally non-PostScript (though some inkjet printers include a PostScript interpreter or can optionally add one).

SEE: • **Chapter 7, "Take Note: Different Types of Printers," for more on printer types**
• **Chapter 10 for more on PostScript graphics**

PostScript Printer Fonts Versus Screen Fonts

A PostScript font is often referred to as a *printer font.* This is because a PostScript font file contains the PostScript instructions needed by a PostScript printer to create text output. However, a printer font is completely unable to create an image of the text on the screen (since only the printer has the PostScript interpreter needed to make use of the PostScript instructions). This makes them fundamentally different from bitmapped and TrueType fonts, which can generate both printed text and screen images.

Of course, in order to use PostScript fonts, you must be able to see the text on the screen. This problem was initially solved by the use of *screen fonts.* The screen font is essentially an ordinary bitmapped font version of the PostScript font's appearance. When you select a PostScript font from a Font menu, it is the screen font that you actually select and see on the screen. However, selecting a given screen font also tells the Macintosh to use the corresponding PostScript printer font when printing to a PostScript printer. The two types of font files work as a pair—both are necessary to use PostScript fonts on a Macintosh (see Figure 9-13).

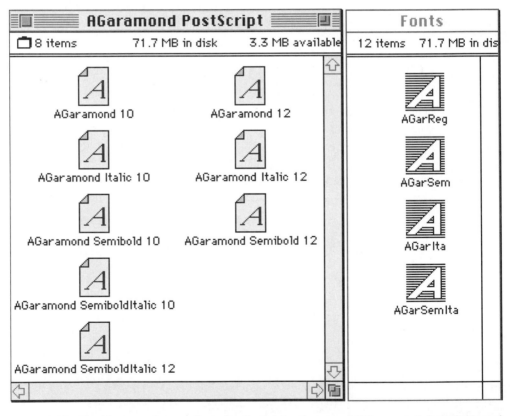

Figure 9-13 The bitmapped screen fonts for the Adobe Garamond (AGaramond) font (left), and the matching printer font files for AGaramond (right)

QuickDraw GX Alert: Things are different if you use QuickDraw GX. See "Post-Script Fonts and QuickDraw GX," later in this chapter (or see Chapter 12), for details.

In general, printer font files are stored in your System Folder (see "Locating, Adding, and Removing PostScript Printer Font Files from your System Folder," later in this chapter, for more details). However, printer font files are also included directly in the (ROM) hardware of PostScript laser printers. For example, most Apple LaserWriters include Avant Garde, Bookman, Courier, Helvetica, Helvetica Narrow, New Century Schoolbook, Palatino, Symbol, Times, Zapf Chancery, and Zapf Dingbats. Thus, you do not need to place separate printer font files in your System Folder to use these fonts. You only need the corresponding screen fonts. If your use of PostScript fonts is restricted to these built-in fonts, you may have never even seen PostScript printer font files!

No printer font files are included with Macintosh system software. You acquire them on your own. Adobe has a slew of excellent PostScript fonts, although at rather high prices. Other companies make less expensive PostScript fonts.

TECHNICALLY SPEAKING ▶

TYPE 1 VERSUS TYPE 3 POSTSCRIPT FONTS

You may occasionally hear reference to Type 1 versus Type 3 PostScript fonts (for some reason, there is no Type 2). These days, you should rarely, if ever, encounter Type 3 fonts. They are a relic from a time when Adobe tried to keep secret some of its ways of improving the appearance of fonts. In particular, Type 1 fonts contained special appearance-enhancing instructions, called hinting, *that could not be used in Type 3 fonts. Only Adobe made Type 1 fonts. Type 3 fonts were for everyone else. Adobe gave up on this restriction several years ago. Now, everyone can create Type 1 fonts and you can pretty much assume that all your PostScript fonts are Type 1.*

PostScript Fonts and Adobe Type Manager (ATM)

Because PostScript was not created by Apple (it was not even developed primarily for the Macintosh), PostScript fonts have not had TrueType's almost seamless integration into the Macintosh system software. Using PostScript for text has traditionally involved several hassles and limitations not found with TrueType. The need for separate printer and screen fonts is one obvious example. (PostScript graphics have their own separate set of problems, as detailed in Chapter 10.)

Fortunately, most of these text-related hassles can be overcome by using a utility called Adobe Type Manager (ATM). ATM is a combination control panel and system extension designed to work exclusively with PostScript fonts. Adobe keeps releasing new versions of ATM, as it tries to keep up with changes in Apple's software and hardware. To avoid problems, make sure you have a recent (ideally, the latest available) version of ATM.

ATM has so many benefits that, if you use PostScript fonts at all, ATM is nearly essential. Fortunately, you can purchase ATM directly from Adobe at a nominal charge (see Appendix). If you see higher-priced versions of ATM, it is typically because additional PostScript fonts are on the disk. ATM also comes with almost every other Adobe product (such as Adobe Illustrator). Other software packages may similarly include ATM. Finally, a special version of ATM is included as part of the QuickDraw GX component of System 7.5 (see "PostScript Fonts and QuickDraw GX," later in this section).

Because of the importance of ATM, it is difficult to describe PostScript fonts and how they work without also describing how ATM modifies this process. So, here is how it all fits together:

- **What about WYSIWYG?**
  Although screen fonts are designed to match what the PostScript printed output looks like, it is almost never a perfect match. This means that the Macintosh's normally close WYSIWYG relationship between the display and the printed output is broken. For example, line breaks might not always appear in the printed copy exactly as they appear on the screen.

  A related problem is the return of the jaggies on the screen. For example, suppose you pick a 17 point font size. Since you probably do not have a 17 point screen font, it will *display* with the jagged look described previously (in the section on bitmapped fonts). However, it will still *print* out smooth as silk to a PostScript printer, because the printer font file is used to create the printed copy and the printer font uses PostScript, which, as with TrueType, is an outline font technology that prints smoothly at any point size.

- **ATM to the rescue (part 1)**
  ATM solves most of the WYSIWYG problems just described. In particular, the main thing that ATM does is use printer font instructions to generate an image of the font on the screen, smoothly scaled to any selected size! The jaggies vanish, much like what happens with TrueType fonts (see Figure 9-14). The WYSIWYG matching of lines breaks and character spacing, while not necessarily perfect (especially because of likely differences in the resolution of the monitor versus the printer), will also be improved.

Bitmapped Palatino 14 point
Bitmapped Palatino 18 point

ATM Palatino 14 point
ATM Palatino 18 point

TrueType Palatino 14 point
TrueType Palatino 18 point

Figure 9-14
Samples of screen displays of bitmapped versus ATM-generated versus TrueType Palatino text; there are no jaggies, but each type looks somewhat different

A minor problem remains with the look of the Size menus. Unlike with TrueType, ATM does not affect what sizes are outlined in Size menus. Thus, if the Palatino 18 screen font is not installed, the 18 in the Size menu will not be outlined. However, don't be fooled! With ATM installed, an 18 point font (or any other size) will still print *and* display without the jaggies.

By the way, given all of this, you may now be asking: If I use ATM, does this mean that I no longer need screen fonts at all? Unfortunately, you still need screen fonts. More precisely, you need at least one point size of a screen font for every PostScript font you use. This is because the screen font is necessary just to get the font name to appear in Font menus. Also, screen fonts at smaller point sizes (12 point or less) generally look better than ATM-generated screen displays. Therefore, it is common to have 9 point, 10 point, and/or 12 point screen fonts in use, even if you have ATM installed.

Finally, note that if you are using the PostScript fonts that are built into your PostScript printer (such as the previously mentioned Times, Helvetica, etc.), you still need to install the corresponding printer font files in your System Folder in order for ATM to create smooth screen displays. ATM cannot access the printer font files in your printer.

- **What if the printer font file is missing?**
  As I have already implied, if you select a presumed PostScript font from a Font menu, but its PostScript font file is missing, it will not print in PostScript, even if you are using a PostScript printer (unless, of course, it is one of the fonts built into the printer). Instead, the screen font prints directly. However, a PostScript printer will still probably do a better job of printing the screen font than a non-PostScript printer would. This is because a PostScript printer generates a temporary outline-like font file for the font when it goes to print it. It won't look nearly as good as if a true printer font was present, but you may find it acceptable if you have no other alternative.

  Similarly, even if you are using ATM, you still need PostScript printer fonts. If you just have the screen font, ATM is irrelevant! The printed output and the screen display will be as if you are not using PostScript fonts at all!

- **What if you don't have a PostScript printer?**
  Another traditional problem with using PostScript fonts, again as already implied, is that they require a PostScript printer. If you try to print PostScript text to a non-PostScript printer, the bitmapped screen font once again prints directly, as if it were an ordinary bitmapped font, whether or not the PostScript printer font is present.

- **ATM to the rescue (part 2)**
  Here is the second major benefit of using ATM: You can use it to print PostScript text even to a non-PostScript printer. In essence, the ATM software substitutes for the printer's PostScript interpreter that would otherwise be needed.

  With ATM, as long as you have the relevant printer font files installed, text output to a non-PostScript printer looks about the same as the output from a Post-Script printer *of the same resolution.* Thus, ImageWriter output never looks as good as LaserWriter output, even with ATM, because the ImageWriter is a lower-resolution printer. However, output from inkjet printers (such as Apple's StyleWriter) and non-PostScript laser printers (such as Apple's LaserWriter Select 300) look almost identical to output from 300-dpi PostScript printers.

  By the way, remember that ATM only affects text. If you plan on printing Post-Script graphics (see Chapter 10), ATM is of no help. For PostScript graphics, you still need a PostScript printer.

ALL IN THE FAMILY

If you have ever purchased a PostScript font and tried to install it, you may notice that things are often a bit more complicated than implied here (as if they weren't already complicated enough!). In particular, you may find that several printer font files exist for the same font family. For example, the Adobe Garamond font includes four printer font files (see Figure 9-13): AGarReg (for plain text), AGarSem (bold), AGarIta (italics), and AGarSemIta (bold and italics combined). All four printer font files are needed for these common styles to appear correctly in printed copy. For example, if you only installed AGarReg, but not the other AGar printer files, Adobe Garamond text will appear correctly in bold or italics on the screen, but will appear as plain text when printed.

This is also why, for example, you can display the Bold style for the Zapf Chancery font (which is a font built into your LaserWriter), but the LaserWriter will not print it as bold. This is because Apple chose to include only the plain text printer font for Zapf Chancery in the printer.

You may also find that a separate set of bitmapped screen fonts is included to match each of the different style variants of the printer font files. For example, there may be screen fonts, at various sizes, for AGaramond (plain text), AGaramond Semibold, AGaramond Italic, and AGaramond SemiboldItalic. If installed, these appear as separate fonts in the Font menu (which can considerably clutter up your Font menu). However, if the font files were created correctly, the Macintosh should still recognize all these variations as belonging to the same font family.

Unlike for the printer fonts, it is usually not necessary to use these screen font style variants. You could still select different styles from the Style menu even without the screen font variants installed, because printed appearance is determined primarily by the presence of the printer files, not of the screen fonts. For example, for printing with most applications, selecting Italic from the Style menu for the AGaramond font usually duplicates the effect of directly selecting the AGaramond Italic font from the Font menu (assuming all the printer font files are installed). Experiment. If your printed output is satisfactory with only the plain text screen font installed, you can skip the others.

Actually, there are advantages to using the Style menu method. For example, if you select Italic from the Style menu for AGaramond text and later change to a different font, the text remains in italics. This would not happen if, instead, you had selected AGaramond Italic from the Font menu.

The main advantage of using the separate style variants of screen fonts is that they typically enhance the WYSIWYG matching of the screen to the printed output, because the Macintosh uses the variant file, when available, to create the screen display rather than trying to approximate it from the plain text file (sometimes called a "false style"). The approximation method usually results in a less accurate matching than using the style variant. For a few applications, character spacing of printed output may also be improved with the use of the style variants.

By the way, don't be surprised if you do not have these variant screen fonts for your PostScript fonts. Not all PostScript fonts come with separate files for different styles. For example, for the PostScript fonts that come with Apple's LaserWriters, Apple includes only the plain text screen fonts, without the other screen font variants. You would have the style variants only if you obtained the font directly from Adobe.

SEE: • **"Technically Speaking: Different Versions of Screen Fonts for the Same PostScript Font," later in this chapter, for related information**
• **"Font Menu Clutter," later in this chapter, for possible problems with using separate screen fonts for different styles of the same font**

PostScript Fonts and QuickDraw GX

Even though I have postponed the primary discussion of QuickDraw GX until Chapter 12, there is an important change in how PostScript fonts work in QuickDraw GX that I should mention right now: You no longer need separate printer fonts and screen fonts with QuickDraw GX! These two components are combined into a single font file that resembles a TrueType font. Though you still need ATM to get everything to work properly, a GX-compatible version of ATM is included with QuickDraw GX. The result is that PostScript fonts in QuickDraw GX work almost indistinguishably from TrueType fonts. Virtually all of the previous "hassles" of using PostScript are gone. Still, because of other overhead associated with QuickDraw GX, users may not rush to adopt this technology (which is why I defer discussing it until Chapter 12).

Locating, Adding, and Removing PostScript Printer Font Files from Your System Folder

In the section on Font Basics, I described the changing location of font files from System 6 to System 7.5. All of that applied both to bitmapped fonts (including the screen fonts of PostScript fonts) and TrueType fonts. However, the PostScript printer font files work a bit differently.

First, unless you are using QuickDraw GX (as mentioned in the previous section), printer font files cannot be included in suitcases, nor can they be installed in a System file (no matter what version of the system software you are using).

Second, the correct location within a System Folder to place printer font files varies a bit from what was true for other font files. In particular, in System 6, printer fonts can be located anywhere at the root level of the System Folder. In System 7.0.x, they should be stored in the Extensions folder. In System 7.1/7.5, they should be stored in the Fonts folder (though they will also work if stored in the Extensions folder). Unlike other font types, you can add or remove printer font files to or from any location in a System Folder without getting any alert messages, even if other applications are open.

TECHNICALLY SPEAKING ▶

AUTOMATIC VERSUS MANUAL DOWNLOADING

When you print a document that uses PostScript fonts that are not built into the printer, the needed information from the relevant printer font files is downloaded to the printer at the time the document is printed. It is then cleared from the printer's memory when the document is finished printing. This means that the next time you print a document that uses the same font, it has to be downloaded again. This repeated automatic downloading takes time and consequently slows down the printing process.

As an alternative, you can manually download a font to the printer, by using the "Download Fonts" command from Apple's LaserWriter Utility. Manually downloaded fonts stay in the printer's memory until you shut down (but you can download only as many fonts as

(continued)

How to Identify a PostScript Font

There is no clear way to know if you are using a PostScript font just by checking an application's Font menu or Size menu. To find out if a given font is a PostScript font, check the System Folder for the presence of PostScript printer font files. There are several different possible icons for PostScript fonts, but they will all have *PostScript font* as their Kind in their Get Info window.

For fonts that are built directly into your PostScript printer, there may not be a printer font file present for you to check. For a list of these built-in fonts, check the manual that came with your printer (for instant help, the family names of the fonts built into most LaserWriters were listed in the previous section, "PostScript Printer Fonts Versus Screen Fonts). Otherwise, you can use LaserWriter Utility. This utility checks a PostScript laser printer and creates a list of all the fonts built into the printer. To do this, select "Display Available Fonts" from the program's File menu.

SEE: • Chapter 7, "By the Way: Help from LaserWriter Utility," for more on this utility

Eventually, you should be able to recall from memory which of your fonts are Post-Script and which are not.

If you use Now Utilities 5.0, its WYSIWYG Menus control panel has a feature that identifies PostScript versus TrueType versus bitmapped fonts from its control panel window.

QuickDraw GX Alert: In QuickDraw GX, PostScript fonts appear exactly like TrueType fonts, even using the same icon. The Get Info window provides no clue as to what type of font it is. In this case, there is no easy way to tell whether a font is a TrueType font or a PostScript font (although you can see Chapter 12 for more help here.)

Combining TrueType, PostScript, and/or Bitmapped Versions of the Same Font

It is entirely permissible to mix font formats for the same font family within the same System Folder. For example, you may have installed the 10 point and 12 point bitmapped versions of the Times to use as screen fonts. You may also install a True-

Type version of the Times font. If you are using a PostScript LaserWriter, you also have the PostScript printer font of Times built into the printer.

Are there problems with doing this? Are there advantages to doing this? The answer is yes to both questions. To understand why, you first need to understand the rules that determine which font is used for the screen display and for printed output when multiple competing types are present.

What Font Format Displays?

What font format displays on the screen when more than one format of the same font is installed is determined according to the following priority list. The Macintosh uses the first format on the list, if it is available, skipping to items lower on the list as necessary:

- Bitmapped font, if the selected size is available
- TrueType font
- ATM-generated PostScript font
- Bitmapped font scaled from a different size (which usually results in the jaggies), if selected size is not available

What Font Format Prints?

What font format prints when more than one format of the same font is installed is governed by a different set of rules from those used for the screen display. Furthermore, the rules vary depending on whether or not you are using a PostScript printer.

PostScript Printers Use, in Order of Preference:

- PostScript fonts built into the printer's ROM
- PostScript fonts contained in the active System Folder (with or without ATM)
- TrueType fonts
- Bitmapped fonts

Non-PostScript Printers Use, in Order of Preference:

- TrueType fonts
- ATM-generated PostScript fonts
- Bitmapped fonts

What It All Means

Bitmapped fonts get the highest priority for screen display but get the lowest priority for printing! Although this may seem illogical at first, it does make sense. Here's why.

Returning to the previous example, if you have Times 10 and Times 12 installed, these bitmapped fonts are used for the screen display at those sizes. This generally offers the best possible screen appearance for these small sizes because, as described in previous sections, even if you use an outline font, the screen display itself remains a bitmap (that is, a collection of dots). The outline font instructions must be converted to a bitmapped approximation in order for it to be displayed. Bitmapped fonts at installed sizes, because they do not depend on any approximation, can best utilize the screen display.

The Times TrueType font kicks in at other sizes. This has the advantage of eliminating the jaggies at these sizes without requiring a separate bitmapped file for each size. (You could have used ATM to obtain this same benefit, but this would have also required installing printer fonts files. In essence, you are using TrueType here, instead of ATM, to avoid the jaggies. The matching TrueType font serves as the screen font for the PostScript font. However, being able to do this assumes that you have a matching TrueType font available. Many times you will not.)

When you go to print to the LaserWriter, the printer's built-in PostScript Times font takes over, overriding both the bitmapped and the TrueType instructions, providing the highest-quality output possible with your PostScript printer.

Still, many experts recommend *not* combining TrueType and PostScript versions of the same font. This is primarily because it may lead to the (TrueType-based) screen display having a different appearance, in terms of line breaks and character spacing, from the (PostScript-based) printed output. Things can get especially complicated, with hard-to-predict results, if you start combining TrueType and PostScript when you have different screen fonts and different TrueType fonts for different styles of the same font (such as Times Bold and Times Italic). However, I made these sorts of combinations in several cases without any problem. So experiment for yourself. In any case, placing TrueType fonts and PostScript fonts from *different* families in the same System Folder is not a problem at all.

Which Font Format Should You Use?

Suppose you have bitmapped, TrueType, and PostScript versions of the same font (such as Times). Assuming you would like to use only one of these formats for creating your text, which should you prefer? Or suppose you are considering purchasing a collection of fonts and you need to decide whether you want them to be TrueType or PostScript. Which should you get? Here are some guidelines for solving these and other similar dilemmas.

Limit Your Use of Bitmapped Fonts

Use bitmapped fonts mainly for display of text at small sizes. They make a clearer display and will redraw faster than TrueType fonts. If possible, use bitmapped fonts only in conjunction with TrueType or PostScript (with ATM) versions of the same font, so that the bitmapped version is not used for printing. Otherwise, try to avoid bitmapped fonts altogether, especially with a high-resolution (300-dpi or higher) printer.

Occasionally, large point sizes of bitmapped fonts may be useful if you're printing to a low-resolution printer, such as an ImageWriter. They may print better than the ATM or TrueType versions.

If you do print bitmapped text to a PostScript LaserWriter, it probably will look better than you might expect. This is because (as mentioned earlier in this chapter in "What If the Printer Font File Is Missing?" in the subsection "PostScript Fonts and Adobe Type Manager (ATM)"), a PostScript LaserWriter creates a temporary outline-like font file for the font, so that any size of the font prints relatively smoothly. Checking the *Smooth Text* option from the Options section of the Page Setup box may also help improve appearance of printed bitmapped fonts (the option is irrelevant for other types of fonts). Still, the converted and smoothed bitmapped output remains inferior to the quality you would get from a true PostScript font.

BY THE WAY ▶

PRINTING SCREEN FONTS AS BITMAPPED FONTS

Screen fonts are not usually printed. They serve only to create the screen display for a matching PostScript printer font. However, if you do not have the matching printer font installed (or if you are using a non-PostScript printer without ATM), the screen font prints directly, just like any other bitmapped font. If you try this, you may find that screen fonts do not print as attractively as bitmapped fonts that are specifically designed to be printed. This is because screen fonts are usually designed with more of an emphasis on how well their screen display matches the related PostScript printed output than on how they actually print out.

Of course, if you are using TrueType or PostScript fonts for printing (as I recommend), all of this is irrelevant!

Decide Between PostScript and TrueType

PostScript (especially with ATM) and TrueType are both excellent font technologies. Which looks better, to a large extent, depends on the design of the particular font, not the technology. If your primary use of text is for minimally formatted documents, such as reports and manuscripts, either type of font is likely to be adequate.

However, PostScript does have some advantages. As a group, PostScript fonts tend to be superior in appearance to the corresponding TrueType fonts. A wider selection of PostScript fonts than TrueType fonts is available, though this gap is rapidly disappearing. Most notable, PostScript is the standard font format used by typesetters and is likely to cause them less problems than TrueType fonts—an important consideration if you plan to have documents printed professionally by a service bureau. Also, if you plan on using PostScript graphics, you will probably prefer to use PostScript fonts as well.

On the other hand, each Macintosh comes with a selection of TrueType fonts at no extra cost. For some people, that alone is reason enough to prefer them. TrueType also has an advantage in its simplicity and better integration with other system software, although using QuickDraw GX sharply reduces this advantage.

With PostScript, you can create special effects, such as rotated text and shading of text, that are not possible (or as easy to do) with standard TrueType. There are also special PostScript fonts (called multiple master fonts) that let you vary the characteristics of a font (such as its weight and width). However, with QuickDraw GX, True-Type can duplicate most, if not all of these effects—as long as your software has been rewritten to be QuickDraw GX-savvy (which is still not common).

Finally, if you are really determined to stick to one format, there are software programs that you can use to convert a PostScript font into a TrueType one, or vice versa.

So, should you use PostScript or TrueType? There is no easy answer. I use them both.

SEE: • Chapter 12 for more on QuickDraw GX

Consider Your Printer

- **For PostScript printers**
  Prefer printing with PostScript fonts. Use ATM to improve screen displays of Post-Script fonts. You can also use TrueType fonts. If you have installed TrueType and PostScript versions of the same font, TrueType is not used for printing.

- **For non-PostScript printers**
  Prefer to use either TrueType fonts or ATM-generated PostScript fonts.

Keep It Simple

Don't overload your System Folder with fonts you rarely or never use. When you must use bitmapped versions of fonts, keep only those sizes that you use frequently.

Summing Up

Table 9-1 presents a summary of much of the information covered so far in this chapter.

Table 9-1 Font Basics Summary*

	BITMAPPED FONT	TRUETYPE FONT	POSTSCRIPT FONT**
Icons	[A] or [A]	[A] or [A]	Several possible icons, including: [A] or [printer]
Location in System 6.0.x System Folder***	System file (via Font/DA Mover)	System file (via Font/DA Mover)****	Any location in System Folder
Location in System 7.0.x System Folder***	System file (can be directly opened)	System file (can be directly opened)	Extensions folder
Location in System 7.1/7.5 System Folder***	Fonts folder	Fonts folder	Fonts folder
Can font be stored in suitcase and/or exist as a separate file?	Font suitcases (in all system versions) or separate files (System 7.x only)	Font suitcases (in all system versions) or separate files (System 7.x only)	Separate files only (unless using QuickDraw GX)
Is screen display smooth?	Smooth only if selected size is installed	Smooth at any size	Smooth only if bitmapped font for selected size is installed or if using ATM
Is PostScript printer output smooth?	Generally smooth, but looks best if selected size is installed	Smooth at any size	Smooth at any size
Is non-PostScript printer output smooth?	Smooth only if selected size is installed	Smooth at any size	Smooth only if bitmap font for selected size is installed or if using ATM

*   Changes due to QuickDraw GX are covered more in Chapter 12.
**   Matching screen font needed to create screen display (except in QuickDraw GX).
*** If you use Suitcase or similar utility, fonts may be stored anywhere on your disk.
****Requires 6.0.7 or a later version and the TrueType INIT extension.

Solve It! Text and Font Problems

This section gives specific advice about various problems with the display and printing of text and with using fonts in general. The emphasis is on problems that can occur with almost all Macintoshes and most printers. However, some advice specific to certain printers, such as LaserWriters and ImageWriters, is also included.

SEE: • Chapter 7 for a more general discussion of printing-related problems
• Chapter 10 for display and printing problems specific to graphics documents

A Document Displays the Wrong Font

Symptoms:

A previously saved text document is opened. The file opens normally, except that the font(s) displayed are different from the ones selected when the document was last saved. For example, the document may have been saved using Garamond, but it now opens using Geneva instead.

Causes:

The Necessary Font Is Not in Your System Folder

This could happen, for example, if you open a document that uses a font you have since deleted from your startup disk. Or perhaps you are using a document obtained from a colleague that contains a font that has never been on your disk.

When this happens, the document typically opens using either a default system font (most likely Geneva or Chicago) or using the application's default font (usually Geneva, New York, or Helvetica). You may also get an alert message warning you of what has happened (see Figure 9-15).

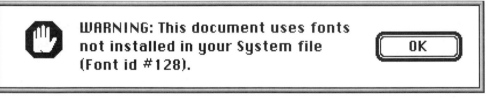

Figure 9-15 The message that appears if you open a document that uses a font not currently installed in your System Folder

By the way, if you click in an area of text and go to the Font menu, the assigned font name for the text where the I-beam is located should have a checkmark in front of it. If no font name is checked, this probably means that the assigned font is not available and a substitute font has been used instead. Thus, even though the text might display in Geneva, the Geneva name will not be checked. However, if you highlight (rather than just click in) an area of text and do not see a checked font in the Font menu, this could also be because the highlighted area includes text of two or more different fonts.

A Font ID Number Conflict Has Occurred

Though you would not normally need to be aware of this, every font file has its own ID number. Initially, it is assigned by the developer who created the font file. The Macintosh uses these numbers to identify the font internally. Within certain limits, what ID number is assigned to a font is arbitrary. Thus, it is possible for two different fonts to wind up with the same ID number.

Two fonts in the same location (the same suitcase file or the same System file) cannot share the same ID number. If you try to install two identically numbered fonts to the same location, the Macintosh automatically assigns a new ID number to one of the fonts to resolve the conflict.

This is not likely to cause any immediate problems—as long as you stick to your own computer and use only documents you've created. Problems occur if you send or receive documents to or from other users. For example, suppose you have two fonts, Futura and Frontier, that initially have the same ID number. When you install them both to your System file, Futura is assigned a new ID number to resolve the conflict. Now you create a document using the Futura font. The document identifies the Futura font by its newly assigned ID number. Later, you take this document to be printed elsewhere. Even though the other computer has the Futura font, it probably uses the font's original ID number. As a result, the other Macintosh does not correctly identify that the document uses Futura and probably displays and prints the document in some other font.

The good news is that this problem is becoming increasingly rare. New ID numbering formats have reduced the probability of two fonts having the same ID number. Similarly, newer software typically identifies fonts by the font's name rather than its ID number. Since names should be unique, conflicts are largely eliminated. However, for people who regularly take their documents to outside sources to be printed, this remains a potential problem.

By the way, a font's ID name is separate from the font's file name in the Finder. This means you could potentially change a font's file name without affecting how the font is listed in a Font menu.

A Font File Is Damaged

If a font file is damaged, text using that font may not display in that font.

What to do:

Check the Font Menu

If a document opens in the wrong font (and you know what the correct font should be), check whether the intended font is listed in the Font menu.

If the Correct Font Is Not Listed in the Font Menu

Check Key Caps   Some applications don't list all installed fonts in their Font menu. You can always use the Key Caps desk accessory to see a complete Font menu list. If the font shows up in Key Caps, check the problem application's manual for how to access the "missing" font.

   If you don't see the font in any Font menu, this probably means that the font is not currently installed. To check and fix this:

Quit Without Saving   Quit the application you are using, but *without* saving the document! This prevents you saving any incorrect font information.

Check Your System Folder   Go to the location in your System Folder where your installed fonts are stored (the System file, Extensions folder, and/or Fonts folder). Check if the font is listed there.

   Make sure you are using the System Folder you think you are! For example, if you are using a startup disk different from the one you normally use, this alone could account for the "missing" fonts.

Get the Font   If the font isn't in your System Folder, the solution is simple. Assuming you have access to the needed font, get it and install it.

SEE: • "Font Basics," earlier in this chapter, for more on where fonts are stored and how to install fonts, if needed

Check for Font Menu Problems   If the font is correctly installed in your System Folder, but still does not appear in the Font menu, check for special problems with Font menu listings.

SEE: • "Fonts Unexpectedly Appear or Disappear from Font Menus," later in this chapter, for more on locating missing font files and related problems

SOLVING FONT PROBLEMS WITH ATM, SUPERATM, ACROBAT, COMMON GROUND, AND QUICKDRAW GX

With Adobe's SuperATM, if a text document includes fonts not currently installed in your System Folder, you can still create a nearly identical substitute version of the font, so that the general appearance and line breaks of the document remain the same. Actually, the most recent versions of the basic ATM control panel also include this previously exclusive SuperATM feature (though you still need a separate ATM Font Database file to use ATM's "Substitute for missing fonts" option). However, this feature can require a lot of disk space and, in any case, only works with PostScript fonts. Also, it only works with certain applications and may actually cause problems with others. So be wary of using it.

More generally, programs like Acrobat or Common Ground, as well as Apple's PPD feature in QuickDraw GX, can create documents that can be viewed and printed in their originally assigned fonts, even if the viewer does not have the needed fonts installed (or even if you are missing the creating application!).

PROBLEMS WITH QUICKDRAW GX FONTS

PostScript fonts files are different in QuickDraw GX and in non-GX systems. If you install a GX PostScript font in an non-GX System Folder, its name should appear in the Font menu. However, if you try to format text with this font, the text will display in Geneva rather than the actual font. You may have similar problems if you install the special TrueType fonts used by QuickDraw GX. Conversely, using a non-GX style PostScript font in a GX system will not work. However, you can use non-GX TrueType fonts in either system.

SEE: • Chapter 12, on QuickDraw GX, for more details on the new font formats

If the Font Is Listed in the Font Menu

Replace a Damaged Font   You may have a damaged font file. If so, replace the font from your backups. This should fix the problem unless your backup copy is also damaged.

SEE: • "Font Basics," earlier in this chapter, for more on deleting and replacing fonts
   • "Solve It! Font File Problems," later in this chapter

Check for Font ID Conflict   Otherwise, you probably have a font ID conflict. The easiest solution for this problem is to select the text with the incorrect font and then select the correct font from the Font menu. The text should now display properly. If this works, you will probably have no further problems. Save the changed document, and it should open properly next time.

Otherwise, go to the System Folder location of your fonts. Delete both the font currently used to display the text and the font that should have been used to display the text. Now reinstall both of them from your backups. Try opening the document again. See if the font now displays as expected.

For Documents Sent to Outside Sources   If you are regularly plagued by ID conflicts because you send documents to outside sources (such as professional typesetters) and the documents you send print in the wrong font, you may need some special solutions. For example, you could include a copy of your System file and related Fonts and Extensions folders to be used when printing your document.

Check for Duplicate ID Numbers   You may encounter a related ID conflict problem if you use a font management utility, such as Suitcase, or if you use System 7.1/7.5. In these cases, fonts can be installed and accessed by the System directly from font suitcase files. Two different fonts in different suitcases may have the same ID number. If so, neither ID number is changed and the conflict remains. The usual result is that you can use only one of the two fonts, even though both may be listed in your Font menu. The solution is to get the Macintosh to renumber the ID of one of the fonts. Typically, this is easily done by combining both fonts into one suitcase, which forces a renumbering.

Utilities such as Suitcase also include special supplemental utilities to resolve this sort of conflict. Suitcase's utility is called Font Harmony.

Seek Outside Help   Dealing with ID conflicts can get messy to diagnose and difficult to solve. If the explanations given in this section are not sufficient to resolve your problem, it's time to seek outside help.

SEE: • Fix-It #18 on seeking outside help

If You Still Can't Use the Font

If none of this works, or you have no idea what the missing font should be or you do not have access to it, you are out of luck. You have to reformat the text using a font that is available.

TAKE NOTE ▶

INCORRECT TEXT CHARACTERS AND INTERNATIONAL KEYBOARD LAYOUTS

If pressing a keyboard key results in an incorrect character appearing on the display (such as "y" appearing when you press the "z" key) or if foreign language characters appear instead of the expected English characters, it probably means that you have inadvertently shifted to an international keyboard layout. Normally you would do this by selecting a layout from the

A Document Prints with a Different Font from the One Displayed

Symptoms:

- A document displays on the screen with the selected font, but a different font is used when printing.
- Specifically for PostScript printers: if the displayed font is Geneva, New York, or Monaco and the printed font is Helvetica, Times, or Courier.
- Specifically for PostScript printers: if the displayed font is any PostScript font and the printed font is Courier.

Causes:

A Font File Is Damaged

If a font file is damaged, text using that font may not print in that font, even if it displays correctly.

Problems Specific to PostScript LaserWriters

Some problems are a direct result of checking a specific option in the Page Setup dialog box (such as fonts changing because the Substitute Fonts option was selected). Others may have a more general cause, such as insufficient memory in the printer.

By the way, the dialog boxes described and pictured here are those of the Laser-Writer 8 driver. Users of previous versions of the LaserWriter driver will have similar options, but with a somewhat different layout of the dialog box (as briefly described in Chapter 7). If you use the QuickDraw GX version of the LaserWriter, check out Chapter 12.

Otherwise . . .

Problems with low memory are usually the cause.

 What to do:

Replace a Damaged Font

You may have a damaged font file. If so, replace the font from your backups. This should fix the problem unless your backup copy is also damaged.

SEE: • "Font Basics," earlier in this chapter, for more on deleting and replacing fonts
• "Solve It! Font File Problems," later in this chapter

StyleWriter: Problems with Low Memory

If a document's font changes about halfway down a page when printing to a StyleWriter or StyleWriter II with background printing on, this is usually a problem with low memory. To solve this problem in the short run, turn background printing off. In the long run, add more memory to your Macintosh. Actually, these same solutions apply to any other printer that exhibits similar problems.

PostScript LaserWriters: Uncheck Substitute Fonts or Change the Font

LaserWriter 8's *Substitute Fonts* option, located in the Options window of the Page Setup dialog box, is usually checked by default (see Figures 9-16 and 9-17). In older LaserWriter driver versions, it is called *Font Substitution* and is found in the main Page Setup dialog box.

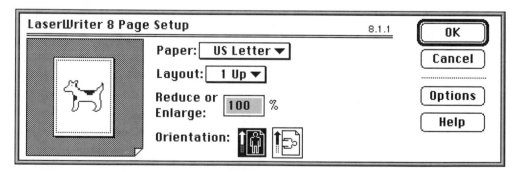

Figure 9-16   A LaserWriter 8 Page Setup dialog box

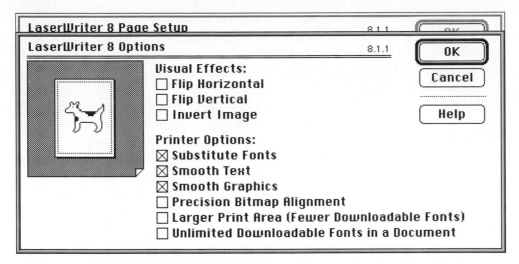

Figure 9-17   The Options window from LaserWriter 8's Page Setup dialog box, accessed by clicking the Options button shown in Figure 9-16. Here is where the Substitute Fonts and Unlimited Downloadable Fonts options are found

If this option is checked, any text displayed in Geneva, New York, or Monaco fonts will be printed in Helvetica, Times, and Courier, respectively. It will do this whether your screen fonts are bitmapped or TrueType. It will not do this for any other fonts. This option will not only cause your display and printout to have different fonts, but it will result in differing line and page breaks as well.

To avoid these problems, uncheck the Substitute Fonts option. This forces the document to print using the actual font displayed on the screen. It uses TrueType if it's available for that font. If not, the bitmapped font prints directly.

Alternatively, if you want to print using a PostScript font, then simply select it for display as well. Thus, for example, select all the Geneva font in your document and change it to Helvetica (or any other PostScript font of your choosing).

By the way, the purpose of Substitute Fonts, which originated before TrueType fonts existed, was to use the higher-quality PostScript fonts for printing instead of the bitmapped fonts that were displayed.

PostScript LaserWriters: Check Unlimited Downloadable Fonts in a Document

Sometimes, especially if your document uses many different PostScript fonts, the document will print out entirely in the Courier font rather than the fonts you selected.

The cause here is usually that there isn't enough memory in the printer (yes, Post-Script printers have their own installed memory!) to hold all the different PostScript information needed to print your document. Usually you should get an alert message informing you of this problem, but sometimes things get mixed up and you get this shift to Courier font instead.

One way to try to solve this problem is to select the Unlimited Downloadable Fonts in a Document option (available from the Options window of the Page Setup dialog box, as seen in Figure 9-17). This doesn't always work, but it is worth a try. It allows the needed font information to be swapped in and out of the printer's memory as needed, rather than be loaded in all at once (as would otherwise be required). Although this permits an unlimited number of fonts to be used, it tends to slow down the printing process.

Simplify the Document   An alternative solution is to simplify the document by using less fonts or by dividing up the document into separately printed segments.

PostScript LaserWriters: Uncheck Unlimited Downloadable Fonts in a Document

Yes, I know. This is the opposite of the previous advice. The resolution of this contradiction is that the advice to *un*check this option only applies when you are printing fonts as part of a graphic (such as an EPS or PICT file) and the fonts print incorrectly. In this case, unchecking this option may help. By the way, printing fonts, especially PostScript fonts, are often a source of trouble with PICT documents. Try to avoid this combination, if possible.

SEE: • "PostScript Fonts Do Not Print Using PostScript" and "The Jaggies Appear Unexpectedly," later in this chapter, for related problems
• Chapter 7 for a more general discussion of memory-related printing problems
• Chapter 10 for more on graphic file formats

BY THE WAY ▶

RIGHT FONT, WRONG CHARACTER

Sometimes, particularly with a PostScript font, your text may correctly print out in the same font as displayed on the screen, except that an occasional character is different, usually some special character accessed via an Option key combination. What is probably going on here is that there is a difference between the character set in the screen font file (used to display the text on the screen) and the printer font file (used to create the printed text). While technically this should not happen, it can occur if, for example, the screen font file is from an older version of the font while the printer font is a newer version (or vice versa). Different versions may have minor differences in their character set. If this happens, there is usually not much you can do about it other than switch to a different font (or font version) that does include the desired character, assuming you can find such a font.

SEE: • "Technically Speaking: Different Versions of Screen Fonts for the Same PostScript Font," in the next section, for related information

A Document Displays or Prints with the Wrong Formatting

Symptoms:

Wrong formatting refers to incorrect margins, line breaks, alignments, or character spacing, often occurring when you change fonts or printers. More specifically:

- A previously saved text document is opened. The file opens normally, except that margin settings and/or line breaks are different from what they were the last time you opened the document.
- Margin settings and/or line breaks shift when you change fonts.
- Vertically aligned columns, such as in tables, lose their alignment when you change fonts.
- Text characters are squeezed too closely together, perhaps even overlapping. Or there may be other unusual irregular spacing. Working with this text may ultimately cause a system crash.
- Formatting (such as bold or italics or spacing) appears correctly on the screen but does not print correctly.

Causes:

- A change in the printer selection from the Chooser can result in unexpected changes in margins and line breaks.
- A change in the fonts used in a document can result in margin and line break shifts, changes in the vertical alignment of text (used in tables), changes in the length of lines created by using the dash or underline keys, and more.
- TrueType fonts may occasionally cause problems with the appearance of text, especially if the application you are using is not a new enough version to recognize and work with TrueType.
- Squeezed-together text, overlapping characters, or solid lines that print as dashed lines are all usually traceable to an option, found in most word processors, called Fractional (Character) Widths.
- Missing printer font files can cause problems with appearance of printed text, such as bold or italics not printing.

- If the wrong font is used when printing, this may be due to options selected from the printer's Page Setup dialog box (see previous section for details).

 What to do:

Line Breaks and Margins Change Due to Changing Printers

When you shift printer drivers via the Chooser, you get a message informing you to select Page Setup for all your open applications. Recall that all you have to do here is to open the Page Setup dialog box and click OK. The readjustment to the new printer is then accomplished.

SEE: • **Chapter 7 for more on Page Setup and using the Chooser**

However, different printers have different page-margin limits. Unfortunately, this often means that if you select a new printer driver, the document's line breaks, page breaks, and tab alignments may all change (see Figure 9-18).

Here are four lines of text using New York 12 point font. Compare the difference between the line breaks for this paragraph when the text is formatted for a LaserWriter (the top paragraph) vs. when it is formatted for an ImageWriter (the bottom paragraph).

Here are four lines of text using New York 12 point font. Compare the difference between the line breaks for this paragraph when the text is formatted for a LaserWriter (the top paragraph) vs. when it is formatted an ImageWriter (the bottom paragraph).

Figure 9-18   Comparing a paragraph formatted for a LaserWriter versus an ImageWriter

There is no quick fix for this. You simply have to manually reformat the document.

The best long-term strategy is to select the printer driver you intend to use *before* you start working on the document. Remember (see Chapter 7), when you select a particular printer driver, the printer itself does not have to be on or even connected to your computer. In such cases, the Macintosh may display an alert box that claims it cannot find the current printer. If so, select Continue rather than Cancel. At this point, the driver is still selected and the document will format correctly for that printer.

If the desired printer driver is not in your System Folder, you obviously cannot select it. In this case, copy it from your system software disks.

Line Breaks Change Due to Changing Fonts

Line breaks can change when you change text to a different font (even if you do not also change the size or style). This can happen because the number of characters that fit on a line can be different with different fonts, even though both the new and the old font are the same size (such as both 12 point). Point size has more to do with the height of the font than the width.

Of particular note, shifting from a *monospaced* font (such as Monaco or Courier) to a *proportional* one (such as Geneva or Times), or vice versa, causes dramatic changes to the layout of your text (see Figure 9-19).

```
Here is a sample of text in Monaco 12 (a monospaced
```

Here is a sample of text in Geneva 12 (a proportional font).

Figure 9-19   A line of text in Monaco (monospaced font) versus Geneva (proportional font)

There is no quick fix for this problem, other than to select Undo and not to use the alternative font. If you need to switch fonts for some reason, you have to manually readjust all the text formatting as needed.

> **TAKE NOTE** ▶
>
> **MONOSPACED VERSUS PROPORTIONAL FONTS**
>
> *Monospaced fonts allocate the same amount of space per letter, regardless of the width of that letter. Thus, an i and a w take up the same space on a line. This simulates how a typical typewriter works and guarantees that each line has the same number of characters on it. However, it tends to have an unattractive, nonprofessional look. Monaco and Courier are examples of monospaced fonts. The alternative is a proportional font, where the space allocated per letter varies appropriately with the width of each letter. Proportional fonts are found in most books, including this one. Most Macintosh fonts are proportional.*

Line Break and Spacing Problems with Downloaded Files   Text files downloaded from online services frequently require a monospaced font (especially Monaco 9 or Courier 9) to display correctly (see Figure 9-19). This sort of problem can be particularly severe for text in the form of a table. While shifting to a monospaced font will usually be a quick fix here, a more general solution is to use tabs, rather than spaces, to create table text (see next section).

Another potential problem with downloaded files is that they may have a line break (an invisible character) at the end of each line. This means that if you reformat a paragraph using a different font, or even just change the margins, the text will not rewrap properly, as it would do with most word-processor created text. Sometimes using a monospaced font will solve the immediate problem. For a more flexible, long-term solution, you will want to get rid of the unnecessary line break characters. You can do this with shareware utilities such as Add/Strip.

Vertical Alignment and Line Length Problems Due to Font Selection

A related problem is shifts in the vertical alignment of columns of text (such as used to create a table) that occur after you change a font. This usually happens if you've used the spacebar to align the columns, rather than the Tab key.

The solution is to use the Tab key. Even better, use your word processor's Table commands, if it has them (Microsoft Word, WordPerfect, and MacWrite Pro all are good at this).

Even if you do not change fonts, the spacebar is a poor choice for aligning columns, especially if you are using a proportional font. The variable width of proportional font characters makes vertical alignment across lines nearly impossible. If you must use the spacebar for such alignments, switch to a monospaced font, such as Monaco or Courier.

Similarly, to create a dotted line of a specific length, do not simply type a series of dots or dashes. Instead, use your word processor's Tab Fill option (if it has one). This causes a series of dots or dashes (usually you have some choice here) to fill in the space between tabs (rather than just having blank space). This method preserves the length of the line even if you change fonts. Consult your word processor's manual for details on this option.

What's the big deal? Does it matter which ones you use? Usually, not much. However, even when using just the plain text style variant (as described earlier in this chapter) the two sets of screen fonts are somewhat different. Some people claim that Adobe's screen fonts are a more accurate match to the printed output than Apple's version. In any case, a document created with one version may format differently if you later substitute the other version in your System Folder. A well-known example of this involves the use of the Palatino font in some versions of HyperCard's tutorial stacks. Palatino text correctly displays in HyperCard's text boxes if you use Apple's screen fonts. But the character spacing is too wide if you use Adobe's screen fonts. You can choose to ignore this, as it is just an aesthetic problem and should not otherwise affect the functioning or printing of the document. Otherwise, you can switch back to Apple's screen fonts.

In another case, if the problem appears after upgrading to System 7.1 or a later version, the problem is that you are using an older incompatible version of the screen fonts. This is especially likely if you are having spacing problems using Helvetica or New Century Schoolbook fonts. The solution is to replace the screen fonts with newer versions, as available from Adobe or Apple.

TrueType Incompatibility Problems

If the version of an application predates the 1991 arrival of TrueType or has not been specifically upgraded to accommodate TrueType, it may have trouble using TrueType fonts. This can lead to problems both with the display and (especially) with printing. Problems may include overlapping characters in display and/or printing. System crashes may even occur.

The short-term solution is to stop using that application or stop using TrueType fonts within that application. The long-term solution is to get a newer version (assuming there is one) of the application, one that can accommodate TrueType.

A different (and less serious) sort of problem can occur whenever TrueType and bitmapped versions of the same font are in use. What happens is that the bitmapped version, when used for the screen display, may lead to different line breaks on screen than will be printed out. Eliminating *all* bitmapped font files for that font will eliminate this problem. It will probably also improve the way italics and bold is formed on the screen (since it will be based on TrueType technology rather than an estimate from the bitmap). However, the appearance of the plain text style of the font will probably appear slightly worse (which is the main reason for retaining the bitmapped fonts in the first place).

Finally, I am also aware of a more general problem that may occur when a selection of text in a TrueType font is included in a paragraph that otherwise uses a PostScript font. While the screen display is fine, when you print this to a PostScript printer, there may be an unusually large space before and after the TrueType font text. Again, the solution here is to not use the TrueType font.

SEE: • **Chapter 7 for more on printing problems with TrueType**

LaserWriter 8 Incompatibility

Some applications may not work correctly with LaserWriter 8, especially early versions of this printer driver. This is especially likely with programs, such as PageMaker, that depend heavily on PostScript. If you are using LaserWriter 8, try switching to Laser-Writer or to a newer version of LaserWriter 8. See if that fixes the problem.

Changes in Appearance Due to Fractional Character Widths

A Fractional Character Widths option, first mentioned in Chapter 7, is found in most text-oriented applications, usually in the Preferences or Page Setup dialog box. Changing its setting from off to on (or vice versa) may change the line breaks and/or character spacing of any text you are currently editing (see Figure 9-20).

With Fractional Character Widths off, the result may be that line breaks are different in the printed output than they are in the display. Here is how the screen display looks with Fractional Character Widths turned OFF.

With Fractional Character Widths off, the result may be that line breaks are different in the printed output than they are in the display. Here is how the screen display looks with Fractional Character Widths turned ON.

Figure 9-20   A sample of text with Fractional Widths turned off (top) and on (bottom)

This option is designed to be used primarily when printing to higher-resolution printers, such as LaserWriters. The reason is that, because of their higher resolution (300 dpi or more), these printers can print thinner (fractional) lines than can be displayed on the screen (which is usually at a 72-dpi resolution). This means that text can be effectively squeezed closer together in the printed copy than is possible on the display.

With Fractional Character Widths off, the result may be that line breaks are different in the printed output from the way they are in the display.

With Fractional Character Widths on, line breaks on the screen and the printed output should now match correctly, but individual characters in the display may be squeezed together too closely for the monitor to display them properly. This is because the option adjusts the spacing on the screen to match the higher-resolution capability of the printer. This is what causes the irregular, less legible, sometimes even overlapping, character display.

Also, if you are using a solid underline and it prints out as a dashed line, turning on fractional character widths should solve the problem.

Turning on Fractional Widths is generally preferred when printing to LaserWriters. If the screen appearance is less than desirable, don't worry. It should all still print okay.

Fractional Widths and ATM

If you are using ATM, the ATM control panel has two check boxes that also influence character and line spacing: Preserve Line Spacing and Preserve Character Shapes (see Figure 9-21). These address the same sort of problems as does Fractional Character Widths. ATM has been known to conflict with Fractional Character Widths, leading to improper spacing of text when both are active! You may need to experiment to see which options produce the most attractive output.

On the other hand, the SuperATM manual specifically recommends keeping the Fractional Widths option turned on when using SuperATM's new ability to create substitute fonts.

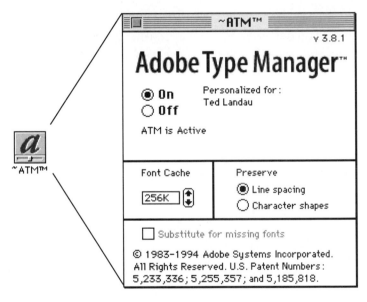

Figure 9-21   The ATM control panel

Style Selection Does Not Print Correctly Because of Missing Printer Font Files

For PostScript fonts, you may find that a style selection, such as Bold or Italics, looks correct on the screen but does not appear in printed output. This is probably because the needed printer font file for that style is not present. It needs to be installed.

SEE: • "Technically Speaking: All in the Family," earlier in this chapter, for more details

Formatting Problems Due to Out-of-Date or Damaged Font Files

If you are having any other font-related formatting problem, or if your problem was not amenable to any of the previously suggested solutions, you may have an out-of-date or damaged font file.

Various versions of the fonts included with LaserWriters have shipped over the years. Earlier versions may not work correctly with current software and hardware. If this seems a possibility in your case, seek the versions from Apple's current software. Otherwise, simply replace damaged fonts with your undamaged backups.

SEE: • "Solve It! Font File Problems," later in this chapter

The Text Is Clipped at the Margins When Printed

 Symptoms:

Text appears fine when displayed on the screen but is clipped (that is, cut off at the margins) when printed. Often, you will get an alert message warning that this may occur, such as one that says *Some margins are smaller than the minimum allowed by the printer. Your document may be clipped.*

 Causes:

This is usually because the top, bottom, left, and/or right margin settings for your document (or for a particular paragraph within a document) are set to smaller than the maximum limit that can be accommodated by your printer. Changes to the default settings are usually made via Document or Paragraph menu commands within your application. Sometimes, margin settings will be in the Page Setup dialog box.

 What to do:

Change the Margin Settings of Your Document

Locate where margins are set for the application in use. Increase their size, as needed.

Select Larger Print Area Option from Page Setup Dialog Box

If your printer supports the Larger Print Area option, select it. For example, for Post-Script LaserWriters it is found in the Options window of the Page Setup dialog box (see Figure 9-17). This allows for narrower margins than the default printer settings. However, this option uses additional memory from the printer and therefore reduces the number of downloadable fonts the printer memory can hold. Thus, if you check this option, it increases the likelihood that you may also want to check the Unlimited Downloadable Fonts option, located in the same dialog box. This option helps prevent memory problems associated with printing documents that use many fonts.

Turn Off Larger Print Area

Some programs do not properly support the Larger Print Area option. In this case, the edges of a document may become clipped only after Larger Print Area is turned *on.* If so, simply turn the option off.

Change or Upgrade Your LaserWriter Driver

The LaserWriter 8 driver allows some printers to print using a larger print area on the page. If your printer does so, you may find that text in some documents reflows or is clipped to fit the new larger area. It may be that an upgraded version of the Laser-Writer 8 driver exists that corrects this problem. Otherwise, you either need to change the margins of your document or to return to using the LaserWriter (not LaserWriter 8!) driver.

SEE: • Chapter 7 for more on LaserWriter 8 and printer drivers in general

PostScript Fonts Do Not Print Using PostScript

Symptoms:

You select a PostScript screen font. It displays correctly, but when you print it, it does not print using PostScript. Typically, the bitmapped screen font version of the PostScript font prints instead.

Causes:

The typical cause is that the needed PostScript hardware and/or software is not in present.

What to do:

- Make sure you are using a PostScript printer and/or ATM software.
- Make sure that the printer font files for the font are either built into the printer (as described in "PostScript Fonts," earlier in this chapter) or that it is in its correct location in the System Folder. For example, for System 7.1/7.5 it should be in the Fonts folder.

- If you are manually downloading a printer font file to the printer (as explained in "Technically Speaking: Automatic Versus Manual Downloading," earlier in this chapter), make sure you downloaded it prior to printing the document.

The Jaggies Appear Unexpectedly

Symptoms:

If text characters display and/or print with ragged, irregular shapes, this is commonly referred to as the *jaggies*. The "expected" reasons for this have been described previously.

SEE: • **"Bitmapped Fonts" and "PostScript Fonts and Adobe Type Manager (ATM)," earlier in this chapter**

However, the jaggies may also appear unexpectedly, such as with a document that previously displayed and/or printed without the jaggies.

Causes:

- A TrueType font was inadvertently deleted.
- ATM was inadvertently turned off or is not working as expected.
- Bitmapped fonts will print with a jagged appearance, even though the correct size is installed, if you use the Best quality option (as selected from the Print dialog box of certain printers, such as the ImageWriter) and you do not have the bitmapped font file installed that is double (or even triple!) the size selected in the Size menu.

What to do:

With TrueType

You may have inadvertently deleted the TrueType file for a font (when updating your system software, for example), leaving behind only a scattered selection of bitmapped files for that same font. If you did, any text in sizes not represented by bitmapped files will now have the jaggies.

To check for this, look in the Fonts folder and/or your System file in the System Folder to determine if you have somehow deleted any TrueType fonts that you expected to still be there. If so, reinstall the TrueType fonts as needed.

If You Use ATM

- Make sure that ATM loaded into memory at startup. (You didn't hold down the Shift key at startup, did you? If you did, this prevents the loading of all startup extensions and control panels, including ATM.)

- The ATM control panel is named deliberately to load near the end of the list of INITs. This is to avoid certain potential INIT conflicts that may prevent ATM from working. So, do not rename the control panel.

SEE: • **Fix-It #4 for more on INIT conflicts**

- Check the ATM control panel to make sure ATM is actually turned on. If it isn't, turn it on (see Figure 9-21). Then restart.

- If you are using a version of ATM prior to 3.7, make sure you have both the ATM control panel (named ~ATM™) *and* the ATM extension (named ~ATM 68000 or ~ATM 68020/030/040 or something similar) installed. The extension should be loose in the System Folder (not in the Extensions folder). Also, make sure you are using the version of the ATM extension that is correct for your hardware (such as using the 68020/030/040 version if you have a 68040 Macintosh).

ATM GX and ATM 3.8 Alert: No ATM extension is used with the initial GX version of ATM (called ATM GX, which is really ATM 3.7). There is only the basic control panel. The other needed information is built directly into the QuickDraw GX system software.

Similarly, starting with ATM 3.8 (which runs in native mode on a Power Mac and works with or without QuickDraw GX), the additional processor-specific extension file is no longer needed. All of the information has been incorporated into the control panel itself. If you use the ATM Installer, the Easy Install option automatically builds in the correct "driver" for your hardware.

By the way, if you click on the version number in the upper right corner of the ATM 3.8 (or later) control panel, you will see one or more letter codes. These indicate the type of support for your version of ATM. For example, "p" means Power Macintosh support, "g" means QuickDraw GX support, and "2" means 68020/030/040 support.

- Make sure that all the needed printer font files are present and in their correct location (typically the Extensions or Fonts folder). ATM will not work for a particular font without the printer font files in your System Folder (even if the fonts are built into your PostScript printer). Remember, printer font files should be stored in the Extensions folder in System 7.0. For System 7.1/7.5, they can be either in the Extensions or the Fonts folder.

- Make sure you are using a version of ATM compatible with the system software. For example, System 7.1 needs at least version 3.0 of ATM (especially important if you are storing printer font files in the Fonts folder).

- If your problem is limited to a specific application and you are using System 7.1 or a later version, make sure you are using an application that is new enough to know to check for printer font files in the Fonts folder. Contact the manufacturer of the application to get this information, if needed.

- If ATM seems to work slowly or improperly when displaying fonts (or if you get a message that says ATM cannot render text because of a low cache size), increase the Font Cache setting in the control panel to as much as 512K, if you can afford the extra memory. The font cache is used to determine how much memory is assigned to ATM at startup. Especially if you are working with a relatively large number of fonts or are using Adobe's multiple master fonts, proper functioning of ATM may require that the cache size be increased from its default setting.

- Finally, replace the ATM file(s), just in case they have gotten corrupted. Restart and try again.

- If you are still having problems getting ATM to work, check the troubleshooting chapter in the ATM manual (if you have one!) for more advice. Also, ATM 3.8 (or a later version) comes with an especially good Read Me file, listing a whole host of compatibility problems and troubleshooting issues. Check it out.

With Bitmapped Fonts Printed at Best Quality

When you print bitmapped fonts using Best quality (as opposed to Faster or Draft), as selected from an ImageWriter's Print dialog box, the Macintosh accesses a font size double the size you selected. It then prints this double-sized font at a 50% reduction. The result is that the font prints at the selected size but at an apparent higher resolution. If the double-sized font is not present, it estimates the size, which can result in the jaggies. For example, to correctly print New York 12 at Best quality, you need the New York 24 font file, not the New York 12 file.

You can avoid this problem by having the double-sized font installed, by using a TrueType version of the font or by using ATM with a PostScript version of the font.

A similar situation exists for StyleWriters, where you may need the triple size font to print bitmapped fonts at Best quality.

Extra Help from PostScript Printers

Some LaserWriters include an option called FinePrint, accessed from the Print dialog box, that helps smooth out jagged edges, especially of text, even beyond what PostScript normally does. This can be useful even if nothing is really wrong with the text.

A Paragraph Unexpectedly Shifts Its Formatting

Symptoms:

In a word processor, a paragraph is typically assigned a specific set of margins, justification, indents, tabs, and line spacing. In some word processors, a paragraph may even have a particular default font, size, and style setting. Taken together, these define a paragraph's formatting. The problem occurs in either of the following cases:

- When you are editing text, a paragraph's formatting suddenly shifts to the format settings of an adjacent paragraph.
- When you are pasting text from one location to another, the formatting of the pasted text is not retained. Instead, the selection adopts the formatting of the surrounding text or uses the application's default format settings.

Causes:

The most likely cause of these problems is the selection (or lack of selection) of special invisible text characters. For example, in a typical word processor, every time you press Return, a special character is created, typically called the *return character* or the *paragraph marker.* This character indicates where a paragraph has ended. It also acts as a marker for all the formatting instructions unique to that paragraph. Other invisible characters are used to identify tabs, page breaks, and paragraph indents.

As implied by their name, these characters are not normally visible on the display or in printouts. However, they can still be deleted, copied, and replaced. Unintended modifications of invisible characters is usually the cause of these unexpected problems. Thus, if you delete a paragraph marker, any customized formatting for that paragraph is lost. Also, the paragraph merges with the adjacent paragraph to form one larger new paragraph.

What to do:

The key to avoiding these problems is to understand the consequences of selecting versus not selecting an invisible character when you make modifications to its related text. Once you understand the consequences, making the appropriate choice is usually easy.

Make Invisible Characters Visible

Showing invisible characters is a key first step whenever you suspect that a problem is caused by invisible characters. Word processors typically include a command, with a name like Show Invisibles or Show ¶ (see Figure 9-22), that makes these characters visible. Select this command. When you are done with your editing, reselect this command to make the characters invisible again.

> Here's a sample of text with normally invisible characters made visible. A tab is inserted here:→   A return character is inserted here:¶
>
> This starts a new paragraph. Note how the selection of text at the end of this paragraph has been extended to include the return character.¶

Figure 9-22   A sample of text from Microsoft Word, with its invisible characters made visible

Be Careful When Copying and Pasting

If you copy the return character along with a paragraph, the text should paste with the same format as it had when you copied it. Depending on exactly how and where you are pasting, it may even cause surrounding text to shift to the format of the newly pasted text. If a pasted selection does not contain a return character, it adopts the format of whatever paragraph now contains the selection.

Be Careful When Deleting Text

If you press the Delete key while the cursor is at the start of a paragraph, you backspace to the end of the previous paragraph. This causes the two paragraphs to merge, with both paragraphs now sharing the formatting of the second paragraph (a similar result occurs if a return character is cut or replaced by any other means).

If, instead, you want the merged paragraphs to share the formatting of the first paragraph, cut the text of the second paragraph (without cutting its paragraph marker), and then paste the text at the end of the previous paragraph. Finally, delete the "empty" line containing the paragraph marker of the second paragraph.

In General: To Correct Unexpected Format Shifts

If pasting or deleting text results in a format change that you did not want:

1. Select Undo immediately! This reverses the undesired change.
2. If you have not already done so, turn on Show Invisibles (or equivalent command), if your program has such a command.
3. With the formerly invisible characters now visible, begin the procedure again. This time, be careful to select or not select the relevant invisible character(s), as desired. Experiment if necessary. Continue to select Undo and try different variations until you get the result you want. For example, to paste text and minimize problems due to merging of formats across paragraphs, press Return immediately prior to selecting Paste. This usually achieves the desired effect.

4. Select Hide Invisibles (or equivalent command) when you are done. This command should have replaced the Show Invisibles command at the same menu location. The so-called invisible characters are now once again invisible.

Problems Copying and Pasting Text Across Applications

Symptoms:

You select a passage of text and cut or copy it to the Clipboard. However, when you attempt to paste the selection into a document of another application, one of the following occurs:

- The Paste command is dimmed and cannot be used.
- Nothing at all appears when you select Paste.
- Something other than what you most recently copied is pasted.
- The text is pasted successfully, but its formatting is incorrect (such as incorrect font and/or style).

Causes:

Assuming that you are working with an application that accepts pasted text, the most likely cause has to do with the operation of the Clipboard. Although this may not be immediately apparent to most users, the Macintosh maintains one Clipboard for use within an application (called the *application Clipboard*) and another for use between applications (called the *system Clipboard*). If you copy and paste within the same application, only the application Clipboard is used. This generally preserves all formatting, and the copy-and-paste transfer works just fine.

However, when you transfer to another application, the copied information is sent to the system Clipboard. This Clipboard does *not* typically retain application-specific text-formatting instructions. This is a major reason why, when text is pasted across applications, formatting information is lost. However, System 7.5 in general, and QuickDraw GX in particular, have new features (such as drag-and-drop clippings) that help minimize this problem.

More to the point, simply switching among two or more open applications is usually sufficient for information in the application Clipboard to pass to the system Clipboard and then to the application Clipboard for the receiving application. That is why you likely never notice the presence of these separate Clipboards. However, the system Clipboard may not always be properly updated. If that happens, whatever is currently present in the system Clipboard (which may be totally different from what you just copied) appears when you select Paste in a second application. If nothing is currently in the system Clipboard, nothing pastes.

Even if the text successfully pastes, it may be incorrectly formatted. This may occur (even if the needed invisible characters are included) either because the pasting application cannot interpret the formatting instructions of the original application or because differences between the application and system Clipboards cause format instructions may get removed during the transfer. In either case, expect pasted text to conform to the format in effect in whatever document is receiving the text.

This section is limited to problems with the transfer of text. Transfer problems with graphics are covered in Chapter 10 (see "Unable to Paste a Graphic Across Applications").

What to do:

If Unable to Paste Text At All

You copy text in one application and select Paste in another. Nothing happens. No text appears. Here's what to try:

- **Select Show Clipboard**
  Select the Show Clipboard command in the Finder's Edit menu. Look in the Clipboard window to see its contents. If the desired selection is not in the Clipboard, you need to update the system Clipboard. To try to do this, go to the next step.

- **Quit the application or go to the Finder**
  Quit the application you were using when you copied the text. (If you get a message such as one that says *Save large clipboard?,* select Yes.) Then return to the receiving application and try pasting again. Alternatively, go to the Finder and then back to the receiving application. Try pasting again. Both of these operations are likely to force an updating of the system Clipboard. If neither of them works, copy the selection a second time and try again. It may work now.

- **Transfer the selection in segments**
  If you are trying to paste a large selection, you may get a message saying that there is not enough memory to copy the selection to the Clipboard. If so, the easiest thing to do here is to transfer the selection in separate segments rather than all at once. Alternatively, you might try importing the selection, instead of pasting, assuming your application supports this option.

- **Make sure the pasting application accepts text**
  If the previous methods all fail, make sure that the pasting application currently accepts text in your selected location. For example, a database does not accept text into numeric or graphic fields.

If Format Shifts When Pasting Text Across Applications

You copy text in one application and select Paste in another. The text appears, but in the incorrect font or style. Here's what to try:

- **Make sure the needed invisible formatting characters were copied**
  It may simply be a case of the pasted text adopting the style of the surrounding text.

SEE: • "A Paragraph Unexpectedly Shifts Its Formatting" in the previous section

- **Import the text rather than paste it**
  In many applications you can directly import text from another document, bypassing the clipboard altogether, either via the Open command or via special Import or Insert commands. Doing this successfully depends on the receiving application having a translator capability for the format you want to import (usually listed in a pop-up menu found in the needed dialog box).

  This method is not guaranteed to work, but is worth a try if the clipboard fails. Try importing even if this means having to transfer more text than you need—you can always delete the unwanted text later.

SEE: • Chapter 6, "When You Can't Open a Document," for more on importing files
• Chapter 10, "Take Note: Foreign Imports"

In General: Use System 7.5/QuickDraw GX Solutions

- **Macintosh drag and drop**
  This System 7.5 feature is an expanded version of the drag-and-drop feature already implemented in System 7.1 (especially System 7 Pro). In System 7.5, it allows you to directly drag a selection from one document to another, even across applications, without needing the intervening copy-and-paste steps traditionally used by the Clipboard.

  You can even drag a selection to the Finder's desktop and create a special *clippings* file, which can be later dragged to another document, largely bypassing the need for the Scrapbook. You can have multiple clippings files on your desk. Double-clicking a clippings file opens up a window showing its contents. You can also drag items to the new System 7.5 Scrapbook.

  Drag and Drop may have no more chance of success than using Copy and Paste, but it's worth a try.

- **More powerful Clipboard**
  Apple claims this new QuickDraw GX feature should lead to more consistent copy-and-paste results. It is especially relevant for graphics, but it also applies here.

Note that using these features requires that the relevant application software be upgraded to be "savvy," "capable," or "aware" of the new feature.

SEE: • Chapter 10, "Unable to Paste a Graphic Across Applications," for more on these features, especially as they apply to graphics
• Chapter 12, for more general information on System 7.5, QuickDraw GX, and requirements for using these features

Otherwise . . . Reformat the Text

The only remaining solution is essentially to give up. Paste or drag the text in whatever fashion it transfers and then reformat it as needed.

Text Turns into Bitmapped Graphics

 Symptoms:

The text is no longer editable in any way. You can't select or otherwise change the text. In addition, the printed output looks distinctly inferior in quality to what you have come to expect from the font and/or printer you have been using. This problem is limited largely to typing text in certain graphics applications.

 Causes:

If you are using a *paint* (not a *draw*) graphics program, any text gets converted to a bitmapped graphic once you finish typing the text and move on to use another tool.

SEE: • Chapter 10 for more on paint versus draw programs

The most immediate consequence is that the text can no longer be edited in any way. In particular, you can no longer delete or add characters or change fonts, styles, or sizes. Instead, the text is treated as another part of the overall bitmap that makes up the picture, as if it were a graphic element drawn by the paint program. For example, it can now be erased using the paint program's Erase tool (see Figure 9-23).

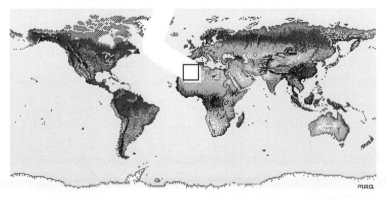

Figure 9-23   If you can erase the text like this, the Macintosh no longer recognizes it as text

Similarly, any TrueType scaling or PostScript instructions that would have been used when printing are now ignored. The text simply prints as a duplicate of the screen display, with any jaggies retained.

What to do:

Start Over and Repaste the Text

If it is necessary to make changes to the text in a paint program, about the only thing you can do is erase the text using the paint program's tools (such as the Eraser). Then start over and repaste the text. Make the needed changes before selecting another tool.

Do Not Use Bitmapped Graphics Programs for Text

Text remains editable in draw programs, similarly to how it would be in a word processor. If it is important that your text remain editable and print in its highest quality, do not use a paint program (or a paint module in a combination paint/draw program) to create the text. Use a draw program or module instead. To see the difference, compare the paint versus draw modules in a program like ClarisWorks. Also avoid image-processing programs (such as Photoshop).

Finally, note that if text has already been converted into a bitmapped graphic, copying and pasting the text into a draw program or word processor does not restore it as editable text.

Solve It! Font File Problems

Damaged Font Files

Symptoms:

A damaged font file should be suspected whenever you have any of the following symptoms (especially if other solutions, as described in previous sections of this chapter, have failed to work):

- Text displays in the wrong font or with otherwise unexpected formatting.
- Any document containing a specific font will not print correctly or will not print at all (see also Chapter 7 on printing errors).
- Whenever you try to open a certain application, a system freeze occurs. This can happen even if you are not using a document that contains the damaged font (see also Chapter 4 on system freezes).

- Every time you open or modify any document that contains a certain font, a system error occurs. Sometimes simply selecting the font from a Font menu will result in a crash.

- Trying to open a font file from the Finder results either in a messages that says the file is damaged or in a system crash.

- An inability to remove a font file from a font suitcase, a Fonts folder, or the System Folder (even if no applications are open). If you try to do so, an error message appears.

- Trying to delete a font file in the Trash results in an error message that says the file could not be deleted.

- The icon for your hard disk looks like a generic text document icon.

 Causes:

A font file can get damaged just like any other file. Damaged font files are a potential cause of incorrect font displays and other symptoms as just listed. These problems can occur not only in text-oriented programs, such as word processors, but in virtually any application.

 What to do:

Locate Any Damaged Font Files

Your first job is to determine if you do indeed have a damaged font file and, if so, which one it is. This can be difficult because the symptoms of a damaged font file are so varied and often have other possible causes.

Thus, your first step should be to rule out other likely causes, such as a damaged document or a damaged application. Use the general guidelines detailed in Chapter 3. For example, try different documents and different applications to see how narrow or widespread the problem is. Replace suspected damaged documents and applications with backup copies. Experiment with changing the font of a problem document, to see if that eliminates the problem. If the printing problem is specific to a certain page of your document, replace fonts that appear only on that page.

Sometimes you may find that symptoms are indeed linked to the use of a certain font. While this suggests (but does not prove) that you have a font problem, the damaged font may not be the one that you think it is. For example, I once had a problem with a calculator desk accessory that displayed its numbers in an incorrect font, making it difficult to read the numbers. The problem did turn out to be caused by a damaged font file. However, the damaged file was neither the correct font nor the one that was incorrectly displaying. It was a totally unrelated font. Yet replacing it remedied the problem.

Remove Fonts from the System Folder   For situations like the one with the calculator, your main hope to isolate the damaged font is to remove fonts from the Fonts folder (or other System Folder locations), one by one, until the problem (hopefully) disappears. Obviously, start with the fonts that appear most likely to be the cause of the problem.

SEE: • "Font Basics," earlier in this chapter, for more on how to remove fonts from a System Folder

To isolate a problem font you can use the same techniques used to identify problem INITs. (For example you can first remove half the fonts and see if the problem goes away. If so, divide that half into two smaller halves and return one of the halves to the Fonts folder. See if the problem reappears or not. And so on.)

SEE: • Fix-It #4 for more details on this procedure

Use WYSIWYG Menus   If you are using Now Utilities' WYSIWYG Menus and a system error occurs as a result of a damaged font, you may get some help with your diagnosis: after you restart, the utility should tell you the name of the font that caused the error. An anti-virus utility, Disinfectant, will also identify font files that appear to be damaged, as part of its normal check for virus infections.

Replace the Damaged Font File(s)

If you do locate a suspected damaged font file, replace it with an undamaged copy from your backups (you do have backups, don't you?). Hopefully, the problem is now gone.

Usually, you have to replace only the exact font file that was causing the problem. You shouldn't need to replace all of the files for other sizes and/or styles that are part of the same font family in addition.

In most cases, replacing a damaged font file should be no different from replacing an undamaged font. Use the procedures as described earlier in this chapter (see "Font Basics"). However, for the sake of clarity, here is a specific example of how to replace a suspected damaged font file (in System 7.1/7.5). Let's assume that the suspected font in this case is a TrueType font called Ashley.

1. First quit all open applications. This is because you cannot remove *any* font files, even undamaged ones, from your active System Folder (or Fonts folder within your active System Folder) if any other applications, besides the Finder, are in use (refer to Figure 9-5).

2. Open the Fonts folder inside your System Folder and locate the Ashley font (see Figure 9-24). In this case, it is a separate font file (not in any suitcase). If it had been in a suitcase file, you would need to open the suitcase (double-click on its icon) to locate the Ashley font file.

3. Drag the Ashley font from its location in the Fonts folder to the Trash. Select Empty Trash. (If the Finder says the font file is "in use" and refuses to delete it, restart and try again. It should delete now.)

4. Locate your undamaged backup copy of Ashley. Drag the backup copy of the Ashley font to the Fonts folder. You are done.

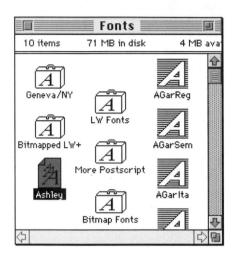

Figure 9-24
The inside of a Fonts folder, with the Ashley font file highlighted

Note that, in this example, I removed the Ashley font from the Fonts folder before adding the new font. I recommend doing the replacement this way. The alternative is to drag the replacement font to the Fonts folder before you remove the damaged font, letting the Macintosh do the replacement in one step (after asking you if you want to replace the font). While the one-step method should work (and may sometimes be necessary if the two-step procedure fails), I don't trust it to be as reliable.

This advice is especially important if your suspected damaged font is stored in a suitcase. In this case, if you drag the replacement font to the System Folder icon or to the Fonts folder, before removing the damaged font, the damaged font will not be replaced! Instead, you will wind up with two versions of the same font stored in your Fonts folder: the problem one in the suitcase and its replacement loose in the Fonts folder. Alternatively, if your replacement font has the same name as its suitcase, dragging the font to the Fonts folder could cause the entire suitcase to be deleted, not just the single font. To replace a font stored in a suitcase, you should remove the font first and directly drag the replacement font to the suitcase! Or, if it makes things simpler, you could remove and replace the entire suitcase, rather than just one font in it.

Problems Removing a Font File from a Fonts Folder

Occasionally, even when all applications are closed, you may be unable to remove or replace a particular font file (or font suitcase) from your Fonts folder. No matter what you try, you probably get an error message like the one in Figure 9-25 (or perhaps like the ones in Figure 9-5). Usually, this is because the font is damaged. If this happens, try the following:

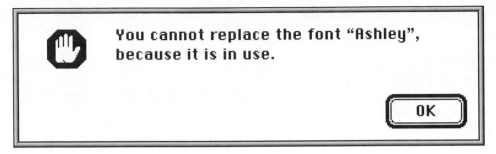

You cannot replace the font "Ashley", because it is in use.

OK

Figure 9-25   This message may appear when you try to remove a damaged font from a Fonts folder, even if all applications are closed

1. Drag the entire Fonts folder from the System Folder to the desktop.

2. Restart the Macintosh, ideally with extensions off.

3. Drag the problem font file(s) to the Trash. It should now delete successfully.

4. Return the Fonts folder to the System Folder.

SEE: • Chapter 6, "When You Can't Delete a File or Folder," for more on this problem

---

TECHNICALLY SPEAKING ▶

THE 31-CHARACTER FONT NAME LIMIT

In System 7, font names cannot have more than 31 characters. If, by some oddity (usually due to a font name assigned in System 6), a font name has more than 31 characters, you may have trouble deleting the font. You may even have problems if and when you try to update your system software. The font name refers to an internally stored ID, used by applications to identify the font. This is not necessarily the same as its file name in the Finder, which means that changing its file name will not help you here. Actually, most fonts have their file "name locked" attribute turned on, so that you could not readily change the name anyway (though see Chapter 8, "Finder Flags," for how to get around this, if you are curious). Your best bet is to open Font/DA Mover 4.1 (or a later version): Locate and select the problem font and click Remove. This should work.

Check for Problems with Other Files

If all else fails to solve your problem, it's time to suspect more generalized problems, such as damaged system files, INIT conflicts, or a bug in the application itself. In the worst-case scenarios, you may have to repair the Directory or reformat the entire drive.

SEE: • Chapter 6 for more general advice on problems with files
  • Fix-It #2 and #3 on application problems
  • Fix-It #4 on INIT conflicts
  • Fix-It #5 on System software problems
  • Fix-It #10 and #13 on Directory problems
  • Fix-It #14 for more Information on damaged files
  • Fix-It #15 on reformatting the drive

Damaged Font Suitcase Files

Symptoms:

You double-click a font suitcase to view its contents, the suitcase will not open. Instead, you get an error message that says the font suitcase cannot open because it is damaged.

Causes:

A variety of causes are possible, most of them rather unlikely these days, and most of them not really a case of a damaged file. For example:

- You have two fonts in a suitcase with names greater than 31 characters (possible in System 6), but with the first 31 characters of each name being identical. In System 7, the Finder only checks the first 31 characters and thus believes that the two fonts are identically named. The Finder will typically react to this by thinking that the font suitcase is damaged.
- The utility, Suitcase, was used to compress font files. This too may fool the Macintosh into thinking a font suitcase is damaged.
- A suitcase file in the Fonts folder is also in use by Suitcase.

Of course, it is also possible that the suitcase file or one or more specific fonts within the suitcase file really are damaged.

What to do:

Delete and Replace the Suitcase File

If you have undamaged backup copies of the fonts, the best thing to do is to simply delete the font suitcase and reinstall fresh copies of the font.

If the Macintosh refuses to let you delete the suitcase file, refer to the previous section, "Damaged Font Files." Follow its advice on how to delete problem font files.

Extract Fonts from the Suitcase File

If you do not have usable backup copies of your fonts, you can try to extract the fonts (assuming they are really not damaged) from the supposedly damaged suitcase. You can do this with a copy of Font/DA Mover (at least version 4.1 if you are using System 7). Otherwise, if you don't care if you save the fonts, just delete the suitcase.

Watch Out for the Suitcase Utility

If the problems seem related to your use of Suitcase, refer to the Suitcase manual for specific advice in order to avoid a repeat of the problem. Alternatively, stop using Suitcase altogether.

Solve It! Font Menu Problems

Fonts Unexpectedly Appear or Disappear from Font Menus

Symptoms:

You check the Font menu of your word processor (or other text application) and find that either of the following occurs:

- One or more new fonts are listed that were never there before and that you do not recall installing.

- One or more fonts that have always been listed are unexpectedly absent, and you do not recall removing them from their System Folder location.

Causes:

There are a variety of probable causes for these Font menu disappearing and reappearing acts, none of them very serious, and all usually easy to correct. These include font differences across startup disks, fonts embedded in an application, fonts installed automatically by Installer utilities, and font management utilities inadvertently turned off. In general, remember that a font will not appear in a Font menu unless it is installed in its proper (usually System Folder) location (as detailed in the beginning of this chapter).

What to do:

Check for Font Differences Among Different Startup Disks

You may be using a different startup disk from the one you normally use. If this new startup disk has different fonts in its System Folder from your normal startup disk, these differences are reflected in the Font menu. The same thing is true, of course, when you are working with someone else's computer. Their fonts are probably different from yours.

Fonts are usually installed in the System file or Fonts folder. As stated earlier in this chapter (in "Font Basics"), fonts are usually not part of the application itself. The fonts listed in an application's Font menu vary, depending on what fonts are installed in the startup disk's System Folder.

If a change in startup disks is the apparent cause of unexpected changes in your Font menu, simply return to your original startup disk, and all will return to normal. If this is not possible for any reason, you have to either give up on using missing fonts or install them into the current startup disk's System Folder.

Check for Embedded Fonts in Applications

You *can* install any font directly into an application (similarly to how you install fonts into the System file). These application-installed fonts are called *embedded fonts.* It is rare to use embedded fonts these days. However, if they are used, they are listed only in the Font menu of the application that contains them. Thus, when you shift to another application, the embedded font seems to have disappeared.

SEE: • Chapter 7, "Technically Speaking: Problems with Embedded Fonts," for a problem with printing documents that use embedded fonts

---

TECHNICALLY SPEAKING ▶

LOCATING AND UNEMBEDDING EMBEDDED FONTS

You can use Font/DA Mover to access embedded fonts. To do so, hold down the Option key and click Font/DA Mover's Open button. The Open dialog box that appears now lists all files on your disk (without using the Option key, it lists only suitcases and System files). Select the application that contains the embedded fonts. The names of the embedded fonts (if any) should now be listed in the Font/DA Mover window. Assuming you are familiar with the use of Font/DA Mover, you can now easily copy these fonts to a suitcase file or even a System file. In this way, you can essentially unembed the font, making it available to all applications, if desired. You can similarly use Font/DA Mover to delete the embedded font from the application.

Check for Fonts Installed by an Installer Utility

If you recently upgraded your system software or installed a new application that uses an Installer utility, you may have automatically installed new fonts without realizing it. Usually, the manual tells you about this, though not all do. Apple's system software Installer, in particular, reinstalls any of Apple's standard fonts that you may have deleted since the previous installation.

If you wish to delete new fonts that have been added by the Installer, it is usually safe to do so.

However, some applications use these fonts for special purposes that may not be immediately apparent. So be careful. Save a copy of the font before you delete it. Be prepared to reinstall it if problems appear when you use the relevant application.

SEE: • "Locating, Adding, and Removing Fonts from Your System Folder" earlier in this chapter

Check If Font/DA Management Utilities Are Turned Off

Font/DA management utilities, such as Suitcase, are system extensions. This means that if you use one of these utilities and you start up with extensions off, such as by holding down the Shift key at startup, any fonts that are accessed through these utilities now do not appear in Font menus. Anything else that you do to turn off these utilities has the same result.

SEE: • "By the Way: Font/DA Mover and Other Font/DA Management Utilities," earlier in this chapter, for more on these utilities

Quit Currently Open Applications

If you just made a change to the fonts in your System Folder, don't expect to see it reflected in any currently open applications. To see the change, you have first to quit the application and relaunch it. Ideally, close all open applications prior to making any changes. In some cases, you may need to restart the Macintosh.

In General: If You Are Having Trouble Finding a Specific Font File

To check if a font file has been inadvertently moved from its proper location or to locate a font file on your startup disk, for any reason, follow these guidelines:

- Check all the relevant System Folder locations. Check the System file, the Extensions folder, and (if present) the Fonts folder. Even in System 7.1, some fonts may be in the System file. Conversely, in System 7.0, some fonts may be in the Extensions folder.

- Otherwise, use the Finder's Find command (or other similar Find utility). Type the likely name or partial name of the font file you wish to locate, and click the Find button.

- You can check for possible embedded fonts using Font/DA Mover.

SEE: • "Technically Speaking: Locating and Unembedding Embedded Fonts" earlier in this section

- Font/DA management utilities, such as Suitcase, can access fonts from anywhere on your disk, not just the System Folder. In these cases, your missing font may be hiding anywhere on your disk. The utilities themselves usually have a function for locating the files that they are accessing. Use it.

SEARCHING FOR RESERVED FONTS IN SYSTEM 7

The Macintosh needs certain fonts for displaying system information such as menus and dialog boxes. These are called reserved fonts. They are: Chicago 12, Geneva 9, Geneva 12, and Monaco 9. Because of their importance, you should never delete these fonts from your System Folder. Usually this is not an option anyway, as the Macintosh does not easily let you do them. In System 7 (all versions), you cannot even find these font files listed anywhere. Even if you were to open a suitcase file that contained these fonts, their names would not appear. In System 7.1/7.5, these fonts are "invisibly" installed in your System file, even though remaining fonts are in your (quite visible) Fonts folder. This certainly makes it difficult to delete reserved fonts. Despite their absence from these Finder-level listings, these fonts still work correctly and appear in Font menus.

A brief aside: Chicago 12 is even more reserved than the other reserved fonts. It is included directly in the Macintosh's ROM hardware. It can therefore never be truly deleted, even if you manage to delete all traces of it from your disk.

You can use Font/DA Mover to view and copy reserved fonts (though you cannot remove them from an active System file).

Font Menu Clutter

Symptoms:

The only symptom here is a Font menu that contains several separate listings that all seem to refer to the same basic font. For example, for the Palatino font, you would see B Palatino Bold, BI Palatino BoldItalic, and I Palatino Italic, as well as Palatino itself (see Figure 9-26).

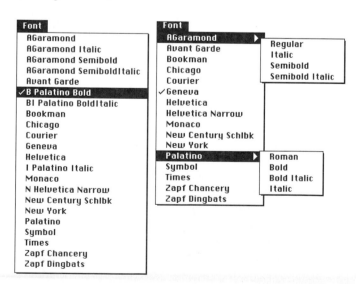

Figure 9-26   Font menu clutter (at left), cleaned up with Now Utilities' WYSIWYG Menus (at right)

If you are lucky, all of these fonts may sort together in the Font menu (as is the case for the AGaramond fonts in Figure 9-26). In the worst cases (as is true for the Palatino fonts in Figure 9-26), the variants of a font are listed in different locations because they do not all start with the same letter. Multiply this by a half dozen or more similarly structured fonts, and you can quickly see the potential scale of this problem. This is Font menu clutter.

Causes:

This is nothing actually wrong here. This is what is supposed to happen, given the nature of these fonts. These are all style variants of screen fonts, designed to match separate PostScript printer font files for each style. Recall that four (or even more) separate printer font files may exist for the same font (either in your System Folder or built into the PostScript printer). In these cases, you may also have a matching set of four screen fonts, one for each printer font.

SEE: • "Technically Speaking: All in the Family," earlier in this chapter, for details on these style variant font files

If this part of the Macintosh interface were perfectly designed, all the different screen fonts would be considered part of the same family and would not result in separate listings in the Font menu. This is how it works with related bitmapped fonts, for example. This is why your Font menu does not separately list Times 10 and Times 12 as different fonts, even though a separate bitmapped font file may be present for each size. Similarly, this problem does not occur when you install different TrueType fonts of the same family, such as Palatino and Palatino (bold).

However, as it turns out, these style variant screen fonts are often considered to be separate families and thus get listed separately. This is the cause of the menu clutter problem.

What to do:

Get Rid of the Style Variant Screen Fonts

If you are not using ATM or a PostScript printer, these style variants are irrelevant. Get rid of them. (How did they get there in the first place?)

Even if you are using ATM and/or a PostScript printer, if the menu clutter bothers you, just remove all the screen fonts for the style variants. Keep only the plain text screen font (such as Palatino and AGaramond). You can even use a TrueType font as a screen font if you have one from the same family (Apple provides a TrueType version of Palatino, for example, as part of System 7). In most cases, this should eliminate the menu clutter without unduly affecting the display or printed output.

SEE: • "Technically Speaking: All in the Family," earlier in this chapter, for more details on pros and cons of eliminating these screen fonts

Use a Utility to Eliminate the Clutter

If you really want to keep the style variant screen fonts, you can use special utilities, such as WYSIWYG Menus (which is part of Now Utilities) and Font Harmony (which comes with Suitcase). These are designed to clean up menu clutter.

WYSIWYG Menus creates a hierarchical menu (off each main font) that lists all the variants (see Figure 9-26). Font Harmony lists the font name only once in the Font menu, no matter how many variants exist. Variants are selected automatically behind the scenes. This is how the whole thing should have been designed in the first place.

Occasional anomalies occur. For example, two common LaserWriter fonts, Helvetica and N Helvetica Narrow, are considered to be from separate families even when you use these utilities.

By the way, another utility in this category is Adobe Type Reunion. However, for some reason, this particular utility causes more compatibility problems than the others. Be wary of using it.

Do Nothing

If you don't like either of those choices, you can just live with the menu clutter. It will do you no harm.

Chapter Summary

Whew! Do you have all that memorized yet? No? Don't worry, this is not the sort of information that needs to be at your fingertips all the time. Keep this chapter handy for those times when you do need it, in particular:

• When you add fonts to or delete fonts from your System Folder

• Whenever the display and/or printing of your text is different from what you expected

Overall, this chapter described the basics of where fonts are stored on your disk, how to install new ones, and how to remove ones that are already there. It detailed the differences among the different font technologies: bitmapped versus outline; PostScript versus TrueType.

It concluded with a broad sampling of problems you may encounter when working with text, both for display and for printing. These ranged, for example, from documents that open using a wrong font, to documents that print in a font different from the one they show on the screen, to problems pasting text across applications.

Chapter 10

Graphics: What's Wrong with This Picture?

Picture This

If you think the graphics features on the Macintosh are just for artists and designers, you are wrong. The Macintosh lives and breathes graphics. From the Finder's icons to a spreadsheet's charts to a word processor's paragraph borders, you are using and creating graphics. Even if you can't draw a straight line, your computer can draw one for you. If you have a scanner, you can use it to convert almost any printed copy into a digitized computer image. Or you can buy prepackaged images, called clip art. You can even have your photographs developed onto a compact disk that can be read by CD-ROM drives.

   This chapter deals with graphics-related issues and problems that are likely to confront even the most casual of users. For better or for worse, this chapter is not designed to meet the specialized needs of graphics professionals. Similar in format to the previous chapter on text problems, this chapter begins with some basics about how graphics are created, stored, displayed, and printed. Then it shifts to specific solutions for a selection of common problems.

Resolution and Display Depth

To solve graphics problems, you first need to understand two issues more fundamental to the operation of the Macintosh: resolution and display depth. While these issues affect all aspects of Macintosh display and printing, they are particularly relevant to graphics.

Understanding Resolution

How does the quality of the image you see, either on the screen or in a printed copy, relate to the resolution of the display or printing device? Here is my attempt to answer this important question, trying to avoid technical jargon as much as possible.

Monitors

All monitor screens are made up of a series of square dots (usually called *pixels*). The combination of dots that are on or off at a particular moment makes up what you see as the screen display. The number of dots that fit across an inch of space is referred to as the *dots per inch (dpi)* of the monitor. The higher the dpi, the more dots you can fit in an inch of space.

   The *resolution* of the screen refers to how clearly we can see images on the screen and how finely detailed those images can be. The most important (but not the only) factor that determines a screen's resolution is its dpi.

To see how this works, let's start by assuming you are comparing two different monitors of exactly the same size. The only difference is in the size of the individual dots or pixels. Let's assume Monitor A has 72 dpi while Monitor B has 144 dpi. Since the screen sizes are the same, this must mean that each dot in Monitor A is twice the size of each dot in Monitor B.

Now, let's further assume that, despite this difference in dpi, a displayed image takes up the same amount of screen real estate on both monitors. Thus, if you displayed the same document on both machines, they would both fit the same amount of the document onto the screen. This means that a object in the document drawn to be 2 inches long, for example, will be 2 inches long on either monitor. Finally, this means that this object will be 144 dots long on Monitor A, but 288 dots long on Monitor B.

As a result of all of this, the object will be seen in *higher resolution* in Monitor B than Monitor A. For example, if the object displayed is an irregularly curved line, the subtle nuances of the curves can be better captured when you have 288 dots to do so than when you only have 144 dots. To see this more clearly, imagine an extreme case of a resolution of 4 dpi. Now try to imagine how you could possibly display an intricately curved 2-inch line with that resolution. You could not.

Higher resolution is generally considered desirable. It offers the potential for smoother, finer, more detailed and more realistic-looking displays. Similarly, since you cannot create a line thinner than the width of a single dot, the higher the resolution of your monitor, the thinner the line you can display.

But beware, dpi is not everything when it comes to screen image quality. You must also consider the size of the screen. For example, let's suppose that the 72-dpi Monitor A we have been considering is a 14" monitor with a typical screen dimension of 640 pixels across by 480 pixels down. But now let's look at a new monitor, Monitor C, with a screen size that is half the size of Monitor A. Monitor C, wanting to maintain consistency with Monitor A, also has dimensions of 640 x 480 pixels. To do this, each pixel in Monitor C must be half the size of those in Monitor A, which means that Monitor C is measured at 144 dpi. Monitor C will thus appear to have higher resolution, with images generally appearing sharper than in Monitor A. But there is a downside here. Unlike with Monitor B (the 144-dpi monitor from the previous example), this 144-dpi resolution has come at the cost of an overall smaller screen. Again assuming that what is displayed on the screen remains the same on all three monitors, this means that everything on Monitor C will be shrunk 50% compared to Monitor A. For example, that 2-inch curved line in Monitor A will now only be 1 inch long in Monitor C, using 144 dots in both cases. This of course makes everything in Monitor C harder to see.

Another alternative would be for Monitor C to have an increased pixel size, so that there would be only 72 dpi. Now the image would appear exactly the same as in Monitor A (a 2-inch line would display at 2 inches in both cases), but because the Monitor C screen is half the size, it could only show half of what Monitor A could show at any one time.

It is this sort of dilemma that has been faced by some PowerBook screens, for example. The screens are smaller than the 14" monitor common on desktop Macs. Despite this, some PowerBook models maintain 72 dpi, and by doing so are unable to show as much on the screen. In particular, these PowerBooks cut off the bottom 80 rows of what would be seen on a desktop screen, using a dimension of 640 x 400, rather than 640 x 480. Other more recent models of PowerBooks duplicate the 640 x 480 dimensions of desktop monitors by making the pixel size smaller. The actual dpi may be as high as 92, which gives images a crisper look. These PowerBooks display identical images to those on the desktop Macs, but everything on the PowerBook is significantly smaller.

Here's one more complication: The original Macintosh monitor had 72 dpi. All applications were written based on this assumption. Thus, a graphics program wanting to draw a 1-inch line would draw a line that was 72 pixels long. Today, many monitors vary from this 72-dpi standard. For example, your monitor may have only 69 dpi. Still, most applications still draw a 72-pixel line for a 1-inch line. With a 69-dpi monitor, this means that a 1-inch line will actually display as slightly longer than 1 inch.

When monitors get much larger than 14 inches (16" to 21" are common these days), they typically still hover close to the 72-dpi standard. This means they have many more pixels on the screen and can thus show much more of an image at one time. You will not need to scroll through a document as often with a larger screen, for example. More recently, *multiscan monitors* have become available for the Macintosh. These allow you to choose from among different pixel sizes (or resolution) of the display. Changing resolution (which is done via the Monitors control panel) will change how much of an image you can see on the screen at one time. You might choose to use a higher resolution when wanting to see a lot on the screen at one time, but shift to a lower resolution when you are more interested in a larger image.

To summarize: as pixel size gets smaller, the number of pixels per inch (dpi) increases. All other things equal, this means a higher resolution. By increasing its dpi, a smaller screen may show exactly the same image (though reduced in size) as a larger screen with a lower dpi. Thus, the size of the screen as well as its pixel dimensions both play a role in resolution. Finally, the depth of the display (described in the next section) has an effect on your perceived resolution.

Printers

Printed images, like their screen display counterparts, are made up of a series of dots. Printer resolution is thus also measured in dots per inch (dpi). Actually, the situation is a lot less complicated with printers than with monitors, because you don't have to deal with an interaction comparable to that of pixel size versus monitor size. With printers dpi *is* the total indication of resolution.

At the low end, Apple's dot matrix ImageWriter printers have a resolution of 72 dpi. This is the same as that of a typical monitor, which (while not very high) is great for having the printed output perfectly duplicate the screen display.

Laser printers have typically had a resolution of 300 dpi, although 600 dpi is now common on newer models. In some printers, you can select what resolution you want to use. Commercial quality printers have even higher resolutions. Inkjet printers have resolutions in the same 300- to 600-dpi range. In other words, most printers in use today have resolutions far higher than that of the monitor display. This is why printed output typically looks much better than what you see on the screen. But the discrepancy in resolution between screen and printer also opens the door to potential problems, as you will soon see.

Understanding Display Depth: Color and Grayscale

What follows is an overview of using color and grayscale on a Macintosh, emphasizing problems common to all levels of Macintosh users.

What Is the Display Depth?

Each pixel of a typical color monitor can be any one of up to millions of different colors. However, because of other hardware restrictions in the Macintosh, a pixel may be able to show only a subset of these millions of colors in a given situation. More precisely, there is usually a limit to the total number of different colors that can appear on the screen—*at any one time.* This is referred to as the *depth* of the display. Noncolor monitors, by definition, have even greater restrictions on their display depth.

In the simplest case, each pixel (or each bit of the bitmap, to phrase it differently) can be in either one of two states: on (white) or off (black). This simplest case produces a *black-and-white* display and is called a *1-bit depth.* A basic black-and-white monitor (such as in a Macintosh SE) is only capable of a 1-bit depth display.

However, with most displays today, each pixel can assume more than just two values. For example, several PowerBook models, such as the PowerBook 180, can have up to 16 different states. This is called a *4-bit display depth.* Each different state of a pixel corresponds to a different shade of gray that the pixel can assume, from very light grays to almost black grays. Thus, a graphic image with gray shadings will appear more accurately on a 4-bit display than on a 1-bit display. However, these Power-Books cannot display color (though other PowerBook models can). Thus, any monitor that can only display different shades of gray is referred to as a *grayscale* (or *monochrome*) *display.*

Most current monitors attached to desktop Macintoshes are *color displays.* Some PowerBooks also have color displays. In these cases, what determines the maximum number of colors you can display at one time is not the display itself, but the hardware on the Macintosh's logic board, the size of your monitor, and the software on your disk.

SEE: • "Problems Displaying at Different Color Depths," later in this chapter, for more on hardware/software requirements for different color depths

These days, the default setting for most color Macintoshes is to display 256 different colors (also called an *8-bit display depth*). If you have the right equipment, you may be able to show millions of colors at one time (over 17 million, to be more precise), a capability referred to as *24-bit color*.

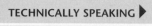

TECHNICALLY SPEAKING ▶

BIT NUMBERS AND COLORS

The relationship between the bit number (such as 8 bits) and the number of colors (such as 256) is determined as follows: Each bit of information can have 2 possible values. The total number of different values is thus 2 raised to an exponent equal to the number of bits. For example, an 8-bit display can have 2^8 (or 256) different values.

The Monitors Control Panel: Setting the Depth of the Display

With a typical grayscale or color display, you have some control over what color depth is actually displayed. You make this selection by using the Monitors control panel (see Figure 10-1).

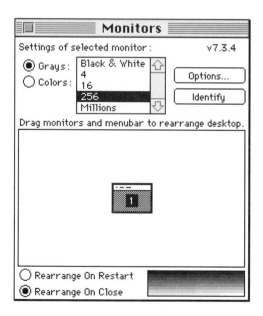

Figure 10-1   The Monitors control panel

You select a bit depth from the scroll box at the top of the control panel. For example, Black & White is a 1-bit display, 256 is an 8-bit display, and Millions is a 24-bit display. To reiterate, these numbers refer to the maximum number of different colors the screen can display at any one time. This means that, with an 8-bit display, you can still vary what 256 colors get displayed. This is in essence what you do when you shift from 256 grays to 256 colors, for example.

Actually, switching between the Grays and Colors options will only make a difference for 4-bit, 16-bit, or 256-bit displays. Black & White is always black and white. Thousands and Millions are always capable of showing color; only those images that do not contain any color will display in all grays at these settings. If your hardware/software is not adequate to display a certain depth (such as Millions), that option will not appear in the scroll box.

A setting of 256 grays is sufficient to display a black and white photograph with smooth gradient transitions and subtle shadings. Overall, the image quality is almost equal to that of a photograph. Note that the term black and white, when used to describe a photograph, is not accurate. These photographs actually contain a multitude of shades of gray. To achieve the same level of image quality for a color photograph, you need 24-bit color.

SEE: • "Technically Speaking: Why 24-bit Color?"
       • "Problems Displaying at Different Color Depths," later in this chapter, for more on color depth problems

Selecting display depth is the main function of the Monitors control panel. Other less commonly used functions include: (1) coordinating displays with multiple monitors attached (described more in Chapter 11), (2) changing resolutions on multiscan monitors (mentioned earlier in this chapter), and (3) accessing other settings via the control panel's Options button.

By the way, if you hold down the Option key when selecting the Options button, you get even more options! For example, you may see a choice of different *gamma corrections* (changing these alters the overall color balance of the display). Still, most users will have little or no need for accessing any of the features available in the Options window. Table 10-1 summarizes the relationship between the Monitors control panel settings and display depth (as measured in bits).

WHY 24-BIT COLOR?

The Millions setting on the Monitors control panel is also referred to as 24-bit color. Assuming you have the necessary hardware to select this setting, why would you want to use it? After all, if you were going to draw a picture with crayons, would you feel a need for 17 million different crayons? Probably not. But the Macintosh is a bit different.

- *The pros of 24-bit color.* Higher depths are especially useful for viewing photographic images, such as those digitized from a scanner or used in QuickTime movies. Twenty-four-bit color gives a subtlety and naturalness that far exceeds what is possible with a 256-color limit. Similarly, the color gradient fill commands, found in many graphics applications, produce a much smoother transition of colors with 24-bit color than with 8-bit color. To see this difference, look at the color bar at the bottom of the Monitors control panel when you shift from 256 to Millions of colors. The difference is dramatic. At 256 colors, distinct bands are visible. With Millions selected, the color transitions are so smooth as to be imperceptible. Twenty-four-bit color also eliminates color shift problems (as described in the Solve It section of this chapter).

- *The cons of 24-bit color.* The speed with which the screen image is updated slows down as the depth level increases. Working with a 24-bit color document can mean, for example, that every time you scroll your image, your computer slows to a crawl (unless you have a lot of RAM, a fast CPU, and/or a graphics accelerator card). Actually, this slowdown occurs even in nongraphics, noncolor documents. Thus, scrolling through a black-and-white text document is faster in 8-bit mode (and faster still in 1-bit mode) than in 24-bit mode. Also, since 24-bit documents contain a lot more information than 8-bit (or other lower-depth) documents, they require much more disk space and need more memory to open than comparable 8-bit documents. By the way, creating 24-bit documents requires more than just a 24-bit display; you also need 24-bit capable software (as explained more in the Solve It section of this chapter).

Display Depth and Dithering

If you have ever looked at a grayscale graphic on a black-and-white monitor, it may appear that you are actually seeing different shades of gray. But you are not. This illusion is achieved by a careful mixing of dots, called *dithering*. For example, alternating black and white pixels, when viewed at a slight distance, simulate the appearance of a medium gray. By altering the proportion of black to white dots in a given area of the screen, as well as by varying the pattern in which the dots are mixed, a range of shades of gray can be simulated.

The Macintosh uses dithering, with reasonable success, when changing display depths. This is needed because the depth level of a document (determined when the file is created) may be greater than the current display depth. Thus, if you display an 8-bit grayscale image at a 1-bit display depth, what you see is a dithered equivalent of the grayscale image (see Figure 10-2). Similarly, if you display a 24-bit color graphic at an 8-bit color depth, you get a dithered approximation of the colors that are outside the 256 color range.

Figure 10-2 At left, a 256 grayscale display of a cat; at right, a dithered display (resulting from shifting to a 1-bit display depth) of the same image

Table 10-1 Display Depth and the Monitors Control Panel

DEPTH (IN NUMBER OF BITS)	DEPTH (AS LISTED IN MONITORS CONTROL PANEL)	DOES SHIFTING FROM COLORS TO GRAYS CHANGE THE DISPLAY?
1	Black-&-White	No
2	4	Yes
4	16	Yes
8	256	Yes
16	Thousands	No
24 (or 32)	Millions	No

Display Depth and Printing

With resolutions of 300 to 600 dpi, most popular printers (such as Apple's LaserWriters) are great for printing text. They can produce finely detailed fonts in almost any variety. They can also print thinner lines, smoother curves, and sharper, more finely detailed graphics than can be seen on the screen. However, most of them are black-and-white printing devices. That is, they have a 1-bit depth. This makes them distinctly limited as devices for reproducing grayscale and color graphics. Any shades of gray that seem to be in an image are accomplished by dithering or by a conceptually similar technique called *halftoning*.

Of course, color printers do exist. However, they vary widely in terms of the color range and quality they can print. At the low end, you have inkjet printers such as the Apple Color StyleWriter Pro and Hewlett-Packard's DeskWriter 560c. They are inexpensive and can produce a rich color printout, even of a 24-bit color image, but their color quality is far from professional. Even the best printers (which use different printing methods and cost thousands of dollars more than inkjets) still have difficulty exactly matching their colors to those on the screen display.

SEE: • **"Problems Printing Color/Grayscale to a Black-and-White Printer," later in this chapter, for more on dithering and halftoning and on color-matching problems**

Types of Graphics, Programs, and Files

Bitmapped Versus Object-Oriented Graphics

The Macintosh uses two basic methods to create graphic images: bitmapped graphics and object-oriented graphics. The differences between these two categories are analogous to the distinction between bitmapped and outline fonts (as described in Chapter 9).

Bitmapped Graphics

A bitmapped graphic is created as a series of individual dots (also called *bits*). A bitmapped graphics file contains the instructions that detail the status of every single bit that makes up the image (which bits are off, which ones are on, and with what color). These instructions are called the *bitmap*.

Technically, the bits in a bitmapped image can be of any size (or *resolution*). However, the most common size is 72 dpi. This is approximately the same as the minimum dot (or pixel) size of most Macintosh monitors.

This similarity is not a coincidence. This matching ensures that a bitmapped graphic file stores *exactly* the information needed to recreate a screen image. When you consider that the Macintosh's first printer, the ImageWriter, also had a 72-dpi resolution, you can clearly see the origins of the WYSIWYG aspect of the Macintosh.

Some applications create bitmapped graphics at higher resolutions, such as at 300 dpi (which conveniently matches the resolution of most LaserWriters). Such images have a greatly improved printed appearance. However, if the monitor's resolution is limited to 72 dpi, this higher-resolution detail cannot be translated to the monitor display image. At best, it can be approximated. In such cases, the WYSIWYG relationship between the display and the printed output is partially broken.

On the other hand, a bitmapped graphic, if it is created at 72 dpi, looks no better in the printed output than it does on the screen. Even if the printer has a higher resolution, bitmapped graphics print only at the resolution with which they were created. Thus, 72-dpi bitmapped graphics print out at 72 dpi even on a 300-dpi or 600-dpi LaserWriter. In some cases, smoothing options are available from the Page Setup dialog box to reduce the jagged look of these images. However, this does not alter the basic resolution.

Object-Oriented Graphics

Object-oriented graphics are defined and stored as individual objects (lines, circles, squares, and so on). A document of this type is typically made up of a collection of these separate objects. Analogous to outline fonts (as described in Chapter 9), this method frees the graphic from dependence on a specific level of resolution. Object-oriented graphics display or print at whatever resolution is used by the output device. For example, an object-oriented graphic prints at a typical LaserWriter's resolution of 300 dpi. On the other hand, the screen display of an object-oriented graphic is still translated into a 72-dpi image, because that is the monitor's resolution. This means that the appearance of printed output is likely to be superior to what you see on the screen.

To further clarify the distinction between bitmapped and object-oriented graphics, consider the differences between a bitmapped versus an object-oriented circle. You create both circles in exactly the same way: Select the relevant application's Circle tool from its tool palette, hold down the mouse button, and drag the mouse (see Figure 10-3). Similarly, if both monitors use a 72-dpi resolution, the display images of both types of circles usually appear indistinguishable from each other (see Figure 10-4, top). The increased resolution capability of the object-oriented circle becomes apparent mainly when you print the circles with a higher-resolution printer (see Figure 10-4, bottom).

Bear in mind that all Macintosh displays and printed output are necessarily bitmapped. The difference between object-oriented versus bitmapped graphics is that bitmapped graphics begin with bitmapped instructions, while object-oriented graphics are converted to a bitmap from the object-oriented instructions.

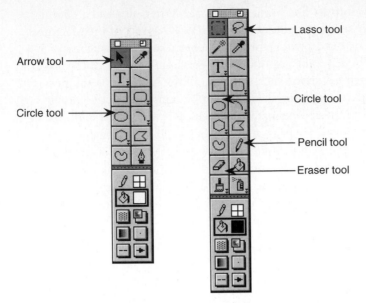

Figure 10-3   At left, a tool palette designed primarily to work with object-oriented graphics (taken from a program's Draw module); at right, a tool palette designed to work with bitmapped graphics (taken from a program's Paint module)

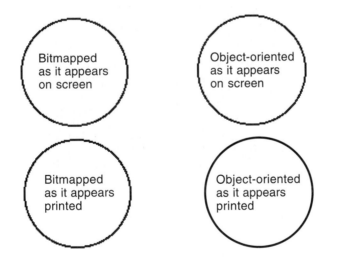

Figure 10-4   At top, a 72-dpi bitmapped circle (left) versus an object-oriented circle (right) as they appear on the screen (note the similarity); at bottom, the same bitmapped circle (left) versus an object-oriented circle (right) as printed by a LaserWriter (note the difference)

Editing Bitmapped Versus Object-Oriented Graphics

A major difference between bitmapped and object-oriented graphics, as explained in the previous section, is that the resolution of objected-oriented graphics is device-independent. Other notable differences become apparent when you edit these graphics.

Selecting and Moving Bits Versus Objects   If you draw a circle directly on top of an object-oriented square, the shape and location of the square (now hidden from view) is still remembered. The circle can be later selected, typically by clicking the mouse while the Arrow tool cursor is over the object. You can then drag the circle to a new location, and the square, now no longer hidden from view, reappears. It is as if the circle had been stacked on top of the square, which is, metaphorically speaking, exactly the case (see Figure 10-5).

When you edit bitmapped graphics, on the other hand, placing a circle on top of a square changes the map of the pixels in that area. There is no separate recognition of a square and a circle. The square (or whatever part of it is now hidden) essentially

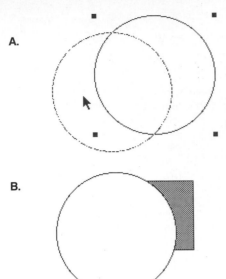

A.

B.

Figure 10-5
At top, an object-oriented circle is selected (indicated by the four "handles" at the corners) and moved (indicated by the dotted-line circle); at bottom, when the move is completed, the square previously hidden underneath the circle is now partially visible

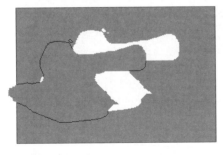

Figure 10-6
Moving this irregularly shaped bitmapped object (selected with a Lasso tool) leaves behind a blank white space; whatever may have been underneath the selection is no longer there

vanishes when the circle is placed on top of it. That is, there is no layering effect. Only one layer of dots exists, and nothing can be hidden underneath it. You can still select the circle, such as with a Lasso tool. However, if you then moved the circle, you would no longer find a square underneath. There would be only white space (see Figure 10-6).

Pixel-by-Pixel Versus Object-by-Object Editing Bitmapped graphics can be edited on a pixel-by-pixel basis. Object-oriented graphics can be edited only on an object-by-object basis. For example, with bitmapped graphics, you can use a Pencil tool to add or delete a single pixel from the circumference of a circle. You can similarly use an Eraser tool to remove part of a bitmapped graphic (see Figure 10-7). This precise editing ability is unique to bitmapped graphics. It is the main reason that bitmapped graphics are the preferred type for creative artwork and image retouching.

With object-oriented graphics, on the other hand, you can make modifications only to an entire object. Thus, you cannot remove one pixel from an object-oriented circle. You must instead erase the entire circle (typically by selecting it and pressing the Delete key). Still, this approach has its advantages. For example, you can change fill patterns and line thicknesses of object-oriented graphics at any time, with a single command. Comparable changes are far less convenient to do with bitmapped graphics.

Reducing, Enlarging, and Rotating Bits Versus Objects For object-oriented graphics, reducing, enlarging, or rotating an object does not alter the quality of the

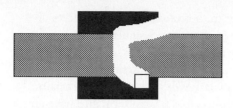

Figure 10-7
Using an Eraser tool to partially erase objects, as shown here, can be done only with bitmapped graphics

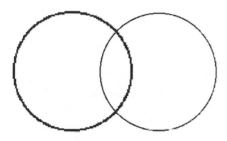

Figure 10-8
At left, the bitmapped circle from Figure 10-4, after enlarging it on the Macintosh; at right, the object-oriented circle from Figure 10-4, similarly enlarged

image. For bitmapped graphics, such operations usually reduce the quality of the selected image (see Figure 10-8).

To change the size of an object-oriented circle, for example, the Macintosh uses an appropriate numeric substitution in the formula used to define the circle. The quality and accuracy of the image are maintained as before. In some cases, the screen display may suffer (because of its 72-dpi bitmapped restriction), but higher-resolution printed output still looks fine.

For bitmapped graphics, however, these same operations are likely to produce distortions in the shape of the image—distortions that affect both the screen display and the printed output. Enlarged images tend to have increased jaggies, reduced images lose fine detail, and rotated images look messier. Reductions are a particular problem for bitmapped graphics, since making the image smaller results in a loss of the number of bits in the bitmap. For example, if you reduce an

irregularly curved line that was 200 dots long to 100 dots long, you have only half as many of the same-size dots to create the same appearance. Some of the details of the original line's twists and turns almost certainly have to be omitted in this smaller image.

Paint Versus Draw Versus PostScript Programs

How do you know whether you are working with bitmapped or object-oriented graphics? Generally, it depends on the application you are using. Programs (or modules of programs) that work with bitmapped images are called *paint* programs, while those that work with object-oriented images are called *draw* programs. Many applications can work with both types of images. Detailed information should be somewhere in the application's manual.

Paint Programs

Paint programs (or modules) work exclusively with bitmapped graphics. The term *paint* is meant to suggest their preferred use for artistic purposes, where the ability to edit pixel by pixel allows for freehand drawing and subtle texture effects that would be impossible with object-oriented graphics. Programs in this broad category range from the minimalist black-and-white approach of MacPaint to the color and texture effects of Painter. Image-processing applications, such as Photoshop, are designed to work primarily with digitized artwork (that is, images typically created by using a scanner). Since digitized artwork uses bitmapped images, these applications are functionally similar to paint programs. Most integrated packages, such as ClarisWorks, include both a paint and a draw module. Some primarily draw programs, such as ClarisDraw, also have an ability to shift to a paint mode so that you can edit bitmapped graphics with them.

Any object-oriented graphics that are pasted into a paint program/module become part of the bitmap and lose their object identity. They can now be edited on a pixel-by-pixel basis.

TAKE NOTE ▶

DIFFERENT TOOLS IN PAINT VERSUS DRAW PROGRAMS

Just as the previous chapter made frequent reference to word-processing programs, this chapter makes reference to graphics applications. In particular, it assumes at least a passing familiarity with the basic array of "tools" used by these programs, such as lasso, eraser, and polygon.

If you don't know whether a program is a paint or a draw program (or whether you are in the paint or draw mode of a program that can do both), you can often figure this out simply by examining the collection of tools currently in its tool bar (see Figure 10-3). For example, paint programs/modules will show an Eraser tool, but draw programs/modules will not. This is because erasing requires editing of individual pixels—something that is possible only with bitmapped graphics in paint programs/modules.

Draw Programs

Applications that use primarily object-oriented graphics are often called *draw* programs. These applications are preferred for architectural and engineering drawings, or any other use where precision and layout are more important than creative touches. However, you can still create some fine artwork with draw programs. Typical programs in this category include ClarisDraw and Canvas.

Draw programs are *not* limited to object-oriented graphics. They can contain bitmapped graphics as well. In "pure" draw programs, the bitmapped graphic simply becomes another separate object. You cannot edit it, on a pixel-by-pixel basis, with paint tools. In some draw programs, you can actually shift into a paint mode to edit it. Again, integrated packages, such as ClarisWorks and Microsoft Works, include separate draw and paint modules.

PostScript Programs

PostScript programs, such as Adobe Illustrator and Freehand, form a special class that doesn't quite fit into either category. In most ways, they are similar to draw programs, because PostScript is basically an object-oriented language. In fact, some draw programs, such as Canvas, incorporate PostScript features. However, with PostScript, what you see on the screen is often only a rough approximation of the printed output, because the PostScript graphic instructions only go to the printer and do not determine the screen display. More details about this distinction are covered in the next section on graphics file formats.

Graphics File Formats

When you save a graphics document, you save it in a particular *file format*. This is really no different from what I have previously described for documents in general, such as with text documents (as described in Chapters 6 and 8). For example, Microsoft Word saves documents in its own Word file format. A generic TEXT format, not tied to any particular application, is also available in almost all text-oriented applications. To open a text file in a format other than the one specific to the application in use generally requires that the application have a translator file for that format. The same general rules apply in the world of graphics.

Generic Graphics File Formats

There is only one generic text format (called TEXT), but there are several different generic graphics formats. Graphics applications do not depend on application-specific formats to nearly the extent that most other categories of applications do. In fact, many graphics applications do not even have an application-specific format, instead relying entirely on generic formats. When things are working well, this considerably simplifies the process of transferring information across applications, reducing the number of translator files needed.

Each of the different generic formats has different limitations and advantages. For example, some are better for bitmapped graphics, and others are better for object-oriented graphics.

The most common generic graphics formats are PNTG, PICT, TIFF, and EPSF.

PNTG or Paint The PNTG format (often referred to as Paint) was originally considered an application-specific format. It is the document type of the Macintosh's first graphics program: MacPaint. It is such a commonly available format today, however, that it is now considered generic.

It is also a limited format and is rarely used anymore. It can store only black-and-white bitmapped information at 72-dpi resolution. This worked well for accurately transferring the screen image from the original 72-dpi black-and-white Macintoshes to the original 72-dpi black-and-white ImageWriters. But it hardly keeps pace with today's color monitors and high-resolution printers.

A common misconception is that all paint programs use the Paint file format. This is not true. What makes a program a paint program is how it works with bitmapped images, not what file format it uses. Paint programs can use any of several formats, especially the PICT format described next.

PICT The PICT format was originally derived from the first object-oriented graphics program for the Macintosh: MacDraw. However, as with PNTG, it is now widely used by many other applications and is considered a generic format.

In fact, PICT is the most versatile and common of all the generic graphics formats. For example, it is the graphics file type used by Apple's TeachText/SimpleText utilities. In this sense, it is the complementary format to the TEXT file type used for text. Also, when you take a picture of your screen (using command-shift-3), the Mac saves the picture as a PICT document.

PICT images can be used by both draw and paint programs and can contain either bitmapped or object-oriented graphics. However, PICT images are notorious for causing problems for PostScript printers, especially those used by professional printers. If you plan to send your documents to a printing service, you will be better off using the TIFF or EPS formats described next.

TIFF   TIFF stands for Tag Image File Format. Like PNTG, it is a bitmapped-only file format. Actually, several different versions of the TIFF format are available. The resolution and color limitations of the format depend on the exact version of TIFF in use (as well as the particular application in use).

TIFF is the preferred format for working with digitized images, particularly scanned photographs. This format is similarly ideal for use in imaging programs, such as Photoshop, that permit brightness and contrast adjustments to a document.

TIFF can save files at very high resolutions, permitting high-quality printouts, but at the cost of requiring enormously large files. Thus, it is common to see special compressed TIFF formats.

EPSF or EPS   EPSF (often called EPS) stands for Encapsulated PostScript File. This file format can be used with either bitmapped or object-oriented graphics. However, the primary reason for using EPS is that it stores the graphic information as PostScript instructions, which are then used to create the graphic on a PostScript printer.

Using EPS files requires an application that supports the use of PostScript instructions. Adobe Illustrator and Freehand are the two best-known examples of graphics applications that have this capability.

EPS files generally include a separate PICT image of the file in addition to the PostScript information. The PICT image—an approximate visual representation of the PostScript commands—is displayed on the monitor. The PostScript information is used only when printing. Thus, as is generally true when using PostScript, the screen display of an EPS file is not identical to the printed output.

You may be able to open an EPSF file with an application that does not support PostScript. If so, the display and printing are generated from the PICT information; the PostScript information is ignored entirely.

By the way, if you are using LaserWriter 8, you can save any file as an EPS file, via the print to disk option in the Print dialog box (as described in Chapter 7, "Technically Speaking: LaserWriter 8 Print Options").

SEE: • **"File Format Shifts When Transferring Graphics Across Applications" and "Problems Printing PostScript Graphics," both later in this chapter**

Application-Specific File Formats

In addition to the generic file formats, some graphics applications have a unique application-specific format, comparable to the specific formats created by most word processors. These unique file formats may allow the creating application to save certain special formatting effects that are not possible with the generic formats. Thus, SuperPaint can maintain a separate bitmapped and object-oriented layer only if the file is saved in SuperPaint format.

Graphics programs with application-specific file formats also have options to save files in generic formats. In fact, you may have to save in a generic format if you wish to transfer the image to another program, such as a word processor or a page-layout program. Word processors and the like rarely have file-translation filters for application-specific graphics formats. They support only generic formats.

How to Determine the File Type of a Graphics Document

Knowing a graphic document's file type can be the key to solving a problem you are having displaying or printing the file. So how can you tell the file type of a specific document?

The Kind description in the file's Get Info window, though useful in identifying file types of most nongraphics documents, is generally not helpful here. It tells you only the name of the application that *created* the document, not necessarily the format (or *file type*) of the document. Thus, for example, a ClarisDraw file saved in ClarisDraw's application-specific format and a ClarisDraw file saved in the PICT2 format are both listed in the Kind description as simply *ClarisDraw document.*

You will have better luck by checking the icons for each document. Many programs, including ClarisDraw, use different Finder icons to indicate the different file formats. For example, Figure 10-9 shows three icons for three different formats of ClarisDraw documents. If checking icons doesn't help, then try one of these options: Determine an assigned format from the Open dialog box, assign a format using the Save As Command, or use a disk-editing utility. Details are given in the following paragraphs.

ClarisDraw format   PICT format   EPSF format

Figure 10-9   Different icons for a ClarisDraw document saved in its application-specific format (left) versus a PICT format (center) versus an EPSF format (right)

Determine an Assigned Format from the Open Dialog Box   Open a graphics application, ideally the application that created the document. Select the Open command. Navigate to the folder where the unidentified file is located. Most graphics applications offer a variety of file format-translation options, typically from a pop-up menu

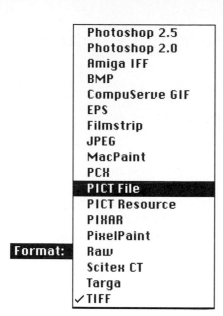

Format:	Photoshop 2.5
	Photoshop 2.0
	Amiga IFF
	BMP
	CompuServe GIF
	EPS
	Filmstrip
	JPEG
	MacPaint
	PCX
	PICT File
	PICT Resource
	PIXAR
	PixelPaint
	Raw
	Scitex CT
	Targa
	✓ TIFF

Figure 10-10
Graphics file formats listed in the Format pop-up menu in Photoshop's Open As and Save As dialog boxes

in the Open and/or Save dialog boxes (see Figure 10-10). Select the different format options listed there one by one. Each time, check whether the file you are interested in is listed in the scroll box. Only those files that match the selected file format appear in the list. Thus, when your file appears, the currently selected format is the one used by your file.

Alternatively, if your document has an All Files option, you might try opening your file using that option. If this works, an alert message may appear that informs you of the file format as the file is being read (such as *Converting TIFF document*).

By the way, an application may not be able to export all the file types it can import. Therefore, the file types listed in its Save (or Export) dialog box may be different from those listed in its Open (or Import) dialog box.

Assign a Format Using the Save As Command   Whenever you first save a graphic (or use the Save As command), you assign a format to the file. Usually, the default format is the application-specific format, if there is one.

If you want to make sure that a file is in a particular format (such as PICT) regardless of what its present format may be, you can assign the file a format with the Save As command. To do so, open the graphics document in a graphics application. Select Save As and choose the desired format from the selection of format options listed there (see Figure 10-10). Click Save. Whatever file format you selected is now assigned to your document. Give the file a new name if you do not want it to replace the original file.

If no selections are given, it usually means that all files in the application are saved in some generic file format (often PICT), with no other options available.

Use a Utility   If the preceding methods do not apply, you can directly read a document's file format using a utility that identifies a document's file type, such as Get More Info. The four-letter name (such as PICT or TIFF) of each generic format is the code you see listed as the file type for these documents. By definition, this tells you the file's format. Application-specific formats have their own unique codes. Generally, do not use this method to change a file's type code. Doing so does not change the format of the file. It only causes problems for subsequent use of the file. Use this method primarily to identify the file's type.

SEE: • Chapter 8 for more details on file type codes and related utilities

Solve It! Problems Transferring Graphics Across Applications

Unable to Paste a Graphic Across Applications

 ### Symptoms:

You copy a selected graphic to the Clipboard and shift to another application (word processor, page-layout program, graphics application, or whatever) to paste the graphic into a document. Unfortunately, one of the following events happens:

- The Paste command is dimmed and cannot be used.
- Nothing at all appears when you select Paste.
- Something other than what you most recently copied is pasted.

These symptoms are not limited to graphics and may occur whenever you use the Clipboard.

SEE: • Chapter 9, "Problems Copying and Pasting Text Across Applications"

 ### Causes:

- **The graphic never copied to the system Clipboard**
  A graphic image will obviously not paste successfully if it was never copied successfully. This can happen for the same general reason first discussed for text transfers in Chapter 9. It involves the distinction between the application versus system Clipboards. To briefly review, there are really two Clipboards: an *application Clipboard* (used in the creating application) and a *system Clipboard* (used when going between applications). Information is supposed to be converted from the application Clipboard to the system Clipboard when you switch applications. However, it does not always work properly, especially with System 7 or MultiFinder, where you can switch to a new application without quitting the old one.
- **The application does not support graphics placement**
  Some applications do not allow pasting of graphics.

If either of these problems occurs, the Paste command will either be dimmed, will paste nothing, or will paste whatever was previously in the system Clipboard.

What to do:

Check Show Clipboard

To check if the graphic was transferred to the system Clipboard, select the Show Clipboard command in the Finder's Edit menu. Look in the Clipboard window to see its contents (see Figure 10-11).

Figure 10-11
The Finder's Show Clipboard command, and the Clipboard window that opens when you select this command

Update the System Clipboard If Necessary

If the image is not in the Clipboard, you need to update the system Clipboard. To do this, try any or all of the following:

1. Quit the application you were using when you copied the graphic. (If you get a message such as one that says *Save large clipboard?*, select Yes.) Then return to the receiving application and try pasting again.

2. Go to the Finder and then back to the receiving application. Try pasting again.

3. Recopy the graphic and paste it to the Scrapbook. Then shift to the application where you wish to paste the graphic. Go to the Scrapbook and copy the desired graphic. Now return to the application and select Paste.

4. Go to the System Folder and locate the file called Clipboard. Drag it to the Trash. A new file will be created automatically, as needed. Now try to recopy and paste your graphic. This may work especially if the Clipboard file was damaged.

5. If none of the above succeeds, keep trying Copy and Paste a few more times. Sometimes, for reasons unknown, it may eventually work.

Check If the Application Supports Graphics Placement

If the image is in the Clipboard but you cannot get it to paste, it is probably because the application doesn't accept graphics. For example, some applications may accept only pasted text, not graphics (such as a spreadsheet that does not accept graphics in its cells). In such cases, when a graphic is on the Clipboard, the Paste command is usually dimmed so that you cannot select it. Even if it is not dimmed, nothing will appear when you select Paste. Check the application's manual for more details as to what can be pasted into it.

Use Drag and Drop and/or QuickDraw GX

If you have had no success using Copy and Paste and you are using system software prior to System 7.5, you may have more success with one or more of these new System 7.5 features. Try them.

- **Macintosh Drag and Drop**
  This System 7.5 feature is an expanded version of the drag-and-drop feature already implemented in System 7.1 (especially System 7 Pro). In System 7.5, it allows you to directly drag a selection from one document to another, even across applications, without needing the intervening copy-and-paste steps traditionally used by the Clipboard.

  You can even drag a selection to the Finder's desktop and create a special *clippings* file that can be later dragged to another document, largely bypassing the need for the Scrapbook (see Figure 10-12). You can have multiple clippings files on your desk. Double-clicking a clippings file opens up a window showing its contents.

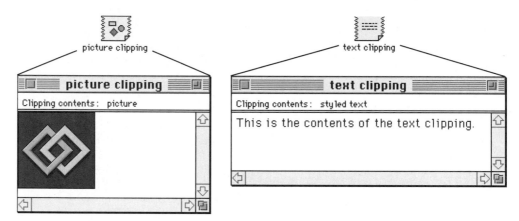

Figure 10-12   Two Drag and Drop clippings files and their contents

**Figure 10-13
The Scrapbook in System 7.5**

- **Enhanced scrapbook**
  The Scrapbook has been improved in System 7.5 (see Figure 10-13). It is now resizable and gives more information about the format of what is stored there. It supports Drag and Drop. However, you may have to allocate more memory to it to cut or paste large images.

- **More powerful Clipboard**
  Apple claims this new QuickDraw GX feature should lead to more consistent copy and paste results. It also simplifies the process of transferring graphics from one

application to another without losing its graphic format (as described in the next section of this chapter).

Using Drag and Drop requires that certain extensions (such as Clipping Extension) be active. Using QuickDraw GX additionally requires its own separate installation of software, including the QuickDraw GX extension. All of this means that these features will not work if you start with extensions off. Finally, note that using these features requires that the relevant application software be upgraded to be "savvy," "capable," or "aware" of the new feature.

SEE: • Chapter 12, for more general information on System 7.5, QuickDraw GX, and require-
       ments for using these features

BY THE WAY ▶

MORE WAYS TO BYPASS THE CLIPBOARD

Drag and Drop is just the latest in a series of different ways that you can transfer data across applications without using copy and paste. They all offer different advantages and/or limitations. They all require that software be written to specifically support the feature.

First, there's System 7's Publish and Subscribe, probably the best-known of the alternatives. It lets you place a copy of your selection into a document while retaining a link to the original. Whenever you update the original, the linked copy can be automatically updated as well, eliminating the need to repaste the modified data. Many applications now support this feature, but it has never become very popular—probably because it is so cumbersome to use.

Another alternative, less well-known and even less often used, is EGO (Embedded Graphic Object). For example, a popular equation editor, Expressionist, uses this method for transferring an equation to other documents, such as a word-processing document. The advantage of an EGO-placed equation is that, if you double-click it from the word processor, it automatically opens Expressionist to allow editing of the equation and then automatically places the modified equation back in the word-processing document. The only trick to doing this is that the object must first be selected with "handles" showing, rather than highlighted. If it is highlighted, you are just selecting it to be cut or copied.

There is another related and very rarely implemented technology, called Word Services, that is specific to text applications. For example, it can allow a stand-alone spelling checker to work within another application, adding its commands to the menubar, as if it were actually part of the other application. If you are interested, WordPerfect can make use of this feature.

In this vein, Microsoft's OLE and Apple's forthcoming OpenDoc technologies break new ground, allowing multiple applications of any type to access the same document, eliminating any need to transfer data at all. You can see OLE in action, for example, in the latest versions of Microsoft Works and Word. Apple has high hopes that OpenDoc will be a major feature of future versions of the system software.

Import the Graphic

If none of the preceding solves the problem, try importing the graphic. This often succeeds even when the Clipboard fails.

Successful importing depends on the receiving application having the relevant file-translation filter for the format of data to be imported. However, even if you have the correct filter, the import may still fail. If so, you typically get an error message (see

Figure 10-14). This is a particularly common problem with the TIFF format, because there are several variations of the format. You can't do much about this, other than return to the original application and see if you can save the file in a different format, one that will be accepted by the importing application. In general, avoid application-specific formats as these are the least likely to be importable. Use generic formats instead.

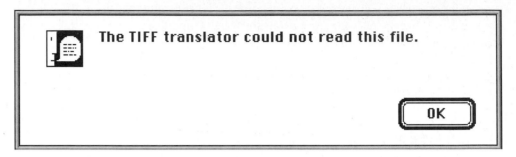

Figure 10-14 This message appeared when a program was unable to import a TIFF file, even though the application had a TIFF format translator

By the way, beware of using Macintosh Easy Open when importing graphics (such as EPS or TIFF files into PageMaker). If you are having problems, turn Easy Open off.

SEE: • Chapter 6 for more on importing problems

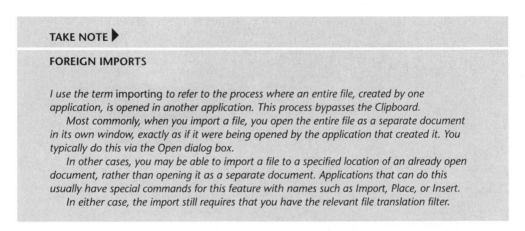

TAKE NOTE ▶

FOREIGN IMPORTS

I use the term importing to refer to the process where an entire file, created by one application, is opened in another application. This process bypasses the Clipboard.

Most commonly, when you import a file, you open the entire file as a separate document in its own window, exactly as if it were being opened by the application that created it. You typically do this via the Open dialog box.

In other cases, you may be able to import a file to a specified location of an already open document, rather than opening it as a separate document. Applications that can do this usually have special commands for this feature with names such as Import, Place, or Insert.

In either case, the import still requires that you have the relevant file translation filter.

Otherwise . . .

If none of the previous suggestions succeed, you are probably stuck and will not be able to transfer the graphic to the application in question. However, if you do finally get the graphic to transfer, you may find that your problems are still not over. In particular, you may find that the graphic is no longer in its original file format. If this happens, check out the next section "File Format Shifts When Transferring Graphics Across Applications."

File Format Shifts When Transferring Graphics Across Applications

Symptoms:

A graphic image is successfully transferred from one application to another (typically by Copy and Paste). However:

- The display quality of the transferred image is poorer than when it is displayed in the original application.

- And/or, when you print the transferred graphic, its quality is distinctly inferior to that obtained when printing it from the original application.

These problems are most common with documents originally formatted in TIFF or EPSF.

Causes:

The primary cause is that when graphics are transferred across applications, they are typically converted to a PICT format, regardless of the format of the document from which they originated. This is especially a problem with TIFF and EPS files, since these formats contain special printing-related information (such as an EPS file's Post-Script instructions) that are lost in the conversion to a PICT format.

Copy and Paste, Publish and Subscribe

This PICT conversion most commonly occurs when using either the Clipboard (Copy and Paste) or Publish and Subscribe commands to transfer a graphic image. For example, if you paste an image from a TIFF file to the Scrapbook, it will be converted to a PICT file. You can confirm this by checking the format of the pasted file in the Scrapbook window. Thus, in the lower left corner of the Scrapbook window shown in Figure 10-13, you can see the graphic's Type indicated as PICT. Fortunately, this conversion problem does not occur when transfers are made within the same application.

Importing

This conversion problem may also occur when you import graphics documents. Don't assume that because an application has a translator for the TIFF format, for example, the imported file is retained in TIFF format. The outcome depends on the features of the importing application.

 What to do:

Use the Option Key to Copy PostScript Code to the Clipboard

If you are trying to transfer EPS images via the Clipboard, note that graphics applications that support this format, such as Adobe Illustrator or Aldus Freehand, can usually copy both the PICT image and the embedded PostScript code. To do this, hold down the Option key when you select Copy. If you then paste this copied image into any other program that can accept the PostScript code, both the image and the PostScript code will paste. Check with the manual of your program to see if it accepts PostScript code.

Import Rather than Copy or Publish

In general, if you were unsuccessful in preserving the format of an image when using either the Clipboard or publish and subscribe, try importing instead (if this option is available). Importing is often more successful in preserving a graphic's format.

SEE: • "Take Note: Foreign Imports," in the previous section, for more details

For LaserWriter Users: Save the Selection as an EPS File

If you want to transfer a graphic to another application with its EPS format preserved and standard importing methods did not or could not work, try selecting Print and saving the selection or file in EPS format (by checking File, rather than Printer, as the Destination). Then try to open the file in the receiving application.

SEE: • Chapter 7, "Technically Speaking: LaserWriter 8 Print Options"

Try a Different Application

If transferring to your first-choice application does not succeed in preserving the format, try transferring to a different application (assuming that you have another one suitable for your needs). Perhaps the alternate application will preserve formats correctly.

For example, page-layout programs (such as PageMaker) tend to preserve most formats they import. Word processors, in contrast, often convert all graphics to a PICT format, though some can preserve EPS format. Graphics programs vary in this regard.

Photoshop is particularly good at being able to open and/or import a variety of graphics formats.

SEE: • Chapter 6 for more general problems opening files

Use Drag and Drop and/or QuickDraw GX

Using System 7.5's Macintosh Drag and Drop, enhanced Scrapbook, and/or Quick-Draw GX Clipboard may succeed in transferring information, where standard methods in earlier versions of the system software would not. In particular, the new Quick-Draw GX Clipboard should retain graphics format information (such as TIFF and EPS) when transferring graphics across applications. Thus, this eliminates the problem of all formats being converted to the PICT format when they are transferred. However, this only works with software upgraded to support this new feature.

SEE: • "Use Drag and Drop and/or QuickDraw GX" in "Unable to Paste a Graphic Across Applications," the previous section of this chapter, for more details
   • Chapter 12 for more on these features and System 7.5 in general

Ignore the Problem

Otherwise, these format shifts, if they occur, cannot be avoided. They are inherent to the operation of the system and/or application software. However, you may choose to ignore this problem. Even in its changed file format, the image may be satisfactory for your needs. In this case, you need do nothing at all. To maintain the original application's format, however, you are limited to editing or printing the file from its original application.

Related Problems

Two other issues, related to this general problem, are discussed in detail elsewhere.

Problems with the Importing Application   When you transfer a graphics selection to another graphics application, its appearance and the methods available to edit the graphic depend on the features of the importing application more than the document itself. For example, a paint program converts all transferred graphics to bitmapped images, regardless of their original format. For PostScript graphics, such as EPS files, other special problems may occur.

SEE: • "Paint Versus Draw Programs" earlier in this chapter
      • "Problems Printing PostScript Graphics" later in this chapter

Color Problems   The displayed colors of a transferred graphic may be different from the way they were in the original application.

SEE: • "Color Shift Problems" in the following section

Solve It! Problems Displaying Color/Grayscale

Color Shift Problems

 Symptoms:

- When you are transferring graphics (such as via the Clipboard, by using publish and subscribe, or by importing), the colors of the image shift such that the transferred graphic now displays in colors different than it did in the creating application.

- If two or more documents are open within a single application, shifting to another document as the active document may cause the displayed colors of the previously active document to temporarily shift.

- When you are using a color graphics program, the colors displayed in other open applications (including the Finder) may temporarily shift to the wrong colors.

 Causes:

This is more of a minor irritation than a real problem. No damage or permanent change has been done to your document. Your graphic remains fully capable of displaying correctly. Often, just closing a window will solve the problem. However, understanding why this happens does provide some useful information about how the Macintosh works. The primary cause, in all of these cases, is a limitation of working in less than 16- or 24-bit color. Here's what's going on.

Color Palettes

Even at an 8-bit color depth, you have access to all the millions of colors possible for a color monitor to display. The problem is that only 256 can be displayed at one time. So the question becomes, what 256 colors get displayed?

The default system-level choice (at 8-bit color depth) is a set of 256 colors called the *system colors* (there is a similar default choice for other depths). Depending on the application in use, your available colors may differ from the system colors. In some cases, you may be able to select from separate sets of 256 colors, called *color palettes*. In such cases the system-color palette becomes just one of many possible palette choices. For example, there may also be palettes for earth tones and pastels (see Figure 10-15). A palette need not fill all 256 available colors. However, no more than one palette can be in use at the same time.

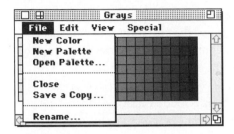

Figure 10-15
A graphic application's color palette window, displaying a palette of different shades of gray

This restriction can lead to what I call *color shift* problems. For example, if you open a document that was created using the system-color palette, while an earth-tone palette is active, the document may display in the wrong colors (that is, in the earth-tones rather than the system colors). Similarly, if two graphics are open at the same time, and they use different palettes, the system may correctly display the active window, leaving the back window to shift colors accordingly. Finally, in some cases, if a graphic uses a palette other than the system palette, it may display in the wrong colors whenever it is opened in an application other than its creating application, no matter what depth setting is in use.

What to do:

Quit and Relaunch the Application

Just quitting and relaunching the same application could solve the problem. This is especially likely to work if your colors changed immediately after changing resolutions with a multiscan monitor.

BY THE WAY ▶

MORE DISPLAY PROBLEMS WITH MULTISCAN MONITORS

With Apple's multiscan monitors, you can change the resolution of your display (via the Monitors control panel) without restarting, even while applications are running. A change in resolution in this way may occasionally lead to problems, such as colors displaying incorrectly or windows that have moved halfway off the screen or are missing altogether. These problems can usually be fixed by quitting and reopening the problem application. Otherwise, you may have to return to your original resolution.

Use Another Application, If Possible

Assuming you have more than one application that can display the graphic, try another application. It may work better. For example, I have found differences among two word processors in their ability to import color TIFF documents. Both word processors opened the TIFF file. However, the colors were correctly displayed with one program but were displayed entirely wrong with the other.

Select the Desired Document to Be the Active Window

At 8-bit (or less) color depths, the display of the entire monitor (all windows from all open applications) typically reflects the color palette of the currently active document. If other open documents use different palettes, they may display incorrectly (using the colors of the active document) when they are not the active document.

This is an aesthetic problem. You can ignore it if you wish. The monitor should shift to display the correct colors when the document is made the active document. However, in some cases you may have to quit the relevant graphics application to get the display of other applications to return to normal. For example, with certain applications open, the Finder's desktop always displays in incorrect colors.

Change to a Higher Color Depth

Shifting to 24-bit (or even 16-bit) color from the Monitors control panel, if this option is available, generally solves all these problems, since this removes the 8-bit restriction of 256 colors. Besides allowing a greater range of colors, these higher depths use a different method of determining what colors to display. This method tends to ensure more accurate matching of colors for graphics transferred across applications. The main potential problem here is if you are using an application that does not run at higher than an 8-bit depth (as explained more in the next section).

Problems Displaying at Different Color Depths

 Symptoms:

- You want to display a document at a high color depth, typically Thousands (16-bit) or Millions (24-bit), but these options are not listed in the Monitors control panel.
- You select Thousands or Millions from the Monitors control panel, but it still does not display in these depths.
- An application will not open in certain color depths.
- A document does not display in the selected color depth.

SEE: • "The Monitors Control Panel: Setting the Depth of the Display," earlier in this chapter

Causes:

Hardware and/or system software that is inadequate to the task is the main cause of this problem. Perhaps you have never attempted to use 24-bit color before. In this case, part of the problem is to determine if your machine can even display in this mode, and if not, why not.

Other causes have to do with software: incorrect settings from the Monitors control panel or problems with the application and/or document itself.

What to do:

Make Sure You Have the Necessary Hardware and System Software

This is not the place to give a complete course in what you need to display at higher color depths. However, here are the main things to consider:

- You need a color monitor.
- You need a Macintosh model with the necessary color display instructions built into its ROM. Virtually all recent models fit this bill.
- If you are still using System 6, you may also need a software extension called 32-bit QuickDraw to access 24-bit color. (Okay, I know. You're asking why is it called 32-bit QuickDraw and not 24-bit QuickDraw? The short answer, which is all you are going to get here, is that you are actually running at a 32-bit level, but only 24 of those bits are used to determine how many colors you can see.)
- You need sufficient video RAM (called VRAM) to display at higher color depths. Some amount of VRAM is included on the logic board of most Macintoshes. If it is not sufficient, you may be able to add more. Otherwise, you will need to add a special *video card* (such as Apple's 8 • 24 Display Card) to increase the available VRAM. These hardware additions will require opening up your Mac.
- You need sufficient ordinary RAM as well. These days, figure on having at least 8Mb of RAM if you regularly use 24-bit color on a 14-inch monitor. If you don't have enough RAM, you usually get an alert message, like the one in Figure 10-16, when you try to open a 24-bit color document. Some Macs make use of a portion of ordinary RAM as a substitute for VRAM. In these cases, your RAM needs will be even higher than on other Macs (though you may be able to bypass this use of RAM by installing a separate VRAM video card).
- The larger the size of your monitor, the more RAM and/or VRAM you will need to achieve a particular color depth. In other words, for a given RAM/VRAM, you may be able to display 24-bit color with a 14-inch monitor, but only up to a maximum of 8-bit color with a 21-inch monitor.

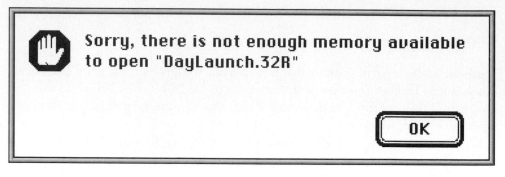

Figure 10-16 An error message that appeared because of insufficient memory to open a 24-bit color document

SEE: • Fix-It #1 for more on hardware incompatibilities

Select the Desired Setting from the Monitors Control Panel

Assuming you now have the appropriate hardware, the higher-depth options in the Monitors control panel should be listed. Still, they don't work unless you select them. If you are not seeing 24-bit color, the solution may be as simple as going to the Monitors control panel and selecting the Millions options.

Allocate Enough Memory to Run in 24-bit (or 16-bit) Mode

If you can't open a document in 24-bit color because of insufficient memory, you may not necessarily need to buy more RAM or VRAM. First try the following:

1. Increase the memory allocation of the application, typically via its Get Info setting. Some applications do not set their default allocation at a high enough level to open 24-bit documents. In some cases, the application may provide its own options for temporarily increasing its allocation.

2. If you don't have enough free RAM available to increase the application's memory allocation, make more memory available by such techniques as quitting other open applications, restarting with extensions off, or using virtual memory (or RAM Doubler).

SEE: • Fix-It #6 for more on these memory enhancing techniques

Make Sure Your Application Can Run in the Desired Display Depth

Some programs will only run at one color depth, such as 256. Using either a lower or a higher depth will not work. Others require a certain minimum depth, such as at least 256. Usually, if there is a problem, you will get an alert message informing you of the situation when you try to launch the application. Use the Monitors control panel to change the depth as needed.

In some cases, the application will successfully launch at a 24-bit Monitors setting even though it is actually incapable of displaying documents in 24-bit color. Check your application's manual for details on this.

These are increasingly rare problems today, as most current software is 24-bit compatible. However, if you want to run at 24-bit depth and the application is incompatible with that setting, there is nothing you can do about this, other than use a different application that is compatible.

Make Sure the Document Can Display in Desired Display Depth

Remember, even if you are at a 24-bit depth setting and using a 24-bit compatible application, it doesn't mean a particular graphic document can take advantage of that level. For example, a document originally created and saved at an 8-bit color depth will not change its appearance if displayed in 24-bit depth. Similarly, a black-and-white image still displays in black and white even if you are using 8-bit color.

Conversely, an image's display cannot exceed the current depth-level setting. Thus, if you open a 24-bit color document, while in 8-bit mode, you will not see all the colors that may have been in the original document, because no more than 256 can be displayed at one time. Typically, what you will see is a 8-bit dithered approximation of the 24-bit image. Similarly, all documents opened in 1-bit mode will display in black and white.

Bear in mind that changing the color depth, via the Monitors control panel, affects only the display. It does not alter the contents of the graphics document itself. The color information is remembered even if it isn't seen. Thus, when you shift back from the 1-bit to the 8-bit depth, an 8-bit color graphic once more displays using its proper colors.

Give Up

If all has gone well, your color image should now be on display in all its spectacular glory. Otherwise, it's time to give up.

Solve It! Problems Printing Graphics

The printer is the final arbiter of what the printed output looks like. No matter what other hardware and software you have, the quality of the printed copy can never exceed the capabilities of the printer.

SEE: • Chapter 7, "Take Note: Different Types of Printers," for an introduction to different types of printers
• Chapter 7, for an introduction to the Page Setup and Print dialog boxes, printer drivers, and problems getting any printout to appear
• Chapter 9, for printing problems specific to formatting of text documents
• "Types of Graphics, Programs, and Files," and "File Format Shifts When Transferring Graphics Across Applications," earlier in this chapter, for printing problems related to different graphic formats

Problems Printing Color/Grayscale to a Black-and-White Printer

 Symptoms:

When you print a grayscale or color image to a black-and-white printer (such as a LaserWriter), the image quality appears distinctly different from the way it appears on the screen (usually worse).

 Causes:

Printing a color or grayscale image to a black-and-white printer requires that the printer try to approximate the look of the image with its limited one-color (black) capability.

Sadly, this approximation is often less than wonderful. The resolution may be great (because it is at 600 dpi instead of the screen's 72 dpi), but the overall image, in worst cases, may still be reduced to an disconcerting set of large black-and-white blotches that render the image almost indiscernible. The quality of the approximation depends on a number of factors, including the particular application in use, the features of the printer, and printer driver.

 What to do:

Short of using a color printer, there is not a perfect solution to this problem. However, here are some partial solutions.

Select Enhancement Options from the Print Dialog Box

The success of these solutions depends partly on whether a particular application is written to be aware of them. So your success may vary across different applications.

- **Color/Grayscale**
  For PostScript LaserWriters, select the Color/Grayscale option (see Figure 10-17), rather than the Black & White option. Doing this causes the printer drivers to generate an improved *dithered* (or *halftone*) output. It does not alter the file or the screen display in any way. This is probably the most important thing you can do to improve print quality. If you leave the setting at Black & White, you will likely get an extremely poor output.

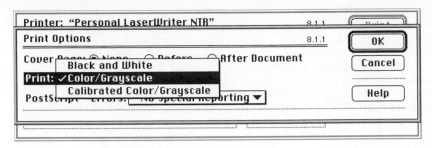

Figure 10-17   The Color/Grayscale selections, as listed in the Options window of the LaserWriter
8 Print dialog box

- **PhotoGrade, FinePrint, and GrayShare**

  Some Apple LaserWriters may include other Print options (see Figure 10-18), such
  as PhotoGrade, that further enhance printing of grayscale images. These printers
  typically have a companion option (useful whether or not you are printing
  grayscale/color), called FinePrint, that helps make edges appear extra smooth.
  Some non-AppleTalk Apple printers have a feature similar to PhotoGrade, called
  GrayShare. (Yes, this is the same GrayShare mentioned in Chapter 7 as a networking utility; hence its two-part name: Gray and Share.) Other printers may have
  their own unique halftone/dither options. These are all printer-dependent
  processes and have no direct relationship to the screen display.

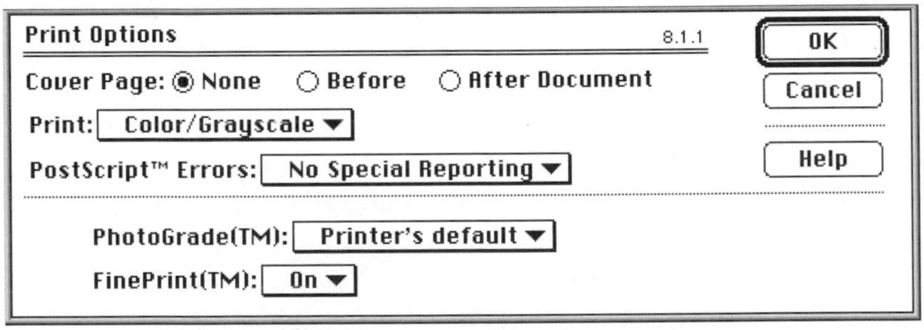

Figure 10-18   Depending on your selected printer, the Print dialog box may have special options
such as the PhotoGrade and FinePrint options seen here

TECHNICALLY SPEAKING ▶

HALFTONES

Halftoning *is the name for a printing process used to simulate the appearance of grays by
printing black-and-white dots. It has the same function as dithering. Technically, halftoning is
based on a special photographic process where the image is broken up into a series of
differently sized dots (small black dots for lighter areas, larger black dots for darker areas).*

(continued)

However, on the printers commonly used with a Macintosh, halftoning is not handled the same way, since these printers can only print dots in a single size such as 300 dpi. Instead, they use digital halftoning, which involves setting up equal-size cells of a given number of dots. The more dots in a cell that are filled in (that is, black instead of white), the darker the shade of gray represented by that cell.

There is a trade-off here. Larger cells allow for more shades of gray (because there are more dots per cell) but result in lower resolution of the image (because the number of cells per inch decreases as cell size gets larger). The result of this trade-off is that, at typical LaserWriter resolutions, halftoning cannot simulate anything close to the full 256 shades of gray seen on an 8-bit display. Under the best circumstances (using Apple's best LaserWriters with PhotoGrade enhancement), you can get only about 90 shades of gray. With other LaserWriters, you may get as few as 36 shades of gray. Still, this may result in satisfactory printouts, at least for nonprofessional uses.

If you need more shades of gray than you can currently get, the best solution is to shift to a printer that has a higher overall resolution. For example, a 600-dpi LaserWriter can simulate more shades of gray than an equally featured 300-dpi LaserWriter. Printers with a resolution higher than 600 dpi can do even better.

This topic is a lot more complex than I have presented here. For example, you soon get into such terms as lines per inch, screen patterns, and screen frequency and angle. For our purposes, it is enough to know that halftoning is a first cousin to dithering—a printing method used to simulate the appearance of shades of gray using only black ink.

Use Halftone Options Built into Specific Applications

Some applications, particularly page-layout programs and image-processing software, have options to override a PostScript LaserWriter's default halftoning routines. Photoshop and ThunderWorks (the imaging software bundled with LightningScan handheld scanners) are two examples. With these applications, for example, you could select a halftone dot pattern different from the LaserWriter's default choice. Depending on the particular graphic, a different pattern can significantly improve the graphic's printed appearance. Experiment with these choices if they are available in your application (see the relevant manuals for more information on how and why to do this).

Using these halftone options typically requires that your image be saved in the TIFF format. Color/Grayscale should also be selected from the Print dialog box.

Dither the Image Prior to Printing

Some graphics applications have an option to create a dithered image from a grayscale or color image. In some cases, the application may automatically do this prior to printing; in other cases, you must manually request for this to be done. For example, in Photoshop, look for the *Bitmap* command in the Mode menu. However, if you want to save the new dithered image, be sure to save it as a separate document and do not discard the original document, because the dithering process strips away all the color/grayscale information from the original image. If you later want to display the dithered image in color, you will not be able to do so.

The printout resulting from a dithered screen image is often better than if you directly print from the grayscale or color image and, thus, depend on the printer's dithering process. However, if you have a PostScript LaserWriter, you will usually be better off using the printer's enhancements, as described in the previous sections.

By the way, do not use the 1-bit (Black & White) setting from the Monitors control panel as a substitute for an application's 1-bit dithering options. These options are by no means equivalent. The printout resulting from shifting to the Monitors' 1-bit setting, while perhaps improved from the original printout, is still distinctly less attractive than an application-generated dithered pattern (see Figure 10-19).

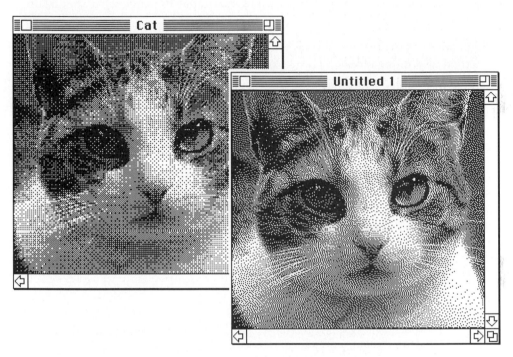

Figure 10-19   At left, the same 1-bit dithered image as shown in Figure 10-2; at right, an application-generated dithered image of the same graphic. Notice the improvement in the image on the right.

Problems Printing Color/Grayscale to a Color Printer

Symptoms:

- A color document displays fine on the screen but prints incorrectly. In particular, either the document prints in wrong colors or the entire image quality is poor.

Causes:

Color printers have difficulty getting their printed output to match what appears on the screen. This is either due to:

- Limitations of the printer (such as the ImageWriter's rather crude color ribbon method of printing color)
- Problems resulting from the fact that screen colors (which are from a light source) are produced differently from printed color (which is from a pigment source)

SEE: • "Technically Speaking: Professional Color Matching" next

By the way, if your problem is not specific to the use of color, then the same causes and solutions described in the previous section, "Problems Printing Color/Grayscale to a Black-and-White Printer," apply here as well. In that case, refer first to that section for advice.

TECHNICALLY SPEAKING ▶

PROFESSIONAL COLOR MATCHING

If you are really serious about color printing, you need to get into color matching techniques that go well beyond the solutions covered in this section. For example:

- *The colors on a monitor are produced by a combination of Red, Green, and Blue lights (RGB), whereas most printers use a combination of Cyan, Yellow, Magenta, and blacK inks (CYMK). Translating an RGB display into a CYMK printed output is not an exact science. The two images are rarely an exact match. Many high-end graphics and page-layout programs have (often complex) features that attempt to compensate for this difference. Apple's ColorSync extension is basically an attempt to make this process more accessible to nonexperts.*
- *Many specialized graphics and page-layout programs can perform a process called color separation. This is where the document is separated into four (or more) separately colored layers that are each separately saved and then combined by a professional printing process to produce the final multicolor output. This process is essential to professional-level full-color printing, as seen in glossy magazines.*

As usual in this area, things are even more complicated than this summary may suggest. You soon find yourself talking about matters such as process versus spot colors, Pantone color selection and more. But take heart! Nonprofessionals often find that the less-than-perfect output they get, without any knowledge of this stuff or any special effort, is still satisfactory for their needs.

What to do:

Select Enhancement Options from the Print Dialog Box

- **Color/Grayscale**
  For PostScript printers, make sure you have selected Color/Grayscale (see Figure 10-17). If you are using LaserWriter 8 driver and have a PostScript Level 2 printer, select Calibrated Color/Grayscale for even better color matching. Changing this setting is probably the most important thing you can do to improve print quality. If you leave the setting at Black & White, you will likely get an extremely poor output.

  SEE: • "LaserWriter Versus LaserWriter 8," in Chapter 7, for more on PostScript Level 2

- **For other printers**
  Check what printer-specific options may be available for enhancing color output. For example, Apple's Color StyleWriter Pro comes with ColorShare, the color equivalent of GrayShare (as described in the previous section).

Use Apple's ColorSync

This extension/control panel combination (see Figure 10-20) is included with System 7.5 (though it can be used with System 7.1). It is designed to work with virtually any color printer, monitor, or scanner, though it needs special device profile files for each hardware component. Currently, these are most readily available for Apple products, as you might guess.

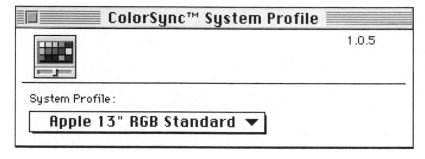

Figure 10-20   Apple's ColorSync System Profile control panel

ColorSync can be used with Apple's Color StyleWriters or Hewlett-Packard's DeskWriter 560c, for example. It also can be used with PostScript LaserWriters. However, there have been some compatibility problems between the LaserWriter driver and ColorSync. These should be no longer an issue if you are using at least version 2.0 of ColorSync and version 8.2 of LaserWriter 8.

ColorSync's sole function is to give the user easy control over color matching by having one simple set of options that will work with all your hardware. You select your hardware in ColorSync's control panel. Other options are selected from the Print dialog box.

By the way, Hewlett-Packard's printer drivers for its current printers also include proprietary color matching software (called ColorSmart).

In either case, check with your Users Guide for detailed instructions on how to use these features.

Special Case: Printing Color with an ImageWriter

ImageWriter IIs and LQs can print in color if you replace their standard black ribbon with the optional color ribbon. The ribbon has three colors plus black. There is no trick to using this ribbon. You install it exactly as you would a black ribbon. However, even with this ribbon installed, you may find that your color image either prints out in the wrong colors or still prints out in black and white. If so:

- **Extend the ImageWriter's range of colors**
  Under standard conditions, ImageWriters can print only eight different colors (including black and white as two). This restriction is a combined function of both the limits of the printer hardware and the ImageWriter's printer driver software. One solution to this is to use a printer driver called MacPalette II (see Figure 10-21). It replaces Apple's ImageWriter driver and uses special printing routines to create dithered output that can simulate up to thousands of colors.

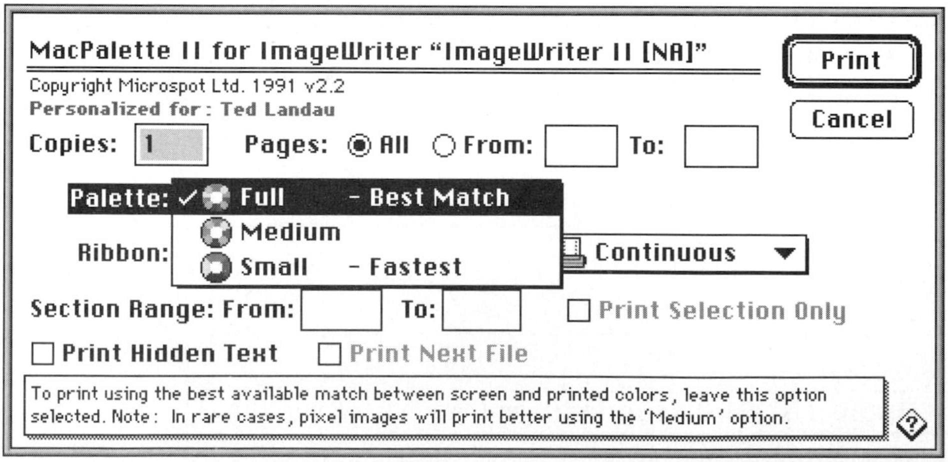

Figure 10-21 MacPalette II's printer driver

Another solution is to use a shareware utility called CheapColor. It takes a color document (such as a PICT2 file that uses no more than 256 colors) and converts it to a file that uses only the eight colors available via the ImageWriter driver. However, by using a dithering technique, it simulates all of the original 256 colors possible in the original document.

Even with these solutions, the printed output is often not a good match to the colors in the screen image. And even if they do generally match, they lack the resolution and richness of output from other higher-quality color printers, including inkjet printers. Nothing can be done about this.

- **Make sure the application supports ImageWriter color printing**
  In order for ImageWriters to print in color, the application in use must be written to be aware of the color-printing option. Otherwise, the printer always prints in black and white. Ideally, the application's manual should inform you about its ImageWriter color support. There is no solution to this problem other than to shift to a application that supports ImageWriter color or get a different printer!

Problems Printing PostScript Graphics

Symptoms:

- You print a document that contains PostScript instructions, such as an EPS file, but it does not print out with the overall image quality you expect.

- Certain graphics objects, such as hairlines, do not print at all.

Causes:

Either you are not using a PostScript printer or you are not using an application that supports PostScript printing. In these cases, what will happen is that you will typically print a less-detailed PICT-based image approximation of the PostScript instructions.

What to do:

Make Sure You Are Using a PostScript Printer

This is obvious of course. With a non-PostScript printer, the printed graphic will be of inferior quality. Certain objects may not print at all. For example, hairline graphics, though probably visible on the screen, may be totally missing from printed output.

This explains why Illustrator and Freehand files will print incorrectly to a StyleWriter, for example. The StyleWriter, at best, prints the PICT version of the file, not the PostScript version (unless you have installed a software PostScript interpreter, such as Freedom of Press or StyleScript, as mentioned earlier in this chapter in "By the Way: PostScript Graphics Without a PostScript Printer").

Make Sure the Application Supports PostScript

Many graphics applications do not support PostScript printing. If you transfer a Post-Script graphic to one of these programs, the PostScript information will not print—even if you have a PostScript printer. Sometimes, this can be a problem for data transferred from programs that you don't think of as PostScript programs but nevertheless use PostScript instructions. For example, Microsoft Word uses PostScript to produce some special effects, such as background watermarks. These effects may not be printed if you import a Microsoft Word file to another non-PostScript supporting application.

Make Sure the File for an Imported EPS Graphic Is Still Available

Some programs, particularly page layout programs such as PageMaker, import EPS graphics in a special way. They do not import the full EPS information from the graphic. Rather, they create a link to the original EPS file. The screen display appears fine, displaying the PICT version of the graphic. However, when printing such a file, PageMaker searches for the original linked graphic. To find it, the graphic file must still be present and with the same name as when it was linked. If the graphic file cannot be found, the graphic will not print correctly.

Avoid PICT Files If Possible

Object-oriented PICT files, though they will normally print fine to your LaserWriter, sometimes cause problems when printing to a PostScript printers, especially those used by professional printing services. The graphic may take unusually long to print or print with inferior quality. Even fonts may print incorrectly when part of a PICT file.

Problems Printing Bitmapped Graphics

Symptoms:

Bitmapped graphics look distinctly inferior to the quality of printed text and/or object-oriented graphics.

Causes:

This is an inevitable consequence of the fact that most bitmapped graphics are at 72 dpi while most printers are at a 300-dpi or higher resolution. Unlike object-oriented graphics, bitmapped images do not change their resolution to match that of the printer.

What to do:

Change the Graphic to Object-Oriented

Redraw the graphic using an object-oriented graphics application. If the graphic is something simple, like a plain circle, this should not be hard to do. Otherwise, this may be impractical. For something like scanned photographic images, this is obviously not relevant advice.

Check If Your Application Supports Higher-Resolution Bitmaps

Some applications can create bitmapped images at higher resolutions, such as 300 dpi.

Use Preferred Formats

For example, for scanned photographs, the TIFF format will generally lead to better results than the PICT format, especially when used in combination with image-processing software such as Photoshop.

Select Enhancements from the Page Setup Dialog Box

Some of these enhancements are available only with PostScript LaserWriters. With LaserWriter 8, they are found in the Options window of the Page Setup dialog box.

- **Select Smooth Graphics**
  Checking the *Smooth Graphics* option (see Figure 10-22) alters the appearance of bitmapped graphics by smoothing out curved lines and reducing jagged edges. This is supposed to improve the appearance of the graphic. However, finely textured artwork may not look any better with this option on. It may even look worse. Similarly, if you selected Color/Grayscale, also selecting Smooth Graphics will probably make things worse. Try it both ways, if in doubt.

  By the way, most LaserWriters also offer *Smooth Text* (for smoothing bitmapped text).

- **Select precision bitmap alignment or Exact Bit Images**
  For PostScript LaserWriters, select *Precision Bitmap Alignment* (see Figure 10-22). Other printers may have an essentially identical option called *Exact Bit Images (Shrink 4%)*. These options reduce the size of the entire document by 4 percent, which generally improves the printed appearance of bitmapped graphics.

  Since it reduces everything by 4 percent, not just bitmapped graphics. This can be a problem if your document is a mixture of text, object-oriented graphics, and/or bitmapped graphics. In these cases, I would avoid this option unless the appearance of your bitmapped graphics are critical.

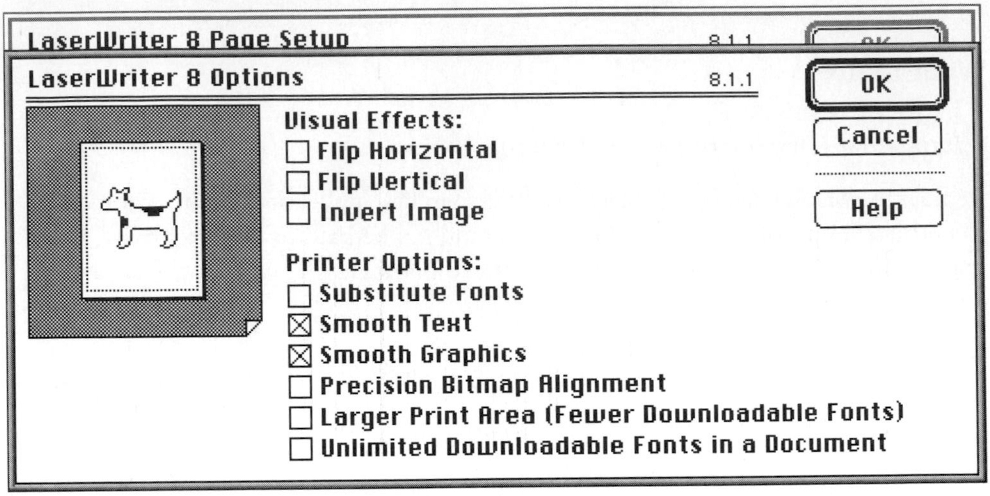

Figure 10-22   This Options dialog box appears after clicking Options in LaserWriter 8's Page Setup dialog box

---

TECHNICALLY SPEAKING ▶

WHY A 4 PERCENT REDUCTION?

Precision Bitmap Alignment appears to be a strange option. Why reduce a document 4 percent and not 5 percent or whatever?

The reason has to do with the 72-dpi resolution of bitmapped graphics. Since the typical LaserWriter prints at 300 dpi, the LaserWriter must adjust the image to match the different resolution. That is, an image that is 1 inch long at 72 dpi contains 72 dots. To remain 1 inch long when it is printed at 300 dpi, it would have to be 300 dots long. The printer handles this conversion.

Because the printer cannot print a fraction of a dot, it does the best job of this conversion if the ratio between the resolution of the bitmapped image and the printer's resolution is a whole number. This is not the case with an image resolution of 72 dpi and a printer resolution of 300 dpi. However, if you reduce the image by 4 percent, the resolution is effectively raised to 75 dpi. Now the conversion process to 300 dpi can work with only whole dots: Put four dots in the printed image for every one dot in the bitmapped image (since 4 x 75 = 300). Thus, the 4 percent reduction eliminates distortions that might otherwise occur. Other reduction percentages that have a whole-number ratio are 72, 48, and 24 percent.

By the way, the StyleWriter printers have no reduction option. It doesn't need one! Why? Because its resolution is 360 dpi. This turns out to be exactly 5 x 72, which means it prints at a whole-number ratio to the screen display without any adjustment needed.

- **Don't select Faster Bitmap Printing**

  This option is of little value and often causes more problems than it solves. It may actually prevent your document from being printed at all, even if your document contains no bitmapped graphics. If you are having any general printing problems with this option on, uncheck this option and try again. This option is no longer included in the LaserWriter 8 driver.

Special Case: Image Quality Problems with ImageWriter Printers

Symptoms:

The quality of an ImageWriter printed graphic is less than you would like. It is either distorted or in an unacceptably poor resolution.

Causes:

The resolution of the ImageWriter is 72 dpi. This is rather paltry compared to the 300 dpi or more of most current printers. No matter what software you use or what Macintosh model you own, you cannot alter this basic fact. This rather low resolution makes the ImageWriter of only limited value for graphics-oriented tasks.

Also, don't forget that you cannot print PostScript graphics to a non-PostScript printer like the ImageWriter (see "Problems Printing PostScript Graphics," earlier in this chapter).

What to do:

There are two options from the ImageWriter's Page Setup dialog box that can help improve the quality of ImageWriter output.

- **Select 50% reduction**
  This option, in effect, simulates raising the resolution to 144 dpi, because you now try to squeeze 144 dots of information into the same space normally occupied by 72 dots (see Figure 10-23).

```
┌────────────────────────────────────────────────────────┐
│ ImageWriter                          7.0.1    ┌────────┐ │
│                                               │   OK   │ │
│ Paper:   ◉ US Letter      ○ A4 Letter         └────────┘ │
│          ○ US Legal       ○ International Fanfold         │
│          ○ Computer Paper                     ┌────────┐ │
│                                               │ Cancel │ │
│ Orientation    Special Effects: ☐ Tall Adjusted └──────┘ │
│  ▐▜▌ ▗▄▖                         ☐ 50 % Reduction        │
│                                 ☐ No Gaps Between Pages  │
└────────────────────────────────────────────────────────┘
```

Figure 10-23   The ImageWriter's Print dialog box

The problem with this solution, however, is that everything is now 50 percent smaller. Aside from the fact that you may not want everything smaller, this technique cannot actually make the size of each dot any smaller. Too often, the result is therefore a packed group of dots that produces little more than an unacceptable blob of black ink.

So, in order for this option to be of much value, you must first double the size of the image, typically by using whatever scaling commands you have available in your graphics application. The 50 percent reduced image then prints at the image's original size.

This is similar to the logic behind the improved appearance of text obtained by using the *Best* quality option from the Print dialog box (as described in Chapter 9). However, shifting from the Faster to the Best option does not affect the appearance of printed graphics. With Draft, of course, the graphic does not print at all.

- **Select Tall Adjusted**
  Macintosh monitors display with an equal number of dpi horizontally and vertically, each dot forming a square (usually at a resolution of about 72 dpi). The ImageWriter's overall resolution is also listed at 72 dpi, but it has a slightly different number of dots per inch in the vertical direction than in the horizontal direction. The result is that printed output has a rectangular appearance, a bit more tall than wide, compared to the screen display. To most people, this effect gives text a more pleasing appearance, and so it is generally ignored rather than considered a problem. However, it causes graphics to print slightly distorted from what you see on the screen. For example, a square on the screen prints as a slight rectangle, and circles appear as ovals.

  If you want graphics printed with correct proportions, select Tall Adjusted (see Figure 10-23). This option compensates for the discrepancy between the screen and the printer. Correct proportions are maintained, and a square prints as a square. Unfortunately, any bitmapped text will probably now look worse.

SEE: • "Problems Printing Color/Grayscale to a Color Printer," earlier in this chapter, for ImageWriter problems specific to color printing

Chapter Summary

This chapter began with an explanation of the terms resolution and display depth and their implications for the display and printing of graphics. It continued with an explanation of one of the most important dichotomies in the world of graphics: bitmapped versus object-oriented graphics. Next, I described the distinctions among paint versus draw versus PostScript programs/modules, as well as among several of the most common file types used for graphics documents (such as PICT and TIFF).

Finally, I delved into a selected range of graphics-related problems. The focus was on general issues involved in working with graphics, rather than on the details of creating particular graphic effects. In particular, I described problems you might have when trying to paste or import graphics across applications, problems getting color graphics to display on the screen correctly, and problems getting graphics (especially color or grayscale images) to print correctly. Special emphasis was given to problems with 24-bit color and with PostScript. Final sections looked briefly at special problems with bitmapped graphics and with ImageWriters.

As with the discussion of fonts and text in Chapter 9, it's easy to get overwhelmed by all of the information here. But take heart. The good news is that, most of the time, things do work out exactly as you expect, without any special effort on your part. For example, despite the discussion of the optional settings in Page Setup dialog boxes, you will usually be okay if you simply accept the default settings and go directly to Print. But then there are inevitably those other times . . .

This chapter—indeed this whole book—is for those other times.

Chapter 11

Trouble To Go:
The PowerBooks

You *Can* Take It with You

Apple's PowerBook line of notebook computers have been an enormous success. Many Mac users now own two Macs—a PowerBook in addition to the traditional desktop machine. Other users find that a PowerBook is all the computing power they need, and make it their only computer.

Fortunately (or unfortunately, depending on your point of view), most of the problems that plague desktop Macintoshes are no different from the ones that travel with you when you use your PowerBook. Thus, most of this book applies equally well to either type of Macintosh. Where important differences do exist, they have probably already been covered (such as in Chapter 4, where I explained the unique variations on how to shut down or restart a PowerBook).

But this still leaves several topics that are only relevant to PowerBook users. Running on battery power and putting the PowerBook to sleep are two obvious examples. Problems with these PowerBook-specific issues are the main focus of this chapter.

Additionally, there are a couple of features that potentially affect all Macintosh users but are still covered primarily in this chapter. This is because I believe that PowerBook users are especially likely to use these features. The most notable example of this is file sharing. While this book has largely avoided networking-specific problems, even users who have never been connected to a multi-Macintosh network may still share files between their PowerBook and desktop machine. Creating RAM disks is another example of this sort. Even if you don't own a PowerBook, you may still find these sections helpful.

BY THE WAY ▶

NEED MORE HELP?

For more help with any of the topics described in this chapter, check your PowerBook's User's Guide, of course. In addition, starting in mid-1994, Apple began including a small book on PowerBook troubleshooting with every PowerBook it sold. With System 7.5 (see Chapter 12), there is a PowerBook Guide Additions file for Apple Guide that includes PowerBook-specific help. For pre–System 7.5 users, some models of PowerBook came with a DA, called Battery Tips, *that outlined the battery conservation options. Also, for instant answers, turn on Balloon Help and moving the cursor over the specific feature of interest. Finally, there are several excellent books on the PowerBook. My favorite is* PowerBook Companion *(by Wolfson and Aker).*

PowerBook Basics

PowerBook Models

You already know that PowerBooks are different from desktop Macintoshes. What you may not know as clearly is that different PowerBook models are often quite different from one another. In particular, there are two main lines of PowerBooks, as presented in the following.

The All-in-One PowerBooks

These PowerBooks, typified by models such as the 180 (which uses a trackball) and the 520 (which uses a trackpad), all include a floppy drive (in addition to their internal hard drive). They also have a full set of connection ports on the back of the machine, such as for SCSI devices, a external modem, a printer, possibly an external monitor, and more. Some models include color displays.

The original Macintosh Portable and the PowerBook 100, while technically in this category, are often an exception to the rules that apply to other all-in-one PowerBooks. This chapter does not describe most of these exceptions.

The Duo PowerBooks

These PowerBooks, typified by models such as the 230 and the 280, do not include the floppy drive or external ports found on the all-in-one PowerBooks. The more general name for this type of computer is *subnotebook*. To access these absent features, you need to connect the Duo to either a Duo Dock or MiniDock. You can also attach a floppy disk drive directly, without a dock, via a special adapter cable.

In particular, if you insert a Duo into a Duo Dock (that has an external monitor and a keyboard attached to it), the unit performs like a desktop Mac, bypassing the Duo's built-in screen and keyboard. This is a main attraction of the Duo. On the one hand, you get the lightest possible portable device. On the other hand, you get a single Mac that can adequately serve as both a portable and a desktop computer. Using a MiniDock is more like turning your Duo into an all-in-one PowerBook rather than a desktop Mac, except that the MiniDock does not include a floppy drive.

The main disadvantage of Duos is that, if you need access to a floppy drive and/or connection ports when you travel, you will need to take additional hardware along (eliminating the lightweight advantage of the Duo).

For better or worse, the Duos are reportedly on the way out. The last of the line are expected to be released in 1995.

PowerBook Control Panels (and Control Strip)

All PowerBooks come with several utilities, primarily control panels, that you use to access and modify features unique to PowerBooks. The layout of these control panels has undergone significant revisions over the years. The descriptions in this chapter assume that you are using the latest versions, as shipped with System 7.5. If you are using earlier versions, you may find that a particular option has a somewhat different name or a different location (possibly even in a different control panel altogether). However, the functions generally remain the same.

PowerBook

This control panel's primary purpose is to set battery conservation options, as described in more detail in "PowerBook Battery Conservation" later in this chapter.

PowerBook Setup

This is used (1) to select whether you are using an internal or external modem, and (2) to select a SCSI ID number for your PowerBook (needed if you are going to use your PowerBook as an external hard drive connected to another Macintosh, as described later in this chapter).

PowerBook Display

This is used primarily to turn video mirroring on and off. This feature (not available in all PowerBooks) is only relevant if you are using an external monitor (as described later in this chapter).

Control Strip

The *Control Strip* is a recent addition to Apple's system software, now included as a standard part of System 7.5. Essentially, it creates a strip of buttons that stay on the screen at all times (see Figure 11-1). To use a button, click and hold down the button. A pop-up menu of choices will appear. Select the desired choice.

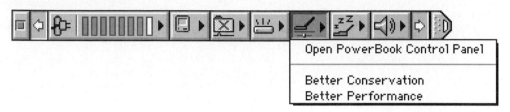

Figure 11-1   The Control Strip, before (top) and after (bottom) clicking a button

The display includes an multibar indicator of the current battery charge level. The fewer number of filled bars, the less battery power you have left. However, this indicator is notoriously inaccurate (especially with NiCad battery PowerBooks). It is common for it to tell you that you have more power left than you really have. Other non-Apple utilities with battery indicators have similar problems.

The battery icon adjacent to the indicator bars changes depending on whether the PowerBook is running on battery (just the battery icon appears) or is fully charged and running on AC power (a plug appears over the battery icon) or whether it is charging (a lightning bolt appears over the battery icon).

Other buttons are used to access the PowerBook control panel, check or change the status of file sharing, or otherwise access features that affect battery conservation (as described in more detail in the next section).

The exact collection of buttons included in the Control Strip is determined by what modules are placed in the Control Strip Modules folder (which is located in the System Folder). Apple includes a basic set of modules with the Control Strip. Many non-Apple modules are now available. Most are shareware. However, even commercial products are joining the Control Strip bandwagon. For example, PBTools has been redesigned to work with the Control Strip. I guess when it comes to competing with free software from Apple, it is wiser to join 'em than try to beat 'em.

Prior to the release of the Control Strip, Apple included a desk accessory, called *Battery,* that was like a limited version of the Control Strip, mainly providing a battery indicator and sleep button.

PowerBook Battery Conservation

Other than their small size, the single most distinguishing feature about PowerBooks is that they can run on batteries. But batteries have a big problem: They can run out of power. If you expect to be away from a convenient power source for any length of time, such as on an airplane, conserving battery power becomes a primary concern. Fortunately, there are a wide assortment of battery conservation options. The more of these features you use, the better your battery savings will be.

Use Features That Conserve Battery Power

- **Sleep: Put the PowerBook to sleep whenever you aren't using it**
  To put a PowerBook to sleep, select Sleep from the Finder's Special menu. Alternatively, you can use the Sleep selection in the Control Strip (see Figure 11-2).

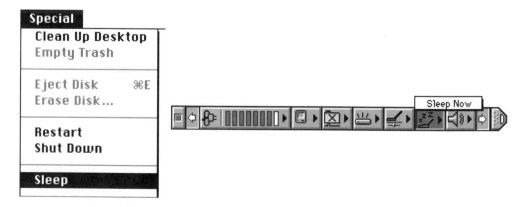

Figure 11-2 Two ways to select Sleep, from the Finder's Special menu (left) and from the Control Strip (right)

To wake up a sleeping PowerBook, press any key except Caps Lock (on some models, you must press the Power On key). The PowerBook will reawaken almost instantly, returning you to where you left off without needing to go through the startup sequence. This is because the RAM contents of a PowerBook is maintained while it is asleep. This is a very convenient way to save battery power without having the hassle of a shut down and restart.

TAKE NOTE ▶

WHY SHUT DOWN WHEN YOU CAN SLEEP INSTEAD?

When you don't plan on using your PowerBook for a while, an obvious alternative to Sleep is to Shut Down (via the Shut Down command in the Finder's Special menu). But why bother with it? Shut Down means that all open applications are quit, all contents of RAM (including RAM disk contents) may be lost, and that you will have to wait to go through a potentially long startup sequence the next time you restart.

You can travel with your PowerBook just as well while it is in sleep mode as when it is shut down. You can even safely connect and disconnect cables (such as modem and printer cables) while in Sleep mode (though you need to shut down to connect a Duo to a Duo Dock).

In fact, the only clear advantage of shutting down a PowerBook, rather than using Sleep, is that a shut down PowerBook drains less battery power than one that is asleep. Shutting down thus makes some sense if you don't expect to use your PowerBook for at least several days.

- **Use an AC outlet, instead of battery power, whenever possible**
  Connect the PowerBook to the Power Adapter (and plug the adapter into a wall outlet). The PowerBook now runs on AC power rather than battery power.

  Even when it is asleep or shut down, a PowerBook's battery is slowing losing power. That's why it pays to keep your PowerBook plugged in whenever possible. While plugged in, the battery will charge until fully charged and then stay fully charged (though it will take longer to reach full charge if the PowerBook is in use instead of sleeping or shut down). You can keep the PowerBook plugged in even if it is fully charged. You cannot "overcharge" a battery.

- **Hard drive Spin Down**
  An active hard drive is one of the two major drains on battery power (the light for the screen is the other). So, to save battery power, temporarily "turn off" the hard drive by selecting the Spin Down button from the Control Strip (see Figure 11-3). This shuts off the motor that otherwise constantly spins the drive.

Figure 11-3   The Control Strip's Spin Down button

A spin down does not prevent you from using your PowerBook. As soon as the PowerBook needs to access any information on the drive, it will automatically turn the drive back on. You will hear the drive spin up, and there will be a slight delay until the PowerBook responds to your command. This delay is normal; do not be concerned.

This option is of little value if you are doing something with an application that keeps turning the hard drive back on every time you turn it off. But if your task is mainly to access information already in RAM, this option allows you to keep working while the hard drive is off for an extended time. This can be an especially effective strategy when used in combination with a RAM disk (as described in "Using RAM Disks," later in this chapter).

Also note that the features of some extensions will force the drive to spin up. For example, the hourly chime of a clock extension will do this whenever the chime sounds. To avoid this, turn such features off or disable the extension altogether.

On a related note, higher disk cache settings, as set from the Memory control panel, (see Fix-It #6), will help minimize how often a hard drive will spin up again after you have selected Spin Down.

- **Screen dimming**
  Screen dimming turns off the light to your screen. Unless you are in a dimly lit area, you can still see the screen images (though dimmed color displays may be hard to see in any light). In fact, it may be possible to continue working while the screen is dimmed, just using external light. Doing this will save considerable battery power. You can dim the screen by turning the Brightness control down to its minimum setting (see next item in this list). Alternatively, several utility programs (I use QuicKeys) include features that let you dim the screen either by pressing a keyboard combination or by clicking on-screen buttons.

BY THE WAY ▶

POWERBOOK FILE ASSISTANT'S ASSISTANT TOOLBOX

If you have PowerBook File Assistant (now included with System 7.5) and install Assistant Toolbox, pressing Command-Shift-Zero puts the PowerBook to sleep. Pressing Command-Shift-Control-Zero spins down the hard disk. Other PowerBook utilities, such as PBTools, provide similar options.

- **Turn down brightness**
  All PowerBook models have some sort of brightness control (typically a slider of some sort) on the front of the PowerBook. On the 100 series, it is near where the top and bottom halves of the PowerBook join. On the 500 series, they are to the right of the screen. Turning down brightness conserves battery power. If you turn it down enough, it is the equivalent of dimming the screen.

- **Use PowerBook control panel options**
  A friendly reminder: The exact locations of the options described here can be quite different in older versions of the system software (and, knowing Apple, they may change again in future versions!).

Easy View: Better Conservation Versus Better Performance   If you open the
PowerBook control panel in Easy view, you simply see a slider control for choosing
along a scale of Better Conservation versus Better Performance (see Figure 11-4).
The reason you have to choose between these alternatives is because most battery
conservation features worsen performance, either by inconveniencing you (such as
by dimming the screen sooner than you would want) or by decreasing the Power-
Book's overall performance speed. You select where on this dimension you want to
be at a given moment.

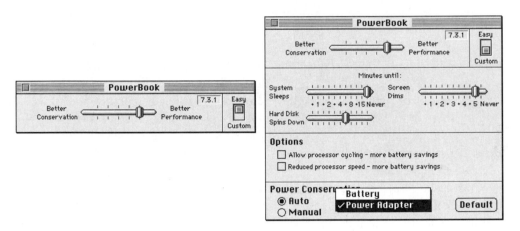

Figure 11-4   The PowerBook control panel Easy view (left) and Custom view (right)

Custom View: Automatic Sleep, Screen Dims, and Hard Disk Spins Down   If
you want to know more exactly what the Easy view's slider control is doing, or if
you want more control over the various settings, switch to the Custom view (see
Figure 11-4). Here you see separate controls that determine how many minutes
until *automatic* onset of Sleep, Screen Dims, or Hard Disk Spins Down (if you
want any of these options to kick in before their automatic time, you can do it
manually, usually from the Control Strip, as previously described). For Sleep and
Screen Dims, the numbers on the sliders refer to minutes of idle activity (that is,
an interval when you are not pressing any keys, clicking any buttons, or otherwise
actively using the PowerBook) that must pass before the automatic kick-in occurs
(at the most extreme, you can select *Never*). For Hard Disk Spins Down, the setting refers to minutes of no hard disk access, even if you are otherwise using the
PowerBook.

   If you move the Easy view slider along you will see how the other three sliders
change accordingly. However, from the Custom view, you can change each separate
slider independently.

Custom View: Power Conservation   As an added bonus, the Power Conservation
feature at the bottom of the window lets you assign one set of options for when
you are running on battery power (*Battery* selected from the popup menu) and

another for when you are using AC power (*Power Adapter* selected). The idea here is that you will probably opt for Better Performance when running from the adapter, while wanting Better Conservation when running on batteries. If you have the Auto button selected, this means that the settings will shift automatically whenever you plug in or unplug the Power Adapter. (By the way, in older versions of the PowerBook control panel, the only option like this was a *Don't sleep when plugged in* checkbox. To mimic this with the new control panel, simply select *Never sleep* as a setting for Power Adapter but not for Battery.)

Custom View: Reduced Processor Speed and Allow Processor Cycling   For most models of PowerBook, the PowerBook Control panel includes two more options: Reduced Processor Speed and Allow Processor Cycling. When turned on, these two options save battery power and help reduce the already small risk of the PowerBook overheating. The first option does exactly what its name implies: reducing the processor's speed, which of course slows down the Mac. The second option allows your processor to "rest" while the PowerBook is idle (though, if you really want to save battery power, you shouldn't let it sit idle very long!). It too will slightly slow down your PowerBook.

Some people leave these options on by default. I don't. I use them only in situations when I know that saving every drop of battery juice is important or if I want to check if persistent system crashes may be due to an overheating problem (see "Defective SIMMs and PowerBook Warmth," later in this chapter).

The Reduced Processor Speed option is not available on 68040 (the 500 series) or PowerPC PowerBooks.

On some PowerBooks you may not see the Allow Processor Cycling option listed. If so, switch to Easy view, then hold down the Option button, and select Custom view again. The option, if it is available for your PowerBook, should now appear. On some PowerBooks, you cannot turn this option off, and so it is never listed.

- **RAM disks**
  Using a RAM disk, especially a RAM startup disk, helps minimize battery-draining access to the hard drive (see "Using RAM Disks," later in this chapter, for details).

- **Add an external battery**
  Several companies market batteries that attach to the PowerBook (via the AC jack) and thereby extend the time (usually at least doubling it) before you run out of battery power.

Don't Use Features That Especially Drain Battery Power

- **Turn AppleTalk off**
  You can do this from the Chooser or from the Control Strip. Just remember not to do it while a shared volume is mounted. First unmount the volume (see "File Sharing: Disconnecting" later in this chapter).

- **Turn off File Sharing**
  Turning off File Sharing also saves battery power. Do this from the Sharing Setup control panel by clicking the Stop button in the File Sharing middle section (refer to Figure 11-18, bottom). If the button says Start, file sharing is already off.
  By the way, by setting up the file sharing software the way I describe later in this chapter (see "File Sharing"), you can share files with a desktop Mac without ever turning on file sharing on your PowerBook.

- **Don't use virtual memory**
  Turn it off from the Memory control panel (see Fix-It #6). Never use virtual memory when running on battery power. If you even try to use it, the PowerBook will give you a warning message (see Figure 11-5). Using virtual memory increases access to the hard disk, one of the bigger eaters of battery power.
  Using RAM Doubler may present similar battery-draining problems, but if you have at least 8Mb of physical RAM, you will probably be okay.

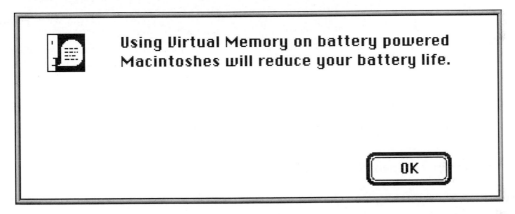

Figure 11-5 Don't use virtual memory when running on battery power

- **Turn modem off: Quit communications software**
  Quit all telecommunications software that you are not using. The modem is on and draining power as long as a telecommunications program is open, even if you are not connected online. Apple does not include a module with the Control Strip that tells you if your modem is on or not, but some other competing utilities, such as PowerStrip, include this feature.

- **Don't use the floppy drive**
  If your PowerBook has a built-in floppy drive, using it will drain battery power.

- **Turn down sound volume**
  Playing sound uses battery power. Keep volume as low as is feasible. Turn it off altogether if you don't need it. You can do all this from the Sound control panel or the Control Strip.

- **Don't plug anything into the PowerBook's ports**
  Almost anything that you plug into a port, such as an external monitor or an external hard drive, will cause the PowerBook's battery to drain faster. In fact, in some PowerBooks, you can't even use an external monitor unless you are running on AC Power.

- **Use a "white" desktop pattern**
  On PowerBooks, a screen pixel is "on" if it is dark. "On" pixels require more energy than "off" ones. Since your Finder's desktop pattern is frequently on the screen, you can probably save a little power by using a pattern of mostly "off" pixels. You choose the pattern via the Desktop Patterns control panel in System 7.5, or via the General Controls control panel in earlier system software versions.

Running out of Battery Power

As you start running low on battery power, a series of three different messages will appear on the screen (such as *You are now running on reserve power and your screen has dimmed, Very little of the battery's reserve power remains,* or *No battery reserve power remains. The Macintosh will go to sleep within 10 seconds to preserve the contents of memory*). Each succeeding message means you have less time left until the PowerBook will automatically go to sleep (see Figure 11-6). At the same time, a battery icon will begin flashing over the Apple icon in the menubar (see Figure 11-7). If you can, plug in the power adapter immediately after the first message. This puts a stop to the messages and starts recharging the battery. Otherwise, if you continue to work on battery power, save your work frequently. Don't wait until the third message to take action . . . you may not even have time to save your work at that point.

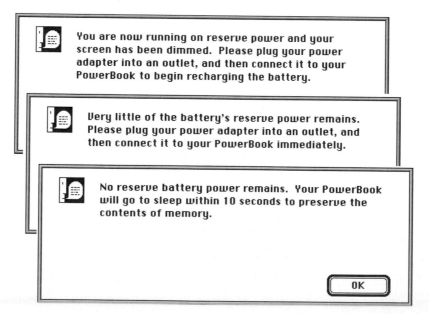

Figure 11-6   The three messages that progressively appear as you run low on battery power

Figure 11-7
The battery icon that appears in the menubar, over the Apple icon, when battery power is low

If you ignore all these warnings and wait until the Macintosh finally is forced to sleep, you have about one to two days to get AC power to the PowerBook and recharge the battery before the battery is totally out of juice. If you wait until this happens, the Mac will need to be restarted from scratch after you recharge the battery; any unsaved data will be lost. If you recharge sooner, the PowerBook will wake up where it left off, as after any other Sleep.

Using RAM Disks

Create and Use a RAM Disk

With the right software, your PowerBook can be "fooled" into thinking that a portion of its RAM is actually a physical disk. This RAM disk appears on the desktop with its own icon, just like any other disk (see Figure 11-8). You can then, for example, copy applications to the RAM disk and launch them just as if they were launched from your hard drive.

RAM Disk

Figure 11-8
A RAM disk icon on the desktop

The software you need to create a RAM disk you already own: it's the Memory control panel. To use it, just click the On button in the RAM disk section of the control panel and use the slider to adjust how large you want the RAM disk to be (see Figure 11-9). Then restart and presto: your RAM disk will appear.

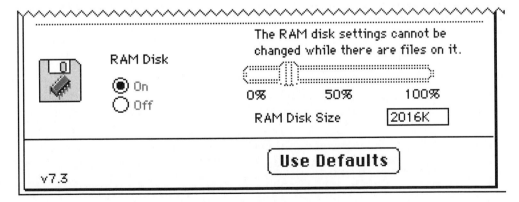

Figure 11-9   The RAM disk settings from the Memory control panel

SEE: • Fix-It #6 for more on creating and removing RAM disks

Why RAM Disks?

The main advantage of a RAM disk for PowerBook users is to save battery power. The more the PowerBook can access information from the RAM disk, rather than the hard drive, the longer the hard drive can remain "spinned down" and the less the hard drive will consume battery power. Since RAM disk access is many times faster than hard disk access, you also get a significant speed boost by doing anything from the RAM disk that would have otherwise been done from your hard drive.

The main disadvantage of using a RAM disk, of course, is that it takes up RAM. Unless you have a lot of RAM installed (typically at least 8Mb, ideally more), you may find that you cannot create a reasonably sized RAM disk and still have enough RAM left over to open the applications you want to run. This is because, even though an application copied to a RAM disk is in RAM, it still additionally requires the same amount of RAM to run as it would ordinarily need.

However, when running an application from a RAM disk, you *can* often lower its memory allocation from its Preferred size to closer to its Minimum size and still not see any speed decrement, because, while lower memory allocations typically mean more frequent access to the disk, the disk in this case is RAM, not the slower hard disk! You change an application's memory allocation from its Get Info window.

SEE: • Chapter 2 and Fix-It #6 for more on the Get Info window

Making a RAM Startup Disk

Suppose you set up a RAM disk and copy your Microsoft Word folder to it (or at least the essential files in the folder; a full installation of Word 6.0 has no chance of making it on to even the largest of PowerBook RAM disks). You now launch Word, expecting that hard disk access will be nil. Wrong. You will find that hard disk access is still annoyingly frequent. This is because most applications, including Word, make frequent calls to System Folder files. And, in any case, the Finder is still accessed from the hard disk's System Folder. Thus, to make really effective use of a RAM disk, you need to create a System Folder for it and use it as a startup disk. (In fact, you will probably access a hard disk less if there is a System Folder on the RAM disk and nothing else, than if there are applications and no System Folder.)

But getting a System Folder onto a RAM disk creates yet another problem. Most users' System Folders are so huge that fitting it on a RAM disk would mean creating a RAM disk so large that there wouldn't be enough RAM left over for other uses. The solution here is to create a minimum System Folder. To do this:

1. Create a RAM disk (as described in the previous section, "Create and Use a RAM Disk"). Set it to at least 4Mb (make it even larger if you can afford to set aside that much RAM). In any case, try to estimate the minimize size disk that you will need and make the RAM disk at least that large, because if you want to change the RAM disk's size after you create it, you will have to start over, deleting everything currently on the RAM disk.

2. Install the minimum version of the system software for your PowerBook, using the Customize option of the Installer (as explained in Chapter 2, for creating an Emergency Toolkit disk, and in Fix-It #5). Alternatively, you can install the minimal floppy disk software from the Disk Tools disk onto a RAM disk to use as a startup disk.

3. **a.** Delete any unneeded control panels, extensions, or other nonessential files you may find on the RAM disk. Finally, copy from your hard disk's System Folder whatever minimum number of control panels, extensions, and fonts that you need (that are not already there). You'll probably want at least the Chooser, a printer driver, and a few key fonts. Remember that control panels that are not INITs (see Chapter 1 and Fix-It #4), such as Startup Disk, work just as well whether or not they are in the startup disk's System Folder. Thus, you don't need to copy these control panels to the RAM disk.

   b. Alternatively, you can save space by creating aliases of your hard disk's control panels and extensions and placing them in the relevant folders within your RAM disk's System Folder. Ideally, the Macintosh should still load these extensions into RAM at startup, as if the original were on the RAM disk. If not, you will need a utility such as Conflict Catcher II. In its Preferences window is an option called *Recognize Aliases*. With this checked, you should definitely have no problems using aliases on your RAM disk. The 5.0 version of Now Utilities' Startup Manager has a similar feature called *Resolve Aliases*.

4. If space permits, copy one or two of your most frequently used applications. Similarly, if your applications access special folders in the System Folder (such as the Claris folder used by Claris applications), copy relevant files from that folder, as space permits.

5. Of course, the whole idea of creating a System Folder on the RAM disk is to use the RAM disk as a startup disk. To do this, select the Startup Disk control panel and select the RAM disk as the startup disk. Then select Restart. The RAM disk will now boot as your startup disk, with all the files you placed there still intact.

   You may get a message at startup saying something to the effect that this system software should only be used on floppy disks. Ignore it. Click OK and all should boot exactly as if the RAM disk were an actual floppy disk. If problems persist, you may have to give up on using the minimal software for your RAM disk (as indicated in step 2). Instead, copy the System and Finder (and Enabler, if needed) directly from your hard disk's System Folder.

Saving the Contents of Your RAM Disk

"But wait!," you may be saying at this point. You have heard that a restart wipes out all RAM, which would seem to imply that the contents of the RAM disk should be lost when you restart. Fortunately, a PowerBook's RAM disk is an important exception to this generally true axiom. *Everything on a RAM disk is preserved when you restart, even if you restart using the reset button after a system crash* (as described in Chapter 4)!

However, your RAM disk's contents are still more vulnerable to being lost than if they were on a hard disk. So here are some tips to help make sure you never lose any valuable data on your RAM disk:

- Never keep documents on your RAM disk that are not backed up elsewhere. This is true even of your hard disk, but is even more true of RAM disks.

- Be careful not to shut down the PowerBook. When you select *Shut Down,* rather than *Restart,* the RAM disk's contents *are* really lost. You will normally get a message warning you of this problem (see Figure 11-10).

    PowerBook users that routinely use the on/off button (rather than the reset button) to restart after a system crash should be especially careful here. While using the reset button preserves the RAM disk's contents, using the on/off button is the equivalent of a shut down and will *not* save the RAM disk's contents.

Figure 11-10   Your RAM disk's contents will be lost if you click OK here

SEE: • "Restarting a PowerBook After a System Error," later in this chapter, for more details

- Happily, you can overcome the previous problem and preserve a RAM disk's contents—even after a shutdown! To do this you need to install the Assistant Toolbox extensions (part of PowerBook File Assistant, now included with System 7.5) or use some similar utility (such as Connectix's Maxima RAM disk). PowerBook File Assistant, for example, writes a copy of the RAM disk's contents to a special file stored in the Preferences folder of the System Folder, called *Persistent RAM Disk.* When you restart after a shutdown, it copies these content's back to the RAM disk.

    If you shut down immediately after a system crash, Assistant Toolbox will be unable to update the Persistent RAM Disk file, as it would do prior to a normal shut down. Even in this case, however, all is not lost. When you next start up, Assistant Toolbox restores your RAM disk to the state it was at the time of your last normal shutdown (not the last time you put the PowerBook to sleep!). Depending on how often you shut down your PowerBook and how often you modify your RAM disk, this could mean that you lost very little (if any) contents of the RAM disk.

SEE: • "Restarting a PowerBook After a System Error," later in this chapter, for more details
• Chapter 4 for more general information on restarting after a system error

• Zapping the Parameter RAM (see Fix-It #11) will erase the contents of a RAM disk.

• If you restart with extensions off (by holding down the Shift key at startup), don't worry. The RAM disk will still appear with its files intact (even though the Memory control panel, used to initially create the RAM disk, is not active!).

TECHNICALLY SPEAKING ▶

AN "UNREADABLE" RAM DISK

Even with an extension like Assistant Toolbox installed, you will get the warning message shown in Figure 11-10 if you shut down during a session where you started up with extensions off. Don't worry; just click OK. When you next restart with extensions on, the RAM disk's contents will appear as normal.

However, here's a strange situation to watch out for: You shut down (not restart!). The next time you start up, you do so with extensions off. As startup is completed you will get a message saying that the RAM disk is "unreadable" and asking if you want to initialize it (see Figure 11-11). If you Click Initialize, a new RAM disk is created, and all the contents of the previous RAM disk are permanently erased. If you click Cancel, the RAM disk will not appear at all for that session, but its contents are still gone forever . . . unless you have previously installed Assistant Toolbox. If you have Assistant Toolbox installed, go ahead and click Cancel. The RAM disk will still not appear this session. But the next time your restart normally, with extensions on, the RAM disk will reappear with its files intact.

Figure 11-11   An "unreadable" RAM disk

- To be extra safe, you should store a copy of at least the RAM disk's System Folder on your hard disk. This will make it convenient to recreate it, should it ever be lost. To avoid any possible problems with two System Folders on your hard disk, as well as to save hard disk space, store your RAM disk's contents as a compressed file (using a utility such as StuffIt or Compact Pro, as described in Chapter 2).

Using an External Monitor

With all but the earliest PowerBook models, you can connect an external monitor to your PowerBook. This section focuses on those setups where both the external monitor and the PowerBook's own screen are active at the same time (with Duos, you do this with the MiniDock). A common reason for doing this is when you want a larger screen for making a presentation on the road.

Problems with connecting external monitors are typically solved by understanding how to use the relevant control panels, especially the Monitors control panel. You also have to make sure the hardware is connected correctly.

Connecting an External Monitor

1. Use AC power to run the PowerBook. Some PowerBooks will not even start up on battery power with an external monitor attached.

2. Put the PowerBook to sleep or shut it down. Connect the monitor to your Power-Book. If you are using a Duo's MiniDock, simply plug the monitor's cable into the video port. For most all-in-one PowerBooks, you need the separate video adapter cable that came with the PowerBook. Plug one end of the adapter into the video port of the PowerBook and the other into the external monitor's video cable.

3. Plug the monitor's power cord directly into an AC outlet. Do not use a monitor with its power cord plugged into a desktop Macintosh. You may have to purchase a separate cord to do this, as the power cord that connects to a Macintosh typically has a hood on it that will prevent you from connecting it to a wall outlet.

4. Turn the monitor on. Turn the PowerBook on.

Activate the External Monitor

Even if you have correctly followed the previous steps, your external monitor will still not show anything other than a blank screen. Don't worry. To get the monitor to actually show something, you need to "activate" it. You do this through the Monitors control panel (see Figure 11-12). On some PowerBooks you only have to do this the first time you attach an external monitor. On others, you have to do it every time you connect an external monitor.

1. Open the Monitors control panel. You will see two rectangles that represent your two monitors. If there is any doubt which one is which, click the Identify button. The number 1 will appear on the screen that corresponds to rectangle 1. If you do

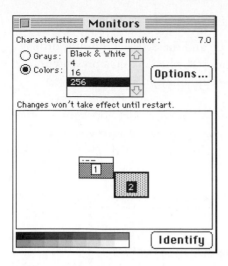

Figure 11-12
The Monitors control panel; the two adjacent rectangles represent the PowerBook screen and an external monitor

not see a number appear over each rectangle, you may have a hardware or cable problem. See if using another video cable works. Otherwise, if cables appear connected correctly, take the monitor in for a possible repair.

2. Click on the rectangle that represents your external monitor. It is now activated. You can select its color depth at this point (via the Monitors control panel of course), which can be set differently from that of the PowerBook screen.

SEE: • Chapter 10 for selecting color depth

3. Close the Monitors control panel. The external screen can now be used. It is probably still empty. But you can now drag items to it from the PowerBook screen, as if the two monitors were one large adjacently connected screen. As you move the cursor, you can see it disappear off one end of the PowerBook screen and reappear on the other end of the external monitor. Unless you have video mirroring turned on (as described shortly), this is how an external monitor works.

4. By the way, you should also turn on processor cycling when using an external monitor. This prevents overheating. (See "PowerBook Battery Conservation: Use PowerBook Control Panel Options" for how to turn this feature on.) If you are using a 16-inch monitor or larger, the PowerBook will automatically turn this feature on.

Other Monitors Control Panel Options

Open the Monitors control panel to access these options.

• To move the menu bar from one monitor to another, drag the menubar image from one monitor's rectangle to the other.

• To change the spatial relationship between the two monitors, move the two rectangles that represent the screens. This determines whether the external monitor acts as if it is to the right, left, above, or below the PowerBook screen. The cursor will only be able to move from one monitor to the other in locations where the two rectangles touch. To minimize the passing of the cursor from one monitor to another, adjust the rectangles so that they only touch in one small area (as done in Figure 11-12).

Depending on your system software, you may have to restart to see these changes.

Video Mirroring

Video mirroring is when both the PowerBook screen and the external monitor display the exact same image. This might be useful, for example, when giving a presentation to a large audience and you want to see on the PowerBook display in front of you exactly what is on a larger screen behind you.

Not all PowerBooks have a video mirroring option. If your model does support this option, you will find it in the PowerBook Display control panel (at least you will if you are using the latest version of this control panel). To get it to work, simply turn it on and restart (see Figure 11-13).

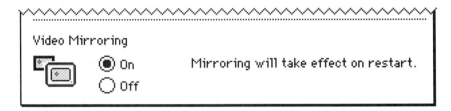

Figure 11-13   The video mirroring option in the PowerBook Display control panel

Disconnecting an External Monitor

When you are ready to disconnect the monitor, shut down the PowerBook. You cannot put a PowerBook to sleep with an external monitor attached. Once you have shut down, simply disconnect the cable(s) and restart.

Solve It! Basic PowerBook Problems

Restarting a PowerBook After a System Error

 Symptoms:

A system crash, system freeze, or other system error has occurred that requires that you restart your PowerBook. You are having trouble figuring out how to do this.

 Causes:

Most causes are the same for PowerBooks as for any other Macintosh. This section focuses specifically on those techniques and problems that are unique to PowerBooks, especially solving the basic problem of just restarting the PowerBook. Most of these techniques were briefly mentioned in Chapter 4, but they are covered in more detail here.

What to do:

Restart the PowerBook. Simply said but not always so simply done. After each step described here. See if the PowerBook now successfully restarts. If not, go on to the next step. The last step considers what to do if the system error recurs after a successful restart.

Try the Finder's Restart or Shut Down Menu Commands

Doing this is called a *soft restart* or *soft shutdown.* After most types of system errors, these probably will not work, but give them a try.

Press the Reset Button or Reset Keyboard Combination

- On the PowerBook 100, the Reset button is on the left side of the machine.

- On all other 100 series PowerBooks, the Reset button is on the rear of the machine recessed into a small hole. It can only be accessed with something like an unbent paper clip. If you don't have a paper clip handy, you may have to pass on this technique.

- On 200 series and 500 series PowerBooks, life is simpler: Just press the Command-Control-Power keyboard buttons at the same time (though this may not work after some particularly nasty system crashes).

Do a Hard Shutdown

This is an almost never-fail technique, but it may result in the loss of a RAM disk's contents that might otherwise have been saved (as mentioned in the previous section on RAM disks). To do a hard shutdown:

- On a PowerBook 100, press the Reset and Interrupt buttons at the same time.

- On a PowerBook 140, 145, or 170, press the Power button on the rear of the machine.

- On any other 100 series PowerBook or any 200 series Duo, press the Power (on/off) button on the rear of the machine and hold it for at least 5 seconds. This initiates a *hard shutdown.* If you hold it for less time, it will attempt the equivalent of a *soft shutdown,* similar to selecting Shut Down from the Finder's Special menu. Unfortunately, a soft shutdown does not work after a system crash. After a system crash, a quick press of the on/off button will do absolutely nothing! Also, don't forget that with Duos, there is a power button on the rear of a Duo Dock.

- On 500 series PowerBooks, press Command-Control-Option-Power all at the same time. This is necessary because the 500 series PowerBooks have no on/off button. If this fails to work, your only other solution is to remove the batteries and disconnect AC power temporarily.

Reset the Power Manager

This is a last resort that should only rarely be necessary to solve a system crash problem (it is more commonly used for battery-related problems, as described in the next section).

1. Shutdown the PowerBook (not just put it to sleep).

2. Disconnect the power adapter and remove the battery. On some PowerBooks, removing the battery is not required to reset the Power Manager. But, if in doubt, play it safe and remove it.

3. Reset the Power Manager. Exactly how to do this step varies with different models of PowerBooks. In particular:

   a. On a PowerBook 100, 140, 145, or 170: Press and hold the Reset and Interrupt buttons for at least 30 seconds (on all but the 100, you'll need two unbent paper clips to do this rather awkward procedure).

   b. On any other 100 series PowerBook or any 200 series Duo: Press the Power button on the rear of the machine and hold it for at least 30 seconds. On Duos, some people have claimed that you should simultaneously press both the Power on/off button on the rear of the machine and the Power On button on the keyboard. Try it.

   c. On a 500 series PowerBook: Press Command-Control-Option-Power keyboard buttons all at the same time (this is the same combination used to initiate a hard shutdown after a system error, as just previously described). You can also try this key combination on other PowerBooks, just to cover all possible bases!

4. Reinstall the battery and turn the PowerBook on.

5. If you still cannot get the PowerBook to start up successfully, remove the battery again and wait at least 15 minutes before you reinstall it. Some people claim that you should leave the battery out overnight to be certain that the procedure has succeeded. If it were me, I'd go for the overnight approach. If you are having this much difficulty, why take chances with shortcuts?

   For 200 series Duos and 500 series PowerBooks, in addition, you may need to remove the backup battery (see "Take Note: What Is the Power Manager?"). Doing this is not that difficult (though accessing the backup battery may require opening up the PowerBook case). For specifics, consult your PowerBook's manual or simply take your PowerBook to an authorized service provider.

6. Reinsert the battery, plug in the power adapter (if desired), and turn the Power-Book on. Hope that your problem is gone.

7. Check your PowerBook control panel. You will have to redo any customized changes you may have made there (because resetting the Power Manager reverts those settings to their default values).

SEE: • "Problems Running on Battery Power," later in this chapter, for another situation where you need to reset the Power Manager
• Chapter 4 for more on reset buttons, power buttons, and what to do to solve system error problems

---

BY THE WAY ▶

A SHORTCUT FOR RESETTING THE POWER MANAGER

There is a freeware utility called ResetPwrMgr that, when launched, resets the Power Manager. It saves you the trouble of having to figure out and remember how to do it for your particular model of PowerBook. The only downside is that it restarts the Mac without the proper checking that is done when you select the Finder's Restart or Shut Down commands. But this is no worse than what happens when you restart after a system crash.

TAKE NOTE ▶

WHAT IS THE POWER MANAGER?

The Power Manager is hardware, sort of like a little microprocessor, located on the PowerBook's logic board. It is used to control most battery- and power-related operations. The Power Manager also maintains some information in memory (such as the time settings used by the PowerBook control panel for automatic sleep and screen dimming). This information is preserved, even when there is no AC or main battery power, via the PowerBook's backup battery. This small battery is also used to maintain the contents of the PRAM, as a similar battery is used in all Macintosh models (see Fix-It #11).

Similarly to what can happen with the PRAM, the Power Manager data can get corrupted. The most common result of this corruption is an inability to start up a PowerBook. Oddly, this may happen even if you are running on AC power. Corrupted Power Manager data may also cause a variety of other symptoms, such as a battery that takes an unusually long time to recharge.

The solution to all of these problems is to reset the Power Manager data (as described in the main text here). For PowerBooks, resetting the Power Manager is one of those generic fix-it procedures, much like zapping the PRAM. It may fix many problems beyond the ones specifically mentioned here.

In the worst case, hardware damage to the Power Manager may cause these same symptoms. Fixing this will require a trip to the repair shop.

If the System Error Recurs After a Successful Restart

Consider the following:

- **Defective SIMMs and PowerBook warmth**
  All PowerBooks get warm as you use them, some more so than others. Color PowerBooks, in particular, get quite warm, almost hot. In most cases, this is normal and not a cause for concern.

  However, if you install a SIMM card that is at or near the maximum possible amount for your PowerBook (typically 10Mb or more), this too adds to the heat level of the PowerBook. If you didn't get the best-quality SIMMs (even though they are not technically defective), the RAM may overheat, causing any number of weird symptoms, including freezes and system crashes. Plain old defective SIMMs, no matter what quantity you have installed, may cause similar symptoms.

  Turning on Processor Cycling (from the PowerBook control panel) helps keep temperatures down. Otherwise, your only cure is to replace the defective SIMMs.

  SEE: • Fix-It #17 for more on SIMMs

- **Screen dimming may not work with certain programs**
  The result can be a system freeze as soon as screen dimming turns on. If you suspect this, turn off screen dimming from the PowerBook control panel prior to using the problem application.

- **PowerBook freezes when hard drive spins up**
  This is probably the result of having rebuilt the desktop while certain problem extensions were turned on (SuperATM is a known example). The solution is to disable all extensions, restart, and rebuild the desktop.

  SEE: • Fix-It #4 on extensions
       • Fix-It #9 on rebuilding the desktop

- **System error may be related to using file sharing**

  SEE: • "Solve It! File Sharing and Modem Problems," later in this chapter, for examples of system errors related to these issues

- **Consider more general causes and solutions**

  SEE: • Chapter 4 for more general information on system errors

Problems Running on Battery Power

Symptoms:

- After following procedures to recharge a battery, the battery remains uncharged.
- The battery indicator in the Control Strip (or other similar utility) indicates that the battery is nearly out of power even though you just recharged it.
- The battery successfully charges but then drains its charge much more rapidly than expected.
- The PowerBook will not start up at all with battery power but works normally when using AC power.

Causes:

- The power adapter may be defective or not plugged in correctly. Or it may be the wrong power adapter for your PowerBook.
- The battery may be dead, or nearly so, and need to be replaced. This is especially likely if the battery either never successfully recharges or loses its charge very rapidly.
- With some types of PowerBook batteries, you may have something called the "memory" effect that causes batteries to discharge rapidly.
- The charger may be stuck in "trickle" mode. This can make it take unusually long to recharge the battery.

TAKE NOTE ▶

WHAT IS TRICKLE MODE?

Recharging a battery, particularly NiCad batteries, is typically divided into two stages. In the first stage, called fast mode, *the charge proceeds at its fastest pace. In the second stage, which typically begins after the battery is more than 80% charged, the remaining charge occurs at a much slower pace, called* trickle mode. *This helps prevent overcharging of the battery. Apple's Control Strip does not have separate icons to indicate which mode you are in, though some competing utilities do.*

Sometimes the charging process may get stuck in trickle mode, never shifting to fast mode when appropriate. This will mean that charging the battery will take an unusually long time. Corrupted Power Manager data can cause this.

- The Power Manager's data may have become corrupted.
- A corrupted PRAM may also cause these symptoms.
- Finally, you may be using your PowerBook in a way that excessively drains battery power.

What to do:

Use Battery Conservation Features

If your battery is simply losing power faster than it typically has in the past and if all battery and charger operations otherwise seem normal, you may be using your Power-Book in a way that drains battery power excessively fast, such as using virtual memory or a modem.

SEE: • "PowerBook Battery Conservation," earlier in this chapter, for details

Check for Power Adapter Problems

The typical way to recharge a battery is to use the power adapter. Just connect it to your PowerBook and you are automatically recharging, even as you continue to use the PowerBook (though using it will lengthen the time needed to recharge). If the Power-Book is asleep or shut down, recharging should only take about 2 to 3 hours. If the power adapter doesn't seem to be doing its job, check for the following possibilities:

- Check that the power adapter plugs are correctly and fully inserted at both the PowerBook end and the wall outlet end.
- Check that the power outlet is working. For example, a wall outlet connected to a wall switch will not work if the wall switch is in the off position.

    Don't trust the on-screen icons as a reliable indicator of a charging battery. For example, the lightning bolt icon (indicating a charging battery) in the Control Strip appears as soon as you plug the adapter into the PowerBook, even if the power outlet end is not plugged into anything! (Eventually, if this condition persists, the PowerBook will figure out it has almost no power left and will inform you of this!)

- Remove the power adapter from its power source, wait briefly, then plug it back in. This may correct a problem with the charger stuck in trickle mode.
- Be sure you are using the power adapter that came with your PowerBook or another compatible one obtained from Apple. Using any other adapter may not work and may potentially damage your PowerBook.
- If possible, check whether the power adapter itself may be broken. Do this by trying to charge the battery with another adapter. If you succeed, this means that the original adapter is broken.

    By the way, Apple sells an optional external charger. This allows you to recharge a battery while it is not in the PowerBook (convenient if you like to keep a spare battery charged at all times). If the charger can recharge the battery but the adapter cannot, this also would indicate a likely defective adapter.

DIFFERENT POWERBOOKS, DIFFERENT BATTERIES, DIFFERENT ENABLERS, DIFFERENT ADAPTERS

Different models of PowerBooks use different types of batteries. When you replace the battery that came with your PowerBook, make sure you replace it with the right one.

All-in-one PowerBooks of the 100 series (such as the 160 and 180) use nickel-cadmium (NiCad) batteries. These are the type susceptible to the "memory effect" problem described in the main text. The newer 500 series PowerBooks use a totally new nickel-metal-hydride (NiMH) battery called the PowerBook Intelligent Battery. It includes a built-in microprocessor that actually sends information to the PowerBook that is used to help conserve battery power.

Duos all use NiMH batteries (but not the Intelligent Battery type found in the 500 series PowerBooks). Depending on the model you have, you may have a Type I, Type II, or Type III NiMH battery. The Type III battery is the newest and lasts the longest. You can use this new type of battery with older Duo models, but only if you first install a special system enabler, called Type III Battery *(a disk with the enabler on it comes with a battery purchase) or if you upgrade to System 7.5. Similarly, upgrading from Type I to Type II batteries on a Duo 210/230 requires using the PowerBook Duo Enabler (if you don't already have it, it's included with System Update 3.0). Using either enabler incorporates the fixes in the* Duo Battery Patch *extension, which should then be deleted.*

By the way, the PowerBook 100 and the original Macintosh Portable used still another type of battery: a lead-acid battery.

Different models of PowerBooks also use different power adapters. In particular, NiCad all-in-one PowerBooks have an entirely different adapter from Duos. The new Intelligent Battery PowerBooks use still another type of adapter. Also, Apple periodically makes minor improvements in their power adapters (and even to the batteries themselves), typically to give them increased power load capacity. For example, Apple has upgraded the adapter used with NiCad PowerBooks several times. While they may look identical, they have different part numbers. Older NiCad PowerBooks will benefit from using the newer adapters. While you can use the older adapters with newer NiCad PowerBooks, try to avoid it. Otherwise, you cannot mix and match different styles of adapters to different PowerBooks.

Check for a Dead or Incorrectly Installed Battery

If your battery will not hold a charge, it may be dead or nearly so. A battery should last for about 500 charges. Under normal use, this may be expected to take about two years. The solution for a dead battery is to replace it.

While you are at it, check that the battery is installed correctly, following the instructions in your PowerBook User's Guide. Sometimes, an improperly installed battery may be the total cause of your problem.

Also make sure you have the right type of battery and software enabler for your PowerBook (see "Technically speaking: Different PowerBooks, Different Batteries, Different Enablers, Different Adapters").

With NiCad Batteries, Check for the "Memory Effect"

If you have a PowerBook that uses NiCad batteries (see "Technically speaking: Different PowerBooks, Different Batteries, Different Adapters"), and your battery seems to lose its charge very quickly after recharging, you may have the mysterious *memory effect* problem. Essentially, the theory goes that if you do not fully discharge a battery before recharging it, it will eventually begin to act as if its total charge is limited to the level it reaches prior to your recharging it. Similarly, if you typically recharge a NiCad battery to less than its full capacity, it may start to "think" of this lesser level as its full capacity and will no longer let you fully charge it. Even in worst-case scenarios, you will probably have to recharge the battery 50 times or more before you start to notice this effect.

The solution to this is to periodically (maybe after every 20 recharges) let the battery completely discharge and then recharge it. To be safe, a regular PowerBook user might do this every month or two, no matter how often the PowerBook is recharged. To do this, simply keep the PowerBook active until it goes past all of its low battery warning messages and finally shuts off. Then recharge it. To speed up the time to fully discharge the battery (and bypass the warning messages), use a shareware utility called Battery Amnesia (called DeepDischarge in older versions).

Newer versions of these NiCad batteries are less subject to this problem. Some experts claim that the memory effect is a myth altogether. You be the judge.

Recondition Duo Batteries

Some Duo models, such as the 270c and the 280, include an application called *Battery Recondition,* that is recommended to use whenever these NiMH battery fails to hold a charge for as long as expected. It is a similar idea to eliminating the memory effect in NiCad batteries. Check with your PowerBook's manual for details. If you are using Type III batteries, make sure you use version 1.1 or later of Battery Recondition. Earlier versions are incompatible.

BY THE WAY ▶

PRESERVING RAM WHEN REPLACING BATTERIES

Suppose you are on an airplane and you run out of battery power for your PowerBook. Fortunately, you have a fully charged spare battery ready to swap with the now discharged one. Great!

To do this with a Duo, first put the PowerBook to sleep. Then swap the batteries. The Duo's backup battery (the small internal one that maintains the contents of PRAM, etc.) will maintain the contents of RAM long enough for you to make the swap. When you wake up the PowerBook, you will be right where you left off.

You can do the same thing with the new 500 series of PowerBooks. In fact, they have an option to hold two batteries at once. In this case, you can swap one battery at any time. You don't even have to put the PowerBook to sleep.

With the 100 series of all-in-one PowerBooks, the backup battery does not maintain the contents of RAM while swapping batteries. Therefore, you must shut down the PowerBook before swapping, rather than just putting it to sleep. This is obviously less convenient. Your only alternatives are to purchase an attachment that provides temporary backup battery power to the PowerBook (sold at most stores that sell Macintoshes) or find a way to get AC

Duos: Special Battery Problem

According to Apple, there is a potential problem "discovered with some PowerBook Duo 210/230/250's, with Express Modems installed, using version 1.0 of the PowerBook Duo Enabler. The problem is that the PowerBook Duo battery won't recharge and the Battery DA shows blank or empty." The original solution to this was to install a special extension, released by Apple, called *Duo Battery Patch*. Subsequently, Apple rolled this bug fix into later versions of the PowerBook Duo Enabler (which is included with System Update 3.0). If you have this Enabler, delete the Battery Patch extension, if still present. Upgrading to System 7.5 also eliminates this problem.

This just reemphasizes a general troubleshooting rule: Use the latest version of system software and install relevant updates and patches.

Recondition Intelligent (500 series) Batteries

Under certain conditions, the information stored in the "intelligent" batteries used by the 500 series PowerBooks (and probably models still to come) can become corrupted and cause the system software to incorrectly report the battery status. The *Intelligent Battery Recondition* software updates this information in the battery and restores normal operation.

Intelligent Batteries: Special Recharging Problem

Intelligent batteries (the ones that come with the 500 series PowerBooks) may have a problem where their charge level is so low that the PowerBook does not recognize its presence and so does not begin to recharge it. There is a procedure you can try that may fix this: Remove and reinsert the battery (preferably in the right-hand compartment with the left compartment empty). Try this several times before giving up. However, it often doesn't work, in which case you will have to get the battery replaced. Your best bet is to call Apple for assistance (1-800-SOS-APPL).

Reset the Power Manager

See the previous section, "Restarting a PowerBook After a System Error," for details on how to do this.

Zap the PRAM

For all PowerBooks running System 7.0 or a later version, you do this by holding down the Command-Option-P-R keys at startup. Obviously, if you can't get the PowerBook to start up from battery power, you will need to do this while running on AC power.

SEE: • Fix-It #11 for more on zapping the Parameter RAM

A Blown Fuse?

Using a damaged power adapter can cause hardware damage to the logic board itself. In particular, it may blow a fuse so that the PowerBook can run on AC power but not on battery power. This is particularly known to happen with the 140, 160, 170, and 180 models of PowerBook. If this happens, replacement of the power adapter is obviously required. Replacement of the main logic board may also be required. Call 800-SOS-APPL for advice here. You should be able to get it repaired at no cost.

PowerBook Appears Dead

 ## Symptoms:

- Whether operating on battery power or with the power adapter, the PowerBook shows no sign of life. You cannot even get it to turn on and begin a startup sequence.

 ## Causes:

- The battery and/or power adapter may be damaged and need to be replaced.
- The Power Manager data may be corrupted.
- Otherwise, the cause is probably a general one not specific to PowerBooks.

 ## What to do:

Check the Battery and Power Adapter

Try another battery, if available. Try a different power adapter, if available. If either of these fix the problem, your old battery may be dead or damaged or your power adapter may be damaged. Replace them.

Reset the Power Manager

Though primarily associated with problems specific to running on battery power, problems here may prevent you from running on AC power as well.

SEE: • "Restarting a PowerBook After a System Error," for details on this topic

Try More General Solutions

Check Chapter 5 ("The Macintosh Is Dead") for other more general possibilities. As a last resort, take the PowerBook in for repair. You may have a damaged Power Manager or other serious problem. If the PowerBook is still under warranty, call 800-SOS-APPL for advice on possible free repairs (see Fix-It #18).

Sleep Problems

Symptoms:

- The PowerBook does not go to sleep automatically.
- The PowerBook automatically goes to sleep sooner (or later) than expected.
- A message appears warning you about some potential problem if your Macintosh goes to sleep.

Causes:

Most of these problems are due to variations in the settings in the PowerBook control panel. Messages warning against putting a PowerBook asleep are usually due to selecting Sleep while AppleTalk is on.

What to do:

Automatic Sleep Disabled

Automatic sleep refers to when the PowerBook goes to sleep without your specifically requesting Sleep. What determines when this happens is the interval set in the Power-Book control panel.

Obviously, if the System Sleeps setting is set to *Never,* there is no automatic sleep. (If you have an older version of this control panel and if your PowerBook is operating on AC power, you get the same result by clicking the Options button and checking *Never Sleep When Plugged In.)*

Similarly, be wary if you use the Manual setting for Power Conservation. In particular, make sure you have not selected Power Adapter mode when you are running from battery power, as the power adapter settings generally uses a longer time (or never) until automatic sleep occurs.

SEE: • **"PowerBook Battery Conservation," earlier in this chapter, for details on the PowerBook control panel**

If your PowerBook control panel settings suggest that you should be getting automatic sleep, but it doesn't happen, check for any of the following possible causes. They all prevent automatic sleep from kicking in.

- AppleTalk is on and the power adapter is plugged in, whether you are actually connected to a network or not.
- You are connected to another volume on a network.
- The modem is on or a document is printing, or a serial port is in use for any other reason.
- Any background activity is occurring.
- An external monitor is in use.
- A Duo is plugged into a Duo Dock or a Duo is plugged into a MiniDock with an external monitor attached.
- An Apple Guide window is open (Apple Guide is a System 7.5 feature, described more in Chapter 1).
- A 500 series PowerBook is connected to an EtherNet network.

Automatic Sleep Works—But Not at the Expected Interval

In some cases, automatic sleep works, but it kicks in sooner (or later) than you expected. A similar problem can occur with automatic screen dimming. If any of this happens, the most likely cause is that the PowerBook control panel settings are not what you think they are. For example, they may somehow have been set to too short a time (or you may be using the Battery setting even though the power adapter is attached).

Manual Sleep: AppleTalk Warning

If you select Sleep manually (such as via the Finder's Sleep command) and AppleTalk is on, you will get a warning message informing you that putting the PowerBook to sleep means you may lose connection to all currently shared volumes on your network (see Figure 11-14, top). You will get this message even if you aren't connected to any volumes at the time.

If you don't care if currently shared volumes get disconnected or if you have no currently shared volumes, just ignore the message and click Sleep.

Otherwise, it is generally advised to unmount networked volumes before selecting Sleep. As another alternative, Apple provides a control panel called AutoRemounter (originally part of the PowerBook File Assistant package, but now available for free and included with System 7.5). You can use it to automatically remount any shared disks after awakening from sleep. However, unless this feature is important to you, I would not use this extension. It has been reported to lead to an increase in system crashes. It also doesn't work on some older models of PowerBook.

By the way, if you find this message annoying and wish to stop it from appearing, you can simply turn AppleTalk off whenever you don't need it to be active. Even better, there are utilities, such as PBTools, that allow you to bypass this message even when AppleTalk is on.

Finally, if shared volumes do get disconnected because of Sleep, you will get another message to that effect when you reawaken the PowerBook (see Figure 11-14, bottom).

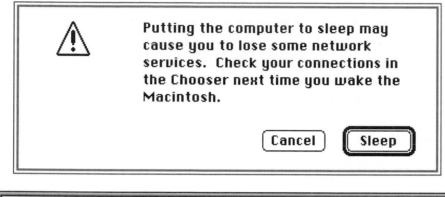

Figure 11-14   Top: A warning message about selecting Sleep while AppleTalk is active; Bottom: A message that may appear when you reawaken

SEE: • "Transfer Files via File Sharing," later in this chapter, for more on shared volumes

PowerBook Quick Fixes

Here are a few miscellaneous, largely unrelated symptoms and solutions, too minor for each one to deserve its own section.

  Symptoms and what to do:

Defective Pixels on Active Matrix Screens

Check for Void or Stuck Pixels   PowerBooks with active matrix screens may have defective pixels (this problem is not relevant to passive matrix screens). To see if you have this problem, turn your PowerBook on and check for either of the following:

- **"Void" pixels**
  This means that the pixel is always off (white). For example, if you look at a screen that should have all dark pixels and one or more pixels are white, staring at you like stars in the night sky, you have void pixels.

- **"Stuck" pixels**
  This means that the pixel is always on (dark). For example, if you look at a screen that should have all white pixels and one or more pixels are dark, looking like periods on a sheet of white paper, you have stuck pixels.

If you have any doubt as to whether you have defective pixels, a simple test is to use a graphics program to create a large black (or large white) rectangle. Then move its window around it until you have tested all of the screen with it, looking for defective pixels as you go (though you may not be able to test the menubar area this way). Even better, Apple Personal Diagnostics (see Fix-It #17) will test the screen by creating both an all-black and all-white display. Programs that can create slide show presentations can do the same thing. This advice applies best to noncolor Macintoshes, though the basic logic is the same in all cases.

Rebuild the Desktop   Rebuilding the desktop (see Fix-It #9) may sometimes fix defective pixels, but don't count on this.

Replace the Screen   Apple's official position is that if you have six or more void pixels, you should replace the screen; if you have even one stuck pixel, you should replace the screen. A stuck pixel is considered more serious because, since it is always in an on position, it is constantly draining power. Fortunately, stuck pixels are less common than void ones.

If your PowerBook is still under warranty, and it is a grayscale (not a color) active matrix display, Apple will replace the screen for free under the following conditions:

"If it has six or more voids or if any two voids are within one inch of each other or if a display has even one stuck pixel." Color active matrix screens are not similarly protected.

Ghosting and Submarining on Passive Matrix Screens

A disadvantage of passive matrix screens is that when you move the cursor rapidly, the cursor may temporarily disappear. This is a symptom of a more general display problem with passive matrix screens, called *ghosting* or *submarining*.

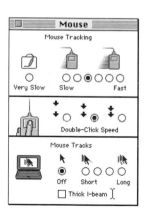

Figure 11-15 The Mouse Tracks options at the bottom of the Mouse control panel

Of course, moving the cursor more slowly helps resolve this problem. However, a better solution is at hand if you have a recent version of Apple's Mouse control panel (it originally was included as part of PowerBook File Assistant). At the bottom of it should be an option called Mouse Tracks (not Mouse Tracking, which is at the top of the control panel). Selecting longer mouse tracks helps keep the arrow cursor in view by leaving a trail behind it. Checking the Thick I-beam option similarly helps make the I-beam more visible (see Figure 11-15). Other PowerBook utilities, such as CPU Tools, have similar options.

Can't Insert a Duo into or Can't Eject a Duo from a Duo Dock

Insert Problems   If you are having problems inserting a Duo into a Duo Dock, check the following:

- Make sure the Duo is off (not just asleep) before trying to insert it into a dock.
- Make sure you are not using a Duo with a cover that is too big for that model of Duo Dock. In particular, some newer Duo models did not fit into older versions of the Duo Dock (check with Apple for details).
- Make sure the Duo Dock is unlocked (the key should be in the vertical position).

Eject Problems   If pressing the Eject button fails to get a Duo to eject from a Duo Dock, check the following:

- Make sure the Duo Dock is unlocked (the key should be in the vertical position).
- Otherwise, you can manually eject the dock by inserting a small screwdriver into the hole on the left side of the Duo Dock. Gently press it in.

Sound Problems

No Sound   If your can't get any sound at all from your PowerBook, try zapping the PRAM (see Fix-It #11).

Too Much Sound   If you are plagued with persistent white noise sound "blips," this is due to a bug in the hardware of some PowerBook models and has no real solution. However, I have found that some extensions seem to particularly aggravate this problem. For example, turning off my fax software made this problem go away in my PowerBook 180.

> SEE: • Chapter 6, "Technically Speaking: A Few Words About Sound and Sound Files," for more on problems with using sound

Transfer Files to and from a PowerBook

If you are fortunate enough to own both a PowerBook and a desktop Macintosh, you will inevitably find yourself wanting to transfer data from one computer to the other. Of course, you can do this by using a floppy disk as an intermediate step. But, except for infrequent transfer of small files, this is slow, tedious, and inefficient. Fortunately, there are better alternatives. This section outlines these alternatives and the problems to avoid when using them.

Transfer Files via the SCSI Port

To Connect an External Hard Drive to Your PowerBook's SCSI Port

You can connect an external drive to your PowerBook in the same way that you do this with any desktop Macintosh. This is an easy way to transfer files from your PowerBook to another Mac. For example, if you have an external hard drive normally connected to a desktop Mac, you can temporarily hook it up to a PowerBook to transfer files to the drive and then reconnect it to your desktop Mac. You need to take the usual precautions here, such as making sure that there are no ID conflicts and that all devices are turned off before you connect or disconnect any cables.

SEE: • Chapter 5 and Fix-It #16 for more on SCSI mounting, connections, cables, IDs, and termination

In addition, there are two special considerations when doing this with a PowerBook:

The PowerBook SCSI Port Is Different from the One on Desktop Macs   The PowerBook's SCSI port is an almost square 30-pin port. A desktop Mac's SCSI port is a larger rectangular 25-pin port. To connect an external drive to the PowerBook port, you need a special cable called the *HDI-30 System Cable.*

As an alternative, you can get a device such as APS's SCSI Boy adapter. It plugs into a PowerBook's SCSI port on one end and leaves an open 25-pin port on the other end. You can now connect an ordinary 25-pin SCSI cable to the PowerBook.

Extra Termination May Be Needed   You may need to insert a terminator at the end of the System Cable that gets connected to the external drive, even if the external drive is already terminated. Do this if you are having any problems getting the hard disk to mount.

To Connect Your PowerBook As an External Drive to a Desktop Mac

There is a special feature of PowerBooks called *SCSI disk mode.* It is available on all PowerBooks except the 140, 145, 145B, 150, and 170. It is available on Duos through use of the MiniDock. In disk mode, the PowerBook acts as if it is just a plain old external drive. With this method, you connect the PowerBook itself to another Macintosh. The PowerBook's drive is then mounted on the other Mac's desktop. You can now transfer files between the two Macintoshes. If you have a lot of data to transfer, this is probably the quickest way to do it. Here's how to set it all up:

1. Before making any connections, open the PowerBook Setup control panel. Select a SCSI ID number from the SCSI Disk Mode section of the control panel (see Figure 11-16). Which ID number you select is not important as long as you make sure it is different from any other number of a SCSI device already on the desktop Mac's SCSI chain. Then close the control panel.

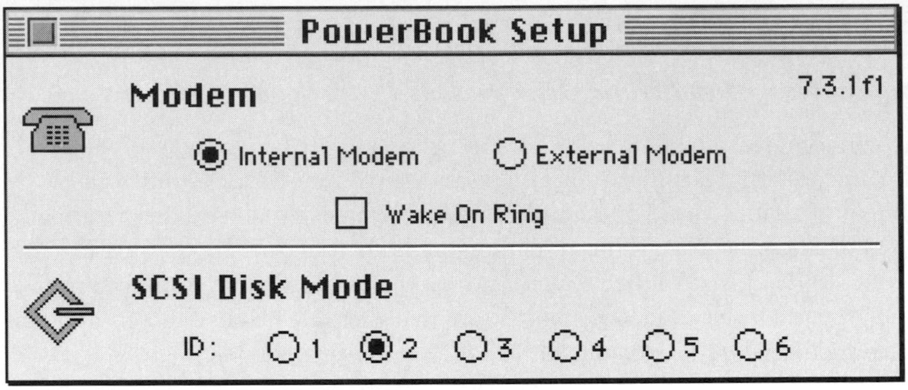

Figure 11-16 SCSI ID number 2 is selected from the PowerBook Setup control panel

2. Turn off all devices. It is especially important to shut down the PowerBook at this point. Just putting it to sleep is not sufficient here.

3. Make the cable connections. For disk mode, you need a special cable that is different from the HDI-30 System Cable described in the previous section. In this case, you need a cable called the *HDI-30 Disk Adapter*. It is dark gray in color, rather than the lighter gray of the System Cable. One end of the Adapter plugs into the PowerBook's SCSI port. The other end does not plug directly into a desktop Mac. Rather you plug it into a 50-pin end of an ordinary SCSI cable. The other end of this second cable then connects either to a desktop Mac or to the *last* device in a desktop Mac's SCSI chain (depending on which you do, the cable will have either a 25-pin or a 50-pin plug on this end). You will probably also need a terminator connected to the SCSI Adapter cable. Consult your PowerBook User's Guide for more details, if needed.

SEE: • Chapter 5 and Fix-It #16 for more on SCSI mounting, connections, cables, IDs, and termination

4. Turn on the PowerBook. You should now see a large SCSI icon (with an ID number inside it). This means you are in SCSI Disk mode.

   If this doesn't happen, immediately disconnect the PowerBook from the desktop Mac and try again, repeating all steps. If you mistakenly connected the cable while the PowerBook was asleep rather than shut down, you should get a warning message when you try to wake it up, telling you *not* to use the PowerBook until you first shutdown (see Figure 11-17). Do what it says!

5. Turn on the desktop Mac. When the desktop Mac finishes starting up you should see the icon for the PowerBook's drive mounted on the desktop Mac's desktop. You can now transfer files.

6. When you are done, turn everything off and disconnect/reconnect cables as needed to return things to how they were when you started.

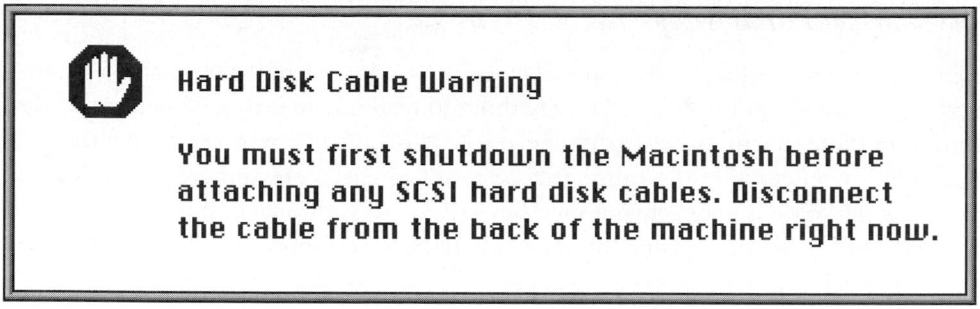

Hard Disk Cable Warning

You must first shutdown the Macintosh before attaching any SCSI hard disk cables. Disconnect the cable from the back of the machine right now.

Figure 11-17 This warning message appears when you awaken a PowerBook after having attached a SCSI cable to it

Transfer Files via File Sharing

With System 7, Apple introduced personal file sharing. This is a method by which up to 10 Macintoshes can share information over a network. For PowerBook users, it means that you can use it to transfer information between your PowerBook and your desktop Mac. Though the transfer rate is slower than via the SCSI connection methods, I prefer the file sharing approach for most transfers (such as copying a few documents from one Mac to the other) because the connection procedure is the quickest and simplest to do: You don't have to shut down your Macs to make the connection and you needn't be concerned about SCSI ID conflicts or termination problems. The lone potential drawback is the required one-time only installation and setup of the file-sharing software.

TAKE NOTE ▶

WHAT IS APPLETALK?

This note is similar to a note that appears in Chapter 7. Because of its direct relevance here, the information seems worth restating.

AppleTalk refers to a method of networking computers and peripherals together. It is the equivalent of the language that is used to send information over the network. All Macintosh computers have AppleTalk support built-in. This makes it easy to connect them together for file sharing.

Making a connection typically requires special networking cables. Apple's cabling system is called LocalTalk. Other companies make competing cabling systems that connect via the same ports. A popular LocalTalk alternative is PhoneNet, which uses ordinary phone wire to make LocalTalk connections. With PhoneNet, the cable connected to the end device at each end of the chain needs a special terminating resistor, plugged into the empty slot in the phone plug.

Once the cables are in place, using a connection also requires turning on AppleTalk and selecting the appropriate driver from the Chooser (as explained in the main text). Finally, if you are using EtherNet or other non-LocalTalk networking system, you will in addition have to open the Network control panel and make the appropriate selection.

File Sharing: Initial Setup

Using file sharing requires several special extensions and control panels that are a standard part of the system software. The key thing to realize here is that 90 percent of the features in these control panels are designed solely for security: to prevent unauthorized users on a network from gaining access to information on your computer. If all you are going to do is connect your own PowerBook to your own desktop Macintosh, security is not an issue. So, what follows is a bare-bones foolproof method of getting file sharing going when security is not a concern. This method eliminates almost all of the hassles you would otherwise have. However, if you ever use this file-sharing software to connect your Mac to a multiuser network, don't use the method described here! For how to do more secure setups, consult System 7 software manuals.

This method assumes that you will be accessing your desktop Mac from your PowerBook (that is, you are going to get the desktop Mac icon to appear on your PowerBook's desktop). It also assumes you will use the built-in LocalTalk (as opposed to EtherTalk or whatever) network.

1. **Make sure you have the needed file-sharing software installed**
   You probably already do. It should have come preinstalled on your hard disk (assuming you have System 7). It also gets installed automatically if you select Easy Install when installing system software yourself. If you have this software installed, you will see files such as Sharing Setup, Users and Groups, File Sharing Extension and Network in your Control Panels and Extensions folders. If not, you need to install them. To do this, launch the Installer utility on your system software disks. Select Customize and then open the Networking Software section and click the File Sharing box. Then click Install. After it is done, restart.

   Install this software both on your PowerBook and your desktop Mac. This will actually install more files than you really need, especially so on your PowerBook. For example, you will need Sharing Setup on your desktop Mac but not on your PowerBook. As you get familiar with the procedure, you can delete the files you know you don't need. In the meantime, it will be easier to just leave everything where it is.

   SEE: • **Fix-It #5 for more details on using the Installer**

2. **From your desktop Mac, select the Chooser**
   Make sure AppleTalk is active. If it isn't, click the Active button. If you are using the Control Strip, you can make AppleTalk active from there.

3. **From your desktop Mac, select Sharing Setup**
   Open the Sharing Setup control panel directly or from the Control Strip (see Figure 11-18).

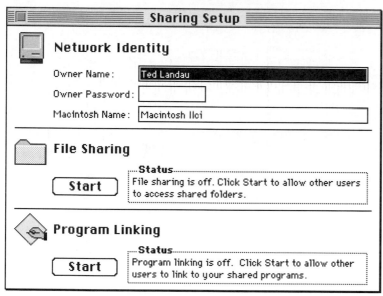

Figure 11-18 Select Open Sharing Setup from the Control Strip (top) and get the Sharing Setup control panel (bottom)

In the Network Identity section, you must type in your name (however you want it to appear) and a name for your computer. Once set, you can change these names, but the Mac will not let you leave these spaces blank. You don't have to type a password, but the Mac will send you a warning message, advising against leaving this blank, if you do not.

From the File Sharing section, click Start. Wait a minute or so until this process finishes.

Leave Program Linking off. Program Linking is a rarely used feature that does not affect what we are trying to do here.

Close the control panel.

4. **From your desktop Mac, highlight the icon of the hard disk you want to share**
   To do this, just click it once.

5. **From your desktop Mac, select "Sharing . . ." from the Finder's File menu**
   After selecting the Sharing command, a dialog box appears. From here, click the check box that says *Share this item and its contents* (see Figure 11-19). At this point,

all the See Files, See Folders, and Make Changes boxes should have X's in them—for all rows, including Everyone. Since we are not worried about security, the simplest thing to do is leave this as it is.

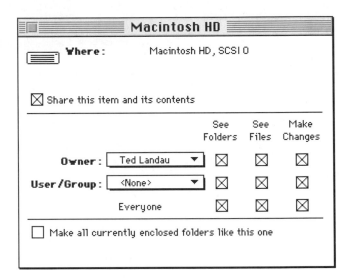

Figure 11-19   The Sharing . . . dialog box. Check "Share item and its contents" to share the disk

File sharing is now enabled for every file and folder on your selected disk. You will be able to tell this is so because the handles of all folder icons on your disk will become double thick (see Figure 11-20). This happens to all shared folders that you "own" (that is, that were placed there by you, not by other users on a network).

Figure 11-20
A folder that you own when file sharing is off (left) versus when it is on (right)

Other changes in folder icons occur if you restrict access to specific folders in any way (or if you let other users on a network create folders on your disk). However, since we won't be doing any of that, I won't bother you with the details here.

Finally, you can repeat Steps 4 and 5 for any additional mounted disks you want to share.

6. **From your desktop Mac, select Users and Group control panel**
   You should see two "face" icons here, one with your name on it (this icon will have a bold outline around it) and the other called Guest (see Figure 11-21). Double-click the Guest icon. From the window that opens, click the *Allow guests to connect* option. Again, be warned that this means that any user on a network to which you

connect will have access to your entire hard drive. As a safer alternative, you can bypass this step and plan to connect using your own name, as listed on the other icon. However, using your name, rather than Guest, may require additional steps to make a file sharing connection.

Close the icon's window and the control panel. You are now done with the desktop Mac side of the setup.

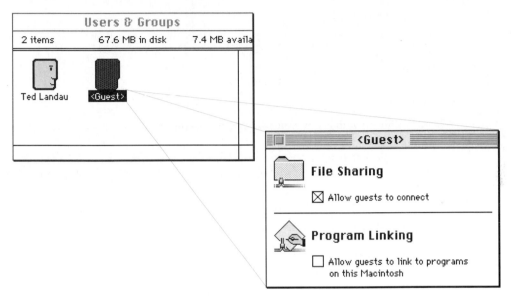

Figure 11-21 **The Users and Groups control panel. Check "Allow guests to connect" to set up a convenient but zero-security connection**

7. **Connect your PowerBook to your desktop Mac**
   To do this, you need a LocalTalk or PhoneNet type cable (see "Take Note: What Is AppleTalk?"). Connect each end of the cable to the printer ports (not the modem port) of each computer. If your PowerBook has only one serial port, it supports AppleTalk and is obviously the one to use. You can make these connections even while both computers are on.

   If you already have a PostScript LaserWriter connected to your Macintosh, you already have such a cable in the printer port. In this case, you can simply unplug it from the back of your printer and plug it into the printer port of your PowerBook (remembering to return the cable to the printer when you are done with file sharing).

SEE: • **Fix-It #17 for more on cables and cable connections**

8. **From your PowerBook, select the Chooser**
   Make AppleTalk active, if it isn't already. Next, select the AppleShare icon. At this point, the name of your desktop Mac should appear in the window on the right (see Figure 11-22). Double-click the name (or single-click the name and click OK).

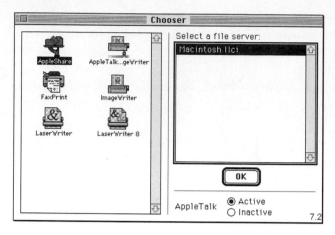

Figure 11-22 The Chooser with my desktop Mac's name highlighted

From the window that next appears, click the Guest button. Click OK (see Figure 11-23, top). Alternatively, if you left Guest access turned off in the Users and Groups control panel (in Step 6), you will need to connect as a registered user, using the name (and password, if you entered one) you entered in the Sharing Setup on your desktop Mac. Guest works more simply . . . but is less secure.

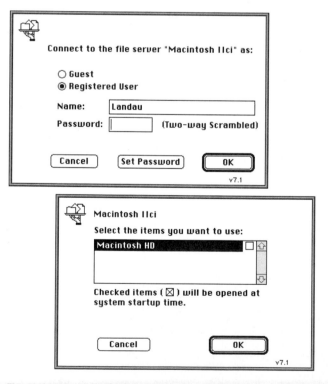

Figure 11-23 The windows that appear when you proceed to mount the desktop Mac from the Chooser

Yet another window will now appear (see Figure 11-23, bottom). The name of the volume(s) you set up for sharing should now appear, already highlighted. (If they are not highlighted, click on them to select them.) Click OK. (Ignore the checkbox about having the item open automatically at startup.)

Close the Chooser. Your desktop Mac's hard disk icon should now appear on your PowerBook's desktop. You are ready to share files. But don't get to work quite yet.

9. **From your PowerBook, select the desktop Mac's disk icon**
After selecting the icon, make an alias of it, using the Make Alias command from the Finder's File menu. Place the alias in any convenient location on your desktop. The advantage of this alias will become clear the next time you want to use file sharing, as is described shortly.

10. **The initial setup is now complete. You can share files**
Any time you access the desktop Mac from the PowerBook, you will see a pair of opposite facing arrows flash on and off in the upper left corner of the menubar, to the left of the Apple icon. This is normal.

Helpful hint: Remember, the previous instructions assume that you intend to share files between a PowerBook and a desktop Mac, that you are the only user doing the sharing, that you intend to share your entire disk, and that you care nothing about security. If you are on a network with other users or if access has been separately set for individual folders for any reason, things can get considerably more complicated. If this is the case, refer to the relevant documentation or other outside help, as needed.

File Sharing: Disconnecting

1. **From your PowerBook, drag the desktop Mac's icon(s) to the Trash**
The icon now vanishes from your desktop. The Macs are no longer connected.

2. **Disconnect the LocalTalk cable**
You don't have to turn off your computers to do this. This is an optional step. You can leave the cable in place if you plan to leave your PowerBook where it is and have no other need for the cable.

3. **If you want, you can now turn file sharing and AppleTalk off**
To do this, select the Sharing Setup control panel on your desktop Mac and click the Stop button. This has the benefit of reducing the amount of RAM used by the system software. You can also turn AppleTalk off if you no longer need it for any other operation. Doing this on your PowerBook helps conserve battery power. But don't forget that you need AppleTalk active to use most PostScript printers. In any case, you will need to make sure these features are on again the next time you want to file share.

SEE: • "Problems with Turning File Sharing or AppleTalk Off," later in this chapter, for more Information

Accessing File Sharing After the Initial Setup

Once you have completed the initial setup, as just described, accessing file sharing on future occasions is much easier. Here's all you have to do:

1. **Connect your PowerBook to your desktop Mac**
   Follow the directions in Step 7 of the Initial Setup section.

2. **From your PowerBook, double-click the alias of the desktop Mac's icon**
   This is the alias you made in Step 8 of the Initial Setup section.

That's it! Assuming that file sharing and AppleTalk are both still on, and all needed extensions and control panels are present and active, the desktop Mac's disk should mount on your PowerBook. You are ready to file-share without any other steps needed. (If you are mounting as a registered user, rather than a guest, you may still get the dialog box, as seen in Figure 11-23, where you need to enter your name and password.)

By the way, the only extensions/control panels you absolutely need at this point are the File Sharing and extensions on your desktop Mac and the AppleShare Chooser extension on your PowerBook. That's right, to use file sharing in the way I have described here, you don't need any other extensions or control panels active. Still, I would keep control panels such as Sharing Setup around, as you may need them to make changes later.

TAKE NOTE ▶

FILE SYNCHRONIZATION

Once you have file sharing setup, one of the best uses you can make of it is to update files that you keep on both disks, so that both computers always have the same version of these files. For example, suppose you are working on a report on your desktop Mac. When you leave for a trip, you copy the report to your PowerBook so you can work on it while you are gone. When you get back home, you want to replace the now-outdated version on your desktop Mac with your newer copy from your PowerBook. If you only do this occasionally, it is easy enough to do by simply dragging the file from one computer to another, via file sharing. However, if you do this frequently and with a variety of files, you will benefit from a method that automates this procedure and makes sure that everything is updated correctly. Doing this is called file synchronization.

There are several utilities that do this. Apple makes a good one called PowerBook File Assistant (see Figure 11-24). Even better, it is now included free with System 7.5.

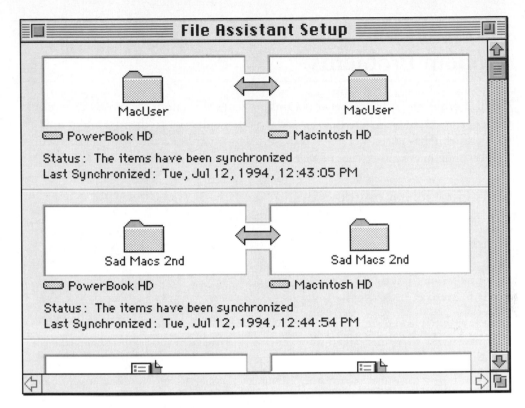

Figure 11-24 PowerBook File Assistant

Transfer Files via a Modem (Apple Remote Access)

If your desktop Macintosh is at home and you are on the road somewhere with your PowerBook, you can still transfer files between machines. To do this, you'll need the same file-sharing software described in the previous section. And both machines will need to be hooked up to a modem. The speed at which information travels over a network or via a modem is called the *baud rate*. Higher numbers mean faster transmission rates. The minimum modem transmission speed you can use for these transfers is 2400 baud, but transfer speed will be much more acceptable if you use at least 9600 baud (though even these higher speeds are slower than the transfer rate used by direct-wired connections, such as LocalTalk or EtherNet). Finally, you need special software, called Apple Remote Access (ARA), formerly called AppleTalk Remote Access, installed on both machines.

For the details on how to setup and use ARA, consult the documentation that comes with the software. Assuming you have ARA installed and ready-to-go, but you are still having some problems, check "Problems Using Apple Remote Access" in the next section. For some more general information on modems, see Fix-It #18.

Solve It! File Sharing and Modem Problems

Detailed problems regarding networks and modem connections are mostly beyond the scope of this book. That said, this section offers solutions to the more common problems you may encounter when using file sharing and/or a modem, whether with a PowerBook or any other type of Macintosh.

Can't Get File Sharing to Work

 ### Symptoms:

- When trying to turn on file sharing, you get a message that says *File sharing could not be enabled,* or the file sharing startup simply never finishes.

- The file sharing option does not appear in the Sharing Setup window.

- When trying to connect to another Macintosh, you get a message that says the shared disk could not be opened because it *could not be found on the network.*

- When trying to connect to another Macintosh, you get a message that says it can't be opened because you do not have enough *access privileges.*

- You cannot enable file sharing or connect to a shared disk for any other reason.

- While sharing information across disks, problems occur, such as system freezes or crashes.

 ### Causes:

Most causes are due to incompatible software, incorrect software settings, bugs in certain software or corrupted data.

 ### What to do:

If You Get a Message That Says "File Sharing Could Not Be Enabled"

In almost all of these cases, the problem is due to a corrupted file that needs to be deleted. By the way, if you succeed in enabling file sharing but still want to delete any of these files, turn off file sharing first.

- **Corrupted Users and Groups data file**
  The Users and Groups data file is located in the Preferences folder. Locate it and delete it. Then restart. A new default version of the file will be created. You will

then need to recreate any custom settings you made in the Users and Groups control panel. After doing so, see if you can now turn file sharing on.

By the way, some versions of AppleShare subtly modify this file so that System 7 file sharing will no longer work if the AppleShare extension is replaced with another version. This too is fixed by deleting the Users and Groups data file and restarting.

- **Corrupted files in File Sharing folder**
  The File Sharing folder is located in the Preferences folder. It may contain corrupted files. To check for this, drag the File Sharing folder from the Preferences folder to the desktop. Restart and try again. If file sharing now succeeds, delete the removed folder; a new one is created automatically and its contents restored as needed. Otherwise, you can return the folder to its original location.

- **Corrupted AppleShare PDS file**
  AppleShare PDS is an invisible file located at the root level of the hard disk. It is used by AppleShare. To check whether the file is corrupted, you need to delete the file. However, since it is an invisible file, you will first need to use a utility, such as DiskTop, that lists and allows you to delete invisible files. Some utilities, such as MacTools, may allow you to make an invisible file visible, but will not be able to delete the file. If you are using this type of utility, make the file visible. Then go to the Finder to locate and delete the file. After deleting the file, restart. The Mac will automatically create a new PDS file. Check if you can now enable file sharing.

  By the way, a corrupted PDS file has also been known to be a cause of unusually long startup times. Deleting the file corrects this problem.

BY THE WAY ▶

WHAT ARE THESE WEIRD RABBIT ICONS?

If you make the invisible AppleShare PDS file visible, you will see that it has a strange-looking rabbit icon, often referred to as the "killer rabbit." For unknown reasons, this icon may occasionally transfer to other files (though rebuilding the desktop should fix the problem). Don't worry, seeing this icon does not mean anything dangerous has invaded your computer.

Less commonly known is that if you have a CD-ROM drive and you use file sharing, you probably have a collection of visible files with killer rabbit icons—right in your System Folder. To find them, go to the Preferences folder and look for a folder called File Sharing. Inside, you will see a collection of files with PDF (not PDS!) at the end of their names, all with the rabbit face and all named after CD-ROM disks that you used while file sharing was turned on (see Figure 11-25). The reason for this is that, since CD-ROM disks are read-only, the Macintosh cannot create the more typical AppleShare PDS file it would otherwise place on the CD-ROM disk. So instead, it creates these PDF files and stores them in your startup disk's System Folder. You can delete them if you wish. The Mac will recreate them if it needs them again.

By the way, speaking of invisible stuff related to file sharing, you may find an invisible folder on your hard disk, called Move & Rename. It too is created and used by AppleShare. Should you delete it by mistake, don't worry. The Mac will yet again create a new one when it needs one.

Figure 11-25
Killer rabbits on the loose

For Other Problems with Enabling File Sharing

You may have problems enabling file sharing that do not result in the *file sharing could not be enabled* message. Here are some common situations and their solutions:

- **AppleTalk is not active**
  If AppleTalk is not active, you should get a message telling you this when you try to turn file sharing on. If so, go to the Chooser (or use the Control Strip) and make it active. While you are at it, make sure *all* needed file-sharing software is installed (as described in "File Sharing: Initial Setup" earlier in this chapter).

- **The Sharing Setup control panel cannot be opened**
  The Sharing Setup control panel will probably not open unless the Network Extension (which is different from the Network control panel) is installed in Extensions folder. If you try to open Sharing Setup without the Network Extension active, you will get a message telling you to install the extension and restart your Mac. Do so.

- **The File Sharing section is missing from the Sharing Setup control panel**
  If this happens, it means that the File Sharing Extension (not the same thing as the Sharing Setup control panel!) is not present or was disabled at startup. Replace it (or reenable it) and restart. Then check the Sharing Setup control panel again.

- **Corrupted PRAM**
  Zap the PRAM (see Fix-It #11). You will probably have to turn on AppleTalk again after this.

- **Disk limitations**
  You should ideally have at least 1Mb of free disk space to use file sharing. Also, some removable cartridge drives do not work with file sharing. Some non-Apple formatting utilities are not compatible with file sharing. Finally, you can't share a PC-formatted volume.

- **Memory limitations**
  You need at least 340K of memory to use file sharing. If you are having problems, restart with some or all non-file-sharing–related extensions off.

- **Problems with the "Sharing" command and dialog box**
  If you select the "Sharing . . ." command for a particular volume from the Finder's File menu and you get a message that says *One or more items could not be shared, because not all items are available for file sharing*, it probably means you are trying to share a removable cartridge (such as in a SyQuest drive) that was mounted after file

sharing was turned on. Try turning file sharing off and then back on again. Otherwise restart, making sure the cartridge is present at startup. Then try the Sharing command again. It should now work.

Once you get the Sharing dialog box to appear and you check the "Share this item and its contents" item for your disk, you may get a message that says the disk *could not be shared because there is a shared folder inside it.* This unlikely event means that sharing has already been turned on for some folder on your disk (see "Technically Speaking: The Sharing Dialog Box for Folders" for information on how this could happen). In this case, select File Sharing Monitor to get a list of currently shared folders. (By the way, this control panel only works if file sharing is first turned on from Sharing Setup.) Then go to the Sharing dialog box for each shared folder and unselect *Share this item and its contents.* You will now be able to select *Share this item and its contents* for the disk.

If You Get a Message That Says That the Shared Disk Could Not Be Opened Because It "Could Not Be Found on the Network"

There are several possible reasons you may get a message like the one in Figure 11-26.

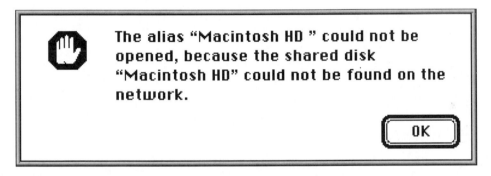

Figure 11-26 Message that indicates a problem accessing a shared disk

- **Cables not connected**
  Make sure that the cable connecting the two computers is present and plugged into the printer ports of each Mac.
- **Needed file-sharing software not installed or not active**
  In general, make sure that all file-sharing–related software is in place. Especially look for AppleShare on the guest machine and for Sharing Setup, File Sharing, and Network (control panel and extension) on the host machine. Make sure AppleTalk is turned on for both machines. Similarly, make sure that File Sharing is turned on for the host machine.

SEE: • **"Transfer Files via File Sharing," earlier in this chapter**

- **Shared disk not finished with its startup sequence**
  Even after the startup sequence appears to be over and the desktop icons appear, it may take a minute or so longer before file sharing is actually enabled. So before trying to mount a shared disk, wait until it completely finishes its startup. You can usually tell this has happened when the noise associated with hard disk access at startup stops and the double thick handles appear on folder icons.

- **Alias no longer works**
  If you are trying to open a shared volume by opening a previously created alias of the volume, the problem may be that something on the shared volume has been modified so that the alias no longer works. The solution is to start over and create a new alias (as described previously in "File Sharing: Initial Setup").

- **CD-ROM disk not mounted at startup**
  If you are trying to use a CD-ROM disk as a shared volume, it may not work if the disk was not present when the Mac started up. If this happens, just restart with the disk inserted.

- **Otherwise . . .**
  Check in the next sections for other possible solutions.

If You Get the Message That Says That the Shared Disk "Could Not Be Opened, Because You Do Not Have Enough Access Privileges"

While trying to connect to a shared disk, you may get a message that says *you do not have enough access privileges* to do so (see Figure 11-27, top). Sometimes, this is simply because file sharing is not turned on or not yet active on the host machine. The obvious solution here is to make sure file sharing is on, using the procedures outlined earlier in this section.

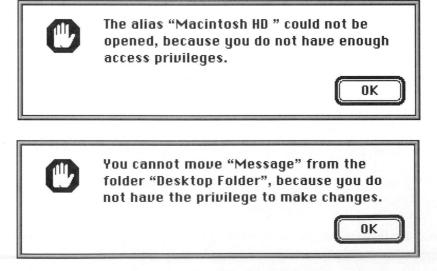

Figure 11-27   Messages indicating insufficient access privileges

SEE: • "Transfer Files via File Sharing," earlier in this chapter

Otherwise, you may have inadvertently limited access privileges via the Finder's Sharing command. To fix this, go to the host machine, not the machine where the error message appeared. Select the icon of the problem disk and then select Sharing from the Finder's File menu. This opens up the Sharing dialog box. Then check for the following:

- **Sharing dialog box: "Share this item and its contents" is unselected**
  If the "Share this item and its contents" option is unchecked (refer to Figure 11-19), it is usually functionally equivalent to having turned off file sharing for the entire disk. When you try to open this as a shared disk, you will get the "insufficient access privileges" message (see Figure 11-27, top). The solution is to turn this option on and try again.

- **Sharing dialog box: "See Folder, See Files, Make Changes" options modified**
  If the "Share this item and its contents" option is checked, you can still separately limit access to Owner, User/Group, or Everyone categories. You do this by unchecking the boxes in the rows following these categories. Normally, for the low-security setups described in this chapter, you would never have reason to do this. But you may find it has happened anyway. If so, here are some basic guidelines:

  In the extreme case, unchecking these boxes can totally block a user's access to the disk. For example, if all three boxes ("See Folders, See Files, Make Changes") are unchecked in the Everyone row (refer to Figure 11-19 again), a Guest user will get the "insufficient access privileges" message when they try to mount the disk (see Figure 11-27, top)—even if access to Guests has been granted in the Users & Groups control panel (refer to Figure 11-21). As another example, if only the Make Changes box is unchecked, the same Guest will be able to mount and view the disk, but will be unable to make any modifications to it. Should they attempt any modifications, such as discarding a file, an alert message will appear (see Figure 11-27, bottom). In any cases of this sort, the solution is to reselect these options and start over again.

SEE: • "Technically Speaking: The Sharing Dialog Box for Folders," for related information
• Chapter 6, "When You Can't Save or Copy a File," for related information, especially regarding a message that says "Illegal Access Permission"

TECHNICALLY SPEAKING ▶

THE SHARING DIALOG BOX FOR FOLDERS

In the main text, I only described selecting the Sharing command for an entire disk. However, you can select any folder on the disk and similarly select Sharing. If you do so (and assuming you have turned on "Share this item and its contents" for the whole disk), you will get a dialog box similar to the one in Figure 11-28. From here, if you uncheck the "Same as

(continued)

enclosing folder" option, you can separately modify the other access options for the folder, overriding what options were selected for the disk as a whole. On the other hand, if "Share this item and its contents" is off for the disk, you can separately turn this option on for individual folders on the disk. Watch for the folder's icon to change as you make these modifications!

There's obviously more to know about how all this works than I have just presented. However, assuming that you are not concerned about limiting file-sharing access to other users (which has been a working assumption throughout this chapter), you should never have any need to alter these settings. Bottom line: Don't bother them and they won't bother you. If you really do need more details on this topic, check out the relevant documentation that came with your system software or seek other outside help.

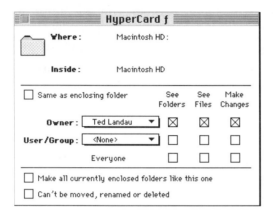

Figure 11-28   The Sharing dialog box for a folder (compare to Figure 11-19)

Problems with Turning File Sharing or AppleTalk Off

If you want to turn file sharing or AppleTalk off, take note of the following:

• When you try to turn AppleTalk on, you get a message reminding you to connect to an AppleTalk network (see Figure 11-29, top). When you turn AppleTalk off (which you may regularly do on a PowerBook to conserve battery power), you are likely to get an alert message (see Figure 11-29, middle) reminding you to make sure you are disconnected from a network. Usually you needn't do anything to respond to these messages. You can turn AppleTalk on or off whether or not you are connected to a network (as long as no shared volumes are mounted). Just click OK and continue.

If you try to turn AppleTalk off when the File Sharing Extension is active, you will in addition get a warning that AppleTalk is in use by that extension (see Figure 11-29, bottom). You can still turn AppleTalk safely off. You just can't use file sharing until you turn it on again.

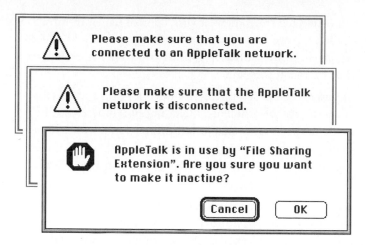

Figure 11-29   Messages that may appear when you turn AppleTalk on (top) or off (middle and bottom)

- Don't turn off AppleTalk while a shared disk is actually mounted. This is almost certain to cause a system freeze or crash.

- You *can* safely turn off file sharing from your desktop Mac, even while its disk is mounted on your PowerBook. If you try to do so, you will first get a message asking you to enter how many minutes until file sharing is disabled (see Figure 11-30). This is just provided as a way of giving other users on the network some advance warning, should they be connected to your computer. If it is just your desktop Mac and PowerBook involved, there are no other users to worry about. In this case, you can safely select zero minutes for immediate disabling. If you do disconnect this way, without first unmounting the shared disk, the PowerBook will eventually display an error message like the bottom one in Figure 11-14.

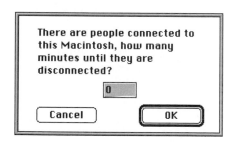

Figure 11-30
This dialog box appears when you try to turn off file sharing from a host Macintosh

Special case: Unexpected disconnection
Actually, the message in Figure 11-14 may occur anytime a file-sharing connection is unexpectedly broken, such as after a system crash on the host machine. If this happens, and you still see the shared volume's icon on your desktop, drag the icon to the Trash before trying to reconnect to the volume.

Other Problems with Using File Sharing . . .

The following is a miscellaneous collection of problems and solutions related to file sharing. Several of these problems involve system freezes and crashes. Read it over to see if your problem is contained here:

- Make sure the correct icon is selected from the Network control panel. In most cases, for connections between a PowerBook and another Mac, you should select LocalTalk (for many users, it will be their only option). If you have connected via an EtherNet network, select that icon instead.

- Make sure connected computers use the same version of networking and file-sharing software. This minimizes the risk of problems, including system freezes. The best policy here is to upgrade to the latest available versions of this software. Networking software in particular may be upgraded separately from other system software (see "Take Note: Upgrade Network and Communications Software," later in this chapter).

- When files are being transferred over the network, other operations are likely to slow down. For example, you will notice that moving icons on the desktop, opening and closing windows, launching applications, and copying files will all take longer. This is normal.

- Try not to have other background activities going while a disk is currently being shared, especially while transferring files over the network, and most especially when the PowerBook is first trying to access and mount the desktop Mac's disk. In particular, don't have other file copying or printing in progress, particularly on the host machine. Neither should you be using your modem. Otherwise, it may lead to a system freeze.

- On Macintosh computers, especially those with a 68040 microprocessor (Quadra, Centris, and Performa 470 series), some programs may quit unexpectedly or cause the computer to freeze when you attempt to open them over the network. This problem is fixed by using the *Network Launch Fix* extension, which is available from online services. This fix is also rolled into the System Update 3.0 and System 7.5; if you have installed the Update or use system 7.5, the Fix file should be deleted.

- Be careful about putting a PowerBook to sleep while a shared disk is mounted. If you do, the connection will be lost (refer to Figure 11-14). If files are currently being transferred, the transfer will halt. A system crash is possible.

- If you try to eject a CD-ROM disk or unmount a hard disk while file sharing is on, you may get a message that says you cannot do it because the disk is being shared or is in use. In this case, turn off file sharing to unmount the disk.

SEE: • Chapter 5 for more on problems ejecting CD-ROM disks

If Any File-Sharing Problems Led to a System Freeze or Crash

If a system freeze occurs while a shared disk is mounted, especially while transferring files, you will likely find that both the host and the guest Macintoshes have frozen. You will usually have no recourse here other than to restart both machines. A forced quit (as described in Chapter 4) will usually have no effect.

If you are transferring files when a freeze occurs, the first symptom that you will probably notice is that the double arrows next to the Apple menu stop their periodic flashing and the watch cursor appears and stays on indefinitely.

If freezes occur often when you use file sharing, the most likely culprit is an extension conflict. Try restarting with extensions off. If the problem goes away, you have an extension conflict. RAM Doubler is particularly known to be a source of these conflicts. Also be suspicious of fax software.

SEE: • Chapter 4 for more on system freezes and crashes
• Fix-It #4 on solving extension conflicts

Can't Get a Modem (or Serial Port) to Work

Symptoms:

- You have installed an internal modem in or connected an external modem to your PowerBook, but you can't get it to work at all.

- You have trouble accessing the serial port to which a modem is typically connected. You may get a message that says the serial port can't be used because it is "in use." Freezes or crashes may occur.

Causes:

Most common causes are either incorrect software settings or corrupted data or a mixup in the signals sent to the serial port, as described in the What to do section.

Problems with setting up a modem's protocol (such as baud rate, stop bits, etc.) are not covered here.

What to do:

If you are having problems, check for the following possibilities:

External Modems

If you use an external modem, select External Modem from the PowerBook Setup control panel (refer to the top part of the control panel in Figure 11-16). Make sure the modem cable is correctly connected and the modem is on. If your PowerBook has only one serial port, you must turn AppleTalk off to use an external modem. Select the Chooser or Control Strip to do this.

Internal Modems

If you have an internal modem, select Internal Modem from the PowerBook Setup control panel (refer again to the top part of the control panel in Figure 11-16). However, for Duos with an internal modem, you may have to switch back to External Modem to use a printer.

If your PowerBook has only one serial port, it acts as a combined printer and modem port. If you have an internal modem, you will probably only use this port to connect a printer. In most cases, you should select the modem port icon from the Chooser even for a printer. If you have an internal Express modem, you may also have to change a control panel setting. If your Express Modem is version 1.5 or later, select "Use Express Modem" from the Express Modem control panel. If the modem is an earlier version, select "Internal" or "Normal" from the PowerBook Setup control panel. Again, you may have to switch these settings when shifting from using the modem to using the printer. There seems to be some inconsistencies about what works here. Experiment. Things are also likely to change as Apple upgrades the Express Modem software.

SEE: • **Chapter 7 for more advice on printing problems**

Communications Software

Many popular communications programs, such as MicroPhone, need special files (modem drivers) that are specific to different modem models. Other special files (called CCLs) may be needed to use Apple Remote Access (as described in more detail shortly). If you don't have the modem file for your modem, the software will not work. You may also have to make a selection such as "Apple Modem Tool" or "Express Modem Tool," from the Method pop-up menu in the Connections or Communications dialog box of your software. Check the documentation that came with your modem and/or your communications software for more details.

Finally, check if you need to upgrade communications-related system software to the latest versions (see "Take Note: Upgrade Network and Communications Software" later in this chapter). They contain bug fixes for problems with previous versions.

Serial Port "In Use"

If you get an alert box message that says you can't use a modem because the serial port is in use (or if the serial port doesn't seem to be working for any other reason), check if you have a file in your Extensions folder called Serial Port Arbitrator (it would normally be installed there by Apple Remote Access software). If so, delete it and restart. This is especially likely to be a problem if you use the Express Modem.

More generally, if the alert box includes an option to reset the port, click OK. If not, try restarting. If that fails, resetting the Power Manager and/or zapping the PRAM should fix the problem. If not, a hardware problem is likely.

SEE: • "Restarting a PowerBook After a System Error," earlier in this chapter, for how to reset the Power Manager
      • "Problems Using Apple Remote Access," later in this chapter, for more on the Serial Port Arbitrator and serial port problems
      • Chapter 4 for what to do after a system freeze or crash
      • Fix-It #11 on zapping the Parameter RAM
      • Fix-It #17 for more on general modem and related hardware problems
      • Fix-It #18, for more advice on using modems

Problems Using Apple Remote Access

Symptoms:

• When trying to set up a connection via Apple Remote Access (ARA), or when trying to access an serial port device (such as a printer) with ARA installed, a message appears that says the "serial port is in use."

• A system freeze or crash occurs when trying to access ARA or when accessing any serial port device while ARA is active.

• You cannot successfully make a connection with ARA for any other reason.

Causes:

Most problems specific to using ARA center around the unusual way ARA works: though you are using ARA to make a networklike connection between two computers, you are not actually using the Mac's networking software. Rather, you are using a modem connection. In fact, in certain cases, when you use ARA, you actually disable the Mac's LocalTalk network connection. In other cases, problems can develop because information from an ARA/modem connection and for another serial port device, such as a printer, are simultaneously trying to transmit through the same port. This can happen, for example, if you connected a modem to the printer port or if you only have one serial port on your PowerBook. In still other cases, you may be connected to a local network while simultaneously accessing a remote network over ARA. In all these cases, there is a potential for the Mac to get confused and for signals to get crossed. ARA software does its best to anticipate and deal with these problems, but is not always successful.

What to do:

Switch Options from the Network Control Panel

With ARA installed, the Network control panel will have at least two icons that you can select: LocalTalk and Remote Only (see Figure 11-31). Which icon should you select? Here's how to decide.

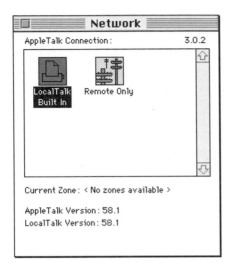

Figure 11-31
The Remote Only and LocalTalk options in the Network control panel

Select the LocalTalk Icon   Selecting the LocalTalk icon obviously permits LocalTalk connections, but also permits remote access. If you aren't having any problems, this is therefore the preferred option. In addition, if you are having trouble accessing a local network, but not a remote network, select LocalTalk.

Select the Remote Only Icon   Selecting Remote Only (an option installed by ARA) turns off LocalTalk at the printer port. You will not be able to use any local network features with this selected (even including a connection to an AppleTalk printer!). Still, this is the preferred option if you were having trouble accessing the remote network with the LocalTalk icon selected. Also select Remote Only if you are having trouble printing to a non-networked local printer, especially while connected to a remote network. When you are done using ARA, you can reselect the LocalTalk icon again, if needed.

Don't Switch Icons While Connected to a Remote Network   If you change the icon selection while connected to a remote network, you will probably get disconnected from the network no matter what icon you select. You should get a message warning about this when you attempt to make the switch (see Figure 11-32).

┌───┐
│   │
│   ⚠   Changing your AppleTalk connection will   │
│   interrupt current network services and   │
│   they will have to be reestablished.   │
│   │
│   Are you sure you want to change from   │
│   LocalTalk to Remote Only?   │
│   │
│   [Cancel]   [OK   ]   │
│   │
└───┘

Figure 11-32   This message appears when you switch from one Network control panel setting to another

Check the Serial Port Arbitrator Extension and Remote Access Setup

Serial Port "In Use" When Remote Connection Is Active   As soon as a remote connection is established, Remote Access prevents other applications from using whatever serial port (printer or modem) you selected in the Remote Access Setup control panel. If a program tries to access that port, you will typically get a message that says the port is "in use."

Serial Port Is "In Use" When "Answer Calls" Is Selected   If you checked "Answer calls" in the Remote Access Setup control panel, Remote Access would ordinarily block other programs from using the serial port, even when ARA is not actually using it. However, this block should not occur if you have also installed a system extension called the Serial Port Arbitrator. This extension is normally installed automatically (in your Extensions folder) when you install Apple Remote Access (and only works if ARA is installed). With this extension in place, other programs are still allowed to use the serial port, even though "Answer calls" is selected. In effect, the "Answer calls" option is temporarily disabled when another program is using the serial port. When the program is finished, Remote Access reenables the Macintosh to answer calls. If you have Serial Port Arbitrator installed and aren't experiencing any serial port problems, leave it installed!

Conflicts with Serial Port Arbitrator   Unfortunately, some programs are not compatible with this extension. In this case, when they try to access a serial port (such as when printing), you will either get the message that says the serial port is "in use" (despite the presence of the Arbitrator extension) or the Macintosh may freeze altogether. In these cases, one of the following options should solve the problem:

- Remove the Serial Port Arbitrator file from the Extensions folder and restart.
- Turn off the "Answer calls" option from the Remote Access Setup control panel, if you don't need that option for the moment (see Figure 11-33).
- Disable the Remote Access Setup control panel altogether, until you plan to use ARA again. Typically, use a startup management utility (such as Extensions Manager) to do this (see Fix-It #4). Then restart.

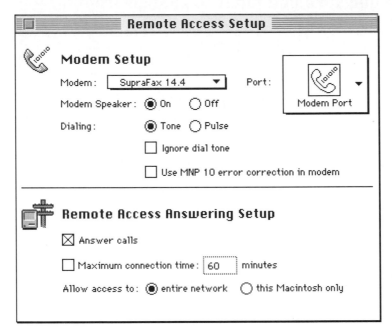

Figure 11-33   The Remote Access Setup control panel. Answer calls option is checked. A Supra modem is selected

Miscellaneous Other Problems

Can't Locate a Communication Command Language (CCL) Script   To use ARA over a modem, you must select the name of your modem from the Modem Setup area of the Remote Access Setup control panel (see Figure 11-33). What modems are listed here are determined by special files, called CCLs, that are located in your Extensions folder. ARA comes with a selection of CCLs and automatically installs them in your Extensions folder when you first install ARA. However, the selection list may not include your particular modem. If this is the case, check the software that came with your modem; it may include a CCL file that you can use. If not, call the modem company for advice. By the way, unless you plan to connect to a variety of different modems on different occasions, you can delete all CCLs other than the one for your modem.

Can't Connect to a Remote Mac Because It Is Turned Off   To use ARA to call your desktop Mac from your PowerBook, your desktop Macintosh must be turned on. But what if you forgot to leave it on when you left your office (or just don't want to leave it on all the time, so as to save energy and money)? Fortunately, there is a solution. There is a device, called PowerKey Remote (from Sophisticated Circuits, 800-827-4669), that will automatically turn on a Macintosh when a phone call comes in and turn it off again when the caller hangs up.

Check for More General File-Sharing or Modem Problems   Your problem may not be specific to ARA.

SEE: • "Can't Get File Sharing to Work" earlier in this chapter
       • "Can't Get a Modem (or Serial Port) to Work" earlier in this chapter

Problems Caused by Incompatible Software   Upgrade the relevant software.

SEE: • Take Note: Upgrade Network and Communications Software

---

TAKE NOTE ▶

UPGRADE NETWORK AND COMMUNICATIONS SOFTWARE

- *File sharing and Apple Remote Access problems*   *AppleTalk is built-in to all system software. There is no AppleTalk file in your System Folder; it is actually contained within the System file itself. However, Apple periodically releases an upgrade disk, called Network Software Installer, available from various online services, which may contain a later version of AppleTalk than the one that came with your system software. If you are having any problems with file sharing or ARA, it's worth using this Installer disk to upgrade your software. For example, early versions of AppleTalk are known not to work with ARA. True, ARA itself installs a version of AppleTalk, which is compatible and should thus solve this problem. However, you may have inadvertently later installed an earlier version via some other communications-related software's Installer. While reinstalling AppleTalk from the ARA disks should solve this particular problem, using the latest version of the Network Software Installer guarantees that you have the least buggy, most generally compatible version available.*

    To find out what version of AppleTalk you have installed, check the listing in the Network control panel (see Figure 11-31 again). For ARA, you need version 57.0.1 or later.

    By the way, should a problem with ARA lead you to decide to remove it from your disk entirely, use the ARA Installer disk to do so. (If it still uses the old-style Installer, you need to select Customize, then hold down the Option key; the Install button should change to a Remove button. For the newer Installer, simply select Custom Remove from the pop-up menu.) This is the safest way to make sure you are removing all relevant software.

- *Modem problems (and more ARA problems)*   *For any modem problems, including those involving ARA, make sure you are using the latest version of the Communications Toolbox extensions. This is software, made by Apple, that provides a standard set of tools for interacting with a modem. You can recognize Toolbox extensions because they typically have icons in the shape of a jigsaw puzzle piece and their names end in the word Tool (such as Serial Tool). Most communication programs now use the Toolbox and include the software as part of their package. However, you may have several applications that use this software, each shipping with a different version of the Toolbox. If so, you may have*

    (continued)

deleted a newer version and installed an older one. To correct this, find the disk with the newest version and reinstall it. Otherwise, you can purchase Toolbox upgrades directly from Apple (see Fix-It #18 for general information on ordering from Apple).

By the way, by the time you read this Apple will have probably completely replaced its Communication Toolbox technology with a newer technology called Open Transport, which is designed to more flexibly accommodate the variety of different types of communication connections now in use.

To avoid problems specific to Apple's Express Modem, make sure you are using the latest version of the Express Modem software (at least version 1.1). For example, with an older version of the Express software, the PowerBook may freeze if it goes to sleep while you are accessing a remote network via ARA. Actually, the Express Modem has been a source of a variety of problems (such as the one corrected by the Duo Battery Patch, as described in the "Problems Running on Battery Power" section earlier in this chapter). These problems have been especially frustrating for many Duo users since, until recently, the Express Modem was the only internal modem they could use. Happily, most of these problems are now solved by using the latest Express software upgrade.

On a related note, users of Apple's GeoPort Telecom Adapter (see Fix-It #1 on AV features) have also had more than their share of problems. This is probably at least partially due to the fact that using the GeoPort as a modem depends on Apple's Express Modem software. That's also why, in order to use the GeoPort as a modem, you need to select Express Modem, rather than External Modem, from the Express Modem control panel.

Chapter Summary

After a brief description of the different types of PowerBooks, this chapter detailed those PowerBook features that either are unique to PowerBooks or are used much more often with PowerBooks than with desktop Macs. These included battery conservation features, using the Control Strip, RAM disks, and connecting an external monitor as a second screen. This was followed by a selection of problems and solutions related to these features.

The chapter concluded with a discussion of how to transfer files between a PowerBook and another Macintosh, as well as the problems that can occur when doing this. This led into explanations of SCSI connections, file sharing, and remote access via a modem. While some of these issues are not entirely specific to PowerBooks, this chapter focused on those aspects that were PowerBook-specific.

Chapter 12

What's New: Power Macs, System 7.5, and Beyond

New Technology, New Problems

Pundits may claim that Apple needs to revamp its operating system by yesterday in order to keep pace with the competition. Critics may carp that Apple is no longer on the cutting edge of computer innovation. My guess is that most end users have a somewhat different view. To them, keeping up with all of Apple's latest developments (assuming they even bother to try) gets more difficult with each year. It's not only that changes are appearing at an ever-increasing rate. It's the exponentially growing number of directions where the changes are going. Want a sampling of what I am talking about? Try these terms out for size: GeoPort, IDE, PCI, built-in Ethernet, PlainTalk, PowerTalk, QuickDraw GX, OpenDoc, Open Transport. If you are still uncertain about what some (or all!) of these terms mean or how they will affect your use of your Macintosh, you are not alone.

The bright side is that you can still buy a Macintosh, easily set it up, and start using it effectively, without ever bothering to learn about most of this stuff. Still, as you start to add peripherals or hook up to a network or get into multimedia applications or expand your use of the Macintosh in almost any way, understanding these new technologies will become increasingly important.

Most of these innovations are at least briefly mentioned elsewhere in this book, as they are relevant to a particular troubleshooting topic. However, there are two particular recent developments, one in hardware and the other in software, that have such far-reaching consequences and affect such a broad range of users, that they demand more in-depth attention: Power Macintoshes and System 7.5 (with a special emphasis on QuickDraw GX). Covering these two topics is the purpose of this chapter. This chapter is not intended to be a general introduction to these topics. The focus, as always, remains on what you need to know for troubleshooting.

Power Macintosh Basics

What Makes a Power Mac Different from Other Macs?

The main thing that is new in a Power Macintosh is its processor. Instead of using the line of Motorola 680x0 processors that have been in every Macintosh from its inception, Power Macs introduce a new line of processors, also developed by Motorola, called *PowerPC processors*. Over time, you will see different variations and generations of the PowerPC processor, just as there were for the 680x0 line. Each variation will have its own unique name: PowerPC 601 versus PowerPC 603 for example.

While we are throwing around new terminology, you might as well know that all PowerPC processors are referred to as RISC processors (which stands for Reduced Instruction Set Computing). The 680x0 processors were CISC (Complex Instruction Set Computing) processors. You might think that CISC is somehow a superior approach (aren't more advanced computers also more complex?), but this is not the case here. The current thought is that the RISC approach is the better alternative. That is why Apple made the switch.

And what makes these PowerPC RISC processors better? Well, for one thing, they tend to be easier and cheaper to manufacture. That's at least great for Apple (and may ultimately translate into lower computer prices for you). More important, they are faster—much faster. For example, the fastest Quadra topped out at about 40 MHz (recall from Chapter 1 that MHz is the measure of a computer's speed). The slowest Power Mac starts at 60 MHz. Actually, the full name of the model gives you its speed. For example, the Power Mac 6100/60 runs at 60 MHz while the 7100/66 runs at 66 MHz. Compared to 680x0 Macintoshes, this speed difference is more than just a marginal increase. It is a quantum leap forward. When performing the same task, a Power Mac can be more than thirty times faster than a Mac Classic, and at least twice as fast as the fastest Quadra.

Now, some of you may say, "So what? What good is a faster Mac for my word processing? My current Mac already works faster than I can type." That's true. But imagine being able to spell-check a long document in one tenth the time it takes now. Or imagine being able to apply a filter in Photoshop in seconds rather than minutes. And most important, imagine being able to do things on a Mac that were previously impossible, because of speed limitations. For example, consider that in the original version of QuickTime, the size of the movie image had to be quite small, because the Macintosh could not process the information produced by a larger image fast enough to get smooth movement. With Power Macs, smooth full-screen video will be common.

BY THE WAY ▶

UPGRADING YOUR 680x0 MAC TO A POWER MAC

Some 680x0 Macintoshes can be upgraded to a Power Mac. There are typically two ways to do this: either via an upgrade card or via a logic board replacement. Both methods, of course, include the essential PowerPC processor. However, the logic board upgrade includes some additional Power Mac features (such as PlainTalk speech recognition) not included with the upgrade card. As you might guess, the logic board upgrade is considerably more expensive.

Running in Emulation Mode Versus Native Mode

To me, the single most amazing thing about Power Macintoshes is that when you first sit down to use one, they do not seem any different from 680x0 Macintoshes. I mean this in the positive sense; that is, the Finder and the desktop are still there and work the same way they always have. Almost all the software that runs on older Macs still runs on Power Macs. At this level, the fact that you are using a completely different processor seems almost irrelevant. In other words, a Power Macintosh is still a Macintosh.

To fully appreciate the significance of this accomplishment, consider this: Software is written to match a particular processor. This means that software written for a

680x0 processor should not be able to run on a machine using a PowerPC processor. Thus, a person upgrading to a Power Macintosh would be faced with the prospect of having to throw out all of his or her existing software. Not at all a happy prospect! Apple solved this dilemma by including a *68040 emulator* in the ROM of all Power Macintoshes. This emulator is essentially a set of instructions that allows the Power Mac, when needed, to imitate a 680x0 Macintosh. This is why a Power Mac can still run almost all of your old software.

When you launch an application, the Power Macintosh automatically determines whether the application is written for a 680x0 Macintosh or a Power Macintosh. If it is a 680x0 application, the Power Mac shifts into *emulation mode.* If it is a Power Mac application (also referred to as a *native code* application), the Power Mac shifts into *native mode.* In native mode, the PowerPC processor is used directly, without any intermediary emulation. The Power Mac can even accommodate software in which part of the software's code is native while other parts are not, again switching modes automatically and transparently as needed. (Unfortunately, this compatibility across machines is a one-way street: There is no way to run Power Mac software on a 680x0 Mac.)

This isn't to say that there is no cost to using emulation mode. The main problem with emulation mode is that you lose the PowerPC processor's speed advantage—which was the primary rationale for developing the Power Mac in the first place. Emulation mode, almost by definition, can be no faster than the speed of the 680x0 Macs that it is emulating. Actually, running software in emulation mode on a Power Mac can result in *slower* speeds than running the same software on a true 68040 Macintosh. This was particularly true of the first generation of Power Macintoshes, released in 1994. However, in 1995, when Apple introduces its new line of Power Macs, it will include an updated version of System 7.5 together with an improved version of the emulator, that will double the speed. This means that Power Macs could equal or outperform all 680x0 Macs, even in emulation mode.

Still, emulation mode can never equal the performance you can get when running in native mode. So ideally, you want all your software to be native code applications. When the Power Mac was first released, there was virtually no native software available. It took until 1995 before the floodgates finally opened. Now, almost all popular software has a native version.

Even if you are running a native application, you will still not necessarily get the maximum speed benefit you might expect. This is because, you may be shifted into emulation mode even when using a native application. There are a two main reasons for this.

First, even in System 7.5, much of the system software is still not written in native code. This is important because system software kicks in regularly while using almost any application. For example, opening and saving documents are typically handled by system software, not by the application itself. Thus, even when running a native application, you will be temporarily switched to emulation mode when you open or save a document. There is a double penalty here. Not only are things slowed down as a result of being in emulation mode, however briefly, but just the act of switching from one mode to another slows things down a bit. The more often you switch back and forth, the more of a slow-down penalty you pay. Also, the Finder is still not written in native code. This means that whenever you go to the desktop (which is almost always lurking behind your application windows), you go into emulation mode.

Second, many third-party extensions and control panels still run in emulation mode. If the extension is active while a native application is in use, this too will result in temporary switches into emulation mode with resulting slow downs.

The ultimate solution here is to wait for all system software and popular extensions to be rewritten in native mode. This is probably still a couple of years away.

Power Macintosh Native Software

Upgrading to Native Software

If you own a 680x0 Macintosh and replace it with a Power Mac, you will likely transfer your current software to your new machine. This means you will be mostly running the Power Mac in emulation mode. Even if you find that a given application runs satisfactorily in emulation mode, you should probably still upgrade to the native version when possible. Otherwise, you are not taking full advantage of what your hardware can do.

Happily, as companies come out with native versions of their software, most of them are making the upgrades available free or at some nominal charge. Others are rolling the native version into their next overall major upgrade and charging no more than they would for any regular upgrade. A couple of companies are not as nice, charging $100 or more for an upgrade that is nothing more than a native code conversion. Oh well.

Of course, you may decide that some rarely used programs are not worth paying to upgrade. And some programs may never get rewritten for the Power Mac. Still, long-time Mac users are likely to be faced with some serious upgrading. Even new Mac users, whose first Mac is a Power Mac, will still likely acquire some non-native software, upgrading it later.

Buying and Installing Native Software

As Power Macs become more prevalent, there will be more and more software that is written just for the Power Mac, with no 680x0-compatible version (especially likely for software that needs the speed of a Power Mac to be effective). However, for now, virtually all software written in native code also has a 680x0 equivalent.

Sometimes, companies sell the two different versions separately—forcing you to make two separate purchases to get both versions (as you might need to do if you own a desktop Power Mac and a 680x0 PowerBook). This approach is thankfully quite rare.

More typically, one purchase gets you both versions. They may come on two separate sets of disks or they may come on a single set with a Installer utility from which you choose which version to install. In the latter case, if you select Easy Install (or an equivalent command), it will automatically install the correct version for your hardware.

In some cases, the Installer may give you the option to install a special version of the application that combines both the 680x0 and Power Mac code. This is called a *fat binary* application. This has the advantage of allowing the same version of the program to run on either type of machine. However, these fat versions, as their name implies, take up more disk space. Some programs may be available only as a fat binary version, in which case you have no choice but to use it.

Is It Native or Not?

Most native code software will identify itself as "Accelerated for Power Macintosh" right on its package and/or manual. But suppose you have an application already installed on your Macintosh and you are not sure whether or not it is native code. How could you quickly find out? Just open its Get Info window. If you see a message at the bottom of the window saying how turning on (or off) virtual memory will decrease (or increase) the memory requirements for the application (see Figure 12-1), the application is native.

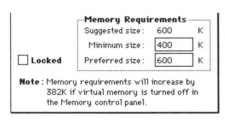

Figure 12-1
A message like the one at the bottom of this Get Info window indicates that you are running in native mode

There is one exception here: The appearance of these messages depends on the presence of the PowerPC Finder Update extension in the Extensions folder of your System Folder. If it is not present, or if you disable it (such as by holding down the Shift key at startup), these messages will not appear.

BY THE WAY ▶

UTILITIES TELL YOU WHEN YOU ARE RUNNING NATIVE

As described in the main text, your Mac can slip back and forth between emulation mode and native mode, even when running a native application. If you want to find out precisely when your Mac is or is not in native mode, check out a freeware extension called PowerPeek. It puts a little "light" in your menu bar that flashes green when the Mac is in native mode and red when it's in emulation mode. This not only gives you an indication of when mode switching occurs, it can confirm whether a supposed native mode application is really running in native mode.

Another shareware utility, PowerPCheck, can check any selected application and report whether or not it contains native PowerPC code.

Virtual Memory and Native Software

Programs running in native mode require significantly *less* RAM (as much as several megabytes less) with virtual memory turned on than they would with it off. This is the implication of the Get Info messages just described in the previous section. You don't need to allocate much virtual memory to achieve this application memory benefit (just 1 or 2MB should be enough; not the double amount that is the Memory control panel's default selection). When you turn on or off virtual memory (and restart), the numbers in the memory requirements boxes will shift accordingly. Check it out.

Helpful Hint: Without the PowerPC Finder Update extension, the numbers listed in the memory requirements boxes will remain the same whether or not virtual memory is on. In particular, these numbers will be incorrect when virtual memory is off; the application will actually need more memory than indicated.

In general, whereas using virtual memory is often of dubious benefit on older Macs (because of disk space requirements and possible slow downs), it is strongly recommended for use on Power Macs. In fact, running a native application on a Power Mac with virtual memory off may require significantly more memory than running the non-native version of the same application! Even with virtual memory on, native versions can be memory hogs (check out Excel 5.0 if you want a dramatic example of this).

By the way, if you use RAM Doubler, it has the same benefit on application memory requirements as does using virtual memory. Even better, because RAM Doubler tries to store information in RAM that System 7's virtual memory stores on disk, you should find RAM Doubler to be faster than using System 7's virtual memory. Just be sure you are using a Power Mac–compatible version of RAM Doubler (version 1.5 or later), and turn off the Mac's virtual memory.

SEE: • Fix-It #6 for more on the Memory control panel, virtual memory, and RAM Doubler

---

TECHNICALLY SPEAKING ▶

WHY DO NATIVE APPLICATIONS NEED LESS RAM WHEN VIRTUAL MEMORY IS ON?

Skipping over some really technical details (which are not relevant to your troubleshooting efforts anyway), here's the basic idea: Native code applications are written in a new way that allows the Mac to perform a neat trick when virtual memory is on. With 680x0 applications, there is a certain amount of data that must be loaded into memory (physical and/or virtual) before the application can even open. There is a similar requirement for native software when launched with virtual memory off. However, with virtual memory on, a significantly smaller portion of this information is loaded into memory (actually it goes exclusively to physical RAM). Additionally, a "map" of the remaining data that would normally be loaded is created

(continued)

on the area of the disk used by virtual memory. This map points to the locations within the application file (as stored on the main part of the disk) that the Mac needs to go to find the data. This map takes up a lot less space than if the actual data had been loaded. This is the source of the memory savings.

A side effect of this is that application developers must now ensure that their applications are not self-modifying in any way. Otherwise, if the file on the disk is altered while the application is open, the map in memory may no longer be accurate. System crashes would likely result.

By the way, the Total Memory size, as listed in the About This Macintosh window, may be larger than expected when virtual memory is on. This is not a cause for concern; everything will still work fine (although you really don't have the extra memory). The mislisting is a consequence of the presence of the 68040 emulator causing the Power Mac to make an incorrect calculation.

Solve It! Power Macintosh Problems

For general problems with running in emulation mode or managing memory, check out the previous section on Power Macintosh Basics. What follows is an assorted collection of more specific problems and solutions.

Compatibility and Memory Problems

 Symptoms:

- A program will not run on any Power Mac, although it appears to run fine on other Macintosh models.

- A program runs slower on a Power Mac than on other types of Macintoshes.

 Causes:

The most likely cause of these problems is that the software in question is a non-native code version, forcing the Mac to run in emulator mode. Even though the Power Mac's 68040 emulator should permit most non-native software to run correctly, some compatibility problems will inevitably occur.

Other related causes include problems with memory management or with special extensions.

Running in emulator mode also means that you will not get the full speed advantage of using a Power Mac. In many cases, the emulator speed may be slower than running the same software on a 68040 Mac.

SEE: • "Running in Emulation Mode Versus Native Mode" earlier in this chapter

 ## What to do:

Emulation Mode Problems

Extensions/Control Panels That Are Not Native   Control panels and extensions running in emulator mode can cause unexpected slow downs. For example, versions of ATM (Adobe Type Manager) prior to 3.8 run in emulator mode. ATM is active any time a program, such as a word processor, needs it for the display or printing of text. This means that the Mac will be shifting into emulator mode for ATM even if the application itself is in native code. This can cause a slow down of as much as 15 percent or more.

The solution is to use native versions of all INITs, whenever possible. In the case of ATM, use version 3.8 or later.

Programs That Need a Math Coprocessor (FPU)   The Power Mac's 68040 emulator is technically a 68LC040 emulator. The relevance of this is that this flavor of 68040 processor does not include an FPU (floating point unit, also called a math coprocessor). This means that non-native versions of programs that use the FPU, such as much statistics and scientific software, will run much slower on a Power Mac than on a 68040 Mac with an FPU. In the worst cases, the program may not run at all, giving you a "No FPU Installed" or "No FPU Present" error message.

You may be able to partially solve this problem by using an FPU emulator called Software FPU (see Fix-It #1), but don't count on it. The best solution is to get the native code upgrade to your problem application (hopefully, there is such an upgrade!).

By the way, your Power Mac does have an FPU. It is built in to all PowerPC processors. But this can only be accessed by programs running in native mode.

Programs That Can't Run with the Modern Memory Manager   Memory management is handled differently by Power Macs from the way it was with previous Mac models. It now uses something called the Modern Memory Manager. Among other benefits, this new manager should reduce memory-related system errors. However, some non-native software is incompatible with this manager. So, if you are having trouble using a particular non-native program, trying turning off the Modern Memory Manager. To do this, open the Memory control panel and click the appropriate off button (see Figure 12-2).

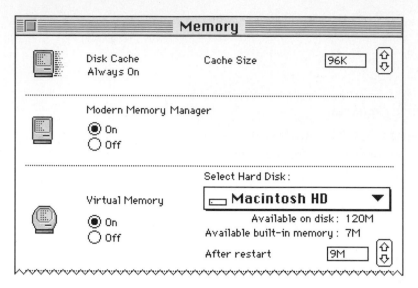

Figure 12-2 Turning off the Memory control panel's Modern Memory Manager may eliminate a compatibility problem

By the way, the Memory control panel for a Power Mac no longer has an option for turning off 32-bit addressing (which has traditionally been another source of memory-related incompatibilities). With a Power Mac, 32-bit addressing is always on.

SEE: • Fix-It #6 for more on the Memory control panel

A "No FPU Present" False Alarm   A program may fail to open or it may unexpectedly quit, followed by a message that identifies the problem as "no FPU present." In most cases this relates to the absence of an FPU in the 68LC040 emulator (as just previously described). However, this can occasionally happen even if the program does not access an FPU. In this case, the problem is most likely related to compatibility problems with the Modern Memory Manager. Once again, the solution is to turn the Modern Memory Manager off.

SEE: • Fix-It #1 for more on FPU problems
      • "Type 11 System Errors" in the next section of this chapter

QuickTime   Playing QuickTime movies on a Power Mac, in addition to requiring the QuickTime extension itself, also requires an extension called QuickTime Power-Plug. Make sure it is installed and enabled.

Totally Incompatible Software   Some software (even ones that don't access an FPU) will just not run in emulator mode under any circumstances. If all previous attempts fail to resolve the problem, you will probably have to give up on the software. If there is a native code upgrade available or coming soon, get it!

The Power Macintosh ReadMe file (it should be on the hard drive of your Power Macintosh) includes a variety of specific incompatibility and related troubleshooting information. Check it out for further advice.

Memory Problems

System software tends to require more memory on a Power Macintosh than it would require on a 680x0 Macintosh. This means that you might find that there is not enough unused memory left to open an application on a Power Mac, even though the same application could open on a 680x0 Mac running the same system software. The standard techniques to make more free memory available (as described in Fix-It #6) may help here, but ultimately this difference across machines will remain.

Also recall that, for a native application, keeping virtual memory off will increase its memory requirements, possibly preventing a given application from opening. So keep virtual memory on. In any case, native software tends to require more memory than the 680x0 version of the same program. Nothing can be done about this. Ultimately, you will have to face the basic fact that Power Macs need more memory than 680x0 Macs.

SEE: • "Virtual Memory and Native Software," earlier in this chapter, for more details

Shared Library Problems

Power Macintosh native applications increasingly use a new technology called *shared* (or *import*) *libraries.* This is a method designed to minimize the need to have the same code in RAM more than once at the same time. Thus, if two programs use essentially the same code, it can be stored in a special shared library file that both programs can access (called *dynamic linking*).

While this should help to reduce the total amount of RAM needed to keep multiple applications open, the memory requirements listed in an application's Get Info don't include any extra memory that may be needed to access a shared library. Thus, you may need more memory to open an application than the Get Info window would suggest. In some cases, this may mean that you do not have enough available memory to open the application.

SEE: • Fix-It #6 on how to solve problems due to insufficient available memory

If a needed shared library file is missing from your hard drive, this too can prevent an application from opening. If this happens, try reinstalling the application software, making sure to use the application's Installer utility (if it includes one) and carefully following the directions given. This should get the needed library file on to your disk.

Shared Library Manager Extension   Prior to System 7.5, using shared libraries required having the Shared Library Manager extension installed. This extension should be in your System Folder if you have installed any software that requires it. Typically it is installed when you run the program's Installer utility. The Installer utility may also make related modifications to the System file itself. So it is important that you use the Installer utility, rather than simply dragging the Shared Library Manager extension to the System Folder.

Starting with System 7.5, the Shared Library Manager code is built into the basic system software and the separate extension is no longer needed.

By the way, there is a similarly named (and similarly functioning) extension called Shared Code Manager. This is not part of Apple's system software, but is a Microsoft extension that is used in conjunction with some Microsoft applications.

Shared Libraries on Power Macs Versus 680x0 Macs   Shared library technology is not limited to use on Power Macs. It can be used by other Mac models as well. However, at least prior to the release of System 7.5, it was used most often in conjunction with Power Macs. This is partially because the design of Power Macintosh native software depends more directly on shared libraries. In fact, you may have library files in your Extensions folder, such as AppleScriptLib and ObjectSupportLib, that are only used by Power Macintoshes.

BY THE WAY ▶

ICONS DISAPPEAR FROM THE FINDER'S DESKTOP

For some reason, Finder icons on a Power Mac's desktop can be moved beyond the edges of the screen, so that you can no longer see them. If you suspect this may have happened, click on any visible icon on the desktop and then select Clean Up Desktop from the Finder's Special menu (with the Option key held down if it doesn't work without it). This should get the icons to return.

Startup and System Crash Problems

 Symptoms:

- A system crash or other unusual event occurs at startup.
- A system crash occurs at any other time.

 Causes:

Power Macs, of course, are subject to the same system crash and startup problems that plague all Macintoshes. Thus, most likely the cause and solution for your problem will be found in the earlier parts of this book that are devoted to these subjects: Chapters 4 and 5.

However, a few startup and system crash problems are unique to Power Macs. Exact causes vary. Several common examples are summarized in the What to do section that follows.

What to do:

Power Macintosh Crashes on Startup

Make sure you are using a compatible version of the system software. The Power Mac requires System 7.1.2 or a later version. Power Macs will not work with earlier versions of the system software. System 7.1.2 is not restricted to use on Power Macs; it will work with any Mac that can run System 7.

BY THE WAY ▶

NEW STARTUP SOUNDS ON POWER MACINTOSHES

As soon as you turn it on, you know you are running a Power Mac because the Welcome to Macintosh screen says Welcome to Power Macintosh. There is also a new startup sound unique to the Power Mac series.

On a less friendly note, Power Macs also have a new startup crash sound, the one usually associated with a sad Mac appearing on your screen. It sounds like a car crash.

SEE: • **Chapter 5 for more on sad Macs and unusual startup sounds**

BY THE WAY ▶

POWER MACINTOSHES AND CD-ROM STARTUP DISKS

Power Macs all ship with a Power Macintosh CD-ROM disk that includes a System Folder and can be used as a startup disk if you have an Apple CD-ROM drive. This disk is especially useful as an alternate startup disk for those times when your hard disk crashes at startup. Your Mac will boot from your Power Macintosh CD-ROM if you insert it at startup and hold down the C key.

SEE: • **Chapter 5 for more on using a CD-ROM disk as an alternate startup disk**

Power Mac Crashes When You Press the Command Key

A Power Mac may crash when you press the Command key, particularly with Power Macs that can be turned on via the Power On keyboard key (such as is the case for the 7100 and 8100). This is indirectly due to a bug that is invoked if you hold down the Power On key too long at startup. This causes the Mac to "see" the Power On key as pressed down all the time. When you later press the Command key, it thus thinks that you have simultaneously pressed the Command and Power On keys. This is one of those key combinations that acts as a substitute for pressing the Interrupt button. The result is not really a system crash. You actually wind up getting the debugger window. If this happens, you can probably exit the debugger simply by pressing G and Return. Otherwise, you will have to restart. In general, to avoid this problem, do not keep your finger down on the Power On button at startup. Press it once lightly and let go.

SEE: • Chapter 4 for more on the Interrupt function

Type 11 (Hardware Exception) System Errors

Type 11 system errors are more common on a Power Macintosh than on other Mac models. This is because a common source for this error is corruption of the Power Mac's 68040 emulator as it loads into RAM. Sometimes simply restarting can cure this problem. However, the emulator can get corrupted by incompatible software, in which case you will not be able to use the problem software. Defective hardware may occasionally be a cause here as well.

PowerPC Enabler and System Errors

If you are using System 7.1.2, your Power Mac needs the *PowerPC Enabler* in order to startup. No enabler is needed in System 7.5 for the first generation of Power Macs. However, for Power Macs released in late 1994 or later, a new version of the PowerPC Enabler (currently version 1.1.1) is required.

If you are using System 7.1.2, be aware that there are several usable versions of the PowerPC Enabler, each newer one designed to fix bugs with the previous version. To avoid trouble, make sure you are using the latest available version. However, truth be told, even the most recent version (as of this writing) is still known to cause problems. For example, the enabler's "video bug" will cause a system crash if you launch Fusion-Recorder on an AV Power Mac, with color level set to its maximum depth.

Also note that the System 7.1 Power Macintosh Disk Tools disk includes a special enabler named Minimal PowerPC Enabler. This is not the same as the standard enabler and should never be used as a substitute for the standard enabler on a hard disk.

SEE: • Fix-It #5 for more on enablers

Monitor Problems

Symptoms:

Your monitor either does not connect to or does not work with a Power Macintosh. No such problem occurs when using the monitor with a 680x0 Macintosh.

Causes:

Causes are described as part of the What to do section that follows.

What to do:

The Ghost Monitor Problem   If you have a Power Macintosh with an AV card installed, and your monitor is attached to the Power Mac's built-in video jack, the Mac may mistakenly think you also have a monitor attached through the AV card input jack. This will be apparent when you open the Monitors control panel and see two monitors indicated. What to do to avoid this ghost monitor is described in the ReadMe file that accompanies all Power Macintoshes. Check it out if needed.

SEE: • Chapter 10 for more on the Monitors control panel

Sync-on-Green Problem   Some non-Apple monitors are incompatible with Power Macintoshes (as well as AV 680x0 Macintoshes) because of something called the "sync-on-green" problem. Ask your dealer about this before purchasing a monitor. Don't buy a monitor that may have this problem.

SEE: • Fix-It #17 for more details on the sync-on-green and other monitor-related problems

Monitor Cable Adapter Needed   Some monitors need a special cable adapter in order to attach to the new monitor port on the back of the Power Macintosh. This adapter should come with your Power Macintosh.

System 7.5 Basics

What's New?

Apple proclaims that System 7.5 adds more than 50 new features to System 7. Despite this, the jump from System 7.1 to System 7.5 is not a difficult one to make. Most software that runs on System 7.0 and System 7.1 will work just as well on System 7.5. The major reason for this is that most of System 7.5's new features are in the form of extensions and control panels, rather than fundamental changes to the basic operating system.

Actually, several of System 7.5's so-called new features were previously available from Apple as optional add-ons for System 7.1. For example, System 7.5 includes AppleScript, PowerTalk, and QuickTime, all previously packaged as part of System 7 Pro (though System 7.5 does add the significant benefit of a scriptable Finder). Similarly, System 7.5's Drag and Drop capability is an expanded version of a feature first introduced in System 7 Pro. System 7.5's General Controls control panel adds "new" features that were already included with the special version of the system software that shipped with Performas (now both standard Macintoshes and Performas use the same version of System 7.5). The PowerBook Control Strip included with System 7.5 was already shipping with several PowerBook models even before the release of System 7.5. And so it goes. PowerBook File Assistant, ColorSync, Macintosh Easy Open, Macintosh PC Exchange, Extensions Manager, and MacTCP are all Apple products that predate the arrival of System 7.5.

Many of the remaining new features of System 7.5 are programs (mostly shareware) that Apple adopted from third parties. These include Find File, Apple Menu Options, the menu-bar clock from Date & Time, and WindowShade.

BY THE WAY ▶

USING SYSTEM 7.5 UTILITIES IN SYSTEM 7.1

Many of the new enhancements in System 7.5 work just as well in System 7.1. These include, for example, the PowerBook Control Strip, the new Find File feature and WindowShade. If you aren't ready to move up to the full System 7.5, but you want some of these features, try using them with your current software. They will probably work (although Apple officially recommends against doing this).

About the only things that are *really* new about System 7.5 are Apple Guide and QuickDraw GX. Still, System 7.5's enhancements (new and old) represent a good value overall and I would recommend that most users upgrade to System 7.5 (especially if you don't already have the previously available software that is now included as standard).

Most of the new features of System 7.5, to the extent that they are relevant to trouble-shooting, have already been described elsewhere in this book (as listed in Table 12-1).

Table 12-1 Where Else to Find Information on "New" System 7.5 Features

Apple Guide	Chapter 1 and later in this chapter
Shut Down Items folder	Chapter 1 (p. 26) and "By the Way: If Items in Your Shutdown Items Folder Do Not Run at Shut Down," later in this chapter (p.550)
Find File	Chapter 2 (p. 47) and Chapter 6 (p. 206)
Shut Down DA	Chapter 4, "Take Note: Power On, Power Off" (p. 101)
WindowShade, Finder Hiding, and Documents Folder	Chapter 6, "Take Note: System 7.5, Now Utilities, and More: Helping You Find Your Way" (p. 210)
Macintosh PC Exchange	Chapter 6 (p. 235) and Fix-It #15 (p. 775)
Macintosh Easy Open	Chapter 6 (p. 229) and Fix-It #9 (p. 708)
Apple Menu Options	Chapter 6 (p. 210)
General Controls control panel	Chapter 6 (pp. 210, 214)
Application Folder Protection and System Folder Protection	Chapter 6, "Take Note: Files Locked by the Performa or by System 7.5's General Control Panel" (p. 244)
Macintosh Drag and Drop and Clippings	Chapters 9 and 10 (pp. 397, 434)
QuickDraw GX printing	Chapter 7 (p. 268) and later in this chapter (pp. 557–570, 578–585)
QuickDraw GX fonts	Chapter 9 (p. 365) and later in this chapter (pp. 571–575, 586–587)
QuickDraw GX Clipboard	Chapters 9 (p. 397) and 10 (p. 434) and later in this chapter (pp. 575–576)
Revised Scrapbook	Chapter 10 (p. 434)
ColorSync	Chapter 10 (p. 451)
Control Strip, File Assistant, revised PowerBook control panels	Chapter 11 (pp. 464–470, 506)
Extensions Manager	Fix-It #4 (pp. 611–613)
New Installer utility	Fix-It #5 (p. 641)
MacTCP	Fix-It #18 (p. 829)

Getting Help from System 7.5

Apple's System 7.5 disks include three important sources of troubleshooting assistance. Before searching through this book for answers regarding problems with System 7.5 (especially to narrowly focused problems not likely to be covered here), check out the following:

Read Me Files

Read Me files have always been included with system software disks. But they are especially relevant here. In particular, there is a "Read Me" file on the "Before You

Install" disk as well as "Urgent Read Me!" files on the QuickDraw GX and PowerTalk Install disks. You should read these files, as advised, before installing. After installing, further Read Me files (such as "System 7.5 Read Me") will appear on your startup disk. Read these as well. These all contain important information (some of which is described in the sections to follow) about System 7.5 incompatibilities and related special problems. In some cases, such as for AppleScript, the primary documentation is contained on disk.

Safe Install Utility

System 7.5 comes with a disk called "Before You Install" (if you have the CD-ROM disk version of System 7.5, look for a folder called "Before You Install"). In it, is a program called Safe Install Utility (see Figure 12-3). Run this before you install System 7.5. It will identify what software in your System Folder may be incompatible with System 7.5 and will offer to remove them from the System Folder. Do so. If desired, you can later return them, one by one, to see if they really do cause a problem (often they will run okay).

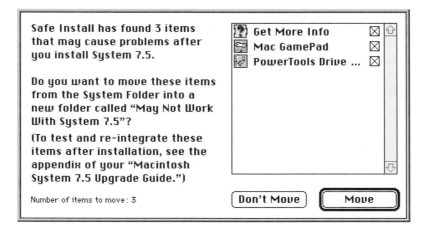

Figure 12-3   The Safe Install Utility

Apple Guide and Balloon Help

The System 7.5 Upgrade Guide is a thin book of just over 100 pages. It is woefully inadequate at describing the new features in System 7.5. I searched in vain for the answers to even simple questions. For example, I went to look for some details on the Input Tray options in QuickDraw GX, but could not even find the term listed in the index, even though it is a menu command in the Printing menu of QuickDraw GX.

Apple's apparent rationale here is to depend on expanded Balloon Help and (especially) on its new Apple Guide interactive help (first described in Chapter 1) rather than on printed documentation. You should be able to get answers to most of your questions from these sources (see Figure 12-4). To access the main Apple Guide listing, go to the Finder and select Macintosh Guide from the Guide menu (formerly called the Balloon Help menu). For some applications (such as PowerBook File Assistant), there are special supplementary Apple Guide files. These files are accessible from the Guide menu only when the relevant application is active.

The easy accessibility and interactive nature of Apple Guide can make it preferable to printed documentation in many situations. Still, there are times that I would prefer printed material. This is primarily because many of Apple Guide's explanations require that you actually carry out an operation in order to find out how to do it. If you just want to learn about something without actually doing it, Apple Guide can be frustrating. It is also quite slow.

Perhaps I shouldn't complain too much. It is just this sort of thing that encourages people to seek out books like this one!

SEE: • Chapter 1 for background on Apple Guide and Balloon Help

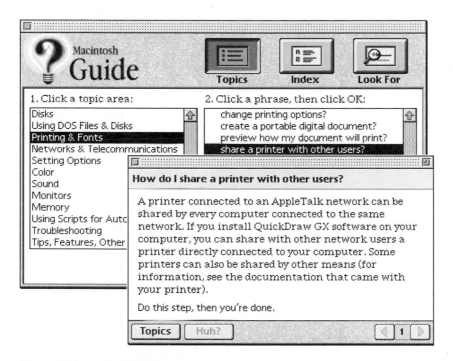

Figure 12-4   Apple Guide

Solve It! System 7.5 Problems

Because System 7.5 (at least without QuickDraw GX installed) is fundamentally not all that different from System 7.1, most of the general troubleshooting advice discussed throughout this book is also relevant to System 7.5. Beyond that, many troubleshooting issues that are unique to System 7.5 are similarly explained in other locations of this book, as indicated in Table 12-1. For example, a problem with Macintosh Easy Open and rebuilding the desktop is covered in Fix-It #9. A problem where PC Exchange may cause a Sad Mac to appear if you also use a removable cartridge drive was mentioned in Chapter 5.

What follows here is troubleshooting advice, specific to System 7.5, that did not fit into these other sections of the book.

Installation Problems

 Symptoms:

The primary symptom is that you are unable to successfully install System 7.5. Related problems that immediately result from a System 7.5 installation are also considered.

 Causes:

This section emphasizes causes that are specific to System 7.5, as detailed in the What to Do section. For more general issues, as well as for explanations of basic concepts (such as clean install and minimal system), see Fix-It #5 on system software problems.

 What to do:

Floppy Disk Versus CD-ROM Versions of the System Software

System 7.5 ships in both a floppy disk and a CD-ROM version. The CD-ROM version includes some bonus software not included on the floppy disk version (none of it essential to the use of System 7.5). Beyond that, the main difference to note in using the CD-ROM disk version is that you do not need to bother inserting and ejecting disks throughout the install process, because the contents of all the floppy disks are stored on the CD-ROM disk in separate folders, accessed by the Installer as needed.

The CD-ROM disk also contains disk images of each floppy disk. You can use these to create a backup set of floppy disks, if desired. You will need Disk Copy to do this (as explained in Fix-It #5, "Take Note: Why Can't I Open the Software I Just Downloaded?").

As of now, the CD-ROM upgrade disk cannot be used as a startup disk (though the CD-ROM disk that comes with a Power Macintosh should be able to act as a startup disk with an Apple CD-ROM). To get around this, the CD-ROM upgrade disk package comes with a Disk Tools floppy disk. You can use this as a startup disk when you can't use or don't wish to use your hard disk as the startup disk.

If, for any reason, you did not get a Disk Tools disk with the System 7.5 CD-ROM disk, you can make your own Disk Tools disk with the Disk Copy utility and the Disk Tools disk image. Both of these files, as well as a text document explaining how to use Disk Copy, are included in the Back-Up CD folder on the System 7.5 CD-ROM disk.

Installing with a Non-Apple CD-ROM Drive

If you are installing System 7.5 from a CD-ROM disk and you do not have an Apple CD-ROM drive, be careful. Normally, you would use your hard disk as a startup disk prior to installation. However, if the installation fails for any reason, you may have to resort to the Disk Tools disk to start up again. If you have an Apple CD-ROM drive, there is no problem, as the CD-ROM driver extension (which is needed to get the Mac to recognize the CD-ROM drive) is included on the Disk Tools disk. However, if you have a non-Apple drive, you may now find that you can no longer access the CD-ROM disk. This would happen if the drive requires its own CD-ROM driver, which of course is not found on the Disk Tools disk. Since you can't access the CD-ROM disk anymore, you can't try again to install System 7.5.

To protect against this happening, make a backup set of System 7.5 floppy disks from the disk image files on the CD-ROM disk (using Disk Copy, as just described in the previous section) before you try to install System 7.5. You can then use these floppy disks if and when you later find that you cannot access the CD-ROM disk. Otherwise, make sure that you have a startup floppy disk that includes the needed CD-ROM driver extension. One way to do this is to delete the Apple CD-ROM extension from the Disk Tools disk and replace it with the driver for your non-Apple CD-ROM.

SEE: • Chapter 5 and Fix-It #16 for more on CD-ROM drivers

Installation Fails

Make Sure You Have Enough Memory and Disk Space   One drawback to System 7.5 is its increased RAM and disk space requirements, as compared to previous versions of the system software. In particular, Apple recommends that you have at least 4Mb of RAM to run System 7.5 (8Mb if you have a Power Macintosh). However, this is just for the basic System 7.5 installation. You have a separate option to install QuickDraw GX and/or PowerTalk. If you install either or both of these, you are expected to have at least 8Mb of RAM (16Mb if you use a Power Mac!). In fact, at least as of this writing, PowerBooks that ship with only 4Mb of RAM still ship with System 7.1 rather than 7.5. You will know immediately if you do not have enough memory to use System 7.5. Without sufficient RAM, the Installer will not even permit the installation to take place, giving you an alert message that informs you of the memory problem. Also, expect a full installation of System 7.5 to take up several more megabytes of disk space than a comparable installation of System 7.1. If you plan to install QuickDraw GX and/or PowerTalk, you will need even more disk space.

Start Up with Extensions Off   If during an installation you have a problem where the Macintosh repeatedly requests that you reinsert Disk 1, restart with extensions off and try again. Similarly, if the Installation fails for any reason, restart with extensions off and try again. Actually, you are best off restarting with extensions off (or starting up from the Install floppy disk, which has no extensions on it) before you try the installation at all!

Turn Off At Ease   If you are using At Ease, turn it off before using the Safe Install Utility as well as before installing System 7.5 and/or QuickDraw GX.

Make Sure System File Can Be Modified   Modifying your System file is required for an update installation (but not a clean install, since this completely replaces the existing System file). Thus, the installation will fail if the System file cannot be modified. If you get a message to this effect, make sure you do not have virus protection on (if you started with all extensions off, this will not be a problem!), because some anti-virus utilities prevent modification of the System file. Otherwise, check if you have the System and/or Finder locked (via the Lock box in the Get Info window) or whether you have Protect System Folder on (as selected in System 7.5's General Controls control panel). If you do, turn these options off in order to unlock/unprotect the files. With these options on, you are prohibited from modifying the System file.

Delete the System File   If the installation still fails, restart from an alternate startup disk (such as the Disk Tools disk), delete the System file and try the installation again. If necessary, do a clean install (by holding down Command-Option-K after the Installer has launched).

Zap the PRAM   How to do this is described in Fix-It #11.

Custom Install Installs Unselected Files

There are reports of a bug in the System 7.5 Installer that results in more files installed than you actually selected to be installed when you do a custom install. If this happens, there is nothing you can do to prevent it. Simply delete the unwanted files from your System Folder when the Installation is complete.

Can't Do a Clean Install

To access the option to initiate a clean reinstall, press Command-Shift-K after the System 7.5 Installer has launched. However, this operation will not succeed if you do not already have a System Folder on your startup disk. Of course, if a System Folder is not on the disk, doing an ordinary install is, in effect, a clean install, so this is not really a problem.

SEE: • Fix-It #5, especially "Take Note: An 'Instant' System 7.5 Clean Reinstall," for more on a clean reinstall

Can't Install on a Floppy Disk

The Minimal System install option on the initial release disks for System 7.5 cannot do an install that is small enough to fit on a 1.44Mb floppy disk. To create a System 7.5 startup floppy disk, copy the System Folder from the Disk Tools disk.

GeoPort Doesn't Work After Upgrading

You need to reinstall the GeoPort software after upgrading to System 7.5.

BY THE WAY ▶

WHERE DID THE NAME OF MY MACINTOSH GO?

After installing System 7.5, you may find that the exact name of your Macintosh model (such as Macintosh IIci or PowerBook 180 or Power Macintosh 6100) is no longer listed in your About This Macintosh window (instead it now simply says: Macintosh, Macintosh PowerBook, or Power Macintosh). Apple says this is a normal consequence of doing a clean install of System 7.5 (using Command-Shift-K, as explained in Fix-It #5), but it is not supposed to happen after a typical update installation. Still, many users report it happens in all cases (see Figure 12-5).

This may seem like a trivial problem (and most often that's all it is). However, some utilities and networking software look for this information to determine model-specific options related to the running of the program. With this information gone, more serious problems can occur. Currently, the best way I know to get the model name back is to use a shareware utility called MacIdentifier.

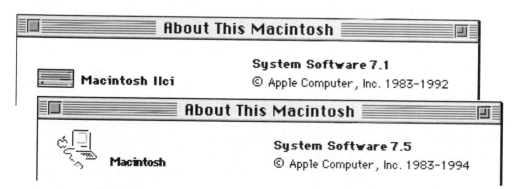

Figure 12-5   The About This Macintosh window before and after upgrading to System 7.5; note that the name of the Macintosh model is missing from the window in System 7.5

Compatibility and Memory Problems

 Symptoms:

- You install System 7.5 but are unable to access certain of its new features. Either the feature simply does not appear or you get an error message when you try to use it (such as an "out of memory" message).
- You have more general trouble using System 7.5, possibly including an inability to startup, even though you had no such problem with your previous version of the system software.

 Causes

In most cases, the problem is due to one of the following causes: insufficient RAM, needed extensions/control panels not installed, applications that are not able to use new System 7.5 features, or conflicts with certain non-Apple extensions and control panels.

 What to do:

Are Extensions and Control Panels Installed (or Deinstalled) as Needed?

The fact that many of System 7.5's new features depend on extensions and control panels can be both a help and a hindrance in troubleshooting. It's helpful in that if you find a problem with almost any of System 7.5's new features, you can probably work around it by disabling the extension or control panel that implements that feature, which is an easier solution than what would be required to solve a problem due to the Finder itself, for example.

SEE: • Fix-It #4 for more on enabling and disabling extensions and control panels

The downside here is that a typical System 7.5 System Folder contains many more extensions and control panels than ever before—and it is not always clear what a particular extension/control panel does or which one(s) you need to include or disable in order to solve a particular problem. To help figure out what an unfamiliar extension does, try turning on Balloon Help and moving the cursor over the extension. If you are lucky, you may get an explanation. *MacUser* and *MacWeek* maintain files in their on-line forums that detail what all the System 7.5 extensions do. Otherwise, here is a sampling of advice that covers some common questions specific to System 7.5.

Make Sure You Have Find File Extension and Finder Scripting Extension   System 7.5 includes a new Find File feature, available both from the Apple menu and from the Finder's File menu. However, to access Find File from the Finder's File menu, you need to have the Find File Extension installed in your Extensions folder.

A slick feature of Find File is that you can drag an item from the Results window list to any location on the desktop. This causes the item to be moved to the new location. However, for this feature to work, you need the Finder Scripting Extension installed in the Extensions folder.

SEE: • Chapter 2 for more on using Find File

Make Sure You Have the Clipping Extension   This is needed to create Clippings files via System 7.5's new Drag and Drop feature (as explained in Chapter 10).

You Don't Need the Shared Library Manager, Thread Manager, or Apple Event Manager Anymore   The Shared Library Manager (used for sharing of data in memory by more than one application), the Thread Manager (used for application multitasking), and Apple Event Manager (used by AppleScript) extensions are no longer needed in System 7.5. They are built into the basic system software. If for some reason you still find these unneeded extensions in your System Folder, it is best to delete them to avoid potential conflicts.

SEE: • "Compatibility Problems," earlier in the "Solve It! Power Macintosh Problems" section of this chapter, for more on the Shared Library Manager

Monitors Extensions Are Not Required   System 7.5 installs an extension specific to your particular model of Macintosh (with names such as IIci/IIsi Monitors Extension, or PowerBook Monitors Extension). These extensions are not essential to use a monitor. Your Mac will still work fine without them. They potentially affect what options are available when you select the Options button from the Monitors control panel.

Don't Use Apple File Exchange   Macintosh PC Exchange (installed as part of System 7.5) is not compatible with Apple File Exchange. If you still have Apple File Exchange on your disk, get rid of it.

Be Careful of SCSI Manager 4.3 Extension   System 7.5 should automatically install SCSI Manager 4.3 Extension on those models that can use it. Normally, this is OK. However, it can cause problems on some Quadra models that should instead use the version that is built in to the ROM. Actually, SCSI Manager 4.3 is associated with a variety of SCSI-related problems. If you are having SCSI problems and this extension is present, try deleting it.

SEE: • Fix-It #16 for more on SCSI Manager 4.3 and SCSI problems in general

Be Careful of Apple Menu Options　The Apple Menu Options control panel adds hierarchical menus off the Apple menu (as described in Chapter 6, "Take Note: System 7.5, Now Utilities and More: Helping You Find Your Way"). However, it is known to conflict with a variety of other non-Apple software as well as to slow down hard disk performance significantly. Most experts suggest not using it and using some comparable alternative program instead (such as Now Menus). Certainly don't use both Apple Menu Options and a program such as Now Menus at the same time.

BY THE WAY ▶

THIRD-PARTY SOFTWARE AND SYSTEM 7.5 CONFLICTS

Problems with Apple Menu Options is only the most notable example of a conflict between a System 7.5 INIT and another third-party software. I could cite numerous other examples. For instance, the PowerBook Control Strip is incompatible with Now Utilities' Now Menus 5.0. You can use one or the other, but not both. However, an exhaustive list of these conflicts would serve no purpose here. These problems tend to get remedied soon after they are identified, usually by upgrades to the third-party software.

Easy Install Doesn't Install Everything　Despite the abundance of extensions included when you install System 7.5, you may find that the one you are looking for was never installed in the first place. In particular, CloseView, Easy Access, and MacTCP do not automatically get installed when you select Easy Install. To use them, you need to do a Custom Install and individually select them.

BY THE WAY ▶

IF ITEMS IN YOUR SHUTDOWN ITEMS FOLDER DO NOT RUN AT SHUT DOWN

Items in the Shutdown Items folder run if Shut Down is selected from the Finder's Special Menu, but do not run if you instead select the Shut Down desk accessory in the Apple menu. This is probably a bug that Apple will eventually fix.

Speaking of the Shutdown Items Folder, an invisible file at the root level of your disk, called Shutdown Check, is used to get this feature to work. The Mac places the file there automatically.

Delete Preferences Files?

Many of the new control panels in System 7.5 have preferences files associated with them. Some problems with a specific control panel may be due to a problem with its preferences file (such as that it is damaged) rather than an actual compatibility problem with the control panel itself. Usually this is remedied by deleting the preferences file. Macintosh PC Exchange is one well-known example. If you are having any problems with this control panel, locate its preferences file in the Preferences folder and delete it. This may cure your problem.

SEE: • Fix-It #2 for more on preferences files

Are Your Applications "Capable," "Savvy," or Not?

Some of the features of System 7.5 (such as Drag and Drop, AppleScript, and Quick-Draw GX) can only be used with software that has been specifically written to support these features. Further complicating matters, there are usually different levels of support possible for each feature. For example, a program may be able to receive data from via the Drag and Drop method, even though it cannot send it. This is called being "Macintosh Drag and Drop aware." If a program can fully use all of the new Drag and Drop features, the program is said to be "Macintosh Drag and Drop capable." A similar distinction is used to differentiate programs that are only "QuickDraw GX-aware" versus "QuickDraw GX-savvy" (a distinction I explore more in the QuickDraw GX section of this chapter).

If you are unable to access a particular System 7.5 feature from within a specific application, it probably means that the application does not yet support this feature. Software that was released prior to 1994 is almost certain not to have this support. In many cases, even more recently released software still lacks the necessary support.

In this regard, one of the as yet unanswered questions about QuickDraw GX is how much and how soon will software developers rewrite their software to support GX's new features. Some developers have claimed that they do not feel it is worth the effort to do this, because they do not expect to see widespread acceptance of Quick-Draw GX. Of course, without the support from developers, this expectation could become a self-fulfilling prophecy!

SEE: • "QuickDraw GX," later in this chapter, for more details

What About Enablers?

When it was first released, System 7.5 did not include any enabler files. All the information contained in the previous enablers were rolled into the basic system software. However, as subsequent Macintosh models are released, new enablers will arrive again (though there is always talk of having just one Universal Enabler, that gets updated as needed). As of this writing, a new PowerPC Enabler has already returned, needed for the latest models of Power Macs released at the end of 1994.

By the way, when selecting Easy Install from the System 7.5 Installer and installing over 7.1 systems, the Installer will fail to remove the PowerBook 150 Enabler, the PowerBook 500 Series Enabler, and the Workgroup Server 9150 Enabler. This is not a problem, as System 7.5 will ignore the enablers. Still, it is best to take the enablers and toss them in the Trash.

System 7.5 Update 1.0 (and Other Updates and Patches)

To address bug-fixes in and add enhancements to the intial release of System 7.5, Apple recently released a four-disk update, called System 7.5 Update 1.0. Other updates may eventually be released as needed. System 7.5 Update 1.0 eliminates the need for the PB150 Modem Patch as well as for assorted other minor updates that had been released prior to Update 1.0.

Helpful hint: If you have used a startup manager (see Fix-It #4) to disable files, turn them all back on (and then restart with extensions off by holding down the Shift key at startup) before running the Update Installer. This assures that all System Folder files are updated properly.

SEE: • Chapter 2, "By the Way: What Exactly Does a System Update Update?," for more details on what System 7.5 Update 1.0 actually updates

Memory Problems

Most memory problems that you will have will not be specific to System 7.5. However, since System 7.5 generally needs more memory than previous systems, you are more likely to have memory problems. Still, there are a few System 7.5–specific memory pitfalls lurking out there. Here are two examples:

Out of Memory Messages (and Other Problems) in the Scrapbook   The new System 7.5 Scrapbook is a genuine application, rather than a desk accessory (as it had previously been). This means that you can change its memory allocation from its Get Info window. It also means that, unless you increase its memory allocation, you are more likely to have memory problems when using it. If you get an out of memory message when trying to cut from or paste to the Scrapbook (or simply cannot get these commands to work), close the Scrapbook, go to its Get Info window, increase its allocation by 100 to 200K, and try again. Otherwise, restarting the Mac should eliminate the problem.

Desktop Patterns out of Memory False Alarm   You can paste your own patterns into the Desktop Patterns control panel window. If and when you try to do this, you may get a message that says *There is not enough memory to complete this operation.* If what you are trying to paste is not very large, the problem may have nothing to do with memory. Rather it probably means that you are trying to paste something that is in an unacceptable format. For example, I got this message when I tried to paste a text selection. When I instead tried to paste a graphic object, everything worked fine.

SEE: • Fix-It #6 for more on the Get Info window and memory problems in general

Apple Guide Does Not Work

Symptoms:

You try to access an Apple Guide file from the Guide menu, but the relevant Guide file is not listed.

Causes:

The most likely causes are that the needed Guide file (or the Apple Guide extension itself) is either not installed or is not in the correct location.

What to do:

Apple Guide Not Installed or Not Enabled

With the Finder as the active application, select the Guide menu. The top line should read "About Apple Guide." If instead, it reads "About Balloon Help" it may mean that the Apple Guide extension (see Figure 12-6) was not installed or has been disabled. Check for this. If this is the case, no Apple Guide files will be accessible, even if they are correctly located.

If Apple Guide was never installed and is thus nowhere on your disk, you need to run the System 7.5 Installer to install it (use Custom Install and select Apple Guide from the Utility Software submenu). If it is disabled, reenable it (such as by using a startup management utility) to get it back in the Extensions folder.

A basic reminder: Apple Guide is disabled if you start with extensions off (by holding down the Shift key at startup). Balloon Help will still work, however.

SEE: • Fix-It #4 on enabling and disabling extensions
• Fix-It #5 on using the Installer

Incorrect Location of Apple Guide Documents

In addition to needing the Apple Guide extension, accessing specific Apple Guide documents from the Guide menu, such as the Finder's Macintosh Guide, requires that the relevant document file be correctly located on your disk. For example, the Macintosh Guide file must be in the Extensions folder (see Figure 12-6).

Apple Guide

Macintosh Guide   About Apple Guide   Shortcuts

Figure 12-6   **The Apple Guide extension with the Macintosh Guide and related documents, all located in the Extensions folder**

Guide documents are only accessible when the appropriate application is active. For example, Macintosh Guide is only available when you are in the Finder. You will not see it listed when another application is active. Similarly, individual applications may have their own Apple Guide documents, which in turn are only available when you are using that application.

Complicating matters a bit more, different Apple Guide documents may need to be stored in different locations in order to be accessible. For example, most of Apple's Guide documents are stored in the Extensions folder. However, most application-specific Guide documents will be found in the same folder as the application itself (thus, you will find File Assistant Guide in the same folder as the File Assistant program). Other Guide documents may need to be at the root level of the System Folder. Generally, if a program uses an Installer utility, it will install its Guide documents in the correct location. If so, do not move them to another location or they will not work!

Apple Guide Document Not Installed

I had one case where an Easy Install of a word processor (WordPerfect) did not install its Apple Guide document. To get it installed, I needed to go back, use Custom Install, and separately select the Guide document option. Check for this possibility if you cannot access an application's Guide document.

Special Case: Apple Guide and At Ease

Apple Guide is not available from At Ease. If At Ease is turned on at startup, Apple Guide is not available from the Finder either (although Guide documents for other applications remain available). This is remedied in System 7.5 Update 1.0.

QuickDraw GX

The first thing to know about QuickDraw GX is that it is entirely optional. Although it is included as part of System 7.5, it is not installed with the basic System 7.5 setup. It has its own separate set of Installer disks. You can happily use the rest of System 7.5 without ever using QuickDraw GX.

However, if you do install QuickDraw GX, it will have more effect on how your Macintosh works than all of the other new features of System 7.5 combined. That is why I am devoting a separate section just to this subject.

QuickDraw GX, as its name implies, is an enhancement to QuickDraw, the set of routines built into your Macintosh's ROM that ultimately determines how almost everything on your Macintosh is displayed and printed (as first described in Chapter 10).

The most immediately obvious change resulting from installing QuickDraw GX is the new way in which printing is handled. It is so completely different that I omitted discussing it in any detail in Chapter 7. Similarly, there are major changes in how fonts, particularly PostScript fonts, are handled with QuickDraw GX. I only briefly described them in Chapter 9. Finally, there are some new graphics-related features associated with QuickDraw GX that were only slightly mentioned in Chapter 10. Here is where I finally go into the details of these matters. In the following sections, I assume that you are at least minimally familiar with non-GX aspects of these topics, as presented in these previous chapters.

BY THE WAY ▶

WHAT ABOUT POWERTALK?

PowerTalk, another feature of System 7.5, also uses a separate optional installation. PowerTalk is mainly a way of setting up a mail system on a network without requiring a mail server. Because of its more narrowly focused applicability, I will not be describing PowerTalk in any detail in this book.

Installing and Using QuickDraw GX

To install QuickDraw GX, use the separate QuickDraw GX Installer. In most cases, you will be best off selecting Easy Install. A couple of cases where you might prefer to use a Custom Install are described later in this chapter. If you ever decide to permanently remove QuickDraw GX software, launch the GX Installer and select Custom Remove.

The key component of the QuickDraw GX software is the QuickDraw GX extension. If this extension is disabled or deleted, you lose access to all QuickDraw GX features, even if all the other GX software remains on your disk.

Simply installing QuickDraw GX does not mean that you can now use all of its features. Some of the features of QuickDraw GX, such as desktop printers and portable documents, are indeed immediately usable with almost all current applications (except a few that are totally incompatible with QuickDraw GX). However, other features (such as the redesigned Page Setup and Print dialog boxes and the improved Clipboard) are available only in programs that are at least "GX-aware" (that is, the programs have been rewritten to permit use of these GX options). Finally, a few remaining features of QuickDraw GX (such as its new font-related features), are only available to programs that have been completely upgraded to be "GX-savvy." Thus, your ability to use the new features of QuickDraw GX will very much depend on the current status of the applications you use. Specific examples of this are cited in the sections that follow.

TAKE NOTE ▶

QUICKDRAW GX 1.1.1

As this book went to press, Apple released QuickDraw GX 1.1.1. This upgrade primarily includes bug-fixes and performance improvements that should reduce problems you might have had using the previous version of QuickDraw GX. It also includes an upgraded version of Adobe Type Manager (3.8.2), installable as either a 680x0 or native PowerPC version. Finally, it adds a few new features.

- *A change in the desktop printer icon variations: After a desktop printer queue is emptied, the page icon goes away rather than turning into the dog-eared page icon.*

- *A new item in the Printing Menu: Disable Manual Feed Alerts turns off the alerts for manual feed printing on PostScript printers.*

- *New menu choices in the PostScript Print dialog box for non-QuickDraw GX applications: they let you select different paper types for the first page versus the remaining pages.*

- *A few new printing-related files: an N-Up Printing Options extension (for printing up to sixteen pages on a sheet of paper); an EPSExtension, relevant if you intend to create PostScript files via the Print dialog box, which may be useful for importing graphics into applications that do not support QuickDraw GX (using this feature requires selecting the PostScript File Options from the Printing menu); and three new paper types (Letterhead, Stationery, and 3-Hole Punch).*

Check the ReadMe file included with the update for more details on these features and for some additional detailed troubleshooting help. Aside from these relatively minor differences, the information in this chapter (which is based on the original version of QuickDraw GX) still applies.

QuickDraw GX and Printing

This section covers what is new and different about printing with QuickDraw GX. As you first read it, it may seem like there is a lot of new things to master. However, once you get things set up and rolling, printing with GX is no more difficult than before (in fact, you may find it even easier). In most cases, you can still simply select Print from within an application and make the standard choices in the Print dialog box. Your document will then print without any further hassle.

QuickDraw GX-Specific Printer Drivers

To print with QuickDraw GX, you need a GX-specific printer driver file for your particular printer (see Figure 12-7). When you install QuickDraw GX, GX-specific drivers for all of Apple's printers are installed in the Extensions folder of your System Folder (non-GX versions of the printer drivers also remain installed).

If you have a non-Apple printer, you will need to get a GX-compatible driver from the company that made the printer. If you do not have a GX-specific driver for your printer, I would recommend against installing QuickDraw GX at all.

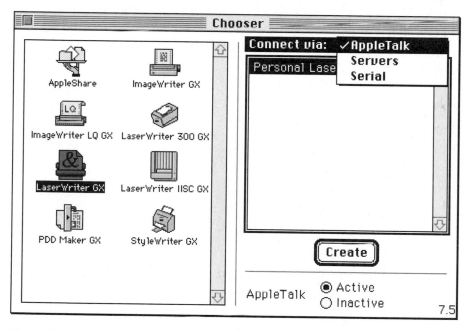

Figure 12-7 The QuickDraw GX Chooser with a selection of GX drivers listed

QuickDraw GX and the Chooser

The first step in setting up to print with QuickDraw GX is to select the Chooser (see Figure 12-7). The Chooser has been redesigned in QuickDraw GX. First, the GX Chooser does not even list non-GX printer drivers in its window. Thus, you will not find LaserWriter 8 listed, even though the driver may be present in your Extensions folder. Instead, to use a PostScript LaserWriter, you must select LaserWriter GX. However, don't be in a hurry to remove the non-GX version of your printer drivers from your System Folder. They may still be needed. For example, if you ever start up with the QuickDraw GX extension disabled, the Chooser will revert to its former non-GX format, and only non-GX printer drivers will be listed. This way you can still print without GX being active.

To use the Chooser in QuickDraw GX:

1. **Select a printer driver**
   Click on the icon for the printer driver you want to use (I will use LaserWriter GX in most examples here, as seen in Figure 12-7).

2. **Select a connection type (and select AppleTalk active or not)**
   From the "Connect via": pop-up menu, select the desired connection type (see Figure 12-7). Typically, you can choose among AppleTalk (used for AppleTalk printers), serial (used primarily for non-AppleTalk printers), or from a server (relevant only if you are on a network that uses a server).

   Thus, there is no longer a need for separate printer drivers for AppleTalk and non-AppleTalk versions of the same printer (such as has been the case for the ImageWriter). The option to switch between AppleTalk and Serial for LaserWriters reflects the fact that there are printers that use this driver (notably the LaserWriter Select 310) that connect via a serial connection rather than the much more typical AppleTalk connection.

   Regardless of your choice here, you still need to separately select whether or not you want AppleTalk active (via the radio buttons at the bottom right of the Chooser).

BY THE WAY ▶

WHAT ABOUT BACKGROUND PRINTING?

There are no longer any on/off buttons for background printing in QuickDraw GX. This is because background printing is automatically always on when using QuickDraw GX. Also, background printing with QuickDraw GX does not use PrintMonitor. Instead, it uses a new method, directly built into QuickDraw GX, that should be faster and more reliable. The PrintMonitor file remains in your System Folder only for those occasions when you choose not to use QuickDraw GX.

---

3. **Create a desktop printer icon for your printer(s)**
   To create a desktop printer icon for an AppleTalk-connected printer, first make sure the printer is on and actually connected to the Macintosh. If so, when you selected the appropriate printer driver, the name of your printer should appear in the right hand side of the Chooser window (just as it does in the non-GX Chooser). At this point, click the Create button (see Figure 12-7). After a few mo-

ments, an icon with the name of your printer will appear on your desktop. This is called, appropriately enough, a desktop printer (see Figure 12-8).

Personal LaserWriter NTR   PDD Maker GX

Figure 12-8   LaserWriter GX and PDD Maker GX desktop printer icons

To create a desktop printer icon for a serial-connected printer, simply select the desired serial port icon (Modem or Printer) and then click Create. There is no named printer to select. For serial-connected printers, the printer does not have to actually be connected to the Macintosh for the desktop printer icon to be created.

Repeat this process for any other printers connected to your Macintosh.

By the way, note that using the Create button does not provide for any optional choices, such as those accessed via the Setup button found in non-GX versions of the Chooser (which is why, for example, GX software does not include printer description files, as used by LaserWriter 8). With GX, all you have to do—indeed all you can do—is click Create. The Macintosh does not actually check what setup options are available with your printer until the first time you print a document. Thus, some printer options may not be immediately accessible for a newly created desktop printer.

Desktop printer icons must remain on the desktop. If you try to move them into any folder, you will get a message saying you cannot do this. However, you can delete them by moving them to the Trash.

4. **Create a PDD Maker GX desktop icon**
   Select the PDD Maker GX driver icon and click Create again (see Figure 12-7). This will create a special desktop icon (see Figure 12-8) whose function I describe more in an upcoming section. This step is optional (and you can always come back to the Chooser and do it later), but I recommend taking care of it right away.

5. **Quit the Chooser**
   Unlike with non-GX systems, after you quit the Chooser, you may never have to select the Chooser again. The only reason to do so would be to create a new desktop printer icon.

Select to Print a Document

You have a choice of two ways to select to print a document with QuickDraw GX:

- **Print from the desktop printer icon**
  To do this, drag the document icon to be printed to the desired desktop printer icon. This will force the selected document to open from within its creating application. If the application is GX-aware, printing will immediately begin at the

current print settings, and the application will quit when done. If the application is not GX-aware, the process will instead halt at the Print dialog box. In this case, select options as desired and click Print.

You can add more documents to the printer's queue via this method, without having to wait for the completion of the current print job. You can even simultaneously assign documents to icons for different printers.

- **Print from within an application**
  To do this, select Print from an application's File menu. Select options, as desired, from the dialog box and then click Print. Just as with non-GX printing, you may first wish to select Page Setup to access other print-related options.

  The exact nature of the Page Setup and Print dialog boxes that appear will vary depending on whether the particular application supports QuickDraw GX or not. If it does not support QuickDraw GX, you will see dialog boxes similar to those that appear in non-GX systems (for example, with LaserWriter GX, you will get dialog boxes that are like those used with LaserWriter 7, as seen in Figure 12-9). If the application does support QuickDraw GX (such as SimpleText), you will get the new GX-specific dialog boxes, as described in the next section.

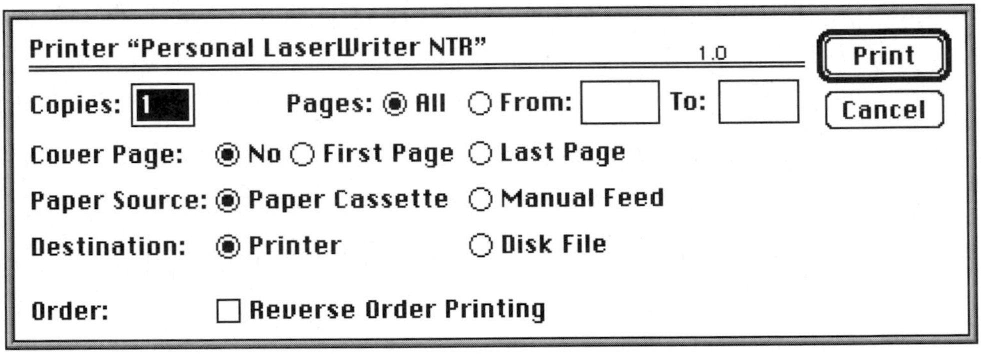

Figure 12-9 The LaserWriter GX Print dialog box, as it appears with QuickDraw GX running, for an application that is not "GX-aware"

If your application supports QuickDraw GX printing, after completing either method of print selection, you will briefly see a Printing Status dialog box appear on the screen as a background-printing spool file is created. Shortly afterward, your printing should begin. However, if you selected manual feed from the Print dialog box, a dialog box will appear in the Finder asking you to confirm that you have inserted paper into the manual feed tray. To print with manual feed, make sure that paper is present, then click Continue.

Respond to Error Messages, If Any Appear

If something goes wrong after selecting to print, an error alert should appear. Although the exact wording of a message may be different from those in non-GX systems, most error messages are similar across both systems. For help in determining the meaning of these general messages, refer to Chapter 7. A selection of GX-specific error messages is covered in the section on QuickDraw GX Problems, later in this chapter.

Generally, error messages appear in the Finder. If you are not in the Finder at the time the message appears, an alert sound occurs. This is the Mac's way of telling you to go to the Finder to view the message. Some errors messages result in your document's being placed on hold. Assuming you fix the cause of the error, you must then separately select to resume printing, either by clicking the Resume button in the Print Queue window or by selecting the Resume command in the Printing menu (details on how to do this are described in following sections).

If your application is not QuickDraw GX-aware, printing will proceed similarly to how it would in a non-GX system (including using PrintMonitor, if available).

TAKE NOTE ▶

FOR APPLICATIONS INCOMPATIBLE WITH QUICKDRAW GX, USE QUICKDRAW GX HELPER

Some applications are incompatible with QuickDraw GX and will not print while QuickDraw GX is active. However, this does not necessarily mean that you have to restart with GX disabled in order to get the document to print. Instead, you can temporarily turn off QuickDraw GX just for that application. To do this, you must first have installed an extension called QuickDraw GX Helper (see Figure 12-10). This is not installed as part of an Easy Install of QuickDraw GX. You have to select Custom Install and then select to install QuickDraw GX Utilities.

With Helper installed, when you select the Apple menu, you will see a new command called "Turn Desktop Printing Off" (see Figure 12-11). Select this when the incompatible application is active. You will then get a dialog box telling you what non-GX driver will be used instead. Click OK. This turns off the GX driver for that application (but not for any other application) and substitutes the non-GX driver.

For this to work, you must have the alternative compatible non-GX driver present in your Extensions folder. For example, if you are turning off LaserWriter GX, either the LaserWriter or LaserWriter 8 driver must be in the Extensions folder (if both are present, LaserWriter will be selected). Without the needed non-GX driver(s), QuickDraw GX Helper will be of no help.

By the way, since Helper enables a non-GX printer driver, you will not have access to GX PostScript fonts. If this is a problem, you will need to install the non-GX PostScript printer font files for those fonts into the Fonts folder (see "QuickDraw GX and Fonts," later in this chapter for more details).

You can later turn GX printing back on for that application (if you wish) by returning to the Apple menu while the relevant application is active and selecting the command which now reads "Turn Desktop Printing On."

If even this technique fails to get your document to print, you will need to restart with the QuickDraw GX extension turned off (use Extensions Manager or other similar utility to do this). You can then select the non-GX driver and print as if you had you never installed QuickDraw GX.

QuickDraw™ GX Helper   PrinterShare GX

Figure 12-10   The QuickDraw GX Helper and PrinterShare GX extensions

Figure 12-11   The "Turn Desktop Printing Off" command appears in the Apple menu when QuickDraw GX Helper is installed

---

BY THE WAY ▶

PRINTER SHARING

With the PrinterShare GX extension installed (see Figure 12-10), and file sharing turned on, you can let other users share your desktop printer icons, in the same way that you can share any other files (as described more generally in Chapter 11). To get the dialog box needed to set access options for the printer icon, select the printer icon and then select Sharing from the File menu.

A printer does not have to be an AppleTalk printer to be shared in this way. Actually, a similar sharing feature is available for non-GX systems via the optional PrinterShare extension. However, to print with QuickDraw GX, the PrinterShare GX extension is required, even if you are not sharing any printers.

QuickDraw GX Page Setup and Print Dialog Boxes

Both the Page Setup and Print dialog boxes have a button to toggle between Fewer Choices and More Choices (see Figure 12-12). Though the Fewer Choices displays should be adequate for most basic printing tasks, the descriptions that follow explain the additional options available via More Choices.

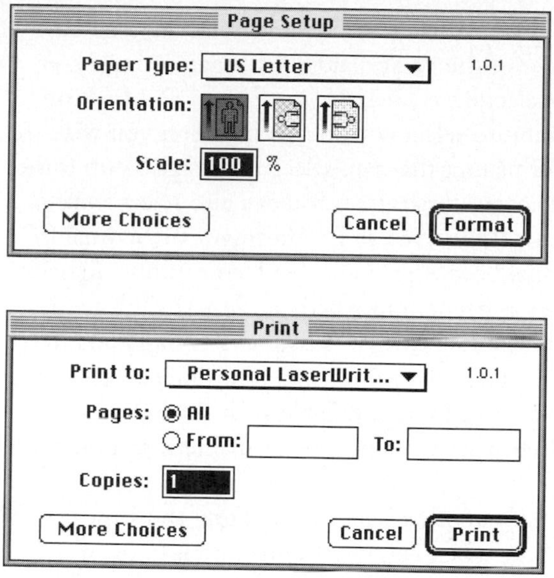

Figure 12-12   The Fewer Choices Page Setup and Print dialog boxes for LaserWriter GX

Page Setup Dialog Box   With More Choices selected, icons appear along the left-hand border of the dialog box. For example, with LaserWriter GX, you should see General and LaserWriter Options icons. General is the one selected by default when you open the Page Setup dialog box (see Figure 12-13). From here, you can select the type of paper and printer that you are formatting for—via the "Paper Type" and "Format for" pop-up menus—even if you do not have the selected paper loaded or selected printer currently attached to your Mac. If you click on the LaserWriter Options icon (see Figure 12-13), the dialog box display shifts to a listing of image manipulation choices similar to (though actually fewer than) what is available with the non-GX LaserWriter driver (such as Flip Horizontal and Invert Image). In any case, when you are done making your choices, click the Format button.

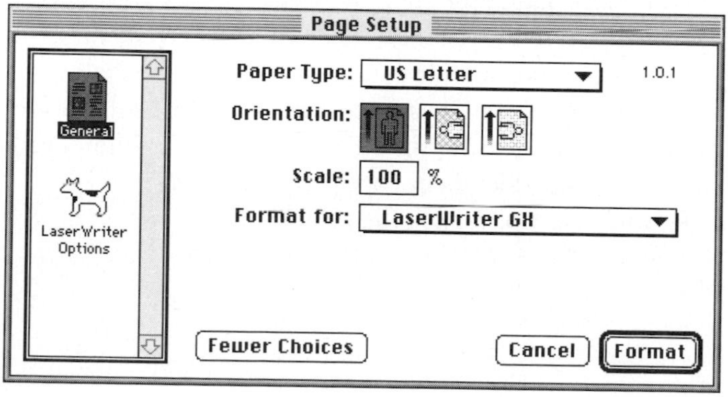

Figure 12-13   The LaserWriter GX Page Setup dialog box, with the General icon selected

Print Dialog Box and Printer Extensions   With More Choices selected, a column of icons appears along the left-hand border of the Print dialog box. Again using Laser-Writer GX as an example, the default selection is General (see Figure 12-14). From here, you use the "Print to" pop-up menu to select what desktop printer you wish to use. Ideally, it should match the type of printer that you selected in Page Setup (otherwise, your document may print with incorrect margins). You can also select from other options, such as whether you want Paper Feed to be Automatic or Manual (if you select Manual, you will get a Manual Feed Alert message when printing actually begins, requesting that you insert paper as needed) or whether you want the document's Destination to be the Printer or a PostScript file (a distinction explained in more detail in Chapter 7). Of course, you also have the standard options to set the number of copies and page range to be printed (also available with Fewer Choices selected). Most of these options are essentially the same ones available with non-GX drivers.

Besides General, you will find at least two other icons: Print Time and Paper Match. Print Time allows you to schedule when you want a document to print (in case you don't want it to print immediately). Paper Match allows you to override the default setting for the size of the paper as set via the Printing menu's Input Tray command (described in the next section). For more details on using these extensions, consult Apple Guide or any of several books on System 7.5. However, I suspect that most users will never have a need for either of these two extensions.

You can further enhance the functions of the Print dialog box by adding optional printer extensions. Currently, these are made by companies other than Apple. You install them by dragging the extension files to the System Folder icon or directly to the Extensions folder. You do not have to restart to begin using them. You can separately select which extensions will be available for a particular printer, via the desktop printer icon's Printing menu (described in the next section).

If you have the CD-ROM version of System 7.5, it comes with two examples of these extensions: Watermark and Paper Saver (see icons in Figure 12-14). These files are not installed as part of a QuickDraw GX installation. You have to separately install them. Actually, they are samples from a larger selection of extensions available in a separate purchasable package called Pierce Print Tools. Details on how to use these sample extensions are explained via the Information button available in the dialog window of each extension. Basically, Watermark is used to add text, such as the words *Draft* or *Confidential,* to the background of each printed page. Paper Saver allows you to print, at a reduced size, more than one document page per printed page.

When you are done making your selections, click the Print button.

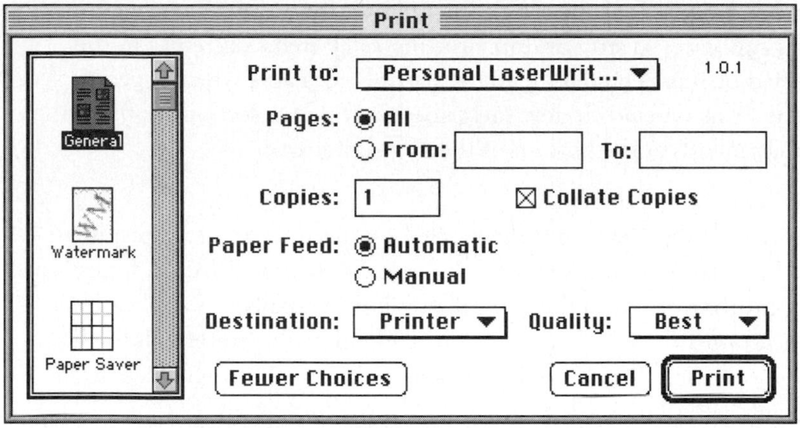

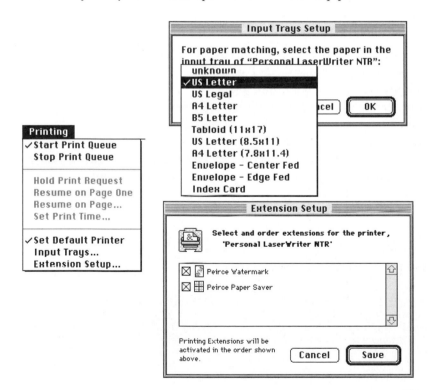

Figure 12-14 The LaserWriter GX Print dialog box, with the General icon selected

The Printing Menu

When you single-click on a desktop printer icon, a Printing menu is added to the menu bar (see Figure 12-15). These commands only apply to the selected printer. You need to separately select these options for each desktop printer icon.

Figure 12-15 Left: The Printing menu as it appears after selecting a LaserWriter GX desktop printer icon; Right: the dialog boxes that appear after selecting the Input Trays and Extension Setup commands from the Printing menu

By using the two commands at the top of the menu (Stop Print Queue and Start Print Queue), you can select to stop or start printing of all items currently in the queue of the selected printer. The middle items are only available when a specific file is selected from the Print Queue window (described in the next section). Finally, there are three special commands at the bottom of the Printing menu:

- **Set Default Printer**

  If you have more than one desktop printer icon, you need to select one as the default printer. This is the one to which all print requests will be directed, unless you specifically select otherwise from the Print dialog box. Actually, for applications that do not yet support the GX Print dialog box, the default printer will be the only printer you can use. To use another printer in this case, you will have to change the default selection.

  To change the default printer for any reason, select the Set Default Printer command from the Printing menu of the desired desktop printer icon (see Figure 12-15). That's it. The Set Default Printer command of the default printer will have a checkmark in front of it. Also, the desktop icon for the default printer will have a bold outline.

- **Input Trays . . .**

  Select the Input Trays command (see Figure 12-15). Select the default size of paper for each tray listed. Typically, you would select the size(s) you most commonly use in your printer's input tray(s).

- **Extension Setup . . .**

  Select the Extension Setup command (see Figure 12-15). You will see a list of all optional extensions available for your printer (such as the Watermark and Paper Saver extensions mentioned previously). To turn off a particular extension (so that it will not be available in the Print dialog box of the selected printer), click the checkbox next to it so as to remove the x. To change the processing order of the extensions, drag an extension up or down the list. This feature is provided because the operation of some extensions may vary depending on which extension is processed first.

TECHNICALLY SPEAKING ▶

SOLVING PAPER SIZE SELECTION CONFUSION

You can select a paper size format from the Page Setup dialog box. You can select the default size of the paper in the input tray from the Input Tray command in the Printing menu. You can then override that selection from the Paper Match extension in the Print dialog box.

All of this can admittedly get a bit confusing. How do you decide what paper size to select and from where do you select it? Here are some simple guidelines: From the Input Trays command for your printer, select the size you most commonly use (US Letter typically). If you ever print at some odd size, such as an envelope, select that size from the Page Setup dialog box. Use the separate manual feed tray, if available, to load the odd-sized paper, rather than

The Print Queue Window

If you double-click on a desktop printer icon, it opens up the printer's Print Queue window (Figure 12-16). The item listed in the top half of the window, if any, is the item currently printing. Items in the bottom half are waiting to be printed.

When a print job is in progress, messages concerning the print job will appear in this window, much as they appeared in the PrintMonitor window of non-GX printers.

Back on the desktop, the desktop printer icon actually changes to reflect changes in current printing status. For example, if there are any documents waiting in the print queue, a mini-picture of a document is added to the icon. If there is currently a printing problem, the triangular yellow alert symbol is added to the icon (see Figure 12-17).

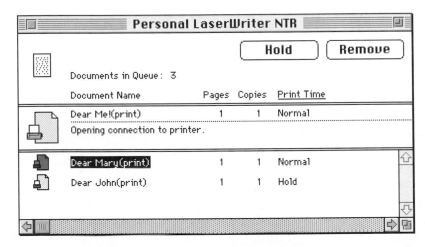

Figure 12-16 A desktop printer's Print Queue window, seen just as the document "Dear Me!" is about to print

Personal LaserWriter NTR   Personal LaserWriter NTR   Personal LaserWriter NTR

Figure 12-17 The changing face of a desktop printer icon: Normal (left), when a document is in the queue (center) and when an alert has occurred (right)

Print Time   Each item has its own Print Time category. Most often it will be Normal. This means that it is scheduled to be printed as soon as the print jobs ahead of it in the queue are completed. Location in the queue is initially determined by the order in which the print requests were made. By default, the list of document names are sorted in the queue based on their Print Time order. You can tell this is so because the word Print Time is underlined (as seen in Figure 12-16). To sort the list based on another column (and have that column name be underlined), simply click that column's name (though this will not change the print order of the listed documents).

If you select an item in the queue and click the Hold button (or select Hold Print Request from the Printing menu), the document's print time will be listed as Hold (see Figure 12-16). These documents are not printed until you again select the document name in the queue and either click the Resume button in the Print Queue window (the Hold button toggles to a Resume button when you select a held document) or select one of the Resume commands from the Printing menu.

Other Print Time options are available by selecting "Set Print Time . . ." from the Printing menu. From here, you can schedule an item as Urgent (so that it jumps to the head of the queue, or set it for delayed printing at some future scheduled time). The functions of the Print Time printer extension (described previously) largely overlap with the Print Time option in the Printing menu. Choose whichever one is more convenient for you.

You can also drag a document from the (lower) queue list area to the (upper) print area of the Print Queue window (or vice versa). This has the similar effect of changing a document's status from Hold to Normal (or vice versa).

You can completely delete an item from the print queue by selecting it and then clicking the Remove button.

Print Preview   If you double-click an item in the queue, it will open up a print preview version of the document in SimpleText. This preview information is taken from a special print version of the file stored in the PrintMonitor Documents folder (similarly to how spooled printing files are stored in the PrintMonitor Documents folder when using background printing in non-GX systems). Actually, you can even directly drag a document out of the Print Queue window altogether. This creates a print file version of the document on the desktop (identical to the type of file in the PrintMonitor Documents folder). You can drag this print file back into a queue when you want to print it (see Figure 12-18). If you double-click the print file while it is out of the queue, it will still open up in SimpleText.

 Print File icon   PDD icon

Figure 12-18   A print file document (left) and a portable digital document (PDD) (right); both function similarly in QuickDraw GX

Special Case: Portable Digital Documents (PDDs)

QuickDraw GX offers a special bonus: the ability to create documents, called Portable Digital Documents (PDDs), that can be viewed and printed on any Macintosh, even if the original document's creating application is missing and even if the fonts that were used to create the document are not available. The display and printed copy of the PDD will be an exact match of the original document. The main limitation is that you cannot edit this document in any way (there had to be some drawback to this!). Still, this means that someone could open or print a PDD file that you created from a PageMaker document, for example, and have it appear exactly as you created it, without needing to have their own copy of PageMaker. All they need is Quick-Draw GX and SimpleText. (But before you run out and install GX just so you can create PDDs, bear in mind that is still more limited than what you can already do with programs such as Adobe Acrobat or Common Ground.)

To create a PDD, use the PDD Maker GX desktop icon (created via the GX Chooser, as described earlier in this chapter). Either drag a document directly to the PDD Maker icon or select PDD Maker GX as the "Print to" location in the Print dialog box of a GX-savvy application. When you do this, a PDD is created (see Figure 12-18).

PDDs only work with QuickDraw GX installed. For example, if you double-click on a PDD icon when GX is not running, you will get an alert message that says *SimpleText cannot display this type of document* (see Figure 12-19). If you try to open the document from within SimpleText, it will not appear in the Open dialog box. Conversely, unlike ordinary text documents, you should use only SimpleText to open a PDD. If you try to open a PDD in another word processor (whether or not GX is installed), it will appear as gibberish.

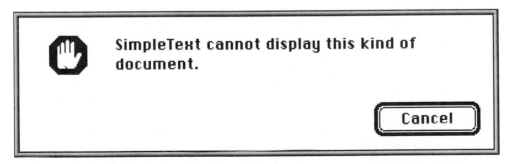

Figure 12-19 **The message that appears if you try to open a PDD when QuickDraw GX is disabled**

Finally, you may be thinking that PDDs sound suspiciously similar to the print file documents you can create with any desktop printer (as described in "Print Preview" in the previous section). If so, you are right. On the other hand, both the PDD files and print files described here are separate from the PostScript print files that you can create by selecting PostScript as the Destination in the LaserWriter GX Print dialog box.

PDD Maker GX and the Printing Menu   The Printing menu for the PDD Maker GX icon is a bit different from that for other desktop printer icons. In particular, it has a special command called "PDD Maker Setup." If you select it, you can designate which folder is the default folder for saving PDDs.

PDDs and SimpleText   What PDD Maker actually does is create a special type of SimpleText document (see "Technically Speaking: The File Types of SimpleText Documents," for more details). Ordinary SimpleText documents are simply plain text documents, such as can be opened by virtually any word processor. When you use the scroll bars for these type of documents, you scroll through the pages of the document.

On the other hand, with PDDs, the scroll bars only take you up and down a single page. To move to another page of a PDD, you have to use SimpleText's page navigation commands, located in the Edit menu: Next Page, Previous Page, and Go to Page (see Figure 12-20). These commands are dimmed and unavailable when you view a plain text document.

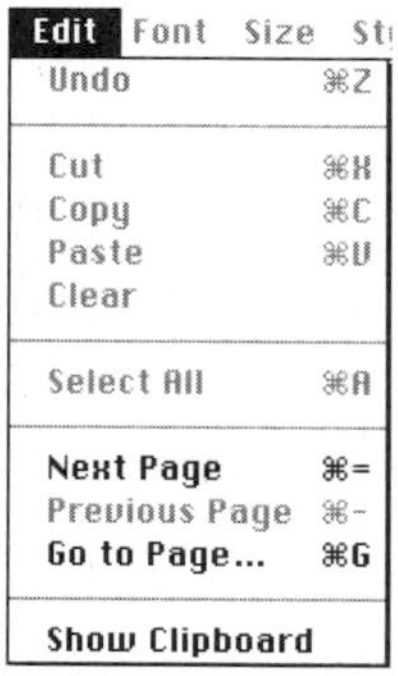

Figure 12-20
SimpleText's page navigation commands become active when you view a PDD file

TECHNICALLY SPEAKING ▶

THE FILE TYPES OF SIMPLETEXT DOCUMENTS

In Chapter 8, I explained the difference between the read-only versus read/write SimpleText (and TeachText) text documents. I explained how each had a different file type (TEXT for read/write versus ttro for read-only). I also explained how you could change a document from the read-only type to read/write type (or vice versa) simply by changing the file's type code (via a utility such as Get More Info).

PDDs, while still listed as SimpleText documents in the Get Info window, have a different file type from either of the previous two text document types. The file type code for a PDD is sjob. Print file documents (the ones that are stored in the PrintMonitor Documents folder or that are created by dragging a file from the Print Queue window to the desktop) have a slightly different file type: tjob. Actually, aside from the fact that sjob and tjob documents have separate icons, they function almost identically. In fact, you can successfully change a document from a PDD (sjob) to a print file (tjob) document just by changing its file type (again via a utility such as Get More Info). However, you cannot change an sjob (or tjob) document into a TEXT (or ttro) document (or vice versa) by changing the document's type code. If you try this, the icon will change correctly, but the document will not open successfully.

QuickDraw GX and Fonts

It's hard to ignore QuickDraw GX's new printing features. You must at least minimally master them in order to print anything. In contrast, it is almost too easy to ignore GX's new methods for handling fonts. You can install and use QuickDraw GX for quite a while without necessarily noticing that anything is different about your fonts. However, significant changes have taken place. And if you don't understand these changes, you will eventually have problems.

This section focuses on the new types of fonts specific to QuickDraw GX: how to recognize them and how they are different from the previous type of fonts. I also explain how you can still use your older styles of fonts in GX. Finally, I explain how to fix things when they go wrong.

Bitmapped Fonts

First the good news: You can still use all your existing bitmapped fonts. There is no change in bitmapped fonts for QuickDraw GX. Bitmapped fonts will work exactly the same in QuickDraw GX as they do in non-GX versions of the system software.

TrueType Fonts

With QuickDraw GX, there are now two types of TrueType fonts. Simple (non-GX) TrueType fonts are the standard types that were around prior to QuickDraw GX. Any TrueType fonts you had prior to the release of System 7.5 are almost certainly non-GX fonts. Still, they can be used equally well in GX or non-GX systems. Complex (GX) TrueType fonts are the ones designed to take advantage of the new capabilities of QuickDraw GX. Installing QuickDraw GX does not convert non-GX TrueType fonts to GX TrueType fonts. The difference is determined by how the font itself was created.

It is best to avoid using complex (GX) TrueType fonts without GX installed. Otherwise, the text may display and/or print incorrectly.

SEE: • "Technically Speaking: A Primer on Using QuickDraw GX Fonts," and "Take Note: Identifying GX Versus non-GX Fonts," next, for more details

---

TECHNICALLY SPEAKING ▶

A PRIMER ON USING QUICKDRAW GX FONTS

New font capabilities with QuickDraw GX You may wonder why Apple bothered to create this new GX-specific font technology. The answer is that QuickDraw GX greatly expands your ability to manipulate the appearance of a font. For example, with non-GX fonts, you can vary the thickness of a character by shifting from plain style to bold. Sometimes, you may find a "light" style that appears thinner than plain style of the same font. But that's about it. With QuickDraw GX, you are able to vary the thickness (technically referred to as the weight) of a character in a virtually limitless series of gradations. You can similarly vary the width of

(continued)

the character set as well as the spacing between characters. You set this for an entire font, using special typographic software. The manipulated font can then be used by any GX-savvy application. These abilities were previously available for PostScript, but only if you had Adobe's Multiple Master PostScript fonts. However, with QuickDraw GX, these abilities are available for virtually all GX TrueType and PostScript fonts.

A technical discussion of the details of these new options is beyond the scope of this book. Suffice it to say that, when you start to explore these new capabilities, you will add a whole new collection of terms to your vocabulary (can you say glyphs and ligatures?). However, there are a couple of basic points that you should be aware of right away:

- Using these new font capabilities requires QuickDraw GX-savvy applications as well as QuickDraw GX fonts. It may also require special typographic software capable of creating the desired modifications to the font. Apple presently is not shipping any such savvy software or typographic applications with System 7.5 (not even SimpleText qualifies). So you may not be able to take advantage of any these new features at first. However, the CD-ROM version of System 7.5 does come with a presentation file (called GX Type Expo) that at least demonstrates all of GX's new font tricks.

    Without GX-savvy applications, GX fonts behave just like non-GX fonts, even though QuickDraw GX is active. However, the good news here is that this means that GX fonts will work, at least at some level, with almost any application, whether the application is GX-savvy or not.

- A primary difference between GX fonts and non-GX fonts is that non-GX font characters are all based on a single keyboard keystroke (or modifier-character keystroke combination). QuickDraw GX fonts no longer have this restriction. Separate characters can be combined into a single character (such as a lower case i with an asterisk for its dot). A more practical example would be to combine the "1," "/," and "2" characters into a new "1/2" character. Thus, QuickDraw GX fonts are referred to as complex fonts while non-GX fonts are referred to as simple fonts.

- When you install QuickDraw GX via Easy Install, it installs the following GX fonts: Apple Chancery, Hoefler Text, Skia, and Tekton Plus. The first three fonts are TrueType fonts. Tekton Plus is a PostScript font (the word Plus is what indicates it is a GX font).

TAKE NOTE ▶

IDENTIFYING GX VERSUS NON-GX FONTS

Given the superficial similarity of the new GX font types, it would be helpful if there was an easy way to identify whether a font is a GX PostScript font versus a GX TrueType font versus a non-GX TrueType font. Unfortunately, there is no easy way to do this. For example, you cannot tell by looking at the font file's Get Info window, or by double-clicking the font file to open its display window, or by seeing how the font is listed in a Font menu.

The only way I know requires using Apple's ResEdit utility. For those who are willing to try it: open up the font file (or suitcase) in ResEdit and then open up its sfnt resource window (this is where the PostScript information that used to be in the printer font file is now stored). Finally, open one of the resources listed in the window. Look in the right-hand column. If the first four letters are "typ1," it is a PostScript font. If the first four letters are "true," it is a GX TrueType font. If the first four letters are anything else, it is probably a non-GX TrueType font. If you can't find an sfnt resource, it is probably a bitmapped font.

The fact that GX PostScript fonts and TrueType fonts now behave almost identically will probably be the most confusing part of shifting to QuickDraw GX. However, the good news

> here is that being able to make this distinction will be less important in QuickDraw GX than it was before. Besides, I predict that some shareware author will soon release a utility that simplifies this identification process.
>
> Also bear in mind that there are really two kinds of GX PostScript fonts. One kind are the fonts converted from non-GX fonts. These are unable to take advantage of the new typographic features possible with GX fonts. The other kind are the fonts specifically designed to be GX fonts and thus can use all of GX's new font features. The identification procedure described here does not distinguish between these two types.

PostScript Fonts

There is no compatibility between the GX and non-GX versions of PostScript fonts. This means that you should not use non-GX PostScript fonts with QuickDraw GX running or use GX PostScript fonts without QuickDraw GX running. Similarly, avoid using GX PostScript fonts in a document if you plan on later opening that document when GX is not running. If you ignore all these warnings, at the very least, text is likely to display and/or print incorrectly. At worst, you may get a system crash.

The main reason for this lack of compatibility is that QuickDraw GX PostScript fonts no longer use separate screen font and printer font files (see Chapter 9 for details on this subject). This is because the printer font file information is now included in the basic font file, just as it always has been for TrueType fonts. In fact, a PostScript font file now looks and behaves on the desktop exactly like a TrueType font.

In this regard, with QuickDraw GX, I would recommend against having a True-Type and a PostScript version of the same font in your Fonts folder. This is more likely to cause problems than it would in non-GX systems.

Ultimately, eliminating the need for printer font files will be a great advantage, as it eliminates many of the hassles and complexities associated with their use. For example, you no longer have to worry that you will select a font based on the presence of its screen font in the Font menu but that it will not print correctly because the matching printer font file is missing.

However, in the short run, you are faced with the problem of making sure that your PostScript fonts are in the right format to be used with the version of the system software you are using. In particular, if you are using QuickDraw GX, you must *enable* your non-GX PostScript fonts before you can use them.

There are two ways to enable a PostScript font:

- **Enable PostScript fonts when you install QuickDraw GX**
  When you install QuickDraw GX, if there are any non-GX PostScript fonts in your Fonts folder, they are automatically converted to the GX format. In addition, all of the now-unneeded screen fonts and printer font files are placed in a special folder inside your System Folder called •Archived Type 1 Fonts• (recall from Chapter 9 that Type 1 fonts are a type of PostScript font; virtually all commonly used PostScript fonts are Type 1). The derived GX version of the font is then placed in the Fonts folder.

This means that, when installing QuickDraw GX, you must have enough free disk space to hold both the existing and converted forms of any PostScript fonts that are currently in your System Folder.

The reason the non-GX version of the fonts is saved is so that you can return to them should you later wish to abandon using QuickDraw GX. This return becomes necessary because, as I stated, you should not use the converted-to-GX form of the PostScript fonts when QuickDraw GX is not running. To reenable the non-GX versions of your fonts, remove the GX version of the fonts from the Fonts folder and drag the files from the •Archived Type 1 Fonts• folder back to the Fonts folder.

Even better, if you reinstall just the non-GX printer font files (and do not remove the matching GX font files), the Mac will be able to access either the GX or non-GX versions of these PostScript fonts as appropriate. (This method also applies to fonts enabled with Type 1 Enabler, described next.) Otherwise, fonts remaining in the •Archived Type 1 Fonts• folder are not used.

- **Enable PostScript fonts with Type 1 Enabler utility**

  Type 1 Enabler (see Figure 12-21) is a utility included with QuickDraw GX. Its function is to convert any non-GX PostScript font to a GX PostScript font. You would use it to convert PostScript fonts that were not present in your System Folder when you first installed QuickDraw GX but that you now want to use. To do this, Apple recommends that you make sure each screen font suitcase contains only one font family. Thus, for example, if Garamond and Hobo font files are in the same suitcase, separate them into two suitcases (see Chapter 9 for more on how to do this if needed). However, when I ignored this recommendation, the conversion still appeared to be successful.

  Type 1 Enabler

  Figure 12-21
  The Type 1 Enabler utility is used to convert non-GX PostScript fonts to the GX format (not needed for fonts that were in your System Folder when you first installed QuickDraw GX)

  After completing any suitcase modifications, launch Type 1 Enabler (and select the Enable command if needed). Locate each font (suitcase) you wish to enable. The utility will ask you for a destination folder for the enabled font (typically, you will choose the Fonts folder of your GX System Folder). After determining this, the enabled font is created (don't forget, you will still need the matching printer font file present, ideally in the same location as the screen font, for this conversion to succeed). The newly created enabled suitcase will contain copies of the preexisting screen fonts plus the newly created PostScript font file (actually it should contain one PostScript font file for every style variant printer font file of the font that was present). The original font files remain unmodified in their original location (or moved to a special folder called Saved Suitcases if you are saving the enabled font to the same location as the original font).

SEE: • "Technically Speaking: A Primer on Using QuickDraw GX Fonts"
• "Take Note: Identifying GX Versus Non-GX Fonts"
• "Take Note: QuickDraw GX and ATM"
• "By the Way: QuickDraw GX Utilities"

TAKE NOTE ▶

QUICKDRAW GX AND ATM

Adobe Type Manager (ATM) is still required for proper display and printing of PostScript fonts (this is one key difference between TrueType and PostScript fonts in QuickDraw GX). A special GX version of Adobe Type Manager is included with QuickDraw GX and is installed when you install QuickDraw GX. However, be aware of the following:

- *ATM 3.7 GX originally shipped with System 7.5. This version does not run in native mode on a Power Macintosh. Power Macintosh users should upgrade to ATM 3.8.1 (or later), which does run in native mode and is compatible with QuickDraw GX and non-GX systems. Be sure to use the ATM Installer to make sure you install the correct version of ATM for your machine. Note that QuickDraw GX 1.1.1 ships with ATM 3.8.2.*

- *You cannot use Adobe Acrobat with ATM 3.7 GX. Acrobat depends on a Font Substitution feature of ATM that is not available in this version of ATM.*

- *Installing some of Adobe's programs, such as Illustrator, may install a pre-3.8, non-GX version of ATM. If so, you need to remove this version in order for the GX version to work. Look for the ~ATM (not ATM GX) control panel (in the Control Panels folder) and a file called something like ~ATM 68020/030/040 (in the root level of the System Folder). Trash them.*

- *ATM 3.7 GX does not work with non-GX system software. Conversely, because GX PostScript fonts do not use separate printer font files, pre-3.8, non-GX versions of ATM cannot access their printer font information. Even with ATM 3.8 (or a later version), you cannot use GX fonts without GX running. Otherwise, at the very least, the fonts' screen displays will be subject to the same jaggies that would occur if you were not using ATM at all. Similarly, unless their printer font file information is built in to the printer's ROM, the fonts will not print correctly.*

- *It might seem that the screen font files in an enabled GX font suitcase are not required anymore (much as they are not required when using TrueType fonts). However, at least one screen font file (typically at 10- or 12-point size) is still needed for ATM to work with the GX font (similar to the ATM requirement for non-GX fonts, as explained more in Chapter 9).*

- *With GX running and ATM installed, PostScript fonts appear as Geneva when displaying a character at a point size less than one half the size of the smallest bitmap available. For example, a font with a single 24-point bitmap would display Geneva at 11 points and lower.*

QuickDraw GX and Graphics

QuickDraw GX has features that assist in better graphic color matching (making use of the ColorSync extension). It also includes built-in routines that will make it easy for almost any application to include enhanced graphics manipulation features, features that were previously only possible with high-end graphics applications and/or PostScript. Finally, as mentioned in Chapter 10, QuickDraw GX improves transfers of graphic images via the Clipboard. In particular, an image's format (such as EPS and TIFF) is more likely to be preserved (rather than converted to a PICT format) when it is copied and pasted. However, as is true for most other GX features, making use of the enhanced Clipboard requires software that is QuickDraw GX-savvy. Apple's Scrapbook is one example of a GX-savvy program.

BY THE WAY ▶

QUICKDRAW GX UTILITIES

There are four QuickDraw GX utilities included with QuickDraw GX. To install them on your hard disk, select Custom Install and then select "QuickDraw GX Utilities." Two of these utilities, QuickDraw GX Helper (used to disable desktop printing) and Type 1 Enabler (used to enable non-GX PostScript fonts), are described in the relevant sections of the main text of this chapter. The other two are Paper Type Editor (used to create extensions that add custom paper sizes to the Paper Type menus in various dialog boxes) and an updated version of LaserWriter Utility (basic functions of which are described in Chapters 7 and 9).

Solve It! QuickDraw GX Problems

Much GX-related troubleshooting advice has already been described in the immediately preceding sections, as part of the general overview of QuickDraw GX. What follows is a more focused look at troubleshooting issues, emphasizing the error messages you may receive.

Remember, most of the error messages described in this section appear in the Finder. If you are not in the Finder at the time, you will have to leave your application and return to the Finder to see the message.

Memory Problems

Symptoms:

- Low memory message alerts appear when running QuickDraw GX.
- More rarely, a memory-related problem may prevent the Macintosh from starting up when GX is active.

Causes:

Almost by definition, the main cause here is insufficient memory to adequately run QuickDraw GX. Recall that running System 7.5 with QuickDraw GX requires a minimum of twice as much memory as you need to run System 7.5 without QuickDraw GX. This means that the absolute minimum required memory to run GX is 8Mb.

What to do:

Problems Running with Only 8Mb of Memory

If you only have the minimally required 8Mb of memory installed (it would have to be 16Mb on a Power Mac), you can still expect to have memory problems when you use QuickDraw GX. For example, Apple claims that in this case you can enable no more than seven printing extensions and seven desktop printers at one time (admittedly not a major concern for most of us). Otherwise, you will get a low memory alert. If you want to have more than seven desktop printers, removing a printing extension may help alleviate memory difficulties (and vice versa).

Personally, I have had problems using QuickDraw GX with only 8Mb of RAM even with just one or two extensions and desktop printers. In one case, I was unable to open any windows in the Finder even though I had several megabytes of unused RAM.

If a low memory alert does appear (see Figure 12-22), try deactivating printing extensions or deleting desktop printers. Also, try closing any open windows in the Finder, close any unneeded documents in any open applications, and (even better) quit any applications that do not need to be open. Using RAM Doubler to double your RAM will also help. As always, adding more SIMMs is the best long-term solution.

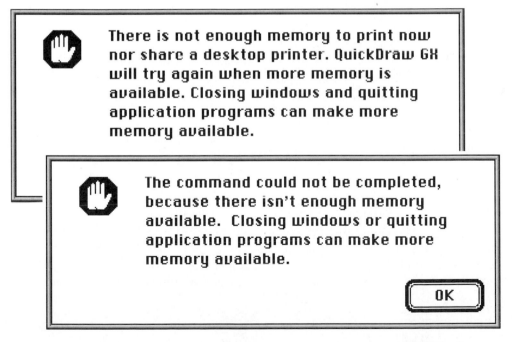

Figure 12-22   Examples of low memory alerts that may appear when running QuickDraw GX

Memory Problems Due to Inactive Desktop Printers

The presence of several inactive desktop printers (those with Xs through the icon, as described in the next section) on the desktop or on disks other than the startup disk can cause low memory alerts to appear. They may also cause your computer to be unable to start up. The solution here is to startup with extensions off (by holding down the Shift key at startup). When startup is over, drag the inactive desktop printers to the Trash and restart normally.

Printing and Printing-Related Problems

 Symptoms:

- Some or all aspects of QuickDraw GX printing features are not usable. In the worst case, all of QuickDraw GX appears disabled. Desktop printer icons may appear with an X over them.

- Page Setup and Print dialog boxes in specific applications are not the expected GX dialogs.

 Causes:

GX-specific causes include needed extensions not loading at startup, desktop printing turned off by QuickDraw GX Helper, a printer driver not selected from the Chooser, no desktop printer created, an incompatible application, a mismatch between selected paper size format and paper size in the printer, or damaged files.

 What to do:

QuickDraw GX Features Are Missing

QuickDraw GX Is Completely Disabled with X's over the Desktop Printer Icons
The most likely reason for the appearance of printer icons with an X over them (see Figure 12-23) is that you started up with extensions off (so that the QuickDraw GX extension is disabled, which effectively disables all of QuickDraw GX, not just the printing features). The obvious solution is to restart with QuickDraw GX active.

Personal LaserWriter NTR

PDD Maker GX

Figure 12-23   Desktop printer icons with an X over them, indicating that you cannot use them for desktop printing

It may also happen if you start up with ColorSync disabled, as this extension (which should load before QuickDraw GX) is needed for QuickDraw GX to load. If ColorSync is missing, you should get a message indicating this (see Figure 12-24) at the end of the startup sequence.

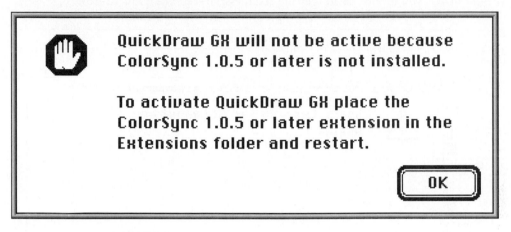

Figure 12-24   This message appears if you try to load QuickDraw GX when ColorSync is missing or disabled

In any case, if you try to open one of these X'd desktop printer icons you will get the message that says it could not be opened because the creating application could not be found (see Figure 12-25).

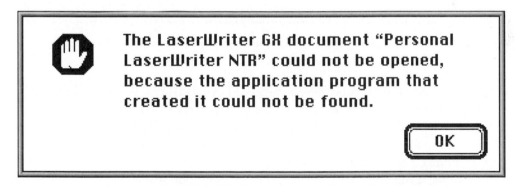

Figure 12-25   This message appears if you try to open the queue window for a desktop printer that has an X over it

By the way, if you copy a desktop printer icon to another disk, the copied icon will probably have an X over it even if the original did not. This is normal and does not affect your use of the original un-X'd desktop printer.

QuickDraw GX Is Enabled at Startup But Does Not Work   In this situation, as in the previous one, desktop printer icons will have an X over them. However, despite this, QuickDraw GX seems enabled because when you select the Chooser, you see the GX printer drivers rather than the non-GX ones. However, if you try to select a GX printer driver, you cannot do so (getting the message seen in Figure 12-26).

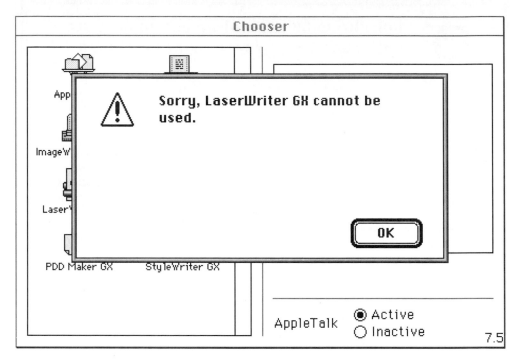

Figure 12-26   Message that may appear in the Chooser if you have damaged GX-related software

If this happens, you probably have a damaged GX-related file. For example, when this happened to me, I ran Norton Disk Doctor and it reported a file length problem with LaserWriter GX. Since this was not a problem that Disk Doctor could fix, the solution was to delete the driver and reinstall a new one (I used the GX Installer to do this). After that, I restarted and everything worked fine.

By the way, if you select Print from within an application before you fix this problem, you will get an error message, probably one of the messages seen in Figure 12-27.

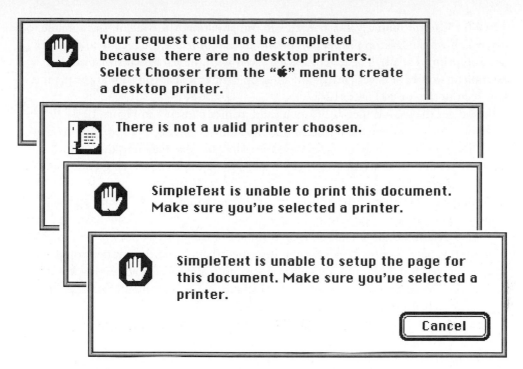

Figure 12-27 These messages appear when the Mac cannot figure out what printer driver or desktop printer to use

QuickDraw GX Page Setup and Print Dialog Boxes Are Missing   This happens when using any application that is not GX-aware. There is nothing you can do to fix this.

It can also happen if you have installed QuickDraw GX Helper and turned off desktop printing for a particular application. To reverse this, go to the Apple menu and select the Turn Desktop Printing On command.

Printing Fails

Sometimes QuickDraw GX appears to be enabled and running correctly (desktop printer icons are not X'd out), yet printing still fails. Typically an alert message appears either as soon as you select Print from an application's File menu or after you click the Print button in a Print dialog box (or after dragging a file to a desktop printer). Occasionally, printing fails without any message appearing (though remember that you may need to go to the Finder to see a particular error message).

As first explained in "The Print Queue Window" section earlier in this chapter, the document that failed to print is likely to be placed on Hold. In this case, after responding to an error message, to get printing to resume, go to the Print Queue window, select the document name, and click the Resume button. Alternatively, you can terminate the print process altogether by clicking the Remove button.

The Mac Cannot Find a Valid Printer   In this situation, the Macintosh is unable to determine which desktop printer you intend to use (or it may be unable to find any desktop printers at all). The exact message varies with the particular situation. For example, if you have never created any desktop printer icons, you should get the message seen in the top of Figure 12-27.

If you get the second message ("not a valid printer chosen") in Figure 12-27, it probably means that you are trying to print without GX being enabled, after having used GX to print in a previous session. As a result, the Mac may not know which non-GX printer driver to use. The simple solution here is to go to the Chooser and select a driver.

A message like either of the bottom two messages in Figure 12-27 may appear when you are using a GX-aware application (such as SimpleText in this case) and it is unable to determine the default desktop printer. For example, I once got the "unable to setup this page" message even though it seemed that a valid default desktop printer was on my desktop. Not quite sure what else to do, I simply clicked on the default desktop printer icon and reselected the Set Default Printer command from the Printing menu. When I tried to print again, it succeeded.

These messages may also appear if any of your printing-related software is damaged or if you have QuickDraw GX disabled (so that the desktop printer icons have X's over them). In these cases, you may alternatively see messages such as those in Figures 12-25 or 12-26.

Print Failure Alert Appears   Most reasons for this are similar to causes described in Chapter 7. For example, if the alert box shown in the top of Figure 12-28 appears, this most likely means that your printer is not turned on, not yet warmed up or cables are not properly connected. The other alert box in Figure 12-28 more likely indicates a PostScript error or similar document-specific error.

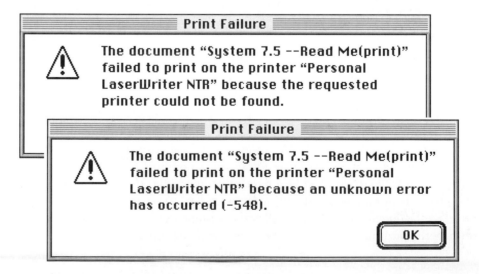

Figure 12-28   Two examples of Print Failure alert messages

Documents May Get Stuck in the Queue   Occasionally, jobs waiting in a desktop printer's queue may not be printed, even though no error message appears. If this happens, check the status of the document in the desktop printer's Print Queue window to ensure that it is not on hold. If it is on hold, select the document name and click the Resume button to change its status. If the current status of the document is Normal and your document is still not printing, this may be due to a system software bug that causes the document to get "stuck." In this case, restart the Macintosh. The document should now print.

PrinterShare GX Is Missing   PrinterShare GX extension is not optional when printing with QuickDraw GX, even if you aren't sharing any printers. If you try to print without PrinterShare GX in your Extensions folder, you will get the message seen in Figure 12-29. The solution is to reenable PrinterShare GX (by getting it to the Extensions folder) if it has been disabled or reinstall it (using the GX Installer disks) if the extension cannot be found anywhere on your startup disk. As always, after making these changes, restart the Mac before trying to print again.

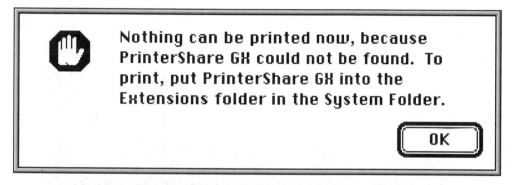

Figure 12-29   This message may appear if you try to print a document without PrinterShare GX in your Extensions folder

Tray Mismatch Alert Appears   When this alert appears (see Figure 12-30), it means that the paper format you have selected for your document (via the Page Setup dialog box) does not match the paper size that the Macintosh believes is in the selected input tray of the printer (as determined via the Input Trays command from the printer's Printing menu or via the setting in the Paper Match extension as selected from the Print dialog box). If you want the printer's paper type selection to change to match the format as selected in Page Setup (presumably because that is the type of paper you are now actually using), click "Manually changed to . . ." (if you have also checked the Save checkbox, the changed selection will become the new default size for the input tray). Otherwise, you can click the "Continue printing" option if it is undimmed (additionally indicating whether you prefer the document to be cropped or scaled, if needed).

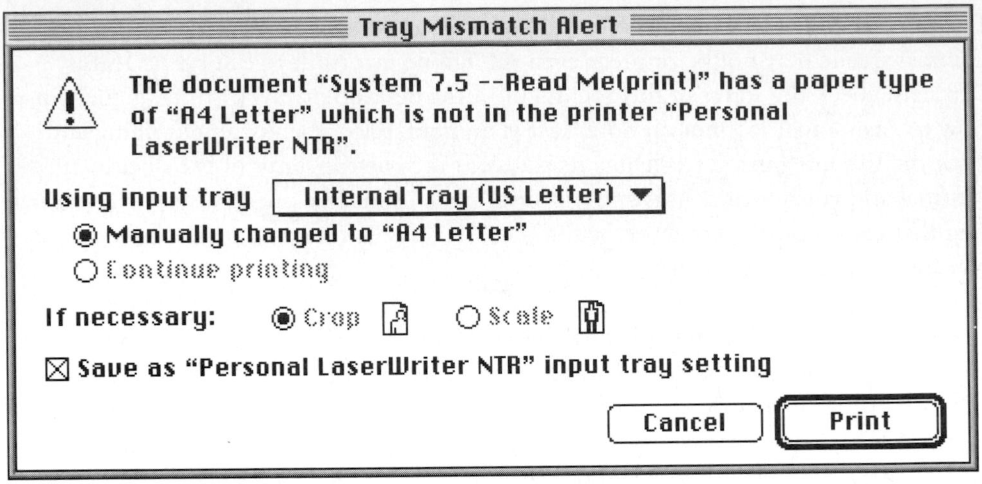

Figure 12-30 Tray Mismatch Alert message may appear just prior to a document beginning to print

A pop-up menu lets you switch to different input trays (which presumably have different sizes of paper), if your printer has this option.

In any case, when you are done, click Print (to continue printing) or Cancel (if you have given up in despair!).

The options in the Tray Mismatch Alert box are not the easiest to understand. When in doubt, you can always experiment with different selections until you get the desired result.

SEE: • "Technically Speaking: Solving Paper Size Selection Confusion," earlier in this chapter, for more on this topic

Otherwise . . . The application you are using may be incompatible with Quick-Draw GX. If so, you may get messages such as *No PostScript fonts are present.* To determine for certain if your application is incompatible, select Turn Desktop Printing Off from the Apple menu (available only if QuickDraw GX Helper is installed) or startup with the QuickDraw GX extension disabled. Now see if your document will print.

SEE: • "Take Note: For Applications Incompatible with QuickDraw GX, Use QuickDraw GX Helper," earlier in this chapter, for more details on QuickDraw GX Helper

"SimpleText Cannot Display This Document" Message

The most common cause of this message is that you are trying to open a PDD document when GX is not active, as explained previously (see "Special Case: Portable Digital Documents (PDDs)" and Figure 12-19).

Desktop Printer-Related System Crashes due to a Locked System File

QuickDraw GX stores the name of the default desktop printer (and the name of its Chooser extension) in the System file. If the System file is locked (which means it cannot be modified), a crash may occur when the Macintosh tries to change any of the contents of the System file (which is what would happen when, for example, you change or delete the default desktop printer). To prevent this, make sure the System file is not locked. To do this, select the System file's icon, choose Get Info from the File menu, and click the Locked checkbox to remove the X (if needed). Similarly, avoid turning on System Folder Protection in the General Controls control panel.

Cannot Delete or Move a Desktop Printer File

If you try to delete a desktop printer file and get the top message seen in Figure 12-31, restart the Macintosh. You should now be able to delete the desktop printer. What's usually going on here is that you cannot delete the desktop printer file (even if you are done printing all the documents that were in its queue) because the Printer-Share GX extension is open (you can see that it is open by going to the Extensions folder and looking at its icon; it has the grayed appearance of an open application). It is this extension that is keeping the desktop printer "busy." The extension opens initially whenever you print a document. The problem is that, once it is open, it apparently remains open even after printing is completed. The only way around this is to restart.

If you get the bottom message seen in Figure 12-31, there is nothing you can do. Currently, QuickDraw GX does not allow you to move a desktop printer icon anywhere except to the desktop, the Trash, or to another volume altogether. You cannot move it to within any folder on the volume from which it was created.

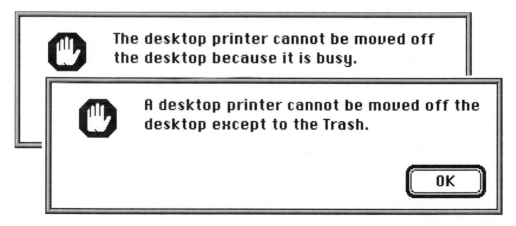

Figure 12-31   Messages that may appear if you try to move a desktop printer icon off of the desktop

Font Problems

Symptoms:

- The display and/or printed font is not the font originally selected for the text.
- A given font displays in some generic font, such as Geneva or Helvetica, rather than in its own font.
- Text unexpectedly displays the "jaggies."
- A system crash occurs shortly after selecting a specific font from a Font menu.

Causes:

If the cause is GX-specific, it is almost assuredly due to some mismatching of the system software and the problem font (such as using GX fonts when not running GX). General guidelines were given in the QuickDraw GX and Fonts section, earlier in this chapter.

SEE: • Chapter 9, for non-GX-related causes of these symptoms

What to do:

Text Displays in Incorrect Font, Displays with "Jaggies," or a System Crash Occurs When Using a Specific Font

In general, try to avoid switching between running with GX on and GX off. Switching back and forth, especially when opening and saving the same document both when GX is on and again when it is off is likely to result in problems, including loss of correct font information.

In one case, for example, I had a document created when a non-GX System Folder was the startup folder. The document contained PostScript fonts that were not present in a separate GX System Folder that I sometimes used. When I later opened the document while the GX System Folder was the startup folder, not surprisingly it displayed in the incorrect font. I made a few minor spelling changes (but no font changes) and saved the document. The real surprise was that when I later opened the document under the original non-GX System Folder, it now displayed in the same wrong font that had appeared when GX was active!

Also, for PostScript fonts, make sure you have at least one size of its matching screen font remaining in the Fonts folder. This is needed for ATM GX to work.

Make Sure Any PostScript Fonts You Use in QuickDraw GX Have Been Enabled

You cannot use non-GX PostScript fonts in QuickDraw GX unless they have been enabled, either when you first installed QuickDraw GX or via the Type I Enabler utility. Even after they have been enabled, they will not acquire the characteristics needed to create special GX font effects. They will only be usable in the same way they were in non-GX systems. To use GX font effects, you need specially designed GX fonts.

SEE: • "QuickDraw GX and Fonts," earlier in this chapter, for more details

And Beyond

Not too long after this book hits the shelves, Apple is expected to come out with System 8. Among other things, expect it to have an improved method of memory management that should result in far less memory-related system errors. It should also incorporate Apple's OpenDoc (which may actually be available prior to System 8). This technology allows a single document to be simultaneously shared by several open applications, each application contributing its part as needed (similar to Microsoft's OLE). This is intended to encourage the development of smaller specialized component applications, designed to be combined/shared with other similar component pieces, allowing you to create your own custom software with just the features you need. This should be a welcome change from the behemoth super-applications that we have today, which often result in users having to pay for and deal with a myriad of features that they never use. System 8 will also have many changes to the operating system's interface, including redesigned Open and Save dialog boxes. A more fundamental restructuring of the entire operating system (System 9?) is expected within a year or so after System 8. Many experts are concerned that System 9 will no longer work with existing Macintoshes (except for perhaps Power Macintoshes). We'll have to wait and see.

On the hardware end, even before System 8 is released, you can expect the arrival of the second generation of Power Macintoshes, which will include numerous changes. For example, they will no longer use NuBus slots as the method for adding cards to the logic board but will instead use a technology called PCI. SCSI may also be on the way out as a method for attaching peripheral devices, to be replaced by something called FireWire. New multimedia and networking-related enhancements are also scheduled. In the world of PowerBooks, you can be certain that the first generation of PowerPC PowerBooks will be released in 1995.

With Apple having licensed its operating system, you can expect to see Macintosh clones hit the market by the summer of 1995. Sometime in 1996, Apple and IBM are expected to jointly release computers that share the same platform (meaning that they will both be capable of running the same software). Currently, these computers are expected to run Macintosh OS as well as IBM's OS/2.

Oops. All this must mean it's time for me to start working on the third edition of *Sad Macs*. See you next time.

Chapter Summary

This chapter focused on recent developments in Macintosh technology, both hardware and software. In terms of hardware, the focus was on the Power Macintosh: what is new about it, what is special about how it works, and some of the unique problems that you may confront when using it. In terms of software, the focus was on System 7.5: what its new features are and the new problems they may present. Extended coverage was given to QuickDraw GX (included as part of System 7.5), especially its new printing features and the new GX-specific fonts. Finally, I took a brief look at what lies ahead in the immediate future of the Macintosh world.

Part III:

Disaster Relief:
The Fix-Its

Meet the Fix-Its. The Fix-Its are a collection of eighteen topics that cover the entire range of problem-solving techniques. Think of them as a set of descriptive troubleshooting tools, the metaphorical equivalent of hardware tools such as a screwdriver or a hammer. Where previous chapters are organized according to symptoms, the Fix-Its are organized according to the tools themselves. There are two ways to use this Fix-It section.

First, and most common, you are sent here via a cross-reference from an earlier chapter of this book. In this case, these Fix-Its are an extension of the step-by-step procedures listed in the previous chapters. Assuming you are still hunting for a solution to your problem, here is where you continue the hunt. These Fix-Its detail frequently cited techniques, avoiding the need to repeat this information every time it is relevant.

Second, I have tried to make each Fix-It stand as a self-contained tutorial on its subject. Thus, if you want to learn about viruses (what they are, how they originate, and how to protect yourself against them), turn to Fix-It #7. This can be useful regardless of whether you are referred there from a previous chapter. To make these Fix-Its independent, some material presented earlier in the book is repeated here, but I have tried to keep this to a minimum.

Each Fix-It is divided into five parts:

1. **Quick Summary.** This briefly describes the key procedure(s) of the Fix-It.

2. **When to Do It.** This section summarizes the common situations and symptoms that suggest the use of the Fix-It. When to Do It is especially useful if you are browsing through the Fix-Its, without having been directed here from a previous chapter.

   Be aware that many of the symptoms described in this section appear in more than one Fix-It. For example, a system crash may point to many different causes, including an extension conflict, a damaged preferences file, a virus, or more. Therefore, when you see your symptom listed for a particular Fix-It, do not immediately assume you have found the cause of your problem. Actually, to diagnose a particular problem, you are better off starting your search in Part II, which also gives suggested sequences for trying the Fix-Its, the precise order varying according to the particular problem at hand.

3. **Why to Do It.** This section briefly summarizes the rationale behind each procedure and what you can expect it to accomplish. Here, more than in the other sections, you can gain insight as to why a given solution works.

4. **What to Do.** This is the main section of each Fix-It. Here is where you'll find the actual procedures and step-by-step instructions. Some of these sections are relatively brief; others are lengthy. In general, they follow the What to Do format of the previous chapters.

5. **For Related Information.** This last section is a list of cross-references that tell you where to go to further investigate selected topics mentioned in the Fix-It.

This Disaster Relief section makes more than occasional reference to utilities needed to assist in repairs, particularly disk-repair and recovery utilities such as MacTools and The Norton Utilities. I go into considerable detail on how to use these utilities—more detail than you are likely to find in other troubleshooting books. Even so, the instructions are not a substitute for the documentation that comes with each utility. If anything here seems unclear, please check your software's manuals before proceeding.

Fix-It #1:
Check for Incompatibilities Between Hardware and Software

QUICK SUMMARY

Read the manuals (as well as any on-disk Read Me files) that come with your software and hardware in order to determine what known incompatibility problems may exist. Check to see if changes to control panel settings can resolve a problem. Otherwise, check if a software upgrade is available that eliminates any incompatibility.

When to do it:

- Before installing or using any new program. Even better, if you can find out incompatibility information before you purchase a program, you may save yourself from buying software you cannot use.

- If an application fails to launch successfully (possibly even causing a system error) the first time you use it.

- Similarly, if an application fails to launch successfully the first time you try it after having made a change in your hardware configuration.

Why to do it:

In the early days of the Macintosh, there was only one model (or at most a few very similar models) of Macintosh available. Unlike other computers at the time, including Apple's own Apple II, Macintoshes were designed to prevent you from accessing the inside of the machine. This was an intentional consequence of the Macintosh vision. The idea was to keep things simple and consistent, so that each software application could be assured that it was interacting with the same hardware, no matter who was using it. This in turn, would make it easy to ensure that all software ran without problem on every Macintosh.

Similarly, the original system software was quite modest and fit entirely on one or two floppy disks. In the same line, when the Macintosh first came out, the only printer that worked with it was the ImageWriter. What you lost in versatility you gained in simplicity.

This is true no more. Yes, I've commented on this before, but it bears repeating here. There are now dozens of Macintosh models, past and present. They vary, right from the factory, on a variety of critical variables: different CPUs, different ROMs, different amounts of RAM preinstalled. With modular Macintoshes, you can add any variety of monitors. The number of possible printers is staggering, from inkjet to laser and beyond. External storage devices are increasingly diverse, from CD-ROMs to SyQuest cartridges. Today's Macintoshes don't even all come with the same system software. Typically, it is specialized for options that are unique to specific models (such as the PowerBook's Control Strip, which is useless for a desktop Macintosh). Prior to System 7.5, Performas came with their own customized system software, somewhat different from what came with other Macintoshes.

The amazing finding, considering all of this diversity, is that most software runs admirably well almost all the time in almost all of the various possible configurations. But "almost" doesn't mean "always." Thus, when things go wrong, one of the first possibilities to consider is that your software is incompatible with your hardware. The most common sources of such problems are as follows.

Application Software Is Too New or Too Powerful for the Hardware

For example, a particular application may require more memory, a faster processor, or a particular color display capability, that your particular Macintosh does not or cannot have. Often, this is because the newer Macintoshes have updated ROMs containing new options not available in the older models.

Hardware Is Too New for the Application Software

Software released prior to the arrival of newer models of Macintosh may have problems due to newer features included in the new hardware. This is often the case when the new hardware includes some significant departure from previous Macintoshes.

For example, many programs initially had problems running on the Macintosh IIci because it was the first Macintosh to include such now common features as 32-bit addressing and 32-bit QuickDraw. More recently, there have been a variety of problems with the AV Macintoshes and again with the Power Macintoshes. Typically, these are temporary problem that are corrected (within less than a year) by upgrades in the problem software.

Hardware Is Too New for the System Software

Typically, you can expect problems, possibly including startup crashes, if you try to use a version of the system software older than the version that was current when your Macintosh model was first released. In particular, most newer models will not run System 6. Increasingly, models will only run on System 7.1 or a later version, and only with the correct System Enabler file installed. Similarly, newer Macintosh models no longer recognize 400K disks.

SEE: • Fix-It #5, for more on System Enablers

 What to do:

General Strategies

1. **Check manuals and Read Me files**
   The main way to discover if a problem is attributable to an incompatibility between a particular application and your hardware configuration is to check the documentation that came with the application. The critical information is usually in the opening pages. Manuals typically inform you of potential incompatibilities as well as minimal hardware requirements. For example, if an application needs a math coprocessor, the manual should tell you that. It should also tell you what models of Macintosh come standard with a math coprocessor.

   Of course, a poorly written manual may omit this information. Similarly, conflicts with hardware that was not released until after the manual was published will not be mentioned. Thus, problems may occur that are not cited in the manuals. Sometimes, Read Me files included on the software disks include information too recent to have made it into the manual.

   If this information cannot be found in the software manual or Read Me files, check the manual(s) that came with your hardware. Also check the documentation included with any peripheral cards you may have added. If you did not set up your Macintosh yourself, and you are not sure what peripheral cards or other add-ons you have, find someone who does know this.

   If you cannot find the relevant manuals, or they don't contain the information you are seeking, call the manufacturer of the program directly.

2. Adjust control panel settings

Some hardware-related incompatibilities can be partially solved by a work-around with your current software. In particular, certain control panels have options that inactivate or modify problem-causing hardware features, enabling you to use otherwise incompatible applications. There is an obvious trade-off here: You lose the advantage of whatever feature you turn off in order to obtain the needed compatibility.

Many of these control panel options are described elsewhere. Here are a few examples:

a. Memory control panel.   A program may be incompatible with 32-bit addressing. To solve this, simply turn off 32-bit addressing from the Memory control panel and restart. On newer Macintoshes, this may not be an option, as they only run in 32-bit mode. On Power Macintoshes, there is an option called Modern Memory Manager. Turning this off solves some incompatibility problems.

b. Monitors control panel.   A program may require a particular color depth to run (such as games that only run in 256 colors). Assuming that your hardware is capable of displaying 256 colors, you simply need to make the proper selection from the Monitors control panel (as described more in Chapter 10).

c. Cache switch control panel.   A program may be incompatible with the special memory cache in 68040 Macintoshes. In this case, use the Cache Switch control panel to turn the cache off (by the way, if you hold down the Option key while turning off the cache, you don't have to restart to have the change take effect). Alternatively, the Compatibility INIT (from Alysis), claims to selectively prevent incompatible applications from being cached. This allows you to have the speed advantage of the cache without having to turn it off for one incompatible application.

3. Upgrade software or hardware, as needed

With luck, a new version of the application software either already exists or will be released shortly that eliminates the incompatibilities. In any case, as a preventative measure, you should keep your software current.

If you have a current version of the application, it may be your system software that is not current (for instance, an application may require System 7.1 or later, and you may be still using System 7.0). If so, upgrade it (as described in Fix-It #5). Be sure to make sure your disk driver is current as well (as described in Fix-It #12).

Otherwise, if it is critical to use the application, you may need to purchase new hardware that eliminates the incompatibilities. This can include anything from a adding more memory to getting a logic board upgrade that essentially transforms your machine into a newer model. You may even have to purchase a new Macintosh. Otherwise, your main remaining choice is simply not to use the problem software.

SEE: • **Chapter 12 on different methods of upgrading to a Power Macintosh**

4. Don't be a pioneer

In general, you can keep compatibility problems to a minimum by not rushing to be the first on your block to purchase a newly released model of Macintosh. I wait at least six months after a machine comes out before I consider buying it. By then, most of the software companies have had a chance to upgrade their software to meet the demands of the new machine, and Apple has had a chance to correct any minor glitches in the hardware.

A Few Common Hardware Incompatibilities

Monitor Incompatibilities

The standard pixel dimensions of a Macintosh 13- or 14-inch monitor is 640 x 480. Many applications are written assuming that the monitor has at least these dimensions. In some cases, if the screen has smaller dimensions, the program can adapt, resizing windows accordingly. However, some programs, especially games, cannot. These games may be unplayable on screens that use lesser dimensions. Certain PowerBooks and Apple's now defunct 12-inch monitor are examples of Macintoshes that have this problem. There is no good solution here other than to avoid those applications that do not work with your monitor size. There are some utilities that fool the Mac into creating a larger screen display (as if it were displaying to a larger monitor). You then need to scroll around to view the parts of the display that are cut off from your monitor. However, I generally do not find this to be a practical solution.

Just remember, it is not the screen size that matters here but the pixel size. That is, a very small screen, with equally small pixels, may still be 640 x 480. In this case, it will display correctly, but everything will be at a reduced size (see Chapter 10 for more on monitor resolutions).

At the other end of the spectrum, larger displays, 16 inches and greater, require more memory than smaller displays to display at the same color depth. Thus, you may find that your Macintosh can display in 24-bit color on a 13-inch monitor but not with a 16-inch monitor. This problem can typically be solved by adding SIMMs, video RAM, and/or special graphics cards to your Macintosh. If you are unfamiliar with the requirements of your particular hardware, seek outside advice.

Card Incompatibilities

With most desktop models of Macintosh, you can insert *cards* into special slots located on the main logic board of the computer. These cards look like smaller versions of the set of integrated circuits found on the main logic board. These cards either add new functions or enhance existing functions of your machine. For example, they may enhance the number of colors that can be displayed, accelerate the speed of the Macintosh, or add video input capabilities. Occasionally, a program may be incompatible with a particular card. If so, you will have to give up either on the application or on the hardware.

Peripheral Hardware Incompatibilities

Every time you connect a peripheral device (such as an external hard drive, scanner or modem), to your Macintosh, some software may be incompatible with it. For example, you may have some imaging or optical character recognition (OCR) software designed to work in conjunction with a scanner. However, it may not work with your particular scanner. This may be because the OCR application requires special software drivers customized for each type of scanner. If the application did not come with a driver for your scanner or cannot recognize the drivers that may have been included with the scanner, the application will not work with the scanner.

No Math Coprocessor

Some programs, especially those that do intensive math calculations, may require a math co-processor. Some Macintosh models ship with a *math coprocessor* (also called a *floating point unit, or FPU*) included, others do not. If you are using a Macintosh that does not have a math co-processor, some math-oriented programs, such as some statistics programs, may not run. If you try, you may get an error message (possibly as part of a system crash!) that says "floating point processor not installed." However, be wary of this message. It can also mistakenly result from causes having nothing to do with an FPU (such as from a bug in the software, an extension conflict, or a call to a memory location that does not exist). In these cases, refer to Chapter 4 for more general advice on system errors. For Power Macintoshes, turning off the Modern Memory Manager from the Memory control panel may eliminate this problem. Installing System 7.5 Update 1.0 will reportedly also reduce the frequency of this type of error in Power Macs.

If you do not know whether an FPU is in your Mac or not, there are various utilities that can tell you, including MacCheck (described in Fix-It #10).

BY THE WAY ▶

SOFTWARE FPU, POWER MACS, AND 68LC040 PROCESSORS

There is a utility called SoftwareFPU that adds FPU capability to Macintoshes that lack it. However, using it is not as fast as using a hardware-based FPU. Many older Macintoshes, such as Mac Plus and SEs, are without an FPU. Prime among more recent FPU-less Macintoshes are those that use a 68LC040 processor (such as the Quadra 605 and 610, and an LC 175). In addition to not having a math coprocessor, these

(continued)

Macs also have a bug in the hardware that prevents SoftwareFPU from working reliably. You know you have this bug if your application crashes on a Mac with a 68LC040 processor with SoftwareFPU installed, but not on a Mac that has a true FPU. There is no current work-around for this bug. Your only options are to (1) use some other alternative application that does not require an FPU, (2) use a different Macintosh that has a true FPU, or (3) wait for a supposedly coming revision to the 68LC040 processor and use it to replace the buggy one in your machine.

Also note that the original 680x0 emulation mode on Power Macs actually emulates a 68LC040. This means that PowerPC Macs running in emulation mode will not work with applications that require an FPU. If you run nonnative software on a Power Mac that requires an FPU, you may get a "No FPU installed" or similar error message.

SEE: • **Chapter 12 for more on Power Macintoshes**

AV Features

The AV (audio-visual) models of 680x0 Macintoshes and all Power Macintoshes (AV models or not) have been plagued by a variety of hardware/software incompatibility problems, most often attributable to the special AV features of these Macintoshes. The GeoPort and the optional GeoPort Telecom Adapter have been a particular sore point. Maybe this is because using the Adapter as a modem requires Apple's Express Modem software, also used in PowerBooks, which itself has been a frequent source of problems. My general recommendation for now would be to avoid the Adapter altogether and just get an ordinary modem.

Some of these problems are addressed by bug-fixed upgraded versions of related software (such as the Express Modem software). If you are having any problems with AV features of your Macintosh, seek outside help for information about what fixes may be available.

Also, depending on what version of the system software you are using, you may benefit from special extensions Apple releases to solve AV-related problems, such as AV Serial Extension. When a new system update or new version of the system software gets released, this type of extension is typically no longer needed (as its information is rolled into the upgrade) and can be discarded. For example, this extension is not needed with System 7.5. Similarly, the extension, !PowerAV Update, which fixes a problem with using 21-inch monitors on certain AV-equipped Power Macintoshes, is no longer needed if you have PowerPC Enabler 1.0.1 or later.

Finally, users of AV Macs may experience an overall performance slow down due to excessive hard disk access. For System 7.1, recent versions of relevant System Enablers (such as Enabler 088) partially fix this. Otherwise, try a freeware extension called sAVe the Disk. This fix should not be needed for System 7.5.

Insufficient RAM

A program may require a minimum of 8 Mb of RAM, and you may only have 4 Mb of SIMMs installed. This is such an important and common problem, that we cover it (and related issues) in a separate Fix-It (#6) on memory problems.

For related information

SEE: • Fix-It #5 on system software problems
       • Fix-It #6 on memory-related problems
       • Fix-It #10 on using MacCheck
       • Fix-It #12 on disk drivers
       • Fix-It #17 on diagnosing hardware problems
       • Fix-It #18 on calling technical support and seeking outside help
       • Chapter 10 on monitor-related problems
       • Chapter 11 on PowerBooks
       • Chapter 12 on Power Macs

Fix-It #2:
Check for Problems with Preferences Files

QUICK SUMMARY

Replace an applications' preferences file and/or system software preferences files (such as Finder Preferences), usually found in the Preferences Folder of the startup disk's System Folder.

When to do it:

• When any changes you have made to preferences settings are unexpectedly lost. For example, customized settings in a word processor, such as fonts and margin settings, may be different from the defaults.

• Whenever you have a problem using a specific feature of an application or control panel, such as a command that does not work or a dialog box that does not appear as expected. Be especially suspicious if that feature had worked properly on previous occasions.

• Whenever an extension does not load or work; especially suspect system software preferences files such as Finder Preferences. Examples of system software known to have preferences file-related problems include the Finder, the Network extension, and PC Exchange.

Why to do it:

Preferences files are used mainly to store customized settings. For example, a word processor may include a checkbox to turn smart quotes on or off. Whichever selection you make, the program remembers it even after you have quit the application. It usually does this by storing your choice in the application's preferences file. This way, you do not have to reselect the desired settings each time you relaunch the application or open a new document.

Preferences files typically have names like Word Settings or Works Preferences (see Figure F2-1) and they are usually located in the System Folder. In System 7, they are usually in a special folder called Preferences. In some cases, preferences files can be stored in the same folder as the application. Usually the program finds its preferences file whether it is with the application or in the System Folder.

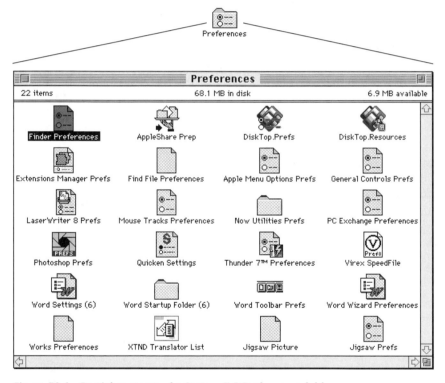

Figure F2-1   Partial contents of a System 7.5 Preferences folder

Not all programs have preference files. But for programs that have them, preferences files are a common source of problems. Problems with preferences files fall into two categories: Customized settings are lost when preferences files are moved or deleted, or various problems occur because of a damaged or upgraded preferences file.

Loss of Customized Settings

Most applications automatically create a preferences file the first time the application is launched. If the preferences file is moved or deleted, the program simply creates a new one the next time you use it. Thus, even if a preferences file was missing or in the wrong place, it is unlikely that you would be alerted to any problem. The real problem here is that, since a newly created preferences file contains the program's default settings, any customized settings you may have previously made are lost.

However, a few programs halt during launch if they cannot locate their preferences files. In most of these cases, an alert message should then appear, requesting that you either locate an existing copy or reinstall a new copy of the preferences file.

Changes in preferences files settings due to unexpectedly "lost" preferences files can occur for numerous reasons. For example, you could shift to a different startup disk, thereby accessing the (newly created default?) preferences file in the alternate disk's System Folder. Or you might completely replace your System Folder, deleting all preferences files that were in it (normally not a recommended procedure), forcing a new preferences file to be created when you next use the application. Similarly, if you use the same application in two different settings, such as at home and at work, each site may have a different customized preferences file.

Corrupted and Upgraded Preferences Files

Preferences files seem particularly susceptible to becoming damaged, often for no discernible cause. When you launch the application that uses a corrupted preferences file, it may refuse to launch. More likely, it opens successfully but exhibits unusual problems, from menu commands that do not work to system crashes. For example, I once had the Save command of a program stop working because of a corrupted preferences file.

A related problem can occur when you upgrade to a new version of a program. Often, even if you exactly follow the program's upgrade instructions, the previous version's preferences file is not replaced during the upgrade procedure. This is fine as long as both versions of the application can read the same preferences file. However, sometimes the new version requires a new format for its preferences file. The existing preferences file is thus incompatible with the upgraded application. If the upgraded program tries to use the previous version's preferences file, results will be similar to using a corrupted file.

Finder Preferences   In System 7, the Finder has its own preferences file (see the highlighted file in Figure F2-1) located in the Preferences folder. It stores settings that affect the Finder's display, such as selections made in the Views control panel. If the Finder's desktop display does not seem consistent with the settings you have selected from the Views control panel, or other Finder-related problems develop, you probably have a corrupted Finder preferences file.

A corrupted Finder Preferences file may sometimes cause problems seemingly unrelated to the Finder. For example, a corrupted Finder Preferences file has been known to prevent the use of the Network extension on Power Macintoshes.

System 7.5 Software Preferences Files   The Finder Preferences file is far from the only preferences file associated with Apple's system software. Especially if you have upgraded to System 7.5, you are likely to find a whole cornucopia of system software preferences files. These include AppleScript Preferences, Find File Preferences, Desktop Pattern Prefs, Apple Menu Options Prefs, Launcher Preferences, and even Jigsaw Preferences (see Figure F2-1). If they get corrupted, they too can be a source of problems.

For example, some cases of an inability to use PC Exchange (now included as a standard part of System 7.5) can be fixed by deleting its Preferences file.

What to do:

1. Quit the problem application (or close the problem control panel)
If a problem is specific to a particular application that is currently open, quit the application before taking any further steps. Relaunch the application only after you have completed these changes.

Similar advice goes for control panels in use. In some cases, you may have to restart with extensions off in order to disable a control panel.

2. Find or replace missing customized preferences files
If you lose an application's customized preferences settings when you switch startup disks, it is because you are now using a different preferences file. The ideal solution is to locate the original customized preferences file, presumably in the System Folder of your original startup disk, and use it to replace the preferences file currently in use. Thus, if your customized settings are on startup disk A but you are using startup disk B, copy the preferences file from disk A to disk B. When the Macintosh asks if you want to replace the existing file, say OK. Make sure you copy the preferences file to its required location. For example, if you place it in the Preferences folder and it seems to have no effect, check whether it needs to be placed in the same folder as the application instead.

If, on the other hand, the problem is that your original customized preferences file has been deleted, the easiest course of action is to simply recreate your customized settings with the new preferences file. In some cases, however, this can be a time-consuming process. For example, Microsoft Word allows you to customize all of its menus. If you make extensive alterations, having to recreate all the changes can be a real annoyance, assuming you can even remember them all. In such cases, if you have installed an undelete utility (described in Chapter 2), use it to try to recover a recently deleted preferences file. Or see if you have a copy on your backup disks.

3. Find and delete (or replace) suspected corrupted or incompatible preferences files
If you suspect a corrupted or incompatible preferences file, delete it. Remember, many control panels now use preferences files. So check for both for application and control panel preference files, as relevant.

If you are having trouble locating a specific preferences file, remember to check for it in both the System Folder (especially in the Preferences folder) and in the folder that contains the application. Also note that, in some cases, preferences files may be contained in a special folder (created by the application) located within the System Folder. A well-known example of this are the preferences files in the Claris folder (a folder created and used by virtually all Claris applications).

For example, suppose you want to check if there is a preferences file for *Busy Works.* First you look, naturally enough, in the Preferences folder. If you are using an icon view, it might help to switch to the By Name view here (from the Finder's View menu). The By Name view lists all files in alphabetical order, making it easier to locate a file that begins with the word *Busy Works* (which is probably the start of the name of the preferences file). Alternatively, you could view files By Kind, looking for files of the kind *Busy Works document* in this case.

What if you come up empty here but you still suspect your sought-after preferences file exists on the disk somewhere? Use the Find command! Simply select Find (or Command-F) and type in any portion of the suspected file name (such as BusyW). Then select Find (or simply press Return). For System 7.0/7.1, the Macintosh locates the first instance of any file that contains that section of text in its name. If the first identified file is not the one you are seeking, you can use Command-G (Find Again) repeatedly to search for more matching files. With System 7.5's Find File, you get a complete list of all files that match the criteria.

If even this fails to locate a specific preferences file (perhaps because it has an unusual name that you do not recognize as belonging to the application), do the following:

a. Get a utility, such as Get More Info, that can list a file's Creator code. Use it to learn the code for your problem application (for example, MSWD is the code for Microsoft Word). See Chapter 8 for more details on doing this.

b. Next, get another utility which can search for files based on Creator codes. In System 7.5, you can do this with same Find File feature you've already been using (as described in Chapter 2). In earlier versions of the system software, the Find function does not include this option. Instead, the best you can do is to search by Kind (such as Kind = "Microsoft Word document"), which is a close, though not quite as reliable, substitute for a search by Creator. Alternatively, you can get any number of other shareware or commercial utilities that can search by Creator (such as DiskTop or FindPro).

c. Use whatever utility you select to search for all files that have the same code as the problem application. Among the found files will almost certainly be the sought-after preferences file.

However you find the file, when you do find the sought after preferences file, delete it. If you find two preferences files with similar names, both apparently for the same application (such as BusyWorks Pref-3 and BusyWorks Pref-4), this probably means that you have upgraded your application and that separate preferences files for both the older and newer versions are present. Check the creation date of both files (using the Get Info command from the Finder). Delete the older of the two files. If this doesn't solve the problem, delete both files.

Normally, this is the end of your problem. A new uncorrupted, compatible preferences file will be created the next time you launch the application. If this does not happen, check the application's original disks for a preferences file. If you find one, copy it from there. In either case, customized settings are lost and need to be recreated.

MORE PROBLEMS DECIDING WHAT PREFERENCES FILE TO DELETE

Deciding what preferences files to delete can get even more complicated than just a difficulty in locating a specific file. For example:

- *Some preferences files are used by several applications (such as XTND Translator List, which is a quasi-preferences file shared by most Claris applications) and Claris Fonts (located in the Claris folder within the System Folder). Conversely, this means that programs may have more than one preferences file. Try deleting these additional preferences files, if you are having any problems associated with an application that you know uses these files.*

- *Some files in the Preferences folder do much more than simply hold an application's Preferences settings (QuicKeys, for example, keeps almost all its accessory files in the Preferences folder). You probably don't want to delete most of these.*

If you have any uncertainty over what can or cannot be deleted, check your application's manual or ask for outside help.

4. **Special case: Delete the Finder Preferences file**

For a suspected corrupted Finder Preferences file, delete it. To do this, drag the Finder Preferences file out of the System Folder, and then restart the Macintosh. A new Finder preferences file is created. You can then delete the old file. This procedure is necessary because the Macintosh does not allow you to delete the Finder preferences file of the current startup disk.

5. **Special case: Delete other system software preferences files**

If you are having any problems with other system software files (such as control panels), check if there is a preferences file associated with the problem software (these preferences files are especially common in System 7.5). If so, delete the relevant preferences file(s). To do this, you may have to drag the files(s) out of the System Folder and restart (as was done with the Finder Preferences file).

6. **Try related solutions**

If the previous steps do not solve the problem, the problem is not with the preferences file. The application itself or its accessory files may be damaged and need to be replaced. Damaged control panels or system software damage are also possible.

For related information

SEE: • Fix-It #3 on replacing accessory files
• Fix-It #5 on replacing system software
• Fix-It #14 on damaged files in general
• Chapter 2 for more on using Find and Find File

Fix-It #3:
Check for Mislocated or Missing Accessory Files

QUICK SUMMARY

Locate and/or move incorrectly located accessory files as needed. If they cannot be located, reinstall them from your backups.

When to do it:

- If an application specifically requests that you locate a missing accessory file either via an Open dialog box or via an alert message.
- If selected features (such as menu commands or dialog box options) of an application are dimmed, missing, or do not work. Rarely, the program may not even launch.

Why to do it:

Most productivity applications use accessory files (such as dictionary files and translator files) as part of their normal operation. Most of these accessory files are optional, and the program launches just fine without them. However, a missing accessory file means that you cannot use the feature or option that requires the file. Thus, for example, a program's spell checker does not work without its dictionary file.

These accessory files often have to reside in specific locations to be recognized by the application. Typically, they have to be either in the same folder as the application or in the System Folder (see Figure F3-1). If they are in the System Folder, they are often in a folder of their own, usually named after the parent application or software company (such as Claris or Aldus). In some cases, these files and/or subfolders are located in the Preferences folder.

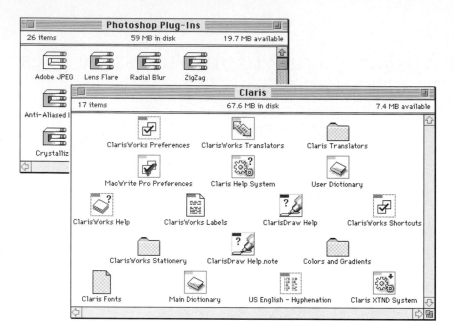

Figure F3-1 Two examples of accessory file folders: at top, Photoshop's Plug-Ins folder, normally located with the Photoshop application; at bottom, the Claris folder, normally located in the System Folder

Normally, if an application comes with an Installer utility, and you use it, all of these accessory files are installed in their proper location. The Installer also creates any needed subfolders. However, the Installer may give you the option to decide which accessory files to install. You may choose not to install some noncritical accessory files in order to save disk space and/or reduce memory requirements. Similarly, if there is no Installer utility, you get to choose which accessory files to install. Finally, you may (inadvertently?) move or delete previously installed accessory files. In any of these cases, the application's functions that depend on these accessory files will not work.

Technically, preferences files (described in Fix-It #2) are also accessory files. However, problems with preferences files are sufficiently different from other accessory file problems that I gave them their own Fix-It.

What to do:

1. Determine if you have missing or mislocated accessory files

a. When an Open dialog box appears.   If an application cannot locate the accessory file needed for a feature you are trying to use, it may present you with an Open dialog box requesting that you locate the file. This could happen, for example, if you select an application's Help command and it cannot locate the needed Help file.

b. When an alert message appears.   If you get an alert message that says an accessory file is missing but you do not get an Open dialog box, this also means the application could not locate the needed file.

c. When no dialog box or message appears.   Missing or mislocated accessory files can cause problems even though no dialog box or alert message appears. For example, a given menu command or a dialog box option may be dimmed or missing. Similarly, if an application does not list as many file-translation formats as the manual says it should, it probably means that the needed translator files are not properly located or were never installed.

2. **Locate missing or mislocated accessory files**

   Try the following suggestions, in the order given, to locate the needed file(s):

   a. Use the Open dialog box.   If you get an Open dialog box and the mislocated file is on your disk, use the dialog box to find the file, select it, and then click Open or Select. This usually solves the problem. If so, the Open dialog box should not reappear the next time you use the feature. If the Open dialog box does reappear, you may have to move the accessory file to a particular location where the program expects to find it (see Step 3). Simply showing the file's location to the program was apparently not good enough.

   b. Go to the expected location.   Otherwise, to find a missing or mislocated accessory file, go to the file's expected location (typically the System Folder or the application folder) as described in the Why to do it section of this Fix-It.

   c. Check other mounted disks with System Folders, if any.   If you have two or more mounted hard disks, both with System Folders, be careful when installing an application onto your nonstartup disk. This is because some Installers automatically place accessory files in the System Folder of the same disk that contains the application, while others place accessory files in the startup disk's System Folder, regardless of where the application is placed. If accessory files wind up in the System Folder of the nonstartup disk, they are not accessed by the application when you launch it (since it looks only in the startup disk's System Folder). If you think this has happened, you have to either reinstall the application to your startup disk or locate the needed accessory files in the secondary disk's System Folder and move them to your startup disk's System Folder.

   d. Use the Finder's Find command.   Follow the same basic procedures as outlined in Fix-It #2 for locating preferences files. If you do not know the accessory file's name, take a guess by using the application's name as a search criterion. This procedure should find most (if not all) accessory files that belong to that application. If not, it should at least bring you to the folder where remaining files are located.

   e. Install it from your backups.   If you still cannot find the file you are seeking, it may not be anywhere on your disk(s). You will need to install it from your backups.

TECHNICALLY SPEAKING ▶

BEYOND TYPICAL ACCESSORY FILES

Some programs require special fonts, sounds, or other special system-related files to work correctly. If the application includes an Installer, it usually properly installs these files for you (often placing them in the Extensions folder). Otherwise, you may be instructed to install them yourself. Check the application's manual for details. Remember that omitting these files or deleting them (which you may be tempted to do if you don't even know how they got on your disk) may present problems when you later use the application.

3. Relocate or replace accessory files, as needed

a. Relocate mislocated accessory files.   If you find mislocated files, move them to their correct location. The manual should tell you where the correct location is, but sometimes it is not clearly stated. If you have found the apparently missing accessory files and they appear to be in the correct location, but they still do not work, you may need to experiment. For example, if an accessory file does not work when it is in the System Folder, make sure that it is in the correct subfolder within the System Folder. Otherwise, try moving it to the same folder that contains the application.

BY THE WAY ▶

LOCATION, LOCATION, LOCATION

I had one unusual variation on this accessory file location problem—one that also involved a preferences file. An application would not list its plug-in modules in the appropriate menu, even though the modules were properly located according to the manual. It turned out that the application's preferences file needed to be placed in the same folder as the modules in order for the application to use the modules. When I moved the preferences file to the plug-in modules folder, the problem was solved.

---

b. Install missing or replace damaged accessory files.   If the accessory file is missing altogether, install it from your original disks. If instead, the file is present and in its correct location, but the problem is still not resolved, you may have a damaged accessory file. Once again the solution is to replace it with a fresh copy from your original disks.

c. Reinstall the application and all of its accessory files.   Finally, if all else fails, it may be that the main application file itself is damaged. At this point, your best bet is to completely replace the application and *all* of its accessory files. Use the Installer utility if one is provided.

For related information

SEE: • Fix-It #2 on preferences files
       • Fix-It #5 on Installer utilities
       • Fix-It #14 on damaged files

Fix-It #4:
Check for Problems with Extensions and Control Panels

QUICK SUMMARY

Temporarily disable all INITs (system extensions and certain control panels that load into memory at startup). In System 7, do this by holding down the shift key at startup. If the symptoms disappear as a result, you have an INIT problem. To solve it, first identify the offending INIT(s). Then you will typically need to either rearrange the loading order of the problem INIT(s), remove the INIT(s) or replace the INIT(s).

When to do it:

- When a system crash occurs at startup, particularly while the Welcome to Macintosh screen (or alternate custom startup screen) is visible. Typically, the crash occurs at exactly the same point (such as just after a certain icon appears along the bottom of the screen) each time you start up.

- When an INIT does not load at startup, even if the startup sequence otherwise proceeds normally.

- When a system error or other disruption occurs while you are using a specific system extension or control panel.

- When a specific command or function in a given application does not work, possibly resulting in a system error. This problem can have numerous causes, an INIT conflict being one of them. An INIT conflict can be the cause even if the problem appears unrelated to the functioning of the INIT.

- When a problem occurs in similar situations across several or all applications, such as when you are trying to save a document. Again, this type of symptom has many possible causes besides problems with INITs.

- Whenever a message appears at startup (from system software or other startup utilities) that indicates that a likely INIT conflict occurred during your previous startup.

- Just about any other time something isn't working as expected. INIT conflicts are one of the most common sources of Macintosh problems.

Why to do it:

Some (but not all) of the extensions and control panels in your System Folder load into memory during the startup sequence. These files perform any number of (largely background) functions, such as placing a clock in your menubar or monitoring for virus infections or enabling file sharing. Apple includes many such extensions and control panels as part of its system software. Some are almost essential to use. Others, including many from third parties, are desirable options because they greatly enhance the capabilities of a bare-bones system.

Even though some of these programs are control panels and even though not all extensions load into memory at startup, Apple generally refers to these programs simply as *extensions*. Is this confusing? You bet it is. To try to disentangle this, I typically still refer to these special programs as *INITs* (Apple's former name for them, as explained in "Take Note: What's an INIT?" in Chapter 1).

On the helpful side, icons for INITs typically appear along the bottom of the Welcome to Macintosh screen as each INIT loads into memory. By identifying the icons, you can get a sense of which extensions and control panels load at startup and which do not (though unfortunately not all INITs display these icons).

INITs, like any software, are subject to the general problems associated with software bugs or corrupted files. However, the two most specific problems associated with INITs are INIT conflicts and INITs that do not load or run.

TECHNICALLY SPEAKING ▶

WHERE IN MEMORY ARE THE INITS?

Applications and documents occupy an area of memory (RAM) referred to as the application heap. *INITs, on the other hand, load into the special area of RAM reserved for the system file and related software called the* system heap. *You can check how the size of the system heap is affected by the presence of INITs. Select About This Macintosh from the Apple menu when you are in the Finder to see a bar representing the amount of memory occupied by the system software (as explained more in Chapter 2). As you add to or subtract from the number of INITs that load at startup, the bar becomes larger or smaller accordingly on subsequent restarts.*

This has some practical implications. For example, if you do not have enough memory available to launch a particular application, you can free more memory by disabling a few rarely needed INITs and restarting. There may now be enough free memory to permit the application to launch. Similarly, the less RAM in your machine, the fewer INITs you can load at startup before you run out of memory. Startup management utilities (as described in this Fix-It) are especially useful for temporarily disabling selected INITs.

SEE: • Fix-It #6 for more on application and system heaps

INIT Conflicts

Most INITs remain in memory, working in the background, from the moment you start up until you shut down. This presents a unique challenge for these programs: They must function smoothly no matter what other INITs or applications you are using at the same time, and they must not prevent the normal functioning of these other INITs or applications. Failure to meet these goals is referred to as an *INIT conflict*.

Sometimes these conflicts are easy to diagnose. Other times, they can be *very* subtle. For example, an application may have some quirk that appears only when you are using a new AutoSaver INIT while running under System 7 with virtual memory turned on and the QuicKeys INIT also installed.

Regardless of the symptoms, the cause of these conflicts is typically a software bug (though developers may argue among themselves whether the source of the bug is in the INIT or in the software with which it conflicts). Three basic types of INIT conflicts occur, as described in the following paragraphs.

1. **Conflict with another INIT**

   Conflicts with another INIT are often the hardest to diagnose because even when you think you have found the problem INIT, another one may be at least partially responsible. This type of conflict is the one most likely to lead to system crashes during the startup sequence.

2. **Conflict with another application**

   The symptoms of a conflict with another application may show up as a malfunction of the INIT or as a problem with the application (often seemingly unrelated to the INIT functioning, such as a menu command that does not work).

3. **Conflicts with system software**

   The worst-case scenario is when the INIT is incompatible with the version of the system software you are using. In this case, problems are likely to occur in a variety of contexts across applications. The INIT may not work at all. Startup problems are also possible.

Although an INIT conflict is not the only possible cause of many of these symptoms, it is usually an easy one to either confirm or eliminate. That's why it should be one of the first things you check.

INITs That Do Not Load or Run

An INIT may simply not work at all—even without any sign of conflict with other software. Typically, this is because the INIT never loaded into memory at startup (which it must do in order to work!). An INIT conflict may still be the underlying cause here, but other causes are possible. For example, remember that you cannot use a newly installed INIT without first placing it in the System Folder (typically in the Control Panels or Extensions folders) and then restarting.

 What to do:

Described here are the three main steps to solving INIT conflicts: (1) Disable INITs to determine if you have an INIT conflict, (2) identify the problem INIT, (3) resolve the conflict. The final section of this Fix-It deals with what to do for an INIT that appears not to load or run at all.

Disable INITs to Determine If You Have an INIT Conflict

The logic is simple. Temporarily disable *all* of your INITs. If the problem goes away, then you know you have an INIT conflict. There are three different ways to disable your INITs: hold down the Shift key during startup, use a startup management utility, or remove all INITs from your System Folder.

To quickly disable all of your INITs, nothing is better than the Shift key method. It is simple, it is easy to do, and it is guaranteed to disable virtually all system extensions and INIT-type control panels in your System Folder.

Using a startup management utility is more likely to leave some INITs enabled (including itself of course!). But it is still fine to use if those remaining INITs are not the source of your problem.

Dragging INITs out of the System Folder is recommended only if you are still using System 6 (since the Shift key method does not work here; at best it disables only some INITs) and if you do not have an effective startup management utility. The only time you may need to use this method in System 7 is to disable unusual INITs that are not disabled by the Shift key or startup management utilities (as described in "Technically Speaking: INITs That Refuse to Be Disabled . . . and Other Oddities," later in this Fix-It).

Here are the details of each method:

Method #1: Disable INITs by Holding Down the Shift Key at Startup

To disable all of your INITs at startup:

1. **Restart the Macintosh**

2. ***Immediately* press and hold down the Shift key**
   If you do not press it soon enough, it will not work. If it fails to work, restart and try again. The first sign that it worked is that, when the Welcome to Macintosh screen is displayed, the words *Extensions off* appear directly below the words *Welcome to Macintosh*. You can now release the Shift key; your INITs have been disabled for this startup. No INIT icons will

appear along the bottom of the startup screen. This is all only a temporary change. Everything returns to its previous condition the next time you start up.

By the way, if you are using a customized startup screen that replaces the Welcome to Macintosh screen, the *Extensions off* message does not appear. To be safe here, hold down the Shift key until the startup screen disappears.

By the way, this shift key technique also bypasses any programs found in your Startup Items folder (which is totally separate from your INITs!). Actually, if you wait to hold down the shift key until just after extensions have loaded, you can bypass Startup Items files without similarly disabling extensions.

Method #2: Disable INITs by Using a Startup Management Utility

Startup management utilities are themselves INIT-type control panels (actually, some of these utilities consist of separate system extension and control panel files). Now Utilities' Startup Manager, Casady & Greene's Conflict Catcher, and Apple's Extensions Manager are three popular examples (see Figures F4-1a and F4-1b).

They all give you a list of the startup extensions and control panels in your System Folder that are INITs. Actually, some may list even more. For example, they may be able to list non-INIT extensions, such as printer drivers, or fonts stored in your Fonts folder.

Apple includes a version of Extensions Manager as part of System 7.5. The System 7.5 version has a few less features than the previous generic version (for example, the System 7.5 version cannot customize what types of files it lists and does not list Apple Menu Items or Fonts), but it includes a new option that lets you start up with all extensions off except those that come with System 7.5 (just select "System 7.5 Only" from the pop-up menu, as seen in Figure F4-1b). This unique feature can help diagnose conflicts specific to non-Apple extensions (especially helpful in System 7.5, because it includes so many extensions and control panels). Otherwise, the generic Extensions Manager version should still be available free from user groups or on-line services (see Appendix). Both versions are less full featured than Startup Manager or Conflict Catcher. For example, Extensions Manager cannot rearrange the loading order of extensions; the others can.

By the way, Conflict Catcher 3 (an upgrade of Conflict Catcher II) was just released as this book went to press. It adds numerous new features, including the ability to display actual INIT names, rather than icons, during startup.

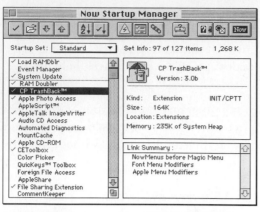

Figure F4-1a   Two popular startup management utilities: Now Utilities' Startup Manager (top) and Casady & Greene's Conflict Catcher II (bottom)

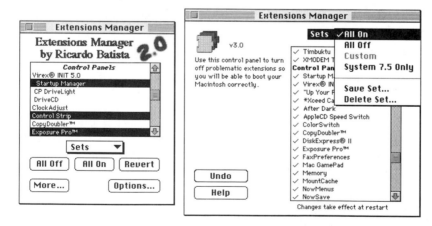

Figure F4-1b   Apple's Extensions Manager: The generic version (left) and the version that comes with System 7.5 (right)

All of these startup management utilities work similarly. Use whichever one you like best, but don't use more than one at the same time! To use them to disable INITs at startup:

1. **Hold down a specified "hot" key at startup**

   Each program has a self-defined hot key—usually the spacebar. When the management utility loads at startup, it detects the held-down hot key. It then halts the startup sequence and opens the utility's dialog box.

   (Alternatively, some startup utilities have an additional hot key that, if held down at startup, immediately instructs the utility to skip all INITs, bypassing the need to access the dialog box.)

2. a. **Select the option to skip loading all INITs**

   The startup management utility's dialog box should have a button or menu command with a name like *Skip All* or *All Off.* Select it. Or:

   b. **Turn off selective INITs.** To help identify a problem INIT (as described in "Identify the Problem INIT," later in this Fix-It), you will want to turn off some INITs but not others. The easiest way to do this is with a startup management utility. In fact, this is the biggest advantage of using a startup management utility over using the Shift key method. For example, with Startup Manager, double-clicking a name in the list of INITs in its dialog box (see Figure F4-1a) places or removes the check in front of its name. Only checked INITs load at startup.

3. **Decide whether the change is to be temporary or permanent**

   Typically, you can choose between having your changes affect only the current startup (a temporary change) or all subsequent startups (a permanent change). For example, with Now Utilities' Startup Manager, you do this by clicking either the *Temporary* or *OK* button at the bottom of the dialog box. The OK button makes the change permanent. When doing this sort of diagnosis, I would preferably make the changes temporary. Extensions Manager, unfortunately, has no temporary option.

   In either case, after selecting the desired button, the startup process now resumes normally, except that all disabled INITs do not load. If you selected to disable an INIT that loaded prior to your extension management utility, the Mac will probably restart at this point (see "Technically Speaking: INITs That Refuse to Be Disabled . . . and Other Oddities," later in this Fix-It.) Actually, with the System 7.5 version of Extensions Manager, restarting appears to be necessary in order to get any changes to take effect immediately.

You are not limited to using these utilities only at startup. You can access them at any other time, as you would any control panel. You can make similar changes at these times. However, changes do not take effect until the next time you start up. Also, the temporary option is not available.

Finally, as an alternative to the temporary option, you can create separate "sets" of extension list settings, selecting among different sets at startup, as desired. Check your manager's documentation for details.

System 6 Alert: If you are using System 6, make sure your startup management utility works with System 6. Now Utilities 4.0 or a later version, for example, works only with System 7.

SEE: • "Technically Speaking: How Do Startup Management Utilities Disable INITs?" and "Technically Speaking: INITs That Refuse to Be Disabled . . . and Other Oddities" for more on disabling INITs

HOW DO STARTUP MANAGEMENT UTILITIES DISABLE INITS?

What exactly does a startup management utility do to an INIT that prevents it from loading at startup? Most management utilities accomplish this feat by either moving the disabled INIT to a special folder or changing the file type of the INIT. Each method has its advantages and disadvantages.

- ***Moving the disabled INIT to a special folder.** The management utility creates folders with names like* Extensions (disabled) *and places these folders in your System Folder. Any INITs that you select to be disabled are then placed in these folders by the management utility. Removed from their normal location, these INITs do not load at the next startup. This works well only in System 7, since System 6 does not support the use of subfolders in the System Folder. Another minor disadvantage is that when you select Control Panels from the Apple menu, disabled control panels do not appear (since they are now in a different folder). At first, you may think they have disappeared. Don't panic. They're still on your disk. They return to the Control Panels folder automatically after you use the management utility to turn them back on. You can also reenable these INITs manually, simply by dragging them back to their previous folder location.*

  All three startup management utilities shown in Figures F4-1a and 1b use this method. It is by far the most prevalent method in use today.

- ***Changing the file type of the INIT.** Every file, when it is first created, is assigned a file type (as explained in Chapter 8). File types help the Macintosh identify the nature and function of a file. For example, there is a unique file type for system extensions and another one for control panels. The system software checks each file's type at startup, thereby identifying those files that act as INITs and properly loading them into memory. With some management utilities, when you disable an INIT, the utility alters its file type. As a result, they are not loaded into memory at startup. For example, an INIT-type control panel's file type may be changed from cdev to xdev. Often, these disabled INITs appear with an X over their icon in the Finder. The file type is returned to normal when you reenable the INIT.*

  The disadvantage of this approach is that a disabled INIT cannot function, under any circumstances, until its file type is returned to normal. Thus, if you stop using the startup management utility before reenabling any disabled INITs, or if you copy a disabled INIT to another disk that does not use the same startup management utility, the disabled INITs will not work. This can be disconcerting, especially if you don't know why it has happened. At worst, if you no longer have access to the management utility, it can put these INITs out of commission indefinitely (unless you know how to alter file types on your own, as explained in Chapter 8). However, the generic version of Apple's Extension Manager includes an option to fix the file type of all extensions that have been disabled by this method. To access this, click the "More . . ." button and then click the "Recover Extensions" button.

One startup management utility, INITPicker, uses a unique method to disable INITs that avoids the pitfalls of both of these other approaches. INITPicker's method neither moves disabled files to a separate folder nor changes their file type.

INITS THAT REFUSE TO BE DISABLED . . . AND OTHER ODDITIES

There are a couple of occasions when the shift key technique and/or startup management utilities will be unable to disable an extension at startup.

For example, some startup managers cannot turn off any INITs that load prior to the manager itself, especially if you are accessing the startup manager during startup. An anti-virus utility is an example of a possible INIT that might load prior to a startup manager. System Updates are another. Some startup managers may not even show such INITs in their list. To get around this problem, you may have to rename the early loading INIT so that it loads later in the sequence, though this is not always advised (see "Take Note: The Loading Order of INITs or What's in a Name?," later in this Fix-it). However, Conflict Catcher II and Startup Manager 5.x, not only list INITs that load before it, but allow you to turn them off—even during the startup sequence. If turned off during startup, they will set the extension to be disabled and then issue a restart command. Extensions Manager has a similar feature, accessed by holding down the Command key when you close its window during a startup access.

A few special extensions and related files load prior to all other extensions and control panels, no matter what they are named. For example, System Enablers load prior to any extensions and cannot be turned off by any startup management technique (including holding down the Shift key). This is because, if the Enabler is needed, the Macintosh will not start up without it. So the Macintosh is intelligent enough not to disable this file.

Similarly, there is a category of extensions with a file type called scri *(as opposed to the more common* INIT *file type). Apple's Event Manager (most commonly found as part of an AppleScript installation) is an example of this type of extension. System Update 3.0 is another example. These load prior to all other extensions. Now Utilities' Startup Manager 5.x and Conflict Catcher II list these INITs and let you turn them on or off—but not change their loading order. Apple's Extension Manager also identifies these files. Holding down the Shift key will also prevent scri files from loading at startup.*

These files are just the start of a growing list of oddities that you are likely to find lurking in your Extensions folder. For example, there is another category of extensions that have a file type of appe. *These are sometimes referred to as background applications. They are sort of a hybrid of extensions and ordinary applications. One example of this, of which I am familiar, is a shareware utility called Folder Watcher. These special extensions do not really launch until the end of the startup sequence, regardless of where their startup icon may appear during the startup process. Again, some startup managers may not even list these extensions and thus you would not be able to selectively disable them. However, holding down the Shift key should disable them.*

Another oddity is an extension such as Network (the extension, not the control panel). This extension is also not listed in the menu of most startup management utilities, and for a very good reason: It is not an INIT (even though it looks for all the world like a system extension). Its file type is text *(not INIT) and its "No INITs" Finder flag is checked (which means it does not load at startup and is thus not listed in most startup management utilities' lists). The extension is actually needed for the File Sharing Monitor, Sharing Setup, and Users and Groups control panels to work correctly. If you get Balloon Help for that extension, you will be informed of this fact (see Figure F4-2). Similarly, if you try to open one of those control panels when the Network extension is not available, you will get a message that tells you that you need the Network extension (see Figure F4-2). It appears to act as a sort of accessory extension, only active when the primary extension is loaded at startup. A similar example is Apple's Shared Library*

(continued)

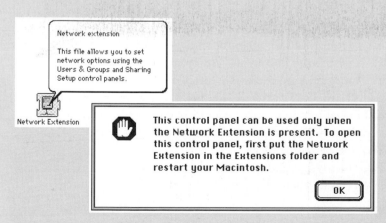

Network extension

This file allows you to set network options using the Users & Groups and Sharing Setup control panels.

Network Extension

This control panel can be used only when the Network Extension is present. To open this control panel, first put the Network Extension in the Extensions folder and restart your Macintosh.

OK

Figure F4-2 Left: Balloon help message for the Network extension; right: The message that appears if you open File Sharing Monitor without the Network extension in the Extensions folder

Method #3: Disable INITs by Removing INITs from Your System Folder

Removing INITs from your System Folder is the least convenient way to disable your INITs. However, it is the only one guaranteed to work under all situations, even in System 6. Here's what to do:

1. **Create a new folder on your desktop (anywhere but in the System Folder)**
   Name it *INITs Folder* (or whatever else you like).

2. **Drag all of the INITs from your System Folder and place them in this newly created folder**
   A potential problem here is that you may not know which of the files in your System Folder are INITs and which are not. To determine this in System 6, open the System Folder and select View by Kind from the Finder's View menu. Locate all files whose Kind is *control panel* (don't worry whether they function as INITs) and *startup document*. Remove them from the System Folder. In System 7, you basically do the same thing, except check for *control panel* and *system extension* (rather than startup document). Also remember to check at the main level of the System Folder as well as in the Extensions and Control Panels folders.

   A few INITs list their kind simply as *document*. These INITs cannot be identified by the technique just described. Thus, if in doubt, also remove unfamiliar files in your System Folder that are identified only as *document*, if they are in the Control Panels or Extensions folder or at the root level of the System Folder.

   This will inevitably catch files (especially control panels and documents) that are not INITs, but there is little you can do about that with this method.

3. **Restart your Macintosh**
   The Macintosh now boots without any INITs loading. If your symptoms disappear, you have an INIT conflict.

Identify the Problem INIT

If your problem disappears as a result of turning off all your INITs, you have an INIT conflict. The next step is to determine which INIT or combination of INITs is the source of the problem. To do this you will have to selectively enable and disable INITs. Of the three methods for disabling INITs described in the previous section, a startup management utility is clearly the best here. It offers the maximum in convenience and flexibility. Dragging INITs in and out of your System Folder from the Finder also works, but it is much more time-consuming. The Shift key technique is useless here; you cannot selectively disable INITs with it.

Bearing this in mind, try the following suggestions, in the order indicated, as appropriate.

Check Recently Added INITs

If you added an INIT to your startup disk just prior to the appearance of a problem, this INIT becomes a prime suspect. To check it out, disable just that INIT. To do this with a startup management utility: Access the list of INITs from the manager's control panel window, enable all the INITs that you normally use, then disable the suspect INIT. Then restart. If the problem disappears, you have identified the likely problem INIT (though the problem may also involve a conflict with another INIT already on your disk).

Check Suspicious INITs

If the symptoms suggest a particular INIT or group of INITs as the cause of the conflict, disable these INITs and restart. For example, if a problem appears across a variety of applications whenever you try to save documents, and you use an autosave control panel, this control panel is a likely source of the problem. Start by disabling it. See if the problem goes away.

Check for Known Incompatibilities and Bugs

Chances are, you are not the first person to experience your particular INIT conflict. If so, others may be able to identify and solve the problem for you. Check the documentation of all of your INITs for any advice. If you discover a likely culprit, disable it to see if the problem goes away. Call the publisher's technical support line for more specific help, if needed.

Similarly, if you are having a problem only with a particular application and you suspect it may be caused by an INIT conflict, call the technical support line for that application. They may be able to identify the problem and offer a solution. However, when there is a conflict between an INIT and an application, it can be hard to determine whether the cause is the INIT or the application. Occasionally, you may get a run-around. For example, if INIT A conflicts with Application X, the INIT developer may blame the application developer for the problem, and vice versa. Unfortunately, while each one waits for the other to correct the problem, you are left without a solution.

Disable and Reenable Individual INITs

If none of the preceding methods succeed, it's time to systematically disable and reenable all your INITs. This is a time-honored method for identifying problem INITs, but it is also a potentially long and tedious one. Not only does it take a long time, but it requires your active involvement throughout the process. This means you can't just walk away for an hour and come back after the procedure is over. You must constantly be present to watch what happens and make changes accordingly. If you use dozens of INITs, as I do, this procedure can take hours.

Unless you only have a few extensions (six or less) or are a masochist, don't try to isolate an extension conflict without some sort of startup management utility. They make the testing process much easier and somewhat faster. It is much more convenient than having to drag files in and out of the System Folder and then restarting. Even with just a few extensions, extension managers help because they typically identify which extensions and control panels really load at startup and which do not, saving you the effort of worrying about files that cannot possibly be the cause of your problem.

1. **Disable all INITs**

   Essentially, start by repeating what you did in the previous section ("Disable INITs to Determine if You Have an INIT Conflict"). Do this either by restarting after dragging all INITs out of your System Folder or by using a startup management utility. Do *not* use the Shift key technique here. As you have presumably already determined that you have an INIT conflict, your problem should now no longer appear.

   If you are using a startup management utility, you may need to disable INITs that normally load before the startup management utility itself (see "Technically Speaking: INITs That Refuse to Be Disabled . . . and Other Oddities" for details). This will be necessary only if it turns out that one of them is the actual culprit. If you cannot get the startup manager to disable them, drag those particular INITs out of the System Folder and test them separately.

   By the way, you could equally well do this whole process in reverse: Start with all INITs enabled and then disable them one by one. However, if your symptom is a system crash, and it keeps recurring until you finally remove the culprit INIT, this can be a more frustrating alternative!

2. Reenable INITs individually, restarting each time

a. If you are using a startup management utility. Access its control panel, either prior to restarting or during the startup process (as described in "Disable INITs to Determine if You Have an INIT Conflict") and use it to turn one INIT back on (start with any one you want). See if your problem has returned.

b. If you are not using a startup management utility. Start by returning one INIT to the System Folder. In System 7, you can do this by dragging the INIT to the System Folder icon. The Macintosh relocates it to the Extensions or Control Panels folder for you. Then restart the Macintosh. See if your problem has returned.

c. In either case, continue to reenable INITs one at a time, restarting each time, until the problem reappears. Hopefully, you had no other plans for the day. The order in which you reenable INITs doesn't matter. When the problem does reappear, you know that the most recently returned INIT is the problem INIT.

d. A possible shortcut if you have a large number of INITs. Start by dividing all your INITs into two groups and then reenable the first half. If the problem reappears, you know that the problem INIT is in this first group. If the problem does not reappear, the problem is presumably in the second group. Reenable the second half to confirm this. Once you have isolated the half that contains the problem INIT, divide that group into two smaller groups and reenable only the first of the two smaller groups. Continue this technique until you have isolated the problem INIT by the process of elimination.

e. Is it the startup management utility itself? If you reach the end of the line here and no problem INIT has been identified, you may have a conflict with your startup management utility itself. After all, these startup managers are themselves INITs. Especially suspect this if the problem goes away if you disable all INITs with the shift key technique but not with your startup management utility. Otherwise, if the manager has a startup hot key that can be used to disable itself, you could conveniently use this to check for a conflict caused by the management utility.

3. Confirm that you have identified the problem INIT

Once you have identified the suspected problem INIT, reenable all INITs except the problem one. Restart. If the problem no longer occurs, the lone disabled INIT is confirmed as the problem INIT.

As an extra check, disable all INITs except the problem INIT. If the problem reappears, this is added confirmation that the lone enabled INIT is the problem.

If these tests do not confirm the identity of the problem INIT, you probably have one of the special cases described in the following sections.

CONFLICT IDENTIFICATION MADE SIMPLE

What if you don't really want to do all the work involved in checking for extension conflicts? You may not have to. Conflict Catcher (as its name implies) and Startup Manager 5.x both provide special help for identifying conflicts. Essentially, they automate the procedure for disabling and reenabling INITs. You simply click a button to start the process, and the utility takes over, telling you what to do and what it all means (see Figure F4-3). They can even diagnose conflicts involving two or more INITs. If you want a no-brainer (though probably not a much faster) approach to resolving INIT conflicts, this is the way to go. However, these automated methods may have problems properly testing codependent INITS (see "Is It a Codependent INIT Problem (or Other INIT Conflict)?," later in this Fix-It).

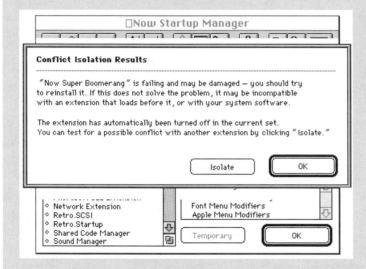

Figure F4-3   Startup Manager's conflict isolation feature isolates a conflict

These utilities also have a separate feature that identifies an INIT that causes a crash at startup. With Startup Manager, it is called "Disable/Isolate crashing extensions" and it is available from the Preferences dialog box. If this option is active, on the next restart after an INIT causes a system crash at startup, the problem INIT is automatically disabled, thereby preventing a recurrence of the system crash. Even more helpful, Startup Manager displays an alert box identifying the name of the disabled INIT. From this alert box you can also click an Isolate button that then takes you directly into Startup Manager's conflict isolation feature (useful to check if the INIT that was turned off was truly the INIT that caused the crash). Conflict Catcher II's similar preferences option is called "Find Startup Crashes."

Special Case: Conflict Between Two INITs

The technique described in "Disable and Reenable Individual INITs" may not succeed if a problem appears only when two INITs are active at the same time. This can be especially problematic if you are using the shortcut grouping method and you have placed two conflicting INITs in separate groups. In this case, you can hopefully still identify one of the likely problem

INITs. You can then repeat the basic technique except leaving the identified INIT always enabled while you begin reenabling others. When the problem reappears you have identified the second problem INIT.

Helpful hint: Make sure you don't install two INITs that do essentially the same thing. For example, don't use two different screen savers or two different INITs that create hierarchical menus off the Apple menu. Doing so will inevitably lead to conflicts.

Special Case: Conflict Occurs Only When Using an INIT

Sometimes a conflict may be apparent only when you actually access an INIT's features (such as selecting a pop-up menu that it creates). If so, you cannot disable the INIT to check if the problem goes away. In this case, restart the Macintosh with *only* the identified problem INIT(s) enabled. Ideally do this by using a startup management utility. If the problem does not now occur, it typically means that the problem is the result of an interaction between that INIT and yet another INIT. Start reenabling INITs, as just described, until the problem reappears. At this point, you have identified the additional conflicting INIT.

On the other hand, if the problem does recur with only the one INIT enabled, treat this situation as an INIT that will not load or run. Refer to the section on this topic, later in this Fix-It.

Special Case: If an INIT Causes a System Crash at Startup

The procedures just described generally apply to all INIT conflict situations, including where an INIT causes a system crash at startup. However, special problems can occur here because a startup conflict prevents the Macintosh from successfully reaching the desktop. For example, without access to the desktop, you cannot drag items into or out of the System Folder.

There is one bit of good news in all this: INITs that cause problems at startup are often the easiest ones to isolate. This is because the crash usually occurs precisely when the problem INIT is loading into memory. Thus, the timing of the crash indicates which is the problem INIT. Here's what to do:

1. **Bypass the system crash at startup**

   a. **If you are using a startup management utility.** When the system crash occurs, restart the Macintosh. Then invoke the startup management utility at startup (as described in previous sections of this Fix-It), using it to disable all INITs. Presumably, you can do this prior to when the system crash would otherwise occur.

BY THE WAY ▶

THE MACINTOSH HELPS OUT

If a system error occurs while INITs are loading during startup, the Macintosh may display an error message with the following advice: To temporarily turn off extensions, restart and hold down the Shift key. *This is the Mac's way of telling you that you have an INIT conflict.*

---

b. If you are not using a startup management utility.   Either hold down the Shift key to bypass all INITs at startup, or start up from an alternate disk that does not contain the problem INIT.

2. **Identify the Problem INIT**

a. Locate the INIT *after* the last one whose icon appeared during startup.   The last icon to appear before the system crash typically indicates the last INIT to have loaded successfully (if you don't recall what icon that was, you will have to restart again with extensions enabled so as to get the system crash to recur). You can usually identify the name of this INIT because the icon is similar to or identical to the icon of the system extension or control panel file as it appears on the desktop. If you do not recognize the icon, go to the System Folder and examine the icons of all INITs until you find the one that matches the icon that last appeared on the startup screen.

But wait! This is not the problem INIT. The next INIT scheduled to load is the likely problem INIT. If you use a startup management utility, you can find out the name of this INIT by checking the list of names in the utility's dialog box. INITs are listed there in the order that they load. Thus, the problem INIT is the one listed immediately below the name you just identified. If you don't use a startup manager, INITs load in alphabetical order (first extensions, then control panels). So examine the names of your INITs to determine which one was scheduled to load when the system crash occurred.

SEE: • "Take Note: The Loading Order of INITs or What's in a Name?," later in this Fix-It, for additional details

b. When the startup icon method does not apply.   A potential pitfall with using startup icons to identify the problem INIT is that not all INITs display an icon during startup. Some have no startup icon to display. In other cases, the INIT icon's display may have been turned off (usually from an optional setting in the INIT's control panel window). In these cases, referring to startup icons may turn out to be of limited value. If so, you will have to determine the likely problem INIT either from the Finder's alphabetical listing of extensions and control panels (view By Name) or, if appropriate, from the loading order as listed in your startup management utility.

c. Use special features of startup management utilities, if available.   Some startup management utilities have special options for dealing with extensions that cause system crashes at startup. In particular, Now Utilities' Startup Manager has an option called "Disable/Isolate crashing extensions" that disables and identifies the name of the INIT that was loading at the time of the crash (see "By the Way: Conflict Identification Made Simple," earlier in this Fix-It, for more details).

3. **Confirm that you have identified the problem INIT**
Once you have identified the suspected problem INIT, reenable all INITs except the problem one. Restart. If the crash no longer occurs, the lone disabled INIT is confirmed as the problem INIT.

However, the problem may still ultimately involve this INIT plus another one that loaded before it. To test for this, disable all INITs that load before the suspected problem

INIT and reenable the problem INIT. If all goes well now, it means that the crash involves at least two INITs. Begin reenabling the early loading INITs one by one, restarting each time, until the crash returns. The INIT that triggers the return of the crash is the second problem INIT.

4. **Expand the search to other INITs if needed**

   If the suspected problem INIT turned out not to be the culprit, successively disable and reenable other INITs that loaded anywhere near when the crash occurred, especially the last INIT that supposedly successfully loaded. If that still fails to isolate the problem INIT, follow the general guidelines given previously to disable all INITs ("Disable and Reenable Individual INITs") and successively reenable them until the problem recurs.

Resolve the Conflict

Once you identify the problem INIT, the simplest solution is to stop using it. Alternatively, if the INIT causes problems only with one application, you might find it preferable to stop using that application. However, the ideal solution is to find a way to continue to use all of your INITs and applications, but minus the problems. This may be possible. Here's how to give it your best shot.

Rearrange the Loading Order of INITs

Sometimes an INIT causes a problem only if it loads before (or after) a certain other INIT. Rearranging the order in which the INITs load can thus eliminate the problem. Typically, to test this out, move a problem INIT toward the start of the loading order or (if that fails to work) toward the end of the loading order. Restart to see if the problem goes away.

The manual that comes with an INIT may offer advice about where the INIT should load and what other common INITs should precede it or come after it (be careful not to reverse the order of codependent INITs, as described in "If the INIT Does Not Load or Run," later in this Fix-It). Otherwise, you have to experiment. Of course, there is no guarantee that any amount of reordering will help. So if a few reshuffles don't seem to do anything, I would give up.

For some INITs, it is critical (from a functional point of view) that they load early in the loading process. For example, you want an anti-virus INIT to load first so that it can detect possible viruses in other INITs. Similarly, you want a startup management utility to load first (or just after an anti-virus INIT) so that it can manage all the remaining INITs. To accomplish this, creators of these INITs give them special names designed to move them to the top of the loading order. A typical trick is to place a blank space in front of the name of the INIT, since the Macintosh considers a blank space to be alphabetically before the letter A.

Adding a blank space to the start of an INIT's name can be tricky, since the Finder does not ordinarily let you type a blank space as a first character. To circumvent this prohibition, select the INIT's name, type any letter as the first character, follow it with a blank space, and then delete the initial letter.

A few INITs (such as startup management and anti-virus utilities) always seem to load near the start of the list, even though they may not appear to have a special character in front of their name. Most often, they do have a special character. Typically, they use a control character. For example, SAM uses Control-A. This loads even before a blank space.

To place a control character in front of any INIT's name, go to the Key Caps desk accessory. Type Control-A (or Control-B, or whatever). Copy the character symbol that appears. Now go to the INIT file in the Finder, select its name, and place the text cursor in front of the first character. Finally, select Paste. To cut a control character from a name, you must also select a character adjacent to the control character.

Other INITs (Adobe Type Manager is one well-known example) work best when they are loaded last (or late) in the loading process. To ensure that this happens, Adobe adds a tilde (~) to the name of its extension, which the Macintosh arranges after the letter Z.

In general, unless you use a startup management utility to maintain the loading order, you should not change the name of INITs that begin with these special characters because you do not want to alter their intended loading order. Finally, note that some special INITs load at the start of the startup sequence, regardless of their name. Typically, you cannot use a startup management utility to rearrange the loading order of these special INITs, even if the utility lists their name.

SEE: • **"Technically Speaking: INITs That Refuse to Be Disabled . . . and Other Oddities," earlier in this Fix-It**

To rearrange the loading order of INITs, try one or more of the following suggestions, as appropriate:

- **Use a startup management utility**
  Using a startup management utility is the preferred method of rearranging INITs. Simply go to the utility's dialog box that lists all INITs. From here, you can usually reorder the names of the INITs by dragging them to a new location in the list. The listed order is the order in which the INITs load, regardless of the names of the INITs and regardless of whether they are in the Extensions or Control Panels folder.

  Apple's Extension Manager does not include this option, which is a major drawback as compared to other competing utilities.

- **Rename the INIT**
  If you don't use a startup manager, you must rename an INIT to change its position in the alphabetical hierarchy. For example, if you want an INIT to load late, go to the Finder, select the INIT's icon, and add a tilde in front of its name. To get it to load early, add a blank space or a control character. Of course, simply putting an extra A or Z in front of the name often works just as well, though it is less aesthetically pleasing.

SEE: • "Take Note: The Loading Order of INITs or What's in a Name?," earlier in this Fix-It, for details on how to add a blank space or control character to a name.

One word of caution, some INITs work only with their original name. Often these INITs have their name "locked" so that you cannot change it. Ideally, the INIT's manual should alert you to this. In any case, I would leave these names alone. However, if you are determined to change it, you can unlock its name (as explained the section on Finder Flags in Chapter 8).

- **Use an alias**
Using an alias is especially useful if you have an INIT located in the Control Panels folder that you want to load prior to an INIT in the Extensions folder. Normally, all items in the Extensions folder load before any items in the Control Panels folder. Simply renaming the INIT, no matter what name you choose, does not change this rule. Of course, you could get the control panel to load earlier by moving the control panel to the Extensions folder. But then it would no longer appear in the Control Panels window.

To solve this dilemma, create an alias for the control panel. Place the control panel in the Extensions folder and the alias in the Control Panels folder. Now it loads the Extensions folder, but the alias shows up in the Control Panels display.

Of course, if you use a startup management utility that permits reordering of loading order, using the utility is more convenient than this alias technique. Still, the alias technique may be useful for establishing the loading order of the startup management utility itself or for a control panel that you want to load prior to the startup management utility (such as an anti-virus utility). In these cases, this alias technique is useful even if you don't have an INIT conflict that you are trying to resolve.

In most cases, utilities that need to be concerned with this dilemma are designed to solve the problem automatically, as part of their installation process. For example, the Extensions Manager control panel uses a companion EM Extension.

SEE: • "Take Note: The Loading Order of INITs or What's in a Name?," earlier in this Fix-It, for more details

System 6 Alert: In System 6, there are no Extensions and Control Panels folders and no aliases. In System 6, all INITs in the System Folder, whatever their location, load in alphabetical order.

BY THE WAY ▶

CREATE LINKS WITH STARTUP MANAGEMENT UTILITIES

Now Utilities' Startup Manager and Conflict Catcher both have a feature that can create special links among any group of INITs. These links can prevent certain INIT conflicts involving two or more INITs. For example, you can create a link that guarantees that one INIT will always load later than another one, that both INITs get turned on (or off) if either one gets turned on (or off), or that certain incompatible pairs of INITs cannot both be on at the same time. Once you identify one of these problems as the cause of your symptoms, these links provide a permanent solution.

Upgrade the Problem INIT or Other Software

Many of these INIT problems are due to bugs in the extension(s) itself (or the application with which it conflicts). If nothing so far has succeeded, check if there is a newer nonconflicting version of the INIT available. If this is the case, get the upgrade and check if it resolves your problem. Upgrading the application, if a newer version is available, may offer another route to a solution.

If the INIT conflict appears to be with the system software, upgrading to a newer version of the system software (or downgrading back to the previous version, if the problem began as a result of an upgrade) can also eliminate the conflict. For example, some newer INITs do not work with System 6, while some older ones do not work with System 7.

SEE: • Fix-It #5 for checking on system software incompatibilities and upgrading system software

Replace Potentially Damaged Files

Conflicts due to damaged files can obviously be resolved by replacing the files with undamaged copies. To check this out:

- **Replace a control panel's preferences file**
  Some control panels have their own preferences files, located in the Preferences Folder. These files may get corrupted and need replacement. To do so, restart with the suspected control panel temporarily disabled. Then delete the potentially corrupted preferences file. The control panel will make a new one automatically, as needed.

- **Replace the INIT or application or system software**
  Delete the problem INIT (as described in the next section) and replace it with a fresh copy from your backups. Alternatively, if the problem only occurs when using a specific application, replace the application software to see if that helps. Some INIT conflicts may be traced to corrupted System and/or Finder files; consider replacing them if all else has failed.

Check for Memory-Related Problems

Some problems involving INITs are not directly caused by the INIT. For example, if you are using many INITs, insufficient memory may be the cause. Memory problems are covered in Fix-It #6. However, for starters, turn off virtual memory (accessed via the Memory control panel) and file sharing (accessed via the Sharing Setup control panel) if they are on. Also, try turning off 32-bit addressing, if you have that option. See if that cures your problem.

Delete the Problem INIT

If nothing so far has helped, you probably do have to stop using the INIT altogether. Sometimes, as previously discussed, a problem may be caused by a conflict between two different INITs. In this case, removing one of the INITs is likely to resolve the problem. If not, remove them both.

Most often, if you decide to permanently stop using an INIT, you want to place it in the Trash and delete it from your disk. However, if the INIT is currently in use (that is, if it was loaded into memory at startup), this may be tricky. If you try to empty the Trash when an active INIT is in it, you may get an alert message that says that the INIT cannot be deleted because it is in use. Even if you can trash the INIT, be careful. The INIT is probably still present in memory and functioning. If it subsequently tries to access its disk file, it will find it missing. This can cause problems, including system crashes.

The safest way to delete an active INIT is: (1) Drag the INIT from the System Folder to the desktop, (2) restart the Macintosh, (3) now drag the INIT to the Trash and discard it.

If the INIT Does Not Load or Run

An INIT may not load at startup, though the startup otherwise proceeds normally. Alternatively, an INIT may appear to load properly, but still not function. For control panels, you may even be unable to open its dialog box. If any of these or similar problems happen, ask yourself the following questions.

Is It a Codependent INIT Problem (or Other INIT Conflict)?

Codependent INITs are two or more INITs, typically from the same software package or same company, that must load in a specific sequence in order to run properly. Typically, one INIT needs to load first in order for the second INIT to function. For example, in order to use CE Software's QuicKeys INIT, you must first load the CEToolbox INIT (QuicKeys ships with both INITs). Similarly, in order to use many of Now Utilities files, you must first load Now Toolbox. Without these toolbox INITs installed, the second INIT of the pair will not load at all.

The solutions to this type of problem are either to install the missing codependent INIT (if only the second INIT is present) or to rearrange the loading order of the INITs (so that the one that needs to load first does).

In the end, this is just a special case of the general problem where any, even unrelated, INIT can cause a conflict if it loads before (or after) a certain other INIT. Thus, sometimes an incompatibility between two INITs is such that if one of the INITs is present (especially if it loads first) the other INIT will not load or function. The quickest way to check this is to disable all INITs except for the one that did not load (see "Special Case: Conflict Between Two INITs" earlier in this Fix-It). Now restart the Macintosh. If the INIT now loads and runs properly, there is a conflict between that INIT and another INIT on your startup disk, probably one that loaded prior to the problem INIT. Often, rearranging the loading order will solve the problem. Otherwise, you may have to disable one of the incompatible INITs.

SEE: • "Resolve the Conflict," earlier in this Fix-It, for more general advice

Did You Restart After Installing the INIT?

Remember, since INITs load into memory at startup, they do not immediately work when they are first installed on your startup disk. To get them to work, restart the Macintosh after installing the INIT.

Is the INIT in the System Folder?

INITs do not disappear from your System Folder by themselves. However, don't forget that if you switch to a different startup disk, the new startup disk may contain different INITs. In this case, some of those you normally expect to see are not present.

Is the INIT in Its Proper Location in the System Folder?

Remember, in System 7, INITs load only if they are in one of the following locations: the Extensions folder, the Control Panels folder, and the root level of the System Folder (that is, not in any subfolder). Some INITs work properly only if they are in one, but not either of the other, of these locations.

   Normally, to add a new INIT to the System Folder, either use the INIT's Installer utility or drag the INIT file to the System Folder icon (*not* the System file icon and *not* the System Folder window). In the latter case, the Finder determines the INIT's correct folder (Extensions or Control Panels) and asks you if you want it to be placed there (see Figure F4-4). If you add INITs by any other method, you may inadvertently place them in a wrong location. In such cases, they may either not work properly or not load at all.

   The solution is to determine the INIT's correct location (check its documentation if needed) and move it there. Then restart the Macintosh.

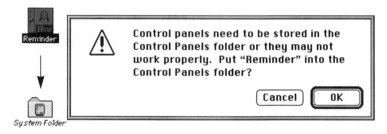

Figure F4-4   Drag a control panel to the System Folder icon and you get this message

Helpful hint: If a control panel is located outside the System Folder, you may still be able to open it successfully. However, if it is an INIT-type control panel, any changes you make to its settings will likely have no effect—until you correctly locate it and then restart.

BY THE WAY ▶

SOME INITS DO NOT WORK IF THEY ARE IN A SUBFOLDER

Some (usually older) INITs may not work properly (or at all) in System 7 if they are placed in the Extensions folder or the Control Panels folder. Often, these INITs still work fine if they are relocated to the main level of the System Folder. If this does not completely resolve the problem, create an alias of the INIT and place the alias in either the Extensions folder or the Control Panels folder, as appropriate. Leave the INIT at the main level of the System Folder. Restart the Macintosh.

For example, I had a system extension that would not load unless it was placed at the main level of the System Folder. Even after it loaded, however, I could not access its preferences settings dialog box. So I placed an alias of the INIT in the Extensions folder, with the original at the root level. After I restarted, everything worked perfectly.

Was the INIT Disabled by Your Startup Manager?

Most startup managers have a user-definable hot key that, when held down at startup, prevents all INITs from loading. This is faster than having to access the manager's control panel at startup. Be careful not to inadvertently press this key at startup. Be especially careful if you define Caps Lock as the hot key, since this can be left locked and will thus prevent your INITs from loading even if you aren't touching the keyboard!

Also recall that you can set your startup manager to disable a particular INIT or automatically skip all INITs (by selecting its Skip All, or equivalent, command). Make sure you do not do this unintentionally.

Similarly, startup managers can save different startup sets (listing which INITs are on or off), which you can then select (making it convenient to selectively turn some INITs on only when you know you will need them). If you do this, make sure you are using the set you think you are.

Finally, be aware that some of these startup managers have an optional preferences setting that automatically disables any newly added INITs. In such cases, you must manually enable the INIT from the startup manager's control panel window before the INIT will load. Then, of course, you still need to restart the Macintosh.

In general, simply make sure that the INIT is not currently disabled by your startup management utility.

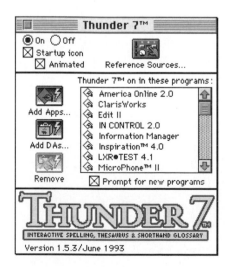

Figure F4-5
The Thunder 7 control panel, with On and Off buttons in the upper left corner

Is the INIT Turned On?

Many control panels have on/off buttons in their dialog box (see Figure F4-5). These buttons must be in the on position for the control panel to work, even if the control panel file is in its proper location at startup. If you discover an INIT in the off position, turn it back on. If this has no immediate effect, restart the Macintosh. This should get it to work again.

Special Case: Startup Icons Appear with an X Over Them or Disappear

Many extensions have an assigned key or key combination that can be used to selectively disable it at startup. No other INIT is affected unless it too uses the same hot key(s). (By the way, although these hot keys can selectively disable INITs, I would avoid using them as a means of diagnosing INIT conflicts. Instead, stick with the other methods described earlier in this Fix-It.)

If you disable an INIT with this hot key method, the startup icon (in the Welcome to Macintosh screen) for the relevant INIT may appear with an X through it, indicating that the INIT did not load. Alternatively, the startup icon may disappear altogether. This is all perfectly normal. Just be careful not to inadvertently hold down these hot keys at startup or you may get a surprise. By the way, sometimes turning off an INIT from its control panel (as described in the previous section) will also cause an X'd icon to appear.

If these possibilities to not account for the X'd icon, consider the following:

- With RAM Doubler (described more in Fix-It #6), this problem can happen the first time you turn RAM Doubler back on after having previously disabled it via the shift key or a startup manager. Skipping over the details, this is due to the fact that RAM Doubler actually loads two separate INITs. The first one has no icon and loads first. If this one does not load at startup (which it may not do after RAM Doubler has been previously disabled and turned back on again), the icon for the second INIT, if present, will appear with an X over it. When startup is complete, you will get a message that says that RAM Doubler did not load but will load correctly the next time you start. To solve this problem, just restart as it suggests.

- You may be trying to use an INIT that does not work on your Macintosh model (such as trying to use the AudioVision INIT on a Mac that does not support this feature). This will typically result in an X'd icon.

- The INIT's preferences file may be damaged. Locate it and delete it (see "Replace Potentially Damaged Files," earlier in this Fix-It.).

- If the problem persists, the INIT itself may be damaged or it may have a bug that has been fixed in an upgraded version. Replace the INIT. If that fails, contact the INIT's publisher for help.

For related information

SEE:
- Fix-It #2 on problems with preferences files
- Fix-It #5 on system software problems
- Fix-It #6 on memory problems
- Fix-It #13 on damaged disks
- Fix-It #14 on damaged files
- Fix-It #18 on seeking outside help
- Chapter 1 on System Folder subfolders
- Chapter 4 on system errors in general
- Chapter 5 on system crashes at startup
- Chapter 11 on file sharing

Fix-It #5:
Check for Problems with System Software

QUICK SUMMARY

If a system software problem is suspected, update or replace the system software files as needed. Generally do a "clean reinstall" of the system software, using the Installer utility that came with your Macintosh system software disks.

When to do it:

- Whenever you have made a change to your system software shortly before the onset of the problem.

- Whenever you have a specific problem using system software (such as a problem with the functioning of the Finder).

- Whenever you have a problem with recently added software that does not appear to be due to the causes described in previous Fix-Its or any other identifiable cause—even if you have made no changes to the system software.

- Whenever a symptom, such as a system crash, occurs in a variety of different contexts or across a variety of applications.

- Whenever you need to upgrade to a newer version of the system software.

For some of these symptoms, other possible causes exist, but system software remains a prime candidate.

Why to do it:

System software, particularly the System and the Finder, forms the essential background against which all other programs must work. It is in use from startup to shutdown. Thus, since the system software is never dormant, you should suspect it as the potential cause of almost any problem—especially one that is not easy to diagnose.

Besides the System file and the Finder, Macintosh system software includes other files normally found in the System Folder, such as various control panels, extensions, and Apple menu items. The definitions and explanations of all categories of system software files, including the distinctions between System 6 and System 7, are described in Chapter 1. If these distinctions are unfamiliar, check Chapter 1 before proceeding.

The bases for most system software problems fall into two familiar categories, as presented next.

Incompatibility Problems   For example, a new upgrade of your favorite application may only work with the latest version of the system software. If you are still using an older version, you have trouble. In particular, many applications now only work with System 7. The severity of the symptoms of any incompatibility can vary from a refusal of a program to launch to minor display problems to system crashes. The primary solution here is to upgrade your system software.

Because the symptoms can be so nonspecific, it can be difficult to know for sure whether a particular problem is due to incompatible system software. Fortunately, there are several ways to get some help (see "Take Note: Identifying System Software Compatibility Problems and Bugs" next).

Damaged File Problems   Any system software file may become damaged. However, the more likely candidates include the System file, the Finder, Enabler files, PrintMonitor, printer drivers, and font files. The System file is particularly prone to damage, mainly because it is modified more often than other files. It gets modified almost every time you use your Macintosh, even though you are not directly made aware of this. Making matters worse, damage to the System file is likely to cause more serious symptoms than damage to other system software files. The main solution in all cases is to replace the corrupted file. If you cannot determine which system software file is the actual culprit, you may have to replace all system software files.

TAKE NOTE ▶

IDENTIFYING SYSTEM SOFTWARE COMPATIBILITY PROBLEMS AND BUGS

You have a problem that may be due to a system software incompatibility, but you are not certain that this is the cause. Before you rush to unnecessarily do a complete system software reinstall, check out the following.

When System 7.0 was released, incompatibility problems with other software were so great that Apple included a special utility called Compatibility Checker. It analyzed the contents of your disk and produced a report of known System 7-incompatible programs present on your disk. This utility is probably not needed anymore, as almost all software has long since been upgraded to be compatible with System 7.

However, System 7.5 comes with a similarly functioning utility called Safe Install. Apple recommends that you run it before you first install System 7.5. It offers to move into a special folder any potentially incompatible files that it finds.

In either case, I find the warnings from these utilities to be overzealous. If a program is listed as incompatible but you don't experience any problem with it, feel free to continue to use it. The problem may be a minor one that may never affect your use of the program or Apple's utility may simply be incorrect in its assessment. However, if an upgrade is available for the program, it probably pays to get it.

Apple's MacCheck application (described more in Fix-It #10) also does some minimal amount of compatibility checking. For example, it might identify an application that is not 32-bit compatible.

Other third-party applications, such as Help!, perform similar functions, identifying conflicts and incompatibilities not only with system software, but with all software and hardware. However, these programs are only as good as the database of information that the program uses as the basis for its decisions. For these databases to remain current, you have to regularly purchase updates.

Don't forget to check any documentation that came with your software for possible advice. Otherwise outside help, in the form of technical support lines, magazines, users groups, and online services may provide the answer (see Fix-It #18 for details).

On a related note, sometimes a problem may be caused by a bug in the system software. Actually, no version of the system software is free of bugs. Apple tries to eradicate bugs, such as via its System Updates (as described more elsewhere in this Fix-It), but it never entirely succeeds. New system software versions, on the other hand, tend to introduce new bugs. Replacing system software will not eliminate bugs inherent in the software itself. Fixing these problems will require waiting for the appropriate bug-fixed upgrade. The best you can do, in the meantime, is to try to stay informed about such bugs, so that you can understand the cause of whatever symptoms they produce.

What to do:

This section is divided into two parts: "Complete Install/Reinstall of System Software" and "Selective Install/Reinstall/Deletion of System Software." The simplest and most direct approach to most system software problems is to completely reinstall the system software. How best to do this is explained in the first part. Sometimes, less drastic solutions are possible, such as just replacing a single file known to be damaged. These solutions are described in the second part.

Complete Install/Reinstall of System Software

Do a Clean Reinstall of System Software

When you use the Installer utility on your system software disks to reinstall system software, the Installer may update an existing file by modifying it rather than by completely replacing it. Similarly, it may fail to modify or replace a file if the new version is not any different from the version already on your drive (that is, if both files are from version 7.5, for example). This is actually preferable in many situations. For example, you may have customized a System file with your own set of sound files. A normal reinstall will update the System file, if needed, but will leave the customized sounds intact. The problem with this approach is that if the System file is damaged, the damage may be left intact. To solve this problem, you need to do what is called a clean reinstall. In this case, you completely replace all existing system software files.

While a clean reinstall is intended primarily to deal with suspected damaged files, doing a clean reinstall will do no harm (other than possibly losing some customized settings) even when no damage is suspected. Actually, I would recommend doing a clean reinstall anytime you make major upgrades to your system software (such as upgrading from System 6 to System 7). Similarly, many experts recommend a clean reinstall of your system software every few months as a preventative measure to forestall any problems caused by unrecognized damage.

However, a clean reinstall is often much more time-consuming, so I would probably skip it for minor upgrades (such as from System 7.0 to 7.1) as long as no damaged files are suspected.

If you want to do a clean reinstall, continue with this section. If instead you simply want to do an ordinary reinstall (or install system software on a disk for the first time), skip ahead to the next section, "Using the System Software Installer."

BY THE WAY ▶

REINSTALLING SYSTEM SOFTWARE ON PERFORMAS

As mentioned in Chapter 1, Macintosh Performas (prior to System 7.5) came with their own unique system software, identified by a P at the end of the version number (e.g., System 7.1P). This is not a problem by itself. However, as of this writing (even with System 7.5), Performas do not ship with a complete set of system software on floppy or CD-ROM disks. Apple does not even sell Performa system software disks as a separately purchasable item. Instead, Performas come with a set of programs, called Apple Backup and Apple Restore, that do what their name implies. Apple advises that you backup your drive when you first get it and then use Apple Restore to restore files, including system software, if needed.

Unfortunately, this is not an ideal solution for doing a clean reinstall or upgrade of your system software. If you contact Apple and tell them that, because of problems with your drive, you need to do a reinstall of your system software, they will probably send you the needed disks. Otherwise, your main alternative is to get the standard version disks and install those instead.

Yes, that's right, the standard version of the system software also works on Performas. However, if you try this, you may need to use a different enabler file. Most Performas are twins of a non-Performa Macintosh model. When you switch to the standard system software, you need to dump your Performa enabler (if any) and use the enabler for its matching twin instead. Unfortunately, figuring out which one to get can get a bit tricky. There is often no relationship between the name of a given Performa and its matching Macintosh. Get outside help here, if needed.

Hopefully, this will all be simpler with System 7.5, since there is no longer a separate Performa (P) version. All Performas and Macintoshes use the same version of System 7.5.

***Helpful hint:** Do not use Performa Enablers with the standard Macintosh system software or use the Macintosh Enablers with the Performa system software, since a particular system enabler may not have system resources that the other operating system needs. Also, do not put a Performa enabler and a Macintosh enabler for a similar machine in the same System Folder, since this may cause unpredictable results.*

Also note that System Updates (discussed more later in the Fix-It) generally do not work with Performa versions of the system software, which is another reason to get the non-P version of the software.

SEE: • **"Take Note: Install Me First Disks and System Enablers," for more on enablers**

TAKE NOTE ▶

AN "INSTANT" SYSTEM 7.5 CLEAN REINSTALL

After launching the Installer, when you get to the window with the Install button, press and hold Command-Shift-K. A new window will open with two additional options: Update Existing System Folder and Install New System Folder (see Figure F5-1). Update Existing Folder is the default option. If you select the Install New System Folder option, the "Install" button will change to read "Clean Install." This sets up the Installer to do a clean reinstall, including an entirely new System and Finder, leaving your old System Folder still intact and renamed as Previous System Folder. After you quit the Installer, you can drag items from the old folder to the new one as needed, discarding the remainder of the old folder. In order to take advantage of this shortcut, you must have enough disk space to hold both System Folders at the same time.

If you use this shortcut, you can skip the entire "Do a Clean Reinstall of System Software" section. Just check the "Using the System Software Installer" section for more detailed instructions, if needed.

Figure F5-1   Press Command-Shift-K to get the Installer's "secret" Clean Install option

One warning: If you cancel this Clean Install in progress, your original System Folder may be left with the name Previous System Folder (with an empty folder named System Folder now on your disk) and it may even be unblessed (that is, the System icon will not be on the folder). This can cause problems for your use of System Folder files and may even prevent you from restarting successfully. The solution is to delete the empty folder, rename your original System Folder correctly, and then open and close the folder (to rebless it if needed).

The logic of a clean reinstall is to delete those files that would not have been replaced by an ordinary reinstall. Then do the ordinary installation. This forces a completely new copy of the software to be installed. It might appear that the simplest way to do this is to delete the entire old System Folder (after restarting with an alternate startup disk). However, if you do this, you will lose the likely dozens of files that are in the System Folder but are not included on the Macintosh system software disks. These include any fonts, Apple menu items, preferences files, extensions, or control panels that did not come from Apple. As mentioned, you will also lose any customized changes to Apple system software files. So, what is needed is an efficient way to delete Apple system software files while preserving all that you want to save. That is what the method described here is designed to do.

You may read about other methods for doing a clean reinstall that are somewhat different from what is given here. Apple even includes instructions for a clean reinstall in the documentation that comes with some Macintoshes. Don't fret about the differences in instructions. They all accomplish the same goal. Here's what to do:

1. **Rename the System Folder**
   Locate the System Folder to be replaced. Rename it *X System Folder* (or any other name of your choosing).

2. **Remove the System file contents**
   Create a new folder and name it *System File Stuff.* Double-click the System file in the X System Folder to view the files within it. Remove all files (such as sound and possibly font files) from within the System file by dragging the files out of the window. Place them in the System File Stuff folder.

BY THE WAY ▶

CUSTOMIZED CHANGES TO YOUR SYSTEM FILE THAT CAN'T BE SAVED

Removing and saving the files from your System file may not save all the customized changes to your System file. In particular, some Installer utilities for other software modify the System file itself, often without telling you they are doing this. For example, you may have used Apple's Network Software Installer (mentioned in Chapter 11) to update the version of AppleTalk built into your System file. No later examination of the System file will directly tell you that this modification has been made. In such cases, when you reinstall the basic system software (assuming that it is the same version you used previously), you will lose these customized changes. If this happens, you may notice that certain systemwide features have disappeared from your Mac. In the AppleTalk example, you may wind up with an older version of AppleTalk than you had been using. The only solution here is to rerun the Installers for the other software (assuming you remember which ones you may need!) when you are done with the system software reinstall.
   For similar reasons, you must reinstall Express modem software after you reinstall system software.

System 6 Alert: You have to use the Font/DA Mover to remove and reinstall files to the System file. You cannot access its contents by double-clicking the file, as you can in System 7.

SEE: • Chapter 9 for more on removing files, especially fonts, from the System file

3. **Remove the Finder from the System Folder**
   One way to do this is to create a new folder called *Old Finder.* Move the Finder to that folder. Now close the X System Folder window; this folder should no longer be a blessed folder (that is, you should no longer see the Macintosh icon on the X System Folder icon). This means that the Mac no longer considers this to be a valid System Folder. When you run the Installer, it should thus create a new System Folder rather than update the X System Folder.

   However, I have found that this method does not always work—the Mac still installs the new software in the X System Folder. In this case, it may be helpful to bury the System file within a folder (such as the Extensions folder) inside the X System Folder, in addition to moving the Finder. It might also help to create a new empty folder at the root level of your disk and name it System Folder.

   However, the surest procedure is to start up with an alternate startup disk and delete the Finder and the System file (and any Enabler file, if present) from your disk altogether (you're going to delete them in the end anyway!). This is my personal recommendation. If you are really the cautious type, you may want to first be certain that these files have been backed up before you delete them (in case something goes wrong with the reinstall and you wish to return to using these files).

4. **Restart the Macintosh**

Restart with no floppy disk inserted or other alternate startup disk mounted. Wait. You should get the blinking question mark icon. This establishes that there are truly no active System Folders on your hard drive.

If a startup does occur at this point, this means you had more than one System Folder on your disk. If so, you should locate (using the Find command, if needed) and delete all System Folders except the one you intended to update. If you need to delete the System Folder that is now active, you will first need to restart from an alternate startup disk.

5. **Insert the relevant system software disk and install a new System Folder**

Follow the directions as detailed in the next section ("Using the System Software Installer"). Briefly: insert the Install 1 disk (or Install Me First disk, if needed). Wait for the Installer to launch. Select Easy Install (or make selections from Custom Install if desired) and click the Install button.

BY THE WAY ▶

WHAT IF YOU DON'T HAVE A NEEDED INSTALL ME FIRST DISK?

If you can't find or don't have the Install Me First disk that contains the Enabler needed for your machine, don't despair. You can still start up from the standard System Software Installer disk. However, to do this you will need the Disk Tools disk that came with your Macintosh (or any other startup disk with the needed Enabler on it). This technique may not work with Power Macs that use a Minimal Enabler on floppy disks. Otherwise, here are the step-by-step instructions:

1. Start up from Disk Tools or any other disk containing the proper System Enabler for your Macintosh.

2. Trash the Finder from the System Folder on your hard disk.

3. Rename the System Folder to X System Folder.

4. Create a new folder on the hard disk and name it "System Folder."

5. Copy the Enabler from the System Folder on your startup disk to the new System Folder on your hard disk.

6. Restart the computer using the Install 1 disk as the startup disk. The Installer will "see" the enabler on the hard disk. This means you won't get the System 7.x does not work on this model error message that you would otherwise see (see "Take Note: Install Me First Disks and System Enablers" later in this Fix-It).

7. Proceed with the installation and install System Software for any Macintosh, using guidelines as given in "Using the System Software Installer," in the main text (you will not have the custom options specific to the enabler-dependent machine when you run the Installer using this method).

8. When finished with the installation, move files from X System Folder to your new System Folder, as needed (see Step 7 of "Do a Clean Reinstall of System Software"). Then delete X System Folder.

---

6. **Restart the Macintosh**

You are probably forced to restart by the Installer when you quit it. But if not, restart anyway. You should now start up from the newly installed System Folder. At this point, check to see if your problem has disappeared. If damaged system software was the cause (or if the cause was due to one of the files now in the X System Folder), your problem should now be gone. If it isn't, you have some other cause for your problem.

7. **Return files from the X System Folder**

Open the X System Folder. Open each subfolder (such as Preferences, Control Panels, and so on) within that folder. Drag all the items in each folder to the identically named folder in the new System Folder. If you get any messages asking whether you want to replace a specific file, say no (click the *Cancel* button)! Otherwise, you will undo the effect of re-installing new copies of those files. If you know which files in X System Folder come from Apple, just delete them rather than dragging them back to the new System Folder. This will avoid repeatedly getting the query about replacing files.

Now drag all other files and folders (except the System and System Enabler files, if still present) from the root level of the X System Folder to the new System Folder.

By the way, if possible, it would be better to install non-Apple files from their original disks rather than from the X System Folder (just in case the version on your hard disk is damaged), but this is not necessary if your primary purpose is to just do a clean reinstall of the Macintosh system software.

8. **Return files from the System File Stuff folder**

Open the System File Stuff folder. Drag these files to the System Folder icon (not the folder window or the System file icon) of the new System Folder. The Macintosh will offer to correctly place these files (returning them to the System file, if appropriate). Accept its offer. Again, if you are asked to replace any files, say no.

As in the previous step, since there is a possibility that one of these files may be the source of the suspected damage, you might prefer to replace any non-Apple files from their original disks rather than from these copies.

9. **Delete the X System Folder, System File Stuff, and Old Finder folders**

Delete the X System Folder, with all its remaining contents, including the System file and Enabler. Delete the System File Stuff folder, with all its remaining contents, and Old Finder folder, which still contains the old Finder.

If you have already deleted the System Finder and Enabler files (optionally suggested in Step 3), you obviously won't need to delete them here.

10. **Restart again**

Restart the Macintosh one more time. You will again start up from the same newly installed System Folder, but now with all your control panels, extensions, and other files returned.

Hopefully, your problem has not returned. If it does, it remains possible that non-Apple files in your System Folder that were not replaced were the source of the problem. For such problems, refer to other relevant Fix-Its, as needed.

Using the System Software Installer

This is the main procedure for installing or reinstalling system software on a disk.

1. Restart with a system software Install 1 disk (or Install Me First disk)

Restart your Macintosh using the system software's Install 1 disk (or Install Me First disk, if needed) as the startup disk. For safety, keep these disks locked (or use backup copies). These disks are part of the set of system software floppy disks that come with your Macintosh (see "By the Way: Reinstalling System Software on Performas," "By the Way: What If You Don't Have a Needed Install Me First Disk?," earlier in this Fix-It, and "By the Way: Installing System Software from a CD-ROM Disk," "Take Note: Install Me First Disks and Enablers," "Take Note: New Versus Old Installer Utility," and "Take Note: System Software Upgrade Blues: Tune-Ups, Updates, and More," later in this Fix-It, for related information).

BY THE WAY ▶

INSTALLING SYSTEM SOFTWARE FROM A CD-ROM DISK

Some Macintosh models, primarily those with internal CD-ROM drives, ship with system software on a CD-ROM disk. You may use such a disk instead of floppy disks to install system software on your hard drive. This simplifies the installation, as you no longer need to deal with swapping multiple floppy disks. In most cases, these special CD-ROM disks can function as startup disks, although you do not need to do this in order to perform an installation. However, if you are doing a clean reinstall, it is probably safer to use the CD-ROM disk as the startup disk (in case a problem with your regular startup disk would interfere with the installation). If you do try to use a CD-ROM system software disk as a startup disk, you may have some trouble getting the Macintosh to accept it. Or you may have trouble getting the disk to eject when you are done with it. For these problems, check out Chapter 5, especially "By the way: CD-ROM Startup Disks" and "A CD-ROM Disk or Removable Cartridge Won't Eject." Also see the section in Chapter 12 on System 7.5 "Installation Problems."

To reinstall system software, it is not required that you use the Install disk as a startup disk. You can use disks while still running from your hard drive as the startup disk (even if you have moved the location of the Finder on your hard disk, as suggested for a clean re-install). You just have to first quit all applications other than the Finder (the Installer will volunteer to do this for you if you have forgotten). However, if you are doing a clean re-install or are having any problems with your hard disk, it is safer to use the system software Install disk as the startup disk. Certainly, if you intend to delete the System and Finder prior to doing a clean reinstall (as optionally suggested in the previous section), you are required to restart from another disk, presumably the Install disk.

INSTALL ME FIRST DISKS AND SYSTEM ENABLERS

Starting with System 7.1, when Apple ships a new model of Macintosh, it does not automatically release a new version of the system software, as it had done in the past. Instead, it includes a special System Enabler file for that model. This provides the special information needed to work with the new model.

The benefit of this is that the same basic version of the system software can remain the current version for all users, despite the release of new hardware. Given the frequency with which Apple releases new machines these days, this is no trivial benefit. However, these Enablers do have their downside. The most notable problem is that a given disk cannot be used as a startup disk unless it contains the Enabler that matches the machine to which it is attached. That is why the first step in upgrading System Software is to run the Install Me First Disk that came with your machine. This installs the Enabler and, when completed, prompts you to insert the standard Install disk and continue with the complete system software installation.

Install Me First disks will also install any control panels, extensions, or related software that are specific to the given model of Macintosh and not included on the universal system software disks. For example, in System 7.1, Install Me First disks for PowerBooks install software, such as the PowerBook control panel, not needed by desktop Macintoshes.

If you try to start up using a disk that does not contain the correct Enabler file, the startup sequence halts with a message such as one that says System 7.x does not work on this model.

The Enabler requirement can lead to a host of other related problems. For example, what if you want to attach your external hard drive to a different model of Macintosh than the one you own? If you don't have the Enabler file for that Macintosh, you can't use the external drive as a startup disk. Similarly, you can't have a floppy Emergency Startup Disk that works with all Macintoshes, unless you have all the needed Enablers on the disk (which may even be too many to fit). To deal with these problems, you can acquire a complete set of all of Apple's Enabler files from various online sources, such as eWorld and CompuServe. You can then place the needed Enabler(s) on the relevant disk (assuming you have room). If you place more than one Enabler on a disk, the Macintosh is smart enough to use only the one that is correct for the particular hardware model in use. The makers of commercial recovery software, such as Norton Utilities, have their own more specialized solutions for creating startup floppy disks, as detailed in Chapter 2.

Complicating matters further, Enabler files are occasionally updated. Thus, the Enabler file that came with your model of Macintosh may no longer be the current version. This means that, when doing a complete reinstall, if you have a more recent version of your Enabler (again available from online services and such), you should replace the Enabler installed by the original Install Me First Disk with the more recent version. Do this after you have completed the installation.

Finally, another quirk of Enabler files is their names. Rather than being named after the model for which they are used, they often have unhelpful names such as Enabler 131. This only makes it more difficult to figure out what machine the Enabler is intended to work with. Such is life. In some cases, the Enabler for a specific machine may be upgraded and given a new name, adding still more confusion for the hapless user trying to stay current. For example, the aforementioned Enabler 131 replaced System Enablers 111 and 121 as the Enabler for PowerBooks 160, 165c, and 180! One optimistic note, the name of the latest version of the Enabler for PowerBook Duos is (ta-da!) PowerBook Duo Enabler. Similarly, there is a PowerPC Enabler.

There is a partial happy ending here. When a new reference version of the system software is released, revisions to the system software should eliminate any need for the existing Enabler files. Such is the case with System 7.5; it needs no Enabler files for any Macintosh or Performa model released prior to the release of System 7.5. However, this is only a temporary benefit. Enablers are needed again for any models released after the arrival of System 7.5.

SEE: • **"By the Way: Reinstalling System Software on Performas" for more on Performas and Enablers**

2. Launch the Installer utility

If it doesn't automatically launch at startup, launch the Installer application. After the Welcome screen, you arrive at the main window (see Figure F5-2).

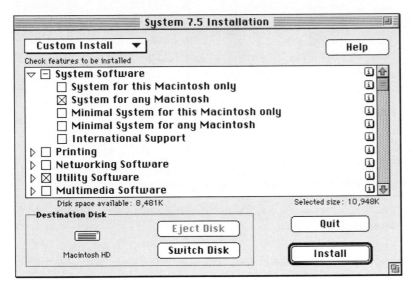

Figure F5-2   The Custom Install view of Apple's latest system software Installer

TAKE NOTE ▶

NEW VERSUS OLD INSTALLER UTILITY

Starting with the System Update 3.0 disks, and continuing with System 7.5, Apple is using an entirely redesigned Installer utility. The instructions in this Fix-It are based on this new Installer. The new version is simpler to use and gives you more flexible control over which options you want to install or remove.

If you are doing an installation with the older Installer, you should still be able to follow along here, especially if you are doing an Easy Install. Although the look and feel are different, the basic capabilities of both versions are the same. For example, in the new version there is a single pop-up menu to choose between Easy Install, Custom Install, and Custom Remove. In the older version, there are separate windows for Easy Install and Customize (see Figure F5-3). You need to select a Customize button to access the Customize window. To access the Remove feature, you need to hold down the Option key when in the Customize window. To make multiple selections from the Customize window, use the shift-click method.

With the older Installer, you have a choice of customizing the system software for a variety of different Macintosh models. The newer version forces you to select between the model currently in use or an "Any Macintosh" option.

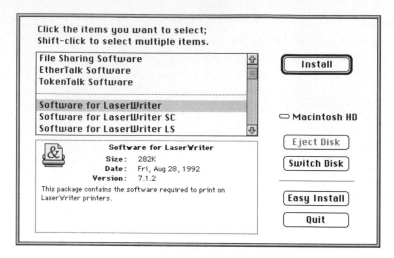

Click the items you want to select;
Shift-click to select multiple items.

| File Sharing Software |
| EtherTalk Software |
| TokenTalk Software |
| |
| **Software for LaserWriter** |
| Software for LaserWriter SC |
| Software for LaserWriter LS |

Install

⊂ Macintosh HD

Eject Disk

Switch Disk

Easy Install

Quit

Software for LaserWriter
Size: 282K
Date: Fri, Aug 28, 1992
Version: 7.1.2
This package contains the software required to print on LaserWriter printers.

Figure F5-3   The Customize window from Apple's previous version of its system software Installer

3. Select the desired destination disk

Click the Switch Disk button until the name of the desired disk is listed. In the event that you are trying to install system software on to a floppy disk, select the Install disk as the destination disk, then click the Eject button. Then insert the desired floppy disk and continue.

TAKE NOTE ▶

MUST YOU USE THE INSTALLER?

The Installer utility is the key to installing your system software. Actually, almost all companies now use some sort of installer utility to install their software. Many use the Apple Installer described here.

You may be wondering, "Must I use an Installer, or could I copy the files directly using the Finder?" It depends. Sometimes, files are stored in a compressed format that renders the files unusable until they are decompressed and only the Installer can decompress them. Also, the Installer may add special resources to the System file or add invisible files to the disk. These would not be installed if you used the Finder. Most Installers also correctly place the files in the proper location on your disk (such as in the System Folder, if necessary). Without the Installer, you would have to do this yourself.

For all these reasons, I strongly recommend using the Installer the first time you install any new software (even if it does not seem required). Later, if you need to replace just one file and the file is uncompressed and accessible from the Finder, you can probably use the Finder to do so. The usual reason to do this is that it saves time. But if any problems appear, replace the file again, this time using the Installer.

Whether for system software or for an application, an Installer is likely to install numerous files across several locations, leaving you uncertain as to what or where all of them are. This can be a hassle if you should ever want to remove the software. Fortunately, the Installer can be helpful here as well. Ideally, it should have an option to remove installed software. Apple's Installer does (see "Take Note: New Versus Old Installer Utility"). Unfortunately, not all other Installer utilities do.

4. Decide whether to use the Easy Install or Custom Install method

Select the desired option from the Installer's pop-up menu. Which one should you use? There is no automatic answer here. Most people are content with the Easy Install option. It automatically installs the correct versions of all system software needed for your hardware.

One disadvantage of this method is that it usually will install a variety of files that you do not want or need. For example, it will install printer drivers for printers that you do not have. You can avoid this sometimes by making more specific selections via the Custom Install option. However, you usually can just as easily delete the undesired files from your hard drive after the installation is complete. If you are a novice user, uncertain of what you want to keep or delete, just do Easy Install and don't worry about it for now. Unless you need the extra disk space that the files occupy, there is no reason to be in a hurry to delete them.

Another potential disadvantage of Easy Install is that it will not install files that are designed for features found on other Macintoshes but not available on your model. Normally, this is what you would want. It avoids adding unneeded files to your disk and unnecessarily increasing the size of your System file. But if you ever plan on using this System Folder with another Macintosh model, Easy Install can present problems. In some cases, it may prevent you from starting up at all from another model. If you see this as a possibility, select Custom Install, go to the System Software category (as described in Step 5) and select "System for any Macintosh" (see Figure F5-2). Even using this option, you will not install Power-Book-specific software on a non-PowerBook Mac. It also will not install any needed Enabler file, unless you started with the Install Me First disk for that model.

By the way, another Custom Install option under System Software is "Minimal System" (see Figure F5-2), which is necessary if you are installing to a floppy disk. However, the initial version of System 7.5 seemed to have a problem here: Its minimal install size was bigger than could fit on a floppy disk! In this case, to create a System Folder on a floppy disk, just copy the System Folder from the Disk Tools disk.

Custom Install is also useful when you are not doing a complete reinstall, but instead want just to add or replace a few selected files (as described in "Selective Install/Reinstall/Deletion of System Software" later in this Fix-It). For example, you can install just printer drivers or just networking-related software without having the hassle of a complete reinstallation. Actually, there are some specialized components of the system software that can only be installed by a Custom Install (such as Mac TCP). Easy Install does not install them.

5. Install the software

a. Easy Install.   Click the Install button. The Installer takes care of the rest, prompting you to insert other disks as required. When it is finished, your installation is complete. A complete new set of system software has been installed.

b. Custom Install.   If you selected this option, a scrollable list of software categories (such as System Software, Printing, and Networking Software) will appear in the center of the window (see Figure F5-2). To the left of each name will be a check box. To the left of some check boxes will be a triangle. Clicking the triangle will reveal a sublist of the files that comprise the larger category (similar to how folders can be manipulated in non-icon views of the System 7 Finder). Click the check box of an item to select it. Each file in the sublist can be selected separately. Selecting the larger category automatically selects all files in the sublist. If you are going to bother to do a Custom Install, I would advise viewing all the sublists and selecting precisely what you want. If you need help deciding what to install, select the "i" button to the right of each name to learn more about what it is. Select the Help button to get more details about what Easy Install does or does not install.

When you are finished with your selections, click the Install button.

6. **Wait and watch while the installation proceeds, inserting disks as requested**

If a problem develops during the installation procedure, an error message typically appears describing the nature of the problem. Usually, it also offers advice about what to do to solve the problem. For example, if there is insufficient room on the destination disk to hold all the system software, you are advised to remove some items from the disk and try again.

If you get bothered by messages from your anti-virus utility while installing, you may find it easier (or even necessary) to halt the installation, temporarily turn off your anti-virus utility, and try again. Doing this is officially recommended anyway.

SEE: • "Take Note: If the Installation Fails," next

TAKE NOTE ▶

IF THE INSTALLATION FAILS

A variety of bugs may occasionally lead to an installation failing. What typically happens is a freeze or a crash occurs prior to the end of an installation. For example, when upgrading to System 7.1, the installation would fail if any existing fonts in your System file had names that were longer than 31 characters (see Chapter 9, "Technically Speaking: The 31-Character Font Name Limit"). Because of a specific bug, a crash may also occur when upgrading from System 7.0.1 to System 7.5. Doing a clean reinstall bypasses these problems.

Related types of problems, such as repeated seemingly endless requests to swap Install disks back and forth during installation, are usually solved by making sure all extensions are off before running the Installer (or by starting up from the Installer floppy disk, which has no extensions).

If none of this succeeds in solving your problem, seek outside help for advice.

SEE: • **Chapter 12 for more advice on installation failure problems that are particularly common with, but not necessarily specific to, System 7.5**

---

7. **Quit the Installer and restart using the destination disk as the new startup disk**

The Installer may force you to restart when you quit it. If it doesn't, restart anyway.

8. **Install/reinstall Updates or other additional system software**

For System 7.5, there are separate Installers for the optional PowerTalk and/or QuickDraw GX software.

For any system software version, you should install files from the latest System Update (or other similar) disks, if the disk has been released since the system software was released.

Of special note: If you had previously installed files from a System Update disk that contains newer versions of files also contained on the system software disks, you will still need to reinstall the newer versions. What will probably happen is that you will get messages during the system software installation asking whether it is OK to replace a newer version of a file (such as one previously placed there by a System Update disk) with an older version (the one now to be installed by the system software disks). Click OK in order to let the installation proceed. If you are doing a clean reinstall, you will not get these messages because all the relevant files are in the X System Folder.

In any case, when you are finished with the system software installation, follow the instructions in the Read Me file on the System Update disk to replace outdated software and install new files, as needed.

SEE: • "Take Note: System Software Upgrade Blues: Tune-Ups, Updates, and More"
          • Chapter 12 for more on QuickDraw GX and PowerTalk

9. Do some final cleanup

If desired, you can do some final cleanup at this point, discarding any files that you do not need. For example, the Installer may have installed some printer drivers, control panels, or Apple menu items that you do not want. If so, delete them. Also check for and delete duplicate copies of fonts that may have been inadvertently installed (as described in Chapter 9).

Helpful hint: This installation does not update the disk driver. For Apple brand disks, you need to use Apple HD SC Setup for that.

SEE: • Fix-It #12 on updating the disk device driver

If you are doing a clean reinstall, return to the previous section for instructions on completing the procedure. Otherwise, you are done.

TAKE NOTE ▶

SYSTEM SOFTWARE UPGRADE BLUES: TUNE-UPS, UPDATES, AND MORE

Apple used to release system software upgrades every few months. Most were designed primarily to fix minor bugs or accommodate new Macintosh models and were distinguished by names such as 6.0.5 versus 6.0.7. With the release of System 7.0, Apple changed the rules. System upgrades are now much less frequent. System Enabler files (as described elsewhere in this Fix-It) handle the problem of new hardware models. Otherwise, Apple releases special disks that upgrade the current system software without actually changing the system version designation.

With System 7.0, these disks were called Tune-Up disks. With System 7.1, they were referred to as Updates, most recently as System Updates. The most critical component on these disks is an extension named similarly to the disk itself. Thus, on the System Update 3.0 disks, there is an extension named System Update. This file, when installed, fixes bugs found in the System and/or Finder files. Unlike most other extensions, this one will load even if you hold down the shift key at startup to disable extensions (see Fix-It #4 for more on this).

The remaining files on Update disks are designed to add to or replace existing files. For example, System Update 3.0 contains, among other files: upgraded Sound Manager extension and Sound control panel, upgraded PowerBook control panels, and new versions of Apple HD SC Setup and Disk First Aid. It also included the latest versions of all the System Enabler files.

(continued)

Detailed installation instructions are contained in a Read Me file included with the Update disk. In some cases, the installation procedure may also directly alter the System file itself.

When a new version of the system software does get released, it incorporates the changes from the previous Tune-Up or Update disks, eliminating the need to use them. Thus, when you upgrade from System 7.0 to System 7.1, you no longer need to worry about the Tune-Up disks specific to System 7.0. Similarly, an upgrade to System 7.5 wipes out the need for all previous updates. If installed correctly, these update disks should delete any out-of-date Tune-Up/Update files currently on your startup disk.

In general, all users of the appropriate version of the system software should use these Update disks. In particular, if you are having any problem that may be caused by a system-level bug, ask your Apple dealer (or other sources of outside help) whether an Update or similar disk is available that corrects the problem. The Read Me file that is included on the disk also gives a detailed list of all of the problems that a particular Update will fix (see Chapter 2, "By the Way: What Exactly Does a System Update Update?" for a sample of these fixes).

Occasional problems may occur. For example, a series of incompatibility problems were reported when Hardware System Update 2.0.1 was first released. One problem was that AV Macintoshes incorporated into their ROM changes that were included in this update. AV Mac users were thus advised not to use the Update file. Other Updates have typically had less problems. In general, follow recommendations in the Update disks' Read Me file. Otherwise, the surest way to learn about these potential problems (other than from your own unfortunate experiences) is by checking outside sources, such as magazines and online services.

While these updates make upgrades a bit more complicated, they would still be manageable if they were the end of the story. Unfortunately, they are not. Apple has continued to compartmentalize its upgrade procedure. For example, there is a disk called Software Utilities Update 1.0 that is separate from the previously described Update disks and is the only Update disk to contain the MacCheck utility (described more in Fix-It #10). When LaserWriter 8 first came out, there was a separate disk for upgrading to this new printer driver (as described more in Chapter 7). There is still another disk, the Network System Installer, needed to upgrade AppleTalk-related software. Prior to System 7.5, QuickTime, AppleScript, and PowerTalk were not part of the standard system software (you needed System 7 Pro), although some of these utilities were available from online services. And so on. . . .

The end result of all of this is that, for many users, it has become almost impossible to know if they are using the latest versions of their system software files. Similarly, the odds that any two people are using an identical system software setup, even if they are using the same hardware, is fairly low. I wish I could offer an easy solution to this problem. But there is none. System 7.5 has temporarily reduced these problems, but they will almost certainly get worse again. If it all gets a bit too bewildering, seek some outside help (see Fix-It #18).

TAKE NOTE ▶

"WHY CAN'T I OPEN THE SYSTEM SOFTWARE I JUST DOWNLOADED?"

Many users acquire supplementary system software, such as Update disks, from on-line services. First, in almost all cases, these files are compressed in some way. Most are self-extracting files, which means that if you try to open them, they automatically decompress their contents and place the uncompressed file(s) on your disk. At this point, you can delete the original compressed file. Sometimes, you may need to have a specific extractor application (especially if the file has a suffix such as .sit or .cpt). A good (and free) general-purpose extractor is StuffIt Expander (itself available from on-line services).

Once you get the decompressed file, you may still not be done. If you double-click the file and it still does not open, you probably have what is called a disk image file (see Figure F5-4). It may have a special suffix, such as .img. If you don't know what's going on, you may begin to worry that an error occurred while downloading and that you have a damaged file. Don't worry, all is fine. Here's what you need to do.

You need a utility called Disk Copy (or another similar copy utility). It is from Apple and should be - available from the same on-line service that you downloaded your Update file. It is also included with the CD-ROM disk version of System 7.5. When you get Disk Copy, launch it. Click the "Load Image File" button. From the Open dialog box, select the file you downloaded. Now click the "Make a Copy" button, and follow the instructions to insert a floppy disk. Remember that some disk images are for 800K disks while others are for 1.44 HD disks (by the way, you may need to increase the memory of Disk Copy to at least 1500K when working with 1.44Mb disk images). Insert the appropriately sized disk. Disk Copy will now create a floppy disk from the disk image that is an exact duplicate of what you would have gotten if you had obtained the disk directly from Apple—down to the precise location of every icon. Quit Disk Copy. All the needed files should now be on the floppy disk, finally in a usable form. If you get a -620 or a -74 error message when using Disk Copy, it probably is due to a conflict with virtual memory. Turn virtual memory off and try again.

If you want, rather than using the floppy disk directly, you can copy the entire floppy disk to your hard drive (by dragging the floppy disk icon to the hard drive) and perform the Update installation from there. Another alternative is to use another Apple utility called MountImage. This control panel allows you to "mount" a disk image file directly, as if it were a real floppy disk, bypassing the need to use Disk Copy. However, I don't trust MountImage to work reliably. Instead, I use an excellent shareware alternative called ShrinkWrap (one of several such alternatives now available).

Disk Tools.image

Figure F5-4
If you see an icon like this, you need a utility like Disk Copy or ShrinkWrap to use it

Selective Install/Reinstall/Deletion of System Software

Basis for a Selective Install/Reinstall

The main purpose of a clean reinstall of your system software is to solve a problem that may be due to damaged or incompatible system software files. However, in some cases, you may be able to solve such problems by replacing only one or a few selected system software files, saving yourself the time and hassle of a complete reinstall. Examples follow.

Selective Damage Suspected   You may suspect, because of the nature of your symptoms, that damage is to a particular file (such as if your problem is just with the Scrapbook). If so, you can choose to just replace that file. More generally, for any system software problem, you may want to start by replacing just the System file, Finder, and Enabler files, as these are the most frequent source of these problems.

By the way, one way to check for potential damage to the System file is to try to open the System suitcase (by double-clicking its icon). If it refuses to open, it is almost certainly damaged and should be replaced. Unfortunately, if it does open, it does not guarantee that it is not damaged. Sometimes, if a Mac cannot maintain the correct date or time, it means a corrupted System file. Of course, to replace the System (or Finder) file on your normal startup disk, you may need to use an alternative startup disk to access and/or delete the problem file(s).

Files or Resources Missing   Some system software problems are not due to damaged software but to missing software. This is especially likely if you initially did a Custom Install. For example, you may not have installed the files needed for file sharing or EtherTalk because, at the time, you did not intend to use these features. If you later try to access these features, you will probably get a message that says that needed resources are missing. Similarly, your System file may have been customized for your particular model of Macintosh. If you later copy the same System file for use on another type of Macintosh, it may not work properly. In this same situation, you may not have the Enabler needed for that Macintosh. In still another common example, if you switch to a different printer, you may find that the System Folder does not contain the printer driver for that printer. Or if you are having a problem getting background printing to work, PrintMonitor may be missing or not in its proper location in the Extensions folder. Last, certain applications expect specific fonts, available from the Macintosh system software disks, to be installed on your startup disk. If these are not installed, you get a message saying that the font is missing. Subsequent screen displays and printed output may not be correct.

Mismatched System and Finder Versions   A mismatch in the version of the System and Finder on your startup disk can cause problems. To check for this:

1. **Check the version number of the System file**
   Open the About This Macintosh window to see the name of the overall System version (such as "System Software 7.1"). Alternatively, the Get Info window of the System file gives this same information, typically in two locations: right underneath the word System and again on the Version line (see Figure F5-5). Wherever you check, you should find the same number.

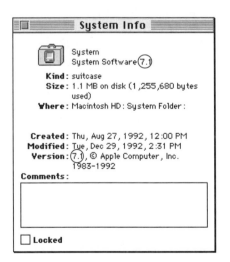

Figure F5-5
The System file's Get Info window with version numbers circled

2. **Check if the version number of the Finder matches that of the System**
   Check the Finder's version number from its Get Info window. The version numbers of the System and Finder files should match. Occasionally, there may be a difference in the digit after the second decimal place (such as Finder 7.1.3 included as part of an overall system version 7.1). This minor difference is usually okay. Otherwise, you have a Finder/System mismatch. One or both of the files need to be replaced.

You can also check to see whether other files in your system software (such as the Chooser or various control panels) match your System file version. However, if you discover a mismatch, it doesn't mean that there is anything wrong. There are numerous reasons (such as files installed by a System Update disk) why the version numbers will be legitimately different. Also, control panels from one version of the system software often work just fine with other versions. Still, if you have a problem with a specific file (such as a Chooser that does not open) and you discover a version number mismatch, consider replacing the file with the matching version on your system software disks.

Install/Reinstall Selected System Software Files

To resolve any of the problems just described in the previous section, you can try installing or reinstalling selected files to your System Folder, rather than doing a complete reinstall. There are three basic ways to do this. Choose the one that is most appropriate for your situation.

Reinstall Files from Your Backups   You can do this if you suspect that, or simply want to check if, a particular file is damaged, as long as you believe that your backup copy is still okay. For System, Finder, and Enabler files, you may even have a special separate set of backups, separate from your system software disks and your hard disk backups, maintained for just this purpose.

By the way, to replace the System, Finder, or Enabler files, you do not need to first start up from another disk. For example, to replace the Finder, drag the Finder from your System Folder to the desktop. Then copy the replacement Finder to your System Folder. Then restart. You will restart using the new Finder. You can now trash the old Finder.

For other system software files, simply replace the file from your backups as you would for any file.

Install/Reinstall Files from Your System Software Disks   Prior to System 7.5, most system software files were stored on your system software disks as ordinary uncompressed files. You could drag any selected file directly from its floppy disk to your hard drive, bypassing the need to use the Installer (the System file is a notable exception here, as the Installer customizes it for your Macintosh). Thus, to replace these files or to add new files not currently in your System Folder, simply copy them as you would any file (to replace the Finder or Enabler, or any file that says it cannot be replaced because it is "in use," follow the special instructions given in "Reinstall Files from your Backups").

Alternatively, you can also install/reinstall selected software directly from the Installer (using the Install Me First or Install 1 disk as needed), via the Custom Install option. Note that, particularly in versions prior to System 7.5, if you scroll to the bottom of the Customize list, there should be an option with a name like *Update Universal System* or *Updates System Software for Any Macintosh.* This option installs or updates the Enabler, control panels, extensions, and desk accessories needed for your Macintosh. It will not modify or replace the System and Finder. To add or replace selected categories of software, such as File Sharing software, the Installer typically has a separate option you can select.

With System 7.5, files are stored in a compressed format (called tomes) so that you cannot copy the files directly from the Finder. Similarly, there is no Update option in the Custom Install view comparable to the *Update Universal System* option. The good news is that, because System 7.5's new Installer utility gives you so much more control over which files you can select to install, you can probably accomplish what you want anyway.

In general, I prefer this method over the previous method of using your backup files, as the files on the system software disks are less likely to be damaged (you may have backed up a file after it was already damaged!). The main advantage of using backups is for files (such as the System file) that you may have customized so that the version on your system software disks is no longer an exact duplicate.

Install/Reinstall Files from Update Disks   Update disks, as described in previous sections of this Fix-It, often contain newer versions of files than those on the system software disks. Use these Update disks, as their name implies, to install the latest updated version of these files.

If you choose a method that does not use an Installer, make sure you install the file(s) in their correct locations. Actually, you might want to first check if an apparent missing file problem is simply due to a file that is mislocated rather than missing (such as a printer driver that is not in the Extensions folder). In this case, you don't have to replace anything. Just move the file to its correct location.

If you replace control panels, you may have to reset any customized preferences you had made to their settings. For files that have separate preferences files, including the Finder, consider replacing the preferences file, if replacing the main file did not solve the problem.

Whatever method you used, restart the Macintosh when you are done, just to be sure that everything new kicks in as expected. If you were using an alternate startup disk, restart with the previous, now modified, startup disk. If the problem is gone, congratulations.

If none of this worked, you probably need to do a complete reinstall of the system software after all (as described in "Complete Install/Reinstall of System Software"). Also, consider checking for media damage, especially if you receive any sort of error message that says the Macintosh was unable to successfully replace a suspected damaged file.

Otherwise, if the problem is due to an incompatibility with a particular application, you may be able to solve it by upgrading to a newer version of the application rather than by dealing with the system software. If the problem is specific to an optional feature of the system software (possibly due to a bug), you may work around the problem by not using that feature (such as turning off a control panel).

SEE: • "Take Note: Identifying System Software Compatibility Problems and Bugs," earlier in this Fix-It

Special Case: Delete Multiple System Folders

Multiple System Folders on your startup disk are a potential source of problems (see "Take Note: The Multiple System Folder Controversy [or Why Worry About More than One System Folder on Your Disk?]"). To eliminate them:

1. **Check for any multiple System Folders on your startup disk**
   The simplest way to locate multiple System Folders is to use the Finder's Find command to search for all files that contain the word *System*. Alternatively, MacCheck (described in Fix-It #10), as part of its diagnostic testing, lists any multiple System Folders on your disk.

   By the way, there is no problem with having another disk with a System Folder on it mounted at the same time as the startup disk. The potential problem is restricted to multiple System Folders on the same startup volume.

2. **Delete any extra System Folders that you find**
   If you find more than one System Folder on your disk (no matter how deep into how many folders they are buried), delete all except the one that you intend to be the startup System Folder. Restart immediately.

If the System Folder you want to delete is currently the blessed System Folder, you may need to change this before you can delete it. To do this, drag either the Finder or the System file out of the folder. Open and then close the System Folder that you want to preserve. This folder should now have a Macintosh icon on it. Restart. The correct System Folder should act as the startup System Folder. You can now delete the unwanted System Folder. Alternatively, you could restart with an alternate startup disk and then discard any System Folders from the original startup disk.

TAKE NOTE ▶

THE MULTIPLE SYSTEM FOLDER CONTROVERSY (OR WHY WORRY ABOUT MORE THAN ONE SYSTEM FOLDER ON YOUR DISK?)

It is best to have only one valid System Folder on your startup disk. Or, more precisely, only one System file and Finder should be on your startup disk.

With more than one System Folder present, you may develop problems with applications that store accessory files and preferences files in the System Folder. If these files are stored in one System Folder, and a second System Folder on the same disk is used for startup, the applications will not access their accessory and preferences files and thus may not function as expected. In general, confusion may develop as to which of the multiple System Folders should be the blessed, or startup, System Folder.

More serious problems, including system crashes, may result when the Macintosh tries to access conflicting information from both System Folders. However, opinions are divided on the likelihood of these more serious problems occurring. Some experts claim that you should absolutely never have two or more System Folders on the same startup disk. Others claim that the predicted dire consequences of doing this are highly exaggerated. Every one seems agreed that problems are especially unlikely if you are using System 6.0.7 or later (including any version of System 7). In these cases, one folder is blessed as the startup System Folder, and any other ones are essentially ignored. All should otherwise proceed as normal. Even Apple now admits that you can (and I quote) "safely store multiple System Folders on your drive."

Nonetheless, my advice is to play it safe: Avoid having extra System Folders on your startup disk, unless you have some deliberate need for them (such as if you wish to be able to switch between two different versions of the system software).

If you are determined to have multiple System Folders on the same disk, a freeware utility called System Picker enables you to easily select or switch which System Folder you intend to use as the startup System Folder.

Sometimes, you may be surprised to find an extra System Folder on your disk in the first place, since you may not recall placing it there. Commonly, this happens when you copy an entire floppy disk to your hard drive, not realizing that there is a System Folder on the floppy disk (in addition to whatever you intended to copy). Certainly get rid of these extraneous System Folders.

 For related information

SEE: • Fix-It #1 on incompatibilities between hardware and software
  • Fix-It #2 for more on replacing preferences files
  • Fix-It #12 on updating the disk device driver
  • Fix-Its #10, #13, #14, and #15 on damaged files, disks, and media
  • Fix-Its #10, #17, and #18 on diagnostic software
  • Chapter 1 for details on the locations of system software files
  • Chapter 5 on startup problems and blessed System Folders
  • Chapter 9 for more on replacing damaged font files
  • Chapter 12 for more on problems specific to System 7.5

Fix-It #6:
Check for Problems with Memory Management

QUICK SUMMARY

Increase free memory by closing unneeded documents and applications, adjust an application's memory allocation from its Get Info window, or make more global adjustments to memory allocation (such as by modifying options in the Memory control panel).

When to do it:

- When you cannot perform a task because of insufficient free memory. Most often this occurs when you are trying to open an application or a document. Usually, you get an alert message such as *There is not enough memory to open <name of application>.*

- Whenever you get an alert message stating that memory is running low.

- Whenever an application suddenly and unexpectedly quits. Insufficient memory is not the only reason for an unexpected quit, but it is a common one.

- Whenever you get a system freeze, a system crash, or any less serious malfunction while using an application, particularly if you were doing a memory-intensive operation at the time (such as making a change to a large area of a complex graphics file). No error message need appear. The only system acknowledgment of the error may be a system beep.

- Whenever applications and/or system software have less (or more) memory assigned to them than you expected.

Why to do it:

No matter how much RAM memory you have, it is not enough. It may seem like enough now, but some day soon, it will not be. As memory becomes cheaper, computers include more and more memory in their standard configurations. But as soon as software developers expect users to have more RAM in their machines, they develop software that requires the additional RAM. The original Apple II computers came standard with as little as 4K of RAM. Today, most Macintoshes come standard with at least 4Mb of RAM (that's a thousandfold increase!).

Yet, programs are already on the market that require more than 8Mb of RAM. This Fix-It can help you deal with the inevitable memory-related problems you will face.

Almost all of your Macintosh's memory is divided into two components: the *system heap* and the *application heap*. The system heap contains the memory needed for the System file as well as for most extensions and control panels. The application heap contains the memory needed by applications and their documents.

TECHNICALLY SPEAKING ▶

SYSTEM HEAP VERSUS SYSTEM SOFTWARE

In the About This Macintosh window (as selected from the Apple menu), there is always a bar representing the size of the memory occupied by the system software. This is not exactly the same as the size of the system heap. In particular, the Finder, as it is technically an application, is located in the application heap. However, its memory size is combined with the system heap size to calculate the system software size in the About This Macintosh window. That's why you don't see the Finder listed as a separate bar. In contrast, in System 6, the Finder and System are listed in separate bars.

In System 7, desk accessories use the application heap. Each open DA is assigned its own bar in the About This Macintosh window. However, in System 6, DAs are included in the size listed for System (because most desk accessories are installed directly in the System file).

By the way, in System 6, the Apple menu selection reads About the Finder rather than About This Macintosh.

The size of the system heap can vary depending on such things as how many extensions are in use. Whatever is left over is assigned to the application heap. For example, suppose you have 8Mb of RAM in your machine and that the system heap is occupying 3Mb. That leaves 5Mb of RAM for all applications. Every application needs a minimum amount of RAM to open and run properly (the amount is listed in the Memory area of the file's Get Info window). If insufficient RAM is available, the application does not open. Thus, in this example, you could never open an application that required more than 5Mb of RAM.

Under System 6's MultiFinder or System 7, multiple applications can be open at the same time. All open applications share the available RAM in the application heap. Each application has a maximum amount of RAM that it occupies. It does not exceed this value even if more memory is available. Again, this limit is determined by the Memory settings in the file's Get Info window. Documents opened within an application use the memory space assigned to the application. So even if an application successfully opens, it may not have sufficient memory for all its documents that you wish to open. In the example, the sum of the RAM requirements of all open applications cannot exceed 5Mb.

Under System 6's Finder, each newly launched application replaces whatever application was previously in RAM and thus would have the entire 5Mb available to it.

If you work at the limits of your total available RAM, you are likely to get frequent memory-related alert messages. Occasionally, you may even get a system error, such as an un-expected quit, a freeze, or a system crash. These errors generally happen when, as a result of the low memory availability, the program gets "confused" and tries to address an area of memory that does not exist or has already been assigned to another use. Ideally, a program should avoid these errors and simply warn you about low memory via an alert message. However, this ideal is often not attained.

SEE: • Take Note: "About 'About This Macintosh' and 'Get Info'," for more on these features

What to do:

This section is divided into four parts: "Memory Problems When Trying to Open an Application," "Memory Problems When Using an Open Application," "Special Case: Finder-Related Memory Problems," and "How to Increase Overall Memory Availability."

TAKE NOTE ▶

ABOUT "ABOUT THIS MACINTOSH" AND "GET INFO"

If you have any problems with memory management, it's useful to assess the allocation of your Macintosh's memory. Details of how and why to do it were first described in Chapter 2. Here's a summary of the essential steps:

1. *Select About This Macintosh from the Finder's Apple menu. Check the size of the Largest Unused Block (see Figure F6-1). The Largest Unused Block is a measure of how much memory is still free to be assigned to applications or other uses. It can never be larger than the Total Memory size minus whatever is used by the system software. Any application that needs more memory than this cannot be opened without first reducing the system software memory size (if possible) or adding more memory.*

2. *Select Get Info (from the Finder's File menu) for the application you wish to open (see Figure F6-1). In the Get Info window, the Minimum size (in System 7.1 or greater) or Current size (in System 7.0) is the minimally required amount of RAM needed to open the application. In System 7.1 and beyond, the application will use more than its Minimum, if memory is available, up until it reaches the Preferred size. The Preferred size is the maximum that the program will use. The more closely a program opens toward its Minimum rather than its Preferred size, the more likely it is to have memory-related problems (such as an inability to open large documents).*

   By the way, desk accessories, though mostly treated like ordinary applications in System 7, do not have these memory allocation options in their Get Info windows.

3. *Compare the information in the application's Get Info window and in About This Macintosh. If the program's Minimum size is larger than the Largest Unused Block, you cannot open the program. This is probably the most common reason for the appearance of memory-related alert messages. Solutions to this are described in the main text of this Fix-It ("Memory Problems When Trying to Open an Application").*

Finally, note that some programs use special memory allocation schemes that differ from the standard procedures outlined here. For example, Adobe's Photoshop has its own virtual memory allocation method that may not be reflected in the About This Macintosh display. Similarly, Deneba's ArtWorks has a special feature that can result in the program using more than its Preferred Memory size (assuming enough free memory is available).

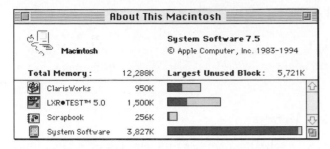

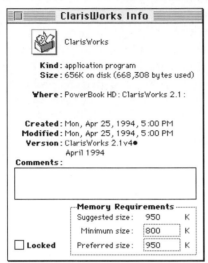

Figure F6-1   Check these windows for helpful information about memory allocation: the About This
Macintosh window (top); an application's (ClarisWorks) Get Info window (bottom)

SEE: • "Take Note: More About 'About This Macintosh': Bar Shading" and "Take Note: Still More About
'About This Macintosh': Built-In Versus Total Memory," later in this Fix-It, for more on this feature

---

TAKE NOTE ▶

QUICK FIXES TO "ABOUT THIS MACINTOSH" ODDITIES

*Occasionally, the information displayed in the About This Macintosh window may suggest that
something is wrong. Here are two common examples and their quick solutions. More details are given in
the relevant sections of this Fix-It:*

- *Problem.   The sum of the memory used by all software together with the Largest Unused Block size
is substantially less than the Total Memory size. Solution.   You have memory fragmentation. Quit
all open applications or restart altogether.*

- *Problem.   You have more than 8Mb of RAM installed, but everything over 8MB is allocated to the
System Software line. Solution.   Turn 32-bit addressing on and restart. If 32-bit addressing is
already on, restart anyway (as this will fix a similar but unrelated problem).*

Memory Problems When Trying to Open an Application

You try to open an application or desk accessory. Instead of opening you are greeted with an alert message that says *There is not enough memory available to open*. When this happens, here's what to do.

Check the Advice, If Any, in the Alert Message

The alert message may offer advice on how to solve the memory problem. For example, it may say *Closing windows or quitting application programs can make more memory available*. If you get such advice, it usually pays to follow it (see Figure F6-2). However, occasionally you may get an alert message that says that less memory is available than a program ideally needs, yet it asks, *Do you want to open it using available memory?* Usually, I would *not* click OK here. Even if the application successfully opens (and it may not), it is likely to give you problems. I prefer to seek other solutions instead.

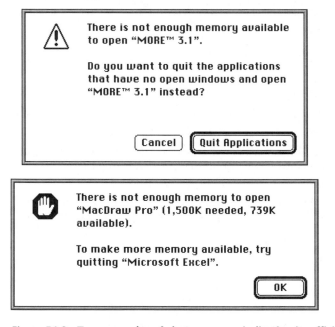

Figure F6-2   Two examples of alert messages indicating insufficient memory to open an application

In particular, the main solutions to any of these problems are either to make more free memory available or to reduce the amount of free memory needed by the application. To do this, try one or more of the following, as appropriate.

Quit One or More Other Open Applications

If you are using MultiFinder or System 7, you can have more than one application open at a time. Quitting open applications frees the memory occupied by those applications. Assuming you have enough total memory available, quit as many programs as necessary to free enough memory to launch the problem application. Now try to relaunch the problem application. If this works, you may also be able to reload the other applications that you have just closed (see "Check for Fragmented Memory Space," shortly, for how this works).

Reduce the Size of a Large Clipboard

Select Show Clipboard from the Finder's Edit menu. If it indicates that a large segment of data is there (such as all of a 50-page document), get rid of the selection. Storing a large selection in the Clipboard can take up extra system heap memory. Reducing its size may increase the Largest Unused Block enough to allow the application to open.

To try this, go to the Finder, select something small (such as one letter of text in a file's name), and copy that selection to the Clipboard. This replaces the large selection, hopefully reducing the Clipboard's memory allocation.

Check for Fragmented Memory Space

What Is Fragmented Memory?   You may find that an application does not open, even though enough unused memory is available to meet the requirements of the application. Here's what is probably happening: Picture the total memory space as a long loaf of bread that gets divided into smaller slices, where each slice represents an open application. Ideally, the slices should be adjacent to each other, so that the remaining unsliced bread forms one big block. However, if for some reason, you removed slices from random locations in the loaf, the unused portion of the bread would be broken into smaller noncontiguous segments.

This can happen with memory, as it can for bread. Normally, applications open into contiguous (that is, adjacent) memory space. However, if you have opened and closed and opened several applications over the course of a session, this adjacency may be gone. Noncontiguous or fragmented memory blocks may exist (note that this is not the same as disk file fragmentation, the subject of Fix-It #8).

The Largest Unused Block size in the About This Macintosh window indicates the largest contiguous block. If memory is fragmented, this amount is less than the amount of unused memory. You can tell that this is the case when the sum of all the memory used by open applications plus the Largest Unused Block size is less than the Total Memory. This is the case, for example, in the displays on the left side of Figure F6-3. After memory is defragmented (by quitting and relaunching Word), the Largest Unused Block increases from 1790K to 2790K (as seen in the right side displays in Figure F6-3). By the way, the top part of Figure F6-3 shows the *memory maps* (taken from the Memory View feature of Now Utilities' NowMenus) that correspond to the change in the size of the Largest Unused Block shown in the bottom part of the figure. The memory map on the left shows unused memory (white space) divided into two separate fragments surrounding Microsoft Word (gray bar). On the right, after defragmenting, Word's location has shifted so that all unused memory is now contiguous.

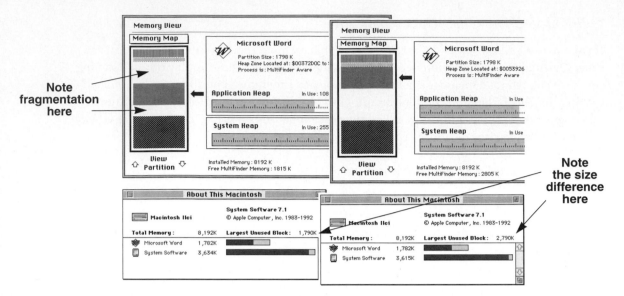

Figure F6-3   An illustration of what happens when memory is fragmented versus unfragmented

By the way, in extreme cases, memory fragmentation can contribute to an insufficient amount of space for the system heap to expand as needed. This can result in system crashes.

How Can You Eliminate Fragmented Memory?   Unlike disk storage, where a file can be stored in fragments, an application must load into RAM as a single contiguous block. Thus, any application you want to open must fit within the Largest Unused Block. So if an application needs 800K of RAM, and only two separate 500K blocks of RAM are currently unused, the application does not open, even though 1000K of memory is available. The solution here is as follows:

1. **Quit *all* open applications, saving your work first**
   Do this even if it seems that this will free far more memory than you need. (This is like returning the loaf to its unsliced form.) Now, when you try to open applications, they load contiguously and they should (assuming sufficient total memory is available) all be able to open. Otherwise, go to step 2.

2. **Restart the Macintosh**
   If quitting open applications does not work, it means that the contiguity of the memory space was somehow not restored. System 7 seems particularly prone to this problem. In this case, restarting the Macintosh completely resets the contents of memory, eliminating any fragmentation, and should allow you to open the desired applications (again, within the constraints of Total Memory size).

With some Macintosh models, particularly compact Macintoshes, some memory fragmentation is related to hardware restrictions. You can't do much about this. If you use virtual memory, still other memory fragmentation problems can occur (see: "Technically Speaking: More on Limitations of Virtual Memory," later in this Fix-It).

Reduce the Minimum/Current Memory Size

In Systems 7.1 and 7.5, what can you do if you want to open an application that has a Minimum size of 750K, but you cannot afford to free more than 680K of memory? You could reduce the application's Minimum size to 680K and see if it now opens (as I try to do in Figure F6-4). Technically, if 750K is truly the minimum needed to open the application, this should not work. In fact, when you try to close the Get Info window, you will get a message warning you about the potential dire consequences of what you are about to do (see Figure F6-4). However, often the posted Minimum is not really the rock-bottom minimum, so the application may successfully open. I would only consider doing this if you do not intend to go very far below the Minimum size (and if the default Minimum size is not too far below the Suggested size). Otherwise, you truly are asking for trouble in the form of an eventual system error.

In System 7.0, you have a better chance for success with this method, because the Memory settings in the Get Info window are set up differently. Here, no separate Minimum and Preferred sizes are listed. Instead, only a Current memory size exists, which is often preset to a size larger than the Suggested size. If so, you can reduce the Current size to match the Suggested size. This often gets the application to open. Again, you may be able to open the application at a memory size below the Suggested memory size, if necessary.

In any version of system software, even if the application opens at reduced memory settings, you may find that not all of its features work. Still, if you only need to do this on rare occasions, it can be preferable to not being able to open the application at all.

By the way, if you do change an application's Minimum (or Preferred or Current) Memory setting, there is no button you can click to get the settings to return to their default values. If you forget the default values, you may need to check with a backup copy to find out what they were (though triggering the message in Figure F6-4 at least tells you the default Minimum value).

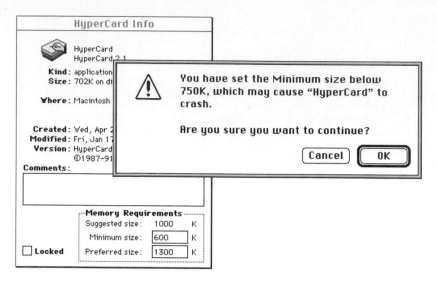

Figure F6-4 The Macintosh warns you not to set the minimum below its preset default value

Power Macintosh Alert: If you have a Power Macintosh, turning on virtual memory may reduce the Minimum size needed to open an application (see "Increase the Total Available Memory," later in this Fix-It, for more details).

Remove Plug-in Modules and Other Accessory Files

If reducing the memory size did not succeed in getting the application to open and if your application uses plug-in modules or other accessory files (such as a grammar checker included as part of a word processor), delete any modules you do not need. Since each of these modules uses a portion of the application's allocated memory, removing them reduces the amount of memory needed to run the program. If so, the application may now open in your reduced memory size setting.

By the way, if an application already successfully opens at a given memory size, you can still decide to remove unneeded modules. Doing this leaves a greater portion of the application's allocated memory available for documents to be opened within the application (a problem discussed more generally later in this Fix-It).

If None of the Preceding Steps Work

If you are using a new, more memory-hungry version of an application, you can return to the previous version, assuming it is compatible with your other software. Alternatively, try methods to increase the amount of unused memory available. For example, eliminate unneeded extensions or turn on virtual memory.

SEE: • "How to Increase Overall Memory Availability" later in this Fix-It

Memory Problems When Using an Open Application (such as an Inability to Open a Document)

There is something of a paradox here. When, as just described, you can't open an application, the solution typically requires freeing up more memory. However, when you can't open a document within an open application, freeing up even an infinite amount of memory is not likely to help. This is because, if the application has already opened in its Preferred memory size, freeing up more memory will not affect how much memory the application can use (barring some rare exceptions). For example, a program that has a Preferred memory size of 1Mb will use no more than 1Mb of memory even if 32Mb of free memory is available. Thus, these problems require a different set of solutions than those just described.

Common memory problems within an application include an inability to open a document or the application's failure to carry out a selected command (such as copy or paste). Typically, these symptoms are signaled by an alert message. For example, you may get a message that says *there is not enough memory . . .* to open a document. Or you may get an alert message that says *out of memory* or *memory low* (see Figure F6-5). Finally, you may simply get a system error (such as an unexpected quit or a system crash).

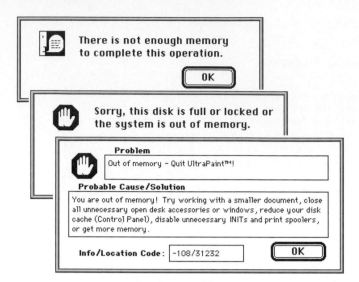

There is not enough memory to complete this operation.

OK

Sorry, this disk is full or locked or the system is out of memory.

Problem

Out of memory – Quit UltraPaint™!

Probable Cause/Solution

You are out of memory! Try working with a smaller document, close all unnecessary open desk accessories or windows, reduce your disk cache (Control Panel), disable unnecessary INITs and print spoolers, or get more memory.

Info/Location Code: -108/31232   OK

Figure F6-5   Three examples of out-of-memory alert messages; the bottom one is unique to a graphics program called UltraPaint

For system errors, see "Take Note: Unexpected Quits and Other System Errors." Otherwise, try one or more of the following solutions, as needed. Then retry opening the document (or carrying out whatever other operation was not working).

Close Any Open Documents That Do Not Need to Be Open

This increases the amount of unused memory available to the application and may permit your requested operation to proceed successfully.

Reduce the Size of the Clipboard

In some cases, the Clipboard uses the application's memory allocation. Reducing the size of the Clipboard is thus another way to increase the unused portion of the application's memory. To do this, select something small (such as one word from an open text document) and copy it to the Clipboard.

Do Not Try to Open the Document from the Finder

When an application's unused memory is low, you may be able to open a document from within the application that would not open if you double-clicked it from the Finder.

Quit the Application and Relaunch It, Restarting If Needed

Select Save and then quit the application. Then relaunch it. Often, this alone will solve the problem. If you are trying this in response to an "out of memory" warning message (see Figure F6-5), do this before trying either of the previous two suggestions. This is because such messages are typically a warning that it is time to bail out immediately. If you ignore this warning, unexpected quits, system freezes, or crashes are likely to occur very soon.

After relaunching, if you had several document windows open previously, work with fewer open documents this time. This will help avoid the return of these memory-related problems.

If relaunching alone does not work, restart the Macintosh and then relaunch. If this still fails to work, you probably don't have enough memory allocated to the application. To correct this, continue to the next step.

Increase the Preferred/Current Memory Size

Allocate *more* memory to the application (assuming you have free memory available). To do this, you need to increase the Preferred (or Current) memory size of the application, as listed in its Get Info window. This is somewhat the reverse of what you try to do when the application cannot open at all. There, you try to reduce the amount of memory the application needs in order to open. Here, you will increase it.

1. **Quit the application**
   You cannot modify the memory size of an application while it is open.

2. **Check the About This Macintosh window**
   Check the About This Macintosh window to see the size of the Largest Unused Block. This tells you the maximum size that you can set as the Preferred size (in System 7.1) or Current size (in System 7.0) of the application.

3. a. **Increase Preferred/Current Memory size**
   Assuming free memory is available, increase the Preferred/Current memory size in the application's Get Info window. To be conservative, unless the program gave you an alert message specifically informing you how much of an increase was needed, I would increase the size by no more than 500K at first (often, 100 to 200K is enough).

   b. **If the application's allocation is less than its Preferred size**
   For System 7.1 or later, the method in Step 3a assumes that the application is currently open at its Preferred memory size. If it isn't, there may be a simpler solution. You can check for this by selecting About This Macintosh before you quit the application. It lists the application's actual memory allocation (see "Take Note: More About ```About This Macintosh': Bar Shading"). Compare this to its Preferred size. If the application's allocation is less than its Preferred size, and other applications are open, it probably means that there was not enough free memory available (when you launched the application) for the program to open at its Preferred size. To remedy this, quit all open applications and launch just the problematic application. It should now open in its Preferred size. You can probably now open the problem document(s). If not, quit the application again and increase the Preferred size, as described in Step 3a.

4. **Repeat the process, if needed**
   Relaunch the application and try opening the document that would not open previously (or try whatever other memory-related problem you were having). If it still does not work, repeat this process, increasing the memory size further, until you succeed or you run out of memory.

   If you do not have enough free memory available to sufficiently increase the application's memory allocation, try to increase free memory availability by using methods described later in this Fix-It.

SEE: • "How to Increase Overall Memory Availability," later in this Fix-It

5. **Divide the document into smaller files**

    If you succeed in getting the application and document to open by increasing the Preferred or Current memory size, consider dividing the document into separate files for future use. For example, if it is a large word-processing document, divide it into two smaller segments and save each one as a separate document. You may now be able to reduce the memory size to its previous level and still avoid a recurrence of this problem. Obviously, this technique does not work as well for graphics files or other documents that do not lend themselves to being subdivided.

6. **Reduce memory demand of graphics files**

    Bitmapped graphics, such as TIFF files, can require a large amount of memory to open. Bear in mind that when creating these files, the lower their depth and resolution, the less memory they will require to open (I am talking here about how they are saved, not how they are displayed). That is, using 256 grays rather than millions of colors, using 72 dpi rather than 300 dpi, and so on, will help reduce memory demands. If you need the higher depth and resolution, so be it. But don't use more than you need. If you succeed in getting the document to open, consider resaving it with a reduced depth or resolution to reduce its memory demands in the future.

SEE: • Chapter 10 for more on depth and resolution

Special Case: Finder-Related Memory Problems

Like every other application, the Finder has a memory size assigned to it. Normally, this size is adequate and does not need readjustment. At times, however, the Finder may have insufficient memory to carry out a request. Most often, this occurs when you are trying to copy files, eject disks, show the Clipboard (see Figure F6-6), or open folder windows. Usually, you get an appropriate alert message informing you of this problem. Here's what to do.

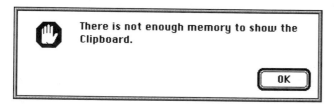

There is not enough memory to show the Clipboard.

OK

Figure F6-6 Message that may appear after the Show Clipboard command is selected from the Finder's Edit menu

Quit Applications and Close Windows

Quit any applications that do not need to be open. Next, close all open Finder windows that you do not currently need. Try again. If this fails to work, restart the Macintosh and try the desired operation again, still maintaining a minimum of open applications and/or Finder windows.

If you get a memory error only when you are trying to copy several files at once, you should also try copying the files in smaller groups. This reduces the memory demand for each copy request.

Increase the Finder's Memory Size

If Finder-related memory problems occur often, you may be able to permanently resolve the problem by increasing the memory allocation of the Finder. Remember that doing so reduces the amount of memory remaining for other applications to use, so don't be in a hurry to do it. In general, Finder-related memory problems occur more often if your total memory is 2Mb or less. They also occur more often in System 6 than in System 7 (especially when you are using MultiFinder rather than the Finder). As a rule, I would not even bother with this technique in System 7 except as a last resort. In fact, some experts claim that increasing the Finder's memory size in System 7 will never make any difference, since the system software should accommodate any needed increase automatically.

Increasing the Finder's Memory Size: System 6

1. Select the Finder's (not MultiFinder's!) Get Info window. It should display an Application memory size of 160K (see Figure F6-7). Increase it to about 240 to 320K.

2. Restart the Macintosh. Your problem should be gone.

3. Alternatively, you could decide to give up on MultiFinder and switch to using the Finder. The Finder uses the entire available memory, rather than a specific portion allocated to it from the Get Info setting. To make this switch, select Finder as the Startup application, using the Set Startup command in the Finder's Special menu. Then restart the Macintosh. Of course, this means giving up on the advantages of using MultiFinder.

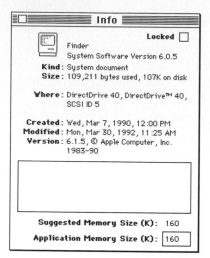

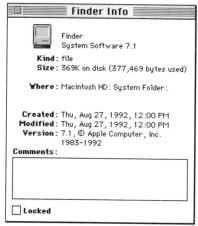

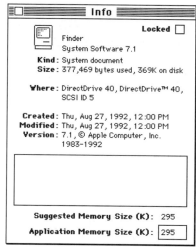

Figure F6-7   Get Info windows from a System 6 Finder (top), a System 7 Finder as it appears when running System 7 (bottom left), and a System 7 Finder as it appears when running System 6 (bottom right)

Increasing the Finder's Memory Size: System 7

1. Restart the Macintosh with a *System 6* startup disk. You must use System 6 because you cannot adjust the Finder's memory size under System 7. No Memory option is listed in the Finder's Get Info window under System 7. If you don't have access to System 6 software or if your Mac does not run under System 6, you can't use this technique.

2. Select Get Info for the Finder on your System 7 disk. Unlike when running System 7, it should now show an Application memory size listing. In Figure F6-7, it lists a size of 295K.

3. Increase the Application memory size by about 100K. This should be enough to solve most problems.

4. Restart your Macintosh with the original System 7 disk.

If the problem persists, repeat the procedure, further increasing the Finder's Application memory size. Go as high as 500 to 750K before giving up, assuming you have enough free memory to do this. However, bear in mind that larger increases reduce the amount of memory for other uses.

SEE: • "Increase the Size of the System Heap (System 7)," later in this Fix-It, for related information

---

BY THE WAY ▶

INCREASE THE FINDER'S MEMORY SIZE WITH FINDER FIXER

A shareware utility called Finder Fixer considerably simplifies the procedure for increasing the Finder's memory size. Just launch the utility, type in your desired memory allocation for the Finder, quit the utility, and restart. That's it! It even works in System 7, so you can use it instead of the method described in the main text.

How to Increase Overall Memory Availability

The previous sections of this Fix-It focus on techniques that affect a single application (such as adjusting Memory settings in the application's Get Info window). If memory problems persist, despite trying those techniques, or if memory problems occur across numerous applications, you need to try more general solutions.

After you try any of the following techniques, relaunch the problem application and/or documents (as well as the other previously opened programs, if enough memory is available). See if all goes well.

TAKE NOTE ▶

THE MEMORY CONTROL PANEL

Many of the solutions described in this section make reference to the Memory control panel (see Figure F6-8). This note serves as a brief and general introduction to how and why to use it.

Always remember, you typically must restart the Macintosh before any changes you make to Memory settings take effect.

The options listed in the Memory control panel window may differ depending on which model of Macintosh you are using. It only displays those options that are applicable to the model in use. The most common ones include:

* ***Disk cache.*** *The disk cache is a specified amount of RAM that has been set aside to hold information that has recently been accessed from your disk. When you access new information from your disk, the new information replaces what is currently in the cache. By itself, this offers no benefit. However, if you request information that is already waiting in the cache, it is accessed directly from the cache rather than from the disk. Theoretically, this speeds up the operation since, as discussed in Chapter 1, RAM access is much faster than disk access. Thus, the disk cache primarily speeds up the performance of operations that would otherwise require repeated reading of the same disk-based data.*

(continued)

You can adjust the size of the disk cache, but you cannot set it to lower than 32K. How much benefit you get will depend on your setting size and the extent to which your use of the computer takes advantage of the cache. Recently, Apple has worked on redesigning the cache to make it generally more effective.

System 6 Alert: For System 6, the cache is (incorrectly) called RAM cache and is found in the General control panel. (Technically, a RAM cache describes a separate hardware addition, so this disk cache option was renamed in System 7.) Unlike in System 7, the System 6 cache can be completely turned off.

- **RAM disk.** A RAM disk is a specified amount of RAM that has been set aside to act as if it were a physical disk mounted on the desktop. A RAM disk's icon, which looks similar to a floppy disk icon, appears on the desktop just like for any other disk. For reasons similar to the rationale for a disk cache, the speed of operations involving files copied to the RAM disk should be greatly increased. The effect can be spectacular, since items on a RAM disk are always accessed from RAM—not just if they are repeatedly accessed. However, since the disk is only in memory, you cannot permanently save files to a RAM disk as you can to a physical disk. Any information on a RAM disk is lost whenever the RAM is cleared. Typically, this will happen every time you shut down or restart. However, as described in Chapters 4 and 11, you can sometimes preserve the contents of a RAM disk after a restart (even after a system crash). Still, be cautious about saving data to a RAM disk.

  The RAM disk option is only available on certain Macintoshes (it's found on almost all Macs from the IIvx onward, including virtually all Quadras, Power Macs, and PowerBooks; the needed information is actually in ROM from Quadras onward). To create a RAM disk, select the disk's size by adjusting the slider in the RAM disk area of the control panel. Then select the On button and restart. To change the size of an existing RAM disk (or to turn it off altogether), you must first delete all files currently on the RAM disk. At a practical level, the size of a RAM disk is limited by your total available memory. Many users will need all the memory they have to adequately run System 7. In such cases, a RAM disk is a dispensable luxury.

  By the way, third-party RAM disk utilities are available that work with any Macintosh, bypassing the Memory control panel altogether.

- **Virtual memory and 32-bit addressing.** While the disk cache and RAM disk options use up available RAM, virtual memory (together with 32-bit addressing) is a way to increase your apparent available RAM. Virtual memory is like the mirror image of a RAM disk. Rather than allocating a portion of RAM to act like a disk (which is what a RAM disk does), virtual memory allocates a portion of a disk to act as if it were RAM. With virtual memory, you can open applications that require more memory than you physically have in memory chips. Using 32-bit addressing lets you use more RAM and/or virtual memory than you otherwise could. To use either of these options, just click their On button. For virtual memory, you also need to select a size. For more details, see "Increase the Total Available Memory" later in this Fix-It.

  On Power Macintoshes, the 32-bit addressing option is gone; 32-bit addressing must always be on.

- **Modern memory manager.** This option appears only on Power Macintoshes. Its practical function is to reduce memory-related problems. However, turning it off may eliminate compatibility problems with particular applications.

SEE: • Chapter 11 for more on RAM disks and PowerBooks
       • Chapter 12 for more on special features of Power Macintoshes

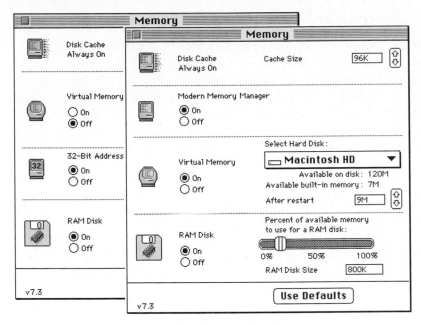

**Figure F6-8   The Memory control panel as viewed from a PowerBook 180 (left) and from a Power
Macintosh 6100 (right)**

Reduce Applications' Preferred/Current Memory Size

Many applications have a Preferred (or Current) size that is larger than the program typically needs in order to run. If you reduce this setting for these applications, they will be assigned less memory when opened, leaving more free memory remaining for other applications to use.

This technique is similar to what was described previously in this Fix-It as a way to get a specific application to open when free memory is low. Here the emphasis is on changing the Preferred size (rather than the Minimum size) in order to allow more applications to stay open at the same time.

To see if this technique is viable for a particular application, check its Get Info window. If its Preferred memory size is set higher than its Suggested size, reduce it to as low as its Suggested size. If this causes no problems with your use of the application, leave it that way. You can get a hint if this is likely to work by initially selecting "About This Macintosh" when the application and a typical number of its documents are open. If the light shaded area of the bar representing the application's memory allocation is quite large, it means that you are not using much of the memory assigned to the program (refer to Figure F6-1 and to "Take Note: More About 'About This Macintosh': Bar Shading," earlier in this Fix-It). If so, reduce it.

If need be, you can reduce the Preferred size all the way down to the Minimum size (though this is more likely to cause other memory-related problems). You shouldn't set the Preferred value below the Minimum (the Macintosh gives you an alert message if you even try).

Reduce the Memory Size Needed by System Software

The system software on your startup disk occupies a portion of memory at all times. Its size varies, depending on the particular activity you are doing each moment, but it generally stays within a relatively narrow range during any one session. To make substantial reductions in the size of the system software requires that you make changes that affect its initial startup size. Doing this should make more memory available for use by applications, which should hopefully solve your problem. In particular, you can turn off or remove nonessential INITs, turn off file sharing, remove unnecessary fonts and sounds, and reduce the size of (or turn off) the disk cache and RAM disks.

Turn Off or Remove Nonessential INITs　INITs take up memory. Turn off INITs that you do not absolutely need. Remember: Simply turning off a control panel by selecting its Off button (assuming it has one) may not free any RAM. To recover any memory, you must disable the INIT at startup (typically via a startup management utility or by dragging the INIT out of the System Folder before you restart). In extreme cases, you may need to disable all INITs (by holding down the Shift key at startup).

Some startup management utilities have a feature that tells you how much memory each INIT occupies. You can use this feature to help determine which INITs require especially large amounts of RAM. Occasionally, a bug in an INIT can cause *out-of-memory* messages to appear even though enough memory is available. Identifying and turning off these buggy INITs solves the memory problem.

SEE:　• Fix-It #4 for more on solving INIT problems

Turn Off File Sharing　File sharing involves several related extensions. When in use, it takes up about 200 to 300K of system software memory. Turning it off recovers this memory for other uses. To turn File Sharing off, you do not have to disable the extensions at startup. Instead, open the Sharing Setup control panel. If File Sharing is on, the button in the File Sharing field of the control panel will read "Stop" and the Status description will say that "File sharing is on." To turn File Sharing off, click Stop (see Figure F6-9). Obviously, you should only do this if you do not plan to use this option for the time being. You typically use File Sharing to connect to other Macintoshes over an AppleTalk network.

Figure F6-9　The File Sharing section of the Sharing Setup control panel, as it appears if File Sharing is currently on

SEE: • Chapter 11 for more on File Sharing, especially as it relates to PowerBooks

Remove Unnecessary Fonts and Sounds   Fonts and sounds require memory. Actually, in System 7.1 or later versions, fonts take up very little system software memory (just enough to keep track of their names), no matter how many fonts you have. However, they may increase the amount of memory needed by any application that includes a Font menu. Sounds, on the other hand, are assigned to system software memory (typically sounds are stored in the System file itself)—so the more sounds you have, the more memory you use. In any case, it is best to delete fonts and sounds that you rarely or never use. Detailed instructions for removing fonts are described in Chapter 9. The procedures for removing sounds are similar.

By the way, there is a bug in System 7.1 that may cause all of your fonts to actually be loaded into system software at startup. This can cause significant swelling of your system software memory allocation. Installing System Update 3.0 (described in Fix-It #5) eliminates this bug.

System 6 Alert: Like sounds, desk accessories take up memory, even when they are not open. Delete unneeded ones.

Reduce the Size of (or Turn off) the Disk Cache and/or RAM Disks   The memory required by these options is included in the system software allocation. Turning them off, while obviously eliminating whatever speed enhancement benefit they had, allows you to recover the memory they would otherwise use. You access these features from the Memory control panel.

- **Disk cache**

  In System 7, the disk cache cannot be turned off. However, you can adjust its size via the arrow keys on the right side of the control panel window, next to the current cache size listing (see Figure F6-8). The minimum size setting is 32K. The larger the size setting, the more RAM it uses, and the more performance benefit you can get—up to a point.

  For system versions prior to System 7.5, there is little or no speed benefit to setting the disk cache larger than 256K. Thus, avoid these higher settings and save your RAM, even if you have plenty of RAM available. Setting the cache size smaller than 256K reduces the effectiveness of the cache, but is still better than no cache at all. If you need extra RAM, reduce the size of the cache accordingly and then restart.

  Note that the RAM cache is less effective when working with applications that read/write mostly nonrepeating data (such as Photoshop's loading and editing of different graphics). If this is your primary use of the Mac, you can set the RAM cache to a near minimum with little or no speed loss.

  System 7.5 Alert: With System 7.5's new memory management, the disk cache reportedly offers better speed benefits the more the cache size increases, no matter how large you make it. Thus, if you have the RAM to spare, try going beyond the 256K cache limit. See if your performance improves. The default setting of the cache is 96K; Apple's official recommendation is 32K per Mb of RAM.

  System 6 Alert: The disk cache (actually named RAM cache and accessed from the General control panel) has a recommended maximum size setting of 128K. Make it lower as needed (you can even reduce it to zero).

- **RAM disks**

  You can reduce the size of a RAM disk or turn it off altogether. Just remember that you must delete *all* files from the RAM disk before you can change its size or turn it off. To do this, drag all files on the RAM disk to the Trash or simply select Erase Disk from the Finder's Special menu (don't worry if you get a message that says "Initialization failed"). Although any modifications to the RAM disk settings should result in the disappearance of the RAM disk icon, you must still restart the Macintosh to see any change in memory allocation.

  If you use some versions of TrashBack, this may create an invisible folder on your RAM disk that must be deleted before you can modify the RAM disk (see Chapter 2, "By the Way: Two Very Different Versions of TrashBack"). Selecting Erase Disk will delete all files, including the TrashBack folder, and allow you to eliminate the RAM disk.

  Finally, other RAM disk utilities are available that do not involve the Memory control panel. If you use one, check its documentation for exact procedures.

BY THE WAY ▶

DRIVER-LEVEL VERSUS SYSTEM-LEVEL DISK CACHES

Disk formatting utilities often have options to create a disk cache separate from the one created by the Memory control panel. If you own a third-party hard drive, cartridge drive, or CD-ROM drive, such a utility may have come with your drive. Drive7 and DriveCD are two such utilities, purchasable independent of any hardware product. The disk cache created by these utilities should show much better performance benefit than Apple's disk cache. This is because they operate at a machine-specific device driver level rather than a more generic system software level. Additionally, to avoid duplication of effort, these utilities come with an option to "Disable System Cache" (essentially preventing data used by the cache from also being sent to Apple's disk cache).

If you are using one of these utilities, be sure to check it, rather than the Memory control panel, to reduce the size of the disk cache, if needed. Also, if you select Disable System Cache (which I recommend), you can lower the size of Apple's disk cache to conserve RAM (though note that Apple's cache will still be used by any devices not using the third-party driver).

BY THE WAY ▶

RUNNING APPLICATIONS FROM RAM DISKS VERSUS HARD DISKS

When an application opens, whether from a hard disk or a RAM disk, it loads into RAM. Thus, you might think that running an application from a RAM disk offers no speed advantage over running it from a hard disk. But this is not the case. In fact, running applications from a hard disk is typically slowed down by frequent required hard disk access. This is because only a portion of the application is in RAM at any one time. Different parts get swapped in and out as needed, accessing the drive each time a swap is made. Some applications do have an option to load entirely into RAM, but this is not common.

Actually, even if you run an application from a RAM disk, it will still access the hard disk whenever it requires information from the System Folder. Avoiding even this access is the rationale behind creating a startup RAM disk.

Increase the Size of the System Heap (System 6)

If you are experiencing periodic system crashes (or other strange and serious symptoms) across a variety of applications, you may have a system heap size problem. Under System 6, the amount of space occupied by the system heap is largely fixed. As you add INITs and fonts to your system, the percentage of the system heap that is unused decreases. You can see this amount in the bar for System memory located in the "About the Finder" window. Once again, the light-shaded portion of the bar represents that portion of the allocated memory that is unused by the system (see "Take Note: More About 'About This Macintosh': Bar Shading," earlier in this Fix-It). If this light area becomes too small (usually less than about 10 to 20 percent of the total size of the bar), a system heap problem may occur. Strange symptoms that start occurring at this point indicate an inadequate system heap size.

A quick solution, as already discussed ("Reduce the Memory Size Needed by System Software"), is to delete some of the INITs, fonts, or desk accessories that are contributing to the system heap size. The disadvantage, of course, is that you lose whatever function was served by the deleted file(s). To work around this, you can increase the size of the system heap. However, be warned that doing this reduces the amount of memory available for applications and may itself sometimes result in more serious problems, including system crashes. If you plan to try this anyway, here's how:

1. Get a utility that can adjust the size of the system heap. CE Software offers one for free, called HeapSizer.

2. Use this utility to enter an increased size for the system heap. Details on how to determine the optimal increase in size are included with the instructions that accompany HeapSizer. Be aware that the number you enter with HeapSizer is typically much larger than the amount of kilobytes that the system heap will actually increase.

3. Restart your Macintosh for the change to take effect.

Increase the Size of the System Heap (System 7)

In System 7, the size of the system heap is dynamically regulated. This means that the Macintosh automatically adjusts the system heap's size as needed to accommodate additional files, theoretically eliminating the need to readjust the heap size yourself. Thus, there would seem to be no need for a utility to change the size of the system heap. However, sometimes this dynamic size readjustment fails because the Mac finds itself needing more system heap space than it can create (this can happen, for example, when several RAM-hungry applications and INITs are all active simultaneously).

As with System 6 (see the previous section), a variety of symptoms including system crashes can result when the system heap runs out of room. To avoid this, you need to set aside more space for the system heap (realizing that this leaves less memory for applications). However, do not use HeapSizer (or other similar utilities) to do this, because they only work with System 6! Instead, your best bet is Now Utilities' Startup Manager. Open it and select its Preferences dialog box. You will find an option there called "Reserve System Heap Space." If you check this, you will have the further option to specify how much of an increase you want (generally 20 percent is a good choice). Read the Now Utilities manual for more details. Crash Barrier has a similar option, accessible from the System Memory Correction dialog box in the Crash Barrier control panel. These are the only two methods (of which I am aware) of increasing the system heap size in System 7.

Some users have reported that increasing system heap size also solves a problem with frequent out-of-memory messages when trying to open at lot of windows in the Finder. This is thus a potential alternative to increasing the size of the Finder's memory, as explained previously (see "Increase the Finder's Memory Size: System 7," earlier in this Fix-It).

Still, if you really load up your system software with extensions and sounds, you will eventually reach a limit beyond which the system heap size cannot reasonably increase. If this becomes a problem, your best immediate alternative is to reduce the system software memory size by eliminating nonessential extensions, fonts, and sounds, as previously described.

Increase the Total Available Memory

To increase the total available memory, you can use virtual memory, use other memory enhancement utilities, or add more physical RAM.

TAKE NOTE: ▶

WHY 32-BIT ADDRESSING?

Every location in memory is given an "address" by the computer. However, there is a maximum number of possible addresses. The original Macs used 24-bit addressing (where the bit number refers to how many digits make up an address). Starting with the Mac IIci, Macs shifted to 32-bit addressing. This increase meant that many more addresses were now available, which in turn meant that the Mac could use more memory. This difference in addressing schemes is determined by information built in to the computer's ROM. A computer that has the necessary ROM is called "32-bit clean." All current Macintosh models are 32-bit clean. From a troubleshooting point of view this has several important consequences:

- *You turn 32-bit addressing on or off from the Memory control panel (see Figure F6-8). The reason you have this option (rather than simply having it on all the time) is because some applications may not be compatible with 32-bit addressing (though recent versions of almost all software are now*

---

compatible). This incompatibility is due to the program's assigning the extra 8 bits to purposes other than an address, which would then be misinterpreted by a 32-bit clean Mac. Using 32-bit addressing with incompatible applications can cause system crashes. There is no sure way to tell whether a program is 32-bit compatible or not, though certain diagnostic utilities, including MacCheck (see Fix-It #10) and Help! (see Fix-It #18) can provide you with some indication. Thus, unless you intend to use memory levels that require 32-bit addressing (as explained later in this note), it is safer to leave it turned off.

- Not all Macintoshes show a 32-bit addressing option in the Memory control panel. Older Macintosh models (prior to the Mac IIci) do not support this option and thus do not list it in the control panel. At the other end, Power Macintoshes similarly do not list this option. In this case, it is because 32-bit addressing is required for these models and cannot be turned off.

- If you want to use 32-bit addressing with a Macintosh II series computer that is not 32-bit clean, such as the Macintosh IIcx, you can get a free system extension from Apple called MODE 32 (developed by Connectix), which simulates 32-bit mode on these machines. There is a new version (MODE 32 7.5) that is necessary to avoid compatibility problems with System 7.5. Apple independently developed a similarly functioning extension called 32-Bit System Enabler. However, Apple has dropped support of this extension and recommends using MODE 32.

- With 32-bit addressing turned off (or not available), the maximum amount of SIMMs that a Mac can address is 8Mb (or up to 14Mb of memory of SIMMs and virtual memory combined). What happens if you install more than 8Mb of physical RAM in your machine, with 32-bit addressing off? Just check the "About This Macintosh" window and you will see. Any additional RAM beyond the 8Mb limit is included in the System Software bar, which will be now larger than it has ever been before. You will thus get no benefit from this extra RAM. Users unaware of the cause may panic, thinking that something is wrong with their hardware. However, the solution is quite simple (for Macs that support 32-bit addressing). Just turn on 32-bit addressing and restart.

- The issue of 24-bit color and 32-bit QuickDraw (as discussed in Chapter 10) is a separate, though related, topic from the one discussed here.

STILL MORE ABOUT "ABOUT THIS MACINTOSH": BUILT-IN VERSUS TOTAL MEMORY

You can of course use the Memory control panel to see if you have virtual memory turned on and, if so, how much virtual memory you have. However, you can also check this from the "About This Macintosh" window (see Figure F6-10). If virtual memory is in use, a new listing called Built-in Memory appears above the Total Memory listing. The difference between these two numbers is how much virtual memory you have. Using RAM Doubler similarly results in the appearance of the Built-in Memory versus Total Memory distinction.

Also, on Power Macs, the Total Memory may be larger than expected when virtual memory is on. This is not a cause for concern; everything will still work fine (although you really don't have the extra memory). Without going into details here, the mislisting is a consequence of how the Power Mac deals with the presence of its 68040 emulator (needed to run non-native applications on a Power Mac).

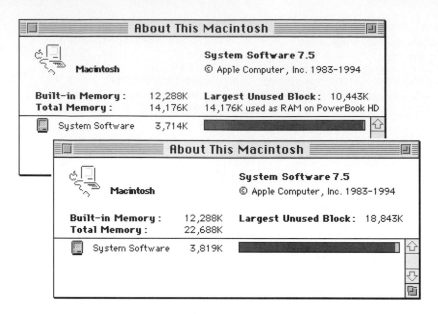

Figure F6-10 The "About This Macintosh" window with virtual memory in use (top) or with RAM Doubler in use (bottom); note the added Built-in Memory line in both cases (compare with Figure F6-1)

Use Virtual Memory   Virtual memory, accessed from the System 7 Memory control panel (see Figure F6-8), fools the Macintosh into treating part of your hard disk space as equivalent to RAM. After you turn it on, select the desired size of total memory (physical plus virtual) by clicking the arrows on the right side of the control panel. It does not let you select a higher value than your Macintosh and disk can accommodate.

Virtual memory is quick and easy to use and is a lot less expensive than buying more SIMMs. However, there are some limitations to using this feature. First, some software may be incompatible with virtual memory (though this is relatively rare now). Second, if you do not have enough unused disk space to accommodate what virtual memory needs (and it usually needs a lot), you cannot use it. Third, your Macintosh will run somewhat slower when it uses virtual memory. Still, as long as no single open application requires more memory than is available with physical (built-in) memory, the slowdown should not be significant. This is because the Macintosh shifts the active application into the faster physical (built-in) memory whenever possible.

Helpful hint: Once virtual memory has been set from the Memory control panel, you can temporarily turn it off by holding down the Command key at startup. This will not disable any other Apple INITs. However, it is possible that some other non-Apple INIT uses the Command key to similarly disable it at startup; so check for this. Virtual memory will return automatically the next time you start up. Thus, this technique allows you to toggle virtual memory on and off without having to go to the Memory control panel each time.

Power Macintosh Alert: If you have a Power Macintosh, you may notice that the Get Info windows for some applications have a message about virtual memory at the bottom of the window (see Figure F6-11). These messages basically tell you that the amount of memory needed to open the application will be less when virtual memory is on. Indeed, if you turn virtual memory on (even using as little as 1 or 2MB), the Suggested, Minimum, and Preferred values will all change to lower numbers (compare the Get Info window on the left side of Figure F6-11 to the partial windows on the right). Thus, for Power Macintoshes, turning on virtual memory has a double benefit: It makes more memory generally available to applications plus it allows each application to open in less memory. All of this is only relevant for applications written in native code. Surprisingly, running native applications on a Power Mac with virtual memory off may require significantly more memory than running a non-native version of the same application on a 680x0 Mac! Even with virtual memory on, native versions can be memory hogs (check out Excel 5.0 if you want a dramatic example of this). If you want to learn more about how and why this all works, check out Chapter 12. By the way, RAM Doubler works similarly to System 7's virtual memory and leads to a similar message in the Get Info window (as indicated in Figure F6-11). Finally, if you should change any Preferred or Minimum values with virtual memory on, the values that appear when you turn virtual memory off will be altered by the same absolute amount (and vice versa).

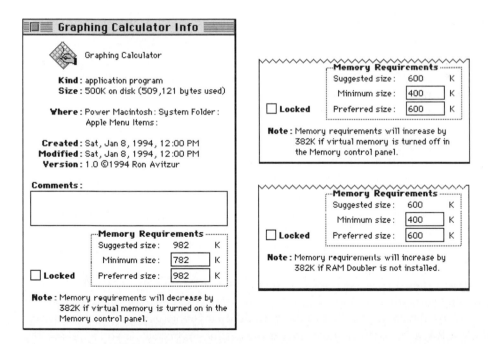

Figure F6-11   Left: The Get Info window for a native code application on a Power Macintosh, with virtual memory off; Right: The bottom of the Get Info windows of the same application when virtual memory is on or RAM Doubler is on

MORE ON LIMITATIONS OF VIRTUAL MEMORY

If you have problems using virtual memory, here's what you need to know to figure out what's going on:

- *Using virtual memory requires that your Macintosh have a Paged Memory Management Unit (PMMU). This is a small piece of hardware that is built into the 68030, 68040, and PowerPC processors. Models using the 68000 and 68020 processor (found in older models such as the Macintosh Plus and SE) do not include a PMMU.*

- *For a given amount of virtual memory, you need disk space equal to the amount of virtual memory you want plus the amount of physical RAM you have installed. Thus, adding 1Mb of virtual memory to a machine that currently has 8Mb of SIMMs requires at least 9Mb of disk space. If your disk space is getting tight, you may not want to give up this much space for use as virtual memory.*

- *As explained in "Take Note: Why 32-Bit Addressing?," without 32-bit addressing turned on, your total memory (built-in and virtual combined) cannot exceed 14Mb. However, this maximum is reduced by 1Mb for each card installed in a NuBus slot. The built-in video hardware, present in most recent models of Macintosh, is considered equivalent to a NuBus slot and thus also reduces the maximum memory by 1Mb (see Fix-It #17 for more on NuBus cards).*

- *To open, an application must load into one block of contiguous RAM. Unfortunately, if you use virtual memory without 32-bit addressing, virtual memory is not considered to be contiguous with your physical (built-in) RAM. For example, if you have 2Mb of physical RAM free and 2Mb of virtual memory free, and you need 3Mb to open an application, the application will not have enough RAM to open even though a total of 4Mb is free! At least 3Mb must be available in either physical or virtual memory. You cannot combine the two for the same application. The use of NuBus cards may result in discontiguous (fragmented) memory within the virtual memory area itself. Compact Macintoshes have other special restrictions that similarly contribute to increased memory fragmentation with virtual memory. Most of these problems are resolved by using 32-bit addressing.*

- *Virtual memory also requires that your disk driver be compatible with this feature. You may need to update your disk driver to use virtual memory (see Fix-It #12 on drivers).*

Use Other Memory-Enhancement Utilities   Some third-party utilities offer competition to virtual memory as a way of increasing your Mac's memory without adding more physical RAM. Two current such products are RAM Doubler and OptiMem. Both depend entirely on software techniques to change the rules for how the Macintosh assigns and uses memory. By doing such things as allowing an application's memory allocation to grow or shrink without having to quit and relaunch the application, or by allowing one application to use memory assigned to, but currently not used by, another application, these utilities effectively increase your apparent RAM.

Of the two utilities, RAM Doubler is preferable, because of its simplicity of operation and greater compatibility with other software. It effectively doubles your apparent RAM, getting your Macintosh to act almost identically to what it would do if you actually added an equivalent amount of physical RAM. Speed decrements may occur at times (especially as you approach the limits of available memory), but they are usually minor. If you have a Power Macintosh, make sure you use the native code (see Chapter 12 for more on this term) version of RAM Doubler (version 1.5 or later). Also note that RAM Doubler works best when you use it to open more programs at once, not to assign increasing amounts of memory to a single program.

RAM Doubler behaves in many ways just like System 7's virtual memory. It even results in the same Built-in Memory versus Total Memory listing appearing in the About This Macintosh window. However, RAM Doubler accesses the hard disk much less than does System 7's virtual memory (which is why it is usually faster than virtual memory) and does not require nearly as much disk space to set up.

By the way, Connectix (the makers of RAM Doubler) also makes a RAM disk utility, called Maxima, that can double the size of a RAM disk in a RAM Doubler-like manner. That is, an 8Mb RAM disk will need only 4 Mb of RAM.

Overall, these utilities are a cheap and effective way to increase your RAM. Just watch out for potential conflicts with your other software (I have had particular problems with RAM Doubler and using file sharing or a modem).

Add More Physical RAM   As a last resort, if memory problems persist, you can solve them by adding more memory chips (SIMMs) to your Macintosh. If you frequently find yourself short of needed RAM, adding SIMMs should not be a last resort! There is no better solution to memory problems. It has no disadvantage other than price, and reaching at least the 8Mb level is no longer prohibitively expensive. If you are having problems working with only 2Mb to 4Mb, moving up to 8Mb or more will make a dramatic difference.

Adding additional SIMMs (or replacing existing ones) is a hardware modification that, depending on your particular model of Macintosh and your willingness to try, can be easy to do yourself or may require that you take your Macintosh to a dealer. Essentially, you insert the SIMMs into special slots located on the computer's main logic board. One important caveat: Whenever you add or replace SIMMs, there is a chance that the SIMM may be of the incorrect type, defective, or incorrectly installed. This can lead to *very* serious problems, including an inability to start up the Macintosh. The details of which types of SIMMs to buy, how to install the SIMMs, how much you can increase your RAM and in what increments, vary significantly among the different Macintosh models. Additional details on these matters are covered in Fix-It #17. If you need still more information, contact an authorized Apple dealer or seek other outside help.

For related information

SEE: • Fix-It #4 on extensions and control panels
        • Fix-It #17 on hardware repairs and upgrades, including adding SIMMs
        • Fix-It #18 on seeking outside help
        • Chapter 1 on hardware terminology (SIMMs, processor, and so on)
        • Chapter 2 on the Get Info command and the About This Macintosh window
        • Chapter 4 on unexpected quits and other system errors
        • Chapter 5 on startup problems
        • Chapter 6 on applications and files that will not open
        • Chapter 9 on installing and removing fonts
        • Chapter 11 on RAM disks and File Sharing
        • Chapter 12 for special memory issues regarding Power Macintoshes

Fix-It #7:
Check for Viruses

QUICK SUMMARY

Use an updated anti-virus utility to scan your disk for viruses. Replace any infected files with clean copies from your backups. If no backup is available, use the anti-virus utility to eradicate the virus and repair the infected file.

When to do it:

- Whenever you get a warning message from your anti-virus utility that a virus attack has occurred.

- If you have frequent and unpredictable system crashes.

- When you replace an apparently corrupted file and it soon becomes damaged again.

- If the Macintosh system beep, or any other sound, occurs at unusual times and for no discernible reason.

- If files have been inexplicably erased from your disk.

- If a strange or nonsensical alert message unexpectedly appears on your screen.

- If you have just installed an anti-virus utility for the first time or are using a new disk that has not been previously checked for viruses.

- When any of an assortment of system-level problems occur, such as: applications take unusually long to open, documents do not print from all (or almost all) applications, cursor movement is erratic, or windows refuse to open or close. These symptoms have several possible causes, as covered in other Fix-Its. The probability that a virus is the cause increases if you have recently engaged in high-risk activity for virus infections (see "Take Note: How to Catch a Virus" later in this Fix-It).

These are just some of the more general symptoms associated with various viruses. For more specifics, see "Technically Speaking: A Few Known Viruses and Their Symptoms."

Why to do it:

A virus is a special type of software program. It has two main purposes in life. Its first (and most critical) is to duplicate itself; in particular, to spread copies of itself to other disks and other computer systems. Its second function is to carry out some activity on each disk where it resides. This activity can be as benign as sending a message that says "Peace" to as vicious as erasing your hard disk.

Viruses duplicate themselves in a variety of ways. The most common method of virus attack is for a newly arriving virus to locate a specific system software file on your disk and infect it (that is, place a copy of itself within some file's code/resources). For example, suppose you install an already infected application on your disk and launch it. This triggers the virus, with the result that it initiates a search for its target file (let's say it's the System file here) and infects it. Now, it uses the System file as a base of operations for further infections (by the way, deleting the original infected application at this point will be of no help). Any other system software file, particularly the Finder, control panels, and extensions, are also potential initial sites of infection (it varies according to the particular virus).

Once the virus has successfully infected a file on your disk, the virus code typically acts as an INIT (see Fix-It #4), loading into memory at startup. From here, it executes its code, with instructions on how and when to duplicate itself as well as whatever else it may have been programmed to do. For example, every time an application on the disk is launched, the virus code is alerted and typically will infect that application. Occasionally, a virus might attach itself to a driver (such as a printer driver) and execute its code when you access the driver (such as when you attempt to print something).

Transfer of the virus to a different disk usually involves some inadvertent help from the user. For example, a virus on a hard disk can transfer to a floppy disk either when you copy an infected file to the floppy disk or if you run an application from the floppy disk while the infected hard disk is mounted. When the newly infected floppy disk is mounted on another computer, the process begins anew with the virus transferring to the startup disk of the other machine.

A few viruses work by attaching themselves to a disk's invisible Desktop file (see Fix-It #9 for more on this file). These viruses spread to other disks as soon as an uninfected disk is inserted and mounted. No copying of files across disks or launching of applications is necessary.

Though a few exceptions exist, most viruses cannot infect an application until it is launched and cannot affect document files at all.

Viruses are created by unscrupulous programmers. Other than a sense of misplaced pride they may give their creators, viruses have no purpose other than to cause trouble for unsuspecting users. Fortunately, most viruses are relatively benign. That is, they do not deliberately alter or damage your software other than to do what is necessary to duplicate the virus. Unfortunately, since legitimate software is not designed to accommodate viruses, even a so-called benign virus can cause problems. Frequent system crashes or damaged files can easily result. Ironically, viruses occasionally have bugs that result in their causing even more harm than their creator intended.

A few viruses are deliberately destructive. Most threatening in this regard is a variation on viruses called a *Trojan horse*. A Trojan horse is a phony program, often disguised as a game. However, the real purpose of the program is to do damage to your disk, often erasing all the files on it. When you launch the program, it begins its insidious task. The only good news is that, unlike a true virus, a Trojan horse cannot replicate itself. To transfer to another disk, it must be deliberately copied by the user.

Virus or Trojan horse, benign or malicious—the bottom line is that you do not want them around.

TAKE NOTE ▶

HOW TO CATCH A VIRUS

The only way your files can get infected by a computer virus is to come in contact with a file that is already infected. The probability that this will happen depends on the nature of your computer activity. Activities that place you at higher risk include the following:

- *Being connected to a network. You are subject to infection anytime someone on the network accesses your disk, even if it is just to send or receive electronic mail.*

- *Using a modem to connect to an electronic bulletin board or information service. You can become infected if you copy or download a file that contains a virus. The major information services, such as CompuServe and America Online, check files for viruses before they list them for downloading, but these services are not guaranteed to be free of viruses.*

> - *Whenever you use a disk given to you by someone else. It doesn't matter whether the person giving you the disk is a close friend or a total stranger. A friend could give you an infected disk without realizing it contains a virus.*
> - *You insert an unlocked floppy disk into a computer other than your own and then later insert it in your computer.*
>
> *Conversely, the odds of coming in contact with a virus are relatively low if you stick to using only shrink-wrapped copies of commercial software, downloaded files from those information services that are known to check their files for viruses, disks from reputable user groups that virus-check their files, and disks from friends that you are confident take adequate precautions against viruses. Also, keep your floppy disks locked as much as possible, especially when taking them from one machine to another.*
>
> *For example, by following this advice, I have not even had an attempted virus infection for several years, even though I work at a university and frequently access a campuswide network.*

 What to do:

Your best defense against viruses is to prevent them from infecting your disks in the first place (see "Take Note: How to Catch a Virus"). Failing that, check for ones that may already be present and get rid of any that you find.

Use an Anti-Virus Utility

Install an Anti-Virus Utility

Your main line of defense against viruses is a current version of a good anti-virus utility. As mentioned in Chapter 2, the four best-known anti-virus utilities are Symantec AntiVirus for Macintosh (SAM), Virex, MacTools' Anti-virus, and Disinfectant (which has the distinct advantage of being free!). Install one of these on your startup disk.

Because of its popularity, I use SAM as the primary basis for examples in this Fix-It. Although other anti-virus utilities work differently, enough similarity exists that these guidelines should be helpful no matter which one you use. One note in this regard: The latest version of Virex includes a new technology called SpeedScan (see Figure F7-1) . It can tremendously shorten the time it takes to scan a disk for viruses. It similarly reduces the time needed to check an application for viruses each time it is launched. Older versions of SAM were particularly slow in doing this (in some cases several times slower). However, starting with version 4.0, SAM includes a QuickScan feature (as listed in Figure F7-3) that competes with Virex's SpeedScan.

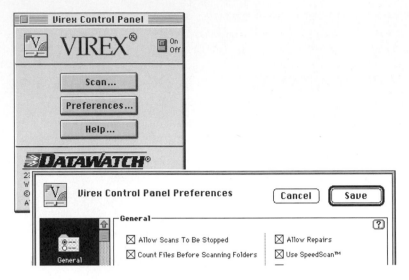

Figure F7-1 The Virex control panel, with the SpeedScan option listed in the partial view of its Preferences dialog box

Most anti-virus utility packages include both an application and a system extension and/or control panel. The application can scan a disk (or just selected folders/files within a disk) and eradicate all copies of any virus it detects, either by deleting or by repairing infected files. SAM's application is simply called SAM (it was called SAM Virus Clinic in older versions).

The extension/control panel is designed primarily to detect a virus before it infects your disk and thereby it stops an infection from occurring. For example, once installed, a typical anti-virus control panel continually monitors for potential attempted infections, working in the background while you do other tasks. It can also be set to trigger a complete scan of a disk, checking for viruses that may somehow already be present. In particular, you can configure it to scan floppy disks immediately after a disk is inserted, before the floppy disk is actually mounted. You can also set it to scan your startup disk every time you start up or shut down your computer.

In versions of SAM prior to 4.0, SAM included a SAM Intercept control panel. From the control panel window, you selected the various background checking options. Starting with version 4.0, the control panel has been eliminated and all its preference options have been incorporated into the SAM application (see Figures F7-2 and F7-3). There is now just a SAM Intercept extension, still needed to permit monitoring of activity in the background. When you install SAM, an alias of the SAM application is placed in the Control Panels folder so that you can access SAM from that location.

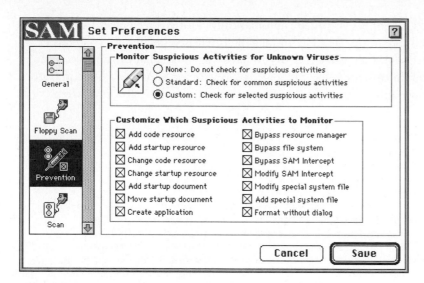

Figure F7-2   SAM's Prevention preferences

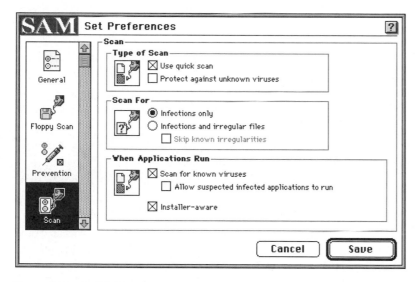

Figure F7-3   SAM's Scan preferences

Keep Your Anti-Virus Utility Up-to-Date

When you install SAM, a file called SAM Virus Definitions is placed in your System Folder. This file contains the information needed by SAM to identify and repair specific viruses. New versions of this file are released every time a new virus is discovered. Thus, if you want to reliably detect new viruses, you need to periodically replace your Definitions file with updated versions.

If you are a registered user of SAM, you are automatically notified (by a postcard) each time a new virus is discovered and an updated Definitions file is released (so be sure you register your anti-virus software!). You then can either pay to have this file mailed to you or you can download it from various information services. The new version of SAM has a built-in feature to assist you in doing this. Other anti-virus programs use similar methods to stay current.

TECHNICALLY SPEAKING ▶

USER DEFINITIONS

Some anti-virus utilities, including SAM, allow the user to directly enter a virus definition. The information about what to type is included on the postcard updates that are mailed to you. The user-entered definitions are saved to a separate file, located in your System Folder, called SAM User Definitions.

This method is a quick and free alternative to obtaining the updated SAM Virus Definitions file. However, with this user definition method, SAM can only detect the new virus. By instead using the updated SAM Virus Definitions file, SAM can both detect and repair the new virus (as explained in the main text). With some other anti-virus utilities, such as MacTool's Antivirus, user definitions can be used both for detection and repair.

Customize Your Anti-Virus Utility

Customization options vary from product to product and include too many to describe them all in this Fix-It. Check your utility's documentation for help. With SAM, you make these selections from the Options menu (or by clicking the Preferences button). Here is a brief look at three of SAM's Preferences options, Prevention, Scan, and Compression.

Prevention   SAM has three levels of Prevention checking (see Figure F7-2). These determine the sort of background monitoring that SAM performs. The lowest level (None) checks only for known viruses. The Standard level additionally checks for certain suspicious activities that may indicate the presence of a currently unknown virus. The third level (Custom) allows you to select which suspicious activities you want checked. The None level is probably sufficient for most situations—as long as you keep your Definitions file up-to-date. Unless you are in a very high high-risk environment (see "Take Note: How to Catch a Virus"), it would be rare to come in contact with a virus not covered by the latest Definitions file.

Scan   From the Scan Preferences window (see Figure F7-3), you select what SAM does when it scans your disk. For example, here is where you select whether or not to use QuickScan. You can also select whether it should "Protect against unknown viruses" and scan for "Infections and irregular files" (you can additionally request that SAM overlook irregularities that are commonly considered "legitimate"). Since irregular files are a signal of a potentially unknown virus, these two options are simply different methods of achieving the same goal. One method may catch something that the other method does not. Similarly, checking for irregular files during a scan checks for the same sort of oddities as does the suspicious activity background monitoring just described. While this overlap of features makes it a bit confusing to figure out which setting does what, don't worry too much: as I have already implied, attacks from unknown viruses are rare and most users can safely leave all of these options off.

Next, you can decide here if you want SAM to scan applications for viruses each time they are launched. This is a good idea, but do not select the suboption to allow infected files to run (otherwise, you run the risk of spreading the infection). Finally, you have a special option here called "Installer-aware" which, when turned on, disables SAM when it detects that Apple's Installer is in use. Unless this is checked, using the Installer is likely to trigger false alarm virus alerts (as described more in "Suspicious Activity False Alarms," later in this Fix-It).

Compression   If you keep compressed files on your disk, such as those created by Disk-Doubler or StuffIt, some anti-virus utilities cannot scan for and detect viruses contained within these files. You would have to decompress the files to check them. Both SAM and Virex, however, can check compressed files. To do this with SAM, go to SAM's Compression options window and select what types of compressed files you want it to check. The downside of doing this is that it slows down the scan.

Prevent a Virus Attack from Infecting Your Disk

A Virus Is Detected

If SAM Intercept detects an attempted infection by a known virus (either while Intercept is scanning an infected disk or when you are launching an infected application), an alert message will appear. The message will tell you the name of the virus and which file is infected. The alert box will also give you the choice to Proceed (thereby ignoring the warning), to Stop (if an application was about to launch, it will not launch if you select this), or to Run SAM (this will launch SAM, assuming it is currently installed on your disk).

In most cases, you should select to stop the process. Definitely do not select to proceed. Using the Proceed button essentially bypasses SAM's anti-virus protection, risking further infection. With some other anti-virus utilities, the equivalent command similarly lets the application launch (if possible) but does so in a manner that supposedly prevents the spread of the virus. Even so, I would avoid using this command—far better to eradicate the virus before proceeding.

Though it is probably safe to do so, I would also avoid going directly to SAM. Instead, when SAM detects a virus and identifies a specific file on your startup disk as the source, immediately go to the desktop, locate the infected file, and delete it. If SAM detects a virus while scanning a floppy disk, immediately eject the disk. In either case, now restart with a locked startup floppy disk that includes SAM. Use this disk to check for and eradicate any remaining virus infections.

By the way, if you have SAM set to protect against unknown viruses, you may get a similar virus alert message that does not include the name of a virus. This does not necessarily mean that you have a virus infection. It could be a damaged file or a false alarm.

If you use Disinfectant, be aware that it may mistakenly report that a damaged font file is infected with a virus.

SEE: • "Eradicate an Existing Virus," later in this Fix-It, for what to do next

A Suspicious Activity Is Detected

SAM can detect a variety of suspicious activities that may or may not indicate an infection attempt by a new or unknown virus. These notifications do not depend on information in the Definitions file. Rather, they are determined by SAM's Prevention settings, as described in "Customize Your Anti-Virus Utility," earlier in this Fix-It (see also Figure F7-2).

When SAM detects a suspicious activity, an alert box appears with buttons to either Allow or Deny the continuation of the activity. If you want to allow the activity, and suspect that this same situation will recur, you can select Remember rather than Allow (the Remember button only appears if you have previously checked the option for it in the Alert preferences window). If you select Remember, it tells SAM not to give you this alert for any future repetition of this suspicious activity. It is up to you to decide what button to press. Make this decision based on whether you believe the alert indicates a real virus threat or a false alarm.

Suspicious Activity False Alarms

A suspicious activity alert does not mean a virus attack is under way. These alerts often occur during normal activities. For example, you can set SAM to alert you every time a new extension or control panel is copied to your disk. The rationale for this is that viruses are often transmitted as extension code.

If a suspicious activity alert message appears when you are intentionally copying a new extension to your disk, there is nothing to worry about. Click the Allow button. However, if this message appears when you are not copying anything, you should probably click the Deny button. This immediately halts the activity. But be aware that clicking Deny short-circuits whatever was going on at the time, which can potentially damage the affected file even if no virus attack was occurring.

Running any Installer utility (as described in Fix-It #5) is another activity that commonly triggers these alert messages. Again, nothing is amiss. Click the Allow button. Suspicious activity alert messages may appear repeatedly while an installation is in progress. In some cases, it can prevent the installation from successfully completing. To avoid this, temporarily turn off your anti-virus utility prior to using the Installer. Even better, if you select SAM's "Installer-aware option" (see Figure F7-3), SAM should temporarily disable itself whenever you run Apple's Installer (in older versions of SAM, you may get an alert message when you launch the Installer, asking if you want SAM Intercept turned off until you are finished).

BY THE WAY ▶

KEEP YOUR FLOPPY DISKS LOCKED

No viruses can infect a locked floppy disk. So if you suspect your hard disk is infected, make sure that all floppy disks inserted into the machine are locked. This prevents transfer of the virus to the floppy disk. After you eradicate the virus, you can use unlocked disks again. Similarly, when you are using a floppy disk on someone else's machine, keep the disk locked if possible. If you need to unlock it (because you want to copy something to the disk), be sure to scan the disk for infection before you use it again on your machine.

Eradicate an Existing Virus

If SAM Intercept (or other similar anti-virus utility) does detect an infected file, your next step should be to get rid of it. However, even if you subsequently delete the identified infected file from the Finder, there may still be other infected files on your disk. Any further activity risks spreading the virus. Thus, with SAM, you should immediately use the SAM application to do a complete scan of all disks that were mounted at the time the alert message appeared. You then delete (or repair) any files that are reported to be infected.

Even if you have not gotten a virus alert message, you may still choose to run your anti-virus utility periodically on a preventative basis. Similarly, if you have just installed your anti-virus utility or are using a new hard disk, you should ideally run the utility before proceeding.

By the way, Virex can repair files directly via its control panel. You don't have to separately open the Virex application.

Scan for and Delete Infected Files

To use the SAM application to scan for and eradicate viruses, do the following:

1. **Restart your Macintosh with a locked copy of a startup floppy disk that contains the SAM application**
   Recall that you may have to customize your startup disk to include any needed Enabler files (as described in Chapter 2 and Fix-It #5). Most anti-virus utilities either include their own startup disk or have procedures to facilitate the creation of such a disk. With SAM, if the included startup disk does not work with your Mac, you can create a workable startup disk via its Startup Disk Builder option.

   If you are just doing a preventative scan, with no virus suspected, you can skip this step and run SAM from your hard disk (assuming you have installed a copy of it there). But be prepared to restart from a floppy disk if any virus is reported.

TECHNICALLY SPEAKING ▶

TAKING EXTRA PRECAUTIONS WITH FLOPPY DISKS

If the disks you need to scan include a floppy disk, scan the floppy disk(s) first, before scanning any hard disks. Ideally, do not have any hard disks mounted when working with infected floppy disk(s). This eliminates the chance of infecting your hard disk while you try to disinfect your floppy disk(s).

To do this with an external hard disk, simply turn it off before you restart with your anti-virus startup floppy disk. For an internal hard disk, insert the startup floppy disk before restarting. Then restart while holding down the Command-Option-Shift-Delete keys. Wait until the Welcome to Macintosh message appears. Then release the keys. Typically, the internal hard disk will not mount. After eliminating problems with floppy disks (by using the methods described in the main text), restart again with any hard disk(s) mounted. Now check the hard disk(s) for virus infection.

2. Launch SAM and select what disk(s) or folders or files you want to check

You do this from the directory listing in the window, much as you would select items from the Finder's similar listing of volumes, folders, and files (see Figure F7-4). Most often you would select an entire disk.

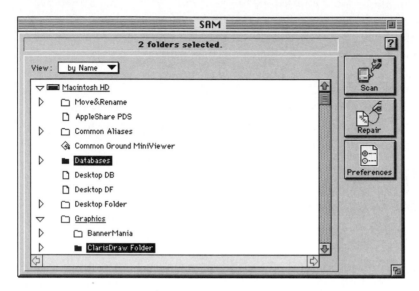

Figure F7-4   Select what items you want SAM to scan

3. Click either the Scan or Repair button to initiate the scan

If you select Scan, SAM will simply report any infected files it finds. If you select Repair, SAM will repair any infected files that it detects (assuming it can successfully do it). If you click Repair, SAM will warn you that you should preferably delete rather than repair infected files. I agree with this advice (for reasons I explain in the next section, "Repair an Infected File?"). Still, if you persist, SAM will allow you to select Repair.

Assuming you selected Scan, when the scan is complete, SAM creates a list of all infected, suspicious, or otherwise problematic files. For example, in Figure F7-5, SAM lists as a problem that a MacTCP Prep file did not have a "valid resource." This message typically means the file is damaged and that SAM was therefore unable to check it. It probably has nothing to do with any virus. Still, because it may be damaged, you should probably delete and replace the file anyway.

4. Delete and replace any reported problem files (or repair infected files)

To delete a file or files, simply select its name(s) from the list and click the Delete button (see Figure F7-5). To attempt to repair a file or files, click the Repair button instead. In either case, you will get a message asking you to confirm what you have selected (see Figure F7-6 for the message that appears if you select Repair). Confirm your choice. Alternatively, you can delete files from the Finder.

For any files you deleted, you will next want to replace them from your uninfected backup copies (ideally from a locked floppy or CD-ROM original disk). Scan the backup disk before making any replacements, if there is any doubt about whether the backup is infected.

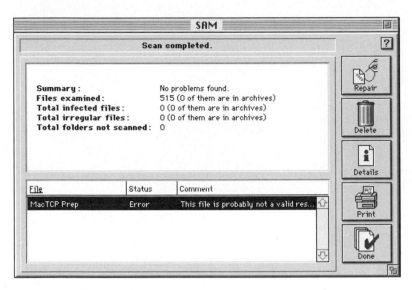

Figure F7-5   Select files to be deleted or repaired

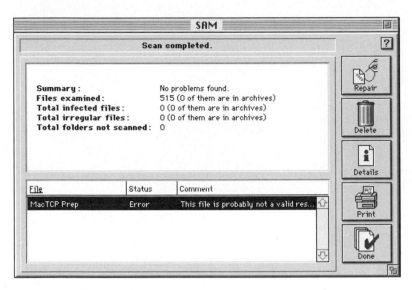

Figure F7-6   This message appears if you select to repair, rather than delete, a file

Replace the deleted files from presumably uninfected backups. Scan the replacement files after you have reinstalled them. If SAM reports a virus is still present, it probably means the backup file(s) are infected and should also be deleted. Other alerts probably mean the problem is not virus related (it could be a damaged file).

5. **Rescan the entire disk**

After completing the previous steps, scan the disk(s) a second time to be certain that no reinfection has occurred.

The previous advice takes a conservative approach. For example, some users would use SAM's Repair function (described next) more freely than I recommend. However, I would rather waste five minutes on a probably unnecessary precaution than risk any chance that the virus is retained on my disk.

TAKE NOTE ▶

INFECTED DESKTOPS

As mentioned in the "Why to do it" section, some viruses attach to the invisible Desktop file on your disk. Anti-virus utilities typically report when this has happened and may automatically disinfect the file. Still, the surest way to eradicate these viruses is to completely rebuild the Desktop file. This creates a new uninfected file.

SEE: • Fix-It #9 on rebuilding the Desktop file

Repair an Infected File?

At times, you may not have a backup available for an infected file. For such occasions, most anti-virus utilities, including SAM, give you the option to repair infected files. This means that the utility removes the virus program from the infected file and attempts to restore the file to its preinfected state.

However, SAM (or any other anti-virus utility) cannot always repair files successfully. Even if the virus is successfully removed from the file, the file may still not function normally. That's why replacing the file with a backup is the preferred method for eradicating a virus.

Trojan horse programs can never be repaired; they must be deleted.

Anti-virus utilities can only, at best, successfully repair damage due to known viruses. To repair any non-virus–related damage, you need to try other types of repair utilities, as described in Fix-It #14.

If the Anti-Virus Utility Didn't Solve Your Problem

If you use your anti-virus utility and update it as needed, you should be safe from almost any type of virus infection. Therefore, if your problem persists despite these efforts, it's probably not a virus-related problem. It's time to look elsewhere. However, you might first call the technical support line for your anti-virus utility and ask if your symptoms indicate an unknown or newly discovered virus.

Otherwise, if you remain concerned that you have an unidentified virus, you could reformat the entire disk and restore it from (what you hope are) your uninfected backups. This should eliminate any virus infections, even if they were not detected by your anti-virus utility. Normally, though, this should not be necessary.

By the way, if a virus or Trojan horse did succeed in infecting your disk and appears to have erased files, don't despair yet (even if the files aren't backed up!). It may only be the disk's Directory that has been damaged or erased. If so, you may be able to repair or restore the disk, as described in Fix-Its #10 and #13.

Determine the Source of Your Virus Infection

Whenever you find a virus on any of your disks, try to determine where the original infected file came from. Use this knowledge to prevent future infections. For example, did symptoms start shortly after you used a particular floppy disk borrowed from a friend? If so, alert your friend to the problem, and be more careful the next time you borrow a disk from him or her!

For related information

SEE: • Fix-It #4 on extensions and control panel problems
   • Fix-Its #10, #13, and #14 on repairing damaged files and disks
   • Chapter 2 on preventative maintenance
   • Chapter 4 on system crashes

Fix-It #8: Defragment/Optimize the Disk

QUICK SUMMARY

Use a disk optimizing utility (such as Speed Disk from Norton Utilities or Optimizer from MacTools) to defragment/optimize the files on your hard disk.

When to do it:

• Whenever the overall speed of operations on your disk slows down significantly.

• Whenever symptoms appear that get worse as less and less free space is available on your disk; especially problems opening or correctly displaying a document.

- Whenever your undelete utility is unable to restore or only able to partially restore even the most recently deleted files.
- Whenever you use a defragmenting utility to analyze a disk and it suggests that defragmenting is desirable.

 Why to do it:

This is the first of a trio of Fix-Its that refer to topics first mentioned in Chapter 2, under the heading "Give Your Macintosh a Tune-Up." At that time, I briefly considered them as preventative maintenance procedures. Now let's look at them, in more detail, as specific problem-solving techniques. For this Fix-It, the problem is file fragmentation.

Suppose that a 50K file is stored on your disk, tucked between two 900K files. If the 50K file is deleted, it leaves a small 50K gap between the two larger files. The larger files cannot automatically slide over to fill in the gap. Files can be moved to different physical locations on a disk only when they are copied or modified. (Remember, *location* refers to the physical area of the disk that the file occupies. This is different from its location on the desktop, which refers to the folder where it resides. It is also different from the area of memory occupied by a file after it is launched.) After you've spent months adding, deleting, and modifying files on your disk, the unused space on your disk may consist mostly of these small gaps.

Now suppose that you want to copy a new 1200K file to your disk but no longer have a single block that large anywhere on the disk. A total of 5000K of unused space may be on the disk, but it is all in blocks smaller than 1200K. By itself, this is not a problem. Fortunately, the Macintosh can divide the physical storage of a file into separate fragments. These fragments, which don't have to be stored near one another on the disk, then fit into the smaller empty blocks. This is called *disk fragmentation,* or (more accurately) *file fragmentation.* Similarly, existing files on your disk can become more fragmented each time they are modified (such as when you save changes to a document file).

The information needed to link together the data from all of a file's fragments is stored in the invisible files that make up the Directory area of the disk (as described more in Chapter 8). By accessing this information, the Macintosh can combine a file's fragmented data as needed (for example, it would do this when opening a file and loading its data into memory). This does not actually eliminate the fragments; it just allows the Mac to work around them. Thus, most of the time, you could not tell the difference between using a file that is stored as a single block versus using the same file stored in fragments.

If the amount of fragmentation gets too great, however, it can become a problem, albeit usually a minor one. Because of the added time needed to skip around the hard drive to find the fragments of a file, the operational speed of the Macintosh may slow down noticeably. Also, especially if an individual file is severely fragmented, you may have trouble using the file. A fragmented word-processing file, for example, may unexpectedly display incorrect formatting. Also, disk-repair utilities and some undelete utilities work less effectively with highly fragmented disks. Finally, if your free space is fragmented, you may have trouble using certain virtual memory utilities that require contiguous free space in order to work (Apple's virtual memory does not have this restriction). If you are experiencing any of these problems, and you haven't defragmented your disk recently, it's time to check it.

What to do:

Optimizing/Defragmenting Basics

Defragmenting and optimizing refer to different but similar operations. *Defragmenting* means to restore fragmented files into single undivided files. *Optimizing* means to rearrange the location of files on your disk so as to minimize future fragmenting. Optimizing works on the principle that files can only get fragmented as they get used and especially as they get modified. Thus, you can minimize fragmenting by locating all rarely modified files (such as most applications) in one location and frequently accessed files (such as most documents) in another. A related optimizing technique is to combine all unused space into one block. In general, when you say you optimized a disk, it implies that you also defragmented it. That's how I will use the term here.

Special utilities are used to optimize a disk. Examples of these utilities are Optimizer (from MacTools Pro), Speed Disk (from Norton Utilities), and Disk Express II (from AlSoft PowerTools).

Disk Express II is noteworthy because it can optimize your disk in the background, working whenever your Macintosh is idle for a few minutes. When you resume work, it halts. At your next break, it returns to where it left off. However, because of their greater popularity, this Fix-It will emphasize the use of MacTools Pro and Norton Utilities.

Before You Optimize

Check for Damage   Optimizing an already damaged disk can further damage files, resulting in irretrievable loss of data that could have otherwise been saved. So before you optimize a disk, first check for possible damage. To do this, run Disk First Aid as well as the relevant utility from your repair package (such as DiskFix from MacTools Pro or Disk Doctor from Norton Utilities). Be especially sure to use these utilities to check for media damage. Some optimizers, particularly Norton Utilities' Speed Disk and Disk Express II, can directly check for media damage. If any damage is reported, repair it before you attempt any defragmentation.

Other Precautions   For reasons explained more in later sections of this Fix-It, you should make sure you have a current backup of the disk to be optimized, that all files on the disk to be optimized are closed, and that you have deleted all unneeded files from the disk. Ideally, start up from a disk other than the disk you want to optimize.

Optimize the Disk

1. Launch your optimizing utility and select the disk you want to optimize

a. With Norton Utilities, click Speed Disk from its Main Menu. From the window that appears (see Figure F8-1) select the disk you want to optimize.

b. With MacTools Pro's Clinic, click the Optimizer button. (If you are using the startup floppy disk with Optimizer on it, you are taken directly to its special Optimizer window at startup.)

2. Select the command to display the current status of the disk

a. For Speed Disk, click the Check Disk button in the Speed Disk window (see Figure F8-1).

b. For Optimizer, click the Analyze button in the window that first appears. This will open up the Map window.

In each case, this creates a graphic map showing the distribution of files across the entire disk (see Figures F8-1 and F8-2). Different types of files are assigned different colors (or shades of gray, as seen here), based on the key shown in each window. The status display also lists the percentage of total files that are fragmented (if you have Fewer Choices selected for Speed Disk, it will describe the fragmentation with words such as "moderate" or "severe," rather than a percentage). Finally, it may suggest whether defragmentation is recommended. As a general guideline, if fragmentation is greater than 5 percent, I would defragment the disk. If in doubt, defragment the disk to be safe.

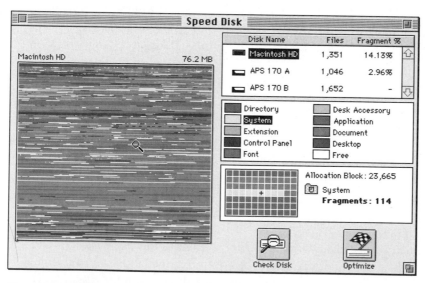

Figure F8-1   Norton Utilities' Speed Disk display

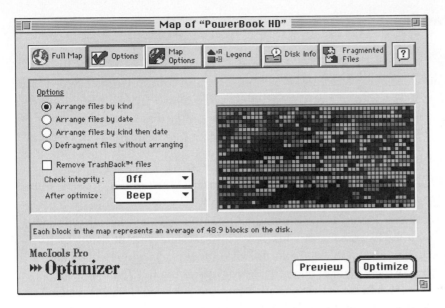

Figure F8-2 MacTools' Optimizer Map window, with the Options button selected

3. Prior to defragmenting/optimizing, select desired options

a. With Speed Disk, you have the option to Prioritize Files. This rearranges the location of files during optimization according to a priority system based on how often the file is likely to be modified (and therefore potentially refragment), as explained in "Why to do it." When you first select Optimize, Speed Disk also gives you the option to Defragment the disk rather than Optimize it. If you choose Defragment, the locations of files are not re-arranged, which means that unused space is not consolidated into one large block.

b. With Optimizer, you make similar choices by clicking the Options button in the Optimizer Map window. Select "Arrange files by kind then date" for maximum prioritizing. Select "Defragment files without arranging" to bypass all prioritization.

From here, you can also select to "Remove TrashBack files" if desired, helpful for freeing up extra space on the disk.

Selecting the options that do more work typically slows down the time it takes for the process to complete. However, as they help minimize the rate of future refragmentation, I recommend using them.

4. Optimize

With either program, click the Optimize button to begin optimization/defragmentation of the disk. Wait until it is finished. This can take quite awhile.

Beyond the Basics

Check for Fragmentation of Individual Files

Prior to defragmenting a disk, both MacTools Pro's Optimizer and Norton Utilities' Speed Disk can report the number of fragments of any specified file. Even if the overall fragmentation percentage for a disk is at an acceptably low level, a particular file on the disk may still be excessively fragmented. If you are having problems with a file, check its fragmentation. To do this:

1. **Display the current status of the disk**

   Follow the instructions in Step 2 of "Optimize the Disk."

2. **Select the option to display fragmentation of individual files**

   a. With Speed Disk, select "More Choices" from the Options menu and then select "Show Fragmented Files" from the Explore menu. This brings up a separate window listing each fragmented file and the number of its fragments. If a file cannot be defragmented because it is currently open or because there is not enough free space ("disk is too full"), this will be indicated as well. From this list, you can select individual files and defragment only those files.

   Alternatively, if you move your cursor over the graphic map of your disk's file fragmentation, the program will identify the name of the file under the cursor's location and the file's number of fragments. For example, in Figure F8-1, Speed Disk shows an impressive 114 fragments for my System file (one fragment of which is located under the magnifying glass cursor).

   b. Optimizer has similar options. If you select its Fragmented Files button (the last button in the row of buttons at the top of Optimizer's Map window, as seen in Figure F8-2), a list of fragmented files appears to the left of the map. However, unlike Speed Disk, you cannot select individual files for defragmentation.

   Clicking on a name in the list results in its fragments displayed in white on the map. Conversely, clicking on a block in the map highlights the file to which that fragment belongs.

3. **Decide whether to defragment/optimize**

   As a general guideline, if a file is divided into more than five or six fragments, and if the file has been causing any problem, strongly consider optimizing the disk (or, with Speed Disk, optimize at least just the problematic files).

Make Sure Files Are Free to Defragment (Startup Disk Problems and More)

Currently open files typically cannot be defragmented. Similarly, the System and the Finder on the startup disk cannot be defragmented, as they are considered to be open files. If you optimize the disk that contains the optimizing utility, the utility itself cannot be defragmented, as it is an open file.

Defragmenting a disk with files that cannot be defragmented reduces the effectiveness of the procedure. Therefore, ideally you should close all files on the disk to be defragmented and not defragment the startup disk or the disk that contains the optimizing utility.

To defragment your normal startup disk, you may need to create a special startup floppy disk that contains the optimizing utility. Norton Utilities and MacTools Pro both give instructions on how to do this. With MacTools Pro, you can also use its new RAMBoot feature (described more in Fix-It #13) to create a startup RAM disk with Optimizer on it.

Disk Express II is an exception. It can effectively defragment the disk that contains it, even if the disk is the startup disk.

Create Free Space

Successful defragmentation requires a minimum amount of free space on your disk. If your hard drive is almost full, you may not be able to completely defragment your disk. In particular, you may not be able to defragment larger files.

The solution is to remove files from your hard disk, to create enough free space for the optimizing utility to work. Ideally, at least 10 percent of your hard drive should remain unused. Delete any and all unneeded files from your disk.

If you are using TrashBack to protect deleted files, MacTools' Optimizer has an option to delete these files as it optimizes. You select it from the Options list (as seen in Figure F8-2). Conversely, MacTools TrashBack (described more in Chapter 2) has an option to prevent fragmentation by preserving unprotected space.

Maximizing the amount of free space available on your disk minimizes future fragmentation. The Macintosh prefers to store files in a single large block. However, as the total amount of free space on your disk declines, large blocks become increasingly rare and file fragmentation becomes increasingly common.

Don't Optimize Floppy Disks

In general, don't bother optimizing floppy disks. They are not large enough for fragmentation to be a significant problem.

A Disk Is Optimized When You Reformat and Restore It

Reformatting a hard drive and restoring its files from backups also completely defragment the disk. I would not usually reformat and restore a disk simply to defragment it. But if you are going to do this, for some other reason, it's nice to know that you are also optimizing the disk.

TECHNICALLY SPEAKING ▶

THE DISK CHECK BUG AND DEFRAGMENTATION

A bug in the Macintosh ROM may, under certain conditions, cause the Macintosh to treat a perfectly okay disk as if it is corrupted. The result is that the disk does not mount. If it is a startup disk, you will not get past the blinking question mark disk icon. If this happens, the only way to mount the disk is with a disk recovery utility such as MacTools or Norton Utilities (as described in Fix-It #13).

Thankfully, this bug (called the disk check bug) is a rare cause for these symptoms. It requires a specific combination of events before it can occur. For starters, it can happen only after a system crash or other improper shutdown. More to the point here, it can occur only if the disk is excessively fragmented. Thus, this is yet another reason to regularly defragment your disk.

A free utility called Disk Bug Checker will tell you if you are susceptible to this bug. The utility is available from the usual online sources. It was also included as part of MacTools 3.x but is no longer included with MacTools Pro. If Disk Bug Checker says you are susceptible, and you are experiencing any unusual

(continued)

symptoms, you should optimize your disk immediately. However, a fix for this problem is supposedly built in to System Update 3.0 and System 7.5. If you use either of these, you can probably ignore this whole issue.

SEE: • Chapter 5 for more general information on start up and disk mounting problems

The Downside of Optimizing and Defragmenting

If you follow the preceding steps, defragmenting/optimizing should proceed smoothly. However, a few cautions to note are described in the following paragraphs.

Defragmenting Takes Time

Defragmentation can take a lonnnnng time. You could easily have time for a leisurely lunch while an 80Mb or larger hard drive is optimized.

Defragmenting Can Erase Files That Otherwise Could Have Been Undeleted

Defragmenting your disk can eliminate the capability of undelete utilities to undelete previously deleted files, because the optimizing process usually overwrites files that have been deleted but that otherwise would have still been recoverable.

MacTools Pro's TrashBack feature avoids this problem (no matter what optimizing utility you use). Public Utilities (now extinct!) also circumvented this problem. However, the problem apparently still exists for Norton Utilities.

With any optimization utility, of course, defragmentation does not prevent the recoverability of files deleted after the defragmentation process is completed.

Defragmenting Can Cause Disk Damage

The optimizing process rearranges and rewrites so much data that, if there is a bug in the optimizing utility, the process could easily damage files on your disk (although the publisher of the utility will almost certainly release upgrades that fix these bugs as soon as they become aware of them). Even without a bug, there is a small risk that damage may occur if there is an unexpected interruption in an optimization, such as from a system crash or a power failure.

To save yourself from potential disaster here, make sure your disk's backups are current before you optimize them.

For related information

SEE: • Fix-Its #10, #13, and #14 for how to check for and repair damaged files and disks
SEE: • Chapters 2 and 6 on using undelete utilities

Fix-It #9:
Rebuild the Desktop

When to do it:

- If a file's desktop icon displays as a blank generic icon rather than its correct custom icon.
- If a file's desktop icon displays an icon for an older version of the software rather than the icon for its current version.
- When you drag a document icon to its application, the drag-and-drop highlighting does not occur and the application does not launch, even though it worked previously.
- When you double-click a document to open it, a message appears saying that the creating application is missing, even though the application is not missing.
- If the overall response speed of the Macintosh slows down significantly.
- If the size of available space on a disk, especially a floppy disk, is considerably less than what you would expect based on the files visibly located on your disk.
- If files are inexplicably missing from the Finder's desktop.
- When you get a message that says *the disk needs minor repairs,* and clicking OK does not remedy the problem.

Why to do it:

The Desktop file is an invisible file created on each disk when the disk is initialized. It stores information about the contents of the disk that is particularly important to the Finder. For example, it keeps track of what custom icons are assigned to files, the links between documents and their creating applications, and the links between aliases and their original files. The text in the Comments boxes of Get Info windows are also stored here. Every time a file is added, deleted or modified, the Desktop file is updated accordingly.

Without the Desktop file, the Finder could not create its desktop display. When you rebuild the desktop, it means that the Desktop file is largely recreated from scratch by scanning the current contents of the disk to get the required information. Here's why you would need to do this.

The Desktop File Can Become Bloated

Even after a file is deleted, the Desktop file retains the information about that file, such as its icon. Particularly because it retains this now-unneeded information, the Desktop file can become quite large over several months of adding and deleting files. Rebuilding the desktop purges unneeded information from the Desktop file and thus reduces the size of the file. This frees up some disk space (especially relevant for floppy disks) and can help speed up Finder operations. You can see exactly how much disk space you recover (it can be as much as several hundred kilobytes) by comparing available disk space immediately before and after rebuilding the desktop.

The Desktop File Can Become Corrupted or Incorrectly Updated

These days, virtually every program and document on your hard drive has its own unique customized icon. These icons give the Finder's desktop a wonderfully varied and colorful appearance, an aesthetic experience that you may miss if you select the "By Name" or other non-icon view from the Finder's View menu (although even these views can show custom icons if you select the relevant option from the Views control panel).

Unfortunately, if the Desktop file is not correctly updated, a file's custom icon may not display. Instead, document(s) may sport the boring generic "blank" document icon or (more rarely) application(s) may display the generic application icon (see Figure F9-1). This is considered a Desktop file, rather than a Finder, problem because the Desktop file is where all of the icon information used by the Finder is stored.

Figure F9-1
The generic document icon (left) and the generic application icon (right)

For example, custom icons often get "lost" when you upgrade to a new version of an application, if the new version uses a different icon from the older version. The Macintosh may get confused about which icons to use. The result is that the new version's files continue to display either the old version's icon or a generic icon.

Happily, rebuilding the desktop updates the Desktop file and usually fixes these icon problems (though some incorrect icon displays can be caused by a problem with a file's bundle bit, as described in Chapter 8).

Like all software, the Desktop file(s) can get corrupted. If this happens, the link between a document and its creating application can get lost. As a result, the *application could not be found* error message can appear when you double-click a document file to open it from the Finder. Occasionally, a damaged Desktop file may cause system crashes. Again, a likely solution to all of these problems is to rebuild the Desktop.

Rebuilding the Desktop is also known to partially remedy a special problem in System 7.0 and 7.0.1, where files mysteriously vanish from the Finder's desktop (described more in Chapter 6, "When You Can't Delete a File or Folder").

What to do:

Rebuilding Basics

The basic procedure for rebuilding the desktop was described in Chapter 2 (in the section called "Give Your Macintosh a Tune-Up"). I explain it in more detail here.

Hold Down the Command and Option Keys

To rebuild the Desktop file on the startup disk (or any other disk mounted at startup), hold down the Command and Option keys during the startup sequence until you see an alert box asking *Are you sure you want to rebuild the desktop file on the disk <name of disk>? Comments in info windows will be lost* (see Figure F9-2).

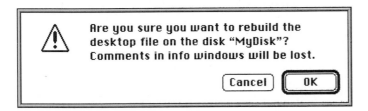

Figure F9 2   The alert box that requests you to confirm that you want to rebuild the Desktop file

To rebuild the Desktop file on any other disk, at any time, hold down the Command and Option keys prior to mounting the disk. For example, for a floppy disk, do it just prior to inserting the disk. If you want to rebuild the Desktop file on a floppy disk that is already mounted, eject the disk using the Put Away command from the Finder's File menu. Then reinsert the disk, while holding down the Command and Option keys. In all cases, wait for the alert box message to appear before releasing the keys.

At Ease Alert: This technique will not work if At Ease is running. You must turn it off and then restart.

System 6 Alert: If you are not using MultiFinder, you can rebuild the Desktop by holding down the Command and Option keys whenever you quit an application. Actually, it pays to turn MultiFinder off, in general, prior to rebuilding the Desktop. Otherwise, you may get a message that says *The desktop file could not be completely rebuilt (out of Finder memory)*. You can turn MultiFinder back on after the rebuild is complete.

SEE: • Fix It #6, "Special Cases: Finder Related Memory Problems," for more on this subject

Click OK to the Alert Box Message

Click the alert box's OK button and wait. A progress bar should appear, monitoring the rebuilding process. Within a minute or two, the Desktop file is rebuilt and the progress bar disappears. You are done.

If you have more than one disk (such as an internal and external hard disk) that gets mounted at startup, you get a separate message request for each disk. You also get separate messages for each partition on a hard disk. Click OK just for the volumes you wish to rebuild. You do not have to rebuild all of them. However, I have occasionally fixed an icon display problem on my internal hard drive by rebuilding the desktop of my external hard drive. This might happen, for example, if a document on my internal drive was created by an application on my external drive. So, it usually pays to rebuild all regularly mounted volumes if you are having problems.

BY THE WAY ▶

REBUILDING THE DESKTOP ON POTENTIALLY DAMAGED DISKS

Just a reminder: If you plan to rebuild the desktop because of symptoms that suggest file damage on the disk, it is a good idea to first run Disk First Aid or a similar utility to check for and repair possible Directory damage (see Fix-It #10). Otherwise, there is a slim chance that rebuilding the desktop can make things worse.

In this regard, note that the desktop is not the primary method by which the Macintosh keeps track of the contents of disks. The Directory is far more critical for this task. The desktop is needed only by the Finder.

Restart Again, If Needed

Restarting may be required to get correct icons to appear. This is especially likely for Desktop files rebuilt at times other than during startup.

Beyond the Basics

Update the Desktop to Fix Icon Problems for Individual Files

As described in the Why to do it section ("The Desktop File Can Become Corrupted or Incorrectly Updated"), rebuilding the desktop can fix problems with incorrect icon displays. However, if you are just having a problem with one or two types of files, you can avoid the time and hassle of rebuilding the desktop and instead selectively update the information for the problem files. With Norton Utilities for Macintosh 3.0, you do this via the Add File to Desktop command in Norton Disk Doctor's Tools menu. Similarly, there is a freeware utility called Fix Icons that does the same thing. In either case, you may need to restart before the change takes effect.

In a related matter, you may be able to fix certain icon problems without rebuilding the desktop or using a utility to update it. For example, if you create a document on your hard disk using an application run from a floppy disk, the document should display the appropriate icon. However, the next time you restart without the floppy disk present, the document may have a blank icon instead (especially if the creating application has never been copied to the hard disk). This is because the icon information on the floppy disk may not have been copied to the Desktop file on your hard drive. A similar situation can occur with any removable media or an external hard drive that you only mount occasionally. The correct icon display typically requires that the needed disk be present at startup. If you mount it later, the correct icon will still not display.

You can usually solve these problems by copying the creating application to the disk that contains the problem document. Then launch the application, open the document, and save it using Save As. The icon should be restored. If not, you need to rebuild the Desktop after all—ideally with all relevant disks mounted. This should almost always work.

If the problem still persists, you may have a more esoteric problem that requires a "complete" rebuild of the desktop (see later in this Fix-It). If even this fails, run a utility such as Norton Disk Doctor or MacTools' DiskFix to check for bundle bit problems or possible damaged files. However, be aware that not all generic icon "problems" mean that some need fixing. For example, I have found that if, after installing QuickDraw GX, I restart without QuickDraw GX, many of the custom icons associated with this feature switch to generic icons. When I return to GX, everything reverts back to its custom icon.

When Rebuilding the Desktop Causes Icon Display Problems

Occasionally, a file may display its correct custom icon and then lose it *as a result* of rebuilding the desktop. Most often, this happens to a document file whose creating application has been deleted prior to rebuilding. Rebuilding the Desktop file purges all information about the deleted application, including what is needed to display the document's custom icon. There is no solution to this other than to return the deleted application to your drive (rebuilding the desktop again if needed). Also, on a Power Mac 7100 or 8100, the System, Finder, and Enabler icons may become generic after a rebuild of the desktop. There is no way to prevent this, but it is only a cosmetic bug that will be remedied in a later release of the system software.

Custom Icons for Folders

Most commonly, custom icons are associated with program and document files. However, folders (and even volumes) can also have custom icons. But, unlike with custom icons for files, information about folder and volume custom icons is *not* maintained by the Desktop file. Instead, the icons are stored as special invisible files, named *icon*, located within each folder that has a custom icon. Thus, rebuilding the Desktop has no effect on these icons.

If a folder with a custom icon unexpectedly displays the generic folder icon, this can mean that the custom icon file is damaged. If so, you may be able to fix or create a new icon via the Get Info window (as explained in "By the Way: Custom Icons Made Easy"). If the file damage prevents you for doing this, try this alternative method: Remove all files from the folder; trash the folder (the invisible icon file goes with it); create a new folder and make a new custom icon.

If you have a missing custom icon for a volume (such as a hard disk), check the disk's formatting utility to see if the icon is selected from there. Otherwise, try using a freeware utility called Disk Rejuvenator. Use a utility to delete the invisible icon file and/or to make sure the volume's "Use Custom Icon" attribute is checked (as generally explained in Chapter 8). As a last resort, you could reformat the entire disk.

Losing (and Saving) Get Info Comments After Rebuilding the Desktop

Rebuilding the Desktop file normally results in the loss of any data in the Comments boxes of all Get Info windows. This is usually of trivial concern, since most users do not store any important information there. However, if you want to save these comments when rebuilding, some utilities can help. One especially slick utility is a system extension called, appropriately enough, CommentKeeper. Just drop it into your Extensions folder and restart. It works automatically the next time you rebuild the desktop (see Figure F9-3).

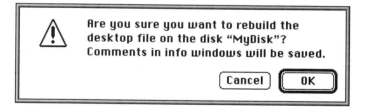

Figure F9-3 **The same alert box as shown in Figure F9-2, but modified by CommentKeeper, so that the last line now says "comments will be saved," instead of "lost"**

Alternatively, Norton Disk Doctor (in its Tools menu) has its own command to rebuild the desktop. If you select it, you will get a dialog box with an option to save comments (see Figure F9-4). If despite all this, you manage to lose comments that you had wanted to save, and if you have FileSaver installed and its Comments option checked (see Chapter 2), you can still restore the lost comments via the "Restore Finder Comments" command in Norton Utilities' Options menu.

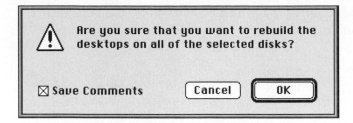

Figure F9-4   Norton Disk Doctor gives you a chance to save comments when rebuilding the desktop

Minor Repairs Alert Message

Occasionally, at startup or whenever you are trying to mount a disk (most often a floppy disk), you may get a message that says that *the disk <name of disk> needs minor repairs* (see Chapter 5, "Problems While Launching the Finder and the Desktop," and Figure 5-11). If you click OK, the problem is typically fixed and that's the end of it.

This message apparently appears either as the result of damage to the Directory or to the desktop. However, it clearly does not rebuild the desktop (it works too fast to have done that). So if the problem persists even after clicking OK, rebuild the desktop. See if that helps. In my experience, this message occurs only rarely, if at all, in System 7.

Don't Bother to Rebuild the Desktop After Initializing a Disk

Any time you reinitialize a disk, it creates a new Desktop file. You do not have to separately rebuild the desktop.

Desktop Files and Reusing Floppy Disks

Many users reuse floppy disks without reinitializing them. That is, they drag all the files on the disk to the Trash and then begin to fill the disk with new files. I don't recommend this. Instead, when you start over with a disk, reinitialize the disk first. Not only does this reconfirm that the disk is not damaged (otherwise, initialization would fail), but it also forces a rebuild of the desktop. This, in turn, purges unneeded information from the Desktop file and may thus reclaim a significant amount of disk space (over a 100K in some cases).

If you don't wish to reinitialize the disk, at least rebuild its desktop (after deleting all items from the disk). However, in System 7, at least one file or folder must be on a floppy disk in order to rebuild its Desktop file. If the disk currently has zero items on it (which it presumably has at this point), create an empty folder on the disk. Then rebuild. The rebuild will be successful and you can then delete the empty folder. By the way, this problem is the result of a bug that may get fixed in newer versions of System 7.

The Desktop Rebuilds Every Time You Start Up

A Desktop Folder on Your Desktop   If you are using System 7 and your Desktop rebuilds every time you start up, check to see if you have created a folder called Desktop. If so, this is the source of your problem. Rename the folder. What is happening is that the Macintosh is confused into thinking that your folder is actually a System 6 Desktop file (as discussed later in this Fix-It). This causes the Macintosh to repeatedly try to rebuild the desktop (among other problems it may cause).

Macintosh Easy Open Problems   Macintosh Easy Open directly modifies the Desktop file. Normally this is not a problem, but conflicts can arise with other programs, leading to an assortment of strange desktop-related symptoms. If you use Easy Open and are experiencing any desktop-related problems, turn it off. Your problems will probably go away.

Of somewhat less concern (but still frustrating), every time you start up with Macintosh Easy Open off (for example, by holding down the shift key at startup to turn all extensions off), the desktop will rebuild (often taking an atypically long time to do so) the next time you restart with Easy Open turned back on again. This appears to be a necessary feature of Easy Open, as it needs to check what might have changed in the desktop file since it was last in use.

Macintosh Easy Open (version 1.1) appears to be a particularly prone to causing rebuilds of the desktop in System 7.5. Some people claim that the desktop rebuilds at every restart with Easy Open on. To solve this, disable Easy Open (such as by dragging it out of your System Folder) and restart. The desktop will rebuild once more, and then not again as long as you leave Easy Open off. Of course, this means you lose the features of Easy Open.

Keep Extensions Off When You Rebuild?

Some extensions may cause problems when you rebuild the desktop, even so far as to prevent the rebuild from successfully completing. For example, with certain anti-virus programs running, rebuilding the desktop may not correct all icon problems. With some versions of Super-ATM turned on, rebuilding the desktop may result in corruption of the Desktop file.

To avoid these, and most other extension problems, the general solution is turn all extensions off prior to rebuilding. To do this, hold down the Shift key at startup until the Extensions Off message appears; then let go of the Shift key and immediately hold down the Command-Options keys to get the desktop to rebuild.

Unfortunately, there are a few exceptions even to this generalization.

Macintosh Easy Open Problems . . . Again   Because Easy Open forces a rebuild of the desktop when you turn it off and then back on again, Apple recommends that you leave Easy Open on when you rebuild.

AutoDoubler Problems   If you use AutoDoubler and rebuild the Desktop without this extension turned on, all files that had been compressed will adopt the AutoDoubler icon. If this happens, rebuild again, with AutoDoubler on.

The ideal way to leave just one or two extensions on and still be able to return to your normal selection of abled/disabled extensions the next time is to use the Temporary feature of a startup manager (as described in Fix-It #4). With Apple's Extensions Manager, which has no Temporary feature, you will need to create a "Set" to store your normal selection.

Otherwise   If none of this works, you probably have a more serious directory-level problem. You will need to try to repair the disk.

SEE: • Fix-Its #10 and #13 on repairing disks

System 6 Versus System 7: More than One Desktop File

System 6 has only one Desktop file, called Desktop. System 7, has two separate Desktop files: Desktop DB and Desktop DF (they contain different information and both are needed; the DB file stores icon information while the DF file stores the information about where on the desktop files are located).

You may occasionally find a System 6 Desktop file on disks running System 7. In such cases, System 7 software still uses only the Desktop DB and Desktop DF files. The Desktop file, if present, is used only when the disk is run under System 6. (If desired, you can view all of these files by using a utility that lists invisible files, as discussed in Chapter 8.)

Normally, you need not be aware of this difference between System 6 and System 7. However, it can be relevant if you switch between System 6 and System 7 (restarting is, of course, required to make this switch). At such times, the Macintosh automatically creates or rebuilds the Desktop files of any disks previously mounted under the alternate System.

For example, maybe your Emergency Toolkit disk runs on System 6, while your hard drive uses System 7. If so, when you start up from your hard drive after having started up with your System 6 Toolkit disk, the hard drive's Desktop files are automatically rebuilt. This is because any changes made to the hard drive while running System 6 were made only to the hard drive's System 6 Desktop file. When you return to System 7, rebuilding is needed to update the System 7 Desktop DB and DF files. Afterward, you may note some minor changes to the desktop display, such as window sizes that are now larger or smaller than they were before or folders that are moved from their prior location. While this may be a minor annoyance, there is nothing more serious to worry about here.

Similarly, when you start up with System 6, using a disk previously run under System 7, you may notice some new folders on the disk, such as Desktop folder and Trash folder. These folders, as described in Chapter 8, are invisible folders that are a normal part of System 7. However, System 6 doesn't know they are supposed to be invisible, and so they appear as visible folders. You should ignore them in System 6. Things will return to normal when you return to System 7.

Floppy disks, even if they were formatted under System 7, don't have Desktop DB and DF files. This is because these files are created only on volumes greater than 2Mb in size. Floppy disks have a maximum size of only 1.44Mb. Thus, all floppy disks use the System 6 single Desktop file.

Really Rebuild the Desktop

The information in this section is sufficiently important that I've separated it out from the rest of Beyond the Basics. When you rebuild the Desktop file(s) using the Command-Option key method, it does not *completely* rebuild the desktop. It is more like a thorough updating of the existing file(s) as opposed to deleting them and replacing them with new ones. This can be a problem if you are rebuilding the desktop because you suspect a corrupted Desktop file. In this case, rebuilding may not repair the damage, and the symptoms may persist. In such cases, it pays to delete the Desktop file(s) and thereby force completely new one(s) to be created (the Mac will create the new ones automatically when it finds the old ones missing). This may solve a problem that a normal rebuild would not.

Completely deleting the Desktop files may also enable you to rebuild the Desktop on those occasions when the standard Command-Option technique does not work.

Of course, reinitializing a disk accomplishes a complete rebuild, but there are less drastic ways to do this. Here's how.

In System 7   Currently, my favorite way of completely rebuilding the Desktop is to use a freeware utility called TechTool. To use it, just launch the utility and click the "Rebuild Desktop" button (see Figure F9-5). TechTool will then ask permission to quit any open applications (and turn off file sharing). Let it do so (by clicking the "Send AE Quit" button). You will then have the option to select which disks to rebuild, if more than one is mounted. After you have made your selection, TechTool deletes the Desktop file(s) and initiates a rebuild. The rebuild occurs without restarting the Macintosh. When the rebuild is finished you are returned to the Finder.

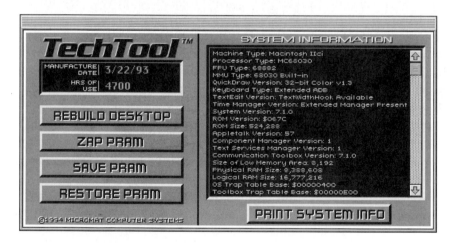

Figure F9-5   The TechTool dialog box

Another solution is to use a freeware system extension called Desktop Reset. When it is installed, you still request a rebuild the normal way—by holding down the Command-Option keys at startup. When you do this, however, the extension intercepts the normal procedure, gives you a slightly different alert message, and (after you click Reset) deletes the Desktop files, initiating the complete rebuild (see Figure F9-6).

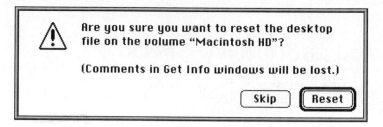

> ⚠️ **Are you sure you want to reset the desktop file on the volume "Macintosh HD"?**
>
> (Comments in Get Info windows will be lost.)
>
> [Skip] [[Reset]]

Figure F9-6   The dialog box that appears instead of the one in the Figure F9-2 when you rebuild the Desktop file with Desktop Reset in effect)

Norton Disk Doctor's Rebuild Desktop command also does a complete rebuild.

In System 6   Use Desktop Reset (as described in the previous section) to rebuild the Desktop. It works in System 6 as well as System 7.

Otherwise, in System 6, start up using the Finder (not MultiFinder). Use a utility (such as DiskTop, as described in Chapter 8) that allows you to view and delete invisible files. Find and select the Desktop file and delete it. When you return to the Finder, a new Desktop file will be built.

This method does not work under System 7 or under MultiFinder in System 6, since the Finder is always open and you cannot delete the Desktop file while the Finder is in use. However, there is a way around this problem. From your utility, you could simply move the Desktop file(s) from their location at the root level of the disk to inside a folder on the disk. This should force a complete rebuild, creating new Desktop file(s) when you restart. After restarting, delete the now obsolete Desktop file(s) from the folder where you moved them. Still, for System 7, the methods I described in the previous section are a lot easier to do.

For related information

SEE: • Fix-It #4 on turning extensions on and off
       • Fix-It #13 on damaged disks
       • Chapter 2 on preventative maintenance
       • Chapter 6 on files that do not open
       • Chapter 8 on invisible files and on icon problems

Fix-It #10:
Run Disk First Aid and/or MacCheck

QUICK SUMMARY

Run Disk First Aid to check for and repair corruption of the Directory area of a disk. If available, run Mac-Check to diagnose possible hardware damage, check for (but not repair) corruption of a disk's Directory and system software, and check for incompatibilities among the other files on a disk.

When to do it:

- Whenever you are unable to get a disk to mount.

- Whenever you have problems related to using files, such as an inability to open, copy, or delete files as well as files that mysteriously disappear.

- Any time you have a problem that is not easily diagnosed or solved. Running MacCheck and (especially!) Disk First Aid is such a simple and effective procedure that it is almost always worth trying.

Why to do it:

MacCheck and Disk First Aid are both part of Apple's system software. Together, these utilities can detect and repair a variety of common problems. Disk First Aid is included with all versions of the system software and with every Mac that is sold (it's on your Disk Tools disk). MacCheck has been included with Performas and with 500 series PowerBooks. MacCheck version 1.04 was available free from online services as part of a disk called Software Utility Update. Version 1.05 (or later?) may also be found on some online services. Sadly, MacCheck was not included with System 7.5, and Apple appears to have dropped all support of it. Still, for those of you who have MacCheck, this Fix-It gives you the lowdown on how to use it.

MacCheck and Disk First Aid are far from the most sophisticated tools of their kind. However, they have three distinct advantages: They are free, they are very easy to use, and (because they are made by Apple and, in the case of Disk First Aid, frequently updated), they sometimes can diagnose or fix problems that the more sophisticated tools cannot. That's why I recommend starting with these tools before moving on to anything more heavy-duty. Disk First Aid should especially be in your first line of defense when anything seems amiss with a hard drive.

MacCheck   MacCheck is primarily a diagnostic utility (which means it can tell you what's wrong but it can't do anything to fix it). First, it profiles your system hardware and software, providing you a detailed list of such things as what processor you have, what ROM version you are using, how much RAM you have installed, what SCSI devices are connected to your machine, the names of all the extensions and control panels on your disk(s), and which ones are currently disabled, what versions of each component of the system software you are using, which of your applications are listed as 32-bit clean—and more. This can be quite useful, especially for novices, in the event that your troubleshooting requires you to know such things as whether or not your Mac has a math coprocessor. With MacCheck, you can easily find this out even if you don't know what a math coprocessor is.

Next MacCheck, as its name implies, checks for a variety of hardware and software problems. For hardware, it primarily checks for potential damage to components on your Mac's logic board (except for SIMMs). For software, MacCheck primarily reports if it finds damage to the System or Finder files, if it finds multiple System Folders on your disk, or if it discovers damage to the disk's Directory. Finally, MacCheck will offer advice as to what to do when it spots trouble. Generally, its advice falls into one of three categories: Run Disk First Aid to try to repair the problem, replace suspected damaged software, or seek help elsewhere. MacCheck cannot make any repairs itself. Additional general troubleshooting advice is included in its help files.

Disk First Aid   Disk First Aid is a repair utility. It checks for possible damage to the Directory, running a series of tests that are virtually identical to MacCheck's examination of the Directory (which are only a subset of MacCheck's tests). The crucial difference is that Disk First Aid can actually fix most of the trouble that it spots.

By the way, because of this overlap between the two utilities, it would seem to make sense for Apple to combine them into one. In a way, they already have, but you can't get it for free. It's a commercial application called Apple Personal Diagnostics (described more in Fix-It #17).

The Directory area of a disk, as detailed in Chapter 8, is a collection of invisible files that contain the essential information that the Macintosh needs to access the disk and the files on it. The Directory maintains a continually updated catalog of exactly what is on a disk, where everything is, and how it is organized. One very important specific function of the Directory is to keep track of the number of fragments of each file (see Fix-It #8) and where each fragment is located. Without this information, fragmented files on the disk are unusable. Each area of the Directory has its own (often esoteric) name, such as *extent BTree* or *catalog hierarchy.*

Because the Directory is continually modified as you change the contents of your disk, and because most disk damage occurs when a file is modified, it is common for the Directory to become corrupted. Minor problems may cause symptoms so subtle that you do not notice them, at least not at first. This is why, in Chapter 2, I recommended using Disk First Aid as a preventative measure even if nothing seems wrong. You should eliminate even the most minor Directory problems as soon as you discover them, because minor problems tend to get more serious if left unfixed. Serious Directory problems can render the files on a disk inaccessible— you may not even be able to mount the disk.

What to do:

You can use these utilities in tandem, starting first with MacCheck and then shifting to Disk First Aid. Theoretically, if you run MacCheck and it reports no problems, you should be able to skip running Disk First Aid at all, since MacCheck's Directory tests (where it says "Checking Directory") are identical to what Disk First Aid checks. In reality, you should run Disk First Aid anyway, particularly if your version of Disk First Aid is more recent than your version of MacCheck (examine the dates in their Get Info windows to find this out). In this case, Disk First Aid may spot problems not reported by MacCheck. Since Disk First Aid gets upgraded more often than MacCheck (especially now that Apple apparently no longer upgrades Mac-Check), this could easily be the case. Eventually, unless Apple changes this policy, MacCheck is likely to disappear from use altogether.

On the other hand, if your version of Disk First Aid happens to be older than your version of MacCheck, it may not be able to repair problems detected by MacCheck. The general advice, of course, is to always use the latest versions of both utilities, as they can spot problems previous versions could not. The utilities that came with your Macintosh may no longer be the latest versions. Check on-line services or related sources (as discussed in Fix-It #18) to find out what the latest versions are.

You may prefer to run Disk First Aid first, using MacCheck only if you want its additional diagnostic and profile information. Actually, if I am having a problem with my disk, I always run Disk First Aid first. Doing so gives you one other immediate advantage: speed. Disk First Aid launches faster than MacCheck and, if you have more than one volume attached, you can select which volume you wish to test (MacCheck always checks all mounted volumes, slowing things down when you don't need to check them all). And of course, if you don't have Mac-Check, you can still use Disk First Aid by itself.

Overall, Disk First Aid is clearly the more essential of the two utilities, and the one you will use most often. For example, for preventative maintenance, I run Disk First Aid about once a month; I would similarly run MacCheck only about two to three times a year, if that.

The next two sections explain how to use Disk First Aid and MacCheck. A final section suggests what to do when neither of these utilities succeed in identifying your problem.

Disk First Aid

Whether you are running Disk First Aid after using MacCheck or just by itself, here's what to do.

Getting Started

1. Before you launch Disk First Aid . . .

While Disk First Aid can always verify a disk (that is, check for problems without making any repairs), repairing a disk requires that certain preconditions be met. In particular, Disk First Aid cannot repair the current startup disk, the disk from which Disk First Aid is running, a write-protected disk (including CD-ROM disks), a disk with any open files on it, or any disk at all while file sharing is active. Thus, to save time, before you even launch Disk First Aid:

a. Restart your Macintosh from a floppy disk (or alternate hard disk) that contains a copy of Disk First Aid (such as the Disk Tools disk that comes with Apple's system software).

b. Make sure file sharing is off (via the Sharing Setup control panel).

c. Make sure any floppy disks or removable cartridges that you want to repair are not locked.

d. Make sure no files are open on the disks you want to repair.

You can choose to bypass these steps for now and just verify a disk. However, if a problem is found, you will have to make these adjustments and start over.

2. Launch Disk First Aid

If you ignored Step 1, you may get warning messages concerning the matters just described (see Figure F10-1). Regardless, you will eventually get to Disk First Aid's window (see Figure F10-2). A brief set of instructions is displayed. If you have not read them yet, do so. You are now ready to begin.

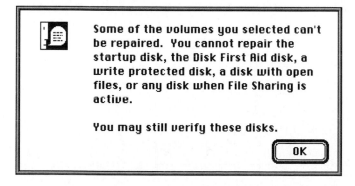

> Some of the volumes you selected can't be repaired. You cannot repair the startup disk, the Disk First Aid disk, a write protected disk, a disk with open files, or any disk when File Sharing is active.
>
> You may still verify these disks.
>
> [OK]

Figure F10-1   Disk First Aid warns you about its limitations

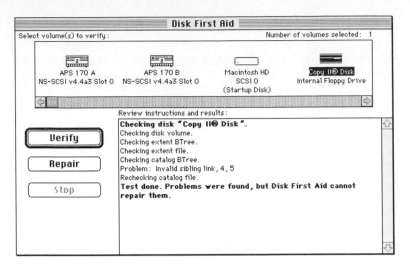

Figure F10-2 The new (version 7.2 and later) Disk First Aid's main screen, indicating it found a problem that it could not repair

BY THE WAY ▶

THE COMPLETELY NEW DISK FIRST AID

Starting with version 7.2, Disk First Aid underwent a major revision in its interface. I am happy to report that the new design makes Disk First Aid significantly easier for novices to understand and use. And, of course, it is capable of fixing problems that previous versions could not. So, while you should always use the latest version of Disk First Aid, make especially sure you are at least using version 7.2. If your Disk First Aid window looks like the one in Figure F10-3, you have an old-style version. This Fix-It only explains how to use the new-style version, If you have some reason to need to know more about the older version, I described it in the first edition of Sad Macs.

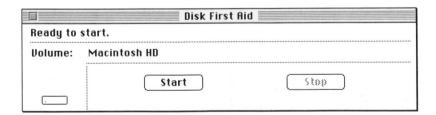

Figure F10-3 The main screen from an older version of Disk First Aid

Verify or Repair a Disk

1. Click the disk icon of the disk you want to check

From the Disk First Aid window, click the icon of each disk you want to check (see Figure F10-2). Shift-click to select more than one volume at once. By the way, if a disk is so damaged that it cannot be mounted from the Finder, Disk First Aid may still list it as openable. Give it a try. (Insert floppy disks that cannot be mounted into a drive only after Disk First Aid is open and currently selected as the active application.) If Disk First Aid cannot access the damaged disk, try other repair utilities, as suggested in the end of this Fix-It.

2. a. Click the Repair button to begin verification and repairs

If the repair button is dimmed, you cannot select it. You can only verify the disk. The reasons this might happen were described in "Getting Started." Or:

b. Click the Verify button to just verify the disk. Most users will do this only if the Repair button is dimmed. However, even if Repair is enabled, you might consider verifying first. This way, if problems are detected, you can back up critical files on the disk before repairing (just in case the repair attempt made things worse).

3. Wait while Disk First Aid goes to work

Whatever you select, Verify or Repair, the instructions will be replaced by a growing list of items that indicate what Disk First Aid is checking (similar to what you see in MacCheck). Don't worry about what any of it means. Just wait for it to finish.

4. If no problems are found

Whether you selected Verify or Repair, you will see a message that says *The volume <volume name> appears to be OK.* for each volume checked. If this happens, you should still run Disk First Aid a second time, just to confirm the diagnosis. If nothing pops up this time, you can quit. Go to Step 6.

5. a. If a problem is found after having selected Repair

If you clicked Repair and Disk First Aid spots problems, one of two outcomes will generally occur:

• **Disk First Aid cannot make repairs.** You get a message (see Figure F10-2) that says *Test done. Problems were found, but Disk First Aid cannot repair them.* This means either that Disk First Aid detects identifiable damage but does not know how to fix it, that the disk has an unfixable problem, or that the disk is sufficiently damaged that Disk First Aid cannot identify the problem.

Similarly, if you get a message such as *Unable to read from disk* or *The disk is damaged,* these imply damage to the disk, probably media damage to the Directory, that prevents Disk First Aid from successfully completing its tests. In these cases, testing is aborted or never begun.

Most likely, Disk First Aid cannot repair such disks no matter what you do. Still, before giving up, try running Disk First Aid a few more times. Sometimes, layers of problems exist, and repairs are made incrementally. Disk First Aid may fix one problem but still report that the disk could not be repaired because of other remaining problems. It may take Disk First Aid several runs before it detects and repairs all problems. With luck, you may eventually get the *OK* message.

- **Disk First Aid successfully repairs the disk.** If this happens, you will get a message something like *Repair done. The disk is OK.* As a precaution, run Disk First Aid a few more times even if you get this sort of message. It may still detect and repair other problems on subsequent runs.

   b. **If a problem is found after having selected Verify.** If you clicked Verify and Disk First Aid spots problems, one of the same basic two outcomes described in Step 5a will occur. The only difference is that Disk First Aid will not attempt a repair when verifying—even if it can fix what is wrong. If Disk First Aid detects a problem, and if it can repair it, you will get a message such as *The volume <name of volume> needs to be repaired* (other messages may appear if Disk First Aid does not know how to make the repair). To make repairs, you will have to click the Repair button. If it is not enabled, you will have to do whatever is necessary to enable it (as described in the Getting Started section). In either case, make sure critical files on your disk are backed up before proceeding with repairs.

6. **If Disk First Aid could not make repairs or if symptoms persist, try other repair procedures** No matter what the outcome of the test, even if Disk First Aid initially or eventually reported no problems, you may still have problems with the disk, because there are many problems that Disk First Aid does not detect. So if symptoms persist despite your use of Disk First Aid, you need to use other procedures to try to fix them (see "What Else Can You Do?," later in this Fix-It, for suggestions).

TECHNICALLY SPEAKING ▶

WHAT DO THOSE SYMPTOM MESSAGES MEAN?

If they find a problem Disk First Aid and MacCheck will often (but not always) include a line describing what it is. For example, it might say Invalid sibling link, 4, 5 *(as in Figure F10-2) or* Invalid PEOF. *Most of the time, these will provide very little insight as to how to solve the problem, should Disk First Aid be unable to do so.*

In case you really want to know: I have no idea what an "invalid sibling link" is. I do know that an "invalid PEOF" refers to an "invalid Physical End of File." This typically means there is a file on the disk that is bigger or smaller than the Mac's Directory thinks it is. More precisely, the Mac makes a distinction between the PEOF and the Logical End of File (LEOF). It is okay for the LEOF to be smaller than the PEOF (since this means the end of the file falls within the physical limit set by the PEOF), but not vice versa. If the PEOF is too small, you will get the invalid PEOF *error message. If you get this message and Disk First Aid cannot fix the problem (and it typically can't), try Norton Utilities and/or MacTools. Even if repairs are successful, you may still need to replace the affected files. Also, rebuild the desktop. If the problem persists, the System or Finder files are probably corrupted and should be replaced. If all else fails, you will have to reformat the drive.*

MacCheck

Whether you are running MacCheck before or after using Disk First Aid, here's what to do.

Getting Started

1. Before you launch MacCheck . . .
Quit all open applications and control panels. Also be sure that the volume you wish to check is unlocked (you cannot check a CD-ROM disk because that is considered to be permanently locked). If you fail to take these steps, MacCheck may give you an error message when you try to run its tests, such as *File system test can't test this kind of volume* or *The system test reports volume is busy.*

2. Launch MacCheck
The first thing you will notice when you launch MacCheck is how long it takes to open. This is because it is collecting all the profile data from your hardware and software before it returns control back to you. This can actually take several minutes. It is annoying, especially if you don't care to check on that information at the moment. But there is little you can do about it (though holding down the spacebar during launch initiates a more limited "quick boot" that may save you a few seconds). Eventually you will get to the main screen (see Figure F10-4).

Figure F10-4   MacCheck's main window (as seen after successfully running its tests)

MacCheck's Profiles

1. Multiple System Folders

MacCheck's main screen will immediately tell you if it found multiple System Folders on your startup disk. To find out the location of any extra copies, check Miscellaneous Boot Volume Statistics list in the Additional System Info window (see next steps).

Even if MacCheck does report multiple System Folders on your disk, you can choose to ignore this, if you intended the folders to be there. However, since these are a potential source of problems (as described in Fix-It #5), you should delete any inadvertently placed extra System Folders.

2. Click the System Info button and/or select items from the Windows menu

Click the System Info button or select "System Info" from the Windows menu. For more information, select "Additional System Info" and/or "Application and Font Info" from the Windows menu. These will result in new windows appearing that contain just about everything you could possibly want to know about the state of your Macintosh, both for hardware and software (examples of what you will find here were described in the "Why to do it" section).

You should browse through these windows at least once, just to get a feel for what they contain. Don't worry if you don't understand what everything in these listings mean. Just know that the information is there if and when you need to know it.

By the way, if your disk has too many files on it, you may get a message that says *Log Full.* In this case, the Profile information may be incomplete.

3. Save this information, if desired

To save this information to a separate file for future reference, simply select "Save Results" from the File menu. This will avoid having to wait for MacCheck to launch just to check on this stuff again (though this assumes that what you need to know has not changed since the last time you saved the file).

MacCheck's Tests

1. Click the Test button

This initiates MacCheck's diagnostic tests. Wait until it is finished running its tests and then read the output in the main window.

2. If no problems are found

If MacCheck found no problems, it will simply report *No trouble found. All tests passed* (see Figure F10-4 again). If this happens, you can now quit MacCheck (though you might want to run the test a second time, just to be sure a problem doesn't get reported that was somehow missed the first time).

3. If a problem is found

If MacCheck does find a problem, it will identify it. It may also offer some brief advice about how to solve the problem (such as recommending running Disk First Aid, as seen in Figure F10-5). In general, do the following:

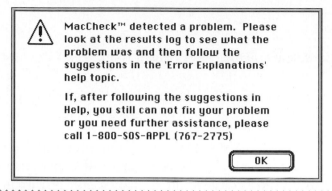

Figure F10-5 Two examples of MacCheck offering advice

a. Logic board failure.   If MacCheck reports a logic board failure, restart your Macintosh with extensions off (by holding down the Shift key at startup). Run MacCheck again. If you still get a logic board failure report, you probably have a hardware problem. It is time to get outside help, such as from an authorized Apple service provider. If the problem goes away with extensions off, you probably have some conflict between an extension and Mac-Check. For example, RAM Doubler is known to cause this problem. If no other symptoms occur, you can probably ignore this. Otherwise, you will need to find the offending extension (see Fix-It #4 for details).

b. System software damage.   If MacCheck reports corruption of your System, Finder, System Enabler, or Launcher files, replace them from your system software disks. By the way, I have not found these checks to be very reliable. For example, MacCheck failed to report damage to a Finder that I had deliberately corrupted.

c. Directory damage.   If MacCheck reports any Directory corruption, you should run Disk First Aid. Actually, for reasons outlined previously, I would run Disk First Aid even if no problems are reported.

d. Other problems.   For any other type of problem (or for more information about any of the previous problems), go to MacCheck's Help files.

MacCheck's Help

1. **Click the Help button**
   This opens up a HyperCard-like stack of help topics (see Figure F10-6).

2. **Select the topic you want**
   If MacCheck reported a problem, the topic that offers the best chance of giving you helpful advice is "Error Explanations." Follow its advice (or, for more detailed help, read the relevant sections of this book!).

   The Help section also has an excellent listing of Sad Mac and System error codes (it lists more codes that I list in Chapters 4 and 5, but it gives less details about what they mean). Some include brief advice about what to do if you get them. If you have been plagued by these errors, you might check here.

Quit MacCheck when you are done. If MacCheck suggested that you run Disk First Aid and you haven't already done so, now is the time to do it!

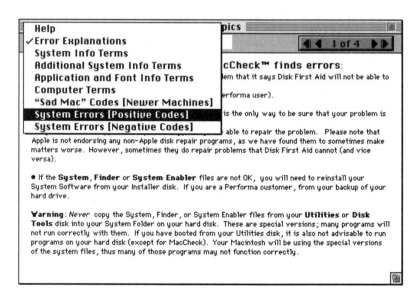

Figure F10-6   MacCheck's Help information

What Else Can You Do?

MacCheck and Disk First Aid are good starting points. But they are not the end of what can be done to solve these problems. Here are some further suggestions:

1. **To check for software damage, use utilities such as MacTools or Norton Utilities**
   These check for similar sorts of damage as does Disk First Aid, but they often can repair problems that Disk First Aid cannot.

2. **To check for hardware damage, use utilities such as Apple Personal Diagnostics or MacEKG**
Apple Personal Diagnostics, a commercial product from Apple, combines the functionality of MacCheck and Disk First Aid into one program and then adds more. In particular, it tests for problems with an extended selection of hardware components, including SIMMs, floppy disks, hard disks, and monitors. MacEKG (and other competing utilities) have even greater diagnostic ability (with more detailed output) but no software-repair functions.

3. **To check for conflicts and incompatibilities, use a utility such as Help!, Conflict Catcher, or Now Utilities' Startup Manager**
Use these to determine if an extension conflict or other type of incompatibility, unrelated to damaged files, is the cause of the problem.

4. **Otherwise, if your symptoms still persist . . .**
If you haven't already done so, try suggestions in other Fix-Its, as appropriate (such as re-building the desktop, zapping the PRAM, or checking for viruses). This statement is more or less true for virtually all Fix-Its, but it applies particularly here because Disk First Aid so often serves as a jumping-off point for further troubleshooting. If all else fails, you will probably have to reformat the disk, using a utility such as Apple HD SC Setup.

For related information

SEE:
- Fix-It #1 on hardware/software incompatibilities
- Fix-It #4 on solving extension conflicts
- Fix-It #5 on system software problems
- Fix-It #7 on checking for viruses
- Fix-It #9 on rebuilding the desktop
- Fix-It #11 on zapping the Parameter RAM
- Fix-It #12 on updating the disk device driver
- Fix-It #13 on disk repair utilities such as MacTools and Norton Utilities
- Fix-It #14 on repairing files
- Fix-It #15 on damaged media and reformatting disks
- Fix-It #17 on Apple Personal Diagnostics and other hardware diagnostic utilities
- Fix-It #18 on Help! and other profile and conflict-reporting utilities
- Chapter 2 on preventative maintenance
- Chapter 5 on startup and disk problems

Fix-It #11:
Zap the Parameter RAM

QUICK SUMMARY

Hold down the Command-Option-P-R keys at startup until the Macintosh restarts itself a second time. Then release the keys and let startup proceed normally. This resets the parameter RAM (PRAM).

When to do it:

- Whenever control panel settings, such as the current date/time and volume level, are inexplicably incorrect (especially if, after you reset these values, the settings are wrong the next time you turn on your Macintosh).

- Whenever you are unable to start up from a hard drive, especially an external hard drive.

- If you cannot mount or otherwise access any externally connected SCSI device.

- Whenever you cannot access a modem because its port is claimed to be in use.

- When you cannot get documents to print at all or if garbage characters print instead of the correct output, especially if an error message appears indicating a problem with the serial port.

- If, in certain PowerBook models, you have a loss of sound from your speakers.

- If, after you select Shut Down from the Finder's Special menu, the Macintosh restarts instead of shutting down.

- If Apple Restore doesn't work and it is a version prior to 7.1P3.

Why to do it:

Parameter RAM, usually referred to as PRAM, is a small amount of RAM maintained by special hardware on the main logic board of the Macintosh. It is separate from both the main memory (see Fix-It #6) and the video memory (see Chapter 10) that I have referred to most often elsewhere in this book.

So, what exactly does PRAM do? Primarily, it stores the settings of several control panels included with the Macintosh system software. Most notably, the PRAM stores the current date and time, the choice of Startup disk (set by the Startup Disk control panel), whether

AppleTalk is active (set by the Chooser desk accessory), as well as settings from the General Controls, Memory, Mouse, Sound, Keyboard, and Color control panels. The PRAM also stores information regarding the status of the serial and SCSI ports of your Macintosh. Some data not technically stored in PRAM are also reset to default values when you zap the PRAM. These include the settings for the desktop pattern and the color depth of the monitor.

The rationale for storing this information in PRAM is that, unlike other forms of RAM, PRAM information is retained after the Macintosh is turned off (or even after you unplug it!). That is why, for example, you do not have to reset the time each time you turn your Macintosh on.

At this point, you may be recalling that I said (in Chapter 1) that RAM gets wiped out when you turn the Macintosh off. This is true. So how is the information in PRAM retained after shut down? The answer is simple enough. The PRAM is saved because a battery inside the Macintosh keeps the PRAM powered at all times (similar to how some bedside alarm clocks use a backup battery to keep going in the event of a power failure).

The problem is that the information stored in PRAM can get corrupted. A good sign that this has happened is if the time and date are suddenly wrong and, even if you reset them, the corrected settings are not retained. If this happens, all other PRAM settings are likely to have the same problem.

A corrupted PRAM can also prevent the Macintosh from transmitting information to or receiving information from the SCSI port and/or serial ports (modem and printer), causing problems with all devices connected to those ports.

BY THE WAY ▶

PRAM VERSUS THE FINDER PREFERENCES FILE

The Finder Preferences file also stores some user-selected settings. In particular, the Finder preferences file stores the settings of the Views control panel and the on or off status of the "Warn Before Emptying" check box (located in the Trash's Get Info window). These settings are separate from PRAM settings and are not reset when you zap the PRAM. Problems with these preferences settings are usually solved by replacing the Finder preferences file, as described in Fix-It #2.

By the way, there are a variety of other system preferences files you may have, especially if you use System 7.5. These include AppleScript preferences, Find File preferences and more. Again, none of these settings are reset when you zap the PRAM.

PRAM problems do not occur often. But when they do, the solution is to "zap the PRAM." This is a cute way of describing the method for erasing the presumably corrupted current PRAM data and returning all PRAM settings to their default values. If zapping the PRAM does not eliminate these symptoms, it may mean you have a dead battery or system software damage.

What to do:

Zapping Basics

How to zap the PRAM varies depending both on the model of Macintosh and the version of the system software you are using. (By the way, if corrupted PRAM is preventing your startup hard disk from mounting, especially if it causes a sad Mac to appear, you may need to start up with a floppy disk, such as your Emergency Toolkit disk, before you can zap the PRAM.)

TAKE NOTE ▶

WARNING FOR POWERBOOK USERS (AND OTHER USERS OF RAM DISKS)

Zapping the PRAM will erase all data on a RAM Disk created via Apple's Memory Control Panel. Be sure to back up any critical data on your RAM disk before you zap!

For System 7, with Any Macintosh Model

1. Simultaneously hold down the Command-Option-P-R keys at startup. Wait until the Macintosh beeps and restarts itself a second time (or a third time on some Macs).
2. Release the keys and let startup proceed as normal. That's it.

For System 6, Macintosh Plus, or Earlier Models

1. Turn your Macintosh off, then remove the battery cover, located in the rear of the Macintosh, and remove the battery from its case. Check the documentation that came with your Macintosh for details on how to do this, if needed.
2. Wait a few minutes to let the capacitor that maintains the PRAM information "drain."
3. Reinsert the battery and replace the cover.

   Note: unlike later models, the Macintosh Plus does not store Startup Disk information in PRAM.

For System 6, All Other Models

1. Press and hold the Shift-Option-Command keys while selecting the Control Panels desk accessory.
2. A special alert box appears and asks whether you want to zap the PRAM. Click the Yes button (see Figure F11-1).

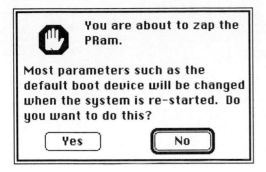

Figure F11-1 The System 6 alert box for zapping the PRAM

After Zapping the PRAM (All Models, All System Software Versions)

1. Zapping the PRAM wipes out any customized changes you may have made to your control panel settings, returning all values to their default state. Thus, you will now need to reset any changes you had previously made. For example, if you use 32-bit addressing, be sure to turn it back on. Otherwise, you will be unable to access more than 8Mb of RAM (as described more in Fix-It #6). Also, reselect "Internal Modem" from the PowerBook Setup control panel if appropriate.

   However, if the time and date were correct before you zapped, you should not have to reset them. These two settings are temporarily stored elsewhere while the PRAM is reset and then written back to the PRAM afterward.

2. If your newly reentered settings are lost again after you turn the Macintosh off, you probably have a weak or dead battery. Replace it.

   In the Macintosh Plus, the battery is stored in a special compartment on the back of the Macintosh and can easily be accessed. Although the battery looks similar to a common AA battery, it is a special 4.5V battery. Make sure you get the right one.

   In recent Macintosh models, a different type of battery is used, and it is located on the logic board inside your Macintosh. In some cases, it is soldered to the board. If so, you need to take the Macintosh in for servicing to get it replaced. But don't worry, a battery should last at least five to seven years. Many users will replace their Macintosh before the battery wears out!

3. If you still have a problem with an incorrect date and/or time, you may have a corrupted System file. Replace it. Also, check the Date & Time control panel to make sure you have actually entered the correct date and time there and have set the formatting for how you want them displayed.

SEE: • Fix-It #5 on replacing system software

Really Zap the PRAM: Use TechTool

Unfortunately, the previous method does not reliably zap *all* the PRAM data. If the remaining unzapped portion of the PRAM is corrupted, the previous zapping of the PRAM will not fix the problem. This seems to happen particularly with the PRAM data that affects the SCSI and serial ports. For example, you may find that, even after zapping the PRAM, you cannot access external SCSI devices or it may be that when you try to use your modem you get an error message that says the serial port is "in use." In these cases, you need to *completely* zap your PRAM.

Fortunately, there is a freeware utility that does this complete zap for you: TechTool! (Yes, this is the same utility used to completely rebuild the desktop, as described in Fix-It #9.) As an added bonus, TechTool will save your PRAM settings before you zap, allowing you to restore them when you are done (refer to Figure F9-5). Here's what to do:

1. **Click the "Save PRAM" button**
   Doing this saves a copy of your current PRAM data for later use by TechTool. Obviously, the ideal time to do this is *before* you suspect that your PRAM is corrupted. Otherwise, you may be saving corrupted data. On the other hand, if you have not previously saved the PRAM before you zap, you might as well do it in any case. If, after you zap, the symptoms still remain, then the PRAM was not the cause. In this case, you can safely restore your just saved PRAM data.

2. **Click the "Zap PRAM" button**
   Active applications must be closed before you can zap the PRAM. If you have any open applications, TechTool will list them after you click the "Zap PRAM" button. Click the "Send AE Quit" button to close them. This will initiate the zap. If you change your mind at this point, click "OK" instead. The Macintosh will restart as part of the zap process.

3. **Click the "Restore PRAM" button**
   If you have previously saved your PRAM (and the saved data appear to be uncorrupted), return to TechTool and click the "Restore PRAM" button (again, active applications must be closed before this can be carried out).

   The PRAM data are now restored to what they were when you last saved them, eliminating the need to manually recreate all of the customized control panel settings that were lost as a result of the zap.

   One caution: never restore data saved from one machine on to another machine. Doing so could prevent your Mac from starting up; you will have to remove the battery to fix the problem.

For related information

SEE: • Fix-It #12 on disk device drivers
       • Fix-It #16 on problems with SCSI devices and connections
       • Chapter 2 on preventative maintenance
       • Chapter 5 on startup and disk mounting problems
       • Chapter 11 on resetting the power manager and on file sharing and modem problems

Fix-It #12:
Update the Disk Device Driver

 QUICK SUMMARY

Use a disk formatting utility to update the device driver on hard disks and removable media cartridges. For Apple hard disks, you can use Apple HD SC Setup. Launch it from its own startup disk and click the Update button.

When to do it:

• Anytime a new version of the driver is released, especially if you have upgraded your hardware or software and the new driver is needed to use selected new features of the upgrade. In this regard, particularly be concerned when upgrading to an AV Mac or a Power Mac.

• To make sure your drive is compatible with SCSI Manager 4.3, if your Macintosh uses this feature, particularly if your machine is running slower than expected.

• If you are using System 7 and cannot get virtual memory to work properly.

• If you are experiencing frequent system crashes or other serious problems, especially if the problems do not occur when you are using a floppy disk as a startup disk.

• If you cannot get your Macintosh to start up. Obviously, this is only one of many possible causes of this symptom.

• If a PowerBook crashes while spinning up after a power down (such as after it has been asleep for awhile).

Why to do it:

A hard disk's *device driver* is software. It is located in a special section of the disk that is created when the disk is first formatted. Thus, virtually any hard disk you own came with a driver already on it. It is normally completely invisible and inaccessible to the user. Even disk-repair utilities, such as MacTools or Norton Utilities, do not directly access it when making disk repairs.

The driver contains critical *low-level* instructions that tell the Macintosh how to initially communicate with the drive. A copy of a disk's driver is loaded into memory whenever the disk is mounted. Without the driver in memory, the disk cannot be mounted.

BY THE WAY ▶

OTHER DEVICE DRIVERS

Most devices connected through the SCSI port, whether or not they are disk drives, have their own drivers. However, this Fix-It focuses only on disk drivers as used for hard disks and removable media cartridges. See Fix-It #16 for more general information on SCSI devices and drivers.

Updating a disk driver requires using the same formatting utility that you would use to reformat the disk (see Fix-It #15). Apple's utility is called Apple HD SC Setup. Different brands of drives typically come with their own formatting utilities that, in turn, install their own disk drivers. The whole updating process takes only a few seconds, and it leaves the rest of your drive untouched. You do not have to reformat the drive in order to update it. This is convenient, because reformatting would erase all the data on the drive (requiring that you restore the files from your backups) and would take much longer to do.

If you "update" your disk driver with the same version of the utility that originally installed it, it will simply replace the existing driver with a duplicate. However, similarly to system software, disk-formatting utilities are periodically upgraded. Updating the driver from a newer version of the formatting utility will replace the older version with the newer one.

In terms of problem solving, there are three basic reasons to update a driver: to accommodate new system software, to accommodate new hardware, or to repair damage to the driver.

Update to Accommodate New System Software

When Apple releases a new version of its system software, newly added features may require changes to disk drivers. For example, when updating from System 6 to System 7, make sure you also update to a System 7-compatible driver, because System 7's virtual memory feature usually does not work with pre–System 7 disk drivers.

Note that when you use the Installer utility to upgrade the system software, this does *not* upgrade the driver, even if you have an Apple hard drive. You need to update the driver separately (see the "What to do" section for details).

Update to Accommodate New Hardware

Occasionally, you may need to update to a new version of a driver in order to accommodate features added to newer Macintosh models.

For example, using a hard disk with Apple's PowerBooks requires special modifications to the disk driver not necessary for use with desktop Macintoshes. If you are using an Apple drive that shipped with your notebook machine, you don't have to worry about this. The preinstalled driver works fine. However, if you bought a third-party drive, it may have shipped with a driver incompatible with the notebook models (though this is less likely now that the PowerBooks have been around for several years). If this happens, you have to either get a newer version of the formatting utility that updates the driver appropriately (call the drive manufacturer for information) or switch to a different driver (one that is already compatible with the PowerBooks).

Similarly, AV and Power Macintoshes (and any other Macintoshes that use Apple's new SCSI Manager 4.3) require an updated driver in order to fully take advantage of the features used by these new machines. The most noticeable symptom of having the wrong driver is slower performance speed. At one time in late 1993, the only driver compatible with SCSI Manager 4.3 was the driver installed by the latest version of Apple's own formatting utility, Apple HD SC Setup. By now, most other major formatting utilities have been updated as well. By the way, some Macintoshes compatible with SCSI Manager 4.3 require a SCSI Manager extension while others have the manager information built into the ROM. So don't depend on seeing the extension as a way of knowing whether or not your Mac uses the new SCSI Manager (see "By the Way: SCSI Manager 4.3 and SCSI-2" in Fix-It #16 for more information).

Update to Repair Damage to the Driver

Despite its relative inaccessibility, the driver (like any software!) can get damaged. For example, sudden power failures, particularly during startup, can cause it to be damaged. A damaged driver usually causes serious problems, including an inability to mount the disk on the desktop. Updating the driver can repair the damage and eliminate the problem.

 What to do:

Get the Latest Version of the Formatting Utility

Always use the latest version of your formatting utility, even if you are not experiencing any of the problems described in "Why to do it." At the very least, the new version probably contains fixes to bugs found in the previous versions.

Apple HD SC Setup   For Apple drives, you typically update the driver via the Apple HD SC Setup application (included on the system software disks). This is what Apple uses to format all SCSI drives that it ships. Do not use a version of HD SC Setup older than the version that came with the system software you are currently using. If you upgrade to a later version of the system software, it should include an upgraded version of Apple HD SC Setup. Use it to update your disk driver. However, Apple periodically releases upgrades to HD SC Setup in between releases of its system software. For example, System Update 3.0 (see Chapter 2 and Fix-It #5) includes a version of HD SC Setup that was newer than the one that originally came with System 7.1. Check with on-line services or other similar sources (see Fix-It #18) to make sure you have the latest version.

Note that Apple HD SC Setup only works with Apple drives (see "By the Way: Switching to a Different Formatting Utility").

BY THE WAY ▶

A TOTALLY NEW FORMATTING UTILITY FROM APPLE?

The rumor mill says that Apple has purchased the rights to the code used by Drive7. The expectation is that Apple will eventually release a redesigned version of its driver that will resemble Drive7. It may already be out by the time you read this.

Custom Formatting Utilities   If your drive is not an Apple drive, it came with its own formatting utility and associated driver. Often, it is a custom utility developed by the maker or reseller or the drive (for example, APS drives come with a utility called APS PowerTools). In this case, contact the company that sold the drive to get information about upgrades to its formatting utility (or check the manual that came with the drive for possible advice). In some cases, these utilities should only be used with drives sold by the same company that makes these utilities.

Universal Formatting Utilities   Finally, you may choose to use a universal formatting utility. These are separately sold software products not associated with Apple system software or any particular drive. As their name implies, they may be used with virtually any drive you own, including Apple drives (but see "By the Way: Switching to a Different Formatting Utility" for a warning regarding Apple drives). Drive7 and Hard Disk ToolKit are two popular examples. In this case, contact the publisher of the utility for upgrade information.

Why would you ever want to use a universal utility? Some users may want advanced features available in the formatting utility that are not present in utilities such as Apple HD SC Setup (which is actually a rather minimal-feature utility). Also, if you have multiple drives connected to your Mac, it is advised that all drives have the same driver. Using a universal formatting utility can simplify doing this. A mix of different drivers on different drives can lead to problems, including system errors. However, this warning may be overstated. I have routinely used mixed drivers connected to the same Mac and have never experienced a problem.

Special Case: Updating Drivers on Removable Media   Each removable media cartridge/disk, such as SyQuest cartridges or optical disks, contains its own disk driver. When updating to a new version of a driver, make sure you update all cartridges that use that driver. If you used different formatting utilities for different cartridges, you should ideally standardize on just one utility. Otherwise, problems may occur, especially when switching from one cartridge to another during a session (see Fix-It #16, "Take Note: Problems Mounting Removable Media Cartridges with Different Drivers" for more details).

BY THE WAY ▶

SWITCHING TO A DIFFERENT FORMATTING UTILITY

You can update a driver using a different formatting utility from that used to format your disk (such as using Drive7 to update a disk formatted by Apple HD SC Setup). This can usually be done without reformatting the disk. Still, as I discuss more in Fix-It #15, I prefer to reformat when switching to a different driver.

However, there is a special problem to watch out for here: Apple HD SC Setup only works with Apple drives. It will not even indicate the presence of non-Apple drives. So you cannot use or switch to this utility for any drive that did not come from Apple. However, you can go in the reverse direction. That is, if you have an Apple drive, you can switch to a formatting utility other than HD SC Setup. But there is a problem here as well. After you switch, you can never switch back to using HD SC Setup, because the switch deletes the special coding information that HD SC Setup uses to recognize that it is an Apple drive.

By the way, the name Apple on a drive doesn't mean that Apple really made the drive. The actual drive mechanism is made by a company that specializes in drive manufacture (such as Quantum). These vendors sell their drives to various other companies who package them and sell them to end users. Thus, both Apple and APS, for example, may use the exact same Quantum manufactured drive (see Fix-It #16 for more on this). Nevertheless, Apple HD SC Setup will recognize only an Apple drive because of the special coding information that Apple places on the drive before it ships.

BY THE WAY ▶

CHECKING THE VERSION NUMBER OF THE DRIVER

If you want to know the version number of your formatting utility, it's simple enough. It is usually present somewhere in the window that appears when you launch the utility (see Figure F12-2). Otherwise, just open the Get Info window and check the line labeled "Version." But what if you can't find this utility anymore? Or what if you want to confirm whether your currently installed driver is the one actually installed by this utility? The solution is to check the version number of the driver itself. You can usually do this by selecting the Get Info window for the disk in question (see Figure F12-1). In the line labeled "Where" you should see a version number. In most cases, it should match the version number of the formatting utility (oddly, drives formatted by Apple HD SC Setup do not show a version number here). In any case, if you call technical support at the company that made the utility, this number should enable them to tell you if you are using the latest version of the driver (or at least a version compatible with the rest of your software and hardware).

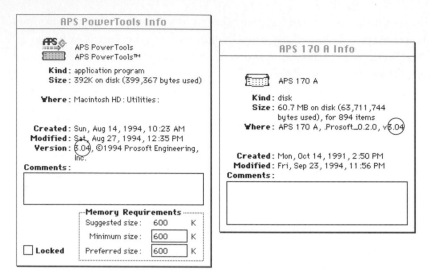

Figure F12-1 The Get Info windows of the APS Power Tools formatting utility (left) and of a disk with a driver updated by this version of APS Power Tools (right); note that both windows list "3.04" as the utility/driver version number

Update the Driver

1. Make sure your data are backed up and your disk is not damaged

As with most of these types of procedures, there is the slim chance that updating will do more harm than good. So, before attempting any updating, make sure all your data are backed up. It is also a good idea to check for possible disk damage (see Fix-Its #10 and #13) before updating or switching drivers.

2. Restart from a startup disk other than the one you want to update

With some formatting utilities, you cannot update the current startup disk or the disk from which you launch the formatting utility. The simplest solution for this problem is to start up with your Emergency Toolkit disk (see Chapter 2) or any other startup floppy disk that contains the formatting utility. If you have more than one startup hard drive, you can startup from an alternate hard drive.

With Apple HD SC Setup, you *can* update the driver on the current startup disk, but you will still have to restart before the new driver is actually used.

(If you are unable to start up because the problem disk causes a crash at startup, even when using an alternate startup disk, check with Chapter 5, "Starting with an Alternate Startup Disk," for advice.)

3. Launch the formatting utility and click the Update button

Most users with Apple hard drives will probably use Apple HD SC Setup. Simply click the Update button (see Figure F12-2, left), wait a few seconds, and you are done. Just remember that HD Setup does not work on non-Apple drives or Apple drives that have been updated and/or reformatted by another utility.

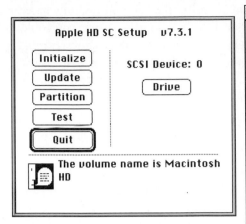
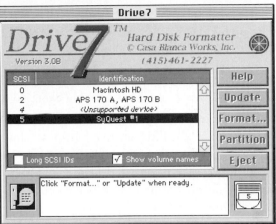

Figure F12-2 The main windows from two hard disk formatting utilities, Apple's HD SC Setup (left) and Drive7 (right)

For most other formatting utilities, such as Drive7, the procedure is essentially the same. Just click the Update button (see Figure F12-2, right).

BY THE WAY ▶

WARNING FOR AT EASE USERS

At Ease for Workgroups includes a security feature that "locks" access to a password-protected disk so that you cannot access the hard drive even if you startup from a floppy disk. It does this by modifying the disk's driver. If you remove At Ease by any method other than via its Installer utility, it may prevent you from starting up from the hard disk at all. The solution at this point is to update the driver.

---

4. **If the Update button is dimmed and cannot be selected (or if the update process fails for any reason) . . .**

If you are using Apple HD SC Setup, it probably means that the drive has been formatted using a different utility. In this case, HD SC Setup does not recognize the drive. The solution here is to use a utility other than Apple HD SC Setup.

Otherwise, for any formatting utility, including Apple HD SC Setup, it may mean that you are using a version of the format utility older than the one used to create the driver now on your disk. (For Apple HD SC Setup, this will happen if the first or second digit of Setup's version number is lower than that of the version that installed the driver currently in use.) Conversely, it can mean that the version of your driver is so old that the newer utility cannot update it. Finally, it may mean that your driver (or partition map, a related low-level area of the drive) is damaged.

To solve these problems, start by making sure you are using the latest version of whatever formatting utility created the driver currently on your disk. If this fails to work, you could try updating with another utility. However, in the end, you will probably need to reformat the disk (especially if the driver or partition map is damaged). Prior to reformatting, use a data recovery package to recover files from the disk, as needed. MacTools, in particular, has special options to mount a disk with a damaged driver (as described in Fix-It #13).

5. **Whatever you do, do *not* click the Format or Initialize buttons!**

   Clicking a format utility's Format button sets up to reformat the entire drive. With Apple HD SC Setup, Initialize is the name of the format button (with other utilities, initialize and format do different things, as explained in Fix-It #15). Reformatting your disk will irretrievably erase all data on the disk, which is probably not what you want to happen when you are just trying to update a driver.

   True, the driver gets updated when you reformat a disk. But reformatting a disk just for this reason is like using a machine gun to swat a fly. However, as noted (see "By the Way: Switching to a Different Formatting Utility"), I would consider selecting Format, rather than Update, if I were switching to a different driver entirely (after first backing up my data, of course).

6. **Quit the utility and restart the Macintosh**

   After updating is complete, quit the format utility. The hard drive may be unmounted as a result of the update, its icon vanished from the desktop. Don't worry. Restart the Macintosh. The hard disk should now mount using the new driver.

For related information

SEE: • Fix-It #15 on reformatting disks, partitioning disks, and formatting utilities in general
       • Fix-It #16 on SCSI problems
       • Chapter 5 on problems mounting disks

Fix-It #13:
Check for Damaged Disks: Repair, Restore, or Recover

QUICK SUMMARY

Use a data recovery utility package (Norton Utilities for Macintosh or MacTools) to repair or restore a damaged disk. If the disk cannot be fixed, recover files from the disk, as needed.

When to do it:

- Whenever you cannot start up your Macintosh with a known startup disk.
- Whenever you are unable to get a properly formatted disk to mount to the Finder's desktop. Especially with floppy disks, you may get a message that says the disk is *unreadable, not a Macintosh disk,* or *damaged* and that asks if you want to initialize it.
- Whenever you have systemwide problems with a particular disk, especially problems related to keeping track of files. These commonly include an inability to open, copy, or delete files/folders on the disk, as well as files/folders that mysteriously disappear.
- If you accidentally erase a hard disk with the Finder's Erase Disk command.
- If you used Disk First Aid and it identified a problem that it could not repair.

Why to do it:

Although utility packages, such as Norton Utilities or MacTools, include dozens of features, their ability to resurrect a damaged disk is undoubtedly the single most important one. These programs accomplish this task in a manner similar to how Disk First Aid works (see Fix-It #10). However, compared to Disk First Aid, these programs do more extensive checks, fix more problems, give you more options, and give more feedback about what they are doing. If you have a disk that will not mount or otherwise seems in serious trouble, and if Disk First Aid could not remedy the problem, these are the utilities to use. If they fail to save the disk, usually your only remaining options are to reformat the disk or (for a floppy disk) discard it.

Similar to Disk First Aid, these utilities check mainly for damage to the invisible Directory files. The Directory area of the disk (as detailed in Chapter 8) contains a continually updated catalog of what is on a disk, where everything is, and how it is organized. This is the essential information that the Macintosh needs to recognize, locate, and access all the files on a disk. For example, if a file is stored on a disk in fragments, the Directory contains the information needed to link all the fragments together when you launch the file. The Directory (together with related "hidden" areas of the disk) also contains the critical information necessary for the Macintosh to recognize whether the disk is a Macintosh-formatted disk as well as whether it is a startup disk. Thus, even a small amount of damage to the Directory can render an entire disk virtually inaccessible.

Fortunately, if Directory damage occurs, there is still a very good chance that your disk, or at least most of the data on it, can be saved, because the remaining areas of the disk, where the documents and applications actually reside, may still be unharmed. The files contained on the disk are often all usable, if only they can be accessed. Working with a disk with a damaged Directory is a bit like trying to use a library without a catalog. The books are all fine, but there may be little hope of finding the ones you want.

The working assumption in this Fix-It is that Directory damage is the cause of a problem mounting a disk (commonly referred to as a *crashed* or *trashed* disk). Related problems are covered in other parts of this book (especially the remaining Fix-Its). This Fix-It covers details of how to use both MacTools and Norton Utilities to fix these problems. The guidelines given here are not intended as a complete substitute for the documentation that accompanies these programs. Still, in many cases, the information in this Fix-It will be sufficient. Additionally, this Fix-It should make clear, in a way often obscured in the manuals, exactly what these recovery utilities can and cannot do.

Disk recovery utilities, such as MacTools or Norton Utilities, provide up to three methods of rescuing these Directory damaged disks: repair, restore, and recover.

Repair

To repair a disk means to return the damaged files to their predamaged state. If the damage to the Directory is simply a garbling of the data stored there, these utilities can often scan the remaining undamaged areas of the disk and determine what the ungarbled data should be. They then recreate it. If this works, it is the ideal solution. It is almost like magic. An apparently dead disk is restored to full working order in a matter of minutes, with no loss of data.

Restore

Sometimes, Directory damage is so extensive that it cannot be repaired, usually resulting in a crashed disk. Similarly, if you accidentally erase a hard disk (via the Finder's Erase Disk command), the original Directory information is hopelessly lost, resulting in the Finder listing the disk as empty. In both cases, however, the rest of the files on your disk may still be perfectly okay (in the case of the "erased" hard disk, this is because the Erase Disk command does not actually erase or reformat a hard disk; it only alters the Directory, as described more in Fix-It #15).

In these cases, you may still be able to resurrect the hard disk by using a utility to completely replace the current presumably damaged or erased Directory with an undamaged backup copy.

Recover

Sometimes a disk cannot be repaired or restored. Among other reasons, this can happen when media damage occurs to the area of the disk where the Directory resides. In these cases, you usually can still use these utilities to recover individual files from the disk (helpful for files that are not backed up elsewhere) because these utilities can identify files (from information that does not depend on the Directory) and then copy these files to a separate disk. Assuming that the files are not themselves damaged, this procedure saves the files from an otherwise unsavable disk. Since recovery does not repair or replace any damage, you will typically have to re-format (or discard) the disk after recovery is completed.

SEE: • **Chapter 2 and Fix-Its #14 and #15 for more on the subject of media damage**

What to do:

This Fix-It describes three main options: repair a damaged disk, restore a damaged or accidentally erased disk, and recover selected files from a damaged disk. This Fix-It further assumes that you are using either MacTools Pro or Norton Utilities 3.x. In the steps that follow, follow directions for (a) MacTools Pro or (b) Norton Utilities, as appropriate. If you are using an earlier version of these programs, be aware that differences in the versions may mean that specific instructions given here do not apply to you.

Repair a Damaged Disk

Before Using Your Repair Utility

1. **Mount the disk from the Finder, if possible, and copy unbacked-up files to another disk**
   If the problem disk mounts on the desktop from the Finder without any problem, you are lucky. Immediately copy any essential unbacked-up files to another disk. This protects them in case your repair attempts make things worse.

   If you cannot mount the problem disk, and it is your normal startup disk, this means you are unable to start up. Thus, you have to restart with an alternate startup disk before you can proceed. Use an alternate disk, such as your Emergency Toolkit disk (as described in Chapters 2 and 5), to start up instead. The problem disk may now mount normally as a secondary disk. If so, now copy essential unbacked-up files to another disk.

   Even if the damaged disk does not mount as a secondary disk, you can still try to recover important unbacked-up files (if any) on the disk before attempting repairs. You do this via the recover capability of the utilities (see "Recover Selected Files from a Damaged Disk" later in this Fix-It).

2. Preferably, start up from an undamaged disk that contains the repair utility

Norton Utilities will let you make repairs to the current startup disk and/or the disk that contains the Norton Utilities application. MacTools Pro (though not earlier versions of MacTools) similarly lets you make many (though not all) of its repairs to the startup disk or the disk that contains MacTools. Still, I recommend avoiding doing this, if possible, because it increases the chance that repairs will be unsuccessful. In the worst case, you may actually precipitate more damage. So to be safe, use an alternate startup disk to repair problems to the startup disk.

If you have two hard drives, an acceptable setup is to start up and run the utility from one hard drive to check the other one for damage. You can also start up from an Emergency Toolkit disk you have created (you may have already started up in this way in Step 1). Or you can use the special Emergency startup disks included with repair utility packages. These special disks contain and automatically launch the relevant repair utility upon startup (see "Take Note: Using MacTools or Norton Utilities to Create Startup Disks" and "Take Note: If You Can't Start Up with Your Emergency Disk").

One advantage of using the special Emergency disks that come with the repair utilities is that there is no Finder on them. Normally, you would not consider this an advantage. However, in System 7 and MultiFinder in System 6, the Finder attempts to mount the disk in the background, even if the data recovery utility is the active application. The Finder is usually less effective in dealing with problem disks than these data recovery utilities. The Finder's difficulties can interfere with the ability of these repair utilities to work, sometimes even causing a crash to occur. By not including a Finder, the Emergency disks bypass this problem.

In this regard, if as a result of inserting a damaged floppy disk when your repair utility is not active, a dialog box appears asking if you want to initialize the disk, do not do so. Eject the disk instead. Then launch the repair utility and insert the floppy disk.

TAKE NOTE ▶

USING MACTOOLS OR NORTON UTILITIES TO CREATE STARTUP DISKS

Current versions of Norton Utilities and MacTools Pro include an Emergency startup disk, ready to use. However, they also have special options for creating custom Emergency Startup floppy disks. These are designed to ensure that your Emergency Startup disk works with your particular hardware (by including needed Enabler files, if any). You will have at least two options: one to create a startup repair disk (as described here) and another to create a startup disk for defragmenting (defragmenting/optimizing is described in Fix-It #8). Ideally, use these options before you run into trouble.

- *MacTools Pro.*   *With MacTools Pro, you are given the option to build an Emergency Startup disk during installation of MacTools on your hard drive. Otherwise, you can select the "Build DiskFix Disk" option from the Clinic menu at any time. New with MacTools Pro, if you have a Macintosh that can create a RAM disk via System 7's Memory control panel, MacTools can automatically create a RAM* disk, copy the needed files to it, and then restart and boot from this RAM disk (assuming that the problem is not so serious as to prevent the RAM disk from setting up). You do this by clicking the "RAMBoot" button in the MacTools Clinic main window (see Figure F13-1). Follow the instructions carefully, as I have had numerous problems getting this RAMBoot option to work. Be especially aware that you will not be able to use RAMBoot unless you have a healthy amount of RAM available (for example, you appear to need more than 8Mb of RAM to use this feature on a Power Mac running System 7.5). Still, when it works, this can be a wonderful convenience, freeing you from the need to have a bootable Emergency disk handy when a problem appears. I have found it especially helpful for when I travel with my PowerBook.

- **The Norton Utilities.** With Norton Utilities, you are similarly given the option to create an Emergency startup disk when you first install Norton Utilities. Otherwise, select "Startup Disk Builder" from the Utilities menu and then select to build a "Norton Disk Doctor/UnErase" disk.

  By the way, when you first install Norton Utilities, you are also given the option to create something called a VIF (Volume Information File) for each currently mounted disk. Otherwise, you can create VIF files at any later time via the "Create VIF Files" command in the Norton Utilities Options menu. These VIF files can help Norton Disk Doctor to identify and recover from certain types of damage to the disk. However, in most cases, you can use Disk Doctor quite successfully without these files. Still, it does no harm to create them.

SEE: • Chapter 2 for more general advice on creating Emergency Startup disks

---

TAKE NOTE ▶

IF YOU CAN'T START UP WITH YOUR EMERGENCY DISK

First of all, before disaster strikes, check whether your Emergency Startup floppy disk will actually work as a startup disk. A hard disk crash is not the ideal time to discover that your startup floppy disk does not start up. If you do have a problem getting the floppy disk to work, make sure the disk was set up properly (see "Take Note: Using MacTools or Norton Utilities to Create Startup Disks"). Otherwise, problems starting up with an Emergency Startup disk are usually indirectly caused by problems mounting the damaged disk you want to repair. To bypass these problems, try the following (more detailed procedures are described in the manual for each utility):

- For damaged floppy disks, do not insert the floppy disk at startup. Insert it after the data recovery utility launches from the Emergency disk.

- For a damaged external hard disk, turn off the disk at startup. Turn it on after the data recovery utility launches.

- For a damaged internal hard disk, hold down the Command-Option-Shift-Delete keys at startup until the Welcome to Macintosh message appears. The Macintosh should bypass the internal drive so that it does not mount. Launch the data recovery utility from the Emergency disk. If this does not work, you may also have to zap the PRAM (see Chapter 5, "By the Way: The Internal Drive May Still Mount When Using Command-Option-Shift-Delete").

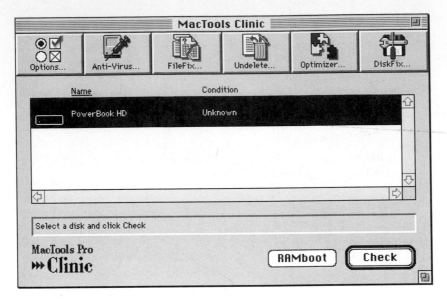

Figure F13-1 MacTools Pro's Clinic window

Make Repairs

1. Launch your repair utility

a. With MacTools Pro, launch MacTools Clinic. A window listing all mounted disks will appear (see Figure F13-1).

Alternatively, you may first be greeted by the MacTools Pro QuickAssist window (see Figure F13-2). If you don't want this window to automatically appear in the future, click the More button and then uncheck "Show this dialog at startup." If you want to skip using this window at the moment and instead proceed to the main Clinic window, click Cancel. Otherwise, put a check next to any symptoms you now have and click the Check button (there is no option here to select which mounted disk to check).

If you are using a MacTools' Emergency floppy disk, it will take you immediately to a special DiskFix window (Figure F13-3). This window is similar to (but has more limited options than) the window of the full MacTools Clinic application.

b. With Norton Utilities, if the Norton Utilities Main Menu window is displayed (as seen in Chapter 2, Figure 2-1), click the Norton Disk Doctor button. Otherwise, from any of Norton Utilities, select Norton Disk Doctor from the Utilities menu. A window listing all mounted disks will appear (see Figure F13-4).

Figure F13-2   MacTools Pro's QuickAssist window

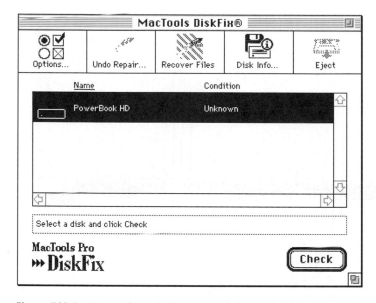

Figure F13-3   MacTools Pro's floppy disk DiskFix window

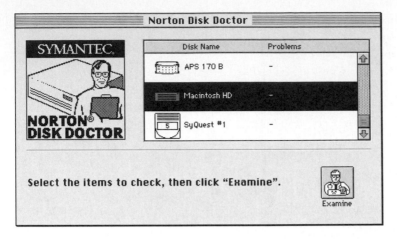

Figure F13-4   Norton Utilities' Norton Disk Doctor window

2. **Set repair options (especially decide whether or not to check for bad blocks)**
   Do this any time you want to change the default preference settings of these applications. Ideally, do it before you check the potentially damaged disk.

   a. With MacTools Pro's Clinic, click the Options button from the top row of buttons. From the Options window that appears, click the DiskFix button if it is not already selected (if you are using the floppy disk version of DiskFix, there is no DiskFix button to select). From here, you can select which tests you wish DiskFix to perform (see Figure F13-5, top). (By the way, a similar set of options are available by clicking the More button when in the QuickAssist window.) Most notably, you can decide whether or not to check for bad blocks (damaged media) on floppy disks and/or hard disks.

b. With Norton Utilities, select the Preferences command from Disk Doctor's Edit menu. From the dialog box that appears (see Figure F13-5, bottom) you use the pop-up menu to additionally select between Repair Preferences and Check Media Preferences. With Repair Preferences, you have the option to select "Check for Defective Media" as part of Norton Disk Doctor's standard checks. The Check Media Preferences selection (not shown) refers to a separate "Check Disk Media" command in Disk Doctor's Tools menu. This command does a more thorough scan of the disk, including making repair attempts as needed.

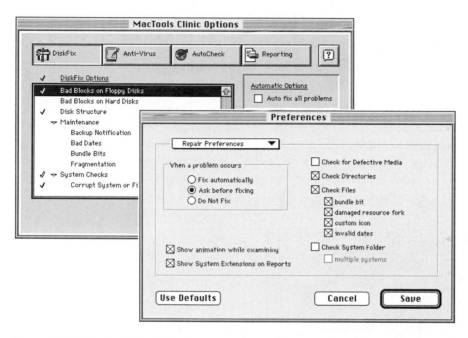

Figure F13-5   MacTools Pro's DiskFix options (top) and Norton Disk Doctor's Preferences dialog box (bottom)

By the way, you can also check for bad blocks from within the Speed Disk utility (see Fix-It #8) by selecting "Check Media" from Speed Disk's Explore menu.

I singled out bad blocks for special mention here because it takes a long time to make this check and it is only rarely the source of a problem (especially for hard disks). Thus, I would typically keep this option off. You might turn on the option to check for bad blocks if a previous check of an apparently damaged disk did not identify any problems. Otherwise, you are most likely to want to check for bad blocks when you are having a problem with a specific file that suggests that bad blocks are the cause (such as a read or write error, when trying to copy a file). What to do in this case is more specifically covered in Fix-It #14 ("Resolve Problems with Bad Blocks").

If bad blocks are located in the critical Directory area of a disk, a repair utility may not even be able to successfully scan the disk. In this case, the only solution is to try to recover files if needed (as described later in this Fix-It) and then reformat the disk. For floppy disks, it is often simpler and safer to discard the disk.

SEE: • Chapter 2 and Fix-Its #14 and #15 for more background information on bad blocks

One other option that I would avoid is to have any damage repaired without having the utility first ask if you want the problem repaired (e.g., "Auto fix all problems"). It's always safer to see what the utility intends to do before it actually does it. There are times when you may even want to skip a particular repair (which you cannot do if "auto fix" is on).

For help in deciding what other options to turn on or off, consult each utility's manual.

3. Attempt to repair the disk

a. From MacTools Clinic (or floppy disk's DiskFix), click on the name of the disk you wish to check and click the Check button (see Figure F13-1 again).

b. With Norton Disk Doctor, click on the name of the disk you wish to check and click the Examine button (see Figure F13-4 again).

In either case, the program now begins to check the disk (see Figure F13-6). If it discovers a problem, it stops to alert you. Under the default options, a window appears that describes the nature of the problem and suggests what to do about it (see Figure F13-7). It usually gives you the choice to repair the problem (if possible) or skip over it (if desired). In general, repair any problem that is detected and can be repaired (though you can ignore minor problems, such as incorrect modification dates, without affecting your ability to use the disk).

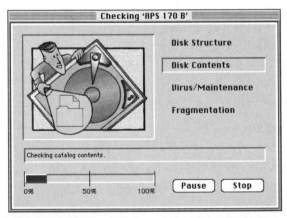

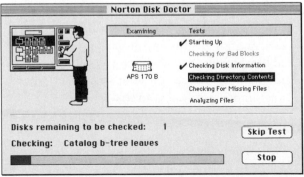

Figure F13-6   MacTools Pro (top) and Norton Disk Doctor (bottom) checking a disk

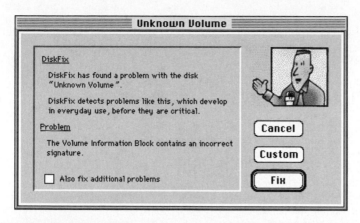

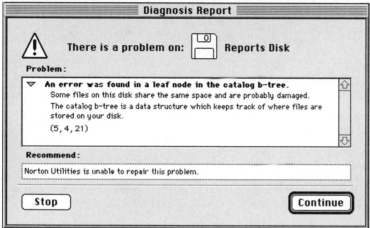

Figure F13-7   MacTools Pro (top) and Norton Disk Doctor (bottom) reporting problems

After making your choice, the analysis then proceeds, pausing again as needed until the entire disk is checked. Normally, that's all there is to doing repairs.

If anything happens that you wish to undo, MacTools gives you the option to undo any repairs that it has made (via the "Undo DiskFix Repair" command in the Clinic (or Disk-Fix) menu. However, to use it, you must first have selected the "Create a file to undo Disk-Fix repairs" option, accessed via clicking the Custom button from the window that appears when a problem is detected. If the repair cannot be undone or if an Undo file is already present, clicking the Custom button, if one even appears, will not list this option. Norton Utilities does not have any Undo option.

If your utility detects a problem that it cannot repair (and especially if the disk analysis halts at that point), skip to Step 6.

4. Check the disk again

If the utility has reported no problems with the disk, or if it has claimed to successfully repair any problems it found, check the disk again anyway. As with Disk First Aid, problems may be detected on subsequent runs that were not spotted or not fixed on the first run. Ideally, check the disk at least until no problems are detected on two consecutive runs.

5. If repairs are successful

If your utility detects no further damage on retesting, your problems should be over. Quit the utility and restart the Mac. Try using the problem disk to see if it now works as expected. If so, you are done.

If the disk seems okay for the moment but the same problem recurs within a few days, you should probably reformat the disk rather than repairing it again. In the meantime, make sure your important files are backed up, just in case disaster strikes.

6. If repairs aren't successful

A data-recovery utility may detect a Directory problem but report that it is unable to repair it. In some cases, a disk is so damaged that the utility either cannot start or cannot complete its analysis of the disk. Rarely, it may claim to have repaired a problem, but when you return to using the disk, the problem remains. For example, you may have *cross-linked files*. This occurs when the Directory indicates that two different files are occupying the same sector of a disk. This usually means that one or both of the files are damaged, with lost data almost a certainty. Although a repair utility may offer to repair the incorrect Directory listing, it can't entirely repair the damaged files.

In some cases, where a repair to a file is impossible, MacTools may give you the option to copy the damaged file to another disk, salvaging whatever possible. Similarly, if Norton Utilities cannot fix a certain problem, it may directly launch its Volume Recover function. Using this is discussed more later in this Fix-It. In other cases, as seen in the bottom of Figure F13-7, it may simply report that it cannot repair the volume.

Whenever you are unable to successfully repair a damaged disk, try to recover any files that you want to save (that have not already been recovered or backed up). After completing any recovery, reformat the disk. After successfully reformatting, restore the data from your backups. You are done.

Using More than One Repair Utility   By the way, if you own both MacTools and Norton Utilities, it pays to try them both. If you have a problem that one can't fix, maybe the other one can.

However, occasionally, one utility may "undo" a repair made by the other, potentially leading to an endless cycle of repairs as you switch back and forth between utilities. For minor problems, such as a bundle bit error, you can probably ignore this and just stop at the end of one utility's analysis. However, for more serious problems (such as a B-Tree Header problem), this situation may result from each utility spotting separate damage to the same area, with neither one able to effect a complete repair (one utility's repair may even allow the other utility to spot damage that it would have otherwise missed). Similar problems can occur between these utilities and Disk First Aid. In these cases, once again, reformatting may be your only solution.

SEE: • "Recover Selected Files from a Damaged Disk," later in this Fix-It, as needed
       • Chapter 2 on restoring from backups
       • Fix-It #15 on reformatting disks

BY THE WAY ▶

AUTOMATED CHECKING AND REPAIRS

Both MacTools Pro and Norton Utilities offer options to periodically scan a disk in the background, while the computer is otherwise idle. Norton Utilities does this via FileSaver. MacTools uses a special AutoCheck extension. With the most recent version of AutoCheck, you can often repair the disk directly, without needing to separately launch the Clinic application.

SEE: • Chapter 2, "Protect Against Disk Damage" in the "Install Protection Utilities" section for
         more on setting up these autoscanning options

Restore a Damaged or Accidentally Erased Disk

You will not often need to restore a disk, maybe never. However, for irreparable Directory damage or an accidentally erased hard disk, this procedure can sometimes save the day (but see "Take Note: Use Backups Instead of Restore or Recover" for some cautions about doing this).

These days, a restore ability is unique to Norton Utilities. Current versions of MacTools no longer support a restore option. Restoring a disk requires using a special feature of FileSaver (a control panel included as part of Norton Utilities, as described more in Chapter 2) that maintains a backup copy of the Directory. This option does not work with floppy disks.

Before Attempting to Restore a Disk

1. Make sure FileSaver is installed and active prior to the onset of the problem
Restoring a disk requires that you have installed and activated Norton Utilities' FileSaver prior to the occurrence of the problem. This creates and updates the needed invisible files. In particular, make sure the On/Off button in the FileSaver control panel is on and that the Protected checkbox is checked next to each disk you want to protect. If you have not already

done this, the best you can do for an immediate problem is to recover files as described in the next section, "Recover Selected Files from a Damaged Disk").

SEE: • Chapter 2 for more on setting up FileSaver

2. Recover recent files that are not already backed up

A restore, even if successful, may not restore your disk to the exact state it was prior to the crash. In particular, recent changes and additions may not get restored (see "Take Note: Use Backups Instead of Restore or Recover" for details). For this reason, before attempting a restore, you should try to recover files that may have been added, modified, or created since FileSaver's most recent update, unless you know that you already have these files backed up elsewhere. To do this, use methods as described in "Recover Selected Files from a Damaged Disk" later in this Fix-It.

When and how often the FileSaver information is updated is set from the FileSaver control panel. If you are unsure when the last update was performed, you will get this information as you carry out the steps in the next section.

TAKE NOTE ▶

USE BACKUPS INSTEAD OF RESTORE OR RECOVER

Central Point's MacTools used to have a control panel, called Mirror, that allowed you to restore a disk much in the same way as you do with Norton Utilities' FileSaver. Central Point dropped this feature from current versions of MacTools because they believed that it would only rarely, if ever, solve a problem that could not be better handled by MacTools' other repair functions. While the overall wisdom of this decision can be debated, Central Point folks do have a valid point. Consider the limitations of and problems with Norton Utilities' FileSaver recover ability:

- *If you have not installed and activated FileSaver prior to the crash, the restore won't work.*

- *Even with FileSaver active, the restore doesn't always work. For example, if the disk damage involves the FileSaver files, they are rendered useless. Also, FileSaver cannot restore files damaged because of bad blocks.*

- *Most notable, these protection files cannot necessarily restore a disk to the state it was at the time of the crash or erasure. This is because the recovery can restore the Directory only to the state it was the last time these protection files were updated. Depending on luck and how you configured FileSaver, the last update may have been made just before the problem occurred, or it may have been made several weeks before. Any changes made since the last time the protection file was updated are not restored. In fact, trying to restore a disk with an out-of-date Directory may cause problems of its own (such as if a file listed in the outdated Directory has since been deleted from the disk).*

  Thus, unless the last update was made relatively close to the occurrence of the problem (or you have made very few recent changes to the contents of your disk), I would not consider using this restore feature. Neither would I want to depend on a utility's recover feature. Frequent backups remain your best protection against data loss (which you should always maintain, whether you use FileSaver or not)! True, backing up also requires regular updating to be effective, and restoring a disk from backups can be time-consuming. But backups are much more reliable than the alternative methods. If you have an up-to-date set of backups, successful recovery is almost guaranteed.

SEE: • Chapter 2 for more on setting up FileSaver and on backing up disks

---

Restore the Disk

1. Access Norton Utilities' Volume Recover
Launch Norton Utilities. From the main menu, click the Volume Recover button. A window listing all mounted volumes will appear.

2. Select the disk to be restored
Select the volume you wish to restore and click the Recover button (see Figure F13-8). You cannot restore the startup disk or the disk that contains the active copy of The Norton Utilities. In these cases, starting up from an alternate disk will be required.

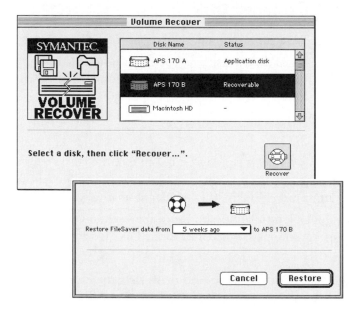

Figure F13-8   Norton Utilities' Volume Recover restores a disk's Directory; first, select a volume (top) and then start the restore (bottom)

3. Attempt to restore the disk
After selecting Recover, Volume Recover searches for the needed FileSaver data. A dialog box then appears with a pop-up menu listing the dates of all available FileSaver files. Generally, pick the most recent date (unless you suspect the damage occurred prior to that date). Then click Restore (see Figure F13-8).

Note that if the FileSaver file's date is much older than the current date, your restore is unlikely to result in a good match to the current status of your disk (as described in "Take Note: Use Backups Instead of Restore or Recover").

If no FileSaver data are found, Volume Recover offers to shift to UnErase to recover files (described more in the next section).

4. a. If the restore is successful
If the restore succeeds, your disk should be returned to normal. Congratulations. Return any separately recovered files (as described in "Before Attempting to Restore a Disk," earlier in this section) that were not restored. To be safe, now go back and check for repair problems,

via Disk Doctor (as described in the previous section). Actually, Norton Utilities will prompt you to run Disk Doctor after completing its Volume Recover.

b. If the restore fails.   If the initial restore attempt fails, you can try to restore again using another FileSaver backup file (if available). Alternatively, you can go to Disk Doctor to see if it can now repair the disk despite the apparently failed restore attempt. Otherwise, recover any unbacked up files that you have not already tried to recover (using methods described in the next section). Then reformat the disk and restore it from your backups and recovered files.

Recover Selected Files from a Damaged Disk

This section emphasizes the general procedure for using MacTools or Norton Utilities to recover unbacked-up files from a severely damaged disk, a disk that could not otherwise be repaired or restored. For more detailed information on this and other ways to recover individual damaged files from any disk, crashed or not, see Fix-It #14.

For Norton Utilities, recovery is facilitated if you have previously installed FileSaver.

1. **Launch your repair utility**

   a. With MacTools Pro, launch MacTools Clinic. A window listing all mounted disks will appear (see Figure F13-1 again). If you are first greeted with the QuickAssist window, click Cancel. If you are running from a floppy disk, DiskFix will launch automatically.

   b. With Norton Utilities, simply launch Norton Utilities to get to the Norton Utilities Main Menu window or (if you are using a floppy startup disk) to the Disk Doctor window.

2. **Generate a list of recoverable files**

   a. With MacTools Pro's Clinic, select the desired volume, and then select the Recover Files command from the Clinic menu. (If you are using the MacTools Emergency floppy disk, select the Recover Files button from the DiskFix window.)

   After scanning the disk, you will be presented with a Recover Files window showing the name of the volume. Click the triangle symbol to the left of the volume name to display the list of recoverable files (see Figure F13-9).

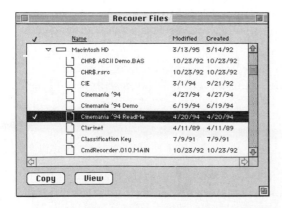

Figure F13-9   MacTools Pro's list of recoverable files

b. With Norton Utilities, select UnErase either from Norton Utilities' Main Menu window (if present) or Utilities menu. A window listing all mounted disks will appear (see Figure 13-10, top). From here, select the name of the desired disk and then click the Search button. This will initially perform a search for erased files based on FileSaver data, if available.

When the initial search is complete, you will see a window similar to the one in the middle of Figure 13-10. From here, click the Search Again button. This will open a dialog box where you will see two checkbox options, one for "erased files" and the other for "real files" (see Figure F13-10, bottom). To recover files from a damaged disk, you want to check the "real files" option. Now once again click Search.

This will give you a list of recoverable files (see Figure 13-10, middle). Actually the list may also include partially recoverable and totally irrecoverable files, unless you select the "Hide Unrecoverable Files" command in the Options menu.

If you are not satisfied that this list contains all the files you wish to recover, click the Search Again button again. Now select a different method from the Method pop-up menu. In particular, try Directory Scan (see Figure F13-10, bottom) if you do not have current FileSaver data. Once more, click Search.

SEE: • Chapter 6, "If the File Was Inadvertently Deleted" in the "When You Can't Locate a File" section, for a related description of undeleting files

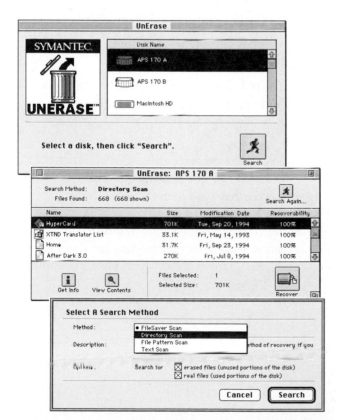

Figure F13-10   Norton Utilities' UnErase windows (top/middle) and Search Method dialog box (bottom)

3. Attempt to recover files

a. With MacTools, select any files you wish to recover (by placing a check mark next to their name) and click the Copy button (see Figure F13-9). For text files, you may first click the View button to see the contents of a file. This may help in your decision as to whether to try to recover it or not.

b. With Norton Utilities' UnErase, select files and click the Recover button (see Figure F13-10, middle). You can click the View Contents button to see the contents of a file (primarily useful for text files) prior to deciding whether to recover it or not.

In either case, be sure to save the files to another disk (not the damaged disk!), when prompted to select a destination disk.

Not all files can be recovered successfully. Some files can only be partially recovered. Also, each program may have different success in recovering a specific file. So if you own both MacTools and Norton Utilities, it is worth trying to recover with both of them. In any case, this sort of file recovery can be long and tedious, especially if you want to recover many files. Thus, try to restrict recovery to essential files not backed up elsewhere (typically, your most recently created files).

4. Check on success or failure of recovered files

When the recovery is done, quit the utility. If possible, go to the Finder (restarting the Mac with an appropriate startup disk, if necessary). Recovered files should be on your selected disk, typically in a folder called Recovered Files. Try to open the files. If documents do not directly open from the Finder's desktop, they usually open from within their creating application (see Chapter 6 for more on how to deal with this problem).

With luck, the files are intact or (for text files) only require minor reformatting. However, some documents may have only partial contents or will be otherwise unusable. In any case, what you now have is the best you are likely to get by this method.

5. Repair and/or reformat

If you have not yet done so, proceed to try to repair the damaged disk. If repair attempts fail, any files that are still unrecovered probably cannot be saved. Some disk repair companies specialize in recovering data from disks that you have given up for dead. If you absolutely must get your data back, this is worth a try.

Otherwise, it is time to reformat the disk (for floppy disks, it's safer to discard the disks rather than reformat them). If the hard disk fails to work after reformatting (or if you can't reformat the disk), you have more serious problems. Hardware damage is a likely possibility.

For related information

MacTools and Norton Utilities can repair minor problems unrelated to Directory damage. Such problems are called "minor" because their symptoms typically do not directly interfere with your use of the Macintosh. Checks for these problems can be done as part of the overall repair examination of the disk, as described in this Fix-It. For example, you can check whether files have invalid creation dates or incorrect bundle bit settings. These utilities can also check for whether your desktop files are corrupted and can rebuild the desktop if needed. However, these problems are not the focus of this Fix-It and are covered elsewhere.

There are also reasons that a disk may not mount that do not involve Directory damage. These too are covered elsewhere, as listed in the following cross-references.

SEE: • Fix-It #9 on rebuilding the desktop
      • Fix-It #14 on recovering damaged files
      • Fix-It #15 on reformatting disks and for problems with floppy disks that appear to be damaged but are really not
      • Fix-It #16 on SCSI-related problems that may prevent a disk from mounting
      • Fix-It #17 on hardware repairs
      • Chapter 2 for information on disk damage, backing up your disks, and installing invisible files needed for restore and recovery
      • Chapter 5 for more details on startup problems and other problems mounting disks
      • Chapter 6 on undeleting files
      • Chapter 8 for more on the disk Directory, bundle bits, and other file attributes

Fix-It #14:
Check for Damaged Files:
Replace or Recover

QUICK SUMMARY

Replace damaged files from backups, if possible. Otherwise, use utilities (such as Norton Utilities for Macintosh, MacTools Pro, and CanOpener) to repair or recover data from damaged files, especially document files. In all cases, check for and "repair" bad blocks.

When to do it:

- Whenever launching an application consistently results in a system crash, freeze, or other serious malfunction.

- Whenever a program's feature that worked correctly on previous occasions now causes problems or simply does not work.

- Whenever opening a document consistently results in a system crash, freeze, or other serious malfunction.

- Whenever a document opens but displays only part of its contents or displays unintelligible gibberish rather than its expected data.

- Whenever specific documents will not print but other similar documents print without a problem.

- Whenever the error message *Unable to read from disk* appears when you try to open a file.

- Whenever you cannot successfully copy a file, especially when attempts to do so result in an error message such as *File could not be read* (or *written* or *verified*) *and was skipped*. These messages indicate bad blocks (media damage) on at least one of the disks involved in the copy operation.

- If you are using a floppy disk, a bad block is also indicated by a distinctive and uncharacteristic whining sound that emanates from the drive as it attempts to read from the defective area of the disk.

Why to do it:

If you have a damaged file, you want to replace it or fix it. In Chapter 2, the causes of damaged files were briefly described in the section entitled "Damage Control." Here is a closer look at how these causes apply to solving problems with damaged documents and applications.

Damaged Files Due to Miscopied Information

Many damaged files appear to be normal on the desktop. They can be moved or copied without any problem. However, when you try to open the file, problems appear. Applications may crash when launched. Documents, if they can be opened at all, display only part of the expected contents or display garbage data. In these cases, the file damage is usually due to some alteration in the data that make up the file. The damage usually originates as an error made when the file is copied, saved, or modified in any way. Since many files, such as the System file, are regularly modified as part of their normal use, this damage can happen to a file without you directly modifying it. This software damage is analogous to a book that has some words misprinted. There is no problem reading the book—it's just that the words don't always make sense.

Damaged Files Due to Bad Blocks

The other common type of damage is usually referred to as *bad blocks*. As indicated in Chapter 2, bad blocks are usually the result of *media damage* (that is, physical damage to the disk media) in a given area (*block* or *sector*) of a disk. Technically, this is not a file-related problem; it is a disk problem. In fact, a bad block can occur in an area of the disk where there is no file at all. Similarly, a bad block can occur in the Directory area of a disk, usually resulting in a crashed disk and almost certainly necessitating reformatting the disk.

SEE: • **Fix-It #13 for more on problems with damaged disks**

However, when a bad block occurs in an area where a document or application file exists, it is also considered a file problem. In these cases, you have two separate problems to solve.

First, the file is damaged. Even small files are usually several blocks in size, so a single bad block damages only a small part of most files. Still, this damage can render an entire file unusable. The information in the bad block region is most often permanently lost in any case. Usual solutions here are either to replace the file, if you have a backup, or (if it is a document file) to try to recover at least some of the data from the damaged file. If the bad block problem is intermittent, which happens occasionally, you may be able to recover the entire file.

Second, regardless of what you do to recover the file, the bad block problem remains and must also be remedied, typically by marking the block so that it will no longer be used. Otherwise, the bad blocks lie in wait, ready to cause problems the next time the Macintosh accesses that area of the disk.

Overall, floppy disks are much more susceptible to bad blocks than hard disks.

TECHNICALLY SPEAKING ▶

WHY ARE MY BLOCKS BAD?

You cannot read any data from a bad block. Often, you cannot write (that is, copy to or save) any data to a bad block. That is why attempts to access these areas of a disk result in error messages that say a file could not be read or written.

Most bad blocks are caused by media damage. This can result from media material flaking off or being scratched or by an assortment of other related possibilities. The probability of media damage increases as a disk ages, even if it is just a floppy disk sitting on a shelf. Other cases of bad blocks are harder to categorize. They are most often the result of a loss or disruption of the magnetic field needed to store data in the block. For example, exposure to strong magnetic fields can cause such bad blocks to appear.

When you first detect a bad block, there is no way to easily identify what type of bad block it is. And it probably isn't worth trying very hard to do so. Whatever the cause of the bad blocks, the symptoms are the same and the solutions are similar. However, the different causes can determine what happens to the bad blocks when you try to fix the disk. If the bad blocks are the result of media damage, they cannot be repaired. They can only be marked to prevent their future use. For other causes of bad blocks, reformatting the disk often returns the blocks to normal.

Intermittent Bad Blocks. *Occasionally, a bad block problem may be intermittent. That is, the damaged area of the block may "flip" back and forth between its correct and incorrect state, such that sometimes the block behaves normally and other times it responds as a bad block. Left alone, the intermittent response usually worsens until it always responds as a bad block. Data written to an intermittent bad block have a reasonably good chance of recovery. The idea is to read the block over and over again until you catch it on one of the times when it reads correctly.*

Caveats

First, several of the situations described in "When to do it" have other causes besides damaged files. So don't automatically assume that if you have one of these symptoms your file is damaged (see Chapter 6 for a more general discussion of file problems). Second, this Fix-It assumes that, despite any potential damage, you can get to the desktop and locate the damaged files. If this is not the case, you should refer first to Fix-It #13.

 What to do:

This section covers three strategies: Replace the damaged file, recover the damaged file, and resolve problems with bad blocks.

Replace the Damaged File

Your first line of defense against damaged files is to replace them, typically from your backup copies.

For Applications

Go to your original backup disks and use them to make a copy of the file(s). If the application came with an Installer utility, use it. If these newly copied files work properly, delete the suspected damaged files from your disk. Remember to consider that the damage may be to associated files, such as preferences files, rather than the application itself (see especially Fix-Its #2 and #3). In that regard, be aware that preferences files may not get replaced when you reinstall the application; instead, you need to separately delete the suspected preferences file.

If you have no replacement copies, order new copies from the company that makes the software. If you are a registered user, you can typically do this for a small fee. Otherwise, particularly if the damage is caused by an intermittent bad block problem, you may still be able to recover the file (as described in the next major section of this Fix-It). Failing that, your application is hopelessly lost.

For Documents

If you have a backup copy of your document, use it. If it works, delete the damaged file.

Even if you are diligent about making backups, you can find yourself without a backup copy for a given document. For example, the document may get damaged after you have saved it but before you have a chance to back it up. Or you may inadvertently back up an already damaged file, leaving your backup copy damaged. In these cases, proceed to the next section on recovering damaged files.

Recover the Damaged File

In some cases, you may be able to totally recover a damaged file back to its original condition. But don't count on this happening often. Partial recovery is usually the best you can hope for, because there is usually no way to figure out exactly what the "correct" data in the damaged area of the file should be.

Most of the techniques here emphasize recovery of document files, because document recovery has a better chance of success (where even partial recovery can be of some value) and is more likely to be needed (for applications, it is more likely that you have a backup copy).

Make a Copy of the Damaged File

Make a copy of the file, ideally to another disk. There are two reasons for this. First, if your recovery attempts make things worse, you have a duplicate copy with which to try again. Second, sometimes copying a file from the Finder succeeds in recovering it, either fully or partially.

1. From the Finder, copy the file to another disk.

2. Try to open the newly copied file.

3. If the copy works normally, make a new backup copy of the now recovered file and delete the damaged copy. You are done.

4. If the copy seems just as "damaged" as the original (or if you get only partial recovery), proceed to the next section, "Try to Open the Damaged Document."

5. If, when you try to make a copy, you get a message that says the file could not be read, this indicates that a bad block is the cause of the damaged file. In this case, proceed to "Resolve Problems with Bad Blocks" later in this Fix-It.

Try to Open the Damaged Document

Sometimes, even though a document appears damaged (as indicated by an inability to copy the document from the Finder), you can still open it. You may find that some data are lost or incorrect when the document is opened, but the document nevertheless opens.

1. Try to open the document. Try first from its creating application. If this does not work, try opening it using another application that reads the damaged file's format (for example, try opening a Word file with MacWrite Pro).

2. If you can get the document to successfully open, even if it displays only partial contents or gibberish, save the contents to a new file, using the Save As command. Now open the newly created file to check if the problem symptoms are gone. As with making a copy of the file from the Finder, this sometimes completely repairs a damaged file.

3. If the Save As technique does not work, copy any usable data from the damaged file to the Clipboard. Open a new document and paste the data into it. Save the new document.

4. For partially recovered or unrecoverable files, if the damage occurred recently and if you have installed a utility such as NowSave or Last Resort, you may be able to find at least some of the missing data in the special recovery files created by these utilities (see Chapters 2 and 4 for details). Even better, if you have a backup copy of the document, but it is insufficient because it is an older version that does not contain recent modifications to the file, you may be able to combine the backup document with the more recent data recovered from Now-Menus or Last Resort files to fully reconstruct the current version of the document.

File Recovery via CanOpener

If all the preceding techniques have failed, you may still be able to use special recovery utilities to extract the text or graphics from the file. However, for text files, even if you succeed in doing this, you will lose all the text's formatting (such as font selections, styles, and margin settings). Still, this is a small price to pay to recover the complete text (or even just part of the text) of a long manuscript.

There are many file recovery utilities on the market. My favorite one is CanOpener. CanOpener works with almost any file—damaged or undamaged, document or application. It can extract graphics (of several different formats) as well as text that may be contained within a file. It can even extract sounds and QuickTime movies. Although utilities such as MacTools Pro and Norton Utilities have some similar features (as described next), CanOpener is generally both more effective and easier to use. To use it:

1. Launch CanOpener.

2. Locate the damaged file in CanOpener's scroll box, much as you would use an Open dialog box.

3. Double-click the damaged file's name. This opens a list of what text, pictures, sounds, and movies are recoverable from that file, each one listed as a separate item (see Figure F14-1).

4. Double-click an item to view its contents. You cannot edit the displayed text or graphic in any way. However, you can view it to check if it is what you want to recover.

5. Once you have found the desired text or graphic, go to the Item menu and select Save As to save the item. This command saves text to a separate plain text file and graphics to a separate PICT file (see Chapter 8 for more on these file formats).

6. Quit CanOpener and access these saved files, for further editing if needed, in other applications (such as word processors or graphics applications). For example, text files may contain extraneous gibberish text that you want to delete.

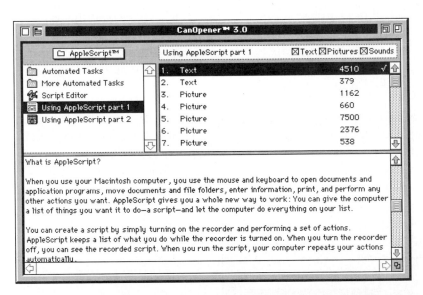

Figure F14-1 **Using CanOpener: Double-clicking the name of the file on the left produces the list of text and picture items on the right; double-clicking the highlighted text item opens the text display below**

If a file contains bad blocks or the disk is severely damaged, CanOpener may not be able to open the file, or the file's name may not even appear in the initial list. If this happens, you have to address the bad blocks problem before you can use CanOpener (see "Resolve Problems with Bad Blocks" later in this Fix-It).

File Recovery with MacTools or Norton Utilities

Both MacTools and Norton Utilities have file recovery capabilities (as described in Fix-It #13, "Recover Selected Files from a Damaged Disk"). If utilities such as CanOpener fail to work, these are your last resort. They can also fix minor file problems, such as incorrect bundle bit settings and incorrect creation and modification dates, that are not addressed by CanOpener. Finally, these utilities have some special file recovery features not mentioned in Fix-It #13. In particular, they do the following.

Norton Utilities   Norton Utilities UnErase is especially good at text recovery. If the text is anywhere on the disk, UnErase is almost certain to find it. However, an often quicker solution for recovery of a single file is to use the Recover File command from Norton Disk Doctor's Tools menu. In either case, Norton does a good job of saving the file with nonprinting characters and other extraneous gibberish stripped out.

MacTools Pro   MacTools Pro includes a utility called FileFix (see Figure F14-2). It has special features for fixing damaged Microsoft Excel and Microsoft Word files. It recovers data from these files and then saves the data to a new file. Check the MacTools Pro manual for details, if needed. FileFix is also an excellent utility for resolving problems with incorrect file type or creator codes (as explained more in Chapter 8).

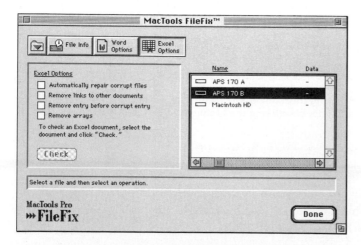

Figure F14-2   MacTools Pro's FileFix, with special options to repair Excel files displayed

Resolve Problems with Bad Blocks

If bad blocks are present in the area of a disk occupied by a file, you typically are unable to open or copy the file. If you try, you get an error message that says a file could not be read. On the other hand, if you get a write or verify error when you try to copy a file, this also indicates bad blocks. However, the file itself is not damaged. Rather, the bad block is in the presently unused destination location for the file copy (though there may also be more bad blocks on this disk, in locations that *are* occupied by files). Fixing bad blocks independently of any specific file problem (such as indicated by a write or verify error) was briefly covered in Fix-It #13. The focus here is on recovering a specific file that is damaged because of bad blocks (as indicated by a read error). In either case, bad block problems need to be resolved before you continue to use the affected disk.

Recover Damaged Files and Repair Bad Blocks

Norton Utilities   Norton Utilities does a decent job of checking for and repairing bad blocks, even attempting to fix files that are damaged due to bad blocks. To initiate all of this, select the Check Disk Media command from Norton Disk Doctor's Tools menu. Norton Utilities can also check for bad blocks as part of its more general analysis of the disk.

SEE: • Fix-It #13, "Set Repair Options (Especially Decide Whether or Not to Check for Bad Blocks)" in "Repair a Damaged Disk," for more details

MacTools Pro   I prefer to use MacTools Pro's DiskFix for dealing with bad blocks problems. Here's what to do:

1. From the MacTools Clinic window, click the Options button at the top of the main window. From the window that next appears, make sure that either or both of "Bad Blocks on Floppy Disks" and "Bad Blocks on Hard Disks" options are checked (refer to Figure F13-5, top).

   If you are running DiskFix from a floppy disk, click its Options button. From the Options window, select the option called "Bad Blocks." (By the way, the instructions in the next steps apply to the full MacTools Pro Clinic application. If you are using the more limited floppy disk DiskFix application, what you see may be a bit different from what is described here.)

   These bad block checking options are off by default. If you want to check only for bad blocks, and not bother with the other analysis, uncheck everything else (but remember to recheck them before you later try to do a more thorough analysis). When you are finished, click OK to return to the main window.

2. Click the Check button. This begins the analysis of the disk. The analysis can take a while, especially for a large hard disk (which is why this option is unchecked by default). If there are any bad blocks on the disk, DiskFix will report them. If so, you will typically see a dialog box as in Figure F14-3.

3. From here, you can click the Fix button to immediately try to repair the bad block. However, you will probably be better off if you select Custom instead. This opens up a new dialog box that identifies which files contain bad blocks as well as indicating bad blocks in unused areas of the disk (see Figure F14-4).

4. DiskFix lists bad blocks in areas of the disk that are currently unused as "Unused bad blocks." To attempt to fix these, select this item and click Repair (see Figure 14-4). What this actually does is to mark the blocks to prevent their future use (see: "Technically Speaking: How Data Recovery Utilities 'Repair' Bad Blocks").

5. For specific files with bad blocks, select the file name(s), so that a checkmark appears before the name, then click Copy (see Figure 14-4). In this case, DiskFix tries to copy the damaged file to a new location. As DiskFix does this, it reads repeatedly from the bad block area. If the bad block problem is intermittent, one of the repeated attempts may successfully read the block. In this case, you may get a fully recovered copy of the file. When done, if Disk-Fix has not reported that it has already marked the bad blocks to prevent their future use, click Repair.

6. If bad blocks are in the Directory, none of this is likely to work. In this case, refer to Fix-It #13, "Recover Selected Files from a Damaged Disk."

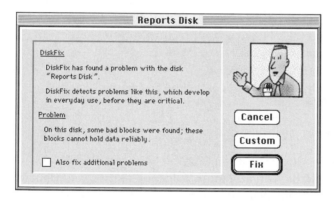

Figure F14-3   DiskFix reports a bad block problem; click the Custom button to get the dialog box in Figure F14-4

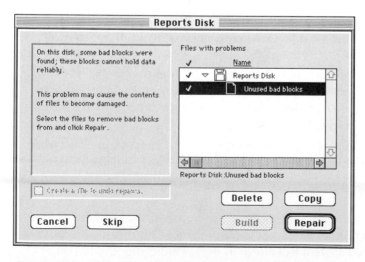

Figure F14-4   DiskFix reports that bad blocks were found in unused areas of the disk

Repairing Bad Blocks: Recovery Utilities Versus Reformatting

After you have recovered files from the damaged disk as best as you are able, there is the separate issue of "repairing" the bad blocks on the disk. While you can use MacTools Pro or Norton Utilities to make these repairs (see "Technically Speaking: How Data Recovery Utilities 'Repair' Bad Blocks"), I usually do not do so.

For hard disks, the best and most reliable way to correct bad block problems (and sometimes the only way, if the recovery utility fails) is to reformat the entire disk using a utility such as Apple HD SC Setup or Drive7. An added advantage of reformatting is that if the bad blocks are *not* due to media damage, reformatting should allow the blocks to be used again, eliminating the need to map them out. On the downside, reformatting erases the entire disk. Thus, when you reformat, you also need to back up and later restore all undamaged files on the disk, which is considerably more time-consuming than using a utility such as DiskFix to mark the bad block. At best, though it is a bit riskier, you can try to repair the bad blocks with DiskFix, resorting to reformatting if problems reoccur. Occasionally, if you need to back up the disk before you reformat it, you may find that the bad blocks prevent a normal backup. In this case, do try to mark the bad blocks with a recovery utility. Then back up the disk (except for files possibly damaged by the bad blocks for which you already have a current backup) and reformat.

For floppy disks with bad blocks, I usually don't even bother with reformatting. I just discard the disk. In any case, to fix bad blocks on floppy disks by reformatting (which can be done only in System 7.x anyway), the Macintosh essentially uses the same method as DiskFix or Norton Utilities.

SEE: • Fix-It #15, "Verifying Disks and Media Damage," for related information

Special Case: Recovering Files from Floppy Disks with Bad Blocks

Use Copy Utilities Using a recovery utility to recover files damaged by bad blocks, as described in the previous section, works equally well for floppy disks or hard disks. For floppy disks, however, an alternative method may be even better (or at least simpler). This method doesn't mark or repair the bad blocks in any way (which is of little consequence, since you should discard the damaged disk after recovery). But it is effective at recovering data from damaged files. At its best, it can recover 100% of the text from a damaged text file. It is also useful for recovering data from floppy disks with bad blocks in the Directory (as such disks likely cannot be mounted or repaired, as described in Fix-It #13). Here's what to do:

1. Copy the entire disk to a new disk, using a special disk-copy utility. For example, use either Norton Utilities' Floppier application or MacTools Pro's FastCopy (see Figure F14-5). These programs have a special feature that copies around bad blocks, so that the bad blocks are not duplicated on the copy.

   With FastCopy, you should turn on the "Skip bad blocks" option, accessed by clicking the Options button at the top of the window. With Floppier, this option is always in effect. With either program, you simply identify a source and destination disk (by inserting the relevant disks) and then click the Copy (with FastCopy) or Start Copy (with Floppier) button. Although these utilities have other option settings, you can ignore them here. Just go with the default settings (except that I would uncheck the "Copy used space only" option in FastCopy).

   Be wary of using other copy utilities. Some may work as well as the ones described here; others may not. For example, with Apple's Disk Copy, I find that it copies too well: It copies the disk exactly, bad block data and all. Also, do not depend on the Finder to make copies. After all, an inability to copy the file from the Finder is often how you discovered the problem in the first place.

   By itself, bypassing the bad blocks does not mean that the damaged file is recovered (the data that were in the bad block area may now be missing), but it's a start. At least you now have a copy of the file that does not contain bad blocks.

2. Try to open the newly created copy of the damaged file from within its creating application. If this does not work (and it usually doesn't), next try to open the damaged file using CanOpener or other comparable utility (this usually works, even if CanOpener could not open the original damaged file).

3. If you succeed in opening the file at all, extract data from it using the methods previously described.

SEE: • "Recover the Damaged File," earlier in this Fix-It

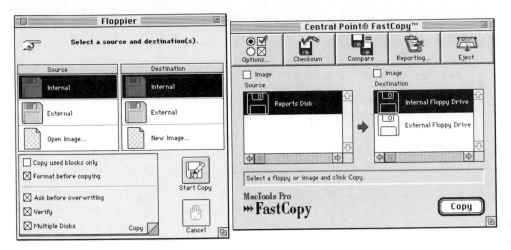

Figure F14-5 Norton Utilities' Floppier (left) and MacTools Pro's FastCopy (right)

Try Apple File Exchange As a completely separate alternative to the previous method, you may be able to copy files from a damaged floppy disk using Apple File Exchange software (included on System 7 software disks prior to System 7.5), even though that is not the main purpose of this software. To do so, follow the same procedures you would use if the file to be copied was on an undamaged non-Mac formatted disk (check your manual for details).

For related information

SEE: • Fix-It #2 for information on corrupted preferences files
       • Fix-It #4 on INIT conflicts
       • Fix-It #5 on replacing damaged system software
       • Fix-It #13 on damaged disks
       • Fix-It #15 on reformatting
       • Chapter 2, "Damage Control," for a general discussion of damage
       • Chapter 4 on system errors
       • Chapter 6 for more on problems opening, copying, and saving files
       • Chapter 8 for more on file types, creators, and bundle bits
       • Chapter 9 for problems with corrupted font files

Fix-It #15:
Format, Initialize, and Verify Disks

QUICK SUMMARY

For floppy disks, use the Finder's *Erase Disk* command to reformat the disk. For hard disks, use a formatting utility (such as Apple HD SC Setup or Drive7) to reformat the disk; launch the utility and click its *Initialize* or *Format* button, as appropriate.

When to do it:

- Whenever everything else you have tried has failed to fix your problem, especially when your recovery utilities (such as Disk First Aid, Norton Utilities, or MacTools) report damage to a disk that they are unable to repair.

- Whenever you have a problem with bad blocks, especially on a hard disk. This usually becomes apparent when you try to copy a file and get a message such as *File could not be read and was skipped.*

- Prior to a complete restoration of your hard disk from your backup files.

- Whenever you want to restore a disk to like-new condition, making sure that virtually all data on it are truly erased.

- Whenever you have an unformatted or incorrectly formatted disk.

Why to do it:

All disks need to be formatted before they can be used. Otherwise, you cannot even mount the disk. So why cover formatting of disks here, near the end of this book? It would appear that formatting should be one of the first things to do, not one of the last things to consider.

The answer is that *re*formatting of disks is an important problem-solving tool. It is an all-purpose last resort for dealing with many of the problems covered in previous Fix-Its. In particular, if you have a damaged disk that cannot be repaired by utilities such as MacTools or Norton Utilities (as described in Fix-It #13), reformatting usually brings the disk back to life. Similarly, if you have a problem with bad blocks on a hard disk (as described primarily in Fix-It #14), reformatting is the most reliable way to solve the problem. Reformatting a disk also rebuilds the desktop (Fix-It #9) and reinstalls the disk driver (Fix-It #12). Finally, when you restore files to a reformatted disk, they are defragmented (Fix-It #8). In other words, in one bold stroke, reformatting can cure a variety of ills. Reformatting is also advised whenever you want to recycle an old floppy disk, even if you do not suspect any problems with it.

The only real disadvantages of reformatting are that it takes a relatively long time (especially for hard disks) and that it erases everything on the disk (requiring you to back up and subsequently restore you disk's contents in order to get back to where you were before reformatting, which adds even more time and hassle to the whole procedure).

The focus of this Fix-It is how and when to reformat problem disks. This Fix-It also tells you when *not* to reformat a disk. In particular, there are several situations where the Macintosh *incorrectly* claims that a perfectly fine floppy disk is unreadable and requests that you reformat it. Don't reformat these disks, or you will unnecessarily erase them. Finally, this Fix-It briefly covers some problems that may occur when you try to format or reformat any disk.

The common use of the term *format* may actually refer to up to six separate processes, only the first of which is what is technically meant by formatting. (1) *Formatting* affects every block on the disk. It lays down the initial background of data that allows a disk to be recognized as a Macintosh disk. (2) For hard disks, the next step (which is optional) is to *partition* the disk, which means to divide the disk into separate volumes, each of which then acts as if it were an independent disk. (3) Again just for hard disks, the third step is to *install the disk's driver,* a critical piece of software that allows the Macintosh to communicate with the disk. (4) *Initializing* the disk occurs next, which primarily means to create a new set of Directory files. (5) Again a sometimes optional step, is to *verify* the disk, which is essentially to check that the preceding steps, especially the formatting step, were successfully carried out. A final check for bad blocks may also occur here. (6) *Mounting* the disk, which means to have the disk appear on the Finder's desktop, comes last.

In some cases, especially when talking about floppy disks, the terms formatting and initializing are used interchangeably to refer to the entire set of steps. Thus, all of these steps are typically performed in response to a single disk-formatting (Format or Initialize) command (although with most hard disk formatting utilities, you can also separately select each step).Verifying a disk can be done separately as a test of an already formatted disk, usually as a way to check for possible media damage.

What to do:

This Fix-It is divided into three topics: floppy disks, hard disks, and verifying disks and media damage.

Floppy Disks

There are three types of floppy disks: 400K (single-sided, rarely seen these days), 800K (double-sided), and 1.44Mb (double-sided HD). The current SuperDrives can recognize and work with any type of floppy disk: 400K, 800K, or HD. However, the older 800K drives cannot format and do not recognize HD disks.

SEE: • Chapter 1 for details on how to identify each type of disk

---

BY THE WAY ▶

VARIATIONS IN MESSAGES FOR FORMATTING DISKS

Many dialog/alert boxes asking whether you want to format/initialize a floppy disk have been redesigned for System 7.5. Thus, if you are using an older version of the system software, some of the messages you see will likely look different from what you see in the figures here.

As described in the main text, these dialog boxes may differ yet again if you are using Macintosh PC Exchange, included as part of System 7.5.

Formatting an Unformatted Disk

When you insert an unformatted floppy disk into a drive, a message appears that says that the disk is unreadable and asks whether you want to initialize it (see Figure F15-1, top). If you insert an HD disk, the format will be listed as "Macintosh 1.4 Mb." If you insert an 800K or a 400K disk, the format will be listed as "Macintosh 800K." If you click the Initialize button, you will next get the alert message seen in the bottom of Figure F15-1. Click the Continue button to begin the format process. That's it. The Macintosh does everything else automatically. During this process the Macintosh gives you feedback on its progress with messages such as *Formatting disk . . . , Verifying format . . . ,* and *Creating directory.* When it is finished, the newly formatted disk appears on the desktop.

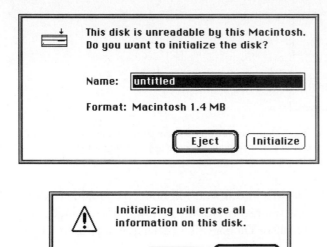

Figure F15-1 **These two messages appear in succession when you format an unformatted floppy disk**

The initial message box gives you a chance to name the disk (it is named "Untitled" by default). Don't worry. Whatever name you give it, you can always change it later.

Clicking the Cancel or Eject buttons in either of these boxes prevents the start of a format. The disk then remains unmodified.

HD Disks in 800K Drives (and Vice Versa)   If you insert an HD disk into an older 800K drive, rather than a SuperDrive, you are given the chance to format the HD disk as an 800K disk. Do *not* do this. *Eject* the disk instead (for more on this, see "Unreadable or Damaged Disks That Really Aren't" later in the section).

Conversely, you may be tempted to figure out a way to get a SuperDrive to format an 800K disk as an HD disk (normally, the Macintosh does not give you an option to do this). Don't try! The 800K disks are physically different from the HD disks, and formatting an 800K disk as an HD disk is asking for trouble. Eventually, the Macintosh is likely to treat the disk as damaged, and you may lose data on this disk.

What Happened to 400K (One-Sided) Format?   In System 7.5, you are not given the option to format a disk as a 400K disk. However, with older versions of the system software, if you try to format or reformat an 800K disk, you should get a message such as the one seen in Figure F15-2. Here you *can* choose to format a disk as a 400K disk. However, the 400K structure is obsolete and should not be used. Not only does an 800K format give you twice as much space, but it is an entirely different and improved format structure.

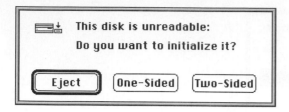

Figure F15-2 This message appears when you insert an unformatted 800K or 400K disk into a disk drive with a system software prior to version 7.5; a similar message appears if you try to erase an already formatted 800K or 400K disk

One exception here: With newer models of Macintosh, you will not get a one-sided (400K) format option no matter what version of the system software you are using. These models no longer support this disk format (see "Unreadable or Damaged Disks That Really Aren't," later in this section).

If you own a bunch of single-sided disks, don't be in too much of a hurry to discard them. You can still choose to (re)format them as 800K disks. These disks really have two sides, despite their name. There is some risk in doing this as, technically, a single-sided disk has only been verified to be without defects on one side. However, if it formats successfully, the media is probably okay on both sides. On the other hand, given how cheap disks are and how important what you put on them is, you may still prefer to throw out these disks.

BY THE WAY ▶

FORMATTING WITH DISK COPYING UTILITIES

Utilities such as MacTools Pro's FastCopy, Norton Utilities Floppier, and Apple's Disk Copy are mainly used (as their names imply) to make copies of floppy disks. If you decide to make a copy to an unformatted disk, they typically first format the disk (eliminating the need to separately use the Macintosh's built-in format functions, as described in the main text). Disk Copy is unusual in that it makes a copy without first separately formatting the disk. In essence, it copies the format information from the original disk as part of the copy process. This saves time when copying to unformatted disks (though at the risk of copying incorrect data if the original disk is damaged).

You can also use these utilities as efficient floppy disk formatters. For example, for FastCopy, select "Format Copies" from the FastCopy menu. With Floppier, click the turned page corner at the bottom of the window to shift from "Copy" mode (as seen in Figure F14-5) to "Format" mode (as seen in Figure F15-10).

Reformatting an Already Formatted Disk

Erase Disk   You can reformat a floppy disk at any time by selecting the disk and then selecting the Erase Disk command from the Finder's Special menu. A message similar to the Format alert message appears, asking you to confirm that you really want to completely erase the disk (see Figure F15-3). You can also rename the disk here. Click the Erase button and the format process begins. This formats the disk in exactly the same way as when the disk was first formatted. All information currently on the disk is completely erased and forever irretrievable! If you got here by mistake, click Cancel.

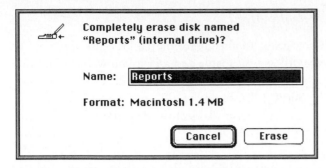

Figure F15-3 This message appears when you select Erase Disk for an already formatted 1.4Mb disk

Command-Option-Tab   As a shortcut to initiate reformatting, hold down the Command-Option-Tab keys prior to inserting a disk. Continue to hold down the keys when you insert the disk, until a message such as the one in Figure F15-4 appears. It appears before the disk is mounted.

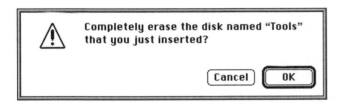

Figure F15-4 This message appears when you insert an already formatted disk while holding down the Command-Option-Tab keys

This shortcut is especially useful if there is a problem with the disk that results in a system crash when the Macintosh tries to mount the disk. By bypassing the mount attempt, you can still reformat the disk.

Reformatting Versus Deleting

Reformatting a floppy disk is an effective way to erase all files on the disk. As an alternative, you can delete all files from a disk by dragging them to the Trash and selecting Empty Trash from the Finder's Special menu. Although this is usually faster than reformatting the disk, I don't recommend it as a method for recycling a disk. Unlike reformatting, using Empty Trash does not rebuild the desktop, nor does it check for bad blocks. Thus, if there are problems with the disk, deleting the files with Empty Trash does not eliminate them—nor does it really erase the files. It only eliminates the references to the files in the disk's Directory, thus allowing the space occupied by the files to be used for new files as needed. This is why you can use undelete utilities (as described in Chapters 2 and 6) to recover files that have been deleted in the Trash.

Thus, in general, use the Erase Disk command to completely erase floppy disks. Only use Empty Trash if you want to preserve the chance to undelete files or if you want to delete selected files.

Unreadable or Damaged Disks That Really Aren't

HD Disk Inserted into 800K Drive   If you insert an already formatted HD disk into an 800K drive, a message appears that says the disk is unreadable and asks if you want to initialize it as an 800K disk (just as would appear if you inserted an unformatted 800K disk). *Don't do it!* Doing so indeed formats the disk (as an 800K disk). However, this means you have just permanently erased any and all the data on the disk. Instead, eject the disk and reinsert it into a SuperDrive. All will be fine.

HD Disk Formatted as an 800K Disk   If you insert an HD disk into an 800K drive and mistakenly format it as an 800K disk, it will perform just fine—as long as it is used in an 800K drive. However, you *cannot* use the disk in a SuperDrive (even though the SuperDrive recognizes ordinary 800K disks)! When you insert such a disk into a SuperDrive, the Macintosh gets confused by the conflicting signals of an 800K format versus the extra hole in the HD disk (which indicates it should be a 1.44Mb formatted disk). The result is that the Macintosh displays an error message saying that the disk is improperly formatted and asking if you want to initialize it (such as the one in Figure F15-5). Do not do this unless you do not care to save the data on the disk!

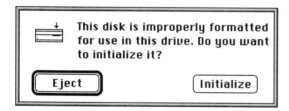

Figure F15-5   This message appears when you insert an HD disk, formatted as an 800K disk, into a SuperDrive

To save data on the disk, eject the disk. The disk still works fine in an 800K drive, so put the disk in an 800K drive and copy any data from the disk to another (properly formatted) disk. Then reinsert the problem disk in a SuperDrive and click Initialize when the message appears. It will now properly format as a 1.44Mb disk.

If you do not have an 800K drive available, you can try an alternative, although somewhat riskier, procedure. *Carefully* tape a piece of paper over the hole that the Macintosh uses to recognize that it is an HD disk (the one without a tab in the rear of the hole). If you now insert it into a SuperDrive, the Macintosh treats it as an ordinary 800K disk. Be careful that the paper or tape does not dislodge and get caught inside the drive! Once again, transfer the data to another disk. Then eject the disk, remove the tape, and reformat the disk as an HD disk.

Macintoshes Unable to Recognize 400K Disks   Newer Macintosh models (from around the Macintosh Classic onward) no longer format or read 400K disks. If you insert a 400K disk into such a computer, it will not mount. If you need to recover the files from this disk, use a Macintosh model that does recognize 400K disks. Once the disk is mounted, transfer the data from the 400K disk to an 800K or HD disk. Then you can discard the 400K disk.

PC-Formatted Disks   PC computers (IBM computers and clones) now use the same HD disks as do Macintoshes. Unless you have special software installed (such as Macintosh PC Exchange), if you insert a PC-formatted HD disk into a disk drive, the Macintosh will not recognize this disk, saying that the disk is unreadable and asking if you want to initialize it. Again, do not initialize the disk or you will erase any data on the disk. If you need to mount this disk on a Macintosh, read on.

Macintosh PC Exchange and PC-Formatted Disks

Macintosh PC Exchange is a control panel that allows PC-formatted disks, when inserted into a SuperDrive, to be mounted on the Finder's desktop just as if they were Macintosh-formatted disks. PC Exchange also allows you to format disks in PC-DOS (as well as Apple II's ProDOS) formats, in case you need to create a disk to be used on these other machines. Thus, when you insert an unformatted HD disk, you will receive the message seen in Figure F15-6. The box is similar to the one in the top of Figure F15-1, except that you now have a pop-up menu of choices for how you want the disk to be formatted (you will get a comparable set of options when inserting an 800K disk). You get these same additional pop-up menu options, in a box similar to the one in Figure F15-3, if you select to erase any already formatted disk via the Erase Disk command.

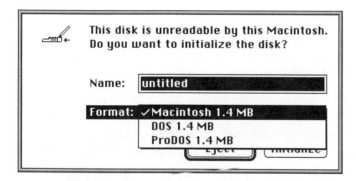

Figure F15-6   This message appears when you insert an unformatted HD disk into a SuperDrive with Macintosh PC Exchange active

Although rarely done, PC Exchange can also be used to mount PC-formatted hard disks. If you need to do this, consult the documentation that came with the software or seek other outside help.

By the way, PC Exchange can also be used to help automate the Finder-level opening of PC-formatted documents into Macintosh applications, assuming that the application in question is capable of reading the particular document. This was described briefly in Chapter 6 (in the "When You Can't Open a Document" section).

Other utilities (such as AccessPC) have similar capabilities to PC Exchange. But, as Macintosh PC Exchange is now included as standard with System 7.5, it will be the method of choice for most users.

Damaged Disks

Occasionally, when you insert a disk, you may get a message that says a disk is *unreadable* (as in Figure F15-1), is *not a Macintosh disk* (see Figure F15-7), is *damaged,* or *cannot be used* (see Chapter 5, Figure 5-14), even though you know you have previously correctly formatted the disk. In this case, you probably do have a damaged disk. If you do not need to recover the data on the disk, you can immediately try to reformat it. If it reformats without a problem, it is probably okay (but see "Verifying Disks and Media Damage," later in this Fix-It). Otherwise, discard the disk. Alternatively, if you do need to recover files from the disk, see Fix-It #14. Also, refer to Chapter 5 for a general discussion of problems with floppy disks that do not mount.

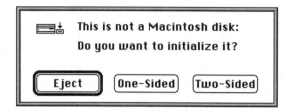

Figure F15-7   One of several messages that may appear when you try to mount a damaged disk

Hard Disks

Formatting and Reformatting in General

You may be surprised to learn that hard disks need to be formatted just like floppy disks. Because most hard disks come preformatted and, in many cases, never have to be reformatted, many users have no experience with formatting hard disks. However, as described in the "Why to do it" section, sometimes you want to reformat a hard disk (for example, if a hard disk is damaged in a way that your data recovery utilities cannot remedy).

To format or reformat a hard disk or removable cartridge, you need a special disk-formatting utility. One such utility, Apple HD SC Setup, is included with the Macintosh system software disks. Typically, if you have a third-party hard drive, you should have received a comparable utility when you purchased the drive unit (such as APS PowerTools, that ships with all APS drives). Finally, you may separately purchase a universal formatting utility, such as Drive7 or Hard Disk ToolKit, which can be used with virtually any drive you own, including Apple drives. All of these alternatives to HD SC Setup offer more options than the rather minimal-feature Apple utility. Using universal utilities can be especially desirable if you own several hard drives from different sources and you want to use the same formatting utility for all of them (which Apple officially recommends that you do).

Always make sure you are using the latest version of these utilities. At the very least, your version of Apple HD SC Setup should come from the same disks that were used to install the system software on your hard disk.

The major functions of these utilities are the same, no matter which one you use. These include formatting the hard drive, updating the device driver, partitioning the disk, and testing the drive for media damage. Additional functions may include checking the performance of the drive and other special features designed to increase speed (such as disk caches) or assist in troubleshooting.

Ideally, you should have a current backup of the data on your disk (as explained in Chapter 2) before reformatting, unless you no longer care to save the data. However, if your disk is damaged, you may not be able to perform a needed backup (in this case, refer to Fix-Its #13 and #14 for advice).

SEE: • Fix-It #12, on updating disk device drivers, for a general introduction to these different types of formatting utilities and why you might switch from one to another

Reformatting Using Apple HD SC Setup

Apple HD SC Setup can be used to format or reformat only an Apple-label disk drive (and even then, only if the disk has not been previously reformatted by some other formatting utility). This is because Apple encodes special instructions on to its hard drives that Apple HD SC Setup then checks when it is launched. If it does not find this code, which is present only on Apple drives, it does not list the drive.

To reformat a disk with Apple HD SC Setup:

1. Start up with a disk other than the disk you want to reformat. If you intend to reformat your normal startup hard disk, restart with the Disk Tools disk that came with your current system software (or your own customized Emergency Toolkit disk or any other startup disk that contains Apple HD SC Setup) as the startup disk.

2. Launch Apple HD SC Setup and select the desired drive, using the Drive button (refer to Figure F12-2).

3. Click Initialize. This selection formats, initializes, and verifies the disk in one step. When it is done, quit Apple HD SC Setup.

4. Most likely, the reformatted disk will not be mounted (that is, it will not yet appear on your desktop). If so, simply restart the Macintosh. The disk should now mount and function normally. If desired, you can instead mount the disk manually prior to restarting, by using a utility such as SCSIProbe (as explained in Chapter 5 and Fix-It #16).

5. If the reformatted disk was your normal startup disk, it obviously needs to have the system software reinstalled before it can serve as a startup disk again. To do this, either restore the contents of the disk from your backups (using a startup disk that contains your backup utility) or start fresh with a new set of system software (using the system software's Installer disk as the startup disk, as detailed in Fix-It #5). In either case, restart when finished.

Reformatting Using Other Formatting Utilities

To reformat non-Apple hard disks, you would usually use the formatting utility that came with your hard drive. Alternatively, you can use a universal formatting utility, as described previously, for almost any hard disk, including Apple disks. All of these utilities tend to work similarly. For example, to use Drive7:

1. Start up with a disk that contains Drive7. This disk should obviously not be the one you want to reformat.

2. Launch Drive7 and select the name of the drive you want to format.

3. Click the Format button (refer to Figure F12-2). That's it. Reformatting also initializes and verifies the drive (as is generally the case with any of these utilities).

4. If needed, select "Mount SCSI Devices" from Drive7's Functions menu in order to mount the reformatted drive. You can then quit Drive7.

To set up the disk as a startup disk, refer to Step 5 in the previous section on Apple HD SC Setup.

TECHNICALLY SPEAKING ▶

TROUBLESHOOTING DRIVE7

If you are having problems using Drive7 to format a drive, here are some suggestions. The logic described here also applies to other formatting utilities:

- *Start up with extensions off (not relevant if you are starting up from a floppy disk).*

- *If a system crash occurs when using Drive7 to format a drive that had been previously formatted with a different utility, restart the Macintosh. This time, do not turn on the drive until after you have launched Drive7. To bypass an internal drive at startup, hold down the Command-Option-Shift-Delete keys at startup (see Chapter 5, "Starting with an Alternate Startup Disk," for more on this). After launching Drive7 (and turning on the drive), if the problem drive's name does not appear in the list, select "Rescan SCSI Bus" from the Functions menu. Once the drive is listed, try to format it as usual.*

- *If Drive7 does not list a drive that has been formatted with a different utility, the drive is probably incompatible with Drive7. In this case, you are out of luck. You cannot reformat this drive with Drive7. Stick to the original utility used to format the drive or try another universal formatting utility.*

Drive7 has numerous other options not covered here; consult the Drive7 manual for details.

TECHNICALLY SPEAKING ▶

FORMATTING IDE DRIVES

IDE (Integrated Drive Electronics) hard drives are a new type of drive that are a lower-cost alternative to SCSI-based drives. They are now showing up on selected models of Macintosh, such as the Macintosh 630 and the PowerBook 150. Newest versions of Apple HD SC Setup may work with these drives. Otherwise, you can format IDE drives with a new Apple utility, called Internal Drive Setup Utility, reportedly included with the Macs that ship with an IDE drive. Also, all of the Macintosh 630 models automatically initialize an uninitialized IDE drive at startup, allowing you to use a non-Apple IDE drive as a replacement for Apple's drive. Other formatting utilities will likely have to be rewritten to accommodate this new drive type. Check with the company that made your utility for specifics.

SEE: • **Fix-It #16 for more on SCSI and IDE drives**

Reformatting Versus Erasing Versus Deleting

Never use the Finder's Erase Disk command to format a fixed or removable cartridge hard disk. If the disk has never been formatted, it will not correctly format the disk. If it has been formatted, it will not truly reformat it. Erase Disk is only for floppy disks.

For formatted hard disks, Erase Disk erases only the Directory, replacing it with an empty one. The net result is that the Macintosh, after checking the Directory, now considers the disk to be empty. This is similar to what would happen if you selected all the files on the disk, placed them in the Trash, and deleted them using "Empty Trash." That's why recovery utilities can restore a hard disk accidentally erased via the Erase Disk command (as explained in Fix-It #13). Restoring an erased hard disk is functionally similar to using a utility (such as Norton Utilities' UnErase) to undelete files deleted via Empty Trash (as discussed in Chapters 2 and 6). In both cases, this is possible because the deleted files are still intact, despite the fact that they are not listed in the Directory.

Partition the Disk

A hard drive can be subdivided into separate *partitions.* These partitions then act as if they are totally separate disks (technically, each partition is referred to as a separate *volume*). Each one mounts separately and has its own icon.

Helpful hint: Partitioning a disk typically requires reformatting the disk and thus erases all data currently on it. So be careful!

Partitioning a disk is not required, and many users choose never to partition their drive. I would not even consider partitioning a drive unless it is at least 160Mb. Still, there are two main advantages to partitioning larger-capacity drives.

Speed   Partitioning can improve disk access speed. For example, a fragmented file (as described in Fix-It #8) always has all of its fragments contained within a single partition. Thus, when trying to open a fragmented file, the Mac will have less "distance" to go to search for fragments if it only has to search within an 80Mb partition of a 250Mb drive than if it has to search within the entire 250Mb drive. However, this speed advantage is diminished if you use your partitions in such a way as to require the Mac to frequently traverse partitions. For example, if your application is in one partition and your document is in another, the speed advantage will be less than if both files are in the same partition.

File Size   A "feature" of the current Macintosh operating system is that the minimum amount of disk space that a file requires gets larger as the size of the drive gets larger. For example, the minimum file size on a 120Mb drive is 2K. For a 720Mb drive, the minimum is 12K. Thus, a 2K text file would take up only 2K of disk space on a 120Mb drive but would require 12K of space on a 720Mb drive (wasting 10K). For any file, no matter what its size, disk space requirements increase in increments of the minimal file size. Thus, a 13K file would require 14K of disk space on a 120Mb drive (2K x 7 = 14K) but would require 24K on a 720Mb drive (12K x 2 = 24K), again wasting 10K. Thus, if you have a large capacity drive with a lot of small files on it, you are probably wasting a significant amount of disk space. The solution to this is to partition the drive. The minimum file size for a partition is a function of the size of the partition, not the size of the entire drive!

If you decide to partition your disk, you cannot use the current version of Apple HD SC Setup. Its Partition button is used to create only a special type of partition that (unless you know about and use A/UX, a Unix-based operating system) you will not want to use. (However, for the more adventuresome among you, there is a freeware utility, called Setup Partitions, with which you can create standard partitions using Apple HD SC Setup).

An updated version of HD SC Setup, expected in the not-too-distant future, should remedy this partition limitation. In the meantime, your only alternative is to use another formatting utility. For example, to use Drive7 to divide a drive into two equal-sized partitions:

1. Start up with a disk that contains Drive7. This disk should not be the one you want to partition.
2. Launch Drive7 and select the name of the drive you want to format/partition.
3. Click the Partition button (refer to Figure F12-2).
4. Select "2 Macintosh OS" from the Partition Style scrollable list (see Figure F15-8) and click OK.
5. Click the Format button.
6. Quit Drive7 and restart. (If you want one of the partitions to be the startup volume, you will next need to install system software on it.)

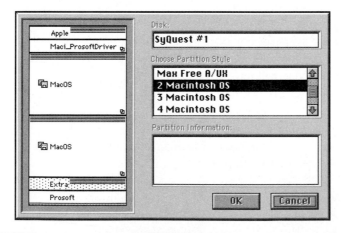

Figure F15-8 Drive7's Partitions dialog box

If you select "Partition Options" from Drive7's Options menu, you can set such options as whether or not you want a partition to mount automatically at startup and which partition you want to be used as the startup partition (should you choose to use the drive as the startup drive). This latter option is needed because Apple's Startup Disk control panel cannot select among partitions of the same drive (as discussed more in Chapter 5, "The Startup Disk Control Panel: Changing the Default Startup Selection" in the "What Determines Which Disk Is the Startup Disk" section). You can change these options, even after partitioning has been completed, without erasing any other data on the drive.

BY THE WAY ▶

HARD AND SOFT PARTITIONS

Formatting utilities like Drive7 create what is called a hard partition. *This requires reformatting the disk (thereby erasing any data on it) and is thus a true format-level dividing up of the disk.*

In contrast, certain partition-making utilities use a soft partition *method to divide the disk. This does not require reformatting the disk (meaning you may not have to erase data to create the partitions). However, these partitions depend on a system extension's being present. This means that the partitions may "disappear" if the extension is not active. Soft partitions are really a way of fooling the Macintosh into thinking that true partitions have been created, when in fact they have not. In general, I would avoid using soft partitions. In any case, this method is no longer popular and utilities that use it appear to be fading from the scene.*

TECHNICALLY SPEAKING ▶

WHAT'S AN INTERLEAVE?

You may have heard that changing something called the interleave factor on your hard disk can improve its speed. The basic idea is this: Hard disks are constantly spinning from the moment they are turned on. A drive "reads" requested data from this spinning disk as the relevant portion of the disk passes by the disk's drive head. In some cases, especially with older drives, the drive cannot read data from the disk as fast as the disk can spin by the drive head. This means the drive has to wait for the next revolution of the disk to read the next sector of data, which can slow things down. Changing the interleave factor alters the way data are written to a disk so that it partially compensates for this problem (essentially, it spaces out data so that the drive does not have to read from contiguous sectors; related sectors are spaced far enough apart so that the drive can read data from them without having to skip over and return to them on subsequent revolutions). The result is that performance speed improves.

The ideal is for the drive to read fast enough to use an interleave factor of 1 (this means that the drive can keep up with the rate of spinning). All current drives are fast enough to do this and come preformatted with a interleave factor of 1. Slower drives similarly come preformatted with an interleave that is optimal for that drive (it could be 2 or 3, for example). When formatting a disk, most utilities are smart enough to pick the optimal factor for that drive. Thus, in most cases, you should be able to ignore this interleave issue entirely.

However, if you have an older model of Mac (especially a Mac Plus), the transfer rate is slowed down by the Mac itself. In such cases, you may get better performance from a fast drive by changing its interleave factor from 1 to a higher (slower) factor. However, even here, the drive may use a "cache" to compensate for the slower transfer rate, eliminating the need to change the interleave factor (see Fix-It #6, "By the Way: Driver-Level Versus System-Level Disk Caches").

If you have determined that changing the interleave factor is desirable for your hardware, you can do so with Apple HD SC Setup by typing Command-I. With Drive7, the interleave setting is accessed via the dialog box that appears after selecting "Format Options" from the Options menu.

Changing the interleave factor requires that you reformat the drive.

Verifying Disks and Media Damage

Verifying a disk means checking each sector (block) on the disk to make sure that no media damage (bad blocks) exists. Usually, this is done automatically whenever a disk is formatted, although there are ways in which you can choose to do this at other times. Typically, if bad blocks are detected, they are *marked (mapped out* or *spared)* so that they cannot be used in the future. If successful, this allows the disk to verify despite the bad blocks. Otherwise, the verification fails. For more specific details, read on.

For Floppy Disks

Using the Macintosh to Verify When you format a floppy disk, such as with the Finder's Erase Disk command, the Macintosh automatically verifies it.

In System 7, if any media damage is detected during the verification, the disk is verified a second time, during which any bad blocks detected are spared. When this happens, a new message appears during the formatting process. In system software versions prior to System 7.5, the message will say *Reverifying the disk.* In System 7.5 or a later version, the message should read *Updating disk.* Reverification takes much longer than the initial verification. Reverification usually succeeds unless there are too many bad blocks or the damage is in the critical area of the disk needed to store the Directory. In these cases, you get a message that says *Initialization failed* (see Figure F15-9). If this happens, it's time to discard this disk. Actually, I take a conservative approach and discard any floppy disk that needs to be reverified, even if it ultimately formats successfully. In my experience, once bad blocks appear on a floppy disk, the probability increases that more will appear soon. Why take chances?

Figure F15-9 **This message appears if the Macintosh is unable to verify a floppy disk that it is attempting to format**

Occasionally, I have had a disk problem that appeared to be due to bad blocks (such as a write error when copying a file). Yet when I reformatted the disk, it surprisingly formatted successfully without any reverification needed. I am more optimistic about the continued use of such a disk than those that require reverification. However, the cause may well be an intermittent bad block problem that will inevitably soon return. So be cautious.

System 6 has no reverification process. Whenever a disk with media damage is detected, you get the *Initialization failed* message. Again, if this happens, discard the disk.

If you begin to have problems with many or all disks failing to verify, there is probably a problem with the floppy drive mechanism.

Using Other Utilities to Verify   Floppy disk formatting utilities (such as Norton Utilities' Floppier or MacTools Pro's FastCopy) also verify a disk when formatting it. They typically do not spare bad blocks. If damage is detected, the initialization fails (as with System 6's Finder). Floppier, however, has an option to format a disk without verifying it. To do this, unmark the Verify checkbox (as marked in Figure F15-10). Generally, I recommend against doing this—it saves time, but it is riskier. Without verifying, you may wind up inadvertently using a damaged disk.

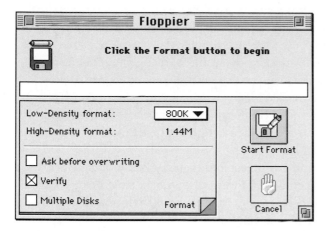

Figure F15-10   Format options for Norton Utilities' Floppier, with the Verify option selected

Conversely, with utilities such as MacTools Pro's DiskFix or Norton Utilities' Disk Doctor, you can verify a disk without having to format it. To do this, use the commands for checking the disk media (as described in Fix-It #14, "Resolve Problems with Bad Blocks"). These utilities *can* mark any detected bad blocks, similarly to how System 7's verification works. Still, if bad blocks are detected, I would discard the disk.

For Hard Disks

Testing a Hard Disk   Most disk-formatting utilities can test a hard disk for bad blocks without having to reformat the disk. To do so with Apple HD SC Setup, click the Test button (refer to Figure F12-2). For Drive7, select "Test Drive" from its Functions menu.

Recovery utilities, such as MacTools Pro's DiskFix or Norton Utilities' Disk Doctor, can similarly check a disk for bad blocks (as described in Fix-It #14, "Resolve Problems with Bad Blocks"). Recovery utilities can map out any bad blocks that they detect. In contrast, the Test functions of format utilities generally can only identify bad blocks. To map out the bad blocks with a format utility, you must reformat the disk (erasing all data on the disk). In any case, testing for bad blocks can take several minutes or more. Be prepared to wait.

Mapping Out Bad Blocks   If media damage is detected with a format utility, you should reformat the disk. Reformatting maps out the damaged areas so that they can no longer be used. When you format a disk with utilities such as Apple HD SC Setup or Drive7, bad blocks are detected and automatically mapped out during the verification stage. Unless an unusually large number of bad blocks exists (which would almost certainly indicate a more serious problem with the disk), the disk successfully formats and verifies.

If your hard disk formatting utility has an option to format without verifying (usually offered to save time), don't take it. Always verify to check for bad blocks when formatting a hard disk.

Although I recommend discarding floppy disks with bad blocks, even if the disk ultimately verifies, I obviously would not recommend this for hard disks! You would not want to discard an expensive drive unit for a single bad block, especially if the block is successfully mapped out.

A few bad blocks on a hard disk are no cause for concern, once they are mapped out. Actually, many new hard drives come with bad blocks already on them (mapped out before they were ever shipped from the factory). Still, if you are careful with the use of your hard drive, you may never have any bad blocks problems. Bad blocks are much more common with floppy disks. However, if new bad blocks frequently appear on a hard disk shortly after you have formatted it, you probably have a hardware problem. In this case, the disk drive needs to be repaired (if possible) or replaced.

Finally, although recovery utilities can similarly detect and map out bad blocks, reformatting is the most reliable method for permanently preventing these blocks from being used again (see Fix-It #14, "Repairing Bad Blocks: Recovery Utilities Versus Reformatting"). After you reformat, restore the disk's contents from your backups.

For related information

SEE: • Fix-It #6 on disk caches
      • Fix-It #12 on using formatting utilities to update the disk driver
      • Fix-Its #13 and #14 for more on bad blocks and using recovery utilities
      • Fix-It #16 on SCSI-related problems
      • Chapter 1 on basic terminology regarding disks
      • Chapter 5 on problems starting up and mounting drives

Fix-It #16:
Check for Problems with SCSI Devices and Connections

QUICK SUMMARY

Use a utility, such as SCSIProbe, to mount a SCSI device that will not otherwise mount. Check for other possible SCSI-related problems, such as ID conflicts, improper termination, or turning the SCSI device on or off improperly.

When to do it:

- When a SCSI device does not mount or does not function as expected. This includes fixed format disk drives, removable media cartridge drives, and CD-ROM drives.

- When multiple copies of the disk icon of a SCSI disk device appear scattered over the desktop.

- When a system crash or freeze occurs as a result of accessing a SCSI device. For example, when trying to open any or almost any file on an external drive or CD-ROM drive results in a system crash.

- When you cannot start up your Macintosh because a sad Mac appears.

- When you cannot start up your Macintosh because a system error occurs, particularly if the error occurs immediately after the Welcome to Macintosh message appears.

- When you lose access to all the external SCSI devices connected to your Macintosh.

- Whenever problems develop immediately after you add, remove, or rearrange the order of externally connected SCSI devices.

Why to do it:

Starting with the Macintosh Plus, all models of Macintosh have a port in the rear of the machine called the *SCSI port* or *SCSI bus* (where SCSI stands for Small Computer Systems Interface and is pronounced "scuzzy"). On desktop Macs, it is usually the large 25-pin port in the rear of the machine, under a symbol shaped like a diamond with a horizontal line drawn through one point (see Figure F16-1). On most PowerBooks it is a smaller, squarish, 30-pin port, under the same symbol.

Figure F16-1
The SCSI symbol

You need a SCSI port to connect certain devices to your Macintosh. These *SCSI devices* include external hard drives, CD-ROMs, tape backup devices, scanners, and certain printers. A special SCSI cable is used to connect the device to the Macintosh. Problems involving these devices can often be traced to problems with how these devices are connected, what cables are used, and settings on the SCSI device itself. These are the major subjects of this Fix-It.

Remember, many of the symptoms described here (such as system crashes) have other causes besides SCSI problems. These other causes are covered throughout this book, as appropriate.

What's a SCSI Chain?

Only one device can be connected directly to the SCSI port on the rear of the Macintosh. However, each external SCSI device is equipped with two SCSI ports. So, for example, if you connect an external hard drive to your Macintosh, this will still leave one SCSI port empty on your external drive. A second SCSI device can be connected to this port. This arrangement can continue, creating a *daisy chain* of SCSI devices. If all devices are connected correctly, the Macintosh will recognize all of them, even though only one device is actually plugged into the Mac.

What's the Problem?

Your Macintosh may be running smoothly right now. But whenever you add or remove a SCSI device, your Macintosh could come to a halt. The probability of this happening multiplies as you attach more devices. The source of most of these problems revolves around two important SCSI requirements: unique ID numbers and proper termination.

SCSI ID Numbers   Each SCSI device has an ID number. The Macintosh uses these numbers to differentiate one SCSI device from another. ID numbers can range from 0 to 7. ID 7 is reserved for the Macintosh (which, despite its number, is technically not part of the SCSI chain). ID 0 is reserved for internal hard drives (which *are* considered part of the SCSI chain).

Thus, you can attach up to *seven* SCSI devices to one Macintosh. With an internal hard drive, you can connect six external SCSI devices, with ID numbers from 1 to 6.

Some Macintoshes can have more than one internal SCSI device (such as both an internal hard drive and a CD-ROM drive). Each device will have its own ID number (internal CD-ROM drives, for example, should have their ID number set to 3).

You assign the ID number to each external device. Usually, you do this by pressing a button located somewhere on the device. Each time you press the button, you cycle to another ID number, which should be indicated in a display next to the button. The number currently in the display is the ID number for that device. These ID numbers do not have to be assigned in the order that the devices are connected. For example, the first external device in a chain could have an ID of 4, and the second device could have an ID of 2.

All other things equal, assign ID numbers based on how often you use a device, giving higher ID numbers (where six is higher than five, for example) to those external devices that you use more often. The device with the higher number is given priority when two devices are simultaneously competing for access to the SCSI bus.

The most important rule to remember is that each device must have a different ID number. To repeat: **No two devices can have the same ID number.** Otherwise, problems will certainly result (as detailed in the "What to do" section).

BY THE WAY ▶

SCSI MANAGER 4.3 AND SCSI-2

- *SCSI Manager 4.3.* SCSI Manager is the name of the instruction set used by the Macintosh to interact with SCSI devices. A version of the Manager is built into the ROM of all Macintoshes. SCSI Manager 4.3 is the latest version of this instruction set. It is included in the ROM of the Macintosh Quadra 660AV, 840AV, all Power Macs, 500 series PowerBooks (and most likely other machines that have been released since I wrote this!). It adds new features to the SCSI bus, including faster data transfer rates.

    Certain other models of Macintosh, including most other Quadra and Centris models, can also use SCSI Manager 4.3. However, they require that you install a SCSI Manager 4.3 extension (which is used instead of the older version in ROM). This extension is available free from Apple. It is also included as part of System 7.5 and with System 7.5 Update 1.0.

    Beyond this, advice about when to use or not use the SCSI Manager 4.3 extension can get murky. Apple has at times advised removing this extension on those Macs that already have SCSI Manager 4.3 in ROM (such as Power Macs), because of possible conflicts. On other occasions, they have stated that leaving the extension should have no effect. Similarly, for those older Macintosh models that cannot use SCSI Manager 4.3, installing the extension should have no effect. The Mac should simply ignore it. But even here, there have been reports of conflicts occurring if you install the extension. Finally, even on those Macs that definitely take advantage of the extension, problems are known to occur. For example, the extension may conflict with the use of virtual memory and with the operation of some formatting utilities.

    Thus, the bottom line here is that unless you have a Mac that can use SCSI Manager 4.3 and doesn't already have it in ROM, your best bet is not to install the extension at all. If you do install it and it appears to precipitate any problems, you should probably get rid of it.

    However, this advice is somewhat tempered by the fact that there are different versions of the SCSI Manager 4.3 extension. The version that ships with System 7.5 is technically an update to the original version in the ROM of the 660AV and 840AV. The version included with System 7.5 Update 1.0 is a still newer version that is an upgrade to the version in ROM for all preexisting Mac models. Conventional wisdom appears to be that you should use these upgraded extensions on models that support SCSI Manager 4.3 to assure that you are using the latest version of the Manager.

    One final caution: SCSI Manager 4.3 is incompatible with early versions of RAM Doubler. Use at least version 1.5.1 of RAM Doubler to avoid this conflict.

- *SCSI-2.* SCSI-2 is a new SCSI standard for data transfer that should also increase transfer speed. This will require a new SCSI-2 port that is included with certain recent models of Macintosh. Another advantage of SCSI-2 is that it allows many more than seven devices to be attached to a chain. The Mac may even have two separate SCSI bus ports. To accommodate this, a new ID numbering system has been introduced. With SCSI-2, each device has a three-digit ID (called the long ID). The old ID numbers are called the short ID. For example, short ID 3 is now long ID 0.3.0.

    To take full advantage of these new features, assuming your Mac has the appropriate hardware, may also require updating your disk device driver (see Fix-It #12).

SCSI Termination   SCSI termination may sound like what you want to do to a drive that has just crashed for the third time this week, but it is nothing of the kind. But SCSI termination is a messy topic, so let me disentangle it for you.

I am the first to admit that I don't really know the nuts and bolts of what termination is all about. Fortunately, to fix most termination problems, you don't have to know very much.

Essentially, termination tells the Mac where a SCSI bus begins and ends, preventing signals from getting mixed up by reaching the end of a chain and bouncing back again. It is also important for keeping signal strength at an appropriate level and maintaining transmission speed at all locations across your cables. The longer your chain, the more likely it is that termination problems will appear.

That said, **the main thing you need to know is that a typical SCSI chain needs to be terminated at both ends of the chain.** Most Macintoshes with internal drives are considered terminated at the Macintosh end. So, in those cases, all you need to do is make sure the opposite (external device) end of the chain is terminated. The most common method to do this is to get a special SCSI plug called a *terminator*. It looks like an ordinary SCSI plug with no cable attached. Simply plug it in to the second (empty) port on the last SCSI device in a chain, and you are done.

If you have no external SCSI devices attached, you can skip this whole discussion. If you have two or more external SCSI devices attached, you will likely need to be concerned about termination issues. More details are given in the "What to do" section of this Fix-It (see "Make Sure All SCSI Devices Are Properly Terminated").

 What to do:

This Fix-It addresses two main topics: Using a SCSI utility and SCSI-related problems.

Using a SCSI Utility

A nearly essential tool when working with SCSI devices is a SCSI utility. An excellent popular (and free!) SCSI utility is the SCSIProbe control panel. I will use it for most of the examples described here. Some hard disk formatting utilities (as described in Fix-It #15) can double as an SCSI utility. These may also include a companion control panel that functions similarly to SCSIProbe.

The primary use of any SCSI utility is to mount SCSI devices. There are two common occasions when you would need to do this: when you need to mount a SCSI device turned on after startup is completed and when a properly connected mountable SCSI device, turned on at startup but not the startup disk, does not mount automatically. Here's how to accomplish these tasks with SCSIProbe.

Mounting SCSI Devices with SCSIProbe

1. Make sure the SCSI device you want to mount is turned on and the cables are securely fastened in their respective ports. SCSIProbe can recognize only devices that are turned on.

   If you are having any trouble securing a plug to a SCSI port, check for bent connecting wires on the end of the plug. If you find any, straighten them and try again. If a wire breaks off, you have to replace the cable. Remember: Only disconnect and connect cables when the Macintosh is off.

2. Open SCSIProbe. A window appears that lists every active device connected to your SCSI chain (see Figure F16-2). Each device is listed next to its assigned ID number. This will help right away to identify a possible ID number conflict!

   All devices, whether mounted or not, should be listed here. SCSIProbe also lists the type of each device, such as whether it is a hard disk *(disk)* or CD-ROM *(ROM)* drive.

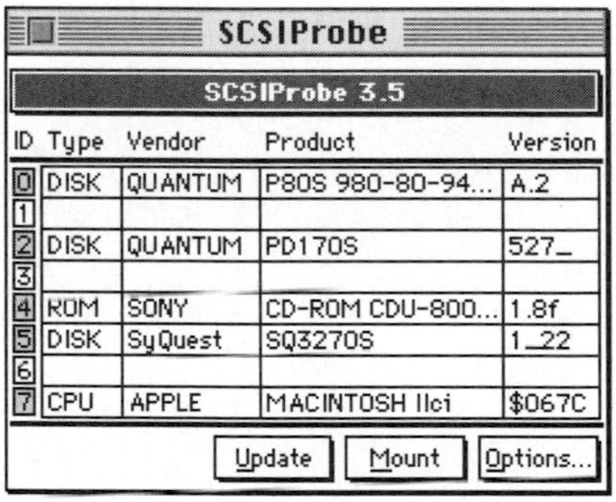

ID	Type	Vendor	Product	Version
0	DISK	QUANTUM	P80S 980-80-94...	A.2
1				
2	DISK	QUANTUM	PD170S	527_
3				
4	ROM	SONY	CD-ROM CDU-800...	1.8f
5	DISK	SyQuest	SQ3270S	1_22
6				
7	CPU	APPLE	MACINTOSH IIci	$067C

Update | Mount | Options...

Figure F16-2 SCSIProbe's main window

BY THE WAY ▶

SCSIPROBE AND SCSI MANAGER 4.3/SCSI-2

For Macintosh models that support multiple SCSI buses via SCSI Manager 4.3/SCSI-2, you can use SCSIProbe to limit your options to just one bus (internal or external) at a time. To choose a bus, click on "ID" and select a bus from the pop-up menu. If the "Both" option is selected, the Mac's SCSI Manager will determine the appropriate bus. If no pop-up menu appears when you click ID, it means your Mac does not support multiple buses.

3. If the device you want to mount is not listed, click the Update button. This button forces SCSIProbe to rescan the SCSI bus and locate any devices that it may have missed when it initially opened. Unless your device is damaged or improperly connected (as described in the next section "SCSI-Related Problems"), it should be listed now.

4. Click the Mount button. Within a few seconds, all SCSI devices in the list that can be mounted should now appear on the desktop.

   By the way, SCSIProbe provides an optional shortcut option for accessing its Mount function. To set this up, first click the Options button. From the dialog box that then appears (see Figure F16-3), select *Install Volume Mounting INIT.* You can then designate your desired Mount Key shortcut in the space provided (Command-Space is the default choice). After this, quit SCSIProbe and restart. Now, whenever you press the Mount Key combination, SCSIProbe immediately (without opening the control panel) attempts to mount all available but presently unmounted devices.

5. Close SCSIProbe. You're done.

Figure F16-3   SCSIProbe's Options window

TECHNICALLY SPEAKING ▶

SCSIPROBE AND PRODUCT LISTINGS

SCSIProbe displays the vendor and product name of each device. These names are not what you might expect to find. For example, Quantum is a popular manufacturer of hard drive devices. Quantum drives are placed in the cases of many different companies that sell hard drives to consumers. Thus, though the outside of your external hard drive may say APS (or whatever other brand you own), the mechanism inside the case may be a Quantum, and the Quantum name is listed as the vendor. Apple's internal drives are often Quantum drives. You may be more surprised to learn that some Apple drives are actually manufactured by IBM!

If SCSIProbe Lists, But Doesn't Mount, a Device

There are two common explanations for why SCSIProbe would list, yet be unable to mount, a SCSI device. These explanations apply to any situation where a SCSI device does not mount as expected, whether you are using SCSIProbe or not.

- **The device isn't supposed to mount**
  Certain SCSI devices, such as scanners and tape backup devices, typically do not mount on the desktop under any circumstances. Clicking SCSIProbe's Mount button does not change this fact. As long as the devices are listed in SCSIProbe's window, they should be okay. In some cases, if SCSIProbe cannot identify the device, it is listed only with the phrase *No Data* for the appropriate ID number line (see Figure F16-4). This does not necessarily indicate any problem.

  When you launch an application designed to work with an unmounted SCSI device, the presence of the device is recognized by the application. Thus, some backup software programs (such as Retrospect) can access an unmounted tape backup device (assuming that the particular brand and model is included among the list of devices compatible with the program). Check your software's manual for details.

- **Problems with the device driver: Hard disks and removable cartridges**
  For a fixed hard disk, or a removable cartridge to mount, it needs a disk driver. Normally, this is not a problem, as the driver is typically installed when the disk is initialized. However, problems mounting the disk can occur if the driver becomes damaged.

SEE: • Fix-It #12 for more on disk drivers, including what to do to fix a suspected damaged driver

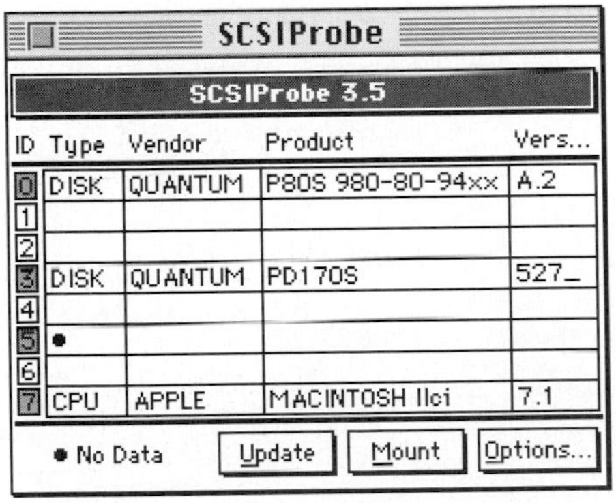

Figure F16-4   SCSIProbe's No Data message means it could not properly identify the device

For removable media disk cartridges, since different cartridges may use different drivers, you may experience special problems when switching from one cartridge to another.

SEE: • "Take Note: Mounting Removable Media Cartridges with Different Drivers" for details

MOUNTING REMOVABLE MEDIA CARTRIDGES WITH DIFFERENT DRIVERS

Removable media cartridges (such as used with SyQuest and Bernoulli drives) present a special problem. As with fixed hard disks, each cartridge contains its own device driver, an invisible software file necessary for the Macintosh to interact with the disk (see Fix-It #12 for more on device drivers).

When you first insert a cartridge into a removable media drive, at startup or afterward, its driver is copied from the disk and loaded into RAM. It is the RAM copy that is actually used. If you switch cartridges after startup, you may be switching to a cartridge that uses a different driver from the one initially present. This could happen if the cartridges were formatted using different format utilities (see Fix-It #15 for more on formatting utilities), as might especially be the case if you are using cartridges obtained from sources other than yourself.

The problem here is that, when you switch cartridges, the Macintosh may not automatically replace the RAM copy of the initial driver with the driver now needed for the newly inserted cartridge. Thus, a conflict occurs because the Macintosh attempts to use the wrong driver (the one from the previous cartridge) to interact with the current cartridge. This can cause various problems, including an inability to mount the cartridge or a loss of data from the cartridge. The simplest solution to this problem is to make sure that all of your cartridges use the same driver. If this is not possible, consider using a utility such as one of the following:

- *SCSIProbe.   Recent versions of SCSIProbe have an Options dialog box that lists an option called Close Driver After Ejecting. This causes the driver from the ejected cartridge to be removed from memory, forcing a newly inserted cartridge's own driver to be used instead. However, note that with some older versions of SCSIProbe, the utility may treat an ejected floppy disk as if it were an ejectable cartridge. This can result in the mistaken closing of the driver for a still remaining drive (fixed or removable), leading to a system crash.*

- *Drive7/Mount Cache.   Drive7, a disk formatting utility from Casa Blanca Works, provides a control panel, called* Mount Cache *(formerly* Drive7rem*). It loads a single driver at startup that is compatible with almost all removable media drives. This driver acts as a universal driver, bypassing a cartridge's own unique driver, thereby preventing the potential conflict. To use Mount Cache most effectively, the removable media drive should be on at startup, but without any cartridges inserted until after startup is over (which is possible only if the drive is not used as a startup drive). This prevents a possible conflict between Mount Cache and the cartridge's own driver both trying to load (though, if this happens, Mount Cache is designed to automatically disable itself). Ideally, to prevent conflicts, Mount Cache should load early in the startup sequence. To do this, either create an alias of Mount Cache and place it in the Extensions folder or use a startup management utility to change its loading order (see Fix-It #4).*

  To activate Mount Cache you must first separately select each drive you wish to use it with. You do this by clicking each desired drive from the control panel (which then places a checkmark next to its name) and then restarting. This allows you to use Mount Cache with any subset of your SCSI devices that you wish.

The formatting software that came with your hard drive may have similar functions to these two utilities. Check it out.

Finally, here's the scoop on a few related problems involving removable cartridge drives:

- *PC-formatted disks and PC Exchange.   If you are trying to use PC Exchange to mount a PC-formatted removable media cartridge (or fixed hard drive for that matter), do not let the disk's driver get installed. Instead, click the Options button from the PC Exchange control panel. Select the relevant SCSI device (such as a SyQuest drive) from the list and then restart. This causes the PC Exchange driver to be used in lieu of the disk's PC-based driver.*

- *Drivers as extensions.   Years ago, some removable cartridge systems used a startup extension (installed in your System Folder) as the disk driver (similar to how CD-ROM drivers work even now), rather than keeping a copy of the driver on the cartridge itself and loading the driver when the cartridge mounts. If you use a cartridge like this, you cannot use a utility such as SCSIProbe to mount the cartridge since these utilities look for a driver on the cartridge. If you have a recent drive but for some reason still need to work with these older-style cartridges, the best solution, if possible, is to reformat the cartridge, updating it to accommodate the new style of driver.*

(continued)

SEE: • Chapter 5, "Special Case: Problems Mounting Removable Media Cartridges" in the "A Hard Disk Won't Mount" section, for a more general discussion of these problems

• **Problems with the device driver: CD-ROM drives and other devices.**   With CD-ROM drives, the device driver is typically a startup extension, installed in the Extensions folder of your System Folder. It remains active no matter what CD-ROM disks you eject or insert. The specific driver needed for your drive should have been included on a floppy disk that accompanied the drive. Apple's driver, appropriately called Apple CD-ROM, is also included as standard with System 7.5. Some drivers, available as a separate software purchase, can be used with a variety of different drive models.

  If the needed extension is not loaded at startup, CD-ROM disks cannot mount. If you find that such a driver extension is missing, install it from the disks that came with your CD-ROM drive and restart (see "Take Note: CD-ROM Drivers and Problems Mounting CD-ROM Disks," for more details).

  Other SCSI devices may similarly use an extension driver. Some SCSI devices, such as scanners, do not require a driver at all. They require only the appropriate application software. Floppy disk drives, which are not an SCSI device anyway, do not require any driver either.

TAKE NOTE ▶

CD-ROM DRIVERS AND PROBLEMS MOUNTING CD-ROM DISKS

As stated in the main text, CD-ROM drives need a driver extension installed, such as Apple CD-ROM, in order for the Macintosh to access the drive. Surprisingly, even if the driver extension is correctly installed, the extension will not load at startup unless the CD-ROM drive itself is first turned on. Thus, if you turn on a CD-ROM drive after startup, any disks inserted in the drive will not mount.

In this case, even though SCSIProbe lists the drive in its control panel window, clicking the Mount button will not remedy the problem. To get the CD-ROM drive to work, you must restart after turning on the CD-ROM drive.

However, if you use DriveCD (an alternative CD-ROM driver from Casa Blanca Works), it can mount CD-ROM disks even if the drive is not turned on until after startup is complete. To do this, you first need to mount the drive, using the DriveCD control panel (which functions similarly to SCSIProbe). After that, inserted disks will mount.

Also, some nonstandard format CD-ROM disks, such as PhotoCD disks, will not mount unless additional extensions are also installed (such as Apple's Apple Photo Access and Foreign File Access extensions). Check your CD-ROM drive's manual for more details. One tip: If you are having problems with an application that is unable to use files from a CD-ROM disk that is in a nonstandard format and you have the needed extensions installed, hold down the Option key when you insert the disk and keep it held down until the disk mounts. This should solve the problem.

Finally, as described in Chapter 5, some Apple CD-ROM disks can act as startup disks, but only with Apple CD-ROM drives. This ability may still strike you as involving a paradox: For a CD-ROM disk to boot at startup, it must load before the supposedly required CD-ROM driver extension has loaded. How can this be? The answer is that, in addition to the required System Folder being on the disk, these CD-ROM disks have special instructions, presumably in the boot blocks, that allow the Mac to mount them as startup disks.

Don't count on all Apple system software CD-ROM disks as being usable as startup disks. For example, the System 7.5 CD-ROM disk cannot serve as a startup disk, but the Power Macintosh disk that includes System 7.5 can act as a startup disk.

If SCSIProbe Doesn't List or Mount the Device

If you cannot mount or even list a connected SCSI device, and SCSIProbe gives a flashing message that says *Bus not terminated,* you may indeed have a termination problem. First make sure you have correctly followed all of the preceding procedures. If so, proceed to the section called "SCSI-Related Problems" later in this Fix-It (especially the subsection titled "Make Sure All SCSI Devices Are Properly Terminated").

If you still cannot mount any SCSI devices, you probably have a dead SCSI controller on the Macintosh's logic board. The logic board will need to be replaced.

SEE: • Fix-It #17 on logic board repairs, if needed

Special Case: Disk Drives That Don't Automatically Mount at Startup

If you are using an internal drive as your startup disk, any external drive that is turned on at startup should mount automatically as a secondary drive. That is, when startup is completed, its icon should appear on your desktop. However, a hard drive needs time to warm up before the Macintosh can detect its presence. If you turn on the external drive too late (such as after the Macintosh is already on and startup has begun), the Macintosh may check for external SCSI devices before the drive is sufficiently warmed up. In this case, the external drive is passed over and does not mount.

Similarly, if the external drive is your default startup disk (as selected by the Startup Disk control panel), and you turn it on too late, the Macintosh will start from its internal drive instead (assuming there is an internal drive and it has a System Folder on it). Again, in such cases, the external drive may not mount at all. SCSI utilities, such as SCSIProbe, are not essential to solving this type of problem. However, they are usually the most convenient solution.

By the way, in some cases, especially with most recent versions of the system software, an external disk may mount even if it warms up too late to be recognized by the Macintosh at its first startup check. This is because the Mac makes a second check later in the startup process. However, the effect of these checks may not be identical. For example, I noted that when mounted via the second check, the custom icon for my disk was absent.

To solve the immediate problem of a disk that does not automatically mount at startup, try one of the following:

- Restart the Macintosh. Assuming they are all turned on, the hard drive(s) will now mount correctly. This is the only solution for an incorrect startup disk selection.

- Mount the disk manually with a utility such as SCSIProbe (as described earlier in this Fix-It). Even if you think the drive had sufficient time to warm up and should have mounted automatically at startup, try using SCSIProbe now. There may have been a one-time glitch. If SCSIProbe mounts the drive, chances are that the next time you restart, the drive will mount automatically as expected. To prevent this problem from recurring, do either of the following.

- Remember to turn the drive on at least several seconds before turning on the Macintosh. This gives the drive enough time to warm up. By the way, if a disk fails to mount even when you gave it sufficient time to warm up, it may be that you are using a disk-formatting utility that has an option (typically called "auto-mount") to turn on or off automatic mounting of a drive. With this option set to off, the drive will only mount manually after startup is over. The solution is to make sure this option is on. Launch your disk-formatting utility or its companion control panel to check.

- Use a special option available with SCSIProbe called *Mount Volumes During Startup* (selected from SCSIProbe's Options dialog box). You also need to turn on the *Install Volume Mounting* INIT option (see Figure F16-3). When both of these are turned on, SCSIProbe scans the SCSI bus at the time that the volume mounting INIT loads at startup. This is significantly later in the startup sequence than when the Macintosh first checks for the presence of SCSI devices. As a result, SCSIProbe recognizes and mounts SCSI devices that are turned on but were skipped over by the Macintosh's initial check. Usually, this is late enough for a hard drive to be detected even if it was not turned on until *after* the Macintosh was turned on. This option is useful only for mounting drives as secondary drives. It does not switch startup disks.

  Various disk-formatting utilities have similar options. Check your manual.

BY THE WAY ▶

SWITCHING STARTUP DISKS AT STARTUP

As discussed at several points in this book, if you hold down the Command-Option-Shift-Delete keys at startup, the Macintosh bypasses the internal hard drive and instead uses an external hard drive as the startup disk, assuming one is available. It does this regardless of the setting in the Startup Disk control panel. Although it is most often used to bypass an internal drive that is crashing at startup, it is also a useful shortcut technique for switching startup disks even if there is no problem with the internal drive. The only inconvenience of this method is that the internal drive may not be mounted during startup. Its icon is absent from the desktop when startup is completed. However, with SCSIProbe installed on your external drive and its Mount Volumes During Startup option selected, the bypassed internal drive does mount automatically as a secondary drive at startup.

As another alternative, Now Utilities' Startup Manager, if accessed at startup (typically done by holding down a specially defined key, as described in Fix-It #4) has an option to switch the assigned startup disk and immediately restart.

If you have an IDE internal drive (see "By the Way: A New IDE" earlier in this Fix-It), you are likely to find that after using Command-Option-Shift-Delete, the internal drive cannot be mounted (since utilities such as SCSIProbe are looking only for SCSI drives). Fortunately, Apple has provided a solution to this: an extension called Mount IDE Drive (available from online services and included as part of System 7.5 Update 1.0). When installed, it mounts an internal IDE drive even if you have initially bypassed it at startup.

SCSI-Related Problems

This section covers cases when you cannot access one or all SCSI devices, often because system freezes or crashes occur at the time of access. In the worst cases, the system crash occurs at startup. Typically, if SCSI problems are the cause of a startup crash, the crash occurs immediately before or after the Welcome to Macintosh message appears, prior to any extensions loading. If the crash is accompanied by a bomb alert box, it probably says that a bus error has occurred.

As mentioned before, other causes can produce similar symptoms. SCSI causes are most likely if the problems occur immediately after you have made some change to your SCSI chain (such as adding a new device).

Fortunately, if you have a relatively simple setup, with no more than one or two external SCSI devices, the chances of confronting these problems are sharply reduced. On the other hand, if you do confront these problems, you will find solving them to be among the most difficult and frustrating of all Macintosh troubleshooting tasks. Don't be shy about seeking outside help (as covered in Fix-It #18).

Very helpful hint: Always shut off the Macintosh and all SCSI devices before disconnecting or reconnecting any SCSI devices. Otherwise, you could damage your hardware. Restart after each change to test its effect.

Make Sure the SCSI Port Is Functioning

If your problem does not prevent a normal startup, checking the SCSI port is a good starting point. Sometimes the SCSI bus stops transferring data correctly. In such cases, all devices on the SCSI chain, with the possible exception of an internal hard drive, no longer function. A variety of causes could be responsible for this, none of which you can directly prevent. To correct this problem, you need to *reset* the bus. Once again, you can do this with utilities such as SCSIProbe. In particular:

1. Open SCSIProbe. Hold down the Option key. The Update button (see Figure F16-2) should change to a Reset button.
2. Click the Reset button.

A corrupted Parameter RAM (PRAM) may also cause this type of problem. Try zapping the PRAM.

SEE: • Fix-It #11 for details on zapping the parameter RAM

If the problem persists, continue to the next sections.

Check If All SCSI Devices in the Chain Are Turned On

You may think that you are safe from SCSI problems if all the devices in your chain are turned off. But this is not the case. If anything, the opposite is closer to the truth. Similarly, if you plan to use only one device on your chain, don't assume that you need to turn on only that device. Often, *all* connected devices must be on for the chain to function properly.

Ideally, turn on all SCSI devices prior to turning on your Macintosh. If you have already started up, the safest course of action is to shut down, turn on all your SCSI devices, and immediately restart.

Of course, there are exceptions. I have five external SCSI devices connected to my Macintosh. I can turn any or all of them on or off at any time during a session without any problem. You may not be so lucky.

Be Careful When Turning Off a Non-Startup Drive

Despite the preceding advice, you may decide to turn off a mounted external secondary drive before shutting down. To do this:

1. Drag the hard disk's icon to the Trash. This unmounts the drive, removing its icon from the desktop. The Finder's Put Away command performs the equivalent action. (At this point, the disk drive is still running. You could remount the drive, using SCSIProbe, if you wanted.)

2. Turn the drive off. If you are as lucky as I have been, this does not cause any problems. If you are unlucky, you cannot do this.

Do not, under any circumstances, turn off a hard drive *before* you drag its icon to the Trash. If you do, *immediately* drag the disk's icon to the Trash. Otherwise, any attempt to use the drive will most often lead to a system freeze or crash!

Similarly, if for any reason the disk icon for a hard disk turns to a shadow icon (similar to what would happen to a floppy disk's icon if you used Command-E to eject the disk), immediately drag the icon to the Trash. Then remount it, using SCSIProbe.

In general, be careful about turning off any SCSI device (scanner, CD-ROM, or whatever) until after you shut down. Doing so may lead to an immediate system crash. You can experiment here. If you do shut off a device and nothing bad happens, great! Otherwise, avoid doing it in the future.

Disconnect All SCSI Devices

If your problem remains, a logical next diagnostic step is to disconnect the SCSI chain from the Macintosh. To do this, simply shut off all devices and unplug the cord that connects the first device in the chain to the rear of the Macintosh. Restart.

If the problem persists, it is probably not an SCSI problem. You can reconnect your SCSI chain and look elsewhere. System software problems loom likely. Check Chapter 5 for a general overview of possible causes.

If the problem vanishes when the chain is disconnected, a SCSI problem is the likely cause. Although the precise problem may be due to a damaged SCSI device, it is more likely a problem with how the SCSI devices are connected (cables, ID numbers, or termination). At this point, dealing with SCSI problems becomes something of a black art. However, most problems will be solved by checking the steps outlined in the following subsections.

TAKE NOTE ▶

READ BEFORE YOU CONTINUE WITH THIS FIX-IT

For the remaining sections of this Fix-It, the solutions apply mainly to situations where you have made a change to the SCSI chain configuration just prior to the onset of your problem. For example, it is unlikely that an ID conflict could be the cause of a new problem if you have not made any recent change to the ID numbers of your devices or added any new devices to your chain (though I suppose you could have accidentally changed the ID number of a device while trying to turn it on or off or whatever).

Make Sure No Two SCSI Devices Have the Same ID Number

If two or more SCSI devices on the chain have the same ID number, you have an ID conflict. If one of the conflicting devices is a hard drive, a likely symptom is the appearance of multiple copies of the disk icon scattered across the desktop. System freezes and crashes are likely to follow. Loss of data on your disk is a real risk. In other cases, the device simply does not mount. In any case, correct this problem immediately!

1. Turn off your Macintosh and all SCSI devices.
2. Check each device's ID number by examining the location on the device where the number is listed. If you cannot locate it, check the device's manual to learn where its ID number is listed.
3. If you find a conflict, change the ID number to correct it. Remember, all external devices should have numbers between 1 and 6.
4. Reconnect SCSI devices to the Macintosh (if necessary) and restart the Macintosh.

Remember to consider the ID number of any internal SCSI devices, beyond the internal hard drive, that may be present. For example, since an internal CD-ROM drive should have an ID of 3, an external device cannot use the same ID number.

While the Macintosh is on, a utility such as SCSIProbe should be able to tell you what these ID numbers are. However, don't rely on it to show an ID conflict, as it may get too confused by the conflict to sort things out. However, you can use SCSIProbe, when you are done with your ID changes, to confirm that all is now well. SCSIProbe lists the ID location of each mounted device. If each device has a unique ID number, the conflict is probably resolved.

Another way to see an SCSI device's ID number, if it is a device that mounts on the desktop, is to select the desktop icon for the device and then select Get Info. The Where listing often (though not always!) lists the device's ID number.

Make Sure All SCSI Devices Are Properly Terminated

Improper termination may leave you unable to access any of the SCSI devices in your chain. However, it does no permanent harm to your hardware. Correctly adjusting the termination should get things working again.

As first explained in the "Why to do it" section of this Fix-It, the last device in an external SCSI chain should be terminated. Sometimes, the first external device also needs to be terminated. Generally, no other external SCSI devices should be terminated. If your chain is not set up this way, you should add or remove termination as appropriate (see "Technically Speaking: SCSI Termination Up Close," for details). However, these rules have exceptions. So be prepared for some experimenting.

SCSI TERMINATION UP CLOSE

Most SCSI devices today use external termination. External terminators are plugs that you insert into the unused port of the SCSI device. They can be easily removed and placed on another device if you need to change a termination setup. However, some SCSI devices are internally terminated. This means the terminator is built into the machine. Usually, there is a way to remove or disable the internal terminator, if necessary. Sometimes it may be as simple as pressing a switch on the rear of the SCSI device. More often, it requires accessing the inside of the case in some way and is thus less convenient than removing an external terminator. In the worst cases, there is no way to remove the built-in terminator. This is undesirable, as it typically requires that the internally terminated device be the last device in the chain (which, if you have two internally terminated devices, can become an impossible problem). Refer to the manuals for your SCSI devices to learn if your device is internally terminated and, if so, how to remove it. Similarly, since exact termination requirements can vary among different models of Macintosh, check with the documentation that came with your Mac for more precise information. Ultimately, you may need to seek outside help here. In the meantime, here is a brief checklist of points to bear in mind:

- *Both ends of a SCSI chain should be terminated.*

- *Macs with an internal drive are typically already terminated. You only need to worry about terminating the far end of the chain.*

- *If your Macintosh does not have an internal drive (which is rare these days), your Macintosh may or may not be considered terminated, depending on the particular model. This difference is irrelevant if you are adding only one external SCSI device—just make sure the added device has a terminator. But if you add two or more SCSI devices to a Macintosh that is not terminated (and does not have an internal drive), both the first and the last device in the chain have to be terminated.*

- *PowerBooks are unusual in that they are not terminated even if they have an internal drive. Thus, even if only one external device is connected, you may need two terminators, one on each end of the device.*

- *If you have an internally terminated device at the end of a chain, you should not also add an external terminator.*

- *Typically, there should be no termination in the middle of a chain. Thus, if you have an internally terminated device as a middle device in a chain, you should typically remove the internal terminator. Alternatively, you can move it to the last device in the chain.*

- *Most terminator plugs are gray in color. A black terminator plug is only for use with SCSI port on the Macintosh IIfx or the LaserWriter IINTX.*

In reality, these rules are often broken. In particular, for short chains (one or two devices with short-length cable), the system may work even without a terminator at the end of the chain (even if your Mac's manual says one is needed). For long chains, a third terminator in the middle of the chain may be required. (Fortunately, in this regard, most external terminators have an outlet on their rear side where another cable can be plugged in, thereby permitting the chain to continue beyond the termination point.) So experiment. If you are having problems that you think may be solved by adding or removing a terminator, try it. Some people may warn you against this, fearing that turning on an improperly terminated system can permanently harm your hardware, but I have never found that to be the case.

Reconnect and Rearrange the Connection Order of SCSI Devices

If the previous solutions have failed to solve your SCSI problem, it's time to delve still deeper into the black art of SCSI problem solving.

If you have more than one external SCSI device, begin by reconnecting them one at a time. If necessary, remove and reconnect them in various combinations (such as only Device 1 connected, then only Device 2 connected, then both connected). Also rearrange the order in which devices are connected along the chain (such as Device 1 followed by Device 2, and then reverse the order). For obscure reasons, a device may work if it is earlier in the chain than another device but not later in the chain (or vice versa). The documentation that came with a given device may offer advice. For example, it may say that the device must be the first in the chain (I hope you don't have two such devices!). Always remember to adjust termination, as needed, when rearranging.

If rearranging devices fails to help, try swapping cables among the various devices. This sometimes works even though the switched cables seem identical. Even shifting ID numbers may help, as long as you make sure that no two devices wind up with the same number. For example, some people claim that it is better to have ID numbers in ascending order as you move to devices further away from the Macintosh.

By the way, the two SCSI ports on SCSI devices are functionally identical. It doesn't matter which port you use as the incoming or outgoing connection.

Overall, explore by trial and error, rearranging until you find a combination that works. There are no hard-and-fast guidelines.

Confront Cable Connection Confusion

If you start rearranging or disconnecting SCSI devices, or whenever you add a new SCSI device, you may find that you do not have the proper cables to accomplish your goal.

This is because there are two main types of SCSI outlets: a 25-pin outlet (in the back of the Macintosh and on some SCSI devices) and a 50-pin outlet (most common on external SCSI devices). Thus, to attach a typical external drive to a Macintosh, you need a cable with a 25-pin plug on one end and a 50-pin plug on the other end. As you add devices, however, you may find that you need a cable with a 50-pin plug on both ends or a 25-pin plug on both ends.

Finally, none of these cables will work directly with PowerBooks, which have an altogether differently sized SCSI outlet, requiring a special matching cable!

Solving these cable problems requires purchasing the correctly configured SCSI cable. In some cases, you can instead buy an adapter that converts a port from one type to another.

SEE: • **Chapter 11 for details on connecting SCSI devices to PowerBooks**

Running with Devices Disconnected

Even if you never find a chain combination that works when *all* of your devices are connected, you may be able to get your chain working with only some of your SCSI devices connected. Obviously, this is less than an ideal solution. But it may be the best you can do for the moment—and is probably a lot better than the alternative of having nothing working!

In the meantime, seek outside help, starting with the manufacturers of your SCSI devices. They may be aware of some way to combine components that you have not yet tried, a way that may yet be successful for connecting all of your devices.

Check for Damage

If all of the above suggestions have failed, and the problem seems specific to one SCSI device, the device may be damaged. Take it in to see if it needs to be repaired or replaced. If the problem occurs across all SCSI devices, the Macintosh itself may be damaged (most likely a component on the logic board). However, software damage is also a possible cause. In particular, for hard drives, there may be software damage to the device driver, the Directory, or related "low-level" areas of the disk. These can often be repaired using a disk repair utility, such as MacTools or Norton Utilities.

For related information

SEE: • Fix-It #1 on hardware and software incompatibilities
      • Fix-It #12 on damaged disk device drivers
      • Fix-It #13 on fixing damaged disks
      • Fix-It #17 on hardware repairs
      • Chapter 5 on startup and disk problems
      • Chapter 11 on SCSI connections and PowerBooks

Fix-It #17:
Check If Hardware Repairs or Replacements Are Needed

QUICK SUMMARY

Switch problem peripherals to another Macintosh to test for the source of the problem. Make sure cards and SIMMs are properly inserted on the Macintosh's main logic board. Check for possible problems due to defective or incorrectly connected cables. Use specialized software to diagnose your hardware. Try other hardware tests as your skills permit.

When to do it:

• If the Macintosh doesn't turn on at all.

• If the sad Mac icon appears at startup (especially if there are no F's in the code numbers below the sad Mac). This symptom is most often caused by defective SIMMs.

• If a Macintosh does not play a normal startup tone when you turn it on, and it subsequently refuses to start up. This is again most likely a SIMM-related problem.

• If you get frequent and apparently unrelated system crashes. This too is most likely a SIMM-related problem.

- If a floppy drive cannot read any disks you insert into it.
- If your monitor display shrinks in size periodically or has a wobbly image. This is often a power supply problem.
- If any peripheral device (monitor, printer, drive, mouse, keyboard, or whatever) is not working as expected (such as a monitor screen that remains constantly dark or a cursor that does not respond to mouse movements).
- If you have any problem with the Macintosh or a peripheral device and you have exhausted all other possible causes, as described throughout this book.

Why to do it:

This book is primarily about problems you can solve at your desktop, mostly just by using the information in this book and some appropriate software. This book is definitely not about making hardware repairs. When it comes to hardware problems, I typically advise you to take your Mac to an authorized repair shop.

So what, you may ask, is a Fix-It about hardware problems doing here? The answer is twofold. First, some problems seem like hardware problems when they really aren't (or vice versa). So, at the very least, it's helpful to know how to diagnose a true hardware problem. Having an accurate diagnosis will also aid in your conversations with a repair technician, should a repair be needed. The second answer is that some hardware "repairs" are so easy and minimal to do that they are worth knowing no matter what the emphasis of this book may be. Similarly, by clearly identifying whether a problem is or is not hardware related, these techniques can save you hundreds of dollars in unneeded trips to a repair shop. These are the goals of this Fix-It.

TECHNICALLY SPEAKING ▶

WORKING INSIDE THE MACINTOSH

Some checks and simple repairs require opening up the Macintosh's case. These include swapping an internal drive, inserting or removing NuBus cards, and adding or removing SIMMs. No matter what you intend to do inside, always unplug the Macintosh before opening its case.

For a few models (especially the compact Macintoshes), opening the case can be somewhat difficult for a untrained person to do. If you are not careful, it can even be dangerous to do. In particular, opening up a compact Macintosh exposes the built-in monitor. Some components associated with the monitor maintain a high voltage even when the machine is unplugged. If you mishandle these components, you risk a serious electrical shock.

At the other extreme, for many models of desktop Macs, opening up the case is quite easy and safe to do. The top of the case snaps off (sometimes you must remove a single screw). The latest models of PowerBooks are similarly designed to make access to its inside easier than in previous models. There is no danger to yourself with working inside any of these models. The more real danger (which applies to compact Macs as well) is that you could damage the internal components. One common way this could happen is via your own static electricity. So discharge this static electricity, by touching a metal object, before you start working inside any Macintosh.

(continued)

This Fix-It gives only rough guidelines for working inside the Macintosh. If you want to add or replace parts, you usually get the details when you make a relevant purchase. For example, if you purchase SIMMs, they should come with detailed instructions on how to install them. Ask about this before you make your purchase. If these instructions are not sufficient, seek outside help. You can always pay to have a service technician do the installation.

Personally, I consider myself to be totally nonskilled when it comes to making any sort of hardware repair. Yet, over the years, I have replaced SIMMs, swapped internal hard drives, installed an internal modem in a PowerBook and more. Believe me, if I can do it, so can you. Still, you may not want to risk trying any of these things. That's fine. That's why they have repair shops.

What to do:

This Fix-It is divided into two topics: (1) Diagnose hardware problems and (2) Repair selected hardware problems.

Diagnose Hardware Problems

Preliminary Checks

If you have reached this Fix-It as a reference from an earlier chapter, you have probably already taken some of the preliminary steps described here. In fact, you have probably taken a host of other steps as well. Generally, unless your symptoms specifically indicate a hardware problem, you should try potential software-based solutions before assuming you have a hardware problem.

Still, a few hardware checks are so simple and basic that it often pays to try them *before* doing anything else, not *after* you have ruled out everything else. For example, if any or all of your devices seem dead, obvious first things to check include:

1. Make sure a device's on/off switch is on.

2. Make sure all cables are plugged in tightly and in their correct port.

3. Make sure devices are connected to an outlet and that, if the outlet is connected to a wall switch, the wall switch is on.

4. If you have a surge suppressor, make sure the fuse is reset.

Use Hardware Diagnostic Utilities

If your symptoms indicate a possible hardware problem, you need not wait for a service technician to confirm your suspicions. Instead, use one of several software utilities designed for the nonexpert that specialize in diagnosing your hardware. The most accessible such utility (because it is free) is MacCheck (see Fix-It #10). However, its capabilities are minimal at best. If you are at all serious about hardware diagnosis, I suggest one of the following alternatives:

- **Apple Personal Diagnostics**

  Apple Personal Diagnostics (see Figure F17-1) is available only as a separate purchase; it is not included with Apple's system software nor is it available from online services. Think of it as an enhanced version of MacCheck. First, it can compare the performance of your Macintosh against benchmarks for other models, allowing you to see if the speed of your Macintosh is consistent with similar models. Second, similar to MacCheck, it provides a detailed accounting of your system information, from what hardware you have to what control panels and extensions are in use. Third, you can perform a series of diagnostic tests of your hardware. In particular, it checks the logic board (including SIMMs), the hard drive, the floppy drive, and the monitor. It is primarily in this area that Apple Personal Diagnostics outperforms Mac-Check. The hardware tests are more extensive and the reporting more detailed. It also includes a test of system software that is similar to what is done by Disk First Aid and MacCheck.

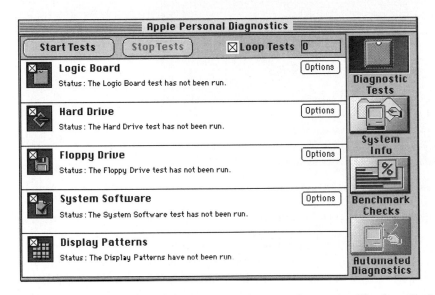

Figure F17-1   Apple Personal Diagnostics, a hardware diagnostic utility from Apple

Finally, it includes an extension called Automated Diagnostics that, when installed, will monitor your Mac's status in the background, checking for potential problems and reporting any problems it finds (as first described in Chapter 2).

Despite all of this, I find Apple Personal Diagnostics to be a mild disappointment: There are too many things it does not check, there is not enough flexibility over choosing what to check, and (most importantly) there is too little reporting of what it finds when it does do a check. It's not bad. It just could be so much better.

- **MacEKG or Peace of Mind**

  MacEKG and Peace of Mind are currently the best available diagnostic utilities. Both include more extensive checks than what you get with Apple Personal Diagnostics (plus their displays are more fun to watch!). MacEKG (Figure F17-2) works as a control panel, checking your Mac each time you start up. Peace of Mind is a separate application that you run as needed.

While both of these utilities are easy to use, they are likely to give you information whose meaning you will not completely understand. Don't worry about this too much. They can at least help you pinpoint the source of a problem (such as logic board versus disk drive), even if the exact cause is not clear. Also, the utility's manual will often provide more details.

Snooper, another excellent diagnostic utility (described in the first edition of this book), is unfortunately no longer available.

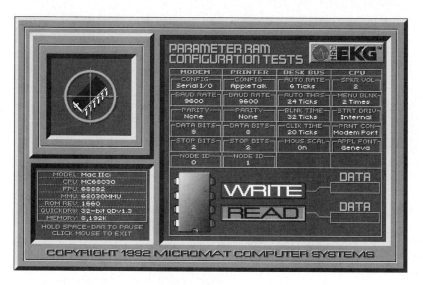

Figure F17-2   MacEKG, an example of a hardware diagnostic utility

- **Other utilities**
  There are utilities whose sole function is to check for problems with a floppy disk drive. They typically also include a floppy drive cleaning kit that may actually be able to "repair" some floppy drive problems. Two such utilities are DriveTech and MacDrive Probe. Most users do not need a separate utility just to check for floppy drive problems, but if you are subject to persistent hassles with your floppy drive(s), they may be worth a look.

  Some hard drive formatting utilities, especially Hard Disk ToolKit, include an array of diagnostic options for your hard drive(s) that typically exceed what other diagnostic utilities can do.

  Norton Utilities can do some diagnostic checking via its System Info module.

  In some cases, freeware or shareware utilities are available that duplicate some of the functions of commercial diagnostic programs. MacCheck, of course, has already been mentioned. A freeware utility called RAM Check will check for defective SIMMs. Other utilities, such as TimeDrive, can specifically check the performance of your hard drive. MacBench and Speedometer perform a more general set of benchmark tests. Profile utilities such as MacEnvy (see Figure F18-1) are a quick way to get a profile of system information, similar to (though less complete than) what you can get using MacCheck or Apple Personal Diagnostics.

SEE: • Fix-It #18 for more on using these utilities to profile your system

The main limitation of all of these hardware diagnostic utilities is that using them assumes that you can successfully start up your Macintosh. This can be a real Catch-22. For example, how can you run a utility to check for defective SIMMs if the defective SIMMs are preventing you from starting up your Mac? You can't! Second, and not surprisingly, these utilities cannot repair any of the hardware problems they discover.

Still, these utilities can be useful as a preventative measure. Often, defective hardware initially produces only minor symptoms, as the component continues to function albeit in a "weakened" state. Major symptoms appear later, when the component fails altogether. These programs can help you detect impending disaster, when the symptoms are still so minor that you may not even notice them and the Mac is still running apparently okay.

Except as described in the next section of the Fix-It, if these programs do spot any hardware problems, my general advice is to take the problem component (or the whole system, if necessary) in for repairs.

Repair Selected Hardware Problems

If you have a likely hardware problem, a critical step is to figure out which hardware component is the culprit. Otherwise, for example, you could waste a good deal of time and money bringing your entire Macintosh system in for diagnosis and repair, when the problem is just a mouse that needs to be replaced. Similarly, if you are having a printing problem, it helps to know whether the printer or the Macintosh is the source of the problem. Sometimes this may not be easy to distinguish.

Using the previously described hardware diagnostic utilities can sometimes help make these determinations. Otherwise, disentangling these possibilities requires applying the general strategies outlined in Chapter 3. The most common strategy is to temporarily swap peripheral components with a second Macintosh to assess if the peripheral device or the Macintosh is the source of the problem. Similarly, swap cables to check for damaged cables. Specific examples follow.

One important reminder: Turn off the Macintosh and all components before attempting any hardware-related repairs. Better yet, unplug them from the wall outlet. Do not even disconnect or reconnect cables, especially SCSI cables, when the Macintosh and/or peripherals are on. Doing so can send a voltage shock to the Macintosh that could damage the machine (though see "Take Note: Hardware Help for Solving SCSI Problems," in Fix-It #16, for a partial exception to this rule).

Hard Drives and Other SCSI Devices

If an external SCSI device refuses to mount or otherwise does not work (and solutions as detailed in Chapter 5 and Fix-It #16 have failed to solve the problem), attach it to another Macintosh. If it exhibits the same symptoms on the second Macintosh, the SCSI device is probably at fault. Take the device in to see if it can be repaired or needs to be replaced. But first, try swapping SCSI cables between the two machines. Sometimes it turns out that just the cable is defective.

For suspected hardware problems with an internal hard drive, swapping drives between two machines requires opening up the Macintosh case. Once the case is open, removing the drive requires unplugging the drive's connecting cables and then prying the drive free of its securing brackets. This is a fairly simple operation that usually requires no tools. Still, if you have never done this before, you should probably get some outside help before attempting it.

One particular hard drive problem, described in more detail in Chapter 5, is called *stiction*. In this case, the drive mechanism gets stuck at startup and never starts spinning. The result is that the disk cannot be accessed in any way. A slap to the side of the drive case may get the drive going, but this is a temporary solution. The symptoms get worse with time. If you succeed in accessing the drive, copy any critical data to other disks, then buy a new drive. Your old one is a goner.

Some hard drive repair facilities specialize in recovering data from a crashed disk, even if the disk cannot be repaired. Seek these out if you have important unbacked up data on a disk that has failed. The best-known and most respected of these repair services is *DriveSavers*. They can be reached at 415-883-4232.

SEE: • **Chapter 5 and Fix-It #16 for more on SCSI devices, including CD-ROM drives**

Floppy Drives

If the Macintosh claims that a formatted disk is *unreadable* or *is not a Macintosh disk* (and you have checked other possible causes, as described in Chapter 5 and Fix-It #15), you may have a defective floppy disk drive. To test this out, insert other disks into the drive.

Does the drive refuse to recognize all disks, or just certain one(s)? If it refuses to recognize all disks, check to see if another floppy disk drive recognizes those same disks. If the disks cause problems with all drives, the disks are the source of the problem. However, if a second drive properly mounts the disks, the original drive may be defective. If so, you need to take it in for repair. A hardware diagnostic utility, especially one specifically designed to check floppy disks (such as DriveTech, as mentioned in the previous section of this Fix-It), can help determine this.

Related points to consider include: offspeed and misaligned drives, intermittent mounting problems, cleaning dust from the disk drive, a disk not automatically inserted, and a disk stuck in the drive.

- **Offspeed and misaligned drives**
  Sometimes, because of minor variations in spinning speed or head alignment among different drives, a floppy drive can read disks that it formatted itself, but not disks formatted by other drives. Similarly, other drives cannot read disks formatted with the offspeed or misaligned drive. If this seems to be the case, take the drive in for repair.

  However, in one special case, floppy drives in newer models of Macintosh (particularly AV models and Power Macs) may have trouble reading mass-duplicated 800K floppy disks. This problem cannot be repaired. Instead, try one of the following work-around solutions: Startup with extensions off, zap the parameter RAM (PRAM), or use another Macintosh to copy the data on the 800K disk to an HD disk.

- **Intermittent mounting problems**
  Sometimes, if you continue to eject and reinsert a disk, the drive may eventually accept and mount the disk correctly. Although the problem may be caused by software damage on the

disk, it is also a potential sign of damage to the drive itself (especially if many disks show this symptom). In this case, do not ignore the problem. It is only likely to get worse. Again, take the drive in for repair.

- **Cleaning dust from the disk drive**
  Because the slot used to insert a disk is uncovered, dirt and dust tend to collect inside a floppy drive. A dirty drive can be the cause of all sorts of unusual symptoms, some of which may seem to have little or nothing to do with the drive.

  To clean the drive, place a portable vacuum cleaner near the disk drive opening and turn it on briefly, to try to draw out the dirt. With luck, this may get things humming again. Disk drive cleaning kits (as mentioned in the previous section on diagnostic utilities) may also help. Otherwise, take the drive to a service technician for cleaning and possible repair.

- **Disk not automatically inserted**
  Older Macintosh floppy disk drives had a feature such that, when you inserted a disk part of the way, the drive grabbed it and inserted it the rest of the way. As a cost-saving measure, newer style SuperDrives no longer do this. They are referred to as "manual inject" drives. All PowerBooks and newer desktop Macs have this type of drive. There is nothing wrong here. You just have to use up an extra half a calorie to get the disk to insert.

- **Disk stuck in the drive**
  Most problems with a disk that will not eject are software related. However, possible hardware causes include a disk label that has come loose and is preventing the eject or a disk's shutter slide that is bent. In most of these cases, you can try to eject the disk by inserting a straightened paper clip into the hole next to the drive opening. If even this fails, you will need to take the drive in for repair.

SEE: • Chapter 5 for more details on different ways to try to eject a disk

Keyboard and Mouse/Trackball

If your keyboard seems dead but your mouse functions fine (or vice versa), switch the keyboard (or mouse) with one from another computer. If the second keyboard (or mouse) works fine on your computer, the original keyboard (or mouse) is probably defective. Usually, these items are not repairable and need to be replaced. However, some problems may be due to a defective keyboard cable or a problem with the ADB ports on the Macintosh. In particular, check for the following:

- **Keyboard cable okay?**
  Be sure to swap the keyboard cable, separately from the hardware. Sometimes just the cable is defective. If the problem disappears when you switch cables, replace your original cable.

  For the Macintosh Plus and earlier models, the keyboard is connected to the Macintosh via a cable that resembles the curly cord used with telephones. If you discover that it needs replacement, do not try an ordinary telephone cord. It is not the same.

- **ADB ports okay?**
  The ports that connect the keyboard and mouse to the Macintosh (on all models from the Macintosh SE to the current models) are called *Apple Desktop Bus (ADB) ports*. Many models of Macintosh have two of these ports. One, but not the other, may be defective. Try

switching cables to see if only one port is associated with the problem. If so, you have a defective port. You need a repair.

Occasionally, an ADB-related problem may be software-based, typically caused by a specific application that somehow conflicts with ADB port communication. Ideally, such applications come with special fixes (usually in the form of an extension, such as one called ADB Fix) that are used to get around this problem. Unfortunately, sometimes the presence of such extensions can be the cause of the problem. In this case, the simple solution is to discard the extension.

- **A false freeze?**
On many Macintosh models, you can choose to attach your mouse to either the ADB port on the rear of the Macintosh or the one on the side of the keyboard.

If you attach the mouse to the side of the keyboard, and the keyboard or keyboard cable is defective, then *both* the mouse and the keyboard cease to function. This may seem to resemble a system freeze (as described in Chapter 4). However, it is really a hardware problem. You can usually spot a false freeze because, with defective hardware, the cursor does not respond to the mouse even in the earliest stages of the startup sequence. In general, if the problem recurs no matter what software techniques you try, suspect a false freeze. Again, the simple solution is to replace the defective cable (or keyboard).

BY THE WAY ▶

ARE INDIVIDUAL KEYS DEFECTIVE?

Sometimes a problem with a keyboard is limited only to specific keys. A quick way to check for this is to use Apple's Key Caps desk accessory. Press the suspected defective key. If the matching screen image of the key darkens, then the key is okay. Conversely, if there is a key in the Key Caps display that is darkened before you press it, this is a stuck key. Depending on what key is stuck, this can cause a variety of different symptoms (imagine, for example, if the Mac thinks the Command key is always depressed!).

- **Cursor doesn't respond to mouse/trackball movements**
The inside of the mouse (or trackball), where the rubber ball lies, collects dust and dirt. Eventually, this may prevent the rollers inside the mouse/trackball from turning properly. The result is that the mouse/trackball responds intermittently, with jerky movements, or not at all. Fortunately, you can easily clean the inside of a mouse or trackball.
Clean the mouse/trackball. On most mice, press on the ring that surrounds the rubber ball and rotate it counterclockwise from its locked to open position. Turn over the mouse and let the ring and the ball fall out into your other hand. On some mouse models, the ring does not rotate; it slides out and snaps back in. In either case, once the mouse is open, blow briefly and strongly into the mouse to remove any loose dust. Use a cotton swab dipped in isopropyl alcohol to clean the rollers. Use tweezers, if necessary, to remove stuck-on dirt. Reverse the steps to reassemble the mouse, making sure the ball is dry and free of dirt.

PowerBooks (other than the newer models that use the TrackPad) have a trackball. As with the mouse, this ball also may need to be cleaned. To do so, turn the ring around the trackball counter clockwise until it pops out. Now you can lift out the ball.

Black ball?   Some mice have inherent problems that prevent them from responding reliably to mouse movement, especially if you use a mouse pad. Mice with a black, rather than a gray, ball are particularly known to have this problem. If you have this type of mouse, try not using a mouse pad. Otherwise, see about getting your mouse replaced.

- **Numeric keypad doesn't work**
  Some applications do not respond to numeric keypad input unless *num lock* is on. To turn it on, on most standard keyboards, press the *num lock/clear* button on the numeric keypad. The num lock light, above the keypad, should now come on. You should now be able to use the numeric keypad. Other programs do not respond to numeric keypad input no matter what you do. There is no fix for this.

- **Adjustable keyboard problems**
  Apple's adjustable keyboard does not work properly without special software installed, provided on a disk that comes with keyboard. Even when installed properly, some applications, particularly games, may not work with the keyboard. A freeware extension called ADB Keyboard INIT may help solve some of these problems.

BY THE WAY ▶

A DEFECTIVE MOUSE PREVENTS A MAC FROM STARTING UP

As described in Chapter 5, sometimes a disk icon with a question mark inside it will appear at startup. The startup sequence halts at this point. This is usually caused by the Mac's failure to find a hard disk with a System Folder on it or by a damaged hard disk. However, I am aware of one unusual case where this was caused by a defective mouse. One clue here was that this Mac would not even start up with a startup floppy disk. The disk was just ejected. However, when a replacement mouse was connected, all worked fine. Go figure.

Monitor I: No Display or Dimmed Display

If a monitor shows no sign of life (or is unusually dim) when you turn on your Macintosh, you should determine whether the problem is with the monitor, the connecting cables, the video display card (if one is used), or the Macintosh itself. Diagnosing these problems is generally easier if you have a Mac that uses an external monitor. In any case, check the following:

- **Adjust brightness and contrast**
  If your monitor has brightness and contrast adjustment knobs, make sure that they are not set so low as to prevent you from seeing the image.

- **Check if the monitor is turned on**
  If your monitor has a small light on its face that lights up when the monitor is on, check this light. If it is off, it means the monitor is off. In any case, check the monitor's on/off switch. Most monitors have an on/off switch that is independent of the Macintosh. If it is off, turn it on, and your problems should be over.

- **Check if you are using an Energy Saver extension**
  If you have an Apple control panel called Monitor Energy Saver, it may be set to automatically turn off the screen display after a specified idle period. If this happens, the monitor is still on and the display will return a short time after you move the mouse or press a key (you may hear a beeping sound before the display returns). Current versions of After Dark have a similar feature. By the way, CPU Energy Saver is a related Apple control panel that will entirely shut off the Macintosh. All of these control panel features only work on certain Macintosh models.

- **Check if connecting cables are working and correctly connected**
  A monitor connects to most Macintoshes with two cables: One carries the display image information and the other carries electrical power. Make sure both are connected. As with all peripherals, also check if cables are defective by swapping them with a matching cable from another Macintosh, if one is available. Replace defective cables.

- **Check the video display card**
  The source of some video problems is inside the Macintosh, not the monitor. For starters, some monitors are connected to the Macintosh via a separate video display card. The card is typically located in one of the NuBus slots on the main logic board of the Macintosh (see "Technically Speaking: Macintosh Slots: NuBus, PDS, PCI" later in this Fix-It). If you set up your system yourself, you would know if you had used such a card. If you do use a display card, it may be defective or improperly inserted.

  To check this, you need to open up the case of the Macintosh. Once it is open, remove the video card (after disconnecting it from the cable). Check for any bent wires. Straighten any that you find. Reinsert the card, making sure it is firmly lodged in its correct slot. If this doesn't work, and if you still believe that the card is the source of your problem, don't immediately assume that the card is defective. Try inserting the card into another slot. Sometimes this solves the problem. If so, you may have a defective slot. In this case, even if everything else is working okay and you don't need to use the defective slot, I'd still recommend taking the Macintosh in for repairs.

- **Check more generally for problems with the Macintosh**
  If all of the previous steps have failed to help, find another Macintosh and hook up your monitor to it. If the monitor works, some component inside your Macintosh is the problem, probably the main logic board. On the other hand, if the monitor does not work on the second Macintosh, the monitor is the defective component. In either case, take your equipment in for repair.

- **Special case: PowerBook display problems**
  PowerBooks have brightness and/or contrast buttons, as do desktop Macintosh monitors. Check these if your screen is too dim. PowerBooks typically also have a feature called *screen dimming* that does what its name implies. If you are unaware of this, it may seem like a hardware problem. Also, don't forget that most PowerBooks are set to automatically go to sleep after a specified period of idle activity. Further, on active-matrix screens, spots on your screen may be due to defective pixels. On passive-matrix screens, a disappearing cursor may be due to something called *ghosting*. All of these problems are discussed in more detail in Chapter 11. Check there.

- **Special case: The "sync-on-green" problem for AV and Power Macintoshes**
"Sync-on-green" is a term used to describe the fact that a special "video synchronization signal" (needed for a monitor to work with a Macintosh) is sent to the monitor together with the green color signal. This has been the default method used by almost all color-capable Macintoshes. However, recent models of Macintosh handle the sync signal differently. These models include the LC III, AV Macs, and Power Macs. Because of this difference, some older non-Apple monitors cannot work with these newer Macintosh models. There is no solution for this other than to get a different monitor.

Monitor II: Quality of Display Problems

This category refers to problems with the quality of the display, rather than the absence of a display.

- **Size and form problems**
A display may shrink in size (horizontally or vertically), or the image may start to flicker. This often indicates a power supply problem. For external monitors, the problem is probably with the monitor's power supply. Otherwise, the problem is with the power supply inside the Macintosh. With compact Macintoshes, the built-in monitor and the computer share the same power supply. In any case, if you have a malfunctioning power supply, it needs to be replaced.

- **Color problems**
If a color display suddenly shows colored blotches on the screen, it is probably *magnetized*. If your monitor has a *degauss switch,* pressing it should fix this problem. You can often resolve other minor display-size and color problems by adjusting convergence controls, if your monitor has them accessible.

   Other color display problems, especially those limited to certain applications and/or documents, are usually software related. Most solutions center on understanding and using the Monitors control panel. This is covered in Chapter 10.

TECHNICALLY SPEAKING ▶

MACINTOSH SLOTS (NUBUS, PDS, PCI)

On the main logic board inside all Macintosh II, Centris, Quadra, and some Power Mac computers, there are special sockets called NuBus slots. These are designed to hold (appropriately enough) NuBus cards. These cards are like mini logic boards and act to extend the functionality of the computer. A video display card is a common example of a NuBus card. On older models of Macintosh (such as the Macintosh IIcx), a video card is required to attach a monitor to the Mac. On others, it is an optional alternative to the Macintosh's built-in video hardware. Using a separate video card usually offers faster displays or greater color depth than the built-in capability. If you use a video display card, your monitor connects directly to the card rather than to any built-in video port.

   Depending on your model of Macintosh, you may have anywhere from one to six NuBus slots. Each slot can hold one card. Each card draws power from the Macintosh's power supply. There is a limit on the total combined power that should be used by all NuBus cards. If you have several NuBus cards, you need to be concerned about exceeding this limit. In rarer cases, even the order in which you fill the slots can be of importance. Check with the documentation that came with your Macintosh and NuBus card(s) for more details, if needed. You should also be able to get help from the manufacturer of your NuBus card(s).

(continued)

Other models of Macintosh use different types of slots. One alternative is called the processor-direct slot (PDS), *available on several usually lower-end models of Macintosh. Power Macintoshes released in 1995 include a new, faster replacement to NuBus slots called* Peripheral Component Interconnect (PCI) *slots. Cards for these other types of slots function in basically the same way as NuBus cards. However, be careful about mixing and matching. When you purchase a card or any device that connects via a card, make sure it is the right type for your machine.*

Accessing these slots requires opening up the Macintosh case. The difficulty of doing this varies among different Macintosh models (as described in "Technically Speaking: Working Inside the Macintosh" earlier in this chapter).

Serial Port Devices: Printers, Modems, and Networks

In the rear of most models of Macintosh are two *serial ports*. These ports are primarily used to connect printers and modems to the Macintosh. A serial port is also used to connect your Macintosh to a network. One port is called the *printer port* and the other the *modem port* (indicated by a printer and a telephone symbol, respectively, above the port). Despite their different names, the two ports are virtually identical and can generally be used interchangeably. Notable exceptions: only use the printer port for AppleTalk connections; only use the modem port for GeoPort connections. Of course, if you have an internal modem (such as used in PowerBooks), you do not connect it to either port. Finally, some Macintoshes, notably certain models of PowerBooks, have only one serial port. It is a combined printer/modem port.

Common problems with devices attached through the serial ports are more often software than hardware related. For example, many printer problems revolve around making the correct selections from the Chooser desk accessory. These, and other printing problems, are explained in Chapter 7. Some problems with modems and with networks (especially as related to file sharing) are covered in Chapter 11. Otherwise, for these problems, you will need to refer to the relevant documentation or seek other outside help.

To check for general hardware problems with devices connected through the serial port, check the serial cables, the serial port, and the serial port peripheral device.

- **Check the serial cables**

  All except the oldest models of Macintosh use round 8-pin serial cables. However, while all of these serial cables may look identical on the outside, they can have quite different wiring inside. For example, a serial cable for non-AppleTalk printers is different from one used for modems. Either cable works correctly with either port. However, printer cables may work only with printers, and modem cables may work only with modems.

  The cables used to connect devices on an AppleTalk network (LocalTalk, PhoneNet, etc.) are a third type of cable that connects via the printer serial port, different from both standard printer and modem cables. Some newer Macintosh models include a separate EtherNet port, using its own type of cable, for connecting to this type of network. Finally, a few printers connect through the SCSI port rather than the serial ports. These, of course, require a SCSI cable.

  If you are having a problem from the first time you connect a serial port device, check to make sure you are using the right cable. If in doubt, consult with the place where you purchased your equipment or seek other outside help. As always, if problems persist even though all cable connections appear correct, you may have a damaged cable. Swap cables from another Macintosh, if possible, to check for this.

SEE: • "Technically Speaking: The GeoPort and Multimedia Features," for information on yet another cable type

- **Check the serial port**
  If you are still unable to get a response from a device connected to a serial port, try restarting the Mac. Also, try turning the serial port device off and back on again. These two techniques should solve most serial port problems (for example, it should reset a modem that is not responding and get it working again). If these fail to solve the problem, you may have a corrupted PRAM. To fix this, zap the PRAM (as described in Fix-It #11).

  Otherwise, one of the two serial ports (assuming your Mac model has two ports; some only have one) may be damaged. To test for this, if your device can work from either serial port, try switching the cable to the other port. To get things to work after switching ports, you probably also have to readjust Chooser settings (as discussed for printers in Chapter 7). If the device now works, the original port is probably damaged. Take the Macintosh in for repair.

- **Check the serial port peripheral device**
  Finally, the peripheral device may be damaged. If so, indicators on the device often provide additional clues. Consult your device's manual for specific details. For example, the different patterns of status lights on Apple LaserWriters indicate different problems. In particular, if both the paper jam and out of paper lights are on at the same time, or are flashing together, a hardware repair is probably needed.

SEE: • Chapter 7, "By the Way: Output Too Light, Too Dark, Streaked, or Smeared?"

TECHNICALLY SPEAKING ▶

THE GEOPORT AND MULTIMEDIA FEATURES

On AV and Power Macs, the modem port is technically also referred to as a GeoPort (it has nine holes rather than the eight holes of a regular serial port). If you connect special GeoPort-capable devices (via a cable that has the needed matching nine pins), you can access special functions built into the Macintosh. For example, the GeoPort Telecom Adapter can be used to access a built-in modem capability. The Adapter acts to connect this built-in modem to your phone line. You can otherwise still use this port as an ordinary modem port for connecting non-GeoPort serial devices.

This is only one of several multimedia features available with the Macintosh. Especially with AV and Power Macs, you can now easily connect a variety of audio/video playback and recording devices (such as microphones, external speakers, and televisions). While this book offers some help for solving problems specific to these features, in many cases you will need to seek outside help.

SEE: • Fix-It #1 for more on software/hardware incompatibilities, especially with AV Macs
• Fix-It #18, "Take Note: Why a Modem?," for more about modems

- Chapter 6, "Technically Speaking: A Few Words About Sound and Sound Files," for more on solving problems using sounds
- Chapter 7 for more specific information on printing problems
- Chapter 11 for more on PowerBook-specific serial port problems, including the Express Modem

The Macintosh

This section deals with the main components of the Macintosh itself: the logic board and the power supply. Problems with SIMMs, which are often considered part of the logic board, are covered separately in the final two sections of this Fix-It.

- **The logic board**
  If you have a hardware problem with the Macintosh itself, this generally means a problem with the circuitry on the main logic board. The symptoms can range from minor to a totally dead Macintosh.

  Logic board problems almost always require taking the Macintosh in for repair. In fact, Apple's official solution to any logic board problem, no matter how trivial, is to replace the entire board. This can be an expensive repair for what may only be a defective resistor somewhere on the board. Still, it's the safest way to go. If you want to risk it, nonauthorized dealers may be willing to replace individual components of the board, at a considerable savings of money.

  Battery problems are one case where even an authorized repair may not mean replacing the logic board. For example, if your Macintosh is one that can be turned on by the keyboard's Power-on button (not all models use this button), a dead internal battery can actually prevent your Macintosh from starting up at all. This can be fixed simply by replacing the battery.

SEE: • Fix-It #11 for information on replacing the Macintosh's internal battery

- **Power supply**
  As cited in this Fix-It, problems with distortions in the monitor display are often an early sign of power supply problems. The ultimate sign of a completely failed power supply is, of course, a dead Macintosh. In either case, get the power supply replaced.

SIMMs I: Adding or Replacing SIMMs

SIMMs are the name for the hardware components that provide the RAM (memory) for your Macintosh (as first described in Chapter 1). Thus, if someone claims to have "eight megs of RAM" in their machine, this means that a total of 8Mb of SIMMs are installed on the Macintosh's main logic board.

Every Macintosh comes with some SIMMs already installed. Otherwise your Macintosh could not work. In some cases, SIMMs are soldered directly to the logic board and cannot be easily removed. More often, they are independent removable minicards that fit into special SIMM slots on the logic board (similar to how NuBus cards work). Some models combine both methods.

In either case, there is almost always some way to add additional SIMMs to your Macintosh. Usually, this is via SIMM slots that are initially empty when you purchase your Macintosh. In PowerBooks (and some other models), there is typically only one location for adding RAM. A special model-specific memory module is inserted in this location; the amount of RAM on the module can vary. (Though the terms memory module and SIMM are technically not synonymous, both are often referred to as SIMMs.)

Exactly how easy it is to add or replace SIMMs yourself depends on which model of Macintosh you have and your own skill levels (see "Technically Speaking: Working Inside the Macintosh" earlier in this Fix-It). For most modular and PowerBook Macintoshes, you can do it yourself fairly easily with just a screwdriver and a set of instructions.

There are two main reasons to add or replace SIMMs in your Macintosh:

- **Add SIMMs in order to increase the RAM capacity of your Macintosh**
  If you find that your available RAM is insufficient to meet your needs (as covered in Fix-It #6), adding more memory is the best long-term solution. Minimum recommended memory requirements get larger every year. These days, 4Mb of RAM is the absolute minimum you need to run current software; 8Mb is a more realistic minimum. If you have a Power Macintosh, you should ideally have at least 16Mb.

- **Replace Defective SIMMs**
  SIMMs may be defective from the moment they are installed or, as with any electronic component, they may go bad over time. Defective SIMMs cause the most serious types of symptoms. Your Macintosh typically will refuse to start up at all, show the Sad Mac icon, and/or sound unusual startup tones (as detailed in Chapter 5, on startup problems). If you do succeed in starting up, despite the bad SIMMs, you will likely be plagued with frequent and apparently unrelated system errors. In such cases, the Macintosh may remain stable long enough for you to use diagnostic utilities, such as Apple Personal Diagnostics or MacEKG (as described earlier in this Fix-It), to determine if a defective SIMM is the cause.

If your Macintosh model is a type that can hold multiple SIMM chips, and if you get a sad Mac at startup, the sad Mac error code can help identify which one is the defective SIMM. Various utilities (such as MacCheck) can help you interpret these codes (see Chapter 5 for more on interpreting sad Mac codes). Otherwise, determining which of your several SIMMs is the defective one typically requires swapping SIMMs in and out of their slots and testing the Macintosh after each swap.

Depending on what model of Macintosh you have, you may be able to remove a SIMM (or a bank of SIMMs) and start up with what SIMMs remain. If the problem goes away, you know that the SIMM(s) you removed were the source of the problem. In other cases, you may need to replace a potentially defective SIMM with a new one before you can even try to start up. If your Macintosh has soldered in SIMMs and they are the cause of the problem, you will want to take the Mac to a service technician to get them replaced. I realize that many users will seek out a service technician to replace SIMMs, no matter what model they own. In any case, if you do have a defective SIMM, it must be replaced. Defective SIMMs cannot be repaired.

SIMMS THAT ONLY SEEM DEFECTIVE

Sometimes a removable SIMM that is not properly seated in its slot will mimic the symptoms of a defective SIMM. To check for this, make sure that each SIMM is firmly in its slot and that its wires are unbent. On some models of Macintosh, SIMMs are held in place by tabs that clip into holes on the SIMM. When you install a SIMM, make sure that the tabs on the slot click into holes at either end of the SIMM. Removing this type of SIMM requires that you carefully pry back the tab without breaking it off. A broken tab can prevent proper seating of the SIMM with the result that the SIMM appears to be defective. So be especially careful when removing these SIMMs. An inexpensive tool, sold by many places that sell SIMMs, can assist in this removal task.

Sometimes (as mentioned in Chapter 4) SIMMs that are merely dirty will behave like defective SIMMs, causing frequent system crashes or startup problems. Using a handheld vacuum cleaner to clean out the inside of your Macintosh may help. Otherwise, you may need to remove each SIMM and clean it. In most cases, just blowing dust off of it and wiping it gently with a soft cloth should be enough. In really bad cases, you may want to apply a specialized cleaning spray (such as one called DeOxIt). Most users should rarely, if ever, find this necessary. In any case, remember to take precautions against static electricity damage (see "Technically Speaking: Working Inside the Macintosh" earlier in this Fix-It).

One more symptom that may fool you into thinking you have defective SIMMs is when you cannot use more than 8Mb of RAM. Actually, the solution here is simply to turn on 32-bit addressing (as discussed more in Fix-It #6).

SIMMs II: Getting the Correct SIMMs for Your Machine

Purchasing SIMMs is yet another area of the Macintosh where the increasing diversity of the hardware has made sweeping generalizations almost impossible. The exact type of SIMM you need, the maximum amount of SIMMs you can add, and how they are added can vary dramatically from one model to another. In fact, the situation has gotten sufficiently out of hand that Apple has created a freeware HyperCard stack, called SIMM Stack (see Figure F17-3), that describes the exact SIMM specifications for each Macintosh model. Apple regularly updates this stack as new models come out. As another alternative, Connectix makes a booklet called *The Macintosh Memory Guide* (available free both in printed and in electronic forms) that provides similar help.

If you intend to add to or replace the SIMMs inside your Mac, I definitely advise getting one of these aids. However, if studying this material seems too daunting, don't fret too much. Reputable sellers of SIMMs are knowledgeable about these matters and should be able to advise you.

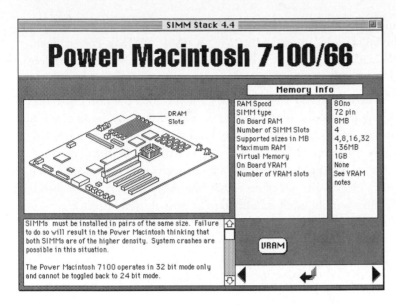

Figure F17-3   SIMM Stack details the SIMM requirements for each Macintosh model

In any case, what follows is a summary of the major issues you need to be concerned about. The specific examples cited are just a sampling of the variety that exists.

- **The maximum allowable RAM**
  Different Macintosh models have different limits on the maximum amount of RAM that they can use. If you install more than this maximum (assuming this is even possible), at best the Macintosh will not recognize it. At worst, it may lead to Sad Macs or system crashes.

  For example, a Macintosh Color Classic can have a maximum of 10Mb. The PowerBook 180 can have a maximum of 14Mb. A Quadra 660AV can have a maximum of 64Mb. A Power Macintosh 6100 can have a maximum of 72Mb.

  Note that if you use virtual memory (as explained in Fix-It #6), the maximum allowable total combined (physical plus virtual) RAM typically exceeds (often by a wide margin) the maximum allowable physical RAM.

- **The size of the SIMM**
  The amount of RAM on an individual SIMM can vary. For example, a single SIMM may hold as little as 1Mb (the common minimum these days) or as much as 64Mb or more. Thus, if your Macintosh has two SIMM slots, and you install two 1Mb SIMMs, you will have a total of 2Mb. But if you install two 64Mb SIMMs into the same two slots, you will have a total of 128Mb.

  SIMM sizes usually double as they increase. Thus typical SIMM sizes are 1, 2, 4, 8, 16, 32, and 64Mb. Replacing existing smaller-capacity SIMMs with larger-capacity ones is a way to increase your Mac's RAM when your Mac has no empty SIMM slots. Note that the word *size* in this context does not refer to the physical dimensions of the SIMM, but rather to its Mb capacity.

Note that each model of Macintosh typically has some restrictions on what sizes of SIMMs it can use. For example, the 660AV cannot use 1Mb, 2Mb, or 64Mb SIMMs. Power Macintoshes cannot use 1Mb SIMMs. Again, using a prohibited size will inevitably cause problems.

- **The speed of the SIMM**
  SIMM speed is measured in nanoseconds (ns)—the lower the number, the faster the speed. Different Macintosh models require a different minimum speed. Generally, faster machines require faster SIMMs. It is okay to add SIMMs that are faster than the minimum needed (though it may cost you more money to do so and will not increase the performance of your Macintosh). However, to avoid problems, do not add a SIMM that runs slower than the minimum required speed. Otherwise, at the very least, the speed of your Macintosh will decline. Currently, 70ns SIMMs should work fine in all or almost all Macintoshes.

  Some PowerBook models require something called *fast RAM*. If you don't use it, performance speed may drop as much as 15%.

  Again, if you purchase SIMMs that are specifically designated for your model, and you stick to reputable dealers, you should not have to worry about getting the wrong SIMM.

BY THE WAY ▶

BEWARE OF COMPOSITE SIMMS

Some large-capacity SIMMs are actually constructed by combining several smaller-capacity SIMMs onto one larger card (this is different from the modules used in PowerBooks). These are called composite SIMMs. Though they may work fine in many cases, Apple advises not to use them. As they are usually larger in physical size than a noncomposite SIMM, there may not be enough room for them to fit along side of the other components inside the Macintosh. Even worse, because of technical issues not worth describing here, composite SIMMs may lead to system crashes or a failure to start up.

- **The type of the SIMM**
  Even if two Macintoshes both use a 4Mb, 80ns SIMM installed in a SIMM slot, there may still be differences in exactly what SIMM each model uses. In particular, as mentioned already, PowerBooks use special memory modules that are different from what desktop Macintoshes use. Also, most older models of desktop Macintosh use a 30-pin SIMM while most newer models use a 72-pin SIMM. Typically, if you don't get the right SIMM, you won't even be able to insert it in the slot of your machine.

- **Other SIMM restrictions**
  If your Macintosh has multiple SIMM slots, it may be that all the SIMMs in all the slots must be the same size. Thus, you could not put a 1Mb SIMM in one slot and a 4 Mb SIMM in the next slot.

  Some, mostly older, models of Macintoshes have two separate *banks* of SIMM slots (called A and B). In this case, all SIMMs within a bank must typically be of the same size, though each bank can have a different size. Sometimes, the slots in a bank must either be all full or all empty in order for the Mac to work properly. The Macintosh IIci is a classic example of this type of Macintosh. It has two banks of 4 slots each.

Some more recent models have a much more flexible memory system. Thus, the Quadra 660AV has two slots. Each slot can hold a different size SIMM. You don't have to have both slots filled, and it doesn't matter which slot you fill. In contrast, the Power Macintoshes (6100, 7100, and 8100) also have two slots, but you cannot leave one empty and they must both be filled with SIMMs of the same size and speed in order for the Macs to work properly.

TECHNICALLY SPEAKING ▶

VIDEO RAM AND PRINTER RAM

For a few models of Macintosh, RAM needed to generate the video display is obtained from the same dynamic RAM (DRAM) used for all other RAM-related functions (this is the same RAM referred to in the main text of this Fix-It). The basic Power Macintosh 6100 is an example of this. However, most models of Macintosh include a separate set of video RAM (VRAM) used just for the display screen. These SIMMs are located in a special area of the logic board, separate from the main SIMMs. The amount of VRAM installed determines, among other things, the maximum number of colors that your monitor can display at one time. For example, without enough VRAM, you cannot get 24 bit color (see Chapter 10). Some models of Macintosh allow you to add additional VRAM SIMMs beyond what comes included with the basic configuration. Otherwise, to get more VRAM, you need to add a special video card (typically a NuBus card), which will include its own VRAM, and bypass the built-in video altogether. Some Power Macintoshes, taking a third hybrid approach, have an option to add a special VRAM Expansion card.

LaserWriters also have their own RAM. On some models, you can add addition printer RAM. Adding RAM will allow the printer to print faster and to better handle complex documents.

For more details and specifications on VRAM and printer RAM, check out SIMM Stack or otherwise get outside help.

 ## For related information

SEE: • Fix-It #1 on incompatibilities between hardware and software
      • Fix-It #6 on memory problems
      • Fix-It #16 on SCSI problems
      • Chapter 4 on system crashes
      • Chapter 5 on startup and disk problems
      • Chapter 7 on printing problems
      • Chapter 11 on PowerBooks
      • Chapter 12 on Power Macintoshes

Fix-It #18:
Seek Technical Support or Other Outside Help

QUICK SUMMARY

If you are unable to solve a specific software or hardware problem, call technical support of the company that makes the product. Otherwise, seek help from users groups, online services, magazines, books, and/or colleagues, as practical.

When to do it:

- Whenever symptoms suggest a bug or incompatibility problem.

- Whenever you have searched the relevant manuals for the answer to a question but were unable to find it.

- Whenever you have a problem that you were unable to solve using the advice given in this book.

Why to do it:

No Macintosh user is an island. Even if you memorize everything in this book, there will still be times when you cannot solve some problem. Perhaps you need some detailed information about your model of Macintosh (such as, "Can I get my Macintosh to display 24-bit color?"). Maybe you want some guidance on a particular procedure you have never tried before (such as installing SIMMs). Or maybe you simply can't find out what to do about some esoteric application- or hardware-specific problem. In all these cases, it's time to seek outside help.

What to do:

This Fix-It divides help into two separate categories: (1) product technical support, and (2) other outside help.

Product Technical Support

Virtually every computer company maintains some sort of technical support line. Basically, it is a help line for problems specific to the company's products. The phone number for technical support should be in the manual that came with the product.

Arrangements for technical support lines vary. Some phone numbers are toll-free, others are not. Sometimes you have to pay an annual fee to gain access to a given technical support line. Many companies also maintain technical support for their products on the major electronic information services, such as America Online or CompuServe (described later in this Fix-It).

Know When to Call Technical Support

At various points throughout this book, I have recommended when to call technical support for a given problem. Here, I offer more general guidelines for when to do this.

Generally, for symptoms that do not clearly point to a likely cause, it pays to call technical support fairly early in the search process. If you are lucky, they already have the answer to your problem. If so, the phone call can save you from wasting a substantial amount of time and effort looking for a solution on your own.

Technical support is especially helpful for problems due to software bugs and incompatibilities with a company's software. The manufacturer is privy to the latest information (and what is being done to resolve the matter). If there is an upgraded version of the program that remedies these problems, you can order it (sometimes you may even get it free of charge!). Occasionally, minor bug-fix upgrades are released that are not generally announced to registered users. Calling and asking for it (or describing a problem that the upgrade version addresses) is the only way to get it. Otherwise, the manufacturer may suggest some way to work around the problem. Technical support is also a good source of information about the obscure features of a program that are not adequately explained in the documentation.

On the other hand, if the technical support people do not know the answer to your problem, all they can do is suggest the same techniques described in this book. That is why it pays to try the simpler solutions before calling technical support. If these techniques succeed, you have saved yourself a call. If not, you are in a more informed position to make your call. Which leads to the next point: be prepared.

Be Prepared Before You Call

The key to getting help from technical support is to be prepared. If the technical personnel don't have an immediate answer to your problem, expect them to ask questions about the circumstances surrounding your problem. You should have answers ready. For example, you should know what model of Macintosh you are using, how much memory you have, what system software version you are running, what extensions you have installed, and exactly what you did immediately prior to the problem. This information is critical for technical support to successfully diagnose the problem.

Similarly, any attempts you made to solve the problem can pay dividends now, even though they were ultimately unsuccessful. The information you gathered helps to isolate the cause. For example, consider these two differing descriptions of the same problem:

- "I don't know what's going on. I was in the middle of writing my report, and all of a sudden the whole application crashed."

- "The application crashes as soon as I attempt to cut a selection of text, but only if I do it immediately after saving the document. At other times, the Cut command works fine. I know this is not an INIT conflict, because it happens even when all of my INITs are turned off. It isn't a damaged document, because it happens with any document I use. I tried replacing the application with a backup copy, and that didn't help either. If you want to know the details of my hardware or system software, I have that available. Just ask what you want to know."

Which statement do *you* think is likely to be more helpful to a tech support person?

As an added bonus, the information in the more detailed statement already provides an initial work-around solution: Do not use the Cut command immediately after you save a document. Type a few characters first. Then cut.

Using Utilities to Help Get Prepared

What if you don't know all the system information you should know before calling technical support? And what if you have no idea where to get this information? Not to worry. Any one of several utilities can come to your rescue. They analyze the current state of your System Folder, examine the overall contents of all your mounted disks, and determine the details of your hardware configuration. When they are finished, they create a report of all this information, which you can then print.

For example, both MacCheck (described in Fix-It #10) and Apple Personal Diagnostics (described in Fix-It #17) can do this. Another alternative is Now Profile, included as part of Now Utilities. For a quick on-screen summary of basic system information (which can be printed if needed), try MacEnvy, a shareware control panel (see Figure F18-1). TechTool (described more in Fix-Its #9 and #11) also includes a system information listing.

A somewhat different alternative is a program like Help! (first mentioned in "Take Note: Identifying System Software Compatibility Problems and Bugs" in Fix-It #5). In addition to giving system information, Help! identifies various known problems, such as software bugs, INIT conflicts, and whether a program is compatible with 32-bit addressing. With Help! you may not even need to call technical support to learn the cause of your problem.

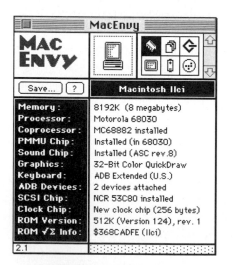

Figure F18-1
The MacEnvy control panel

REGISTRATION AND UPGRADES

Whenever you purchase a computer product, you almost always find a registration card enclosed. Fill it out and mail it back! You will not regret it. Registering computer products, especially software, is more valuable to you than for almost any other type of product you purchase. Here's why:

- *Some companies provide technical support only to registered users. (Otherwise, if you haven't registered, they may require that you tell them the serial number of your software before they help you.)*

- *Registering your product puts you on the company's mailing list. This means you get the company's newsletter, if any, which often contains useful hints and tips about the product. Similarly, registered owners of anti-virus software are alerted to newly discovered viruses.*

- *Finally, when an upgrade to the software is released, registered users are given an opportunity to purchase it at a substantially reduced cost. Usually, you will be automatically mailed a notification about the upgrade offer. This is by far the greatest benefit of registering your product. It's like being able to get a new car at a fraction of its normal selling price, simply because you own an older model of the same car. Sometimes, especially if the upgrade is released primarily to fix bugs in the previous version, the upgrade is free and sent to all registered users.*

   It is true that not all upgrades are worth buying. Some add more style than substance, primarily making the product larger, more RAM-hungry, and slower to use. If you are content with your present version, there may be little to gain by upgrading. More often, however, the upgrade adds significant and valuable new features, fixes bugs, and generally addresses user complaints about the previous version. It also may be the only version compatible with Apple's most recent system software version, which is important if you are staying current with system software.

   In most cases, getting an upgrade is worth the cost. However, registering the software is always free and at least gives you the option to decide about the purchase of any upgrades. So register your product!

Make the Call

When calling technical support, make sure you are dialing the technical support number, not the customer service number. The two services are entirely different. Customer service deals primarily with sales and generally knows little or nothing about technical problems. Some companies offer only one phone number. In this case, there is usually an automated system for making a choice after the call is answered.

When you get to the technical support location, you will probably be placed on hold. Be patient. Depending on the company's staffing and the popularity of the product, you may be on hold for a minute or for half the day. Sometimes, if the hold promises to be a long one, you are asked to leave a recorded message and wait to be called back. This is still another reason to try to solve the problem yourself before calling.

When you finally get to speak to someone, be courteous but be persistent. Restate your question if the initial answer was not helpful. While most technical support people are knowledgeable about their company's product, some may seem like they were just hired yesterday. If the person answering the phone seems incapable or unwilling to help, ask to speak to someone else. You should eventually get transferred to someone who knows the product well enough to answer your question.

GETTING HELP FROM APPLE

Traditionally, Apple has had a poor reputation for providing technical support for its products. Happily, there have been significant improvements in the past few years.

- *The most notable improvement is 800-767-2775 (SOS-APPL), your best bet number to call for Apple technical assistance. This number is also useful if you are having hardware problems with certain Apple products (most notably PowerBooks), especially if they are still under warranty. In this case, Apple may actually send someone to your door to pick up the equipment, have it repaired, and return it to you within a few days. However, after being connected to SOS-APPL's automated answering system, be prepared to wait a while before a real person answers. Users have reported waits of 30 minutes or more before they get through.*

- *Apple's complete selection of free software updates is now available through most on-line services or the Internet. Check in one of these locations to find out what's new. By the way, most users will find Apple's eWorld on-line service to be a definite improvement over its more stodgy older cousin, AppleLink (see "On-Line Information Services," later in this Fix-It, for more details).*

- *Apple also maintains a toll-free order center where, for a usually nominal charge, you can order all updates directly. The number is 800-769-2775. Of course, it helps to know that an update is available so that you know when to call to ask for it. This is still a weak link in Apple's support structure. Unlike almost every other computer company, it does not reliably notify you of upgrades to its products, even if you are a registered user.*

- *If you are more technically inclined, you can order a subscription to the same monthly developer's CD-ROM disk that gets sent to Apple developers. It is full of the latest information and software available from Apple. To order it, call APDA (Apple Programmers and Developers Association) at 800-282-2732. APDA also sells many other developer-oriented products.*

- *Just about anything else, software or hardware, that Apple sells can be ordered directly from the Apple Catalog at 800-795-1000 (but don't expect to get a discount price).*

- *Apple currently publishes a twice-monthly on-line magazine called* Information Alley *that is available from all on-line services. It is an excellent source of troubleshooting and support information designed for nonexpert users.*

- *Apple maintains still other customer support numbers. However, rather than list them all here (which may be futile, since they keep changing anyway), I recommend trying either 408-996-1010 or 800-538-9696 for any assistance beyond what you can get from the numbers already listed. Also, Apple now includes a pamphlet, listing many of its customer service phone numbers, as part of the documentation that comes with each Macintosh.*

Seeking Other Outside Help

Product technical support, by definition, is focused on the product the company publishes. It is not prepared to answer questions about more general problems you may have. Occasionally, technical support people may even be unaware of some esoteric problem with their own software. At these times, look elsewhere for help.

Try any or all of the following suggestions, as suits your style for seeking help. The solution is almost always available somewhere.

User Groups

Macintosh User Groups (MUGs) are independent groups formed by and for people who use a Macintosh. You may think that user groups are not for you. You may think they are only for hobbyists and experts. You may think that, by itself, owning a Macintosh is no more reason to join a MUG than simply owning a camera is a reason to join a photography club. If so, you may very well be wrong. Don't be too quick to dismiss the benefits of user group membership.

User groups have something for every level of Macintosh user. Besides having regular meetings, many larger groups maintain a telephone help line for answering questions. It's like a super technical support line, not limited to any particular product. Most MUGs also maintain a software library of shareware and freeware programs. Also common is a user group newsletter, with useful tips and advice on Macintosh-related topics.

If you don't have a user group near you, don't worry. The larger groups, such as Berkeley Macintosh User Group (BMUG), cater to a national membership. If you join a faraway user group, you won't be attending their meetings, but you can still get the other benefits.

On-Line Information Services

If you have a modem, you can use your Macintosh to connect to any one of several on-line information services. Though options vary somewhat from service to service, you can use them for everything from playing games to ordering clothes. However, for Macintosh problem solving, they have two main uses:

- **Bulletin boards**
  On-line services maintain electronic *bulletin boards,* where you can post messages for other users to read. Anyone can then reply to your message. If you have a question, leave it as a message on a bulletin board. Within a few hours to days, you should get an answer—often several answers—from some of the most knowledgeable Macintosh users in the country. Actually, just by browsing through existing messages, you may find that the answer to your question is already there.

  Many on-line bulletin boards are independent of any particular product. However, software and hardware companies often maintain product-specific message areas where you can leave messages for their technical support staff. If you are having trouble getting past hold on the technical support phone line, this is a good alternative. You should get an answer within 24 to 48 hours.

- **Download libraries**
  On-line services maintain libraries of shareware and freeware that you can directly transfer *(download)* to your computer over the phone. This is an alternative to obtaining the same software from user groups. Actually, some of the larger user groups, such as BMUG, maintain their own on-line library, free to members (except for the cost of the toll call).

  Again, the major download libraries are independent of any one company. However, the same areas that contain company-maintained bulletin boards may also have special product-specific software libraries. The software in these libraries typically includes files that can be used to update the company's software to a newer version as well as other supplementary software that does not come with the purchased product.

For Macintosh users, the best-known on-line services are CompuServe, America Online, eWorld, and GEnie. If you have never used an on-line service before, America Online is probably the best service to get. It offers a wide selection of features, with a pleasant graphical interface at a relatively low cost. More experienced users are likely to prefer CompuServe. It has the best organized and most comprehensive selection of software and related features, but it costs a bit more. If you are interested primarily in getting updates and related information directly from Apple, eWorld is your best bet. Because eWorld is maintained by Apple, it is often the first service to make Apple system software updates available and is more likely to have files detailing Apple's official position on troubleshooting issues (see Figure F18-2). Also, eWorld's interface is derived from America Online, so it shares many of the same ease-of-use advantages.

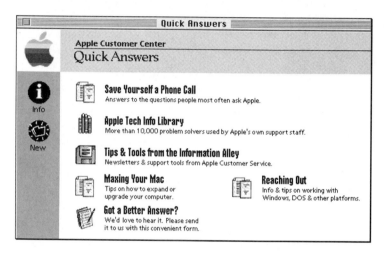

Figure F18-2   Getting troubleshooting help from Apple at eWorld

Besides eWorld, Apple maintains another on-line service, called AppleLink. It has traditionally been targeted mainly for developers and other more advanced users. It does not have the non-computer–related features of the other services. However, AppleLink may no longer be around by the time you read this. Apple is expected to phase out AppleLink and to convert to eWorld exclusively.

By the way, if you are hooked up to the Internet, you will find that most of the same shareware and freeware found on the commercial services are also lurking somewhere on the information superhighway. For example, to find Apple on the Internet, check out ftp.info.apple.com or (via the World Wide Web) http://www.info.apple.com. Actually most commercial services now give you at least partial access to the Internet, combining the best of both worlds.

Before you can effectively use any of these services, you need to learn how on-line communications works. This means learning how to set up a modem, run the telecommunications software, navigate around the service, leave messages, and download files. While this is all much easier to do than it used to be, you may not yet be ready to make the necessary commitment. That's fine. Other options for getting help are available, as described in this Fix-It. But if you already know how to telecommunicate, or you are inclined to learn, by all means take advantage of this invaluable resource.

SEE: • "Take Note: Why a Modem?" and "Technically Speaking: Hooking Up to the Internet," for some background on modems and communications software
• Fix-It #5, "Take Note: "Why Can't I Open the System Software I Just Downloaded?," for help in using downloaded files
• Chapter 11, "Can't Get a Modem (or Serial Port) to Work," for problem-solving advice on setting up a modem

---

TAKE NOTE ▶

WHY A MODEM?

A modem is a hardware device that connects to the serial port of your Macintosh on one end and to your telephone line on the other end. With the right software, you can use these devices to connect to other computers or to computerized information services anywhere in the world. To use any of the major services described here, you are required to pay either a monthly fee or an hourly rate or both.

Modems run at different maximum speeds, referred to as the baud rate. These days, 2400, 9600 and 14400 baud rates are common. Modems with fast maximum speeds can also run at slower speeds if required. Faster baud rates mean that, for example, you can download a file in less time, which also potentially saves you money in on-line charges. However, some services charge more for using a faster rate, partially offsetting the potential money-saving benefit of the higher rate. Also, to use a given baud rate, the connection on the receiving end must also be using that rate. Thus, if your 9600 baud modem connects to a service over a 2400 baud line, you will actually connect at 2400 baud. On-line services typically have different phone numbers to call for accessing different baud rates.

The more user-friendly services today, such as America Online and eWorld, have their own communications software. Getting started using this software requires almost no understanding of how modems or communications software work. Otherwise, you will need some general communications software (such as MicroPhone or the communications module of ClarisWorks or any one of several shareware programs). For a more general background on on-line communications, check out your modem's and/or communication software's manuals or seek other outside help.

TECHNICALLY SPEAKING ▶

HOOKING UP TO THE INTERNET

While many users access the Internet via the popular on-line services (such as America Online), more and more users are logging on to the Internet directly. Should you want to do this, be aware that it requires special communications software. In particular, you will need a file from Apple called MacTCP. It is included with System 7.5 or can be purchased separately. For direct access to the Internet over a modem (as opposed to a hard-wired connection at a university or workplace), you will need still other specialized setup software (such as MacPPP or InterSLIP). Finally, for any type of direct connection, you will want additional software for surfing the 'Net, such as a program for downloading files from ftp sites (Anarchie is a popular one) and a web browser for navigating the World Wide Web (Mosaic and Netscape are two popular examples).

If you are new to the Internet and all of this jargon is making little or no sense, don't despair. If you are on a network at work, there is probably a network administrator that can help you get all this set up and running. Otherwise, there are a host of Macintosh-specific books on this subject. Buy one.

Magazines

Similar to user groups, Macintosh magazines often have a reputation as being only for the most devoted of Macintosh users. This may be true in certain cases, but the most popular magazines offer something for everyone. Because they publish monthly, or even weekly, magazines are a good place to get late-breaking information about software bugs, upgrades, and new products. Their product reviews are among the best sources of critical information on which products to buy. Finally, regular columns offer help and advice on almost every imaginable topic related to the Macintosh.

MacUser and *Macworld* are the best of the monthly magazines. They are available on most newsstands. *MacWeek* is another superior publication, though more industry-oriented than *MacUser* or *Macworld* and only available by (a potentially free!) subscription.

Books

Since you are reading this book, you presumably already know that there are books on the Macintosh. What you may not know is that Macintosh books are available for virtually every skill level and almost every specialized interest. Some books are devoted to a single popular program, such as Excel or Photoshop. Others are on some specialized topic, such as how to use the Macintosh to create newsletters. Some are for experts who need help with their programming skills. Still others are a general introduction designed for the first-time user.

Visit a bookstore and check them out. You may find a book on exactly the topic you need.

Other Options

If you have a friend or colleague who is more knowledgeable about the Macintosh than you are, you don't need me to tell you how valuable a resource this can be. Not only can this person usually solve your immediate crisis, but he or she can teach you enough so that the next time the same or a similar problem happens, you can solve it on your own!

If you don't have a friend who is a Macintosh expert, you could hire a consultant or attend special training seminars. These are usually too expensive for an individual user, but they are viable for corporate use. Finally, although their advice is often unreliable, you could ask for help from the sales staff of computer retail stores or mail-order outlets.

 For related information

SEE: • Chapter 3 on general problem-solving strategies
• Chapter 11 for more on using modems
• Appendix for the phone numbers of all the services and publications cited here, as well as an explanation of exactly what is meant by shareware and freeware

A Final Note

I encourage you to send me your comments about this book. I would really like to get the feedback. Did you find the book helpful? Was the information easily accessible? Were you disappointed that certain topics were omitted? Were some topics covered in too little or too much detail? Or were you impressed with the breadth and depth of the coverage? Were you pleased to find just what you were seeking in just the right amount of detail? Any suggestions, criticisms, or compliments are welcome. This second edition was, in part, shaped by comments from readers of the first edition. Your comments can play a role in determining the direction of the third edition.

For those who would want to send me email, I am most easily reached on CompuServe at 72511,337 or on America Online at Ted Landau. You can also reach me on the Internet at landau@oakland.edu. For regular mail, you can write to me in care of Department of Psychology, Oakland University, Rochester, MI 48309.

Appendix

Stocking Your
Troubleshooter's Toolkit

Throughout this book, I have described and recommended a variety of troubleshooting software. If you're interested in getting any of these products, but don't know how to obtain them, this appendix will help. The first part explains the different ways that software is distributed—and where best to go to get each different type (including a special offer just for readers of this book). The second section lists the names, vendors, and phone numbers of all the commercial troubleshooting software products mentioned in this book.

Where to Get Software

Commercial Software

Commercial software is the most commonly available and widely used category of software. These products are sold in retail stores and through mail-order outlets. Many of the companies that publish them are probably familiar to you: Claris (ClarisWorks, ClarisDraw), Microsoft (Word, Excel, Works), and Adobe (Illustrator, Photoshop).

Among troubleshooting utilities, Norton Utilities, SAM, MacTools, Now Utilities, Retrospect, CanOpener, and Drive7 are just a few of the popular commercial products mentioned throughout this book.

For purchasing commercial software, I strongly recommend using mail-order outlets. They almost always have the best prices and the widest selection of products, and they keep most current with the latest upgrades. And if they have it in stock, your order is delivered overnight. In contrast, most computer stores carry a more limited selection of Macintosh products, often with out-of-date versions on the shelves.

Over the past few years, I have ordered from three different mail order firms. I have been satisfied with the service from all three:

- MacConnection: 800-800-3333
- The Mac Zone: 800-248-0800
- MacWarehouse: 800-255-6227

If you work for an educational institution, they may sell products at special discounts that beat even mail-order prices. Check it out.

Shareware and Freeware

Shareware and freeware typically include utilities, games, and other specialized products. They do not usually include the word processors and spreadsheets that would otherwise directly compete with commercial software. Shareware and freeware are not often even sold in the same outlets that sell commercial software. Although this may make them a bit harder to find, the best ones are well worth the effort. They offer professional-quality features often not available from any other product at a fraction of what a comparable commercial software program would cost.

SCSIProbe (mentioned in Chapter 5 and Fix-It #16) and Disinfectant (the anti-virus utility cited in Chapter 2 and Fix-It #7), are two popular freeware troubleshooting utilities. Get More Info (described in Chapter 8) is an example of a shareware utility. Most of the more specialized utilities mentioned in this book, such as TechTool or ShortFinder, are also shareware/freeware.

Freeware and shareware are similar in most ways. The difference is only in how and how much you pay for them. Since it is perfectly legal to make copies of these programs to give to others, one common way to get shareware/freeware is from a friend who already has the program. Alternatively, you can get these programs from any of several services (as described below). While there may be a minimal charge involved in obtaining the software from these services, it is important to understand that this payment goes to the service distributing the software, not to the creators of the programs. It is at this point that shareware and freeware differ.

For shareware, you are obligated to pay an additional fee (usually about $10 to $40) directly to the author of the program. But you need to pay this fee only if you continue to use the program. The idea is that you get to try out the software for a limited time risk-free. It is a sort of honor system: If you use the program, you pay for it; otherwise, you don't. You pay the shareware fee by mailing a check directly to the software developer. The instructions on how to do this are invariably included with the program. After you pay this fee, you may get an immediate bonus in return: a set of printed documentation or a copy of the latest version of the program (in case your version is not the newest one). In some cases, shareware products are distributed in a restricted form. For example, you may need a password to access the full program. To obtain the password, you must pay the shareware fee.

Let me be as clear as possible here: The fee to the author is the true shareware fee. You are obligated to pay this if you continue to use the program. Otherwise, the author gets no money at all and you are essentially cheating the author.

For freeware, there is no additional fee to pay. That's why it's called freeware.

Popular sources of shareware/freeware programs include on-line services, Macintosh user groups, the Internet, and mail-order outlets.

SEE: • Fix-It #18 for more general information on on-line services and user groups

THE *SAD MACS UTILITIES DISK* BONUS OFFER

Even with all the information provided in this appendix, I know it can sometimes be a hassle to locate and obtain many of the freeware or shareware products mentioned in this book. So, as a helpful shortcut, I have created a disk that contains many of these troubleshooting utilities: the Sad Macs Utilities Disk. On this disk, you will find SCSIProbe, TechTool, ShortFinder, Get More Info, MacErrors, and more. The disk will be updated periodically to make sure that it always contains the latest and best shareware/freeware troubleshooting software currently out there. Documentation on how to use these programs is provided on the disk.

The disk is available for a small fee to everyone who purchases this book. To get it, just mail in the coupon located on the last page.

On-Line Services

If you own a modem and telecommunications software, you can download shareware and freeware products from various on-line services. The services usually charge you an hourly rate for your connect time. The best services for Macintosh software are the following:

- America Online: 800-827-6364
- AppleLink: 408-974-3309
- CompuServe: 800-848-8990
- eWorld: 800-775-4556
- GEnie: 800-638-9636

The phone numbers listed here are for getting more information about how to sign up for these services. These are not the numbers used to log onto the service with your computer. Most of these services require that you use special communications software, which they supply at a minimal (or no) charge.

Internet

The files available for downloading from on-line services are also available in various locations on the Internet. While you can access at least some parts of the Internet via the on-line services just described, the best way to use the Internet is with direct access, either via an account where you work or via an account you set up yourself to work over a modem. For more information about this, see Fix-It #18, especially "Technically Speaking: Hooking Up to the Internet."

Macintosh User Groups

Many larger user groups maintain a library of shareware and freeware, with programs available for purchase at a cost of a few dollars per disk (where each disk may contain a dozen or more programs, depending on their size). If you don't live near where one of these groups is based, they will mail your order. Some groups also maintain an on-line service for downloading software. The best known of these user groups are:

- Berkeley Macintosh User Group (BMUG): 510-549-2684
- Boston Computer Society's Macintosh User Group (BCS•Mac): 617-846-1700

Mail-Order Outlets That Specialize in Shareware/Freeware

Some mail-order companies specialize in selling shareware and freeware products (some may also sell some commercial software). The pricing policy is similar to that of user groups. Typically, they have catalogs from which you order what you want. Two of the better known such companies are:

- EduCorp: 800-843-9497
- Diskette Gazette: 800-222-6032

Apple's Macintosh System Software

The distribution of Macintosh system software doesn't quite fit into either of the two previous categories. Your first set of Macintosh system software comes included with the purchase of your Macintosh. After that, if you want to stay current with each upgrade, you must obtain it on your own.

Upgrades (such as to System 7.5) are sold as retail products. They are usually available from the same sources that sell commercial software. In the past, system software (without the printed documentation) was available at no charge. You could get it from any authorized Apple dealer, from on-line services, or from user groups. Starting with System 7.1, however, Apple has discontinued this policy. Now the only way to get the latest system software is to buy it, either directly from Apple or from commercial software outlets.

Several other Apple products, such as Apple Personal Diagnostics and Apple Remote Access, are sold as separate packages, independent of system software.

On the other hand, many Apple updates (such as System Update disks) and utilities (such as Disk Copy and ResEdit) remain available at no charge through typical freeware/shareware outlets, especially AppleLink, eWorld, and Apple locations on the Internet.

Finally, you can order almost any Apple product directly from Apple. Call one of the following numbers:

- Apple Catalog (for most hardware or software): 800-795-1000

- Apple Order Center (especially for updates): 800-769-2775

- Apple Programmers and Developers Association (for more technical products): 800-282-2732

SEE: • "Take Note: Getting Help from Apple," in Fix-It #18 for more on calling Apple for assistance

Product Directory

The following is a list of the name, vendor, and phone number of every troubleshooting-related commercial software product (as well as a couple of hardware products) mentioned in this book. You can use these phone numbers to contact a vendor for more information about a specific program. Shareware and freeware products are not listed here, as they typically do not have a phone number you can call. Apple products (such as System 7.5 and Apple Personal Diagnostics) are not listed here. Refer to the previous section for information about them. Also not listed here are software products mentioned in this book but not directly related to problem solving (such as word processors and graphics programs).

- AccessPC (Insignia Solutions, Inc., 800-848-7677)
- Acrobat (Adobe Systems, 800-833-6687)
- Adobe Type Manager (ATM) (Adobe Systems, 800-833-6687)
- Adobe Type Reunion (Adobe Systems, 800-833-6687)
- ALLRight Utilities (Management Science Associates, 800-366-4622)
- ALSoft Power Utilities (ALSoft, Inc., 800-257-6381)
- APS Power Tools (APS Technologies, 800-233-7550)
- AutoDoubler (Symantec, 800-441-7234)
- CanOpener (Abbott Systems, 800-552-9157)
- Common Ground (No Hands Software, 800-598-3821)
- Compatibility INIT (Alysis Software Corp., 800-825-9747)
- Conflict Catcher II (Casady & Greene, 800-359-4920)
- CopyDoubler (Symantec, 800-441-7234)
- CPU Tools (Connectix, 800-950-5880)
- Crash Barrier (Casady & Greene, 800-359-4920)
- DiskDoubler Pro (with AutoDoubler and CopyDoubler) (Symantec, 800-441-7234)
- DiskExpress II (ALSoft, Inc., 800-257-6381)
- Diskfit Pro (Dantz Development Corp., 800-225-4880)
- DiskTop (PrairieSoft, 515-255-3720)

- Drive7 (Casa Blanca Works, Inc., 415-461-2227)
- DriveCD (Casa Blanca Works, Inc., 415-461-2227
- DriveTech (MicroMat Computer Systems, 800-829-6227)
- eDisk (Alysis Software Corp., 800-825-9747)
- Freedom of Press (Custom Applications, Inc., 800-873-4367)
- GOfer (included with DiskTop), (PrairieSoft, 515-255-3720)
- Hard Disk ToolKit (FWB, Inc., 415-474-8055)
- Help! (Teknosys, 800-873-3494)
- INITPicker (Inline Design/Focus, 800-453-7671)
- Last Resort (Working Software, Inc. 800-229-9675)
- MacDrive Probe (Accurite Technologies, 408-433-1980)
- MacEKG (MicroMat Computer Systems, 800-829-6227)
- MacLinkPlus (DataViz, 800-733-0030)
- MacPalette II (Microspot Limited, 800-422-7568)
- MacTools Pro (Central Point Division of Symantec, 800-964-6896)
- Maxima (Connectix, 800-950-5880)
- Norton Utilities for the Macintosh (Symantec, 800-441-7234)
- Now Utilities (Now Software, 800-689-9427)
- OptiMem RAM Charger (Jump Development Group, 412-681-0544)
- PBTools (VST Power Systems, 508-287-4600)
- Peace of Mind (DiagSoft, 408-438-8247)
- QuicKeys (CE Software, 800-523-7638)
- RAM Doubler (Connectix, 800-950-5880)
- Redux (Inline Design/Focus, 800-453-7671)
- Retrospect (Dantz Development Corp., 800-225-4880)
- SCSI PowerPlug (ADCON, 203-761-0651)
- SCSI Sentry (APS Technologies, 800-233-7550)
- Silverlining (LaCie Ltd., 800-999-0143)
- SpaceSaver (Aladdin Systems 800-732-8881)
- Stacker (Stac Electronics, 800-522-7822)
- StuffIt Deluxe (with SpaceSaver) (Aladdin Systems, 800-732-8881)
- Suitcase (Symantec, 800-441-7234)
- SuperATM (Adobe Systems, 800-833-6687)
- Symantec Antivirus for Macintosh (SAM) (Symantec, 800-441-7234)
- Thunder 7 (Baseline Publishing, 800-454-9333)
- Virex (Datawatch, 919-549-0711)
- Word for Word (Mastersoft, 800-624-6107)

Symptom Index

What follows is an index of all major symptoms and symptom-related alert messages described in this book. Alert messages cited in the text that do not imply any problem (such as *Please name this disk*) are typically *not* listed here. Conversely, a few of the alert messages listed here are not specifically mentioned in the text; in these cases, the page citations refer to the section in the text that describes the problem that would result in the alert message.

Alert/error messages are listed in italics. Other symptoms appear as plain text. The words *A, An, The,* or *This,* if they would normally appear as the first word of a message, are typically omitted from this listing.

In general, this index cites only the primary location(s) in the book where a symptom is described and/or where a figure showing the error/alert message is found. Further, if a symptom is discussed over several consecutive pages or as part of a particular section or Fix-It, this index often cites only the first page of that section or Fix-It.

Finally, this index is not exhaustive. If you don't find precisely what you are looking for here, go to the topic that seems most closely related. You may yet find the answer you are seeking!

Index

Desktop file(s)
  bloated, 702
  corrupted or incorrectly updated, 702
  in System 6, 709
  in System 7, 709
  viruses in, 692
Desktop Folder, 212, 339
Desktop Patterns, out of memory false
    alarm, 552
Desktop printer file, deleting or moving,
    585
Desktop Reset extension, 710–711
DeskWriter 560c, 420
Device driver(s). *See also* Disk driver(s);
    Printer driver(s)
  for CD-ROM drives, 183–184, 793
  for removable media, 792
Device independence, 356
Diagnostic utilities, 35
Digital Active Termination (DAT), 800
Directory, 713–714
  damaged, 120, 721, 738
  recurring system errors and, 124
  repairing, 144
  viewing and editing, 339–341
Directory object, 340
Disinfectant, 34, 63, 683, 687, 834
Disk(s), 9–15, 737–755. *See also* CD-ROM
    disks; Defragmentation; Disk-related
    problems; Floppy disk(s); Formatting,
    disk; Hard disk(s); Optimization, disk;
    RAM disk; Reformatting, disk; Re-
    movable media
  access speed of, 779
  crashed, 169, 738
  damaged, 30–31, 153, 160–161, 774
  deleting, 773, 779
  full, 254–255
  HD, 774
  initializing, 769
  locked, 40, 254–255, 688
  logical, 341
  mounting, 135, 769
  optical drives, 15
  PC (DOS)-formatted, 171, 236, 775,
    792
  permanence of storage, 11
  physical, 341
  recovery, 739, 752–755
  reinitializing, 171
  repairing, 738, 739–749
  restoring, 738, 749–752
  SCSI, 497, 744
  storage capacity of, 10
  trashed, 738
  unformatted, 167, 171

  unreadable, 774
  verifying, 769, 782–784
Disk Bug Checker, 151, 699
Disk cache, 667–668
  driver-level versus system-level, 672
  memory conservation and, 671
Disk check bug, 699
Disk Copy, 34, 647, 772
Disk directory, restarting failure and, 191
DiskDoubler, 62
Disk driver(s), 125, 729–736
  damage to, 120
  as extensions, 792
  installing, 769
  system performance and, 197
  updating, 144
Disk drives, non-automatically mounting,
    794–795
Disk errors, 253, 257–258
Diskette Gazette, 836
Disk Express II, 35, 695, 699
Disk First Aid, 34, 73, 144, 193, 249,
    712–718, 737–738
  major revision of, 716
  for verifying or repairing disk, 717–718
DiskFix, 746
DiskFix Pro, 35
Disk icon, 147–152
  dragging to trash, 188, 189
  removing, 187–188
  shadow, 175
Disk-level compression, 62
Disk-related problems, 163–199. *See also*
    Disk First Aid
  categories and, 128
  disk icon and cycling happy Mac icon
    from, 150–151
  files missing from Desktop, 192–194
  Finder and, 740
  Macintosh runs slower, 194–197
  missing files due to, 216
  repeated requests to reinsert floppy disk,
    179–181
  Restart, Shut Down, or Sleep problems
    and, 189–191
  system crashes from, 197–199
Disk space
  file sharing and, 510
  printing and, 306–307
  System 7.5 installation and, 545–546
Disk Tools, 50–51, 52, 54
DiskTop utility, 326, 333, 337
Display depth, 415–420
  defined, 415–416
  dithering and, 418–419
  printing and, 420

  setting, 416–418
  system performance and, 196
Displays. *See* Monitors
Dithering, 446–449
  display depth and, 418–419
Divide by zero error, 95
Document(s), 28
  backing up, 58
  color depth capacity of, 445
  conflict with PrintMonitor and, 310
  creator code missing or corrupted, 320
  damaged, 123, 240–241, 759, 760
  deleting, 246
  duplicates of, 85
  graphics, 445–458
  graphics in text, 437
  importing to application, 232, 233, 235
  printer halted by, 301
  sent to outside sources, 376
  SimpleText, 570
  simplifying, 308–309
  startup, 21
  stuck in queue, 583
  type codes for, 318
  unable to open, 227–241
  wrong font displayed in, 372–377
  wrong formatting in, 381–389
  wrong icon for, 320
Dot-matrix printers, 267
Dots per inch (dpi), 412–413
Dotted lines, 384
Double-sided disks, 12, 13, 770–774
Download libraries, 827–828
Drag and Drop, 203, 397, 434–435, 439
Draw programs, 425, 426
Drive7, 35, 166, 778, 780–781, 792
DriveCD, 793
Driver descriptor map, 341–342
Driver-level disk cache, 672
Drivers. *See* Device driver(s)
DriveSavers, 808
DriveTech, 806
DropStuff, 62
Duo Dock, 464
Duos
  Duo PowerBooks, 463–464
  inserting into or ejecting from Duo
    Dock, 496
  models, 488–489
Duplicates, working only with, 85
Dynamic linking, 535

Easy Install, 550, 551, 643
Easy Open, 34, 229–230, 237, 436, 708
eDisk, 62
EduCorp, 836

Sad Macs Utilities Disk

When your Mac misbehaves, the only thing more helpful than a copy of *Sad Macs, Bombs, and Other Disasters* on your bookshelf is a copy of the *Sad Macs Utilities Disk* in your drive!

Updated regularly, this disk is full of indispensable freeware and shareware tools for preventing disasters, diagnosing problems, and recovering from mistakes, including:

Bomb Shelter	CommentKeeper	Desktop Reset
Disinfectant	Extensions Manager	Finder Fixer
Get More Info	Mac Identifier	MacErrors
ResetPwrMgr	SCSIProbe	ShortFinder
TechTool	Zap!	***and more!***

Don't wait; order the *Sad Macs Utilities Disk* today.
The Mac you save may be your own.

☐ ***Yes***, please send me the *Sad Macs Utilities Disk!*
I've enclosed $5* cash, check, or money order (purchase orders and CODs not accepted) to cover materials, shipping, and handling.

☐ ***No thanks***, but keep me informed of updates and special offers.

Company _____
Name _____
Address _____
City _____
State _____
ZIP _____
Country _____

MAIL TO: **OWEN INK**

2227 15TH AVENUE
SAN FRANCISCO, CA 94116

* For orders from outside the United States, please add $2 to cover additional costs, and make sure your payment is denominated in U.S. funds.

(If you don't want to cut up your book, mail a copy of this page or any piece of paper with the necessary info.)

MACINTOSH

Praise for the first edition of

Sad Macs, BOMBS, and Other Disasters

"I know of no other resource, book, or software that explains system errors, what causes them, and what to do about them as completely and cogently as *Sad Macs, Bombs, and Other Disasters*. Having saved my bacon several times over, it has earned a permanent place of honor on my bookshelf."
—Bob "Dr. Macintosh" LeVitus, Mac book author and *MacUser* columnist

"Choice Product for 1994 and 1995. The best book for finding out what is wrong with your Mac and dealing with it. A book that every Mac owner will need sooner or later."
—*BMUG Newsletter*

Does your Mac ever freeze, failing to respond to any keyboard input? Have you been plagued by the infamous system bomb alert box? Or maybe it's just that your Mac can't find your printer, or a file refuses to be deleted. Solutions to these and hundreds of other problems—including the very latest ones caused by Power Macs, PowerBooks, and System 7.5—are covered in this completely updated edition of *Sad Macs, Bombs, and Other Disasters*.

Symptom by symptom, Macintosh expert Ted Landau walks you through exactly what can go wrong and how to fix it. Inside, you'll find:

- the latest information (almost every page has been rewritten for this edition) about how to diagnose and solve the problems that can occur while using a Mac
- two entirely new chapters that detail problems and solutions specific to PowerBooks, Power Macs, System 7.5, QuickDraw GX, file sharing, and more
- a Symptom Index listing every error message and major symptom discussed in the book
- self-contained Fix-It sections that delve into the det 07/29/95 and useful techniques for solving problems

Using a nontechnical, step-by-step approach, *Sad Macs,* provides disaster relief at its finest. Whether you're a new the first edition of *Sad Macs,* or otherwise, this new bool vital fix-it information you can't survive without!

Ted Landau is a contributing editor for *MacUser*. He has published more than sixty Macintosh-related articles, and currently teaches at Oakland University in Michigan.

Cover design and art by Jean Seal

Addison-Wesley Publishing Company

53495
9 780201 409581
ISBN 0-201-40958-5
$34.95 **US**
$48.00 CANADA